CRIMINAL JUSTICE

A Brief Introduction
FOURTH EDITION UPDATE

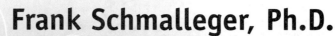

Frank Schmalleger, Ph.D.
Director, The Justice Research Association
and Professor Emeritus
The University of North Carolina at Pembroke

Police

Courts

Correction

Prentice Hall, Upper Saddle River, New Jersey 07458

Library of Congress Cataloging-in-Publication Data

Schmalleger, Frank.
    Criminal justice: a brief introduction / Frank Schmalleger.—4th ed. update
        p. cm.
    Includes bibliographical references and index.
    ISBN 0-13-093350-3
    1. Criminal justice, Administration of—United States.   I. Title.

HV9950 .S34 2002
364.973—dc21   2001034593

Publisher: Jeff Johnston
Executive Assistant: Brenda Rock
Executive Acquisitions Editor: Kim Davies
Assistant Editor: Sarah Holle
Managing Editor: Mary Carnis
Production Management: North Market Street Graphics
Interior Design: Lorraine Castellano
Production Liaison: Adele M. Kupchik
Director of Manufacturing and Production: Bruce Johnson
Manufacturing Manager: Ilene Sanford
Creative Director: Cheryl Asherman
Senior Design Coordinator: Miguel Ortiz
Cover Illustration: Leza Anthenien
Cover Design: Cheryl Asherman
Typesetting: North Market Street Graphics
**Director of Marketing Communication
    and New Media:** Frank Mortimer, Jr.
Marketing Manager: Ramona Sherman
Printer/Binder: Banta Company, Menasha

Pearson Education LTD.
Pearson Education Australia PTY, Limited
Pearson Education Singapore, Pte. Ltd
Pearson Education North Asia Ltd
Pearson Education Canada, Ltd.
Pearson Educación de Mexico, S.A. de C.V.
Pearson Education—Japan
Pearson Education Malaysia, Pte. Ltd

10 9 8 7 6 5 4 3 2
ISBN 0-13-093350-3

FOR
Nicole "Ariel" Schmalleger,
*who has always been
the apple of her father's eye*

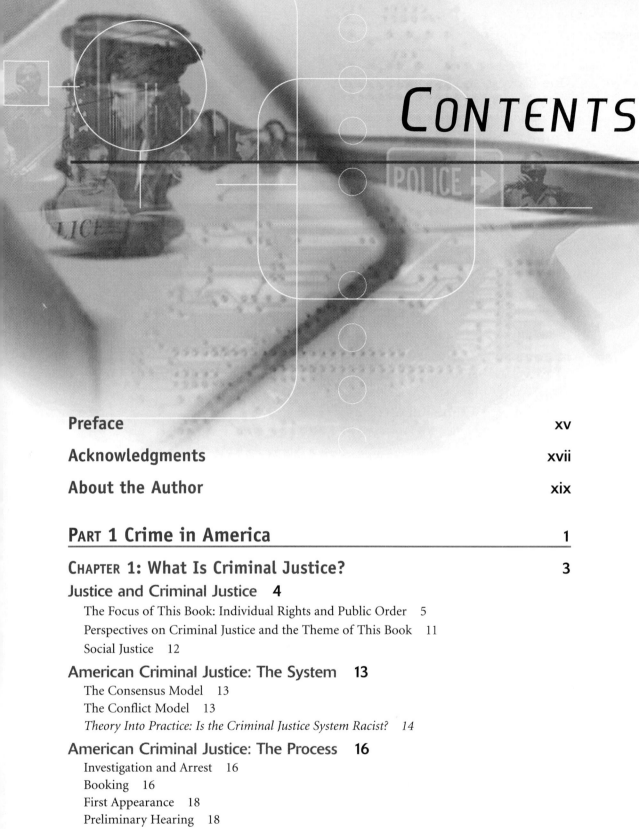

CONTENTS

The publisher and the author of this book
jointly donate a portion of proceeds from all sales
to research in the field of crime and justice.

PREFACE

Criminal justice is a dynamic and fluid field of study. Ever changing crime statistics, newsworthy events involving American law enforcement, precedent-setting U.S. Supreme Court decisions, and rapidly breaking innovations in correctional practice all challenge instructors and students alike to keep pace with a field undergoing constant modification.

As the floodgates to the twenty-first century open wider, and accelerated change engulfs American society, it is appropriate that a streamlined and up-to-date book such as this should be in the hands of students. The information age and all that it has wrought is here, and the quick dissemination of information has become a vital part of contemporary life.

Criminal Justice: A Brief Introduction results from the realization that today's justice students need to have the latest quality information available to them in a concise and affordable source. The paperback format of this book has made it possible to quickly translate the latest happenings in the justice field into a pragmatic textbook that is both inexpensive and easy to read.

Criminal Justice: A Brief Introduction focuses directly on the crime picture in America and the three traditional elements of the criminal justice system: police, courts, and corrections. The text is enhanced by the addition of career boxes that can assist today's pragmatically minded students in making appropriate career choices. Colorful photographs, charts, graphs, and other visual aids help keep student attention and add variety to the text. Twenty-First Century Criminal Justice boxes, which are placed strategically throughout the book, draw attention to the many exciting possibilities facing the justice system as it realizes the possibilities held out by the new millennium. Crime in the News! stories, an added feature in this edition, bring a true-to-life dimension to the text, and allow insight into the everyday workings of the justice system.

As the author of numerous books on criminal justice, I have often been amazed at how the end result of the justice process is sometimes barely recognizable to anyone involved in the process as *justice* in any practical sense of the word. It is my sincere hope that the technological and publishing revolutions that have contributed to this book will combine with a growing social awareness to facilitate needed changes in our system; and that that will help supplant what have at times appeared as self-serving, system-perpetuated injustices with new standards of equity, compassion, understanding, fairness, and heartfelt justice for all.

Frank Schmalleger, Ph.D.
Director, The Justice Research Association
and Professor Emeritus
The University of North Carolina at Pembroke
April 2001

Accessing the *Criminal Justice: A Brief Introduction* World Wide Web Site

Anyone using this book is encouraged to visit the award-winning *Criminal Justice: A Brief Introduction* site on the World Wide Web. This book's companion Web site provides a broad range of materials of relevance to the study of criminal justice and has links to a vast number of other criminal justice-related sites. Through the many Audio Extras!, WebExtras!, and Library Extras! that are built into this text, and via the Web Quests! found at the end of every chapter, the companion Web site provides substantially enhanced learning opportunities. Students and instructors can use the site to interact with one another, and with others interested in the study of justice around the world. Electronic homework, Web searches, and a comprehensive glossary are among the many other features of the companion Web site. An integrated resource, "Dr. Frank Schmalleger's Criminal Justice Cybrary" (http://talkjustice .com/cybrary.asp) provides thousands of links to criminal justice agencies and resources that can be easily searched and visited.

If you have a personal computer, a modem, an Internet account, and Web browser software, you can easily access the *Criminal Justice: A Brief Introduction* home page. Point your Web browser at www.prenhall.com/schmalleger and get ready for a cyberspace excursion through the halls of *Criminal Justice* online!

ACKNOWLEDGMENTS

Many thanks go to all who assisted in so many different ways in the development of this textbook. Manuscript reviewers, Taylor Davis at Georgia Southern University, Joan Luxenburg at the University of Central Oklahoma, Gary J. Prawel at Keuka College, Carl E. Russell at Scottsdale Community College, and Kevin M. Thompson at North Dakota State University, should know how grateful I am to them for their helpful comments and valuable insights. I appreciate the many valuable comments made by Kevin Barret, Derald D. Hunt, Rick Michaelson, Morgan Peterson, and Jim Smith. I wish to thank Prentice-Hall's Mary Carnis, Cheryl Asherman, Miguel Ortiz, and Adele Kupchik, as well as the North Market Street Graphics team, especially Christine Furry and Mary Jo Fostina. All are recognized and appreciated. Special thanks go to Kim Davies, who is that perfect combination of editor and friend, and to marketing manager Ramona Sherman, without whom this book would never have seen the light of day. Frank "Krazy Elvis" Mortimer—who lives up to his nickname—deserves an exceptional "thank you" for his diligence and insight into educational technologies—and for using his skills to blend them with this text. Thank you also to my beautiful wife Harmonie Star-Schmalleger, for the personal support she has offered, and to my daughter, Nicole, to whom this book is dedicated, and who has always had the courage to follow her heart.

Frank Schmalleger, Ph.D.
Director, The Justice Research Association
and Professor Emeritus
The University of North Carolina at Pembroke

ABOUT THE AUTHOR

*F*rank Schmalleger, Ph.D., is director of the Justice Research Association, a private consulting firm and think tank focusing on issues of crime and justice. The Justice Research Association, which is based in Hilton Head Island, South Carolina, serves the needs of the nation's civil and criminal justice planners and administrators through workshops, conferences, and grant-writing and program evaluation support. JRA also sponsors the Criminal Justice Distance Learning Consortium (CJDLC). CJDLC resides on the Web at http://cjentral.com/cjdlc.

Dr. Schmalleger holds degrees from the University of Notre Dame and Ohio State University, having earned both a master's (1970) and a doctorate in sociology (1974) from Ohio State University with a special emphasis in criminology. From 1976 to 1994, he taught criminal justice courses at the University of North Carolina at Pembroke. For the last 16 of those years, he chaired the university's Department of Sociology, Social Work, and Criminal Justice. In 2001 he was named Professor Emeritus at the University of North Carolina at Pembroke.

As an adjunct professor with Webster University in St. Louis, Missouri, Schmalleger helped develop the university's graduate program in security administration and loss prevention. He taught courses in that curriculum for more than a decade. Schmalleger has also taught in the online graduate program of the New School for Social Research, helping to build the world's first electronic classrooms in support of distance learning through computer telecommunications. An avid Web surfer, Schmalleger is also the creator of a number of award-winning World Wide Web sites, including one that supports this textbook (www.prenhall.com/schmalleger).

Frank Schmalleger is the author of numerous articles and many books, including the widely used *Criminology Today* (Prentice Hall, 2002); *Criminal Justice Today* (Prentice Hall, 2001); *Criminal Law Today* (Prentice Hall, 2002); *Corrections in the Twenty-First Century* (Glencoe, 2001); *Crime and the Justice System in America: An Encyclopedia* (Greenwood Publishing Group, 1997); *Trial of the Century: People of the State of California vs. Orenthal James Simpson* (Prentice Hall, 1996); *Computers in Criminal Justice* (Wyndham Hall Press, 1991); *Career Paths: A Guide to Jobs in Federal Law Enforcement* (Regents/Prentice Hall, 1994); *Criminal Justice Ethics* (Greenwood Press, 1991); *Finding Criminal Justice in the Library* (Wyndham Hall Press, 1991); *Ethics in Criminal Justice* (Wyndham Hall Press, 1990);

A History of Corrections (Foundations Press of Notre Dame, 1983); and *The Social Basis of Criminal Justice* (University Press of America, 1981).

Schmalleger is also founding editor of the journal, *The Justice Professional.* He serves as editor for the Prentice Hall series *Criminal Justice in the Twenty-First Century,* and as Imprint Advisor for Greenwood Publishing Group's criminal justice reference series.

Schmalleger's philosophy of both teaching and writing can be summed up in these words: "In order to communicate knowledge we must first catch, then hold, a person's interest—be it student, colleague, or policymaker. Our writing, our speaking, and our teaching must be relevant to the problems facing people today, and they must—in some way—help solve those problems."

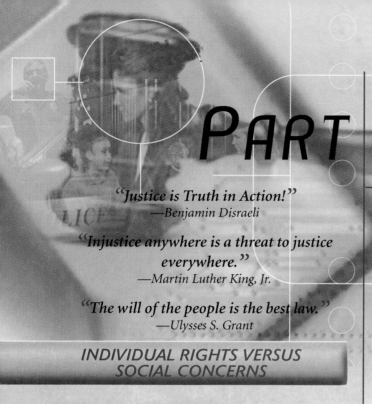

PART 1

"Justice is Truth in Action!"
—Benjamin Disraeli

"Injustice anywhere is a threat to justice everywhere."
—Martin Luther King, Jr.

"The will of the people is the best law."
—Ulysses S. Grant

INDIVIDUAL RIGHTS VERSUS SOCIAL CONCERNS

GOALS OF THE CRIMINAL JUSTICE SYSTEM

Common law, constitutional, statutory, and humanitarian rights of the accused:

◆ Justice for the Individual
◆ Personal Liberty
◆ Dignity as a Human Being
◆ The Right to Due Process

These individual rights must be effectively balanced against these community concerns:

◆ Social Justice
◆ Equality before the Law
◆ The Protection of Society
◆ Freedom from Fear

How does our system of justice work toward balance?

CRIME IN AMERICA

1	2	3
What Is Criminal Justice?	The Crime Picture	Criminal Law

The great American statesman and orator Daniel Webster (1782–1852) once wrote: "Justice is the great interest of man on earth. It is the ligament which holds civilized beings and civilized nations together." While Webster may have lived in a relatively simple time with few problems and many shared rules, justice has never been easily won. Unlike Webster's era, society today is highly complex and populated by groups with a wide diversity of interests. It is within that challenging context that the daily practice of American criminal justice occurs.

The criminal justice system has three central components: police, courts, and corrections. The activities and the legal environment surrounding the police are discussed in Part 2 of this book. Part 3 describes courts, and Part 4 deals with prisons, probation, and parole. We begin here in Part 1, however, with an overview of that grand ideal which we call *justice*—and we consider how the justice ideal relates to the everyday practice of criminal justice in the United States today. To that end, in the three chapters that comprise this section, we will examine how and why laws are made. We will look at the wide array of interests which impinge upon the justice system, and we will examine closely the dichotomy which distinguishes citizens who are primarily concerned with individual rights from those who emphasize the need for individual responsibility and social accountability. In the pages that follow we will see how justice can mean protection from the power of the state to some, and vengeance to others. In this section we will also lay the groundwork for the rest of the text by painting a picture of crime in America today, suggesting possible causes for it, and showing how policies for dealing with crime have evolved.

As you read about the complex tapestry that is the practice of criminal justice in America today, you will see a system in flux, perhaps less sure of its values and purpose than at any time in its history. You may also catch the sense, however, that very soon a new and reborn institution of justice may emerge from the ferment that now exists. Whatever the final outcome, it can only be hoped that *justice,* as proffered by the American system of criminal justice, will be sufficient to hold our civilization together—and to allow it to prosper well into the twenty-first century.

Police

Courts

Corrections

CHAPTER 1

What Is Criminal Justice?

"Crime does more than expose the weakness in social relationships; it undermines the social order itself, by destroying the assumptions on which it is based."
—Charles E. Silberman[1]

"If you break the law, we're going to hold you accountable, and there will be tough consequences for your actions."
—North Carolina Governor Jim Hunt[2]

CHAPTER OUTLINE

- ◆ Justice and Criminal Justice
- ◆ American Criminal Justice: The System
- ◆ American Criminal Justice: The Process
- ◆ Due Process and Individual Rights
- ◆ Criminal Justice and Criminology

—Jeffry Scott, PictureQuest Vienna

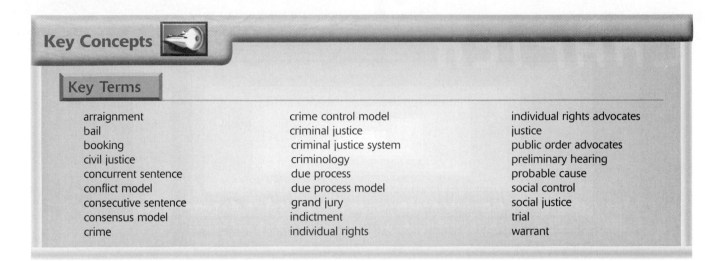

Key Concepts

Key Terms

arraignment	crime control model	individual rights advocates
bail	criminal justice	justice
booking	criminal justice system	public order advocates
civil justice	criminology	preliminary hearing
concurrent sentence	due process	probable cause
conflict model	due process model	social control
consecutive sentence	grand jury	social justice
consensus model	indictment	trial
crime	individual rights	warrant

Justice and Criminal Justice

Hear the author discuss this chapter at **cjtoday.com**

Most students who major in criminal justice seek to dedicate their professional careers to crime fighting. That was not true in the case of Benjamin Nathaniel Smith, a 21-year-old former criminal justice major at Indiana University in Bloomington. On Fourth of July weekend, 1999, Smith went on a 36-hour drive-by shooting spree that spanned the states of Illinois and Indiana. When it was over, two people were dead and many more injured. Smith's targets appear to have been Hispanics, blacks, Orientals, and Jews. Killed in the rampage were former Northwestern University basketball coach Ricky Byrdsong and Won-Joon Yoon, a South Korean doctoral student at Indiana University. Byrdsong, who was black, was gunned down as he walked with his children. Yoon was killed outside of Bloomington's Korean United Methodist Church. Eight other people, including six Orthodox Jews, were shot and wounded as a result of the shooting spree. Another nine people were shot at but not physically injured.[3]

Media reports claimed that Smith's one-man crime spree was related to his membership in a white supremacist group called the World Church of the Creator. Founded in 1973, the group is often mentioned as one of the most dangerous hate groups in the country. Its Web site, which was shut down shortly after Smith's shooting spree, exhorted its members to "gird for a total war against Jews and the rest of the goddamned mud races of the world." Church leader, 27-year-old Matt Hale, had been using the Web in what he called "Internet blitzkrieg" to promote the group's racist policies.

Crime

Conduct in violation of the criminal laws of a state, the federal government, or of a local jurisdiction, for which there is no legally acceptable justification or excuse.

Hate crime experts believe that Smith saw himself as a soldier in RAHOWA—the racial holy war movement that is driving members of some underground groups into committing a wide variety of hate-motivated crimes.[4] During his time at IU-Bloomington, Smith had become well known for his habit of littering the campus with racist leaflets and for discussing his racist views openly in class.[5]

Smith's shooting spree ended on the evening of July 4, 1999. As officers pursued him down a highway in southern Illinois, Smith apparently tried to kill himself—firing two shots into his body as he drove. Soon afterward his vehicle crashed into a tree. As officers surrounded the car and struggled with Smith, he managed to fire one more shot—this one into his own heart. Officers were able to positively identify their quarry when they saw the tattoo "Sabbath Breaker" on Smith's chest.

Another infamous crime, the Columbine High School massacre, in which 13 people died and 20 more were injured, also took place in 1999. The shootings, which happened on April 20, 1999, in Littleton, Colorado, were the work of 18-year-old Eric Harris and 17-year-old Dylan Klebold, both of whom were students at the school. After police arrived, the attackers killed themselves. As of this writing, the Columbine shooting still stands as the worst incident of student violence in U.S. history. See WebExtra! 1-1 at CJToday.com for multimedia coverage of the Columbine shooting.

Nathaniel Smith (top left) the hate-crime shooting spree killer, whose murderous 1999 rampage through Illinois and Indiana left two people dead and many others injured.
Chicago Police Department, AP/Wide World Photos.

Killed in the rampage were 26-year-old Won-Joon Yoon (top right), and former Northwestern University basketball coach, Ricky Byrdsong (bottom photo).
HO, AP/Wide World Photos and Fred Jewell, AP/Wide World Photos, respectively.

Half a year later, 47-year-old Larry Gene Ashbrook opened fire at a crowded Christian music concert at Wedgwood Baptist Church in Fort Worth, Texas, taking the lives of seven people, including four teenagers. Seven others were wounded before the gunman took his own life.[6]

Crimes like these—in which seemingly random violence unexpectedly claims the lives of well-meaning citizens going about their daily routines—have shaken American confidence in the criminal justice system, and have greatly enhanced the fear of crime that so many Americans have come to feel. Because of such crimes, a growing fear of crime persists—even amidst today's falling official crime rates. Such crimes also challenge long-cherished beliefs about **social control** in American society and call into question a number of basic values centered on the family, children, violence in the media, public safety, and social equality.

The Focus of This Book: Individual Rights and Public Order

This book, which is about the American system of criminal justice and the agencies and processes which constitute it, has an orientation which we think is especially valuable for studying criminal justice today. For many years the dominant philosophy in American criminal justice focused on guaranteeing the rights of criminal defendants while seeking to understand the root causes of crime and violence. During the last decade, however, a grow-

Social Control

The use of sanctions and rewards available through a group to influence and shape the behavior of individual members of that group. Social control is a primary concern of social groups and communities, and it is the interest that human groups hold in the exercise of social control that leads to the creation of both criminal and civil statutes.

A visitor pauses at a cross bearing the name of 17-year-old Dylan Klebold. The cross was one of many erected at a makeshift memorial near Littleton, Colorado, after Klebold and 18-year-old Eric Harris carried out a planned attack on their classmates and teachers at Columbine High School in 1999. The attack left 13 dead and 20 others injured. The crosses for Klebold and Harris were removed by irate survivors not long after this picture was taken.
Kevin Moloney, Liaison Agency, Inc.

ing conservative emphasis has concerned itself with the interests of an ordered society and with the rights of crime victims. This newly popular perspective has called into question some of the fundamental premises upon which the American system of criminal justice rests. In attempting to balance both points of view, the materials presented in this text are built around the following theme:

> There is increasing recognition in contemporary society of the need to balance (1) the respect accorded the rights of individuals faced with criminal prosecution against (2) the valid interests of society in preventing future crimes and in reducing the harm caused by criminal activity. While the personal freedoms guaranteed to criminal suspects by the Constitution, as interpreted by the U.S. Supreme Court, must be closely guarded, so, too, the urgent social needs of local communities for controlling unacceptable behavior and protecting law-abiding citizens from harm must be recognized. Still to be adequately addressed are the needs and interests of victims and the fear of crime now so prevalent in the minds of many law-abiding citizens.

Figure 1-1 represents our theme diagrammatically. Most people today who intelligently consider the criminal justice system assume either one or the other of these two perspectives. We shall refer to those who seek to protect personal freedoms and civil rights within the criminal justice process as **individual rights advocates.** Those who suggest that under certain circumstances involving criminal threats to public safety, the interests of society (especially crime control) should take precedence over individual rights, will be called **public order advocates.** In this book we seek to look at ways that the individual rights and the public order perspectives can be balanced to serve both sets of needs.

Both points of view have their roots in the values which formed our nation. However, the past 30 years have been especially important in clarifying the differences between the two points of view. The 1960s and 1970s saw a burgeoning concern with the rights of ethnic minorities, women, the physically and mentally challenged, and many other groups. The civil rights movement of the period emphasized equality of opportunity and respect for individuals regardless of race, color, creed, or personal attributes. As new laws were passed and suits filed, court involvement in the movement grew. Soon a plethora of hard-won individual rights and prerogatives, based upon the U.S. Constitution and the Bill of Rights, were recognized and guaranteed. By the 1980s the civil rights movement had profoundly affected all areas of social life—from education through employment to the activities of the criminal justice system.

Individual Rights Advocates

Those who seek to protect personal freedoms within the process of criminal justice.

Public Order Advocates

Those who suggest that, under certain circumstances involving a criminal threat to public safety, the interests of society should take precedence over individual rights.

FIGURE 1-1 ■ *The theme of this book: balancing the concern for individual rights with the need for public order through the administration of criminal justice.*

This emphasis on **individual rights** was accompanied by a dramatic increase in criminal activity. "Traditional" crimes, such as murder, rape, and assault, as reported by the FBI, increased astronomically during the 1970s and into the 1980s. Many theories were advanced to explain this virtual explosion of observed criminality. A few doubted the accuracy of "official" accounts, claiming that any actual rise in crime was much less than that portrayed in the reports. Some analysts of American culture, however, suggested that increased criminality was the result of newfound freedoms which combined with the long-pent-up hostilities of the socially and economically deprived to produce social disorganization.

By the mid-1980s, popular perceptions identified one particularly insidious form of criminal activity—the dramatic increase in the sale and use of illicit drugs—as a threat to the very fabric of American society. Cocaine, in particular, and later, laboratory-processed "crack," had spread to every corner of America. The country's borders were inundated with smugglers intent on reaping quick fortunes. Large cities became havens for drug gangs, and many inner-city areas were all but abandoned to highly armed and well-financed racketeers. Some famous personalities succumbed to the allure of drugs, and athletic teams and sporting events became focal points for drug busts. Like wildfire, drugs soon spread to younger users. Even small-town elementary schools found themselves facing the specter of campus drug dealing and associated violence.

Worse still were the seemingly ineffective governmental measures intended to stem the drug tide. Drug peddlers, because of the huge reserves of money available to them, were often able to escape prosecution or wrangle plea bargains to avoid imprisonment. Media coverage of such "miscarriages of justice" became epidemic and public anger grew.

By the close of the 1980s, neighborhoods and towns felt themselves fighting for their communal lives. City businesses faced dramatic declines in property values, and residents wrestled with the eroding quality of life. Huge rents had been torn in the national social fabric. The American way of life, long taken for granted, was under the gun. Traditional values appeared in danger of going up in smoke along with the crack now being smoked openly in some parks and resorts. Looking for a way to stem the tide, many took up the call for "law and order." In response, then-President Reagan initiated a "War on Drugs" and created a "drug czar" cabinet-level post to coordinate the war. Careful thought was given at the highest levels to using the military to patrol the sea lanes and air corridors through which many of the illegal drugs entered the country. President Bush, who followed President Reagan into office, quickly embraced and expanded the government's antidrug efforts.

The 1990s began with the arrest of serial murderer Jeffrey Dahmer (in 1991) and the shocking details of his crimes which later became public. Dahmer, who killed as many as 15 young men in sexually motivated encounters, cannibalized some of his victims and kept the body parts of others in his refrigerator. Dahmer's crimes, along with those of other serial killers, are discussed in more detail in Chapter 2.

Individual Rights

Those rights guaranteed to all members of American society by the U.S. Constitution (especially as found in the first 10 amendments to the Constitution, known as the Bill of Rights). These rights are especially important to criminal defendants facing formal processing by the criminal justice system.

In 1992, the videotaped beating of Rodney King, a black motorist, at the hands of Los Angeles–area police officers, splashed across TV screens throughout the country and shifted the public's focus onto issues of police brutality and the effective management of law enforcement personnel. As the King incident seemed to show, when financially impoverished members of "underrepresented groups" come face to face with agents of the American criminal justice system, something less than justice may be the result. Although initially acquitted by a California jury—which contained no black members—two of the officers who beat King were convicted in a 1993 federal courtroom of violating his civil rights.[7] The incident is described in more detail in Chapter 5.

The year 1993 saw an especially violent encounter in Waco, Texas, among agents of the Bureau of Alcohol, Tobacco, and Firearms, the FBI, and members of cult leader David Koresh's Branch Davidian. The fray, which began when ATF agents assaulted Koresh's fortresslike compound, leaving four agents and six cultists dead, ended 51 days later with the fiery deaths of Koresh and 71 of his followers. Many of them were children. The assault on Koresh's compound led to a congressional investigation and charges that the ATF and FBI had been ill-prepared to deal successfully with large-scale domestic resistance and had reacted more out of alarm and frustration than wisdom. Janet Reno, attorney general under President Clinton, refused to blame agents for misjudging Koresh's intentions, although 11 Davidians were later acquitted of charges that they murdered the agents.

By the mid-1990s, however, a strong shift away from the claimed misdeeds of the criminal justice system began, and a newfound emphasis on individual accountability began to blossom among an American public fed up with crime and fearful of their own victimization. Growing calls for enhanced responsibility began to quickly replace the previous emphasis on individual rights. As a juggernaut of conservative opinion made itself felt on the political scene, Texas Senator Phil Gramm observed that the public wants to "grab violent criminals by the throat, put them in prison [and] stop building prisons like Holiday Inns."[8]

It was probably the public's perception of growing crime rates, coupled with a belief that offenders frequently went unpunished or that many received only judicial slaps on the wrists, that led to the burgeoning emphasis on responsibility and punishment. However, a few spectacular crimes which received widespread coverage in the news media heightened the public's sense that crime in the United States was out of hand and that new measures were needed to combat it. In 1993, for example, James Jordan, father of Chicago Bulls' basketball superstar Michael Jordan, was killed in a cold-blooded robbery by two young men with long criminal records. Jordan's death, which seemed the result of a chance encounter, helped rivet the nation's attention on what appeared to be the increasing frequency of random and senseless violence.

In that same year, a powerful bomb ripped apart the basement of one of the twin World Trade Center buildings in New York City. The explosion, which killed five and opened a 100-foot crater through four sublevels of concrete, displaced 50,000 workers, including employees at the commodities exchanges that handle billions of dollars worth of trade in oil, gold, coffee, and sugar. The product of terrorists with foreign links, the bombing highlighted the susceptibility of the American infrastructure to terrorist activity.[9]

Similarly, in 1993 the heart-wrenching story of Polly Klaas splashed across the national media. Twelve-year-old Polly was kidnapped from a slumber party at her home while her mother and little sister slept in the next room. Two other girls were left bound and gagged after a bearded stranger broke into the Klaas home in Petaluma, California. Despite efforts by hundreds of uniformed officers and 4,000 volunteers, attempts to find the girl proved fruitless. Nine weeks later, just before Christmas, an ex-con named Richard Allen Davis was arrested and charged with Polly's murder. Investigators found that Davis's life read like a litany of criminal activity and that Polly's death was due at least partially to failure of the criminal justice system to keep a dangerous Davis behind bars. Three years later, in 1996, Davis was convicted of Polly's murder and sentenced to death.

In 1994, the attention of the nation was riveted on proceedings in the Susan Smith case. Smith, a South Carolina mother, confessed to drowning her two young boys (ages one and three at the time) by strapping them into child-safety seats and rolling the family station wagon off a pier and into a lake. Smith, who appears to have been motivated by the demands of an extramarital love affair, had originally claimed a black man carjacked her vehicle with the boys still inside. 1994 was also the year in which seven-year-old Megan Kanka was brutally murdered by previously convicted sex offender Jesse K. Timmendequas.

Senseless violence linked to racial hatred stunned the nation during the 1995 trial of Colin Ferguson. Ferguson, who was eventually convicted of killing six passengers and wounding 19 others during what prosecutors claimed was a racially motivated shooting rampage on a Long Island Rail Road commuter train in 1993, maintained his innocence throughout the trial, despite the fact he was identified by more than a dozen eyewitnesses, including some he had shot. "This is a case of stereotyped victimization of a black man and subsequent conspiracy to destroy him—nothing more," Ferguson told the jury. Many were offended by the fact that Ferguson declared himself the victim when the real victims were either dead or seriously injured. Famed defense attorney William Kunstler suggested that Ferguson plead not guilty by reason of insanity, which, Kunstler argued, had been caused by "black rage" at racial injustice in America. Instead, Ferguson claimed that he had dozed off on the train and that a white man had stolen his gun and shot the passengers. Public backlash at the increasing willingness of defense attorneys to use an "offender as victim" defense contributed to growing disgust with what many saw as a hamstrung and ineffective criminal justice system.

In 1995, the double-murder trial of former football superstar and media personality O. J. Simpson received much national exposure, with daily reports on the trial appearing on television and in newspapers throughout the country. Simpson was acquitted of the brutal murders of his ex-wife, Nicole, and her associate, Ronald Goldman, after hiring a team of lawyers whom some referred to as "the million-dollar defense"—an action which many saw as akin to buying justice. In a 1997 civil trial, however, a California jury found Simpson liable for the death of Goldman and the "battery" of his former wife, and he was ordered to pay $33.5 million in damages.

Perhaps no one criminal incident gripped the psyche of the American people, and was to later galvanize the policy-making efforts of legislators, more than the 1995 bombing of the Alfred P. Murrah Federal Building in Oklahoma City by right-wing extremists. One hundred

"The horrific events in Oklahoma City . . . show the high price we pay for our liberties."

—Senator Orrin Hatch, *Chairman of the Senate Judiciary Committee, commenting on the 1995 bombing of the Alfred P. Murrah Federal Building*

Two women embrace at a makeshift memorial at the Wedgwood Baptist Church in Fort Worth, Texas. In 1999 a gunman killed seven people attending a Christian music festival at the church.
J. Pat Carter, AP/Wide World Photos.

sixty-eight people died in the bombing, 19 of them children. Hundreds more were wounded and millions of dollars worth of property damage occurred. The bombing had the added impact of demonstrating just how vulnerable the United States is to terrorist assault. That attack, and a bombing during the 1996 Atlanta Olympics which killed one person and injured 111, caused many Americans to realize that the very freedoms which allow the United States to serve as a model of democracy to the rest of the world make it possible for terrorist or terrorist-affiliated groups to operate within the country relatively unencumbered.

The strangulation murder of six-year-old JonBenet Ramsey, the young "beauty queen" killed at Christmastime 1996 in her family's Boulder, Colorado, home added to the national sense that no one is safe. (See WebExtra! 1-2 at CJToday.com for more information.) In 1997, the roadside murder of 27-year-old Ennis Cosby, son of well-known entertainer Bill Cosby, heightened the public's fear of random violence. A 1997 killing spree attributed to Andrew Cunanan, which ended in his suicide (and which claimed the life of world-renowned fashion designer Gianni Versace and five other men), galvanized the nation as the public participated in a media-led hunt for the alleged killer.

In 1998, 21-year-old Matthew Shepard, a shy and slightly built University of Wyoming college student was savagely beaten to death by two men, Aaron James McKinney and Russell Arthur Henderson—both of whom were also 21.[10] Shepard, who was gay, had been lured from a bar to a remote location outside of town. He suffered 18 blows to the head and had been pistol whipped with a .357-caliber Magnum revolver. Shepard's body had been tied so tightly to a barbed wire fence that sheriff's deputies had trouble cutting it free. The blood on Shepard's face had been partially washed away by tears—a sign that he had lived for some time after the beating. The killing outraged the gay community and helped focus the nation's attention on hate crimes.

The Columbine High School shooting and the Wedgwood Baptist Church shootings in Ft. Worth, Texas, mentioned at the start of this chapter, provided a stunningly violent backdrop to 1999. A check of local or national newspapers, TV news show, or news-oriented Web sites will show that crimes, especially shocking, violent, personal, and seemingly random, crimes continue unabated.

Violent crimes, punctuated with seemingly random cruelty, have changed the mood of the American public or, perhaps more accurately, have accelerated what was an already changing mood. A growing national frustration with the apparent inability of our society and its justice system to prevent crimes and to consistently hold offenders who are identified and then arrested to heartfelt standards of right and wrong has led to increased conservatism in the public policy arena. That conservative tendency, which continues to thrive today, was already in place by the time of the 1994 congressional elections, where get-tough-on-crime

"When you know both the accuser and the accused, as we so often do, the conflict between civil rights and victims' rights is seldom completely black or white. And it is the gray areas in between that make the debate so difficult."

—*Columnist Vicki Williams,* writing on crime in a small American town

"People expect both safety and justice and do not want to sacrifice one for the other."

—*Christopher Stone,* President and Director, the Vera Institute of Justice

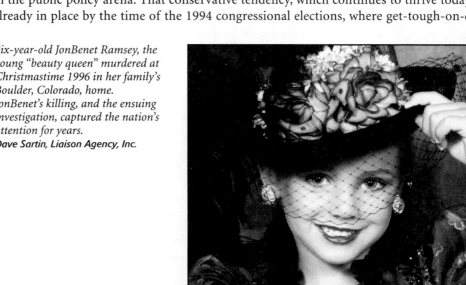

Six-year-old JonBenet Ramsey, the young "beauty queen" murdered at Christmastime 1996 in her family's Boulder, Colorado, home. JonBenet's killing, and the ensuing investigation, captured the nation's attention for years.
Dave Sartin, Liaison Agency, Inc.

policies won the day. Since that time, numerous other public officials have joined the get-tough bandwagon. Many have stopped asking what society can do to protect individuals accused of crimes and demand to know instead how offenders can better be held accountable for violations of the criminal law. As we begin the twenty-first century, public perspectives have largely shifted away from seeing the criminal as an unfortunate victim of poor social and personal circumstances, to seeing the criminal as a dangerous social predator. Learn more about the most infamous crimes of the last century at WebExtra! 1-3.

Perspectives on Criminal Justice and the Theme of This Book

While conservative sentiments very much influence today's public policy, it is important to recognize that national feelings, however strong, have historically been somewhat akin to the swings of a pendulum. Hence, although the emphasis on individual rights, which rose to ascendancy a few decades ago, now appears to have been eclipsed by calls for social and individual responsibility, the tension between the two perspectives still forms the basis for most policy-making activity in the criminal justice arena. Rights advocates continue to carry on the fight for an expansion of civil and criminal rights, seeing both as necessary to an equitable and just social order. The treatment of the accused, they argue, mirrors basic cultural values. The purpose of any civilized society, they claim, should be to secure rights and freedoms for each of its citizens—including the criminally accused. Rights advocates fear unnecessarily restrictive government action and view it as an assault upon basic human dignity and individual liberty. In defense of their principles, criminal rights activists tend to recognize that it is sometimes necessary to sacrifice some degree of public safety and predictability in order to guarantee basic freedoms. Hence, rights advocates are content with a justice system which limits police powers and which holds justice agencies accountable to the highest evidentiary standards. An example of the kind of criminal justice outcome feared by individual rights advocates is the case of James Richardson, who served 21 years in a Florida prison for a crime he did not commit.[11] Following perjured testimony, Richardson was convicted in 1968 of the poisoning deaths of his seven children. He was released many years later after a babysitter confessed to poisoning the children's last meal because of personal jealousies. The criminal rights perspective holds that it is necessary to allow some guilty people to go free in order to reduce the likelihood of convicting the innocent.

In the present conservative environment, however, calls for system accountability are often tempered with new demands to unfetter the criminal justice system in order to make arrests easier and punishments swift and harsh. Advocates of law and order, wanting ever greater police powers, have mounted an effective drive to abandon some of the gains made in support of the rights of criminal defendants during the civil rights era. Citing high rates of recidivism, uncertain punishments, and an inefficient courtroom maze, they claim that the criminal justice system has coddled offenders and encouraged continued law violation. Society, they say, if it is to survive, can no longer afford to accord too many rights to the individual or place the interests of any one person over that of the group.

As we begin the twenty-first century, the trick, it seems, is to balance individual rights and personal freedoms with social responsibility and respect for authority. At a conference sponsored by the *New York Post,* New York City Mayor Rudolph W. Giuliani identified the tension between personal freedoms and individual responsibilities as the crux of the crime problem facing his city and the nation. We mistakenly look to government and elected officials, Giuliani said, to assume responsibility for solving the problem of crime when, instead, it is each individual citizen who must become accountable for fixing what is wrong with our society. In the mayor's words, "We only see the oppressive side of authority. . . . What we don't see is that freedom is not a concept in which people can do anything they want, be anything they can be. Freedom is about authority. Freedom is about the willingness of every single human being to cede to lawful authority a great deal of discretion about what you do."

This text has two basic purposes: (1) to describe in detail the criminal justice system, while (2) helping students develop an appreciation for the delicacy of the balancing act now facing it. The question for the future will be how to ensure the existence of, and effectively

"I hope somewhere down the road I will be forgotten . . . that I will just be able to live the life I had before jail, a quiet life unknown to the world, and I'll be satisfied with that."

—*Long Island shooter* Colin Ferguson's comment before sentencing

"It is commonly assumed that these three components—law enforcement (police, sheriffs, marshals), the judicial process (judges, prosecutors, defense lawyers) and corrections (prison officials, probation and parole officers)—add up to a "system" of criminal justice. A system implies some unity of purpose and organized interrelationship among component parts. In the typical American city and state, and under federal jurisdiction as well, no such relationship exists. There is, instead, a reasonably well-defined criminal *process,* a continuum through which each accused offender may pass: from the hands of the police, to the jurisdiction of the courts, behind the walls of a prison, then back onto the street. The inefficiency, fall-out, and failure of purpose during this process is notorious."

—*National Commission* on the Causes and Prevention of Violence

manage, a justice system which is as fair to the individual as it is supportive of the needs of society. Is "justice for all" a reasonable expectation of today's system of criminal justice? As this book will show, the question is complicated by the fact that individual interests and social needs frequently diverge, while at other times they parallel one another.

Social Justice

Justice

The principle of fairness; the ideal of moral equity.

Criminal Justice

The criminal law, the law of criminal procedure, and that array of procedures and activities having to do with the enforcement of the criminal law. Criminal justice cannot be separated from social justice because the kind of justice enacted in our nation's criminal courts is a reflection of basic American understandings of right and wrong.

Civil Justice

The civil law, the law of civil procedure, and that array of procedures and activities having to do with private rights and remedies sought by civil action. Civil justice cannot be separated from social justice because the kind of justice enacted in our nation's civil courts is a reflection of basic American understandings of right and wrong.

Social Justice

An ideal which embraces all aspects of civilized life and which is linked to fundamental notions of fairness and to cultural beliefs about right and wrong.

The well-known British philosopher and statesman Benjamin Disraeli (1804–1881) once defined **justice** as "truth in action." One popular dictionary definition of *justice* says that it is "the principle of moral rightness, or conformity to truth."[12]

Of special concern to anyone seeking to enact justice are **criminal justice** and **civil justice**—both of which are aspects of a wider form of equity termed **social justice**. Social justice is a concept that embraces all aspects of civilized life. It is linked to notions of fairness and to cultural beliefs about right and wrong. Questions of social justice can arise about relationships between individuals and between parties (such as corporations and agencies of government), between the rich and the poor, between the sexes, between ethnic groups and minorities, and about social linkages of all sorts. In the abstract, the concept of social justice embodies the highest personal and cultural ideals.

Civil justice, the first subcomponent of social justice, concerns itself with fairness in relationships between citizens, government agencies, and businesses in private matters—such as those involving contractual obligations, business dealings, hiring, equality of treatment, and so on. Criminal justice, in its broadest sense, refers to those aspects of social justice which concern violations of the criminal law. As mentioned earlier, community interests in the criminal justice sphere demand the apprehension and punishment of law violators. At the same time, criminal justice ideals extend to the protection of the innocent, the fair treatment of offenders, and fair play by the agencies of law enforcement, including courts and correctional institutions. Criminal justice, ideally speaking, is "truth in action" within the process that we call "the administration of justice." It is, therefore, vital to remember that *justice,* in the truest and most satisfying sense of the word, is the ultimate goal of criminal justice—and of the day-to-day practices and challenges which characterize the American criminal justice system.

Reality, unfortunately, typically falls short of the ideal and is severely complicated by the fact that justice seems to wear different guises when viewed from diverse social vantage points. To many people, the criminal justice system and criminal justice agencies often seem biased in favor of the powerful. The laws they enforce seem to emanate more from well-financed, organized, and vocal interest groups than they do from any idealized sense of social justice. As a consequence, disenfranchised groups, those who do not feel as though they share in the political and economic power of society, are often wary of the agencies of justice, seeing them more as enemies than as benefactors.

On the other hand, justice practitioners, including police officers, prosecutors, judges, and correctional officials, frequently complain of unfair criticism of their efforts to uphold the law. The "realities" of law enforcement, they say, and of justice itself, are often overlooked by critics of the system who have little experience in dealing with offenders and victims. We must recognize, practitioners often tell us, that those accused of violating the criminal law face an elaborate process built around numerous legislative, administrative, and organizational concerns. Viewed realistically, the criminal justice process, while it can be fine-tuned in order to take into consideration the interests of ever wider numbers of people, rarely pleases everyone. The outcome of the criminal justice process in any particular case is a social product and, like any product which is the result of group effort, it must inevitably be a patchwork quilt of human emotions, reasoning, and concerns.

Whichever side we choose in the ongoing debate over the nature and quality of criminal justice in America,[13] it is vital that we recognize the plethora of pragmatic issues involved in the administration of justice, while also keeping a clear focus on the justice ideal. Was justice done, for example, in the criminal trial of O. J. Simpson or in the trials of the Los Angeles police officers who beat Rodney King? While answers to such questions may reveal a great deal about the American criminal justice system, they also have much to say about the perspective of those who provide them.

American Criminal Justice: The System

The Consensus Model

So far we have described the agencies of law enforcement, the courts, and corrections as a **system of criminal justice.**[14] Those who speak of a system of criminal justice usually define it as consisting of the agencies of police, courts, and corrections. Each of these agencies can, in turn, be described in terms of their subsystems. Corrections, for example, includes jails, prisons, community-based treatment programs such as halfway houses, and programs for probation and parole. Each sub-area contains still more components. Prisons, for example, can be described in terms of custody levels, inmate programs, health care, security procedures, and so on. Some prisons operate as "boot camp" facilities, designed to shock offenders into quick rehabilitation, while others are long-term confinement facilities designed for the most hard-core criminals who are likely to return to crime quickly if released. Students of corrections also study the process of sentencing, through which an offender's fate is decided by the justice system, and examine the role of jails in holding prisoners prior to conviction and sentencing.

The systems model of criminal justice is characterized primarily by its assumption that the various parts of the justice system work together by design in order to achieve the wider purpose we have been calling *justice.* Hence, the systems perspective on criminal justice generally encompasses a larger point of view called the **consensus model.** The consensus model assumes that all the component parts of the criminal justice system strive toward a common goal and that the movement of cases and people through the system is smooth due to cooperation between the various components of the system.

The systems model of criminal justice, however, is more an analytical tool than it is a reality. Any analytical model, be it in the so-called hard sciences or in the social sciences, is simply a convention chosen for its explanatory power. By explaining the actions of criminal justice officials (such as arrest, prosecution, sentencing, etc.) as though they are systematically related, we are able to envision a fairly smooth and predictable process (which is described in more detail later in this chapter). The advantage we gain from this convention is a reduction in complexity, which allows us to describe the totality of criminal justice at a conceptually manageable level.

The systems model has been criticized for implying a greater level of organization and cooperation among the various agencies of justice than actually exists. The word *system* calls to mind a near-perfect form of social organization. The modern mind associates the idea of a system with machinelike precision in which wasted effort, redundancy, and conflicting actions are quickly abandoned and their causes repaired. The justice system has nowhere near this level of perfection and the systems model is admittedly an oversimplification which is primarily useful for analytical purposes. Conflicts among and within agencies are rife; immediate goals are often not shared by individual actors in the system; and the system may move in different directions depending upon political currents, informal arrangements, and personal discretionary decisions.

The Conflict Model

The **conflict model** provides another approach to the study of American criminal justice. The conflict model says that criminal justice agency interests tend to make actors within the system self-serving. Pressures for success, promotion, pay increases, and general accountability, according to this model, fragment the efforts of the system as a whole, leading to a criminal justice *non*system.[15]

Jerome Skolnick's classic study of clearance rates provides support for the idea of a criminal justice nonsystem.[16] *Clearance rates* are a measure of crimes solved by the police. The more crimes the police can show they have solved, the happier is the public they serve.

Skolnick discovered an instance in which an individual burglar was caught "red-handed" during the commission of a burglary. After his arrest, the police suggested that he should confess to many unsolved burglaries which they knew he had not committed. In effect they

---

Criminal Justice System

The aggregate of all operating and administrative or technical support agencies that perform criminal justice functions. The basic divisions of the operational aspects of criminal justice are law enforcement, courts, and corrections.

Consensus Model

A perspective on the study of criminal justice which assumes that the system's subcomponents work together harmoniously to achieve that social product we call justice.

"Criminal justice cannot be achieved in the absence of social justice...."

—*Struggle for Justice,* American Friends' Service Committee

Conflict Model

A perspective on the study of criminal justice which assumes that the system's subcomponents function primarily to serve their own interests. According to this theoretical framework, justice is more a product of conflicts among agencies within the system than it is the result of cooperation among component agencies.

Is the Criminal Justice System Racist?

A few years ago, Professor Lani Guinier of the University of Pennsylvania School of Law was interviewed on *Think Tank,* a public television show. Guinier was asked by Ben Wattenberg, the program's moderator, "When we talk about crime, crime, crime, are we really using a code for black, black, black?" Guinier responded this way: "To a great extent, yes, and I think that's a problem, not because we shouldn't deal with the disproportionate number of crimes that young black men may be committing, but because if we can't talk about race, then when we talk about crime, we're really talking about other things, and it means that we're not being honest in terms of acknowledging what the problem is and then trying to deal with it. . . ."[1]

Crimes, of course, are committed by individuals of all races. The link between crime—especially violent, street, and predatory crimes—and race, however, shows a pattern that is striking in terms of its ethnic dimensions. In many crime categories, arrests of black offenders equal or exceed arrests of whites. In any given year arrests of black persons account for more than 50 percent of all arrests for violent crimes. Blacks, however, comprise only 12 percent of the U.S. population, and when *rates* (which are based upon the relative proportion of racial groups) are examined, the statistics are even more striking. The murder *rate* among blacks, for example, is 10 times that of whites. Similar rate comparisons, when calculated for other violent crimes, show that far more blacks than whites are involved in other street crimes, such as assault, burglary, and robbery. Related studies show that 30 percent of all the young black men in America are under correctional supervision on any given *day*—far more than members of any other race in the country.

The real question for anyone interested in the justice system is how to explain such huge racial disparities. Some authors maintain that racial differences in arrest and in rates of imprisonment are due to the differential treatment of blacks at the hands of a discriminatory criminal justice system. Marvin D. Free, Jr.,[2] for example, says that the fact that blacks are *underrepresented* as criminal justice professionals results in their being *overrepresented* in arrest and confinement statistics. Some police officers, says Free, may be more prone to arrest blacks than whites, may frequently arrest blacks without sufficient evidence to support criminal charges, and may overcharge in criminal cases involving black defendants—leading to unfair and misleading statistical tabulations which depict blacks as responsible for a greater proportion of crime than is, in fact, the case.

Other writers disagree. In *The Myth of a Racist Criminal Justice System,*[3] for example, William Wilbanks claims that while the practice of American criminal justice may have been significantly racist in the past, and while some vestiges of racism may indeed remain, the system is today by-and-large objective in its processing of criminal defendants. Using statistical data, Wilbanks shows that "[a]t every point from arrest to parole there is little or no evidence of an overall racial effect, in that percentage outcomes for blacks and whites are not very different."[4] Wilbanks claims to have reviewed "all the available studies that have examined the possible existence of racial discrimination from arrest to parole." In essence, he says, "this examination of the available evidence indicates that support for the 'discrimination thesis' is sparse, inconsistent, and frequently contradictory."

Wilbanks is careful to counter arguments advanced by those who continue to suggest the system is racist. He writes, for example, ". . . perhaps the black/white gap at arrest is a product of racial bias by the police in that the police are more likely to select and arrest black than white offenders. The best evidence on this question comes from the National Crime Survey which interviews 130,000 Americans each year about crime victimization. . . . The percent of offenders described by victims as being black is generally consistent with the percent of offenders who are black according to arrest figures."

A fundamental critique of Wilbanks' thesis comes from Coramae Richey Mann,[5] who says that his overreliance on quantitative or statistical data fails to capture the reality of racial discrimination within the justice system. White victims, says Mann, tend to overreport being victimized by black offenders because they often misperceive Hispanic and other minority offenders as black. Similarly, says Mann, black victims are sometimes reluctant to report victimization—especially at the hands of whites. Moreover, says Mann, statistics on specific crimes, such as rape, may include false accusations by white women in order to hide their involvement with black lovers. And finally, says Mann, a greater integration of black neighborhoods (in the sense that whites are less reluctant to enter black neighborhoods than blacks are to enter white neighborhoods) may result in a disproportionate but misleading number of reports by white victims.

Mann's arguments are discounted by those who point out that the statistics appear to be overwhelming. *If* they are accurate, then another question emerges: Why do blacks commit more crimes? Wilbanks says, "The assertion that the criminal justice system is not racist does not address the reasons why blacks appear to offend at higher rates than whites before coming into contact with the criminal justice system. . . . It may be," he suggests, "that racial discrimination in American society has been responsible for conditions (for example, discrimination in employ-

(Continued)

Theory Into Practice

Is the Criminal Justice System Racist?

ment, housing, and education) that lead to higher rates of offending by blacks."

Marvin Free, Jr., suggests that blacks are still systematically denied equal access to societal resources which would allow for full participation in American society—resulting in a higher rate of law violation. In a recent work that considers such issues in great detail, John Hagan and Ruth D. Peterson acknowledge the reality of higher crime rates among ethnic minorities and attribute them to (1) concentrated poverty, (2) joblessness, (3) family disruption, and (4) racial segregation.[6]

The question of *actual* fairness (of the justice system) can be quite different from one of *perceived* fairness. As University of Maryland Professor Kathryn K. Russell[7] points out, "Study after study has shown that blacks and whites hold contrary views on the fairness of the criminal justice system's operation; blacks tend to be more cautious in their praise and frequently view the system as unfair and racially biased; by contrast whites have a favorable impression of the justice system. . . . The point is not that whites are completely satisfied with the justice system, but rather that, relative to blacks, they have faith in the system." One reason for such differences may be that blacks are more likely to be victims of police harassment and brutality or may know someone who has been. Even if blacks do engage in more criminal activity than whites, says one author,[8] higher

rates of offending may be due, at least in part, to their perception that members of their group have historically been treated unfairly by agents of social control—resulting in anger and defiance which express themselves in criminal activity. From this vantage point, crime—at least crimes committed by minority group members—becomes a kind of protest against a system which is perceived as fundamentally unfair.

According to Russell, inequities in the existing system may propel blacks into crime and combine with stereotypical images in the popular media to perpetuate what she calls a *criminalblackman* myth. The *criminalblackman* myth, says Russell, is a stereotypical portrayal of black men as *inherently* more sinister, evil, and dangerous than their white counterparts. The myth of the *criminalblackman*, adds Russell, is self-perpetuating—resulting in continued frustration, more crime, and growing alienation among black Americans.

? QUESTIONS FOR DISCUSSION

1. What does Guinier mean when she says that if we can't talk about race, then we can't talk about crime? Is there a reluctance in our society to deal squarely with issues of race and crime? If so, why?
2. Do you think that the American criminal justice system is discriminatory? Why or why not?

3. If you think the justice system is discriminatory, what would you do to change it?
4. What is the *criminalblackman* myth? Do you think that such a myth exists in American culture? What basis, if any, does it have in reality?

[1]*"For the Record,"* Washington Post *wire services, March 3, 1994.*

[2]*Marvin D. Free, Jr.,* African-Americans and the Criminal Justice System *(New York: Garland, 1996).*

[3]*William Wilbanks,* The Myth of a Racist Criminal Justice System *(Monterey, CA: Brooks/Cole, 1987).*

[4]*William Wilbanks, "The Myth of a Racist Criminal Justice System,"* Criminal Justice Research Bulletin, *vol. 3, no. 5 (Huntsville, TX: Sam Houston State University, 1987), p. 2.*

[5]*Coramae Richey Mann, "The Reality of a Racist Criminal Justice System," in Barry W. Hancock and Paul M. Sharp,* Criminal Justice in America: Theory, Practice, and Policy *(Upper Saddle River, NJ: Prentice Hall, 1996), pp. 51–59.*

[6]*John Hagan and Ruth D. Peterson,* Crime and Inequality *(Stanford, CA: Stanford University Press, 1995).*

[7]*Katheryn K. Russell, "The Racial Hoax as Crime: The Law as Affirmation,"* Indiana Law Journal, *vol. 71 (1996), pp. 593–621.*

[8]*Thomas J. Bernard, "Angry Aggression Among the 'Truly Disadvantaged,'"* Criminology, *vol. 28, no. 1 (1990), pp. 73–96.*

said, "Help us out, and we will try to help you out!" The burglar did confess—to over 400 other burglaries. Following the confession, the police were satisfied because they could say they had "solved" many burglaries, and the suspect was pleased as well because the police had agreed to speak on his behalf before the judge.

Both models have something to tell us. Agencies of justice with a diversity of functions (police, courts, and corrections) and at all levels (federal, state, and local) are linked closely enough for the term *system* to be meaningfully applied to them. On the other hand, the very size of the criminal justice undertaking makes effective cooperation between component agencies difficult. The police, for example, may have an interest in seeing offenders put behind bars. Prison officials, on the other hand, may be working with extremely overcrowded facilities. They may desire to see early release programs for certain categories of offenders, such as those who are judged to be nonviolent. Who wins out in the long run could be just a matter of internal politics. Everyone should be concerned, however; when the goal of justice is impacted, and sometimes even sacrificed, because of conflicts within the system.

American Criminal Justice: The Process

Structurally, as we have discussed, the criminal justice system can be described in terms of its component agencies: police, courts, and corrections. Functionally, the components of the system may work together well or they may be in conflict. Whether system or nonsystem, however, the agencies of criminal justice must process cases which come before them. An analysis of case processing within the system provides both a useful guide to this book and a road map to the criminal justice system itself. Beginning with the investigation of reported crimes, Figure 1-2 illustrates the processing of a criminal case through the federal justice system.

Investigation and Arrest

The modern justice process begins with investigation. When a crime has been committed, it is often discovered and reported to the police. On occasion, a police officer on routine patrol discovers the crime while it is still in progress. Evidence will be gathered on the scene when possible, and a follow-up investigation will attempt to reconstruct the likely sequence of activities. A few offenders are arrested at the scene of the crime, while some are apprehended only after an extensive investigation. In such cases, arrest **warrants** issued by magistrates or other judges provide the legal basis for an apprehension by police.

An arrest involves taking a person into custody and limiting his or her freedom. Arrest is a serious step in the process of justice and involves a discretionary decision made by the police seeking to bring criminal sanctions to bear. Most arrests are made peacefully, but some involve force when the suspect tries to resist. Only about 50 percent of all persons arrested are eventually convicted, and of those, only about 25 percent are sentenced to a year or more in prison.

During arrest and prior to questioning, defendants are usually advised of their constitutional rights as enumerated in the famous Supreme Court decision of *Miranda* v. *Arizona*.[17] Defendants are told the following:

> (1) "You have the right to remain silent." (2) "Anything you say can and will be used against you in court." (3) "You have the right to talk to a lawyer for advice before we ask you any questions, and to have a lawyer with you during questioning." (4) "If you cannot afford a lawyer, one will be appointed for you before any questioning if you wish." (5) "If you decide to answer questions now without a lawyer present, you will still have the right to stop answering at any time. You also have the right to stop answering at any time and may talk with a lawyer before deciding to speak again." (6) "Do you wish to talk or not?" and (7) "Do you want a lawyer?"[18]

It is important to realize that although popular television programs almost always show a rights advisement at the time of arrest, the *Miranda* decision only requires police personnel to advise a person of his or her rights prior to questioning. An arrest without questioning can occur in the absence of any warning. When an officer interrupts a crime in progress, public safety considerations may make it reasonable for the officer to ask a few questions prior to a rights advisement. Many officers, however, feel on sound legal ground only by immediately following an arrest with an advisement of rights. Investigation and arrest are discussed in detail in Chapter 5, Policing: Legal Aspects.

Booking

During the arrest process suspects are *booked*—pictures are taken, fingerprints are made, and personal information, such as address, date of birth, weight, and height, is gathered. Details of the charges are recorded, and an administrative record of the arrest is created.

Warrant

Any of a number of writs issued by a judicial officer that direct a law enforcement officer to perform a specified act and affords protection from damages if he or she performs it.

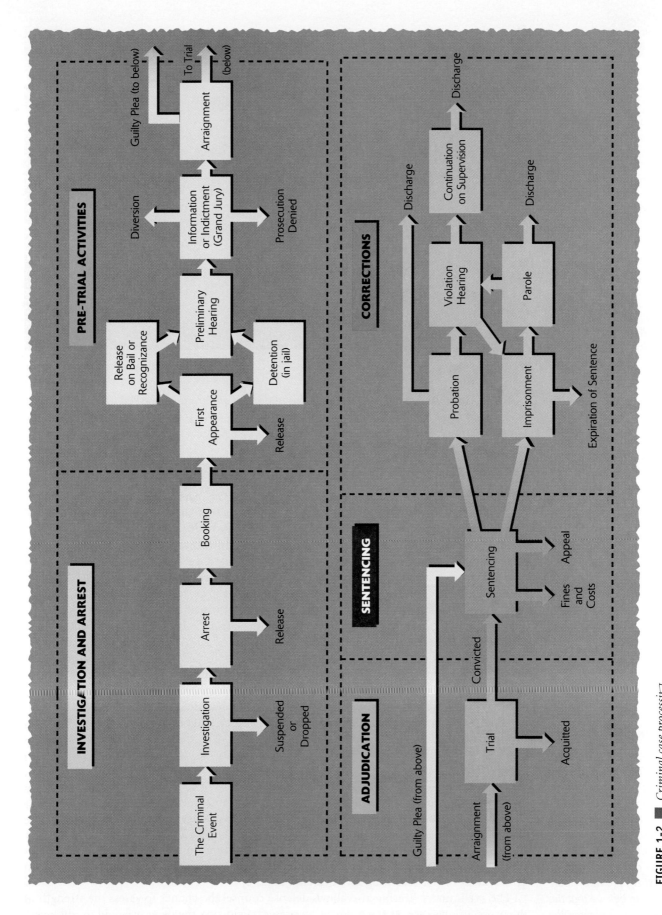

FIGURE 1-2 ■ *Criminal case processing.*

Source: *Adapted from U.S. Department of Justice, Compendium of Federal Justice Statistics 1989 (Washington, D.C.: Bureau of Justice Statistics, 1992), p. 3.*

Darrel Frank, the founder of Dead Serious, Incorporated, shown with the organization's official vehicle. Reflecting the "get tough" on crime and criminals attitude now so prevalent in American society, Dead Serious offers a $5,000 reward to members who legally kill a criminal.
Fort Worth Star-Telegram.

Booking

A law enforcement or correctional administrative process officially recording an entry into detention after arrest and identifying the person, the place, time, and reason for the arrest, and the arresting authority.

During **booking,** suspects are again advised of their rights and are asked to sign a form on which each right is written. The written form generally contains a statement acknowledging the rights advisement and attesting to the fact that the suspect understands them.

First Appearance

Within hours of arrest, suspects must be brought before a magistrate (a judicial officer) for a first or initial appearance. The judge will tell suspects of the charges against them, will again advise them of their rights, and may sometimes provide the opportunity for **bail.**

Bail

The money or property pledged to the court or actually deposited with the court to effect the release of a person from legal custody.

Most defendants are released on recognizance (into their own care or the care of another) or given the chance to post bond during their first appearance. A bond may take the form of a cash deposit or a property bond in which a house or other property can serve as collateral against flight. Those who flee may be ordered to forfeit the posted cash or property. Suspects who either are not afforded the opportunity for bail because their crimes are very serious or who do not have the needed financial resources are taken to jail to await the next stage in the justice process.

If a defendant doesn't have a lawyer, one will be appointed at the first appearance. The defendant may actually have to demonstrate financial hardship or be ordered to pay for counsel. The names of assigned lawyers are usually drawn off the roster of practicing defense attorneys in the county. Some jurisdictions utilize public defenders to represent indigent defendants. All aspects of the first appearance, including bail bonds and appointed counsel, are discussed in detail in Chapter 7, The Courts.

Preliminary Hearing

The proceeding before a judicial officer in which three matters must be decided: whether a crime was committed, whether the crime occurred within the territorial jurisdiction of the court, and whether there are reasonable grounds to believe that the defendant committed the crime.

Preliminary Hearing

The primary purpose of a **preliminary hearing,** also sometimes called a preliminary examination, is to establish whether sufficient evidence exists against a person to continue the justice process. At the preliminary hearing, the hearing judge will seek to determine whether there is **probable cause** to believe that (1) a crime has been committed and (2) the defendant committed it. The decision is a judicial one, but the process provides the prosecutor with an opportunity to test the strength of evidence at his or her disposal.

The preliminary hearing also allows defense counsel the chance to assess the strength of the prosecution's case. As the prosecution presents evidence, the defense is said to "discover" what it is. Hence, the preliminary hearing serves a *discovery* function for the defense. If the defense attorney thinks the evidence is strong, he or she may suggest that a plea bargain be arranged. Indigent defendants have a right to be represented by counsel at the preliminary hearing.

Information or Indictment

In some states the prosecutor may seek to continue the case against a defendant by filing an "information" with the court. An information is filed on the basis of the outcome of the preliminary hearing.

Other states require an **indictment** be returned by a **grand jury** before prosecution can proceed. The grand jury hears evidence from the prosecutor and decides whether a case should go to trial. In effect, the grand jury is the formal indicting authority. It determines whether probable cause exists to charge a defendant formally with a crime. Grand juries can return an indictment on less than a unanimous vote.

The grand jury system has been criticized because it is one-sided. The defense has no opportunity to present evidence; the grand jury is led only by the prosecutor, often through an appeal to emotions or in ways which will not be permitted in a trial.

At the same time, the grand jury is less bound by specific rules than a jury in a trial. For example, one member of a grand jury told the author that a rape case had been dismissed because the man had taken the woman to dinner first. Personal ignorance and subcultural biases are far more likely to be decisive in grand jury hearings than in criminal trials.

In defense of the grand jury, however, we should recognize that defendants who are clearly innocent will likely not be indicted. A refusal to indict can save considerable time and money by diverting poorly prepared cases from further processing by the system.

Arraignment

The **arraignment** is "the first appearance of the defendant before the court that has the authority to conduct a trial."[19] At arraignment the accused stands before a judge and hears the information, or indictment, against him or her as it is read. Defendants will again be notified of their rights and will be asked to enter a plea. Acceptable pleas generally include (1) "Not guilty"; (2) "Guilty"; and (3) "No contest" (*nolo contendere*), which may result in conviction but which can't be used later as an admission of guilt in civil proceedings. Civil proceedings, while not covered in detail in this book, provide an additional avenue of relief for victims or their survivors. Convicted offenders increasingly find themselves facing suits brought against them by victims seeking to collect monetary damages.

Federal rules of criminal procedure specify that "arraignment shall be conducted in open court and shall consist of reading the indictment or information to the defendant or stating to him the substance of the charge and calling on him to plead thereto. He shall be given a copy of the indictment or information before he is called upon to plead."[20]

Guilty pleas are not always accepted by the judge. If the judge feels a guilty plea was made under duress or because of a lack of knowledge on the part of the defendant, the plea will be rejected and a plea of "not guilty" will be substituted for it. Sometimes defendants "stand mute"; that is, they refuse to speak or enter a plea of any kind. In that case, the judge will enter a plea of "not guilty" on their behalf. The arraignment process, including pretrial motions made by the defense, is discussed in detail in Chapter 7, The Courts.

Trial

Every criminal defendant has a right under the Sixth Amendment to the U.S. Constitution to a **trial** by jury. The U.S. Supreme Court, however, has held that petty offenses are not covered by the Sixth Amendment guarantee and that the seriousness of a case is determined by the way in which "society regards the offense." For the most part, "offenses for which the maximum period of incarceration is six months or less are presumptively petty."[21] In *Blanton* v. *North Las Vegas* (1989),[22] the Court held that "a defendant can overcome this presumption and become entitled to a jury trial, only by showing that . . . additional penalties [such as fines and community service] viewed together with the maximum prison term, are so severe

---

Probable Cause

A legal criterion residing in a set of facts and circumstances which would cause a reasonable person to believe that a particular other person has committed a specific crime. Probable cause refers to the necessary level of belief which would allow for police seizures (arrests) of individuals and searches of dwellings, vehicles, and possessions.

Indictment

A formal, written accusation submitted to the court by a grand jury, alleging that a specified person(s) has committed a specified offense(s), usually a felony.

Grand Jury

A body of persons who have been selected according to law and sworn to hear the evidence against accused persons and to determine whether there is sufficient evidence to bring those persons to trial, to investigate criminal activity generally, and to investigate the conduct of public agencies and officials.

Arraignment

(1) The hearing before a court having jurisdiction in a criminal case, in which the identity of the defendant is established, the defendant is informed of the charge(s) and of his or her rights, and the defendant is required to enter a plea. (2) In some usages, any appearance in court prior to trial in criminal proceedings.

Trial

The examination in a court of the issues of fact and law in a case for the purpose of reaching a judgment of conviction or acquittal of the defendant(s).

that the legislature clearly determined that the offense is a serious one." The *Blanton* decision was further reinforced in the case of *U.S.* v. *Nachtigal* (1993).[23]

In most jurisdictions, many criminal cases never come to trial. The majority are "pled out" (that is, dispensed of as the result of a bargained plea) or dismissed for a variety of reasons. Some studies have found that as many as 82 percent of all sentences are imposed in criminal cases because of guilty pleas rather than trials.[24]

In cases which do come to trial, the procedures which govern the submission of evidence are tightly controlled by procedural law and precedent. Procedural law specifies what type of evidence may be submitted, what the credentials of those allowed to represent the state or the defendant must be, and what a jury is allowed to hear.

Precedent refers to understandings built up through common usage and also to decisions rendered by courts in previous cases. Precedent in the courtroom, for example, requires that lawyers request permission from the judge before approaching a witness. It also can mean that excessively gruesome items of evidence may not be used or must be altered in some way so that their factual value is not lost in the strong emotional reactions they may create.

Some states allow trials for less serious offenses to occur before a judge if defendants waive their right to a trial by jury. This is called a *bench trial.* Other states require a jury trial for all serious criminal offenses.

Trials are expensive and time consuming. They pit defense attorneys against prosecutors. Regulated conflict is the rule, and juries are required to decide the facts and apply the law as it is explained to them by the judge. In some cases, however, a jury may be unable to decide. In such cases, it is said to be deadlocked, resulting in a mistrial being declared. The defendant may then be tried again when a new jury is empanelled. The criminal trial and its participants are described fully in Chapter 8, The Courtroom Work Group and the Criminal Trial.

Sentencing

Consecutive Sentence

(1) A sentence that is one of two or more sentences imposed at the same time, after conviction for more than one offense, and that is served in sequence with the other sentences, or (2) a new sentence for a new conviction, imposed upon a person already under sentence(s) for previous offense(s), which is added to a previous sentence(s), thus increasing the maximum time the offender may be confined or under supervision.

Once a person is convicted it becomes the responsibility of the judge to impose some form of punishment. The sentence may take the form of supervised probation in the community, a fine, a prison term, or some combination of these. Defendants will often be ordered to pay the costs of court or of their own defense if they are able.

Prior to sentencing, a sentencing hearing may be held in which lawyers on both sides present information concerning the defendant. The judge may also request that a presentence report be compiled by a probation or parole officer. The report will contain information on the defendant's family and business situation, emotional state, social background, and criminal history. It will be used to assist the judge in making an appropriate sentencing decision.

Judges traditionally have had considerable discretion in sentencing, although new state and federal laws now place limits on judicial discretion in some cases, requiring that a sentence "presumed" by law be imposed. Judges still retain enormous discretion, however, in specifying whether sentences on multiple charges are to run consecutively or concurrently. Offenders found guilty of more than one charge may be ordered to serve one sentence after another is completed (a **consecutive sentence**) or be told that their sentences will run at the same time (a **concurrent sentence**).

Many sentences are appealed. The appeals process can be complex, involving both state and federal judiciaries. It is based upon the defendant's claim that rules of procedure were not properly followed at some earlier stage in the justice process or that the defendant was denied the rights accorded him or her by the U.S. Constitution. Chapter 9, Sentencing, outlines modern sentencing practices and describes the many modern alternatives to imprisonment.

Corrections

Concurrent Sentence

(1) A sentence that is one of two or more sentences imposed at the same time after conviction for more than one offense and to be served at the same time; or (2) a new sentence imposed upon a person already under sentence(s) for a previous offense(s) to be served at the same time as one or more of the previous sentences.

Once an offender has been sentenced, the stage of corrections begins. Some offenders are sentenced to prison where they "do time for their crimes." Once in the correctional system, they are classified according to local procedures and assigned to confinement facilities and treatment programs. Newer prisons today bear little resemblance to the massive bastions of the past which isolated offenders from society behind huge stone walls. Many modern prisons, however, still suffer from a "lock psychosis" among top- and midlevel administrators as well as a lack of significant rehabilitation programs. Chapter 11, Prisons and Jails, discusses the philosophy behind prisons and sketches their historical development. Chapter 12, Prison Life, portrays life on the inside and delineates the social structures which develop as a response to the pains of imprisonment.

Probation and Parole

Not everyone who is convicted of a crime and sentenced ends up in prison. Some offenders are ordered to prison only to have their sentences suspended and a probationary term imposed. They may also be ordered to perform community service activities as a condition of their probation. During the term of probation these offenders are required to submit to supervision by a probation officer and to meet other conditions set by the court. Failure to do so results in revocation of probation and imposition of the original prison sentence. Other offenders, who have served a portion of their prison sentences, may be freed on parole. They will be supervised by parole officers and assisted in their readjustment to society. As in the case of probation, failure to meet the conditions of parole may result in parole revocation and a return to prison. Chapter 9, Sentencing, and Chapter 10, Probation, Parole, and Community Corrections, deal with the practice of probation and parole and with the issues surrounding it.

> "African-American men comprise less than 6% of the U.S. population and almost one-half of its criminal prisoners."
> —*Bureau of Justice Statistics*

Due Process and Individual Rights

Imposed upon criminal justice case processing is the constitutional requirement of fairness and equity. Guaranteed by the Fifth, Sixth, and Fourteenth Amendments to the U.S. Constitution, this requirement is referred to as **due process.** The due process clause of the U.S. Constitution is succinctly stated in the Fifth Amendment, which reads "No person shall be . . . deprived of life, liberty, or property, without due process of law." The constitutional requirement of due process mandates the recognition of individual rights in the processing of criminal defendants when they are faced with prosecution by the states or the federal government. The guarantee of due process is found not just in the Fifth Amendment, but underlies the first 10 amendments to the U.S. Constitution, which are collectively known as the Bill of Rights. The Fourteenth Amendment is of special importance, however, for it makes due process binding upon the states—that is, it requires individual states in the union to respect the due process rights of U.S. citizens who come under their jurisdiction.

The fundamental guarantees of the Bill of Rights have been interpreted and clarified by courts (especially the U.S. Supreme Court) over time. The due process standard became reality following a number of far-reaching Supreme Court decisions affecting criminal procedure which were made during the 1960s. That period was the era of the Warren Court (1953–1969), led by Chief Justice Earl Warren, a Supreme Court which is remembered for its concern with protecting the innocent against the massive power of the state in criminal proceedings. As a result of the tireless efforts of the Warren Court to institutionalize the Bill of Rights, the daily practice of modern American criminal justice is now set squarely upon the due process standard. Due process requires that agencies of justice recognize these rights in their enforcement of the law, and under the due process standard, rights violations may become the basis for the dismissal of evidence or criminal charges, especially at the appellate level. Table 1-1 outlines the basic rights to which defendants in criminal proceedings are generally entitled.

Due Process

A right guaranteed by the Fifth, Sixth, and Fourteenth Amendments of the U.S. Constitution and generally understood, in legal contexts, to mean the due course of legal proceedings according to the rules and forms which have been established for the protection of private rights. Annotation: Due process of law, in criminal proceedings, is generally understood to include the following basic elements: a law creating and defining the offense, an impartial tribunal having jurisdictional authority over the case, accusation in proper form, notice and opportunity to defend, trial according to established procedure, and discharge from all restraints or obligations unless convicted.

The Role of the Courts in Defining Rights

Although the Constitution deals with many issues, what we have been calling *rights* is open to interpretation. Many modern rights, although written into the Constitution, would not exist in practice were it not for the fact that the U.S. Supreme Court decided, at some point in history, to recognize them in cases brought before it. The well-known Supreme Court case of *Gideon* v. *Wainwright* (1963),[26] for example (which is discussed in detail in Chapter 8), found the Court embracing the Sixth Amendment guarantee of a right to a lawyer for all

TABLE 1-1 ■ Individual Rights Guaranteed by the Bill of Rights*
A Right to be Assumed Innocent Until Proven Guilty
A Right Against Unreasonable Searches of Person and Place of Residence
A Right Against Arrest Without Probable Cause
A Right Against Unreasonable Seizures of Personal Property
A Right Against Self-Incrimination
A Right to Fair Questioning by the Police
A Right to Protection from Physical Harm Throughout the Justice Process
A Right to an Attorney
A Right to Trial by Jury
A Right to Know the Charges
A Right to Cross-Examine Prosecution Witnesses
A Right to Speak and Present Witnesses
A Right Not to Be Tried Twice for the Same Crime
A Right Against Cruel or Unusual Punishment
A Right to Due Process
A Right to a Speedy Trial
A Right Against Excessive Bail
A Right Against Excessive Fines
A Right to Be Treated the Same as Others, Regardless of Race, Sex, Religious Preference, and Other Personal Attributes

* As interpreted by the U.S. Supreme Court.

criminal defendants and mandating that states provide lawyers for defendants who are unable to pay for them. Prior to *Gideon*, court-appointed attorneys for defendants unable to afford their own counsel were practically unknown, except in capital cases and in some federal courts. After the *Gideon* decision, court-appointed counsel became commonplace, and measures were instituted in jurisdictions across the nation to select attorneys fairly for indigent defendants. It is important to note, however, that while the Sixth Amendment specifically says, among other things, that "In all criminal prosecutions, the accused shall enjoy the right to . . . have the Assistance of Counsel for his defence," it does *not* say, *in so many words,* that the state is *required to provide* counsel. It is the U.S. Supreme Court which, interpreting the Constitution, has said that.

Unlike the high courts of many other nations, the U.S. Supreme Court is very powerful, and its decisions often have far-reaching consequences. The decisions rendered by the justices in cases like *Gideon* become, in effect, the law of the land. For all practical purposes, such decisions often carry as much weight as legislative action. For this reason some writers speak of "judge-made law" (rather than legislated law) in describing judicial precedents which impact the process of justice.

Rights which have been recognized by Court decision are often subject to continual refinement. New interpretations may broaden or narrow the scope of applicability accorded to constitutional guarantees. Although the process of change is usually very slow, we should recognize that any right is subject to continual interpretation by the courts—and especially by the U.S. Supreme Court.

Crime Control through Due Process

Crime Control Model

A criminal justice perspective that emphasizes the efficient arrest and conviction of criminal offenders.

Two primary goals were identified at the start of this chapter: (1) the need to enforce the law and maintain social order, and (2) the need to protect individuals from injustice. The first of these principles values the efficient arrest and conviction of criminal offenders. It is often referred to as the **crime control model** of justice. The crime control model was first brought to the attention of the academic community in Herbert Packer's cogent analysis of the state of criminal justice in the late 1960s.[27] For that reason it is sometimes referred to as Packer's crime control model.

The second principle is called the **due process model** because of its emphasis on individual rights. Due process is a central and necessary part of American criminal justice. It requires a careful and informed consideration of the facts of each individual case. Under the model, police are required to recognize the rights of suspects during arrest, questioning, and handling. Prosecutors and judges must recognize constitutional and other guarantees during trial and the presentation of evidence. Due process is intended to ensure that innocent people are not convicted of crimes.

Up until now we have suggested that the dual goals of crime control and due process are in constant and unavoidable opposition to one another. Some critics of American criminal justice have argued that the practice of justice is too often concerned with crime control at the expense of due process. Other conservative analysts of the American scene maintain that our type of justice coddles offenders and does too little to protect the innocent.

While it is impossible to avoid ideological conflicts such as these, it is also realistic to think of the American system of justice as representative of *crime control through due process.* It is this model of law enforcement infused with the recognition of individual rights that provides a workable conceptual framework for understanding the American system of criminal justice—both now and into the future.

| **Due Process Model** |
| *A criminal justice perspective that emphasizes individual rights at all stages of justice system processing.* |

Criminal Justice and Criminology

The study of criminal justice as an academic discipline began in this country in the 1920s when August Vollmer, the former police chief of Berkeley, California, persuaded the University of California to offer courses on the subject.[28] Vollmer was joined by his student Orlando W. Wilson and by William H. Parker in calling for increased professionalism in police work through better training.[29] Early criminal justice education was practice oriented; it was a kind of extension of on-the-job training for working practitioners.

While criminal justice was often seen as a technical subject, **criminology,** on the other hand, had a firm academic base. Criminology is the interdisciplinary study of the causes of crime and of criminal motivation. It combines the academic disciplines of sociology, psychology, biology, economics, and political science in an effort to explore the mind of the offender and the social and economic conditions which give rise to criminality. The study of criminology is central to the criminal justice discipline, and courses in criminology are almost always found in criminal justice programs. Victimology is a subfield of criminology, which seeks answers to the question of why some people are victimized while others are not.

| **Criminology** |
| *The scientific study of crime causation, prevention, and the rehabilitation and punishment of offenders.* |

As a separate field of study, criminal justice had fewer than 1,000 students before 1950.[30] The turbulent 1960s and 1970s brought an increasing concern with social issues and, in particular, justice. Drug use, social protests, and dramatically increasing crime rates turned the nation's attention to the criminal justice system. During the period, Congress passed two significant pieces of legislation: (1) the Law Enforcement Assistance Act of 1965, which created the Law Enforcement Assistance Administrator (LEAA), and (2) the Omnibus Crime Control and Safe Streets Act of 1968. Through LEAA, vast amounts of monies were funneled into fighting crime. Law enforcement agencies received a great deal of technical assistance and new crime-fighting hardware. Students interested in the study of criminal justice often found themselves eligible for financial help under the Law Enforcement Education Program (LEEP).

LEEP monies funded a rapid growth in criminal justice offerings nationwide. In the first year of its existence, the LEEP program spent $6.5 million on 20,602 students in 485 schools around the country. By 1975, more than one hundred thousand students were studying criminal justice at 1,065 schools with assistance from LEEP. The federal government in that year spent in excess of $40 million on criminal justice education.[31]

LEEP funding began to decline in 1979. Meanwhile, criminal justice programs nationwide were undergoing considerable self-examination. The direction of justice studies and the future of the discipline were open to debate. The resultant clarification of criminal justice as a discipline, combined with the recent resurgence of federal funding initiatives through the

"The criminal justice system is composed of a sprawling bureaucracy with many separate agencies that are largely autonomous and independent."
—*Gary LaFree,* Ph.D.,
University of New Mexico

Violent Crime Control and Law Enforcement Act of 1994, and the "block grants" and other programs it and later legislation provided, has made the field stronger and more professional than ever before. WebExtra! 1-4 at CJToday.com contains the full text of the 1994 legislation.

To meet the growing needs of police officers for college-level training, the International Association of Police Professors (IAPP) was formed in 1963. The IAPP later changed its name to the Academy of Criminal Justice Sciences (ACJS) and widened its focus to include all aspects of criminal justice education. Today ACJS and its sister organization, the American Society of Criminology (ASC), are the two largest associations of community college- and university-based criminal justice trainers and educators in the world. A few years ago, ACJS formed an Academic Review Committee charged with conducting peer reviews of academic criminal justice programs upon request. Although ACJS does not offer accreditation through its peer review process, university and community college criminal justice programs undertaking self-studies or participating in a state or regional accreditation process may find the review process helpful.[32] Learn more about ACJS and ASC via WebExtra! 1-5 and 1-6 at CJToday.com.

Today criminal justice is well established as an academic discipline and is offered as a major course of study in well over a thousand colleges and universities across the country. Freda Adler, a well-known criminal justice academician, notes that "[f]rom an obscure discipline scorned by most academics with only two small doctoral programs as recently as 1970, criminal justice has exploded to 350,000 undergraduate majors at colleges and universities."[33]

The largest criminal justice program in the United States is offered at the John Jay College of Criminal Justice in New York City. "John Jay," as the school is called, serves over ten thousand students studying in the criminal justice area and conducts research in criminal justice organization, law enforcement, and forensic science. Other well-known criminal justice programs can be found at Sam Houston State University, the University of Illinois at Chicago, Rutgers (New Jersey), Florida State University, the State University of New York at Albany, Michigan State University, the University of Louisville, the University of Maryland, the University of Illinois, Ohio State University, East Tennessee State University, and the University of California at Irvine.[34] In addition to campus-based programs, distance learning and Web-based criminal justice programs are quickly becoming popular. Learn more about such programs via WebExtra! 1-7 at CJToday.com.

Summary

In this chapter the process of American criminal justice and the agencies that contribute to it have been described as a system with three major components: police, courts, corrections. As we have warned, however, such a viewpoint is useful primarily for the reduction in complexity it provides. A more realistic approach to understanding criminal justice may be the nonsystem approach. As a nonsystem, criminal justice is depicted as a fragmented activity in which individuals and agencies within the process have interests and goals which at times coincide, but often conflict.

Defendants processed by the system come into contact with numerous workers in the justice process whose duty it is to enforce the law, but who also have a stake in the agencies which employ them and who hold their own personal interests and values. As they wend their way through the system, defendants may be held accountable to the law, but in the process they will also be buffeted by the personal whims of "officials," as well as by the practical needs of the system itself. A complete view of American criminal justice needs to recognize that the final outcome of any encounter with the criminal justice system will be a consequence of decisions made not just at the legislative level, but in the day-to-day activities undertaken by everyone involved in the system. Hence, in a very real sense, justice is a product whose quality depends just as much upon practical considerations as it does upon idealistic notions of right and wrong.

An alternative way of viewing the practice of criminal justice is in terms of its two goals: crime control and due process. The crime control perspective urges rapid and effective law enforcement and calls for the stiff punishment of law breakers. Due process, on the other hand, requires a recognition of the defendant's rights and holds the agents of justice accountable for any actions which might contravene those rights.

"Everywhere across the Nation, we are more concerned with ensuring that criminal activity does not repeat itself, rather than keeping criminal activity from occurring in the first place."

—*Tony Fabelo*, *Executive Director, Texas Criminal Justice Policy Council*

21st Century CJ

Research and Professionalism

As an academic discipline, criminal justice made its debut in the 1930s, beginning with the work of August Vollmer (1876–1955) and continuing with the writings of his student Orlando Wilson (1900–1972). Vollmer, Wilson, and their followers were primarily interested in the application of general management principles to the administration of police agencies. Hence, in its early days, criminal justice was primarily a practical field of study—concerned with issues of organizational effectiveness. By the 1960s, however, students of criminal justice were beginning to apply the techniques of social scientific research—many of them borrowed from sister disciplines such as criminology, sociology, psychology, and political science—to the study of all aspects of the justice system. Scientific research into the operation of the criminal justice system was encouraged by the 1967 President's Commission on Law Enforcement and Administration of Justice, which influenced passage of the Safe Streets and Crime Control Act of 1968. The Safe Streets Act led to the creation of the National Institute of Law Enforcement and Criminal Justice, which later became the National Institute of Justice (NIJ). As a central part of its mission, NIJ continues to support research in the criminal justice field through substantial funding for scientific explorations into all aspects of the discipline—and funnels much of the $3 billion spent annually by the Department of Justice to help local communities fight crime.

Many early government-funded scientific studies in the criminal justice field focused on police management practices and are discussed in more detail in Chapter 5. Scientific research has since become characteristic of the entire criminal justice discipline—with studies of all aspects of criminal justice administration, practice, and ideology now routinely undertaken as well as

reported at academic conferences and professional meetings and in journals focusing on the profession. Such research has become a major element in the increasing professionalization of criminal justice, both as a career field and as a field of study, and can be expected to play an ever widening role in the twenty-first century.

While space doesn't permit discussion of most scientific studies in the justice field, a recent report by Lawrence Sherman and his colleagues at the University of Maryland stands out as one of the most definitive criminal justice studies of recent times. The *New York Times* calls the "Sherman report" "the most comprehensive study ever" of the criminal justice system in this country. The Sherman study, which may set the tone for research throughout the early part of the twenty-first century, is a "meta-analysis"—or a study of other studies. Conducted at the request of the U.S. Congress and released in 1997, the report analyzes the results of hundreds of other studies conducted throughout the criminal justice enterprise over the past few decades. Entitled, "Preventing Crime: What Works, What Doesn't, What's Promising," the massive survey examined independent studies of more than 500 local crime prevention programs throughout the country in an effort to determine what programs and practices are effective at preventing or reducing crime. The study surveyed literature on gang violence prevention programs, community-based mentoring programs, after-school recreational programs, family-based crime prevention programs, school-based programs, policing programs such as neighborhood watch and community policing, drug treatment programs, and get-tough sentencing initiatives such as prison boot camps and home confinement and electronic monitoring (all of which are discussed later in this book).

The report concluded that some of the most popular programs now in widespread use, including prison boot camps, midnight basketball, neighborhood watches, and drug education classes, have little impact on crime rates in the United States. The study did find some promising results for certain programs, especially intensified police patrols in high-crime areas, drug treatment in prisons, and home visits by nurses, social workers, and others for infants in troubled families.

The most important finding of the study, however, was its conclusion that it remains difficult to assess federally funded crime-prevention programs because there is far too little ongoing rigorous, scientific evaluation of such programs. As the study's lead author, Lawrence W. Sherman, says, "The most important finding is that we really can't tell how a majority of funding is affecting crime." The major reason for that problem, Sherman says, is that Congress has never insisted on the same kind of scientific evaluation of crime prevention programs that it does, for example, in testing new drugs before they are approved for public consumption.

The Sherman study, and others like it, hold the potential to significantly influence criminal justice research well into the next century. By pointing out the importance of rigorous and well-focused research, it is likely that Sherman's research will help move Congress to soon require well-tuned evaluations as part of the accountability process imposed upon all recipients of federal crime-fighting monies.

Source: Fox Butterfield (no headline), New York Times *News Service, April 16, 1997; Lawrence W. Sherman, Denise Gottfredson, Doris MacKenzie, John Eck, Peter Reuter, Shawn Bushway, et al.,* Preventing Crime: What Works, What Doesn't, What's Promising—A Report to the United States Congress *(Washington, D.C.: National Institute of Justice, 1997).*

CRIME IN THE NEWS

Genetic Crime: Body Parts, Cloned Children For Sale!

London—With new discoveries in genetic research, law enforcers are girding themselves for a new type of criminal, one that deals in genetically manufactured body parts—or even offers to clone a human being.

"Selling body parts—what a thought," Robert Hall, head of analysis for Britain's National Criminal Intelligence Service (NCIS), said at a crime intelligence conference here. "But there is lucrative potential for the criminal who may wish to make easy money."

Describing what he called the "sinister side" of genetic commerce, Hall spoke of a cash-rich biotechnology business that could attract rogue scientists cloning humans for a fee or selling body parts over the Internet.

Harvesting Plastic Plants

Within a few years, biotech scientists will be able to implant a plastic-manufacturing gene into plants and harvest the plastic, Hall said, citing a report. Within 20 years, technology will be able to clone 95 percent of human body parts, he said.

Firms such as the Monsanto Corp. have been researching and developing genetically engineered products that they hope to sell at great profit, said Hall. "The criminal will try to step in and take some of that profit," he said.

Clones for $160,000

For now, Hall told intelligence analysts at the NCIS-sponsored International Criminal Intelligence Conference, law enforcement authorities need to monitor the growth of genetic commerce—

if only to understand it and predict the criminality that will emerge.

"We need to be ahead of the criminal, so that action may be taken, even if it is only legislative action," he told audience members, most of whom work in law enforcement in Europe and North America.

Though he knows of no biotechnology crimes yet committed, Hall said, "It doesn't take a lot of imagination to think what would happen if a thief got a hold of It."

Rogue scientists have already said they're prepared to clone a human child for 100,000 British pounds (about $160,000), he said.

Source: Jim Krane, "Genetic Crime: Body Parts, Cloned Children for Sale," APB News, March 2, 1999. Reprinted with permission.

The goals of due process and crime control are often in conflict. Popular opinion may even see them as mutually exclusive. As we describe the agencies of justice in the chapters which follow, the goals of crime control and due process will appear again and again. Often they will be phrased in terms of the theme of this book, which contrasts the need to balance the rights of individuals against other valid social interests. We have presented this theme as represented by two opposing groups: individual rights advocates and public order advocates. As we shall see, however, the most fundamental challenge facing the practice of American criminal justice is one of achieving efficient enforcement of the laws while recognizing and supporting the rights of individuals. This mandate of crime control through effective due process ensures that criminal justice will remain an exciting and ever evolving undertaking—well into the twenty-first century and beyond.

Discussion Questions

1. What are the two models of the criminal justice process which this chapter describes? Which model do you think is more useful? Which is more accurate? Why?
2. What have we suggested are the primary goals of the criminal justice system? Do you think any one goal is more important than another? If so, which one(s)? Why?
3. What do we mean when we say that the "primary purpose of law is the maintenance of order"? Why is social order necessary? What would life be like without it?
4. Do we have too many criminal laws? Too few? Do we have enough social order or too little? How can we improve on the present situation, if at all?
5. What might a large, complex society such as our own be like without laws? Without a system of criminal justice? Would you want to live in such a society? Why or why not?

CAREERS IN JUSTICE

Working for the FBI

TYPICAL POSITIONS

Special agent, crime laboratory technician, ballistics technician, computer operator, fingerprint specialist, explosives examiner, document expert, and other nonagent technical positions.

EMPLOYMENT REQUIREMENTS

General employment requirements include (1) an age of between 23 and 37; (2) excellent physical health; (3) uncorrected vision of not less than 20/200, correctable to 20/20 in one eye, and at least 20/40 in the other eye; (4) good hearing; (5) U.S. citizenship; (6) a valid driver's license; (7) successful completion of a background investigation; (8) a law degree or a Bachelor's degree from an accredited college or university; (9) successful completion of an initial written examination; (10) an intensive formal inter-view; and (11) urinalysis. A polygraph examination may also be required.

OTHER REQUIREMENTS

Five special-agent entry programs exist in the areas of law, accounting, languages, engineering/science, and a general "diversified" area, which requires a minimum of three years of full-time work experience, preferably with a law enforcement agency. The FBI emphasizes education and especially values degrees in law, graduate studies, and business and accounting. Most nonagent technical career paths also require Bachelor's or advanced degrees and U.S. citizenship.

SALARY

Special agents enter the bureau in Government Service (GS) grade 10 and can advance to grade GS-13 in field assignments and GS-15 or higher in supervisory and management positions. A high-cost area supplement ranging from 4 to 16 percent is paid in specified geographic areas.

BENEFITS

Benefits include (1) 13 days of sick leave annually, (2) $2\frac{1}{2}$ to 5 weeks of annual paid vacation and 10 paid federal holidays each year, (3) federal health and life insurance, and (4) a comprehensive retirement program.

DIRECT INQUIRIES TO:

Federal Bureau of Investigation, U.S. Department of Justice, 9th Street and Pennsylvania Ave., N.W., Washington, D.C. 20535. Phone: (202) 324-3000, or check your local telephone book. Web site:www.fbi.gov.

---

6. What do we, as individuals, have to give up to facilitate social order? Do we ever give up too much in the interest of social order? If so, when?

Web Quest!

Familiarize yourself with the *Criminal Justice: A Brief Introduction* Web site and with its many features. To get there point your browser at www.prenhall.com/schmalleger. Once you've opened the site, you'll be able to read the latest crime and justice news, explore student-oriented message boards, join the criminal justice e-mail discussion list, and sign up to receive announcements of late-breaking crime stories. You can learn about your textbook's chapter objectives, practice with online review questions, preview chapter summaries, submit electronic homework to your instructor, and enjoy many Web-based criminal justice projects. (Remember that if your instructor decides to use the electronic homework feature of the site, it's always a good idea to keep a copy of any materials that you submit.) The site also allows you to listen to the author introduce each chapter.

Unique WebExtras! and book-specific Library Extras! substantially enhance the learning opportunities available with your text. WebExtras! bring the justice system to life by providing a wealth of links to relevant and informative sites. Library Extras! help you learn more about important topics in the justice field via the *Criminal Justice: A Brief Introduction* electronic library. Library Extras! include the latest reports and bulletins from the Bureau of Justice Statistics, the National Institute of Justice, the Bureau of Justice Assistance, the FBI, and other agencies. Each report has been specially selected by your author to complement the textbook and to enhance your learning experience.

One Web resource of special importance is Dr. Frank Schmalleger's Cybrary of Criminal

Justice links (the word *Cybrary* means cyber-library). Known to justice professionals as the "World's Criminal Justice Site Directory," Dr. Schmalleger's Cybrary contains links to more than 12,000 crime and justice sites, and to justice-related documents throughout the nation and around the world. Because it is continuously updated and fully searchable, the Cybrary can be an invaluable tool when writing term papers or doing Web-based research on crime and justice.

Library Extras!

The Library Extras! listed here complement the WebExtras! found throughout this chapter. Library Extras! may be accessed on the Web at CJToday.com.

Library Extra! 1-1. *The Challenge of Crime in a Free Society: Looking Back Looking Forward* (USDOJ, May 1998).
Library Extra! 1-2. *Perspectives on Crime and Justice: 1996–1997 Lecture Series* (NIJ, 1998).
Library Extra! 1-3. *Perspectives on Crime and Justice: 1998–1999 Lecture Series* (NIJ, 1999).
Library Extra! 1-4. "Race, Crime, and the Administration of Justice: A Summary of the Available Facts," from *The National Institute of Justice Journal* (NIJ, April 1999).
Library Extra! 1-5. *Women in Criminal Justice: A Twenty Year Update* (NIJ, 1998).
Library Extra! 1-6. The Violent Crime Control and Law Enforcement Act of 1994.

References

1. Charles E. Silberman, *Criminal Violence, Criminal Justice* (New York: Random House, 1978), p. 12.
2. *Criminal Justice Newsletter,* September 16, 1997, p. 1.
3. "Weekend of Terror," APB Online, July 5, 1999. Web posted at www.apbonline.com/911/1999/07/05/chicago0705_02.html.
4. Amy Worden, "FBI Eyes Link to Hate Shootings, California Fires," APB Online, July 7, 1999. Web posted at www.apbonline.com/911/1999/07/07/hate0707_01.html. Citing David Goldman, executive director of Hatewatch.
5. "Gunman's Racial Outrage was Building," APB Online, July 6, 1999. Web posted at www.apbonline.com/911/1999/07/06/chicago_suspect0706_01.html.
6. "Mourners Remember Shooting Victims," *USA Today* online, September 19, 1999. Web posted at www.usatoday.com/news/nphoto.htm.
7. See, "Cries of Relief," *Time,* April 26, 1993, p. 18, and "King II: What Made the Difference?" *Newsweek,* April 26, 1993, p. 26.
8. Ibid.
9. "FBI: Definitely a Bomb," *USA Today,* March 1, 1993, p. 1A.
10. "Gay Victim Was Tortured for Information," APB Online, November 19, 1998. Web posted at www.apbonline.com/911/1998/11/19/gay1119_1.html.
11. "A Free Man," *USA Today,* April 27, 1989, p. 13A.
12. *The American Heritage Dictionary on CD-ROM* (Boston: Houghton Mifflin, 1991).
13. For a good overview of the issues involved, see, for example, Judge Harold J. Rothwax, *Guilty: The Collapse of Criminal Justice* (New York: Random House, 1996).
14. The systems model of criminal justice is often attributed to the frequent use of the term *system* by the 1967 Presidential Commission in its report, *The Challenge of Crime in a Free Society* (Washington, D.C.: U.S. Government Printing Office, 1967).
15. One of the first published works to utilize the nonsystems approach to criminal justice was the American Bar Association's *New Perspective on Urban Crime* (Washington, D.C.: ABA Special Committee on Crime Prevention and Control, 1972).
16. Jerome H. Skolnick, *Justice Without Trial* (New York: John Wiley, 1966), p. 179.
17. *Miranda v. Arizona,* 384 U.S. 436, 86 S.Ct. 1602, 16 L. Ed. 2d 694 (1966).
18. North Carolina Justice Academy, *Miranda Warning Card* (Salemburg, N.C.).
19. John M. Scheb and John M. Scheb II, *American Criminal Law* (St. Paul, MN: West, 1996), p. 32.
20. Federal Rules of Criminal Procedure, 10.
21. *Blanton v. City of North Las Vegas,* 489 U.S. 538, 103 L. Ed. 2d 550, 109 S. Ct. 1289 (1989).
22. Ibid.
23. *U.S. v. Nachtigal,* 122 L. Ed. 2d 374, 113 S. Ct. 1072, 1073 (1993), *per curiam.*
24. Barbara Borland and Ronald Sones, *Prosecution of Felony Arrests, 1981* (Washington, D.C.: Bureau of Justice Statistics, 1986).
25. For a complete analysis of the impact of decisions made by the Warren Court, see Fred P. Graham, *The Due Process Revolution: The Warren Court's Impact on Criminal Law* (New York: Hayden Press, 1970).
26. *Gideon v. Wainwright,* 372 U.S. 353 (1963).
27. Herbert Packer, *The Limits of the Criminal Sanction* (Stanford, CA: Stanford University Press, 1968).
28. For an excellent history of policing in the United States, see Edward A. Farris, "Five Decades of American Policing: 1932–1982," *The Police Chief,* November 1982, pp. 30–36.

29. Gene Edward Carte, "August Vollmer and the Origins of Police Professionalism," *Journal of Police Science and Administration,* vol. 1, no. 1 (1973), pp. 274–281.

30. Larry L. Gaines, "Criminal Justice Education Marches On!" in Roslyn Muraskin, ed., *The Future of Criminal Justice Education* (New York: Criminal Justice Institute, Long Island University, C. W. Post Campus, 1987).

31. Ibid.

32. For more information, contact ACJS at 1500 North Beauregard St., Suite 101, Alexandria, VA 22311 (800-757-ACJS), or see "Academic Review of Programs," *ACJS Today* (November/December 1996), p. 9. ASC can be contacted at 1314 Kinnear Road, Suite 212, Columbus, OH 43212. Visit the *Criminal Justice Cybrary* Web site at http://talkjustice.com/cybrary.asp for links to these and other professional organizations in the field.

33. Fox Butterfield, "A Newcomer Breaks into the Liberal Arts," the *New York Times,* December 5, 1998.

34. This list includes schools that are well known for producing graduate students specializing in either criminal justice or criminology. Because of the liberal arts emphasis at many of the schools in the list, however, programs may be officially designated as "criminology" or even "sociology" rather than "criminal justice." One (at the University of California at Irvine) is housed within the "Program in Social Ecology."

CHAPTER 2

The Crime Picture

"It may turn out that a free society cannot really prevent crime. Perhaps its causes are locked so deeply into the human personality, the intimate processes of family life, and the subtlest aspects of the popular culture that coping is the best that we can hope for. . . ."
—*James Q. Wilson, UCLA*[1]

"No one way of describing crime describes it well enough."
—*The President's Commission on Law Enforcement and Administration of Justice*

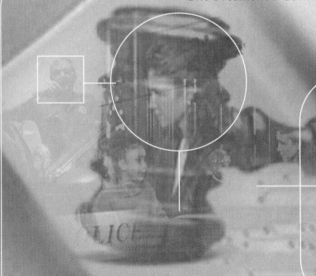

CHAPTER OUTLINE

- Introduction: Sources of Data
- The *Uniform Crime Reports*
- The National Crime Victimization Survey
- Emerging Patterns of Criminal Activity

—*Ed Bailey, AP/Wide World Photos.*

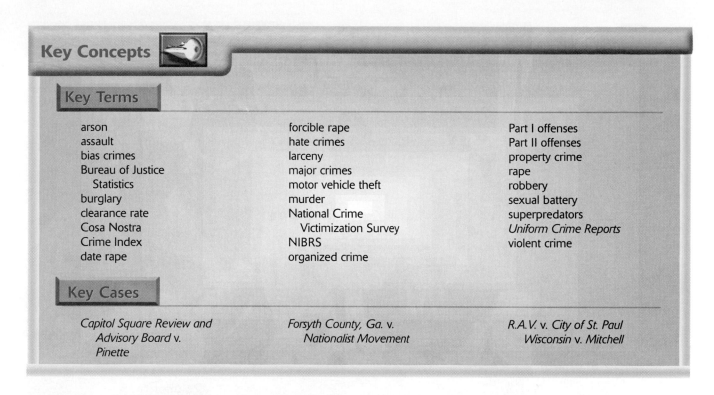

Key Concepts

Key Terms

arson
assault
bias crimes
Bureau of Justice
    Statistics
burglary
clearance rate
Cosa Nostra
Crime Index
date rape

forcible rape
hate crimes
larceny
major crimes
motor vehicle theft
murder
National Crime
    Victimization Survey
NIBRS
organized crime

Part I offenses
Part II offenses
property crime
rape
robbery
sexual battery
superpredators
Uniform Crime Reports
violent crime

Key Cases

*Capitol Square Review and
    Advisory Board* v.
    Pinette

Forsyth County, Ga. v.
    Nationalist Movement

R.A.V. v. *City of St. Paul*
Wisconsin v. *Mitchell*

Introduction: Sources of Data

Hear the author
discuss this
chapter at
cjtoday.com

On a hot July afternoon in 1999, Atlanta's Buckhead financial district was shaken by a work-place shooting that ultimately left 10 dead and 13 injured.[2] The alleged killer, 44-year-old Mark O. Barton, reportedly walked into the office of Momentum Securities—a brokerage house used by day traders (people who buy and sell stock throughout the day as a way of making a living). Barton was heard to say: "I hope this doesn't ruin your trading day,"[3] before he pulled out two powerful handguns and started shooting. Within minutes four people lay dead. Barton then walked across a busy six-lane highway and into the offices of All-Tech Investment Group, another day-trading firm. Five people died there. Witnesses to the gun-fire said that Barton told his victims that he had been distressed over heavy trading losses. Media reports later said that he had lost $105,000 trading stocks in the two months preced-ing the rampage.[4] After the shootings, Barton fled in a green Ford Aerostar van, taking the time to buckle himself in before driving off.

A college graduate, Barton seemed an unlikely killer. His career included work as a chemist and salesman, and he had recently moved back in with his second wife, 27-year-old Leigh Ann. The two had been legally separated only months before. Barton also had custody of his two young children by a former marriage—Elizabeth Mychelle, 7, and Matthew, 11. When officers went to the Barton residence, they found the dead bodies of Barton's wife and children. All three had suffered hammer blows to the head, and the children had been placed face down in a filled bathtub to prevent any chance of reviving.

Soon after Barton fled, investigators learned that he had been the primary suspect in the 1993 murders of his first wife, 36-year-old Deborah Spivey Barton, and her mother, Eloise Powell Spivey, 59.[5] The bodies of both women were found beaten to death at Riverside Campground on Weiss Lake in northeastern Alabama. They had been spending Labor Day weekend in a camper at the lake with Barton. The camper showed no signs of forced entry, and no one was ever arrested in the killings. Barton had taken out a $600,000 life insurance policy on his first wife shortly before her death.

Four hours after the Atlanta shootings, Georgia officers spotted Barton's vehicle in Acworth—a town 30 miles northwest of Atlanta. Police corralled the vehicle in at a service station. The incident ended when Barton shot and killed himself. He had left four notes at his apartment for investigators to read. You can view their contents by visiting WebExtra! 2-1 at CJToday.com.

The dead Barton family. Left to right: daughter Mychelle Elizabeth (7), wife Leigh Ann, Mark Barton, and son Matthew (11). Barton killed his wife and children before going on a shooting spree in two Atlanta offices in 1999 that claimed the lives of 10 people and injured 13 others.
Reuters/HO, Archive Photos.

Bureau of Justice Statistics (BJS)

A U.S. Department of Justice agency responsible for criminal justice data collection, including the annual NCVS.

This chapter provides a statistical picture of crime in America today. It does so by examining information on reported crimes from the FBI's *Uniform Crime Reports* (UCR), as well as data from the door-to-door National Crime Victimization Survey (NCVS) conducted by the **Bureau of Justice Statistics** (BJS). Not all crimes are as newsworthy as the Atlanta killings. While reading this chapter, however, it is important to keep in mind that statistical aggregates of reported crime, whatever their source, do not readily reveal the human suffering, lost lives, lessened productivity, and reduced quality of life that crime causes. Although every murder victim, like the people killed by Mark Barton, led an intricate life and had a family, dreams, and desires, their death at the hands of another person is routinely recorded only as a numerical count in statistical reports. Such information does not contain details on the personal lives of crime victims, but represents merely a numerical compilation of reported law violations.

Crime Data and Social Policy

Crime statistics render a comprehensive picture of crime in this country. If used properly they can provide one of the most powerful tools for social policy creation. Decision makers at all levels, including legislators, elected public officials, and administrators throughout the criminal justice system, rely on crime data to analyze and evaluate existing programs, fashion and design new crime-control initiatives, develop funding requests, and plan new laws and crime-control legislation. The "get-tough" policies described in the last chapter, for example, are in large part based upon the public's perception of increasing crime rates and the measured ineffectiveness of existing programs to reduce the incidence of repeat offending.

Some, however, question just how "objective"—and therefore how useful—crime statistics are. Social events, including crime, are complex and difficult to quantify. Even the choice of which crimes should be included in statistical reports, and which should be excluded, is itself a judgment reflecting the interests and biases of policymakers.

Moreover, public opinion about crime is not always realistic—nor is it always based on a careful consideration of statistics. As well-known criminologist Norval Morris points out, the news media does more to influence public perceptions of crime than any official data.[6]

Between 1991 and 1995, for example, the frequency of crime stories reported in the national media increased by a factor of 4. From 1993 to 1995 crime was at the top of the list in subject matter covered in news stories at both the local and national levels. "Please note," says Morris, "that the grossly increasing preoccupation with crime stories came at a time of steadily declining crime and violence." However, as Morris adds: "Aided and abetted by this flood of misinformation, the politicians, federal and state, and local, foster the view that the public demands our present get-tough policies." As a new millenium begins, Morris' observations seem as true as ever.

Collecting Crime Data

Nationally crime statistics come from two major sources: (1) the FBI's Uniform Crime Reporting Program (UCR), and (2) the Bureau of Justice Statistics' National Crime Victimization Survey (NCVS). The most widely quoted numbers purporting to describe crime in America today probably come from the FBI's *Uniform Crime Reports* and depend upon reports to the police by victims of crime. One problem with such summaries is that citizens do not always make official reports, sometimes because they are afraid to contact the police, or perhaps because they don't think the police can do anything about the offense. Even when reports are made, they are filtered through a number of bureaucratic levels. As noted methodologist Frank Hagan points out, "The government is very keen on amassing statistics. They collect them, add to them, raise them to the nth power, take the cube root, and prepare wonderful diagrams. But what you must never forget is that every one of these figures comes in the first instance from the *chowty dar* (village watchman), who puts down what he damn pleases."[7]

Another problem with the UCR comes from the fact that certain kinds of crimes are rarely reported, if at all. These include "victimless crimes," or crimes which, by their nature, involve willing participants. Victimless crimes (also known as social order offenses) include such things as drug use, prostitution, and gambling. Similarly, white-collar and high-technology offenses, such as embezzlement, computer crime, and corporate misdeeds, probably only rarely enter the official statistics. Hence, a relatively large amount of criminal activity in the United States likely remains unreported in the UCR, while those types of crimes that are reported may paint a misleading picture of the true nature of criminal activity by virtue of the publicity accorded to them.

A second data collection format is typified by the Bureau of Justice Statistics' (BJS) National Crime Victimization Survey (NCVS). It relies upon personal interpretations of what may (or may not) have been criminal events, and upon quasiconfidential surveys, which may selectively include data from those most willing to answer interviewer's questions. Unfortunately, the survey tends to exclude information from less gregarious and more reclusive respondents.

The NCVS suffers from other shortcomings, as well. Some victims are afraid to report crimes, even to nonpolice interviewers. Others may inaccurately interpret their own experiences or may be tempted to invent victimizations for the sake of interviewers. As the first page of the NCVS admits, "Details about the crimes come directly from the victims, and no attempt is made to validate the information against police records or any other source."[8]

Another source of crime data can be found in offender self-reports based upon surveys that ask respondents to reveal any illegal activity in which they have been involved. Offender self-reports are not discussed in detail in this chapter since surveys utilizing them are not national in scope. Similarly, offenders are often reluctant to accurately report ongoing or recent criminal involvement, making information derived from such surveys somewhat unreliable and less than current. Where information from such surveys is available, however, it tends to show that criminal activity is more widespread than most "official" surveys show.

Finally, although the FBI's UCR and the BJS's NCVS are the country's major sources of crime data, other regular publications contribute to our knowledge of crime patterns throughout the nation. Available yearly is the *Sourcebook of Criminal Justice Statistics,* a compilation of national information on crime and on the criminal justice system. The *Sourcebook* is published by BJS through support provided by the Justice System Improvement Act of 1979. A Web-based version of the *Sourcebook* is continually updated as data become available. The

"We talk about the criminal justice system, but rarely does it perform as a system."

—Samuel F. Saxton,
Director Prince George's County (Maryland) Dept. of Corrections

Uniform Crime Reports (UCR)

An annual FBI publication series that summarizes the incidence and rate of reported crimes throughout the United States.

National Institute of Justice (NIJ), the primary research arm of the U.S. Department of Justice, the Office of Juvenile Justice and Delinquency Prevention (OJJDP), the Federal Justice Research Program, and the National Victim's Resource Center, provide still more information on crime patterns. Visit CJToday.com and view WebExtra! 2-2 for an overview of the many sources of crime data.

The *Uniform Crime Reports*

Development of the UCR Program

Crime Index

An inclusive measure of the violent and property crime categories of the UCR, also known as Part I offenses. The Crime Index has been a useful tool for geographic (state-to-state) and historical (year-to-year) comparative purposes because it employs the concept of a crime rate (the number of crimes per unit of population). However, the recent addition of arson as an eighth index offense and the new executive branch requirements with regard to the gathering of hate crime statistics have the potential to result in new crime index measurements, which may provide less than ideal comparisons.

In 1930 Congress authorized the attorney general of the United States to survey crime in America, and the FBI was designated to implement the program. The Bureau quickly built upon earlier efforts by the International Association of Chiefs of Police (IACP) to create a national system of uniform crime statistics. As a practical measure, IACP recommendations had utilized readily available information, and so it was that citizens' reports of crimes to the police became the basis of the plan.[9]

During its first year of operation the FBI's Uniform Crime Reporting Program received reports from 400 cities in 43 states. Twenty million people were covered by that first comprehensive survey. Today, approximately 16,000 law enforcement agencies provide crime information for the program, with data coming from city, state, and county departments. To assure uniformity in reporting, the FBI has developed standardized definitions of offenses and terminologies used in the program. A number of publications, including the *Uniform Crime Reporting Handbook* and *Manual of Law Enforcement Records,* are supplied to participating agencies, and training for effective reporting is made available through FBI-sponsored seminars and instructional literature.

Following IACP recommendations, the original UCR Program was designed to permit comparisons over time through construction of a **Crime Index.** The Index summed the total of seven major offenses—murder, forcible rape, robbery, aggravated assault, burglary, larceny-theft, and motor vehicle theft—and expressed the result as a crime rate based on population. In 1979, by congressional mandate, an eighth offense—arson—was added to the Index. Although UCR categories today parallel statutory definitions of criminal behavior, they are not legal classifications, only conveniences created for statistical reporting purposes. Because many of the definitions of crime used in this textbook are derived from official UCR terminology, it is important to remember that UCR terminology may differ from statutory definitions of crime.

Historical Trends

"In a field like criminal justice, where sensitive issues abound, none is more sensitive than the issue of race and gender bias."

—*Gary LaFree,* Ph.D.
University of New Mexico

Most UCR information is reported as a *rate* of crime. Rates are computed as the number of crimes *per* some unit of population. National reports generally make use of large units of population, such as 100,000 persons. Hence, the rate of rape reported by the UCR for 1999 was 32.7 forcible rapes per every 100,000 inhabitants of the United States.[10] Rates allow for a meaningful comparison over areas and across time. The rate of reported rape for 1960, for example, was only about 10 per 100,000. We expect the number of crimes to increase as population grows, but rate increases are cause for concern because they indicate that crimes are increasing faster than the population is growing. Rates, however, require interpretation. Since the FBI definition of rape includes only female victims, for example, the rate of victimization might be more meaningfully expressed in terms of every 100,000 female inhabitants. Similarly, although there is a tendency to judge an individual's risk of victimization based upon rates, such judgments tend to be inaccurate since they are based purely on averages and do not take into consideration individual life circumstances, such as place of residence, wealth, and educational level. While rates may tell us about aggregate conditions and trends, we must be very careful in applying them to individual cases.

Since the UCR Program began, there have been two major shifts in crime rates—and we are in the middle of what is now a third. The first occurred during the early 1940s, when crime decreased sharply due to the large number of young men who entered military service during World War II. Young males comprise the most "crime-prone" segment of the population, and their removal to the European and Pacific theaters of war did much to lower crime rates at home. From 1933 to 1941, the crime index declined from 770 to 508 offenses per every 100,000 members of the American population.[11]

The second noteworthy shift in offense statistics—a dramatic increase in most forms of crime beginning in the 1960s and culminating only recently—also had a link to World War II. With the end of the war and the return of millions of young men to civilian life, birth rates skyrocketed during the period 1945–1955, creating a postwar "baby boom." By 1960, baby boomers were entering their teenage years. A disproportionate number of young people produced a dramatic increase in most major crimes as the baby boom generation swelled the proportion of the American population in the crime-prone age range.

Other factors contributed to the increase in reported crime during the same period. Modified reporting requirements, which reduced victims' stress associated with filing police reports, and the publicity associated with the rise in crime, sensitized victims to the importance of reporting. Crimes which may have gone undetected in the past began to figure more prominently in official statistics. Similarly, the growing professionalization of some police departments resulted in more accurate and increased data collection, making some of the most progressive departments appear to be associated with the largest crime increases.[12]

The 1960s were tumultuous years. The Vietnam war, a vibrant civil rights struggle, the heady growth of secularism, dramatic increases in the divorce rate, diverse forms of "liberation," and the influx of psychedelic and other drugs, all combined to fragment existing institutions. Social norms were blurred, and group control over individual behavior declined substantially. The "normless" quality of American society in the 1960s contributed greatly to the rise in crime. From 1960 to 1980 crime rates rose from 1,887 to 5,950 offenses per every 100,000 members of the U.S. population.

Crime rates continued their upward swing, with a brief respite in the early 1980s when postwar boomers began to age out of the crime-prone years and American society emerged from the cultural drift which had characterized the previous 20 years. About the same time, however, an increase in drug-related criminal activity led crime rates to soar once again, especially in the area of violent crime. Crime rates peaked about 1991 and have since begun to show a third major shift—with decreases in the rate of most major crimes being reported. Between 1991 and 1999 the Crime Index decreased from 5,897 to 4,267 offenses per every 100,000 citizens—sending it down to levels not seen since 1973. Recent decreases in crime, however, while they are noteworthy, do not even begin to bring the overall rate of crime in this country anywhere close to the low crime rates characteristic of the early 1940s, and 1950s. From a long-term perspective, even with recent declines, crime rates in this country remain more than seven times what they were in 1940.

A fourth (and coming) shift may be discernable on the horizon—as the size of an increasingly violent teenage population is anticipated to grow over the next decade or two. John J. DiIulio, Jr., for example, warns of a coming generation of **superpredators**—young violent offenders bereft of any moral sense and steeped in violent traditions. Superpredators, according to DiIulio, are juveniles "who are coming of age in actual and 'moral poverty' without the benefits of parents, teachers, coaches, or clergy to teach them right from wrong and show them 'unconditional love.' "[13]

Supporting DiIulio, James A. Fox notes that, "[b]y the year 2005, the number of teens, ages 14–17, will increase significantly, with a larger increase among blacks in this age group."[14] Such an observation, says Fox, is especially worrisome because, over the past 10 years, "the rate of murder committed by teens, ages 14–17, [has] increased 172 percent." Indicative of a significant trend, says Fox, "black males aged 14–24," although comprising only 1 percent of the population, "now constitute 17 percent of the victims of homicide and over 30 percent of the perpetrators." Also, says Fox, "the differential trends by age of offender observed for homicide generalize to other violent offenses." During the last five years, for example, "the arrest rate for violent crimes (murder, rape, robbery, and aggravated assault) rose over 46 percent among teenagers, but only 12 percent among adults." Writers like DiIulio and Fox predict that the coming crime wave will peak around 2010. See Figure 2-1, which shows both historical rates of crime and projected rates through 2010. When viewing the figure, keep in mind that official crime rates are based upon the FBI eight major crimes, and do not include drug offenses. Hence, as we shall see in Chapter 11, while

Superpredators

Juveniles who are coming of age in actual and moral poverty without the benefits of parents, teachers, coaches, or clergy to teach them right from wrong. The term is often applied to inner-city youth, socialized in violent settings without the benefit of wholesome life experiences—and who hold considerable potential for violence.

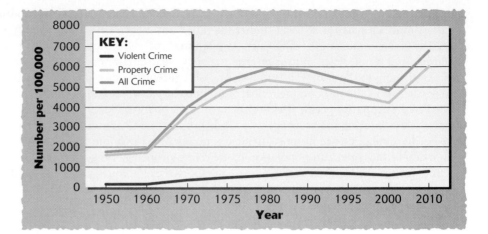

FIGURE 2-1 ▪ *Actual and projected rates of crime in the United States (per 100,000 inhabitants), 1950–2010.*

Source: *Federal Bureau of Investigation,* Uniform Crime Reports, *various years.*

official rates of crime appear to be down, drug offenses continue to increase—accounting for much of the huge growth in prison populations our country has experienced over the past two decades.

UCR Terminology

Figure 2-2 shows the UCR crime clock, which is calculated yearly as a shorthand way of diagramming crime severity in the United States. It is important to remember, however, that crime clock data imply a regularity to crime that, in reality, does not exist.[15] Also, while the crime clock, although a useful diagrammatic tool, is not a rate-based measure of criminal

FIGURE 2-2 ▪ *FBI crime clock, 1999, showing the frequency of major crime commission.*

Source: *Adapted from Federal Bureau of Investigation,* Uniform Crime Reports for the United States, 1999 *(Washington, D.C.: U.S. Government Printing Office, 2000).*

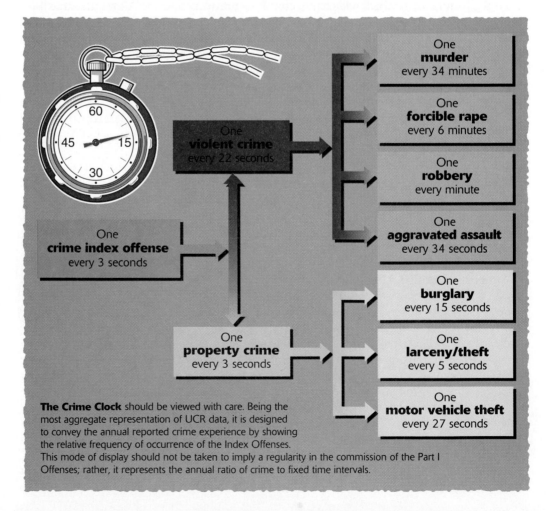

activity and does not allow easy comparisons over time. Eight **Part I offenses,** also called **major crimes,** are listed in the right-hand margin of the figure. Part I offenses are (1) murder, (2) rape, (3) robbery, (4) aggravated assault, (5) burglary, (6) larceny, (7) motor vehicle theft, and (8) arson. As noted earlier, the sum total of all Part I offenses, divided by the nation's population, comprise the UCR's widely reported Crime Index, which facilitates comparisons of crime rates over time. Since, however, arson was added as a Part I offense relatively late in the history of the UCR program, it is sometimes excluded from official crime index calculations.

The crime clock distinguishes between two categories of Part I crime: **violent** (or **personal**) **crime** and **property crime.** Violent crimes include murder, forcible rape, robbery, and aggravated assault. Property crimes, as the figure shows, are burglary, larceny, and motor vehicle theft. Other than for the use of such a simple dichotomy, UCR data do not provide a clear measure of the severity of the crimes they cover.

Crime clock data are based, as are most UCR statistics, upon crimes reported to (or discovered by) the police. For a few offenses the numbers reported are probably close to the numbers which actually occur. Murder, for example, is a crime that is difficult to conceal because of its seriousness. Even where the crime is not immediately discovered, the victim is often quickly missed by friends and associates and a "missing persons" report is filed with the police.

Auto theft is another crime that is reported in numbers similar to its actual rate of occurrence, probably because insurance companies require that a police report be filed before any claims can be collected. Unfortunately, most crimes other than murder and auto theft appear to be seriously underreported. Victims may not report for various reasons, including (1) the belief that the police can't do anything; (2) a fear of reprisal; (3) embarrassment about the crime itself or a fear of being embarrassed during the reporting process; and (4) an acceptance of criminal victimization as a normal part of life.

UCR data tend to underestimate the amount of crime which actually occurs for another reason: Built into the reporting system is the hierarchy rule—a way of "counting" crime reports such that only the most serious out of a series of events is scored. If a man and woman go on a picnic, for example, and their party is set upon by a criminal who kills the man, rapes the woman, steals the couple's car, and later burns the vehicle, the hierarchy rule dictates that only one crime will be reported in official statistics—that of murder. The offender, if apprehended, may later be charged with each of the offenses listed, but only one report of murder will appear in UCR data.

Violent Crime

An offense category which, according to the FBI's Uniform Crime Reports (UCR), includes murder, rape, robbery, and aggravated assault. Because the UCR depends upon reports (to the police) of crimes, the official statistics on these offenses are apt to inaccurately reflect the actual incidence of such crimes.

Property Crime

An offense category which, according to the FBI's UCR program, includes burglary, larceny, auto theft, and arson. Since citizen reports of criminal incidents figure heavily in the compilation of official statistics, the same critiques apply to tallies of these crimes as to the category of violent crime.

Victimless crimes, such as prostitution, are rarely reported. As a consequence, they are likely to be seriously underrepresented in the FBI's Uniform Crime Reports. Here, teenage prostitutes solicit a "John." **John Maher, Stock Boston.**

TABLE 2-1 ◼ Major Crimes Known to the Police 1999 (Part I Offenses from the UCR)			
OFFENSE	NUMBER	RATE PER 100,000	CLEARANCE RATE (%)
Personal/Violent Crimes			
Murder	15,533	5.7	69
Forcible rape	89,107	32.7	49
Robbery	409,670	150.2	29
Aggravated assault	916,383	336.1	59
Property Crimes			
Burglary	2,099,739	770.0	14
Larceny	6,957,412	2551.4	19
Motor vehicle theft	1,147,305	420.7	15
Arson[1]	66,321	35.0	17
U.S. total	11,635,149	4266.8	21

[1] *Arson can be classified as either a property crime or a violent crime, depending upon whether personal injury or loss of life results from its commission. It is generally classified as a property crime, however. Arson statistics are incomplete for 1999 and do not enter in the "total" tabulations.*

Source: *Adapted from Federal Bureau of Investigation,* Uniform Crime Reports for the United States, 1999 *(Washington, D.C.: U.S. Government Printing Office, 2000).*

Clearance Rate

A traditional measure of investigative effectiveness that compares the number of crimes reported and/or discovered to the number of crimes solved through arrest or other means (such as the death of a suspect).

Part I Offenses (also called Major Crimes)

Includes murder, rape, robbery, aggravated assault, burglary, larceny, and motor vehicle theft as defined under the FBI's Uniform Crime Reporting Program.

A commonly used term in today's UCRs is **clearance rate,** which refers to the proportion of reported crimes which have been "solved." Clearances are judged primarily on the basis of arrests and do not involve judicial disposition. Once an arrest has been made, a crime is regarded as "cleared" for purposes of reporting in the UCR Program. Exceptional clearances (sometimes called clearances by exceptional means) can result when law enforcement authorities believe they know who the perpetrator of a crime is but cannot make an arrest. The perpetrator may, for example, flee the country, commit suicide, or die.

For data gathering and reporting purposes, the UCR Program divides the country into four geographic regions: the Northeast, West, South, and Midwest. Unfortunately, no real attempt has been made to create divisions with nearly equal populations or similar demographic characteristics, and it is difficult to meaningfully compare one region of the country to another. Table 2-1 summarizes UCR statistics for 1999. For a detailed overview of the most recent UCR data see Web Extra! 2-3 at CJToday.com.

Part I Offenses

Murder

Murder is the unlawful killing of one human being by another.[16] UCR statistics on murder describe the yearly incidence of all willful and unlawful homicides within the United States. Included in the count are all cases of nonnegligent manslaughter which have been reported or discovered by the police. Not included in the count are suicides, justifiable homicides (that is, self-defense), deaths caused by negligence or accident, and attempts to murder. In 1999, some 15,533 murders came to the attention of police departments across the United States.[17] *First-degree murder* is a term which describes criminal homicide which is planned or involves premeditation. *Second-degree murder* is an intentional and unlawful killing, but one which is generally unplanned and which may happen "in the heat of passion."

Murder is the smallest numerical category in the Part I offenses. The 1999 murder rate was 5.7 homicides for every 100,000 persons in the country—a decrease of 9 percent over the previous year. Murder rates tend to peak annually in the warmest months. In many years, July and August show the highest number of homicides. Typically, in 1999 the month of August showed the highest number of murders.

Geographically, murder is most common in the southern states. However, because they are also the most populous, a meaningful comparison across regions of the country is difficult.

Age is no barrier to murder. Statistics for 1999 reveal that 205 infants (under the age of one) were victims of homicide, as were 281 persons aged 75 and over.[18] Persons aged 20–24 were the most likely to be murdered. Murder perpetrators were also most common in the 20- to 24-year-old age group.

Firearms are the weapon of choice in most murders. Ours is a well-armed society, and guns accounted for 65 percent of all killings in 1999. Handguns outnumbered shotguns 18 to 1 in the murder statistics, while rifles were a distant third. Knives were used in approximately 13 percent of all murders. Other weapons included explosives; poisons; narcotics overdoses; blunt objects, such as clubs; hands; feet; and fists.

Few murders are committed by strangers. Only 12 percent of all murders in 1999 were perpetrated by persons classified as "strangers." In 34 percent of all killings the relationship between the parties had not yet been determined. The largest category of killers was officially listed as "acquaintances," which probably includes a large number of former "friends." Arguments cause most murders (30 percent), but murders occur during commission of other crimes, such as robbery, rape, and burglary. Homicides which follow from other crimes are more likely to be impulsive rather than planned.

Murders may occur in sprees, which "involve killings at two or more locations with almost no time break between murders."[19] Andrew Cunanan, who killed fashion designer Gianni Versace in 1997, provides an example of a spree killer. Cunanan's killing spree lasted three months and claimed five victims.[20] He was put on the FBI's "Ten Most Wanted" list before committing suicide aboard a Miami yacht where he had hidden. In contrast to spree killing, mass murder entails "the killing of four or more victims at one location, within one event."[21] Yet another kind of murder, serial murder, happens over time and is officially defined to "involve the killing of several victims in three or more separate events."[22] In cases of serial murder, days, months, or even years may elapse between killings. Serial killers have been frequently portrayed in the media.[23] Some of the more infamous serial killers of recent years include Jeffrey Dahmer, who received 936 years in prison for the homosexual dismemberment murders of 15 young men (and who was himself later murdered in prison); Ted Bundy, who killed many college-aged women; Henry Lee Lucas, now in a Texas prison, who confessed to 600 murders but later recanted (yet was convicted of 11 murders and linked to at least 140 others);[24] Ottis Toole, Lucas's partner in crime; Charles Manson, still serving time for ordering followers to kill seven Californians, including famed actress Sharon Tate; Andrei Chikatilo, the Russian "Hannibal Lecter," who killed 52 people—mostly school children;[25] and David Berkowitz, also known as the "Son of Sam," who killed six people and wounded seven on lover's lanes around New York City.

Because murder is such a serious crime, it consumes substantial police resources. Consequently, over the years the offense has shown the highest clearance rate of any index crime. Sixty-nine percent of all homicides were cleared in 1999. Figure 2-3 shows clearance rates for all Part I offenses.

Murder

The unlawful killing of a human being. Murder *is a generic term which, in common usage, may include first- and second-degree murder, as well as manslaughter, involuntary manslaughter, and other similar kinds of offenses.*

"We are the most violent and self-destructive nation on earth. . . . In 1990, no nation had a higher murder rate than the United States. What is worse, no nation was even close."

—From a 1991 report released by Joseph R. Biden, Jr., U.S. Senate Judiciary Committee Chairman

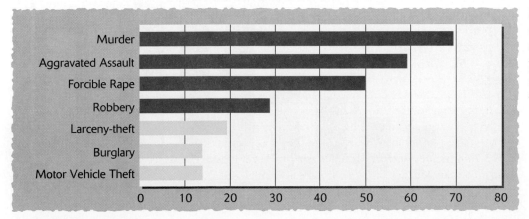

FIGURE 2-3 ■ *Crimes cleared by arrest, 1999.*

Source: *Federal Bureau of Investigation,* Crime in the United States 1999 *(Washington, D.C.: Government Printing Office, 2000).*

Forcible Rape

Rape (generic)

Unlawful sexual intercourse, achieved through force and without consent. Broadly speaking, the term rape has been applied to a wide variety of sexual attacks and may include same-sex rape and the rape of a male by a female. Some jurisdictions refer to same-sex rape as sexual battery.

Forcible Rape (UCR)

The carnal knowledge of a female forcibly and against her will. For statistical reporting purposes, however, the FBI defines forcible rape as "unlawful sexual intercourse with a female, by force and against her will, or without legal or factual consent." Statutory rape differs from forcible rape in that it involves sexual intercourse with a person who is under the age of consent—regardless of whether he or she is a willing partner. Date rape, or acquaintance rape, is a subcategory of rape which is of special concern today.

Broadly speaking, the term **rape** has been applied to a wide variety of sexual attacks and, in popular terminology, may include same-sex rape and the rape of a male by a female. Use of the term **forcible rape** for statistical reporting purposes by law enforcement agencies, however, has a specific and somewhat different meaning. The *Uniform Crime Reports* defines forcible rape as "the carnal knowledge of a female forcibly and against her will."[26] In contrast to what may be emerging social convention, in which homosexual rape is a widely recognized form of sexual assault, the latest edition of the *Uniform Crime Reporting Handbook,* which serves as a statistical reporting guide for law enforcement agencies, says: "By definition, sex attacks on males are excluded [from the crime of forcible rape] and should be classified as assaults or 'other sex offenses,' depending on the nature of the crime and the extent of the injury."[27] Although not part of UCR terminology, some jurisdictions refer to same-sex rape as "sexual battery." **Sexual battery,** which is not included in the UCR tally of reported rapes, is intentional and wrongful physical contact with a person without his or her consent that entails a sexual component or purpose.

Forcible rape is the least reported of all violent crimes. Typical estimates are that only one out of every four forcible rapes which actually occur are reported to the police. An even lower figure was reported by a 1992 government-sponsored study, which found that only 16 percent of rapes were reported.[28] The victim's fear of embarrassment has been cited as the reason most often given for nonreports. In the past, reports of rape were usually taken by seemingly hardened desk sergeants or male detectives who may not have been sensitive to the needs of the victim. In addition, the physical examination which victims had to endure was often a traumatizing experience in itself. Finally, many states routinely permitted the woman's past sexual history to be revealed in detail in the courtroom if a trial ensued. All these practices contributed to a considerable hesitancy on the part of rape victims to report their victimizations.

The last few decades have seen many changes designed to facilitate accurate reporting of rape and other sex offenses. Trained female detectives often act as victim interviewers, physicians have been better educated in handling the psychological needs of victims, and sexual histories are no longer regarded as relevant in most trials.

UCR statistics show 89,107 reported forcible rapes for 1999 (Figure 2-4), a 5 percent decrease over the number of offenses reported for the previous year. Rape is a crime which has generally shown an increase in reporting, even in years when other personal crimes have been on the decline. By definition, rapes reported under the UCR Program are always of females. Homosexual rape is excluded from the count, as are instances of forced oral copulation, but attempts to commit rape by force or the threat of force are included. Statutory rape, where no force is involved but the female is below the age of consent, is not included in rape statistics.

The offense of rape follows homicide in its seasonal variation. The greatest number of forcible rapes in 1999 were reported in the hot summer months, while January, February, November, and December recorded the lowest number of reports.

FIGURE 2-4 ■ *Rate of reported rape, 1960–1999.*

Source: *Federal Bureau of Investigation,* Crime in the United States *(Washington, D.C.: U.S. Government Printing Office, various years).*

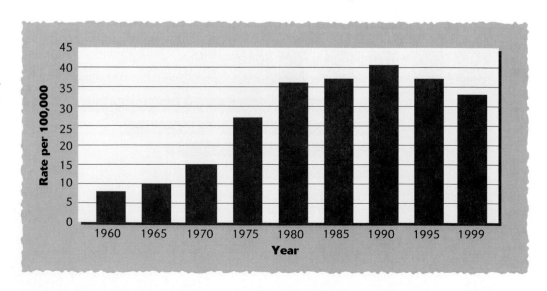

CRIME IN THE NEWS

One in 5 U.S. Women Faces Rape

NEW YORK—The problem of rape in America may be more prevalent than previously thought, according to new data released by the U.S. Justice Department.

The National Violence Against Women (NVAW) Survey, funded by the Department and conducted by the nonprofit Center for Policy Research (CPR) in Denver, reports that nearly 1 in 5 American women has at some point in her life been the victim of rape or attempted rape.

For the purpose of the study, "rape" was defined as an act or attempted act of vaginal, anal, or oral sexual penetration performed without the victim's consent under force or threat of force.

8,000 Women Surveyed

Interviewers talked by phone with 8,000 randomly selected women around the U.S. during 1995–1996, and 18 percent of those women said they had been raped or were the target of an attempted rape.

If the survey accurately reflects the whole country, it means that about 18 million American women—or a number of people equivalent to the total population of Australia—have been the victim of a rapist.

"There is no question that rape and attempted rape are more prevalent than we had initially believed. . . ." says Jean O'Neil, director of research for the National Crime Prevention Council.

Husbands, Boyfriends, and Dates

More than 40 percent of the women who said they were the victims of an attempted or completed sexual assault said the rapist was a current or former intimate partner, such as a husband, boyfriend, or date.

Half of Rape Victims Are Minors

About a quarter of all the women who had been raped said they were first sexually attacked when they were 12 or younger, while a third said they were first sexually assaulted as teens before they turned 18. That means more than half of all rape victims are minors.

Patricia Tjaden, who co-authored the report, said that "the evidence is growing that rape is prevalent and that it's a crime committed primarily against young people."

David Beatty, director of public policy for the National Victim Center (NVC), said the report's results match those of a study his group published five years ago.

"Almost point-by-point, it validated the legitimacy of our report," Beatty said, adding that his organization's report showed only 1 in 5 rape victims reported the crime.

"If we aren't making it easier for woman who come in and report these crimes, we're making it easier for perpetrators to go and do it again," Beatty added.

More Specific Questions

The federally sponsored NVAW Survey sought to get better information on crimes against women by asking more explicit questions. Interviewers never used the word "rape." Instead, they described in detail a forced sexual act and asked women if they had been subjected to it.

In comparison, a prominent Justice Department study of victims, known as the National Crime Victimization Survey, is less specific. It asks women if they've been sexually attacked without defining what that means.

O'Neil said the survey shows that women are more willing today to talk about rape. "There is much less of a social stigma against rape victims then there was even fifteen or ten years ago, so women are much more comfortable stating that something happened and feeling that they don't have to take the blame on themselves, that they can place the blame where it belongs, on the attacker. . . ."

Report Recommendations

The report recommends that the medical community receive comprehensive training about the medical needs of female victims of crime, and that a greater awareness by the public of the problem of rape and assault against women be fostered.

O'Neil says, "There's a need for services beyond what probably is currently available to help people deal with some of these traumas, many of which are long-lasting." She calls for more counseling to be provided for rape victims.

The NVAW study was released during the bi-annual meeting of the Violence Against Women Advisory Council chaired by Attorney General Janet Reno and Health & Human Services Secretary Donna Shalala on November 17th.

Source: Robert Wang, "One In 5 U.S. Women Faces Rape," APB News, Nov. 20, 1998. Reprinted with permission.

Rape is frequently committed by a man known to the victim—as in the case of date rape. Victims may be held captive and subjected to repeated assaults.[29] In the crime of heterosexual rape, any female—regardless of age, appearance, or occupation—is a potential victim. Through personal violation, humiliation, and physical battering, rapists seek a sense of personal aggrandizement and dominance. In contrast, victims of rape often experience a lessened sense of personal worth; increased feelings of despair, helplessness,

Sexual Battery

Intentional and wrongful physical contact with a person without his or her consent that entails a sexual component or purpose.

Date Rape

Unlawful forced sexual intercourse that occurs within the context of a dating relationship.

and vulnerability; a misplaced sense of guilt; and a lack of control over their personal lives.

Contemporary wisdom holds that forcible rape is often a planned violent crime which serves the offender's need for power rather than sexual gratification.[30] The "power thesis" had its origins in the writings of Susan Brownmiller, who, in 1975, argued that the primary motivation leading to rape is the male desire to "keep women in their place" and to preserve sexual role inequality through violence.[31] Although many writers on the subject of forcible rape have generally accepted the power thesis, recent studies have caused some to rethink it. In a 1995 survey of the motives of serial rapists, for example, Dennis J. Stevens found that 41 percent of imprisoned rapists—the largest category of all—reported that "lust" was "the primary motive for predatory rape."[32]

Statistically speaking, however, most rapes are committed by acquaintances of the victims and often betray a trust or friendship. **Date rape,** which falls into this category, appears to be far more common than previously believed. Recently, the growing number of rapes perpetrated with the use of the "date rape drug" Rohypnol have alarmed law enforcement personnel. Rohypnol, which is discussed in more detail in Chapter 3, is an illegal pharmaceutical substance that is virtually tasteless. Available on the black market, it dissolves easily in drinks and can leave anyone who unknowingly consumes it unconscious for hours—making them vulnerable to sexual assault.

Date rape is unlawful sexual intercourse with a female against her will which occurs within the context of a dating relationship. A number of "date rape drugs," such as Rohypnol, are sometimes secretly placed in women's drinks—rendering them unable to resist sexual advances.
Courtesy of Index Stock Imagery, Inc.

Theory Into Practice

Guns, Crime, and Gun Control

The Second Amendment to the U.S. Constitution reads, "A well regulated Militia, being necessary to the security of a free State, the right of the people to keep and bear Arms, shall not be infringed." Constitutional guarantees have combined with historical circumstances to make ours a well-armed society. In a typical year approximately 10,000 murders are committed in the United States with firearms—most with handguns. Handguns are also used in many other crimes. Approximately 1 million serious violations of the law—ranging from homicide through rape, robbery, and assault—occur each year in which a handgun is used.

A 1999 Pew Research Center poll found that two-thirds of all Americans—including three out of four women—believe that increasing restrictions on guns will prevent crime and is more important than protecting the rights of people to own them.[1] The federal government and the states have already responded to growing public concern over the easy availability of handguns. In 1994, the U.S. Congress passed, and President Clinton signed, the Brady Handgun Violence Prevention Act. The law was named for Reagan-era press secretary James Brady, who was shot and severely wounded in an attempt on the president's life on March 30, 1981. It provides for a five-day waiting period before the purchase of a handgun and for the establishment of a national instant criminal background checking system to be contacted by firearms dealers before the transfer of any firearm. Applications are to be checked to determine whether receipt or possession of a handgun would be in violation of federal, state, or local law.[2] (The national instant criminal background check system should be fully in place by the time this book goes to press.) Under the system, a licensed importer, licensed manufacturer, or licensed dealer is required to verify the

identity of a firearm purchaser using a valid photo ID (such as a driver's license) and to contact the system in order to receive a unique identification number authorizing the purchase before transfer of the handgun can be made.

The Violent Crime Control and Law Enforcement Act of 1994 further regulated the sale of firearms within the United States, banning the manufacture of 19 military-style assault weapons, including those with specific combat features, such as high-capacity ammunition clips capable of holding more than 10 rounds. The 1994 law also prohibits the sale or transfer of a gun to a juvenile, as well as the possession of a gun by a juvenile, and it prohibits gun sales to, and possession by, persons subject to family violence restraining orders.

Following the 1999 Columbine High School shooting, a number of states moved to tighten controls over handguns and assault weapons. The California legislature, for example, restricted gun purchases to one per month, and tightened a 10-year-old ban on assault weapons. Similarly, Illinois passed a law requiring that gun owners lock weapons away from anyone under 14.

Not everyone agrees that gun sales and gun ownership should be subject to additional regulation. The National Rifle Association (NRA), the Citizen's Committee for the Right to Keep and Bear Arms, and other pro-gun ownership groups have filed lawsuits to derail enforcement of the Brady act and the assault weapons provisions of the Violent Crime Control and Law Enforcement Act. In the combined cases of *Printz* v. *U.S.* (1997)[3] and *Mack* v. *U.S.* (1997),[4] for example the U.S. Supreme Court held that *state* officials could not be required to perform background checks on gun buyers under *federal* law (a requirement originally imposed by the Brady law). The NRA continues to maintain that many existing gun

control laws violate the Constitution's Second Amendment. Similarly, the NRA criticizes a federally proposed ban on guns in housing projects, arguing that the ban would be "discriminatory" and would disarm and "single-out low-income citizens."

Prior to the recent spate of high school shootings around the country, the U.S. Supreme Court, in the case of *U.S.* v. *Alfonso Lopez, Jr.* (1995),[5] upheld a lower court ruling dismissing charges against a 12th-grade student who had carried a concealed .38-caliber handgun and five bullets into Edison High School in San Antonio, Texas. The student was charged with violating the federal Gun-Free School Zones Act of 1990, which forbids "any individual knowingly to possess a firearm at a place that [he or she] knows . . . is a school zone." The law had been passed to assuage parents' concerns that their children might be in mortal danger due to the presence of guns in the hands of school-aged children and interlopers on school property. The Court ruled that education and the administration of educational facilities was a local and not a national function, effectively invalidating the law.

The 1996 Domestic Violence Offender Gun Ban[6] is a relatively new tool in the federal gun control arsenal. The ban prohibits individuals convicted of misdemeanor domestic violence offenses from owning or using firearms. Soon after the law was passed, however, it became embroiled in controversy when hundreds of police officers across the country who had been convicted of domestic violence offenses were found to be in violation of the ban. A number of officers lost their jobs, while others were placed in positions that did not require the carrying of firearms. Beth Weaver, a spokeswoman for the National Association of Police Organizations, noted that "the [ban] is causing more chaos than almost anything I've

(Continued)

Theory Into Practice

Guns, Crime, and Gun Control

ever seen in law enforcement...."[7] While some legislators pushed to exempt police officers and military personnel from the ban's provisions, others argued that they should be included. Feminist Majority President Eleanor Smeal was angered. "Rather than trying to seek an exemption for police officers and military personnel who are abusers, we should be concerned with why we are recruiting so many abusers for these positions," she said.[8]

? QUESTIONS FOR DISCUSSION

1. This box says that "not everyone agrees that gun sales and gun ownership should be subject to additional regulation." How do you feel? Why?
2. Do you believe that regulating the sale of handguns will lower the crime rate in the United States? Why or why not?
3. Should the Domestic Violence Offender Gun Ban be applied to police officers who have been convicted of domestic violence offenses? Why or why not?

[1]"Two-Thirds of Americans Support Gun Control," APB Online. Web posted at www.apbonline.com/911/1999/05/20/gunpoll0520_01.html. Accessed January 20, 2000.

[2]18 U.S.C., Section 922(q)(1)(A).

[3]*Printz v. U.S.* (1997), 521 U.S. 98 (1997).

[4]*Mack v. U.S.* (1997). Combined with *Printz v. U.S.* op. cit.

[5]*U.S. v. Alfonso Lopez, Jr.,* 115 S.Ct. 1624, 131 L. Ed. 2d 626 (1995).

[6]PL 104-208. An amendment to Section 921(a) of Title 18, USC. Also known as the Lautenberg Amendment.

[7]Jacob R. Clark, "Police Careers May Take a Beating from Fed Domestic-Violence Law," *Law Enforcement News,* vol. 23, no. 461 (February 14, 1997), p. 1.

[8]Ibid.

Rape within marriage, which has not always been recognized as a crime, is a growing area of concern in American criminal justice, and many laws have been enacted over the past few decades to deter it. Similarly, even though UCR statistics report only the rape or attempted rape of females,[33] some state statutes, by definition, allow for the rape of a male by a female. Such an offense, when it occurs, however, is typically of the statutory variety. In late 1993, for example, 24-year-old Fairfax County, Virginia, swimming coach Jean-Michelle Whitiak pleaded guilty to one count of statutory rape, admitting an affair with a 13-year-old boy. When the boy ended the relationship, Whitiak said, she had sex with two of his friends.[34] Similarly, in 1997, sixth-grade schoolteacher Mary Kay LeTourneau, a 35-year-old married mother of four, pled guilty in Burien, Washington, to second-degree child rape after having a child by one of her students—a 13-year-old boy named Vili Fualuaau. Ms. LeTourneau had known the boy since he was in the second grade. "When the sexual relationship started," she told reporters, "it seemed natural. What didn't seem natural was that there was a law forbidding such a natural thing."[35] She was sentenced to six months in jail and banned from seeing the boy or their child. Following her release after a brief jail stay, LeTourneau became known as "America's most famous pedophile" after she had a second child by her teenage lover. In 1998 she was sentenced to a 7½-year prison term for violating probation.[36]

Robbery

Robbery, sometimes confused with burglary, is a personal crime and involves a face-to-face confrontation between victim and perpetrator. Weapons may be used, or strong-armed robbery may occur through intimidation, especially where gangs threaten victims by their sheer number. Purse snatching and pocket picking are not classified as robbery by the UCR Program, but are included under the category "larceny-theft."

In 1999 individuals (versus businesses and banks) were typical targets of robbers. Banks, gas stations, convenience stores, and other businesses were the second most common target of robbers, with residential robberies accounting for only 12 percent of the total. In 1999, 409,670 robberies were reported to the police, and 48 percent of them were highway rob-

Robbery

The unlawful taking or attempted taking of property that is in the immediate possession of another, by force or the threat of force. Armed robbery differs from unarmed or strong-armed robbery with regard to the presence of a weapon. Contrary to popular conceptions, highway robbery does not necessarily occur on a street—and rarely in a vehicle. Highway robbery is a term applicable to any form of robbery which occurs in a public place and out of doors.

New York City police officials examine some of the weapons turned over to police under a program in which local businesses exchanged a $100 toy store gift coupon for each gun received. Over 1,000 weapons were collected by the program—one of many similar programs across the country that work to remove guns from the streets.
Ed Bailey, AP/Wide World Photos.

beries (meaning that they occurred outdoors, probably as the victim was walking) or muggings. Strong-armed robberies accounted for 42 percent of total robberies reported. Guns were used in 40 percent of all robberies and knives in 8 percent.

Armed robbers are dangerous. Guns are actually discharged in 20 percent of all robberies.[37] Whenever a robbery occurs, the UCR Program scores the event as one robbery, even though there may have been a number of victims who were robbed during the event. With the move toward incident-driven reporting (discussed later in this chapter), however, the UCRs will soon make data available on the number of individuals robbed in each instance of robbery. Because statistics on crime show only the most serious offense which occurred during a particular episode, robberies are often hidden when they occur in conjunction with other, more serious, crimes. For example, in a recent year 3 percent of robbery victims were also raped, and a large number of homicide victims were robbed.[38]

Robbery is primarily an urban offense, and most arrestees are young males who are members of minority groups. The robbery rate in large cities in 1999 was 477 (per every 100,000 inhabitants) while it was only 15 in rural areas. Ninety percent of those arrested in 1999 were male, 62 percent were under the age of 25, and 56 percent were minorities.[39]

Aggravated Assault

Assaults are of two types: aggravated and simple. For statistical reporting purposes, simple assaults may involve pushing and shoving or even fistfights (although, technically speaking, the correct legal term used to describe such incidents is actually *battery*). Aggravated assaults are distinguished from simple assaults by the fact that they either include the use of a weapon, or the assault victim requires medical assistance. When deadly weapons are employed, even though no injury may result, aggravated assaults may be chargeable as attempted murder.[40] Hence, because of their potentially serious consequences, the UCR Program scores some cases of attempted assault as aggravated assaults.

In 1999, 916,383 cases of aggravated assault were reported to law enforcement agencies in the United States. The summer months evidenced the greatest frequency of assault, while February, November, and December were the months with the lowest number of reports. Most aggravated assaults were committed with blunt objects or objects near at hand (35 percent), while hands, feet, and fists were also commonly used (29 percent). Less frequent were knives and firearms (18 percent each), as Figure 2-5 shows. Because those who commit assaults are often known to their victims, aggravated assaults are relatively easy to solve. Fifty-nine percent of all aggravated assaults reported to the police in 1999 were cleared by arrest.

Assault

The unlawful, intentional inflicting, or attempted or threatened inflicting, of injury upon the person of another. Historically, assault meant only the attempt to inflict injury on another person. A completed act constituted the separate offense of battery. Under modern crime statistics, however, attempted and completed acts are put together under the generic term assault. *While the terms* aggravated assault *and* simple assault *are standard terms for reporting purposes, most state penal codes use labels such as "first degree," "second degree," and so on to make such distinctions.*

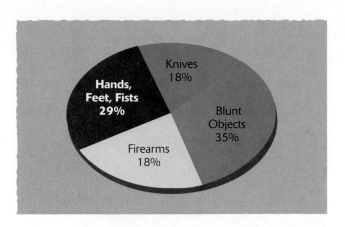

FIGURE 2-5 ■ *Aggravated assault—weapons used, 1999.*

Source: *Federal Bureau of Investigation,* Crime in the United States 1999 *(Washington, D.C.: U.S. Government Printing Office, 2000).*

Burglary

Burglary

The unlawful entry of any fixed structure, vehicle, or vessel used for regular residence, industry, or business, with or without force, with intent to commit a felony or larceny. For UCR purposes, the crime of burglary can be reported if (1) an unlawful entry of an unlocked structure has occurred, (2) a breaking and entering (of a secured structure) has taken place, or (3) a burglary has been attempted.

Although it may involve personal and even violent confrontations, **burglary** is primarily a property crime. Burglars are interested in financial gain and usually fence (that is, illegally sell) stolen items in order to recover a fraction of their cash value. About 2.1 million burglaries were reported to the police in 1999. Dollar losses to burglary victims totaled over $3.1 billion, with an average loss per offense of $1458.

Many people fear nighttime burglary of their residences. They imagine themselves asleep in bed as a stranger breaks into their home and then conjure up visions of a violent confrontation. While such scenarios do occur, daytime burglary is more common. Many families now have two or more breadwinners, and since children are in school during the day, some homes—and even entire neighborhoods—are virtually unoccupied during daylight hours. This shift in patterns of social activity has led to a growing burglary threat against residences during daytime.

The UCR Program employs three classifications of burglary: (1) forcible entry, (2) unlawful entry where no force is used, and (3) attempted forcible entry. In most jurisdictions, force need not be employed for a crime to be classified as burglary. Unlocked doors and open windows are invitations to burglars, and the crime of burglary consists not so much in a forcible entry as it does in the intent of the offender to trespass and steal. In 1999, 29 percent of all burglaries were unlawful entries, 64 percent were forcible entries, and 7 percent were attempted forcible entries.[41] The most dangerous burglaries were those in which a household member was home (about 10 percent of all burglaries).[42] Residents who were home during a burglary suffered a greater than 30 percent chance of becoming the victim of a violent crime.[43]

Property crimes generally involve low rates of clearance. Burglary is no exception. The clearance rate for burglary in 1999 was only 14 percent. Burglars are usually unknown to their victims, and, even if known, they conceal their identity by committing their crime when the victim is not present.

Larceny

Larceny

The unlawful taking or attempted taking of property other than a motor vehicle from the possession of another, by stealth, without force and without deceit, with intent to permanently deprive the owner of the property. Larceny is the most common of the eight major offenses—although probably only a small percentage of all larcenies which occur are actually reported to the police because of the small dollar amounts involved.

Larceny is another name for theft. Some states distinguish between simple larceny and grand larceny. *Grand larceny* is usually defined as theft of valuables in excess of a certain set dollar amount, such as $200. Categorizing the crime by dollar amount, however, can present unique problems, as during the high fiscal inflation periods of the 1970s, when legislatures found themselves unable to enact statutory revisions fast enough to keep pace with inflation.

Larceny, as defined by the UCR Program, includes thefts of any amount. The reports specifically list the following offenses as types of larceny (listed here in order of declining frequency):

■ Thefts from motor vehicles

■ Shoplifting

■ Thefts of motor vehicle parts and accessories

■ Thefts from buildings

■ Bicycle thefts

- Pocket picking
- Purse snatching
- Thefts from coin-operated machines

Thefts of farm animals (known as rustling) and thefts of most types of farm machinery also fall into the larceny category. In fact, larceny is such a broad category that it serves as a kind of "catchall" in the UCR. In 1995, for example, Yale University officials filed larceny charges against 25-year-old student Lon Grammer, claiming that he had fraudulently obtained university monies.[44] The university maintained that Grammer stole his education by forging college and high-school transcripts and concocting letters of recommendation prior to admission. Grammer's alleged misdeeds, which Yale University officials said misled them into thinking that Grammer, a poor student before attending Yale, had an exceptional scholastic record, permitted him to receive $61,475 in grants and loans during the time he attended the school. Grammer was also expelled.

Reported thefts can involve a wide diversity of materials with values that range anywhere from pocket change to the stealing of a $100 million aircraft. Specifically excluded from the count of larceny for reporting purposes are crimes of embezzlement, "con" games, forgery, and worthless checks. Larceny has been traditionally thought of as a crime which requires physical possession of the item appropriated. Hence, most computer crimes, including thefts engineered through online access or thefts of software and information itself, have typically not been scored as larcenies—unless electronic circuitry, disks, or machines themselves were actually stolen. On the other hand, the crime of larceny may count other types of high-technology thefts. In 1995, for example, Dr. Ricardo Asch, a world-renowned fertility doctor working at the University of California-Irvine's Center for Reproductive Health, was accused of stealing frozen human embryos and implanting them into infertile women. After fleeing to Mexico, Asch gave a videotaped deposition from a Tijuana hotel room, where he testified that he never stopped to determine if legal consent to donate had been given when he transferred eggs and embryos from one woman to another.[45] He was soon indicted on 35 counts of criminal activity, including using the mail to steal from insurance companies through the filing of false claims. The center at which Asch had worked closed after more than 50 suits were filed against it.

Reports to the police in 1999 showed 6,957,412 larcenies nationwide, with the total value of property stolen placed at $4.7 billion. The most common form of larceny in recent years has been theft of motor vehicle parts, accessories, and contents. Tires, wheels, stereos, hubcaps, radar detectors, CB radios, cassette tapes, compact discs, and cellular phones account for many of the items reported stolen.

Larceny is the most frequently reported major crime according to the UCR. It may also be the UCR's most underreported crime category because small thefts rarely come to the attention of the police. The average value of items reported stolen in 1999 was about $6678.

Motor Vehicle Theft

For record-keeping purposes, the UCR Program defines motor vehicles as self-propelled vehicles which run on the ground and not on rails. Included in the definition are automobiles, motorcycles, motorscooters, trucks, buses, and snowmobiles. Excluded are trains, airplanes, bulldozers, most farm and construction machinery, ships, boats, and spacecraft—whose theft would be scored as larceny.[46] Vehicles that are temporarily taken by individuals who have lawful access to them are not scored as thefts. Hence, spouses who jointly own most property may drive the family car, even though one spouse may think of the vehicle as his or her exclusive personal property.

As mentioned earlier, **motor vehicle theft** is a crime in which most occurrences are reported to law enforcement agencies. Insurance companies require police reports before they will reimburse car owners for their losses. Some reports of motor vehicle thefts, however, may be false. People who have damaged their own vehicles in solitary crashes, or who have been unable to sell them, may try to force insurance companies to "buy" them through reports of theft.

In 1999, 1.1 million motor vehicles were reported stolen. The average value per vehicle stolen was $6,104, making motor vehicle theft a $7 billion crime. The clearance rate for

Motor Vehicle Theft

The unlawful taking or attempted taking of a self-propelled road vehicle owned by another with the intent to deprive him or her of it permanently or temporarily. The stealing of trains, planes, boats, construction equipment, and most farm machinery is classified as larceny under the UCR reporting program, not as motor vehicle theft.

motor vehicle theft was only 15 percent in 1999. City agencies reported the lowest rates of clearance (9 percent), while rural counties had the highest rate (30 percent). Many stolen vehicles are routinely and quickly disassembled, with parts being resold through chop shops. Auto parts are, of course, much more difficult to identify and trace than are intact vehicles. In some parts of the country, chop shops operate like big businesses, and one shop may strip a dozen or more cars per day.

Motor vehicle theft can turn violent, such as in cases of "carjacking"—a crime in which offenders force the occupants of a car onto the street before stealing the vehicle. In an incident that brought carjacking to national prominence some years ago, Pamela Basu of Savage, Maryland, was dragged 2 miles to her death when she became entangled in her seat belt after being pushed from her car as the carjackers drove off. The thieves had to sideswipe a chainlink fence in order to finally dislodge her. Her 2-year-old daughter, still strapped into her carseat, was apparently later tossed from the vehicle. The FBI estimates that carjackings account for slightly more than 1 percent of all motor vehicle thefts.[47]

Arrest reports for motor vehicle theft show that the typical offender is a young male. Sixty-seven percent of all arrestees in 1999 were under the age of 25, and 84 percent were male.

Arson

Arson

The burning or attempted burning of property with or without intent to defraud. Some instances of arson are the result of malicious mischief, while others involve attempts to claim insurance monies. Still others are committed in an effort to disguise other crimes, such as murder, burglary, and larceny.

The UCR Program received crime reports from more than 16,000 law enforcement agencies in 1999.[48] Of these, only 8,061 submitted **arson** reports for all 12 months of the year. Few agencies provided complete data as to the type of arson (nature of the item burned), the estimated monetary value of the property damaged, ownership of the property, and so on.

Current arson data include only those fires which, through investigation, are determined to have been willfully or maliciously set. Fires of unknown or suspicious origin are excluded from arson statistics.[49]

The intentional and unlawful burning of structures (houses, storage buildings, manufacturing facilities, etc.) was the type of arson most often reported in 1999 (29,934 instances). The arson of vehicles was the second most common category, with 19,965 such burnings reported. The average dollar loss per instance of arson in 1999 was $10,882, and the estimated total nationwide property damage was placed at close to $1 billion.[50] As with most property crimes, the clearance rate for arson was low—only 17 percent nationally.

The crime of arson exists in a kind of statistical limbo. In 1979 Congress ordered that it be added as an eighth Index offense. To date, however, the UCR Program has been unable to integrate statistics on arson successfully into the yearly Crime Index. The problem is twofold: (1) many law enforcement agencies have not yet begun making regular reports to the FBI on arson offenses which come under their jurisdiction, and (2) any change in the number of index offenses produces a Crime Index which will not permit meaningful comparisons to earlier crime data.

The Crime Index is a composite offense rate which provides for useful comparisons over time and between jurisdictions, so long as it retains definitional consistency. Adding a new offense to the Index, or substantially changing the definition of any of its categories, still provides a measure of *crime,* but it changes the meaning of the term.

Some of these difficulties may eventually be resolved through the Special Arson Program, authorized by Congress in 1982. The FBI, in conjunction with the National Fire Data Center, now operates a Special Arson Reporting System, which focuses upon fire departments across the nation. The Arson Reporting system is designed to provide data which supplements yearly UCR arson tabulations.[51]

Part II Offenses

Part II Offenses

In UCR terminology, a set of categories used to report data concerning arrests for less-serious offenses.

The *Uniform Crime Reports* also include information on what the FBI calls Part II offenses. **Part II offenses** are generally less serious than those that make up the Crime Index and include a number of social order, or so-called victimless, crimes. The statistics on Part II offenses are for recorded arrests, not crimes reported to the police. The logic inherent in this form of scoring is that most Part II offenses would never come to the attention of the police

TABLE 2-2 ■ UCR Part II Offenses, 1999

OFFENSE CATEGORY	NUMBER OF ARRESTS
Simple assault	1,294,400
Forgery and counterfeiting	106,900
Fraud	363,800
Embezzlement	17,100
Stolen property (receiving, etc.)	121,900
Vandalism	278,200
Weapons (carrying, etc.)	172,400
Prostitution and related offenses	92,100
Sex offenses (statutory rape, etc.)	92,400
Drug law violations	1,532,200
Gambling	10,400
Offenses against the family (nonsupport, etc.)	151,200
Driving under the influence	1,511,300
Liquor law violations	657,900
Public drunkenness	656,100
Disorderly conduct	633,100
Vagrancy	30,000
Curfew/loitering	167,200
Runaways	148,300
Total	8,036,900

Source: *Federal Bureau of Investigation,* Uniform Crime Reports for the United States, 1999 *(Washington, D.C.: U.S. Government Printing Office, 2000).*

were it not for arrests. Included in the Part II category are the crimes shown in Table 2-2 with the number of estimated arrests made in each category for 1999.

Part II arrests are counted each time a person is taken into custody. As a result, the statistics in Table 2-2 do not measure the number of persons arrested, but rather the number of arrests made. Some persons were arrested more than once.

NIBRS: The New UCR

NIBRS

The National Incident Based Reporting System, soon to become part of the FBI's Uniform Crime Reports.

The *Uniform Crime Reports* are undergoing significant changes in the way in which data are gathered and reported. From 1985 to 1992 the UCR Program was comprehensively evaluated under federal contract by ABT Associates of Cambridge, Massachusetts. The final report of the UCR study group, entitled *A Blueprint for the Future of the Uniform Crime Reporting System,* recommended a number of sweeping changes. Among them were the following:

■ Each category of offense should clearly distinguish statistics on attempts versus actual commissions.

■ The rape category should be broadened to include all forcible sex offenses. Sexual battery, sodomy, and oral copulation—accomplished through the use of force—should be included.

■ The hierarchy rule should be modified so as to count the most serious offense *for each individual victim* during an incident.[52]

■ Crimes against individuals, households, and businesses should be more clearly distinguished in most categories.

■ Aggravated assault should be more clearly defined in terms of the weapons used and the degree of injury suffered.

■ A code of professional standards should be developed for reporting agencies and for the system as a whole.

■ The UCR should be modified so as to permit easier and more meaningful comparisons with the NCVS and with Offender-Based Transaction Statistics (OBTS).

Many of these changes are now being implemented. Whereas the original UCR system was "summary based," the new enhanced UCR, called the National Incident-Based Reporting System, or NIBRS, is a national incident-based reporting system. Under NIBRS, city, county, state, and federal law enforcement agencies throughout the country furnish detailed data on crime and arrest activities at the incident level to either the individual state IBR programs or directly to the Federal NIBRS Program.

The old (UCR) system depended upon statistical tabulations of crime data which were often little more than frequency counts. In contrast, NIBRS is "incident driven." Under the new system, many details will be gathered about each criminal incident. Included among them will be information on place of occurrence, weapon used, type and value of property damaged or stolen, the personal characteristics of the offender and the victim, the nature of any relationship between the two, nature of the disposition of the complaint, and so on. The new reporting system replaces the old Part I and Part II offenses with 22 general offenses, including arson, assault, bribery, burglary, counterfeiting, vandalism, narcotic offenses, embezzlement, extortion, fraud, gambling, homicide, kidnapping, larceny, motor vehicle theft, pornography, prostitution, robbery, forcible sex offenses, nonforcible sex offenses, receiving stolen property, and weapons violations. Other offenses on which data will be gathered include bad checks, vagrancy, disorderly conduct, driving under the influence, drunkenness, nonviolent family offenses, liquor law violations, "peeping Tom" activity, runaway, trespass, and a general category of all "other" criminal law violations. Definitional differences in major crime categories for the UCR and NIBRS are shown in Table 2-3.

NIBRS eliminates the need for the hierarchy rule (because multiple types of crimes can be reported within a single incident) and collects an expanded array of attributes involved in the commission of offenses, including whether the offender is suspected of using alcohol, drugs or narcotics, and/or a computer in the commission of the offense. The FBI began accepting crime data in NIBRS format in January 1989. Although NIBRS was intended to be fully in place by 1999, delays have been routine. A recent evaluation of the status of NIBRS implementation reported that "[a]lthough it has been a full decade since publication of the *Blueprint* recommending incident-based reporting, less than 6 percent of the U.S. population is represented by NIBRS contributing agencies."[53] A 1999 report by the Bureau of Justice Statistics found that law enforcement agencies in 14 states were contributing UCR data using the NIBRS format. Remaining agencies were continuing to report crime incident data under the old format. A separate study concluded that for many law enforcement "agencies, the costs of implementing changes in reporting practices to make their systems NIBRS-compliant (for example, revising offense reporting forms, department-wide training, and software reprogramming), compounded by concerns over the impact NIBRS will have on the department's reported crime rate and a lack of understanding on how the data will be used at state and federal levels, create formidable impediments to NIBRS implementation."[54] For additional information on NIBRS see WebExtra! 2-4 at CJToday.com.

Other reporting changes, however, have already occurred. The 1990 Crime Awareness and Campus Security Act, for example, required college campuses to commence publishing annual "security reports." Although campuses are not required by the law to share crime data directly with the FBI, many have begun doing just that—increasing the reported national incidence of a variety of offenses. In May 1999, the *Chronicle of Higher Education* reported that 13 murders and 1,053 forcible sex offenses occurred at public and private four-year institutions with 5,000 or more students during 1997—the most recent year for which data were available. Another 890 robberies, 2,071 aggravated assaults, 13,947 burglaries, and 3,957 motor vehicle thefts were reported at those schools.[55]

Hate Crimes

A final change in reporting practices followed from the Hate Crime Statistics Act, signed into law by President Bush in April 1990. The act mandates a statistical tally of "hate crimes," and data collection under the law began in January 1991.

TABLE 2-3 ■ UCR and NIBRS Offense Classifications

OFFENSE	UCR	NIBRS
Homicide	The classification of this offense, as for all other Crime Index offenses, is based solely on police investigation as opposed to the determination of a court, medical examiner, coroner, jury, or other judicial body; these are law enforcement statistics. Not included in the count for this offense classification are deaths caused by negligence, suicide, or accident; and attempts to murder or assaults to murder, which are scored as aggravated assaults.	
	Murder and nonnegligent manslaughter: The willful (nonnegligent) killing of one human being by another.	**Murder and nonnegligent manslaughter:** The willful (nonnegligent) killing of one human being by another.
	Also excluded in the count for this offense classification are deaths caused by justifiable homicides, which are recorded as murder and then unfounded.	
	As a general rule, any death due to injuries received in a fight, argument, quarrel, assault, or commission of a crime is classified in this category. Although offenders may be charged with lesser offenses, e.g., manslaughter, if the killing was "willful" or intentional it must be reported in this category.	
	Manslaughter by negligence: The killing of another person through gross negligence.	**Negligent manslaughter:** The killing of another person through negligence.
	Does not include traffic fatalities. However, arrests in connection with traffic fatalities should be counted on the Age, Sex, Race, and Ethnic Origin of Persons Arrested form as manslaughter by negligence.	Does not include accidental traffic fatalities.
	Not included in this category are deaths of persons due to their own negligence; accidental deaths not resulting from gross negligence.	
	Justifiable homicide: The killing of a felon by a peace officer in the line of duty, or the killing (during the commission of a felony) of a felon by a private citizen.	**Justifiable homicide:** The killing of a perpetrator of a serious criminal offense by a peace officer in the line of duty; or the killing, during the commission of a serious criminal offense, of a perpetrator by a private individual.
	Recorded as murder and then unfounded, no actual offenses will be counted or recorded for justifiable homicides.	Justifiable homicide is not an actual "offense" and is not included in an agency's crime counts. The crime that was being committed when the justifiable homicide took place must be reported as a separate incident.
	In cases of justifiable homicide, a second offense, the crime the felon was committing at the time of death, must also be recorded and cleared by exceptional means.	
Forcible Sex Offenses (NIBRS)		**Forcible sex offenses:** Any sexual act directed against another person, forcibly, and/or against that person's will; or not forcibly or against the person's will where the victim is incapable of giving consent. Forcible rape, forcible sodomy, sexual assault with an object, and forcible fondling are included in this category.
Forcible Rape	**Forcible rape:** The carnal knowledge of a female forcibly and against her will. a) rape by force b) attempts to commit forcible rape Includes female victims only.	**Forcible rape:** The carnal knowledge of a person, forcibly, and/or against that person's will, or not forcibly or against the person's will where the victim is incapable of giving consent because of his/her temporary or permanent mental or physical incapacity (or because of his/her youth). Includes male and female victims. Cases where victim and offender are of the same sex are classified under forcible sodomy.
	In cases where several offenders rape one person, one forcible rape is reported. The number of offenders is not counted. Assaults or attempts to commit rape by force or threat of force are also included; however, statutory rape (without force) and other sex offenses are excluded from this classification.	

(Continued)

TABLE 2-3 ■ UCR and NIBRS Offense Classifications

OFFENSE	UCR	NIBRS
Robbery	**Robbery:** The taking or attempting to take anything of value from the care, custody, or control of a person or persons by force or threat of force or violence and/or by putting the victim in fear. a) firearm b) knife or cutting instrument c) other dangerous weapon d) strong-arm—hands, fists, feet, etc.	**Robbery:** The taking, or attempting to take, anything of value under confrontational circumstances from the control, custody, or care of another person by force or threat of force or violence and/or by putting the victim in fear of immediate harm. Because some type of assault is an element of the crime of robbery, an assault should not be reported as a separate crime as long as it was performed in the furtherance of the robbery. However, if the injury results in death, a homicide offense must also be reported.
	In any instance of robbery, one offense is scored for *each distinct operation* including attempts. Not counted are the number of victims robbed, those present at the robbery, or the number of offenders. In cases involving pretended weapons or those in which the weapon is not seen by the victim but the robber claims to possess one, the incident is classified as armed robbery.	
Assault	**Assault:** An unlawful attack by one person upon another. **Aggravated assault:** An unlawful attack by one person upon another for the purpose of inflicting severe or aggravated bodily injury; this type of assault usually is accompanied by the use of a weapon or by means likely to produce death or great bodily harm. a) firearm b) knife or cutting instrument c) other dangerous weapon d) hands, fists, feet, etc. (aggravated injury) e) other—simple, not aggravated (see below)	**Assault:** An unlawful attack by one person upon another. **Aggravated assault:** An unlawful attack by one person upon another wherein the offender uses a weapon or displays it in a threatening manner, or the victim suffers obvious severe or aggravated bodily injury involving apparent broken bones, loss of teeth, possible internal injury, severe laceration, or loss of consciousness. This also includes assault with disease (as in cases when the offender is aware that he/she is infected with a deadly disease and deliberately attempts to inflict the disease by biting, spitting, etc.).
	It is not necessary that an injury result when a gun, knife, or other weapon is used which could and probably would result in serious personal injury.	
	Other assault: e) other—simple, not aggravated Include in this category all assaults which do not involve the use of a firearm, knife, cutting instrument, or other dangerous weapon and in which there were no serious or aggravated injuries to the victims. Include such offenses as simple assault, assault and battery, injury caused by culpable negligence, intimidation, coercion, and all attempts to commit these offenses. Simple assault is not within the Crime Index—it is a Part IIoffense but is collected as a quality control matter and for the purpose of looking at total assault violence.	**Simple assault:** An unlawful physical attack by one person upon another where neither the offender displays a weapon, nor the victim suffers obvious severe or aggravated bodily injury involving apparent broken bones, loss of teeth, possible internal injury, severe laceration or loss of consciousness. **Intimidation:** To unlawfully place another person in reasonable fear of bodily harm through the use of threatening words and/or other conduct, but without displaying a weapon or subjecting the victim to actual physical attack.
Burglary	**Burglary:** The unlawful entry of a structure to commit a felony or a theft (excludes tents, trailers, and other mobile units used for recreational purposes). The use of force to gain entry is not required to classify an offense as burglary. Burglary in this Program is categorized into three subclassifications: a) forcible entry b) unlawful entry—no force c) attempted forcible entry	**Burglary:** The unlawful entry into a building or other structure with the intent to commit a felony or a theft (excludes tents, trailers, and other mobile units used for recreational purposes). Because burglary is defined in terms of theft, only the burglary is to be reported, and not the accompanying larceny. Expands the *hotel rule* to include temporary rental storage facilities, i.e., "mini-storage" and "self-storage" buildings.
	Burglaries of hotels, motels, lodging houses, and other places where lodging of transients is the main purpose are scored under provisions of the "Hotel Rule." This principle of scoring dictates that if a number of dwelling units under a single manager are burglarized and the offenses are most likely to be reported to the police by the manager rather than the individual tenants, the burglary should be scored as one offense.	

(Continued)

TABLE 2-3 ■ UCR and NIBRS Offense Classifications

OFFENSE	UCR	NIBRS
Larceny	**Larceny:** The unlawful taking, carrying, leading, or riding away of property from the possession, or constructive possession, of another.	**Larceny:** The unlawful taking, carrying, leading, or riding away of property from the possession, or constructive possession, of another person.
	Larceny and theft mean the same thing in Uniform Crime Reporting. Motor vehicle theft is not included and is counted as a separate offense because of the great volume of thefts in that particular category. All thefts and attempted thefts are counted. This crime category does not include embezzlement, confidence games, forgery, and worthless checks.	
	Pocket-picking: The theft of articles from a person by stealth where the victim usually does not become immediately aware of the theft.	**Pocket-picking:** The theft of articles from another person's physical possession by stealth where the victim usually does not become immediately aware of the theft.
	Purse-snatching: The grabbing or snatching of a purse, handbag, etc. from the custody of an individual.	**Purse-snatching:** The grabbing or snatching of a purse, handbag, etc., from the physical possession of another person.
	Shoplifting: The theft by a person (other than an employee) of goods or merchandise exposed for sale.	**Shoplifting:** The theft, by someone other than an employee of the victim, of goods or merchandise exposed for sale.
	Thefts from motor vehicles: Except theft of motor vehicle parts and accessories, the theft of articles from a motor vehicle, whether locked or unlocked.	**Theft from motor vehicle:** The theft of articles from a motor vehicle, whether locked or unlocked.
	Theft of motor vehicle parts and accessories: The theft of any part or accessory attached to the interior or exterior of a motor vehicle in a manner that would make the part an attachment to the vehicle or necessary for the operation of the vehicle.	**Theft of motor vehicle parts or accessories:** The theft of any part or accessory affixed to the interior or exterior of a motor vehicle in a manner that would make the item an attachment of the vehicle or necessary for its operation.
	Thefts of bicycles: The unlawful taking of any bicycle, tandem bicycle, unicycle, etc.	**Theft of bicycles:** NIBRS does not classify theft of bicycles as a separate type of larceny. Bicycles can be identified by the Property Type data element.
	Thefts from buildings: A theft from within a building that is open to the general public and where the offender has legal access.	**Theft from building:** A theft from within a building that is either open to the general public or where the offender has legal access.
	Thefts from coin-operated device or machine: A theft from a device or machine which is operated or activated by the use of a coin.	**Theft from coin-operated machine or device:** A theft from a machine or device that is operated or activated by the use of coins.
	All other larceny—theft not specifically classified: All thefts that do not fit the definition of the specific categories of larceny listed above.	**All other larceny:** All thefts that do not fit any of the definitions of the specific subcategories of Larceny/Theft listed above.
Motor Vehicle Theft	**Motor vehicle theft:** The theft or attempted theft of a motor vehicle.	**Motor vehicle theft:** The theft of a motor vehicle.
	Motor vehicle theft includes joyriding, excludes the taking of a motor vehicle for temporary use by those persons having lawful access. A "motor vehicle" is defined for UCR purposes as a self-propelled vehicle that runs on land surface and not on rails. This offense category includes the stealing of automobiles, trucks, buses, motorcycles, motor scooters, snowmobiles, etc. It does not include farm equipment, bulldozers, airplanes, construction equipment, or motorboats.	
	Autos: All sedans, station wagons, coupes, convertibles, and other similar motor vehicles that serve the primary purpose of transporting people from one place to another; also include automobiles used as taxis.	**Automobiles:** Sedans, coupes, station wagons, convertibles, taxicabs, or other similar motor vehicles that serve the primary purpose of transporting people.
	Trucks and buses: Vehicles specifically designed to transport people on a commercial basis and to transport cargo; includes pickup trucks and vans regardless of their use; in UCR the self-propelled motor home is a truck.	**Trucks:** Motor vehicles that are specifically designed (but not necessarily used) to transport cargo on a commercial basis. **Buses:** Motor vehicles that are specifically designed (but not necessarily used) to transport groups of people on a commercial basis.

(Continued)

TABLE 2-3 ■ UCR and NIBRS Offense Classifications

OFFENSE	UCR	NIBRS
	Recreational vehicles are included with trucks and buses.	Recreational vehicles: Motor vehicles that are specifically designed (but not necessarily used) to transport people and also provide them temporary lodging for recreational purposes.
	Other vehicles: All other vehicles limited by the UCR definition, such as snowmobiles, motorcycles, motor scooters, trail bikes, mopeds, golf carts, etc.	Other motor vehicles: Any other motor vehicles, e.g., motorcycles, motor scooters, trail bikes, mopeds, snowmobiles, golfcarts, whose primary purpose is to transport people.

Source: Uniform Crime Reporting Handbook *(FBI, 1984);* Crime in the United States, 1998 *(FBI, 1999);* Uniform Crime Reporting Handbook NIBRS Edition *(FBI, 1992);* Uniform Crime Reporting, National Incident-Based Reporting System, Volume 1, Data Collection Guidelines *(FBI, 1996).*

Hate Crimes

Criminal offenses in which the defendant's conduct was motivated by hatred, bias, or prejudice, based on the actual or perceived race, color, religion, national origin, ethnicity, gender, or sexual orientation of another individual or group of individuals.

Hate crimes have been defined by Congress as offenses "in which the defendant's conduct was motivated by hatred, bias, or prejudice, based on the actual or perceived race, color, religion, national origin, ethnicity, gender, or sexual orientation of another individual or group of individuals."[56] In 1999 police agencies reported a total of 7,876 hate crime incidents, including 17 murders, across the country. Sixteen percent of the incidents were motivated by religious bias, while 56 percent were caused by racial hatred. Sixteen percent of all hate crimes were based on sexual orientation, and most of those were committed against males believed by their victimizers to be homosexuals.[57] Most hate crimes fell into the category of "intimidation," although vandalism, simple assault, and aggravated assault also accounted for a fair number of hate crime offenses. Notable in recent years has been a spate of church burnings throughout the South where congregations have been predominantly African American. A few robberies and rapes were also classified under the hate crime umbrella in 1999.

One particularly heinous and widely publicized hate crime[58] culminated in death sentences for white Jasper County, Texas, residents 24-year old John William King and 32-year-old Lawrence Russell Brewer. In 1999 King and Brewer were found guilty in separate trials of capital murder for lashing James Byrd, Jr., a 49-year-old black man, to a pickup truck with a chain and dragging him to his death over 3 miles of rural Texas asphalt. Byrd, who was tied by his ankles, died after his right arm and head were severed when his body struck the edge of a culvert. If executed, King or Brewer will become only the second white person ever put to death in Texas for killing a black person. A third white supremacist, 24-year-old Shawn Allen Berry, was tried on the same charges.

Although hate crimes are popularly conceived of as crimes motivated by racial enmity, the Violent Crime Control and Law Enforcement Act of 1994 created a new definitional category of "crimes of violence motivated by gender." Congress defined a gender-motivated crime of violence to mean "a crime of violence committed because of gender or on the basis of gender, and due, at least in part, to an animus based on the victim's gender. . . ." Additionally, the act mandated the addition to the hate crimes category of crimes motivated by biases against persons with disabilities.

Bias Crimes

Another term for hate crimes.

Hate crimes are sometimes called **bias crimes.** One form of bias crime that bears special mention is homophobic homicide. Homophobic homicide is a term that refers to the murder of homosexuals by those opposed to their lifestyles. A 1997 movie, *Licensed to Kill,* by producer/director Arthur Dong, for example, tells a harrowing story about homophobia and murder using police interrogation videos, crime scene photos, and courtroom footage of real-life events. Included in the movie is a detailed description of how former U.S. Army Sergeant Kenneth French, Jr., randomly killed four people in a Fayetteville, North Carolina, restaurant in response to President Clinton's decision to allow gays into the military. According to witnesses, French shouted, "I'll show you, Clinton, about letting gays into the army," as he fired at patrons and the restaurant's owner.[59]

Even more worrisome to many enforcement agencies is the continued growth of separatist groups with their own vision of a future America. Some, such as the White Aryan

Convicted killers John William King, 25 (front, left photo), and Lawrence Russell Brewer, 32, are escorted from the Jasper County, Texas, Courthouse. King and Brewer were convicted of the 1998 pickup truck dragging death of James Byrd, Jr. (right). Both men received death sentences. A third defendant, Shawn Allen Berry, 24 (not pictured), was sentenced to serve at least 40 years in prison.
Left: *Courtesy of David J. Phillip, AP/Wide World Photos.* **Right:** *Liaison Agency, Inc.*

Resistance (WAR), hope for the start of RAHOWA, or racial holy war. RAHOWA was mentioned in the opening story of Chapter 1, where the term was associated with the World Church of the Creator—the group to which 1999 hate crime shooter Benjamin Nathaniel Smith belonged. In another 1999 case, Buford Oneal Furrow, Jr., a 37-year-old mechanic was charged with multiple counts of attempted murder in an armed attack on a day care facility in Los Angeles run by the North Valley Jewish Community Center. The attack injured three little boys, a counselor, and a receptionist. Furrow, a member of the supremacist group known as Aryan Nations, was also charged with the murder of a postal employee. A year earlier he had told police: "I am a white separatist." The declaration came as Furrow waved a knife in a Seattle-area psychiatric hospital where he tried to have himself committed.

Other supremacist groups include the White Patriot Party; Posse Comitatus; the Covenant, the Sword, and the Arm of the Lord; the Ku Klux Klan; the Order; and umbrella organizations such as the Christian Conservative Church. Described variously as the "radical right," "neo-Nazis," "skinheads," "white supremacists," and "racial hate groups," indications are that these groups are organized, well financed, and extremely well armed. John R. Harrell, leader of the Christian Conservative Church, preaches that the nation is on the eve of destruction. According to some authorities, Christian patriots are exhorted to stand ready to seize control of the nation before leadership can fall into the "wrong hands."[60] Such extremist groups adhere to identity theology, a religion which claims that members of the white race are God's chosen people. Identity theology envisions an America ruled exclusively by white people under "God's law."[61] Figure 2-6 shows the location of various supremacist and survivalist groups in the United States.

Whatever we may think of them, the activities of supremacist groups may be constitutionally protected, at least in some instances. Recent authors[62] suggest, for example, that statutes intended to control hate crimes may run afoul of constitutional considerations insofar as they (1) are too vague, (2) criminalize thought more than action, (3) attempt to control what would otherwise be free speech, and (4) deny equal protection of the laws to those who wish to express their personal biases. The U.S. Supreme Court would seem to agree. In the 1992 case of *R.A.V.* v. *City of St. Paul,*[63] which involved a burning cross on the front lawn of a black family, the Court struck down a city ordinance designed to prevent the bias-motivated display of symbols or objects, such as Nazi swastikas or burning crosses. In the same year, in the case of *Forsyth County, Ga.* v. *Nationalist Movement,*[64] the Court held that a

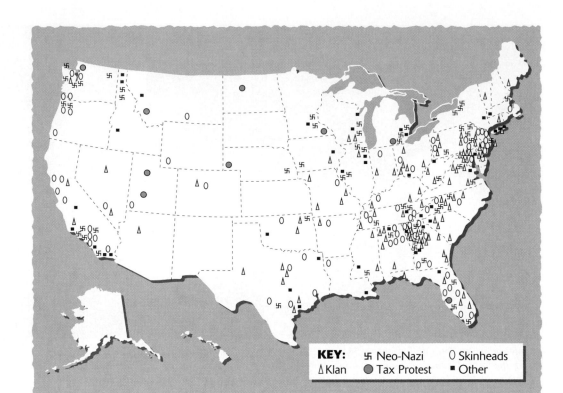

FIGURE 2-6 ■ *White supremacist groups in the United States.*
Source: *Klanwatch Project. Reprinted with permission.*

KEY: ᛋ Neo-Nazi   O Skinheads
△ Klan   ⬤ Tax Protest   ■ Other

Theory Into Practice

Hate Crimes

A decade ago, Glenn Miller, then leader of the White Patriot Party in North Carolina, declared war on ZOG—the "Zionist Occupational Government"—a conspiratorial coalition that Miller and his followers believed held the true reins of power in the United States. What follows is a portion of that strongly worded original document— authentically reproduced here to include the misspellings and typographical errors found in the original. Not long after the declaration was issued, Miller was arrested and sent to prison for his part in various crimes against the government.

Declaration of War

Dear White Patriots:
All 5,000 White Patriots are now honor bound and duty bound to pick up the sword and do battle against the forces of evil. In the name of our Aryan God, thru His beloved son, I Glenn Miller now this 6th day of April 1987 do hereby declare total war. I ask for no quarter. I will give none. I declare war against Niggers, Jews, Queers, assorted Mongrels, White Race traitors and despicable informants. We White Patriots will now begin the Race War and it will spread gloriously thru-out the nation. We will cleanse the land of evil, corruption, and mongrels. And, we will build a glorious future and a nation in which all our People can scream proudly, and honestly, "This is our Land. This is our People. This is our God, and this we will defend." War is the only way now, brothers and sisters. ZOG has pointed the way for us. He has left us no other choice. And, so fellow Aryan Warriors strike now. Strike for your home land. Strike for your Southern honor. Strike for the little chil-

dren. Strike for your wives and loved ones. Strike for sweet Mother Dixie. Strike for the 16 million innocent White babies murdered by Jew-legalized abortion and who cry out from their graves for vengeance. Strike for the millions of your People who have been raped, assaulted, and murdered by niggers and other mongrels. Strike in vengence against the Jews for all the millions of our Race slaughtered in Jew-Wars. Strike my brothers and sisters, strike, for all the outrages committed against our People....

For God, Race, Nation and Southern Honor

Glenn Miller, Leader White Patriot Party and Loyal member of "The Order"

"THE ORDER WILL LIVE SO LONG AS ONE OF US BREATHES"

county requirement regulating parades was unconstitutional because it regulated freedom of speech—in this case a plan by an affiliate of the Ku Klux Klan to parade in opposition to a Martin Luther King birthday celebration. In 1995, in the case of *Capitol Square Review* and *Advisory Board* v. *Pinette,* the Court reiterated its position, saying that KKK organizers in Ohio could legitimately erect an unattended cross on the Statehouse Plaza in Columbus's Capitol Square. Some laws intended to reduce the incidence of hate crimes appear to pass Supreme Court muster, however. In 1993, in the case of *Wisconsin* v. *Mitchell,*[65] for example, the Court held that Mitchell, a black man whose severe beating of a white boy was racially motivated, could be punished with additional severity as permitted by Wisconsin law because he acted out of race hatred. The Court called the assault "conduct unprotected by the First Amendment" and upheld the Wisconsin statute saying, "[since] the statute has no 'chilling effect' on free speech, it is not unconstitutionally overbroad."

The National Crime Victimization Survey

As mentioned near the beginning of this chapter, a second major source of statistical data about crime in the United States is the National Crime Victimization Survey (NCVS), which is based upon victim self-reports rather than on police reports. The NCVS began operation in 1972 and built upon earlier efforts by both the National Opinion Research Center and the President's Commission on Law Enforcement and the Administration of Justice in the late 1960s to uncover what some had been calling the "dark figure" (or unreported offenses) of crime.

Early data from the NCVS changed the way criminologists thought about crime in the United States. The use of victim self-reports led to the discovery that crime of all types was more prevalent than UCR statistics indicated. Many cities were shown to have victimization rates more than twice the rate of reported offenses. Others, such as St. Louis, Missouri, and Newark, New Jersey, were found to have rates of victimization which very nearly approximated reported crime. New York, often thought of as a "high-crime" city, was discovered to have one of the lowest rates of self-reported victimization.

NCVS data are gathered by the Bureau of Justice Statistics (BJS) through a cooperative arrangement with the U.S. Census Bureau.[66] NCVS interviewers work with a national sample of more than 50,000 households which are interviewed twice each year. Household lists are completely revised at the end of every three-year period. BJS statistics are published as research briefs called "Criminal Victimization," and an annual report entitled *Criminal Victimization in the United States.*

Using definitions similar to those used by the UCR Program, the NCVS includes data on the national incidence of rape, robbery, assault, burglary, personal and household larceny, and motor vehicle theft. Not included are murder, kidnapping, and victimless crimes. Commercial robbery and the burglary of businesses were dropped from NCVS reports in 1977. The NCVS employs a hierarchical counting system similar to that of the pre-NIBRS system: It counts only the most "serious" incident in any series of criminal events perpetrated against the same individual. Both completed and attempted offenses are counted, although only persons 12 years of age and older are included in household surveys. Highlights of NCVS statistics for the 1990s reveal the following:

- Approximately 23 million American households per year are touched by crime—or 25 percent of all households.
- Nearly 31 million victimizations are reported to the NCVS per year.
- City residents are about twice as likely as rural residents to be victims of crime.
- About half of all violent crimes, two-fifths of all household crimes, and slightly more than one-fourth of all crimes of personal theft are reported to police.[67]
- The total "personal cost" of crime to victims is about $13 billion per year for the United States as a whole.
- Victims of crime are more often men than women.
- Younger people are more likely than the elderly to be victims of crime.

National Crime Victimization Survey (NCVS)

An annual survey of selected American households conducted by the Bureau of Justice Statistics (BJS) in order to determine the extent of criminal victimization throughout the United States—especially unreported victimization.

TABLE 2-4 ■ A Comparison of UCR and NCVS Data, 1999

OFFENSE	UCR	NCVS[1]
Violent Crime		
Homicide[2]	15,533	—
Forcible rape	89,107	383,000
Robbery	409,670	810,000
Aggravated assault	916,383	1,503,000
Property Crime		
Burglary	2,099,739	3,652,000
Larceny	6,957,412	16,495,000
Motor vehicle theft	1,147,305	1,068,000
Arson[3]	66,321	—
Total of all crimes recorded[4]	11,635,149	28,780,000

[1] NCVS data covers "households touched by crime," not absolute numbers of crime occurrences. More than one victimization may occur per household, but only the number of households in which victimizations occur enter the tabulations.
[2] Homicide statistics are not maintained by the NCVS.
[3] Arson data are incomplete in the UCR and not reported by NCVS.
[4] NCVS numbers include other crimes not shown in the table.

Sources: Compiled from the U.S. Department of Justice, Criminal Victimization 1999 (Washington, D.C.: Bureau of Justice Statistics, 2000); Federal Bureau of Investigation, Crime in the United States, 1999 (Washington, D.C.: U.S. Government Printing Office, 2000).

■ Blacks are more likely than whites or members of other racial groups to be victims of violent crimes.[68]

■ Violent victimization rates are higher among people in lower-income families.

■ Young males have the highest violent victimization rates; elderly females have the lowest.

■ The chance of violent criminal victimization is much higher for young black males than for any other segment of the population. (The life chances of murder run from a high of 1 in 21 for a black male to a low of 1 in 369 for a white female.)[69]

A comparison of NCVS and UCR data for 1999 can be found in Table 2-4. Explore the latest NCVS data via WebExtra! 2-5 at CJToday.com.

Problems with the NCVS

Because most researchers believe that self-reports provide a more accurate gauge of criminal incidents than do police reports, many tend to accept NCVS data over that which is provided by the UCR program. The NCVS, however, is not without its problems. Primary among them is the potential for false or exaggerated reports. False reports may be generated by overzealous interviewers or self-aggrandizing respondents and are difficult to filter out. There are no reliable estimates as to the proportion of such responses which make up NCVS totals. Unintentional inaccuracies create other problems. Respondents may suffer from faulty memories, they may misinterpret events, and they may ascribe criminal intent to accidents and mistakes. Likewise, the lapse of time between the event itself and the conduct of the interview may cause some crimes to be forgotten and others to be inaccurately reported.

Comparisons of the UCR and NCVS

Table 2-5 summarizes the differences between the UCR and the NCVS. Both provide estimates of crime in America. Both are limited by the type of crimes they choose to measure, by those they exclude from measurement, and by the methods they use to gather crime data.

TABLE 2-5 ■ How Do the UCR and NCVS Compare?

	UNIFORM CRIME REPORTS	NATIONAL CRIME VICTIMIZATION SURVEY
Offenses measured	Homicide Rape Robbery (personal and commercial) Assault (aggravated) Burglary (commercial and household) Larceny (commercial and household) Motor vehicle theft Arson	Rape Robbery (personal) Assault (aggravated and simple) Household burglary Larceny (personal and household) Motor vehicle theft
Scope	Crimes reported to the police in most jurisdictions; considerable flexibility	Crimes both reported and not reported to police; all data are available for a few large geographic areas
Collection method	Police department reports to FBI or to centralized state agencies that then report to FBI	Survey interviews; periodically measures the total number of crimes committed by asking a national sample of 49,000 households encompassing 101,000 persons age 12 and over about their experiences as victims of crime during a specified period
Kinds of information	In addition to offense counts, provides information on crime clearances, persons arrested, persons charged, law enforcement officers killed and assaulted, and characteristics of homicide victims	Provides details about victims (such as age, race, sex, education, income, and whether the victim and offender were related to each other) and about crimes (such as time and place of occurrence, whether or not reported to police, use of weapons, occurrence of injury, and economic consequences)
Sponsor	U.S. Department of Justice; Federal Bureau of Investigation	U.S. Department of Justice; Bureau of Justice Statistics

Source: *Bureau of Justice Statistics,* Report to the Nation on Crime and Justice, *2nd ed. (Washington, D.C.: U.S. Department of Justice, 1988), p. 11.*

Crime statistics from the UCR and NCVS are often used in building explanations for criminal behavior. Unfortunately, however, researchers too often forget that statistics which are merely descriptive can be weak in explanatory power. For example, NCVS data show that "household crime rates" are highest for households (1) headed by blacks, (2) headed by younger people, (3) with six or more members, (4) headed by renters, and (5) in central cities.[70] Such findings, combined with statistics which show that most crime occurs among members of the same race, have led some researchers to conclude that values among certain black subcultural group members both propel them into crime and make them targets of criminal victimization. The truth may be, however, that crime is more a function of geography (inner-city location) than of culture. From simple descriptive statistics, it is difficult to know which is the case. Learn more about how the UCR and NCVS compare by viewing **WebExtra!** 2-6 at CJToday.com

Emerging Patterns of Criminal Activity

Planned revisions in both the NCVS and the UCR reflect the fact that patterns of criminal activity in the United States are changing. Georgette Bennett has termed the shift in crime patterns "crimewarps."[71] Crimewarps, says Bennett, represent major changes in both what society considers criminal and in who future criminal offenders will be. Some areas of coming change that she predicts are[72]

■ The decline of street crime

■ The growth of white-collar crime

■ Increasing female involvement in crime

■ Increased crime commission by the elderly

■ A shift in high crime rates from the "Frost Belt" to the "Sun Belt"

■ Safer cities, with increasing criminal activity in rural areas

■ The growth of high-technology crimes

The anticipated growth of the superpredator population, mentioned earlier in this chapter, holds potentially great significance for future crime rates and for the types of crime that will be committed in the future. If a superpredator population truly develops, as some suggest, we can expect to see a dramatic rise in both violent and property crimes by the end of the first decade of the twenty-first century. Street crime will rise once again, and cities will become less safe places in which to live and work.

The Fear of Crime

Although we may read in newspapers or in books that violent street crime is decreasing, we may not fully believe it. In fact we may be just as afraid as ever. As some authors point out,[73] the fear of crime is often out of proportion to the likelihood of criminal victimization. Table 2-6 compares the chance of death from homicide with other causes of death for persons in this country aged 14–25. For most people, regardless of age, the chance of accidental death is far greater than the chance of being murdered.

The Bureau of Justice Statistics says that "fear of crime affects many people, including some who have never been victims of crime."[74] Sources of fear are diverse. Some flow from personal experience with victimization, but most people fear crime because of dramatizations of criminal activity on television and in movies and because of frequent newspaper and media reports of crime. Feelings of vulnerability may result from learning that a friend has been victimized or from hearing that a neighbor's home has been burglarized.

Speaking to a session of the American Psychiatric Association in 1999, following the Columbine High School shootings, Kathleen M. Fisher of Pennsylvania State University said that schools are much safer today than they were 10 years ago. "Schools are safe, that is the reality," said Fisher. Still, she noted, the fear generated by high school shootings makes parents everywhere afraid for the safety of their children, and contributes to the general perception in American society that violent crime is out of control.[75]

TABLE 2-6 ■ Deaths and Death Rates for the 10 Leading Causes of Death, for Americans Aged 15–24

CAUSES OF DEATH	NUMBER OF DEATHS	RATE PER 100,000
Total: all causes	32,699	90.3
Accidents (except motor vehicle)	17,120	47.3
Motor vehicle accidents	10,624	29.3
Homicide	6,548	18.1
Suicide	4,369	12.1
Cancer	1,642	4.5
Heart disease	920	2.5
HIV/AIDS	420	1.2
Congenital anomalies	387	1.1
Lung Disease/Asthma	230	0.6
Pneumonia and influenza	197	0.5
Stroke/Brain hemorrhage	174	0.5
All other causes	3,940	10.9

Source: National Center for Health Statistics, Annual Report *(Washington, D.C.: U.S. Government Printing Office, 2000).*

At least one social commentator suggests that fear of crime is directly related to the amount and type of crime presented by the news media. Indira Lakshmanan, a columnist for the *Boston Globe*, says, "How about this for a theory: crime news is a product. Like all manufacturers, the makers of crime news strive to constantly broaden their market. They try to diversify their product line, increase public awareness of its existence, raise its quality, and increase its quantity."[76] It may be that what people fear the most is the chance of becoming the victim of a random act of violence. As a consequence, even in an environment where crime rates are falling, fear of crime remains high—and may be increasing.

Interestingly, the groups at highest risk of becoming crime victims are not the ones who experience the greatest fear. The elderly and women report the greatest fear of victimization, even though they are among the lowest-risk groups for violent crimes. Young males, on the other hand, who stand the greatest statistical risk of victimization, often report feeling the least fear.[77] Similarly, although people most fear violent victimization by strangers, many such crimes are committed by nonstrangers or by people known to victims by sight. For current opinion poll data on crime issues view **WebExtra!** 2-7 at CJToday.com.

Women and Crime

Women Victims

Women are victimized far less frequently than are men in every major crime category other than rape.[78] When women are victimized, however, they are more likely than men to be injured.[79] Even though experiencing lower rates of victimization, it is realistic to acknowledge that a larger proportion of women than men make modifications in the way they live because of the threat of crime.[80] Reflecting the growing fear of crime now so pervasive in America, women, especially those living in cities, are increasingly careful about where they travel and the time of day they leave their homes—particularly if unaccompanied—and are often wary of unfamiliar males in a diversity of settings.

As in other crime-related areas, the popular media, special interest groups, and even the government have contributed to a certain degree of confusion about women's victimization.[81] Very real concerns reflected in movies, television programs, and newspaper editorial pages have properly identified date rape, familial incest, spouse abuse, and the exploitation of women through social order offenses such as prostitution and pornography as major issues facing American society today. Testimony before Congress has tagged domestic violence as the largest cause of injury to American women,[82] and former Surgeon General C. Everett Koop identified violence against women by their partners as the number one health problem facing women in America today.[83] Some years ago, the 1995 murder trial of O. J. Simpson focused national concerns on issues of spousal abuse and on the victimization of women by spouses and ex-husbands.

In November 2000, the National Institute of Justice,[84] in conjunction with the Centers for Disease Control and Prevention (CDC), published findings from the National Violence Against Women Survey (NVAWS).[85] Analysis of the survey, which was based upon two years of national telephone interviews with both men and women, found that

> "If people here were not getting killed on the job in homicides, we would have quite a low rate of fatalities."
>
> —*Samuel Ehrenhalt*, Labor Department official commenting on findings that show murder to be the top cause of on-the-job deaths in New York City

■ Physical assault is widespread among American women. Fifty-two percent of surveyed women said that they were physically assaulted as a child or as an adult.

■ Approximately 1.9 million women are physically assaulted in the United States each year.

■ Eighteen percent of women experienced a completed or attempted rape at some time in their life.

■ Of those reporting rape, 22 percent were under 12 years old, and 32 percent were between 12 to 17 years old when they were first raped.

■ American Indian and Alaska Native women were most likely to report rape and physical assault victimization, while Asian/Pacific Islander women were least likely to report such victimization. Hispanic women were also less likely to report rape victimization than non-Hispanic women.

■ Women experience significantly more partner violence than do men. Twenty-five percent of surveyed women, compared with 8 percent of surveyed men, said they were raped and/or physically assaulted by a current or former spouse, cohabiting partner, or date in their lifetime.

■ Violence against women is primarily partner violence. Seventy-four percent of the women who were raped and/or physically assaulted since age 18 were assaulted by a current or former husband, cohabiting partner, or date, compared with 18 percent of the men.

■ Women are significantly more likely than men to be injured during an assault. Thirty-two percent of the women and 16 percent of the men who were raped since age 18 were injured during their most recent rape; 39 percent of the women and 25 percent of the men who were physically assaulted since age 18 were injured during their most recent physical assault.

■ Stalking is more prevalent than previously thought. Eight percent of surveyed women and 2 percent of surveyed men said they were stalked at some time in their lives. According to survey estimates, approximately 1 million women and 371,000 men are stalked annually in the United States.

A detailed BJS analysis[86] of female victims of violent crime found that about twice as many women who are victims of violent crimes are likely to be victimized by strangers than by people whom they know. However, when women do fall victim to violent crime, they are far more likely than men to be victimized by individuals with whom they are (or have been) in intimate relationships. When the perpetrators are known to them, women are most likely to be violently victimized by ex-spouses, boyfriends, and spouses, (in descending order of incidence). The BJS study also found that separated or divorced women are six times more likely to be victims of violent crime than widows, four and a half times more likely than married women, and three times more likely than widowers and married men. Other findings indicated that (1) women living in central-city areas are considerably more likely to be victimized than women residing in the suburbs; (2) suburban women, in turn, are more likely to be victimized than women living in rural areas; (3) women from low-income families experience the highest amount of violent crime; (4) the victimization of women falls as family income rises; (5) unemployed women, female students, and those in the armed forces are the most likely of all women to experience violent victimization; (6) black women are victims of violent crimes more frequently than are women of any other race; (7) Hispanic women find themselves victimized more frequently than white women; and (8) women in the age range 20–24 are most at risk for violent victimization, while those aged 16–19 comprise the second most likely group of victims.

These findings show that greater emphasis needs to be placed on alleviating the social conditions that victimize women. Suggestions already under consideration call for expansion in the number of federal and state laws designed to control domestic violence, a broad-

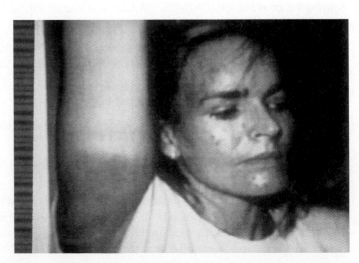

A bruised Nicole Brown Simpson after one of many alleged attacks by her husband, O. J. Simpson. According to sociologists, violence against women is perpetuated by social conditions which devalue females.
AVR, Corbis.

ening of the federal Family Violence Prevention and Services Act, federal help in setting up state advocacy offices for battered women, increased funding for battered women's shelters, and additional monies for prosecutors and courts to develop spouse abuse units. The federal Violent Crime Control and Law Enforcement Act of 1994 was designed to meet many of these needs through a subsection entitled the Violence Against Women Act (VAWA). That act allocated $1.6 billion to fight violence against women. Included are funds to (1) educate police, prosecutors, and judges about the special needs of women victims; (2) encourage pro-arrest policies in cases of domestic abuse; (3) provide specialized services for female victims of crime; (4) fund battered women's shelters across the country; and (5) support rape education in a variety of settings nationwide. The law also provides for new civil rights remedies for victims of felonies motivated by gender bias[87] and extends "rape shield law" protections to civil cases and to all criminal cases in order to bar irrelevant inquiries into a victim's sexual history. Read the text of the original VAWA legislation at WebExtra! 2-8 at CJToday.com.

Women Offenders

In 1999 Susan Eubanks, a 35-year-old mother, was convicted in Vista, California, of shooting each of her four sons to death at their home. Authorities found the body of 14-year-old Brandon Armstrong, a well-liked football player at the local junior high, lying found face down on the living room floor with two bullets in his head. Spilled breakfast cereal was next to his body. In a nearby bedroom, Brandon's seven-year-old brother, Austin, was found sitting upright on the top level of his bunk bed, dead from two shots to the head. Two younger brothers, six-year-old Brigham and four-year-old Matthew, were found on the bottom bunk—also dead from gunshot wounds to the head.[88] Eubanks shot her sons after an argument with her boyfriend. She stopped once to reload the 38-caliber revolver she was using, and then shot herself in the stomach. Police found her crying on a bedroom floor. At trial, prosecutors argued that Eubanks deliberately plotted to kill her sons in order to torment her boyfriend and the boys' fathers (two ex-husbands). Gruesome as her story may be, however, Eubanks was just the latest in a string of news-making female killers.

In 1992, Aileen Carol Wuornos, a 35-year-old former prostitute, received multiple death sentences in Florida after confessing to a string of seven murders. Wuornos, labeled by the FBI as the "first textbook female serial killer,"[89] preyed upon men who offered her rides as she hitchhiked. Property belonging to all seven victims—most of whom were robbed, killed, and left naked—was found in a storage unit rented by Ms. Wuornos. One victim was a former police chief, another a security guard. All were white, middle-aged men with blue-collar jobs who were traveling alone. Each was killed with a small-caliber handgun.[90] In 1996 the U.S. Supreme Court turned down an appeal by Wuornos who argued that claims that she killed the men in self-defense when they became violent, raped her, and did not pay for sexual services, were not given sufficient weight before sentencing.[91]

In 1995 another woman, Susan Smith of Union, South Carolina, rose to prominence in the national media after she confessed to the drowning murders of her two young sons, Alex, 1, and Michael, 3. The boys died after their mother rolled their car off the end of a pier and into a lake, leaving her sons strapped in their safety seats. Smith's confession came after investigators found a letter from Smith's adulterous lover, suggesting that he felt unable to continue the relationship because of the children.

The crimes committed by Eubanks, Wuornos, and Smith, ghastly as they are, fall outside what we know of as the pattern for female criminality. Although the popular media has sometimes portrayed female criminals as similar to their male counterparts in motivation and behavior, that image is misleading. Similarly, the academic study of women's criminality has been fraught with misconceptions.

One of the first writers to attempt a definitive explanation of the criminality of women was Otto Pollak. Pollak's book, *The Criminality of Women*,[92] written in 1950, suggested that women commit the same number of offenses as men—but that most of their criminality is hidden. Pollak claimed that women's roles (at the time, primarily those of homemaker and mother) served to disguise the criminal undertakings of women. He also proposed that chivalrous treatment by a male-dominated justice system acted to bias every stage of crimi-

"The public is properly obsessed with safety. Of industrialized countries, the U.S. has the highest rate of violent crime...."

—*Bob Moffitt,* The Heritage Foundation

nal justice processing in favor of women. Hence, according to Pollak, although women are just as criminal as men, they are rarely arrested, tried, or imprisoned. In fact, while the criminality of women may approach or exceed that of men in selected offense categories, it is safe to say today that Pollak was incorrect in his assessment of the degree of female criminality.

Contemporary statistics tell us that, although females comprise 51 percent of the population of the United States, they are arrested for only 17 percent of all violent crimes and 29 percent of property crimes. The relatively small amount of reported female involvement in the FBI's eight major crimes can be seen in Table 2-7. The number of women committing crimes appears to be increasing faster than the number of male offenders, however. Between 1970 and 1999, crimes committed by men grew by 45 percent, while crimes reported to have been committed by women increased 135 percent. Violent crimes by males increased 88 percent during the period; by women 255 percent.[93] Property crimes perpetrated by men grew by 10 percent; by women 88 percent. Nonetheless, as the table shows, female offenders still account for only a small proportion of all reported crimes.

Statistics on the FBI's Part II offenses tell a somewhat different story. Arrests of women for embezzlement, for example, increased by more than 167 percent between 1970 and 1999, arrests of females for drug abuse grew by 268 percent, and liquor law violations by women increased 215 percent (versus 76 percent for men).[94] Such statistics are difficult to interpret, however, since reports of female involvement in crime may reflect more the growing equality of treatment accorded women in contemporary society than they do actual increases in criminal activity. In the past, when women committed crimes, they have been dealt with less officiously than is likely to be the case today. In only two officially reported categories—prostitution and runaways—do women outnumber men in the volume of offenses committed.[95] Other crimes in which significant numbers of women (relative to men) are involved include larceny-theft (where 35 percent of reported crimes are committed by women), forgery and counterfeiting (38 percent), fraud (44 percent), and embezzlement (49 percent).

Even when women commit crimes, however, they are more often followers than leaders. A 1996 study[96] of women in correctional settings, for example, found that women are far more likely to assume "secondary follower rules during criminal events," than "dominant leadership roles." Only 14 percent of women surveyed played primary roles, but those that did "felt that men had little influence in initiating or leading them into crime." African-American women, however, were found to be more likely to play "primary and equal crime roles" with

TABLE 2-7 ■ Male/Female Involvement in Crime: Offense Patterns Differ

UCR INDEX CRIMES	Percentage of All Arrests		GENDER DIFFERENCES
	MALES	**FEMALES**	
Murder and nonnegligent manslaughter	88.6	11.4	Men are more likely than women to be arrested for more serious crimes, such as murder, rape, robbery, or burglary
Rape	98.7	1.3	
Robbery	89.9	10.1	
Aggravated assault	80.3	19.7	
Burglary	87.1	12.9	Arrest, jail, and prison data all suggest that more women than men who commit crimes are involved in property crimes, such as larceny, forgery, fraud, and embezzlement, and in drug offenses.
Larceny-theft	64.5	35.5	
Motor vehicle theft	84.4	15.6	
Arson	85.6	14.4	

Source: Federal Bureau of Investigation, Crime in the United States, 1999 *(Washington, D.C.: U.S. Government Printing Office, 2000).*

men or with women accomplices than were white or Hispanic women. Statistics such as these dispel the myth that the female criminal in America has taken her place alongside male offenders—either in terms of leadership roles or the absolute number of crimes committed.

The Economic Cost of Crime

Some years ago, Florida state officials came face to face with the economic consequences of criminal activity: Three robbery-related killings of foreign visitors near Miami in the summer of 1993 caused many potential "Sunshine State" tourists to cancel their reservations and stay home. Tourism is Florida's number one industry. In a typical year, more than 40 million tourists visit the state, including 7 million foreigners. All told, they spend over $31 billion on their Florida vacations.

Following the highly publicized robbery-murder incidents, European tabloids labeled the "Sunshine State" the "State of Terror," and the British newspaper *Independent* called Florida "the main danger area" in the United States. Indicative of media sentiment across Europe, the London *Times* ran a cartoon picturing a revolver shaped like the state of Florida, and Britain's largest newspaper, the *Sun,* ran a headline advising Florida tourists to "Get Your Butts Outta Here." The image portrayed by the media was one of a state and a nation where crime—and guns—are out of control. In response, then-Governor Lawton Chiles canceled state-sponsored foreign advertising, fearing that it would provoke only further cynicism. Although the tourism industry in Florida has recovered, the summer of 1993 showed officials across the nation just how costly crime can be in terms of lost tourist dollars.

The national costs of crime are difficult to measure. The Bureau of Justice Statistics estimates the personal cost of crime (direct dollar losses to individuals, not including criminal justice system costs) at around $17.6 billion per year.[97] Robberies cost the nation about $500 million annually, burglaries nearly $4 billion, and larceny-thefts account for approximately $4 billion in losses per year. Not included in the Bureau's figures are the costs to crime victims of lost work, needed medical care, and the expense of new security measures they may implement. Lost work time, for example, was reported in 12 percent of aggravated assaults and 17 percent of rapes.

In 1996 the National Institute of Justice attempted to calculate both the direct and indirect costs of criminal victimization. NIJ researchers concluded that when crimes of all types are counted "victimizations generate $105 billion annually in property and productivity losses and outlays for medical expenses. This amounts to an annual "crime tax" of roughly $425 per man, woman, and child in the United States. When the values of pain, long-term emotional trauma, disability, and risk of death are put in dollar terms, the costs rise to $450 billion annually (or $1,800 per person)."[98] Overall, said the study authors, "rape is the costliest crime: With annual victim costs at $127 billion, it exacts a higher price than murder."[99]

The economic impact of crime is different for different groups. In 1999, for example, households reporting an annual family income of less than $7,500 suffered more than twice the rate of burglary as did households reporting incomes over $35,000. In fact, as family income rose, the rate of reported burglaries steadily declined. The opposite was true of auto theft, where rates of auto vehicle theft rose in direct proportion to household income.[100]

The commercial costs of crime are substantial as well. Losses from commercial robberies (including bank robberies) and business burglaries have been put at $1.2 billion per year.[101] Frauds perpetrated against financial institutions in 1999 numbered 8,799 discovered cases with an associated dollar loss of nearly $3 billion.[102] The cost to businesses of white-collar crime is not known, but is thought to be substantial. To guard against crimes by employees and members of the public, private businesses spend in excess of $21 billion per year for alarms, surveillance, and private security operations.[103]

Costs to the government for the apprehension, prosecution, and disposition of offenders, including crime prevention efforts by the police, far outstrip the known dollar losses to all criminal enterprises other than drugs. Federal criminal justice expenditures for fiscal year 1996 were in excess of $16.5 billion,[104] while federal, state, and local expenditures totaled over $80 billion.[105] Nonetheless, government spending on criminal justice services amounts to only about 5 percent of all governmental expenditures. State and local governments absorb most of the costs of criminal justice-related activity.

Media Impact on the Public's Fear of Crime

Turn on nightly television in the United States on a typical day and you will see killing after killing, frequent acts of gruesome violence, and murder and mayhem as typical prime-time fare. The same is true whether you choose to view one of the major networks, a pay-per-view channel, or a premium service such as Home Box Office, Cinemax, or Showtime. Only a few specialized forms of programming, such as the Home Shopping Network, the Disney Channel, and Public Broadcasting, are relatively violence free.

Many argue that the networks and cable companies are simply giving viewers what they want. Violence (often tinged with sexuality or combined with explicit sexual behavior), because it is exciting, attracts audiences. And, of course, large audiences attract advertisers whose fees support the networks.

Not to be outdone by their highly visual counterparts, newspapers and newsmagazines depict real-life episodes of violent crime in every issue. For a year following the highly publicized murders of Nicole Brown Simpson and Ronald Goldman, for example, it was almost impossible to find a newspaper in the country which wasn't running a daily story about some aspect of the case, especially when O. J. Simpson, charged in the murders, went to trial. Even computer-based services, among them CompuServe and America Online, set up special O. J. Simpson sections to attract subscribers. Simpson's 1997 civil trial received almost as much publicity—limited only by the fact that the judge banned television cameras from the courtroom.

Unfortunately, what some have called the overemphasis on crime and violence, now so characteristic of the media in this country, makes it extremely difficult to separate crime fiction from crime fact. If media emphasis is any guide, it would appear that the United States is awash in crime, especially violent personal crime. The impression given is that crime is likely to strike almost anyone when they least expect it—devastating their lives (should

they survive) irreparably. In fact, while there are many victims of violent crime in this country, the media's preoccupation with crime and violence is much overdone. Worse still, such preoccupation has led to an enormous fear of crime among the American public, which, for at least a substantial segment of the population, is probably misplaced.

As one social commentator points out, "Anxiety about crime grips the land but, looking at federal statistics, you have to wonder why. The FBI reports crime is merely crawling upward. Victim surveys show crime actually falling. Yet for many people, an evening stroll, an unlocked car, or going alone to the mall hint at lunacy. After tucking in their children, many parents bolt the doors, check the alarms, and pat the guns under their beds goodnight."[1] According to William Chambliss, past president of the American Society of Criminology, "[t]he best scientific evidence we have clearly shows there is no increase in crime or violent crime in the last 20 years.... The fact is, even if the crime rate was going up, the victims who were the victims remain the victims."[2]

Realistically, crime—especially violent personal crime—while it may be on the rise, appears concentrated in certain poverty-stricken population-dense regions of the nation. That is not to say that crime does not make an appearance in affluent neighborhoods and rural areas. It certainly does, but the nature and extent of criminal activity in such areas is a far cry from the inner-city areas where the daily threat of crime is a hard reality for most residents.

Yet, when surveys reporting the fear of crime are examined, Americans everywhere appear to be on guard. Fear of crime festers in people's minds like a specter haunting the land, and frightened residents routinely report taking self-protective steps. Statistics from the most recent *U.S. News*/CNN poll[3] on neighborhood crime, for example, show 37 percent of Americans own a gun for protection and 45 percent think it's unsafe to let children play unsupervised where they live. Thirty-one percent of

respondents also report that there are areas within a mile of their home in which they would be afraid to walk alone at night. Other surveys, however, have found that those most afraid of crime spend more time watching television than those who are less fearful[4]—lending support to the notion that media portrayals of criminal activity lead to a heightened fear of victimization.

Efforts are currently underway to reduce the degree of crime fear induced by the mass media.[5] A recent U.S. Senate hearing, for example, stressed the need for television producers and network executives to assume a socially responsible role by lowering the amount of violence in aired programming. Unfortunately, no one knows for sure whether television merely broadcasts what viewers most want to see, or whether it presages and helps to determine what we, as a nation, are becoming.

❓ QUESTIONS FOR DISCUSSION

1. To what extent does television influence what people think about crime? What they do?
2. Does television help shape our culture, or does it merely reflect what we, as a nation, already are?
3. Would you be supportive of more "socially responsible" television programming? Why or why not? If so, how would you change the content of television shows?

[1] Arlene Levinson, "America Behind Bars—Crime, Wanted: The True Crime Rate," the Associated Press wire services, northern edition, May 8, 1994.
[2] Ibid.
[3] CNN Online, April 2, 1995.
[4] See Arthur Spiegelman, "America's Year in Crime—Enough to Scare Anyone," Reuters wire services, December 15, 1994.
[5] For a good collection of articles detailing the role of the media in crime causation and social policy creation, see Ray Surette, *The Media and Criminal Justice Policy: Recent Research and Social Effects* (Springfield, IL: Charles C. Thomas, 1990), and Steven M. Chermak, *Victims in the News: Crime and the American News Media* (San Francisco: Westview Press, 1995).

21st Century CJ

Gender Issues: The Growing Recognition of Women's Rights and Gender-Based Violence

As mentioned earlier in this chapter, the Violent Crime Control and Law Enforcement Act of 1994 included significant provisions intended to enhance gender equality throughout the criminal justice system. Section 40301, the "Civil Rights Remedies for Gender-Motivated Violence Act," is discussed in an earlier box in this chapter. Other especially notable provisions of the act are discussed here.

TITLE IV of the Violent Crime Control and Law Enforcement Act of 1994 is known as the Violence Against Women Act of 1994 (VAWA). VAWA also contains the Safe Streets for Women Act of 1994. The Safe Streets for Women Act increases federal penalties for repeat sex offenders and requires mandatory restitution for sex crimes including costs related to medical services (including physical, psychiatric, or psychological care); physical and occupational therapy or rehabilitation; necessary transportation, temporary housing, and child care expenses; lost income; attorneys' fees, plus any costs incurred in obtaining a civil protection order; and any other losses suffered by the victim as a result of the offense. The act also requires that compliance with a restitution order be made a condition of probation or supervised release (if such a sentence is imposed by the court) and provides that violation of such an order shall result in the offender's imprisonment.

Chapter 2 of the Violence Against Women Act provides funds for grants to combat violent crimes against women. The purpose of funding is to assist states "and units of local government to develop and strengthen effective law enforcement and prosecution strategies to combat violent crimes against women, and to develop and strengthen victim services in cases involving violent crimes against women." The law also provides funds for the "training of law enforcement officers and prosecutors to more effectively identify and respond to violent crimes against women, including the crimes of sexual assault and domestic violence"; for the purpose of "developing, installing, or expanding data collection and communication systems, including computerized systems, linking police, prosecutors, and courts or for the purpose of identifying and tracking arrests, protection orders, violations of protection orders, prosecutions, and convictions for violent crimes against women, including the crimes of sexual assault and domestic violence"; and to develop and strengthen "victim services programs, including sexual assault and domestic violence programs." The act also creates the crime of crossing state lines in violation of a protection order, and another crime of crossing state lines to commit assault on a domestic partner—and sets out federal penalties for the offense of up to life in prison in cases where death results.

Chapter 3 of the Violence Against Women Act provides for monies to increase the "safety for women in public transit and public parks." The chapter authorizes up to $10 million in grants through the Department of Transportation to enhance lighting, camera surveillance, and security telephones in public transportation systems used by women.

Chapter 5 of the Violence Against Women Act provides for the creation of hotlines, educational seminars, the preparation of informational materials, and training programs for professionals intended to provide assistance to victims of sexual assault, and for the operation of a national, toll-free telephone hotline to provide information and assistance to victims of domestic violence. Another portion of the law, titled the "Safe Homes for Women Act," increases grants for battered women's shelters, encourages arrest in cases of domestic violence, and provides for the creation of a national domestic violence hotline to provide counseling, information, and assistance to victims of domestic violence. The act also orders that any protection order issued by a state court must be recognized by another state and by the federal government, and enforced "as if it were the order of the enforcing state."

SEC. 40401, known as the "Equal Justice for Women in the Courts Act of 1994," provides monies "for the purpose of developing, testing, presenting, and disseminating model programs" to be used by states in training judges and court personnel in the laws "on rape, sexual assault, domestic violence, and other crimes of violence motivated by the victim's gender." Training is to recognize the underreporting of rape, sexual assault, and child sexual abuse; the physical, psychological, and economic impact of rape and sexual assault on the victim; and the psychology of sex offenders, their high rate of recidivism, and implications for sentencing.

VAWA was renewed by Congressional action in 2000.

Drugs and Crime

Drug law violations do not figure into crime index calculations. Unlike index crimes, however, they continue to increase, lending support to those who feel that this country is experiencing more crime than traditional index tabulations show. The relentless increase in drug violations largely accounts for the fact that America's prison populations have continued to grow, even when official crime rates (i.e., index offenses) are declining. Figure 2-7 shows the number of persons arrested for drug law violations in the United States between 1975 and

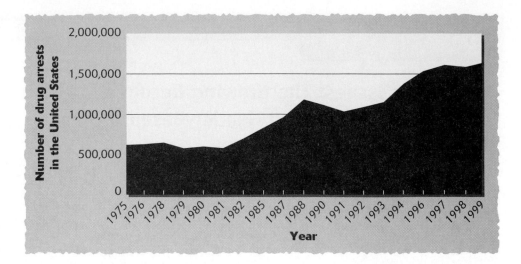

FIGURE 2-7 ■ *Drug arrests in the United States, 1975–1999.*
Source: *The* Uniform Crime Reports, *various years.*

1999. Compare Figure 2-7 with Figure 2-1 (earlier in this chapter) to see how drug arrests show a far different pattern over time than do index offenses. Note, however, that while Figure 2-1 depicts the *rate* of crime, Figure 2-7 shows only the raw number of arrestees for given years. Even so, when rates are computed, it is easy to see that the number of drug crimes per 100,000 Americans has more than doubled since 1975.

Drugs and other forms of crime are often found together. Drug law violations are themselves criminal, but more and more studies are linking drug abuse to other serious crimes. A study by the Rand Corporation found that most of the "violent predators" among prisoners had extensive histories of heroin abuse, often in combination with alcohol and other drugs.[106] Some cities report that a large percentage of their homicides are drug related.[107] Many property crimes are committed to sustain "habits," and the numbers of both violent and property crimes committed by drug users have been shown to be directly related to the level at which they use drugs.[108] Substance abuse may well be the most expensive of all illegal activities. The social cost of drug abuse has been estimated at nearly $60 billion per year, with half of that amount being in lost job productivity.[109] Drunk driving alone is thought to cost over $13 billion in property losses and medical expenses yearly.[110]

The Elderly and Crime

UCR statistics define "older offenders" as those over 55 years of age. Relative to other age groups, older offenders rarely appear in the crime statistics. Criminality seems to decline with age, suggesting that a burnout factor applies to criminal behavior as it does to many other areas of life. In 1999 persons age 65 and over accounted for less than 1 percent of all arrests.[111]

The type and number of crimes committed by older people, however, appear to be changing. According to the UCR, arrests of the elderly for serious crimes decreased slightly between 1975 and 1999.[112] Overall, arrests of persons 65 and older declined by about 30 percent during the period.[113] On the other hand, when elderly people are sent to prison, it is usually for violent crimes, though violent crimes account for far less than 50 percent of prison admissions among younger people.

Although crimes committed by older persons may be on the decline, the relatively serious nature of such crimes has led to an increase in the number of elderly persons behind bars. The population of prisoners age 55 and over has steadily increased, having risen from 13,800 inmates nationally in mid-1988 to 39,000 by mid-1998, an increase of nearly 200 percent.[114]

Some authors have interpreted these statistics to presage the growth of a "geriatric delinquent" population, freed by age and retirement from jobs and responsibilities. Such people, say these authors, may turn to crime as one way of averting boredom and adding a little spice to life.[115] Statistics on geriatric offenders, however, probably require a more cautious interpretation. They are based upon relatively small numbers, and to say that "serious crime among the elderly doubled" does not mean that a geriatric crime wave is upon us. The apparent increase in criminal activity among the elderly may be due to the fact that the older pop-

CAREERS IN JUSTICE

Working for the Drug Enforcement Administration

TYPICAL POSITIONS:

Special agent, criminal investigator, chemist, diversion investigator, and intelligence research specialist.

EMPLOYMENT REQUIREMENTS:

Applicants for GS-5 levels must (1) be U.S. citizens, (2) be between the ages of 21 and 36 at time of hiring, (3) hold a four-year college degree, (4) be in good health, (5) pass a comprehensive background investigation, (6) hold a valid driver's license, (7) possess effective oral and written communications skills, and (8) have three years of general job experience. Applicants for GS-7 levels must also demonstrate *one* of the following: (1) a 2.9 overall college average, (2) a 3.5 grade point average in the applicant's major field of study, (3) a standing in the upper one-third of the applicant's graduating class, (4) membership in a national honorary scholastic society, (5) one year of successful graduate study, or (6) one year of specialized experience (defined as "progressively responsible investigative experience").

OTHER REQUIREMENTS:

Applicants must (1) be willing to travel frequently, (2) submit to a urinalysis test designed to detect the presence of controlled substances, and (3) successfully complete a two-month formal training program at the FBI's Training Center in Quantico, Virginia. Special-agent applicants must be in excellent physical condition, possess sharp hearing, and have uncorrected vision of at least 20/200 and corrected vision of 20/20 in one eye, and at least 20/40 in the other.

SALARY:

Entry-level positions for individuals with four-year college degrees begin at the GS-7 level. Appointments are made at higher pay grades for individuals possessing additional education and experience.

BENEFITS:

Benefits include (1) 13 days of sick leave annually, (2) 2½ to 5 weeks of annual paid vacation and 10 paid federal holidays each year, (3) federal health and life insurance, and (4) a comprehensive retirement program.

DIRECT INQUIRIES TO:

Drug Enforcement Administration, 700 Army-Navy Drive, Arlington, VA 22202. Phone: (800) DEA-4288. Web site: www.usdoj.gov/dea.

---

ulation in this country is growing substantially, with even greater increases expected over the next three decades. Advances in health care have increased life expectancy and have made the added years more productive than ever before. World War II baby boomers are now reaching their late middle years, and present trends in criminal involvement among the elderly can be expected to continue. Hence, it may not be that elderly individuals in this country are committing crimes more frequently than before, but rather that the greater number of elderly in the population make for a greater prevalence of crimes committed by the elderly in the official statistics.

The elderly are also victims of crime. Although persons age 65 and older generally experience the lowest rate of victimization of any age group,[116] some aspects of serious crime against older people are worth noting. Elderly violent crime victims are more likely than younger victims to

1. Face offenders armed with guns
2. Be victimized by total strangers
3. Be victimized in or near their homes
4. Report their victimization to the police

Older victims are also less likely to attempt to protect themselves than are younger ones. The older the victim, the greater the likelihood of physical injury.

Elderly people are victimized disproportionately if they fall into certain categories. Relative to their numbers in the elderly population, black men are overrepresented as victims. Similarly, separated or divorced persons and urban residents have higher rates of victimization than do other elderly persons. As observed earlier, older people live in greater fear of crime than do younger people, even though their risk of victimization is considerably less. Elderly people, however, are less likely to take crime preventive measures than are any other age group. Only 6 percent of households headed by persons over the age of 65 have an alarm, and only 16 percent engrave their valuables (versus a 25 percent national average).

Organized Crime

Organized Crime

The unlawful activities of the members of a highly organized, disciplined association engaged in supplying illegal goods and services, including but not limited to gambling, prostitution, loansharking, narcotics, labor racketeering, and other unlawful activities of members of such organizations. Source: *The Organized Crime Control Act of 1970.*

Cosa Nostra

Organized crime of Sicilian origin. Another word for Mafia.

Organized crime has been defined by the Organized Crime Control Act of 1970 as "the unlawful activities of the members of a highly organized, disciplined association engaged in supplying illegal goods and services, including but not limited to gambling, prostitution, loansharking, narcotics, labor racketeering, and other unlawful activities of members of such organizations."[117] Criminal organizations have existed in America since before the turn of the twentieth century. Contemporary organized crime groups are involved to some degree in just about every aspect of American life, but the manufacture, transportation, and sale of controlled substances has provided an especially lucrative form of illegal enterprise for many of them. A few such groups are thought to be among the largest businesslike enterprises in the world.

The Mafia, perhaps the best-known criminal organization in the United States, rose to power in this country largely through its exploitation of the widespread demand for consumable alcohol during prohibition years. The Mafia, now called the **Cosa Nostra,** came into existence when a group of small-time hoods, largely of Italian descent, began selling "protection" and other services, such as gambling and prostitution, in turn-of-the-century New York City. With the advent of prohibition, financial opportunities became enormous for those willing to circumvent the law, and organized gang activity spread. Soon Chicago, Detroit, Miami, San Francisco, and other major cities became gang havens. It was during this period that infamous gangsters such as Lucky Luciano and Al Capone were catapulted to the forefront of popular attention.

Today, the Cosa Nostra consists of 24 families based in various cities across the country. Their illegal take is estimated at around $60 billion per year.[118]

Families are involved in a variety of illegal activities, including drug trafficking, loansharking, gambling, shakedowns of drug dealers, killings-for-hire, and the infiltration of various labor unions. Many run legitimate businesses as fronts for money laundering and other financial activities. Such businesses are often rife with "ghost workers," paid at high rates, but who actually do no work at all. Organized crime families will stop at little to increase their influence. Nicholas Caramandi, a former member of the Philadelphia mob led by Nicodemo Scarfo, responded to a question about how high the mob reaches into American society this way: "If politicians, doctors, lawyers, entertainment people all come to us for favors, there's got to be a reason. It's because we're the best. There are no favors we can't do."[119]

The Cosa Nostra requires new members to undergo an initiation ritual, which has changed little since the days it was brought to American shores by Sicilian immigrants more than a hundred years ago. During a secretly recorded candlelit Cosa Nostra induction ceremony held in Medford, Massachusetts, for example, new members were required to hold a burning picture of a Catholic saint in their cupped palms and made to swear to uphold the code of *omerta* (silence). "*Come si brucia questa santa, cosi si brucera la mia anima,*" the men repeated, which means, "As burns this saint, so will burn my soul." Anyone violating the Cosa Nostra's code of silence recognizes that death is the penalty.

Crime families are hierarchically organized under a boss and consist of a number of levels, each with varying authority. Bosses exercise their power through underbosses and lieutenants. Lieutenants pass orders along to soldiers. Soldiers, the lowest level of mob operatives, are charged with directly carrying out the activities of their families. In doing so they often make use of local community members, allowing organized crime to seamlessly integrate itself into almost any locale. Hierarchical organization has frequently allowed many Cosa Nostra higher-ups to avoid arrest and prosecution. Recently, however, federal agents armed with new statutes have been able to make inroads into many such operations. For example, John Gotti, leader of New York City's infamous Gambino crime family (and once known as the "Teflon Don" for being able to beat criminal charges), was finally sent to federal prison in 1992, along with underboss Frank Locascio. Although Gotti passed control of his crime syndicate on to his son, John A. "Junior" Gotti, the younger Gotti pleaded guilty in 1999 to charges of racketeering, bribery, extortion, fraud, and gambling and was sentenced to 6½ years in prison.[120]

Although most people think of the Mafia (or Cosa Nostra) when "organized crime" is mentioned, the term actually includes a wide variety of types of groups and associated activities. Here reputed Mafia boss and head of New York's Genovese crime family, Vincent "The Chin" Gigante, leaves his New York residence on June 25, 1997. Gigante was convicted a month later of conspiracy to murder and racketeering. Accused of ordering the execution of seven fellow gangsters and plotting to kill three others, Gigante was dubbed the "The Oddfather" for previously appearing disheveled and for sometimes wearing a bathrobe in public. Prosecutors claimed that he was faking mental illness.
Michael Schmelling, AP/Wide World Photos.

During the past decade or so, well over one thousand Cosa Nostra bosses, soldiers, and associates across the nation have been convicted and sentenced.[121] Peter Milano, once the crime boss of Los Angeles, is in prison. So, too, are leaders of Kansas City's Civella family, and a few years ago 13 members of New England's Patriarca family were convicted of murdering one of their underbosses.

In 1997, a federal jury convicted 69-year-old Vincent "The Chin" Gigante, head of New York's Genovese crime family—and one of the nation's most powerful mobsters—of racketeering and two murder conspiracies.[122] Gigante had sought to avoid prosecution by feigning mental illness, a strategy that earned him the nickname "The Oddfather." Growing disorganization among Cosa Nostra families was evident at Gigante's trial, which featured a parade

---

CAREERS IN JUSTICE

Working as a Deputy U.S. Marshal

TYPICAL POSITIONS:

Deputy U.S. marshals are involved in the following activities: (1) court security, (2) fugitive investigations, (3) personal and witness security, (4) asset seizure, (5) special operations, and (6) transportation and custody of federal prisoners.

EMPLOYMENT REQUIREMENTS:

General employment requirements with the Marshals Service include (1) a comprehensive written exam, (2) a complete background investigation, (3) an oral interview, (4) excellent

physical condition, and (5) a bachelor's degree or three years of "responsible experience." Applicants must be between 21 and 36 years of age and be U.S. citizens with valid driver's licenses.

OTHER REQUIREMENTS:

Successful applicants must complete 16 weeks of training at the Federal Law Enforcement Training Center (FLETC) at Glynco, Georgia.

SALARY:

Deputy U.S. marshals are typically hired at federal pay grade GS-5 or

GS-7, depending on education and prior work history.

BENEFITS:

Benefits include (1) 13 days of sick leave annually, (2) 2½ to 5 weeks of annual paid vacation and 10 paid federal holidays each year, (3) federal health and life insurance, and (4) a comprehensive retirement program.

DIRECT INQUIRIES TO:

U.S. Marshals Service, 600 Army-Navy Drive, Arlington, VA 22202. Phone: (202) 307-9600. Web site: www.usdoj.gov/marshals.

of turncoat gangsters testifying for the government. Witnesses against Gigante included ex-underbosses Salvatore "Sammy the Bull" Gravano, Alphonse "Little Al" D'Arco, Philip "Crazy Phil" Leonetti, and Peter Savino, a one-time Genovese associate.

Even as the power of the Cosa Nostra wanes, other groups stand ready to take its place. There is historical precedent for such a transition. Italian-led gangs were preceded in New York City and other places by Jewish criminal organizations. One infamous Jewish gang, for example, was headed at the start of the century by Arnold Rothstein, who dreamed of becoming kingpin of all organized criminal activity in America. Ethnic succession has typified organized criminal activity. Today, gangs of Hispanics, Chinese, Japanese, Vietnamese, Puerto Ricans, Mexicans, Colombians, and African Americans have usurped power traditionally held by the Cosa Nostra in many parts of the country. Similarly, Russian-led and Arabic-speaking gangs have moved into New York and other major American cities.

Summary

Two major national comprehensive crime data-gathering programs are in operation in the United States today: the FBI's *Uniform Crime Reports* (UCR) and the National Institute of Justice's National Crime Victimization Survey (NCVS). These programs provide a picture of victim characteristics through self-reports (NCVS) and reports to the police (UCR) and allow for a tabulation of the dollar costs of crime. Both programs also permit historical comparisons in crime rates and allow for some degree of predictability as to trends in crime. It is important to realize, however, that all statistics, including crime statistics, are inherently limited by the way in which they are gathered. Statistics can only portray the extent of crime according to the categories they are designed to measure and in terms understood by those whose responses they include.

Lacking in most of the crime statistics that are gathered today is any realistic appraisal of the human costs of crime—although some recent efforts by researchers at the National Institute of Justice have attempted to address this shortcoming. The trauma suffered by victims and survivors, the lowered sense of security experienced after victimization, the loss of human productivity, and reduced quality of life caused by crime are still difficult to gauge.

On the other side of the balance sheet, statistics fail to adequately identify the social costs suffered by offenders and their families. The social deprivation which may lead to crime, the fragmentation of private lives following conviction, and the loss of individuality which comes with confinement are all costs in which society must share, just as they are the culturally imposed consequences of crime and failure. Except for numbers on crimes committed, arrests, and figures on persons incarcerated, today's data-gathering strategies fall far short of gauging the human suffering and wasted human potential which both causes and follows from crime.

Even when reports do provide victim-impact measures, they may still fail to assess some of the objective costs of crime, including lowered property values in high-crime areas and inflated prices for consumer goods caused by the underground economy in stolen goods. White-collar crimes in particular are often well hidden and difficult to measure, yet many produce the largest direct dollar losses of any type of criminal activity. Hence, although modern crime statistics are useful, they do not provide the whole picture. Students of criminal justice need to be continually aware of aspects of the crime picture that fall outside of official data.

Discussion Questions

1. What are the two major sources of crime statistics for the United States? How do they differ? How are they alike?
2. What can crime statistics tell us about the crime "picture" in America? How has that picture changed over time?
3. What are the potential sources of error in the major reports on crime? Can you think of some popular usage of those statistics that might be especially misleading?

4. Why are many crime statistics expressed as a *rate*? How does the use of crime rates improve the reporting of crime data (over a simple numerical tabulation)?

5. What is the Crime Index? What crimes comprise the Crime Index. How is it computed? Why is it difficult to add offenses to (or remove them from) the Index and still have it retain its value as a comparative tool?

6. What are the two major offense categories in Part I crimes? Are there some property crimes that might have a violent aspect? Are there any personal crimes that could be nonviolent? If so, what might they be?

7. What is the hierarchy rule in crime-reporting programs? What purpose does it serve? What do you think of modifications in the hierarchy rule now occurring under NIBRS?

8. What does it mean to say that a crime has been *cleared*? Can you imagine a better way of reporting clearances?

Web Quest!

Visit "Dr. Frank Schmalleger's Cybrary of Criminal Justice Links" on the Web at http://talkjustice.com/cybrary.asp in order to familiarize yourself with the Cybrary's features. Note that a number of general categories are listed on the home page. The power of the Cybrary, however, lies in its advanced search capabilities. Practice using the Cybrary's search feature. Once you have become familiar with how the search feature works, use it to find links to the *Uniform Crime Reports* (hint: look for the FBI's home page), the *Sourcebook of Criminal Justice Statistics,* and the Bureau of Justice Statistics. Visit all three sites in order to gather information on the crime of rape.

What are the similarities and the differences in the availability of information on the crime of rape between these three sites? What are some of the other differences between these sites? Which do you find most useful? Why?

Submit the answers to these questions to your instructor if asked to do so.

Library Extras!

The Library Extras! listed here complement the WebExtras! found throughout this chapter. Library Extras! may be accessed on the Web at CJToday.com.

Library Extra! 2-1. *Age Patterns of Victims of Serious Violent Crime* (BJS, September 1997).

Library Extra! 2-2. "Crime's Decline—Why?" *The National Institute of Justice Journal* (NIJ, October 1998).

Library Extra! 2-3. *Criminal Victimization* (BJS, current volume).

Library Extra! 2-4. *Prevalence, Incidence, and Consequences of Violence Against Women: Findings from the National Violence Against Women Survey* (NIJ, November 1998).

Library Extra! 2-5. *Preventing Crime: What Works, What Doesn't, What's Promising* (NIJ, 1998).

Library Extra! 2-6. *Promising Strategies to Reduce Gun Violence* (NIJ, 1999).

Library Extra! 2-7. *Stalking in America: Findings from the National Violence Against Women Survey* (NIJ, April 1998).

Library Extra! 2-8. *Violence by Intimates: Analysis of Data on Crime by Current or Former Spouses, Boyfriends, and Girlfriends* (BJS, March 1998).

Library Extra! 2-9. *Women Offenders* (BJS, December 1999).

References

1. "Point of View," *The Chronicle of Higher Education,* June 10, 1992, p. A40.
2. The dead included the shooter and three members of his family.
3. Laura Parker, Gary Fields, and Scott Bowles, "Average Neighbor Lived with a Dark Past," *USA Today* online, July 30, 1999.
4. Mark Krantz, "Even for Day Trader, Killer Lost Big Money," *USA Today* online, August 1, 1999.

5. "Gunman was Suspect in 1993 Murder," *USA Today* online, July 30, 1999.

6. Norval Morris, "Crime, the Media, and Our Public Discourse," National Institute of Justice, *Perspectives on Crime and Justice* video series, recorded May 13, 1997.

7. As quoted in Frank Hagan, *Research Methods in Criminal Justice* (New York: Macmillan, 1982), from Eugene Webb et al., *Nonreactive Measures in the Social Sciences,* 2nd ed. (Boston: Houghton Mifflin, 1981), p. 89.

8. U.S. Bureau of Justice Statistics (BJS), *Criminal Victimization in the United States, 1985* (Washington, D.C.: U.S. Government Printing Office, 1987), p. 1.

9. Federal Bureau of Investigation (FBI), *Uniform Crime Reports for the United States, 1987* (Washington, D.C.: U.S. Government Printing Office, 1988), p. 1.

10. Federal Bureau of Investigation (FBI), *Uniform Crime Reports for the United States, 1999* (Washington, D.C.: U.S. Government Printing Office, 2000), p. 16.

11. The President's Commission on Law Enforcement and Administration of Justice, *The Challenge of Crime in a Free Society* (Washington, D.C.: U.S. Government Printing Office, 1967). The President's Commission relied on *Uniform Crime Reports* data, and the other crime statistics reported in this section come from UCRs for various years.

12. Hagan, *Research Methods in Criminal Justice and Criminology.*

13. John J. DiIulio, Jr., "The Question of Black Crime," *The Public Interest,* fall 1994, pp. 3–12.

14. James Alan Fox, *Trends in Juvenile Violence: A Report to the United States Attorney General on Current and Future Rates of Juvenile Offending* (Washington, D.C.: Bureau of Justice Statistics, 1996).

15. That is, while crime clock data may imply that one murder occurs every half hour or so, most murders actually occur during the evening and only a very few around sunrise.

16. Most offense definitions in this chapter are derived from those used by the UCR reporting program and are taken from the FBI, *Uniform Crime Reports: Crime in the United States, 1999* (hereafter referred to as the *Uniform Crime Reports*), or from BJS, *Criminal Justice Data Terminology,* 2nd ed. (Washington, D.C.: Bureau of Justice Statistics, 1981).

17. FBI, *Uniform Crime Reports, 1999.*

18. These and other statistics in this chapter are derived primarily from the *Uniform Crime Reports, 1999.*

19. Bureau of Justice Statistics (BJS), *Report to the Nation on Crime and Justice,* 2nd ed. (Washington, D.C.: U.S. Government Printing Office, 1988), p. 4.

20. There is no definitive cut-off between serial killing and spree killing in terms of time. Cunanan's three-month spree might qualify him as a serial killer in the minds of some criminologists. Nonetheless, renowned homicide investigators Robert Ressler (a former FBI criminal profiler) and Vernon Geberth (a retired New York commander of homicide investigations and noted forensic expert) both classify him as a spree killer. (See Michael Grunwald, "Cunanan Leaves Experts at Loss," *Boston Globe* via Simon and Schuster *Newslink,* July 28, 1997.

21. Bureau of Justice Statistics, *Report to the Nation on Crime and Justice,* 28, p. 4.

22. Ibid.

23. For excellent coverage of serial killers see, Steven Egger, *The Killers Among Us: An Examination of Serial Murder and Its Investigation* (Upper Saddle River, NJ: Prentice Hall, 1998); Steven A. Egger, *Serial Murder: An Elusive Phenomenon* (Westport, CT: Praeger Publishers, 1990); and, Stephen J. Giannangelo, *The Psychopathology of Serial Murder: A Theory of Violence* (New York: Praeger Publishers, 1996).

24. A few years ago Lucas recanted all of his confessions, saying he never killed anyone—except possibly his mother (a killing which he said he didn't remember). See "Condemned Killer Admits Lying, Denies Slayings," the *Washington Post,* October 1, 1995.

25. Chikatilo was executed in 1994.

26. FBI, *Uniform Crime Reports, 1999.*

27. Federal Bureau of Investigation, *Uniform Crime Reporting Handbook* (Washington, D.C.: FBI, 1984), p. 10.

28. "Study: Rape Vastly Underreported," *Fayetteville Observer-Times* (North Carolina), April 26, 1992, p. 16A.

29. Ronald Barri Flowers, *Women and Criminality: The Woman as Victim, Offender and Practitioner* (Westport, CT: Greenwood Press, 1987), p. 36.

30. A. Nichols Groth, *Men Who Rape: The Psychology of the Offender* (New York: Plenum Press, 1979).

31. Susan Brownmiller, *Against Our Will: Men, Women, and Rape* (New York: Simon and Schuster, 1975).

32. Dennis J. Stevens, "Motives of Social Rapists," Free Inquiry in *Creative Sociology,* vol. 23, no. 2 (November 1995), pp. 117–126.

33. The latest edition of the *Uniform Crime Reporting Handbook,* which serves as a statistical reporting guide for law enforcement agencies, says, for example, "By definition, sex attacks on males are excluded and should be classified as assaults or 'other sex offenses,' depending on the nature of the crime and the extent of the injury." *Uniform Crime Reporting Handbook* (Washington, D.C.: FBI, 1984), p. 10.

34. "Swim Coach Guilty of Statutory Rape," *USA Today,* August 13, 1993, p. 3A.

35. "Teen: Teacher's Pregnancy Planned," the Associated Press wire services, August 22, 1997.

36. *Washington* v. *LeTourneau,* Court TV Online, March 18, 1998. Web posted at www.courttv.com/trials/letourneau/031898.html.

37. BJS, *Report to the Nation on Crime and Justice,* 2nd ed., p. 5.

38. Ibid.

39. FBI, *Uniform Crime Reports, 1999.* For UCR reporting purposes, *minorities* are defined as blacks, Native Americans, Asians, Pacific Islanders, and Alaskan Natives.

40. Sometimes called assault with a deadly weapon with intent to kill, or AWDWWIK.

41. FBI, *Uniform Crime Reports 1999.*

42. BJS, *Report to the Nation on Crime and Justice,* 2nd ed., p. 6.

43. Ibid.

44. "Yale Says Student Stole His Education," *USA Today,* April 12, 1995, p. 3A.

45. Jim Mulvaney and Susan Kelleher, "Doctor Continues Deposition," *Orange County Register,* Web posted at www.ocregister.com/clinic/tlr/ 0121dep.htm. Viewed May 20, 1999.

46. Federal Bureau of Investigation (FBI), *Uniform Crime Reporting Handbook* (Washington, D.C.: U.S. Department of Justice, 1984), p. 28.

47. "Carjacking Case Goes to Trial," *USA Today,* April 13, 1993, p. 2A.

48. FBI, *Uniform Crime Reports, 1999.*

49. As indicated in the UCR definition of arson, *Uniform Crime Reports, 1999.*

50. FBI, *Uniform Crime Reports, 1999.*

51. Ibid.

52. While the old rule would have counted only one murder when a woman was raped and her husband murdered in the same criminal incident, the new rule would report both a murder and a rape.

53. Bureau of Justice Statistics, *Implementing the National Incident-Based Reporting System: A Project Status Report* (Washington, D.C.: BJS, July 1997).

54. The SEARCH Project Web Site, *NIBRS Overview,* www.nibrs.search.org.

55. "Crimes on 483 Campuses with more than 5,000 Students," *Chronicle of Higher Education,* May 28, 1999. Web posted at http://chronicle. com/free/v45/i38/stats/1year.htm. Accessed January 3, 2000.

56. H.R. 4797, 102d Cong. 2d Sess. (1992).

57. FBI, *Uniform Crime Reports, 1999.*

58. See www.apbonline.com/911/1999/02/25/ drag0225_01pm.html. Accessed May 20, 1999.

59. "Grim Portraits of Homophobic Killers," *Boston Globe* online, May 10, 1997.

60. Michael E. Wiggins, "Societal Changes and Right Wing Membership," paper presented at the Academy of Criminal Justice Sciences Annual Meeting, San Francisco, California, April 1988.

61. Richard Holden, "God's Law: Criminal Process and Right Wing Extremism in America," paper presented at the annual meeting of the Academy of Criminal Justice Sciences, San Francisco, California, April 1988.

62. John Kleinig, "Penalty Enhancements for Hate Crimes," *Criminal Justice Ethics* (summer/fall 1992), pp. 3–6.

63. *R.A.V. v. City of St. Paul, Minn.,* 112 S.Ct. 2538 (1992).

64. *Forsyth County, Ga. v. Nationalist Movement,* 112 S.Ct. 2395 (1992).

65. *Wisconsin v. Mitchell,* 508 U.S. 47 (1993).

66. For additional information, see Bureau of Justice Statistics, *Criminal Victimization 1999: Changes 1998–99 with Trends 1993–99* (Washington, D.C.: BJS, 2000).

67. Ibid.

68. Bureau of Justice Statistics, *Report to the Nation on Crime and Justice,* 2nd ed., p. 26.

69. Bureau of Justice Statistics, *Criminal Victimization 1999.*

70. Bureau of Justice Statistics, *Report to the Nation on Crime and Justice,* 2nd ed., p. 27.

71. Georgette Bennett, *Crimewarps: The Future of Crime in America* (Garden City, NY: Anchor/ Doubleday, 1987).

72. Ibid.

73. Ibid., p. xiv.

74. BJS, *Report to the Nation on Crime and Justice,* 2nd ed., p. 24.

75. "School Killings Drop, But Gang Activity Rises," APB Online; www.apbonline.com/911/1999/ 05/19/schools0519_01.html. Accessed May 20, 1999.

76. Indira A. R. Lakshmanan, "Fear Goes Up As Crime Goes Down," *Boston Globe,* August 18, 1994. Web posted at http://world.std.com/ ~jlr/comment/crime.htm. Accessed May 20, 1999.

77. Bureau of Justice Statistics, *Report to the Nation on Crime and Justice,* 2nd ed., p. 32.

78. The definition of rape employed by the UCR, however, automatically excludes crimes of homosexual rape such as might occur in prisons and jails. As a consequence, the rape of males is excluded from the official count for crimes of rape.

79. Bureau of Justice Statistics, *Report to the Nation on Crime and Justice,* 2nd ed., p. 25.

80. See, for example, Elizabeth Stanko, "When Precaution Is Normal: A Feminist Critique of Crime Prevention," in Loraine Gelsthorpe and Allison Morris, *Feminist Perspectives in Criminology* (Philadelphia: Open University Press, 1990).

81. For excellent coverage of women's issues in all areas of criminal justice, see Alida V. Merlo and Joycelyn M. Pollock, eds., *Women, Law, and Social Control* (Needham Heights, MA: Allyn and Bacon, 1995), and Donna C. Hale, ed., the journal *Women and Criminal Justice,* (Binghamton, NY: The Haworth Press).

82. For more information, see Eve S. Buzawa and Carl G. Buzawa, *Domestic Violence: The Criminal Justice Response* (Thousand Oaks, CA: Sage, 1996).

83. "Battered Women Tell Their Stories to the Senate," *Charlotte Observer* (North Carolina), July 10, 1991, p. 3A.

84. U.S. Department of Justice family violence publications can be found at www.otp.usdoj.gov/ familyviolence/whats_new.htm.

85. Patricia Tjaden and Nancy Thoennes, *Prevalence, Incidence, and Consequences of Violence Against Women: Findings from the National Violence Against Women Survey* (Washington, D.C.: National Institute of Justice, November 2000).

86. Caroline Wolf Harlow, *Female Victims of Violent Crime* (Washington, D.C.: BJS, 1991).

87. This aspect of the law is currently facing legal challenges. See, for example, *Brzonkala v. Virginia Polytechnic Institute and State University, et al.* 4th Cir. (No. 96-1814), 1999.

88. "Woman Convicted of Murdering Four Sons," APB Online, August 19, 1999. Web posted at www .apbonline.com/911/1999/08/19/foursons0819_ 01.html. Accessed January 2, 2000.

89. "Florida Woman Sentenced to Death," *USA Today,* February 1, 1992, p. 3A.

90. "Fla. Slayings: Men Beware," *USA Today,* December 17, 1990, p. 3A.

91. *Wuornos* v. *Florida,* No. 96-5766.

92. Otto Pollak, *The Criminality of Women* (Philadelphia: University of Pennsylvania Press, 1950).

93. FBI, *Uniform Crime Reports, 1970* and *1999.*

94. Ibid.

95. FBI, *Uniform Crime Reports, 1999.*

96. Leanne Fiftal Alarid, James W. Marquart, Velmer S. Burton, Jr., Francis T. Cullen, and Steven J. Cuvelier, "Women's Roles in Serious Offenses: A Study of Adult Felons," *Justice Quarterly,* vol. 13, no. 3 (September 1996), pp. 432–454.

97. Patsy A. Klaus, "The Costs of Crime to Victims," a Bureau of Justice Statistics Crime Data Brief, 1994.

98. Ted R. Miller, Mark A. Cohen, and Brian Wiersema, *Victim Costs and Consequences: A New Look* (Washington, D.C.: National Institute of Justice, February 1996).

99. Ibid.

100. Bureau of Justice Statistics, *Criminal Victimization 1999.*

101. Bureau of Justice Statistics, *Report to the Nation on Crime and Justice,* 2nd ed.

102. Kathleen Maguire and Ann L. Pastore, eds., *Sourcebook of Criminal Justice Statistics, 1999* (Washington, D.C.: Bureau of Justice Statistics, 2000).

103. Bureau of Justice Statistics, *Report to the Nation on Crime and Justice,* 2nd ed., p. 114.

104. "President Asks for 20% Growth in Justice Department Funding," *Criminal Justice Newsletter,* February 1, 1995, p. 1.

105. Ibid.

106. J. M. Chaiken and M. R. Chaiken, *Varieties of Criminal Behavior* (Santa Monica, CA: The Rand Corporation, 1982).

107. D. McBride, "Trends in Drugs and Death," paper presented at American Society of Criminology annual meeting, Denver, Colorado, 1983.

108. B. Johnson et al., *Taking Care of Business: The Economics of Crime by Heroin Abusers* (Lexington, MA: Lexington Books, 1985). See also Bernard A. Grooper, *Research in Brief: Probing the Links Between Drugs and Crime* (Washington, D.C.: National Institute of Justice, February 1985).

109. Bureau of Justice Statistics, *Report to the Nation on Crime and Justice,* 2nd ed., p. 114.

110. Ibid.

111. FBI, *Uniform Crime Reports, 1999.*

112. FBI, *Uniform Crime Reports, 1975* and *1999.*

113. Ibid.

114. Maguire and Pastore, *Sourcebook of Criminal Justice Statistics, 2000.*

115. Bennett, *Crimewarps,* p. 61.

116. Much of the data in this section comes from Bureau of Justice Statistics, "Elderly Crime Victims," March 1994. See also Catherine J. Whitaker, *BJS Special Report: Elderly Victims* (Rockville, MD: Bureau of Justice Statistics, November 1987).

117. The Organized Crime Control Act of 1970.

118. Bonnie Angelo, "Wanted: A New Godfather," *Time,* April 13, 1992, vol. 139, no. 15, p. 30.

119. Richard Behar, "In the Grip of Treachery," *Playboy,* November 1991, vol. 38, no. 11, p. 92.

120. " 'Junior' Gotti Gets Nearly 6½ Years," APB Online. Web posted at www.apbnews.com/911/1999/09/03/gotti0903_01.html. Accessed January 4, 2000.

121. William Sherman, "Kingpins of the Underworld," *Cosmopolitan,* March 1992, vol. 212, no. 3, p. 158.

122. Some reports claim that Dominick Cirillo, 67—known as "Quiet Dom"—has emerged as the heir to Gigante.

CHAPTER 3

Criminal Law

"Law is the art of the good and the fair."
—Ulpian, Roman Judge (Circa 200 a.d.)

"Every law is an infraction of liberty."
—Jeremy Bentham (1784–1832)

"Law should be like death, which spares no one."
—Montesquieu (1689–1755)

CHAPTER OUTLINE

- Sources of Modern Criminal Law
- The Rule of Law
- Types of Law
- General Categories of Crime
- General Features of Crime
- Elements of a Specific Criminal Offense
- Types of Defenses to a Criminal Charge

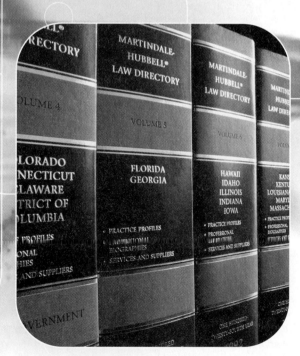

—Bill Gallery/Stock Boston

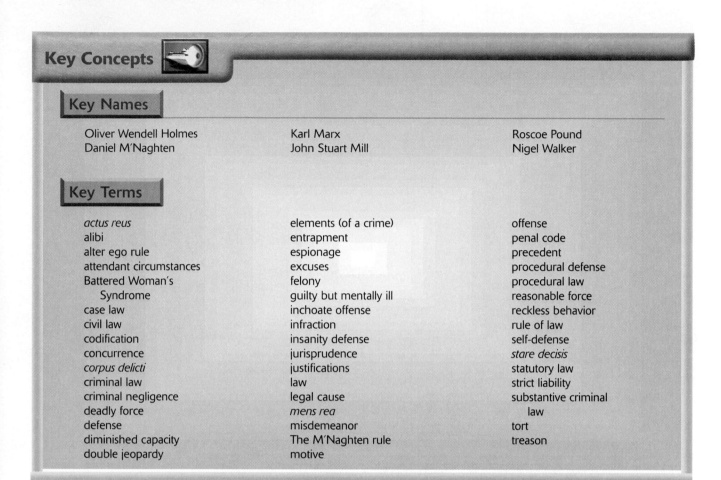

Key Concepts

Key Names

Oliver Wendell Holmes   Karl Marx   Roscoe Pound
Daniel M'Naghten   John Stuart Mill   Nigel Walker

Key Terms

actus reus	elements (of a crime)	offense
alibi	entrapment	penal code
alter ego rule	espionage	precedent
attendant circumstances	excuses	procedural defense
Battered Woman's	felony	procedural law
Syndrome	guilty but mentally ill	reasonable force
case law	inchoate offense	reckless behavior
civil law	infraction	rule of law
codification	insanity defense	self-defense
concurrence	jurisprudence	*stare decisis*
corpus delicti	justifications	statutory law
criminal law	law	strict liability
criminal negligence	legal cause	substantive criminal
deadly force	*mens rea*	law
defense	misdemeanor	tort
diminished capacity	The M'Naghten rule	treason
double jeopardy	motive	

AUDIO EXTRA! *Hear the author discuss this chapter at* **cjtoday.com**

Sources of Modern Criminal Law

Twenty years ago, as South American jungles were being cleared to make way for farmers and other settlers, a group of mercenaries brutally attacked and wiped out a small tribe of local Indians. About two dozen native men, women, and children were either hacked to death with machetes or shot. The Indians had refused to give up their land and would not move. At their arrest the killers uttered something that, to our ears, sounds frightening: "How can you arrest us?" they said. "We didn't know it was illegal to kill Indians!"

These men killed many people. But, they claimed, they were ignorant of the fact that the law forbade such a thing. In this case, these killers didn't consider their victims "human." It may seem obvious to us that what they had done was commit murder, but to them it was something else. Nevertheless, their ignorance of the law was rejected as a defense at their trial, and they were convicted of murder. All received lengthy prison sentences.

The men in this story were hardly literate, with almost no formal education. They knew very little about the law and, apparently, even less about basic moral principles. We, on the other hand, living in a modern society with highly developed means of communication, much formal schooling, and a large workforce of professionals skilled in interpreting the law, usually know what the law *says*. But do we really know what the law *is*? The job of this chapter is to discuss the law both as a product of rule creation and as a guide for behavior. We will also examine criminal law in some detail, as well as discuss defenses commonly used by defendants charged with violations of the criminal law.

The Nature of Law

Practically speaking, **laws** regulate relationships between people and also between parties (such as agencies of government and individuals). Most of us would probably agree that the law is whatever legislators, through the exercise of their politically sanctioned wisdom,

Law

A rule of conduct, generally found enacted in the form of a statute, which proscribes and/or mandates certain forms of behavior. Statutory law is often the result of moral enterprise by interest groups which, through the exercise of political power, are successful in seeing their valuative perspectives enacted into law.

tell us it is. If we hold to that belief, we would expect to be able to find the law unambiguously specified in a set of books or codes. As we shall see, however, such is not always the case.

The laws of our nation, or of a state, are found in **statutory provisions** and constitutional enactments,[1] as well as in hundreds of years of rulings by courts at all levels. According to the authoritative *Black's Law Dictionary,* the word *law* "generally contemplates both statutory and **case law.**"[2] If "the law" could be found entirely ensconced in written legal codes, it would be plain to nearly everyone, and we would need far fewer lawyers than we find practicing today. But some laws (in the sense of precedents established by courts) do not exist "on the books," and even those that do are open to interpretation.

The Rule of Law

The social, economic, and political stability of any society depends largely upon the development and institutionalization of a predictable system of laws. Western democratic societies adhere to the **rule of law,** which is sometimes also referred to as "the supremacy of law."

The rule of law concept centers around the belief that an orderly society must be governed by established principles and known codes which are applied uniformly and fairly to all of its members. Under the rule of law no one is above the law, and those who enforce the law must abide by it.

The rule of law has been called "the greatest political achievement of our culture." Without it few other human achievements—especially those which require the efforts of a large number of people working together in coordinated fashion—would be possible.

President John F. Kennedy eloquently explained the rule of law, saying: "Americans are free to disagree with the law, but not to disobey it; for a government of laws and not of men, no man, however prominent and powerful, no mob, however unruly or boisterous, is entitled to defy a court of law."

The American Bar Association notes that the rule of law includes[3]

- Freedom from private lawlessness provided by the legal system of a politically organized society;
- A relatively high degree of objectivity in the formulation of legal norms and a like degree of evenhandedness in their application;
- Legal ideas and juristic devices for the attainment of individual and group objectives within the bounds of ordered liberty;
- Substantive and procedural limitations on governmental power in the interest of the individual for the enforcement of which there are appropriate legal institutions and machinery.

To learn more about the rule of law visit WebExtra! 3-1 at CJToday.com.

Types of Law

"Criminal" and "civil" law are the best-known types of modern law. However, scholars and philosophers have drawn numerous distinctions between categories of the law which rest upon their source, intent, and application. Laws in modern societies can be usefully described in terms of the following groups:

- Criminal law
- Civil law
- Administrative law
- Case law
- Procedural law

This typology is helpful in understanding and thinking about the law, and we will now discuss each type of law in some detail.

Statutory Law

Written or codified law. The "law on the books," as enacted by a governmental body or agency having the power to make laws.

Case Law

That body of judicial precedent, historically built upon legal reasoning and past interpretations of statutory laws, which serves as a guide to decision making, especially in the courts.

Codification

The act or process of rendering laws in written form.

Rule of Law

The maxim that an orderly society must be governed by established principles and known codes, which are applied uniformly and fairly to all of its members.

"If this country should ever reach the point where any man or group of men, by force or threat of force, could long defy the commands of our courts and our Constitution, then no law would stand free from doubt, no judge would be sure of his writ, and no citizen would be safe from its neighbors."

—U.S. Representative Bob Barr
Speaking at the 1998 impeachment hearings of President Bill Clinton

Theory Into Practice

What Does Law Do? The Functions of Law

◆ Laws maintain order in society.

◆ Laws regulate human interaction.

◆ Laws enforce moral beliefs.

◆ Laws define the economic environment.

◆ Laws enhance predictability.

◆ Laws support the powerful.

◆ Laws promote orderly social change.

◆ Laws sustain individual rights.

◆ Laws redress wrongs.

◆ Laws identify evildoers.

◆ Laws mandate punishment and retribution.

Criminal Law

Criminal Law

That branch of modern law which concerns itself with offenses committed against society, members thereof, their property, and the social order. Another term for criminal law is penal law.

Fundamental to the concept of **criminal law** is the assumption that criminal acts injure not just individuals, but society as a whole. Hence, we can define criminal law as that body of rules and regulations which defines and specifies punishments for offenses of a public nature or for wrongs committed against the state or society. Criminal law is also called penal law.

Social order, as reflected in the values supported by statute, is reduced to some degree whenever a criminal act occurs. In old England (from which much of American legal tradition devolves) offenders were said to violate the "King's Peace" when they committed a crime. They offended not just their victims, but contravened the peaceful order established under the rule of the monarch. For this reason, in criminal cases, the state, as the injured party, begins the official process of bringing the offender to justice. Even if the victim is dead and has no one to speak on his or her behalf, the agencies of justice will investigate the crime and file charges against the offender. Because crimes injure the fabric of society, the state, not the individual victim, becomes the plaintiff in criminal proceedings. Cases in criminal court reflect this fact by being cited as follows: *State of New York* v. *Smith* (where state law has been violated) or *U.S.* v. *Smith* (where the federal government is the injured party).

"EQUAL JUSTICE UNDER LAW"

Words inscribed above the entrance to the U.S. Supreme Court building

Violations of the criminal law result in the imposition of punishment. Punishment is philosophically justified by the fact that the criminal *intended* the harm and is responsible for it. Punishment serves a variety of purposes, which we will discuss later in the chapter on sentencing. When punishment is imposed in a criminal case, however, it is for one basic reason: to express society's fundamental displeasure with the offensive behavior and to hold the offender accountable for it.

Criminal law, which is built upon constitutional principles and operates within an established set of procedures applicable to the criminal justice system, is composed of both statutory and case law. Statutory law is the "law on the books." It is the result of legislative action and is often thought of as the "law of the land." Written laws exist in both criminal and civil areas and are called codes. Once laws have been written down in organized fashion, they are said to be "codified." Federal statutes are compiled in the United States Code (U.S.C.). State codes and municipal ordinances are also readily available in written, or statutory, form. The written form of the criminal law is called the **penal code.**

Penal Code

The written, organized, and compiled form of the criminal laws of a jurisdiction.

Substantive Criminal Law

That part of the law that defines crimes and specifies punishments.

Written law is of two types: substantive and procedural. Substantive law deals directly with specifying the nature of, and appropriate punishment for, particular offenses. For example, every state in our country has laws against murder, rape, robbery, and assault. Differences in the law among these various jurisdictions can be studied in detail because each offense and the punishments associated with it are available in the **substantive criminal law** in written form. Procedural laws, on the other hand, specify acceptable methods for dealing with violations of substantive laws, especially within the context of a judicial setting.

Civil Law

Civil law provides a formal means for regulating noncriminal relationships between and among persons, businesses and other organizations, and agencies of government. In contrast to the criminal law, whose violation is an offense against the state or against the nation, civil law governs relationships between parties. Civil law contains rules for contracts, divorce, child support and custody, the creation of wills, property transfers, negligence, libel, unfair practices in hiring, the manufacture and sale of consumer goods with hidden hazards for the user, and many other contractual and social obligations. When the civil law is violated, a civil suit may follow.

Civil suits seek not punishment, but compensation, usually in the form of property or monetary damages. They may also be filed in order to achieve an injunction or a kind of judicial cease-and-desist order. A violation of the civil law may be a **tort** (a wrongful act, damage, or injury not involving a breach of contract) or a contract violation, but it is not a crime. A tort, involving, say, an automobile accident, may give rise to civil liability under which the injured party may sue the person or entity who caused the injury and ask that the offending party be ordered to pay damages directly to injured party. Because a tort is a personal wrong, however, it is left to the aggrieved individual to set the machinery of the court in motion—that is, to bring a suit.

Civil law is more concerned with assessing liability than it is with intent. Civil suits arising from automobile crashes, for example, do not allege that either driver intended to inflict bodily harm. Nor do they claim that it was the intent of the driver to damage either vehicle. However, when someone is injured, or property damage occurs, even in an accident, civil procedures make it possible to gauge responsibility and assign liability to one party or the other. The parties to a civil suit are referred to as the plaintiff (who seeks relief) and the defendant (against whom relief is sought).

In 1999, for example, jurors in Pontiac, Michigan, decided that the producers of the Jenny Jones television talk show would have to pay more than $25 million in damages associated with the slaying of a guest who had appeared on the show. Scott Amendure was killed by Jonathan Schmitz after revealing on national television that he had a crush on Schmitz. Jurors found the producers liable because they created the situation which led to Amendure's death, and because they misled Schmitz into thinking he was about to meet a woman. Amendure's family was ordered to receive $5 million in damages for the suffering Amendure endured before his death, $10 million for the loss of a loved one's companionship, and another $10 million for the loss of money Amendure would have earned during his lifetime.[4]

Currently, many states award punitive damages (for example, those intended to compensate for mental anguish, degradation, shame, or hurt feelings suffered by the plaintiff) when jurors determine that the chances were better than 50 percent that the defendant acted with gross negligence (where gross negligence is defined as "the intentional failure to perform a manifest duty in reckless disregard of the consequences as affecting the life or property of another"[5]). Punitive damage awards may be huge. In 1996, for example, an Alabama jury awarded 37-year-old Alex Hardy $50 million in compensatory damages and $100 million in punitive damages after he was left partially paralyzed in the crash of his Chevrolet Blazer. Jurors found that door latches on the vehicle were defective, causing Hardy to be thrown from the vehicle.[6]

That amount pales, however, beside the $4.9 billion civil judgment against General Motors awarded to six people by a Los Angeles jury in 1999. The case, the biggest personal-injury award in U.S. history, involved an exploding gas tank on a 1979 Chevrolet Malibu, a problem which General Motors apparently knew about, but refused to fix. Only $107 million of the judgment was awarded for compensatory damages in the 1993 accident. The other $4.8 billion consisted of punitive damages. Los Angeles Superior Court Judge Ernest Williams later reduced the punitive damage award to $1.1 billion. General Motors is appealing the judgment further as this book goes to press.[7]

Civil Law

That part of the law that governs relationships between parties.

Tort

A wrongful act, damage, or injury not involving a breach of contract. A private or civil wrong or injury.

Auto accident burn victim Alisha Parker, 11, sits with a Los Angeles County Sheriff's deputy. In 1999 a California jury ordered General Motors to pay Alisha and five other burn victims $4.9 billion as the result of a 1993 car crash in which the gas tank on their 1979 Chevrolet Malibu exploded. The personal-injury award is the biggest in U.S. history. Only $107 million of the judgment was awarded for compensatory damages. The rest of the judgment—$4.8 billion—consisted of punitive damages. Upon appeal, the amount was reduced to $1.1 billion.

Nick Ut, AP/Wide World Photos.

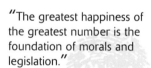

"The greatest happiness of the greatest number is the foundation of morals and legislation."

—Jeremy Bentham

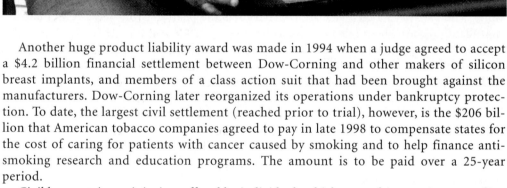

Another huge product liability award was made in 1994 when a judge agreed to accept a $4.2 billion financial settlement between Dow-Corning and other makers of silicon breast implants, and members of a class action suit that had been brought against the manufacturers. Dow-Corning later reorganized its operations under bankruptcy protection. To date, the largest civil settlement (reached prior to trial), however, is the $206 billion that American tobacco companies agreed to pay in late 1998 to compensate states for the cost of caring for patients with cancer caused by smoking and to help finance anti-smoking research and education programs. The amount is to be paid over a 25-year period.

Civil law pertains to injuries suffered by individuals which are unfair or unjust according to the standards operative in the social group. Breaches of contract, unfair practices in hiring, the manufacture and sale of consumer goods with hidden hazards for the user, and slanderous comments made about others have all been grounds for civil suits. Suits may, on occasion, arise as extensions of criminal action. Monetary compensation, for example, may be sought through our system of civil laws by a victim of a criminal assault after a criminal conviction has been obtained.

Following the murder a few years ago of Sandra Black, for example, her son and mother successfully sued *Soldier of Fortune* magazine, winning damages of $9.4 million.[8] *Soldier of Fortune* had printed a classified advertisement by a "mercenary" who, as a result of the ad, eventually contracted with Mrs. Black's husband to commit the murder. In a quite different type of civil suit, Robert McLaughlin was awarded $1.9 million by a New York State Court of Claims in October 1989, after having spent six and one-half years in prison for a murder and robbery he did not commit.[9]

A 1993 civil case, which may hold considerable significance for the criminal justice system, found a Florida jury holding K-Mart stores liable for selling a gun to a drunken man. The buyer, Thomas W. Knapp, used the weapon a half hour later to shoot his girl-friend, Deborah Kitchen, in the neck—leaving her permanently paralyzed. Knapp had consumed 24 beers and nearly 25 shots of whiskey prior to purchasing the weapon. He was convicted of attempted first-degree murder and is serving a 40-year prison term. Following a civil suit brought by Kitchen, K-Mart was ordered to pay her $12 million, sending a message to gun retailers across the nation. In 1997 the Florida supreme court upheld the award.[10]

In a precedent-setting 1995 case, a San Francisco judge ruled that a lawsuit brought by a widow of a man slain by gunfire was based upon solid legal principles and could proceed.[11] At issue was whether the handgun maker, Miami-based Navegar, Incorporated, could be sued under a legal theory which holds manufacturers liable for injuries caused by their products. In this case, Michelle Scully sued the gun manufacturer after her husband, John, was killed by an assailant who opened fire on workers in a California law office in 1993. As the shooting started, John Scully threw himself over his wife and shielded her with his body. Some criticized the judge's ruling, saying that it opened a Pandora's box of potential suits against manufacturers of all kinds of products—since lawsuits targeting products which are not defective and which function precisely as intended might result in suits against automobile manufacturers; makers of alcohol, insecticides, and high-cholesterol foods; and even against companies which make knives, gasoline, candles, cigarette lighters, and flammable materials when irresponsible individuals choose to use those products to harm others.

Suits against gun manufacturers continue to proliferate. In 1999 and 2000, a number of cities, including Atlanta, Miami, Bridgeport, New Orleans, Chicago, Cleveland, and Boston, sued the firearms industry to recoup municipal monies spent on gun crime. The suits sought to recover costs for city-supported services utilized in instances of gun crime. Expenses for EMS (emergency medical service) personnel and equipment, city-run hospitals, and police investigations were all covered by the suits (most of which are ongoing as this book goes to press).

Not all suits against gun makers seek monetary damages. In 1999, for example, the NAACP (National Association for the Advancement of Colored People) announced that it would sue handgun manufacturers, distributors, and importers, in a bid to impose restrictions on the marketing and sale of firearms.[12] The NAACP's goal is to keep guns out of the hands of criminals. In place of money, the suit seeks court orders that would force gun manufacturers to monitor where the guns they produce are distributed. Another portion of the suit would place limits on multiple handgun purchases by the same individual.

Criminal action, not otherwise excusable, may even be grounds for a civil suit by the offender. Some years ago, for example, a civil jury awarded $2.15 million to convicted murderer William Freeman and his family. Freeman, a former assistant chief of police from Fort Stockton, Texas, is serving a life term in prison for killing his friend, Donnie Hazelwood. A jury agreed with Freeman's claim that the sleeping pill Halcion altered his personality and caused him to kill Hazelwood.[13]

Some claim that civil suits seeking monetary damages have taken on the characteristics of a lottery—offering instant riches to those "lucky" enough to win them. In a typical year 100 million lawsuits are filed in this country—approximately one for every two living Americans. While most of these suits, which may involve divorces, wills, and bad debts, are legitimate, some are simply shots in the dark, taken by lawsuit-happy citizens hoping to win at least some limited type of fame or fortune through the courts. It is becoming increasingly clear to critics of the current system that American civil courts can unwittingly serve the get-rich-quick schemes of the greedy who feign injury.

The largest civil suit ever filed, for example, was brought by Allen and Kathy Wilson in 1994.[14] The Wilsons filed suit in Carson City, Nevada, asking the state to pay them $657 trillion—the amount the couple said they were owed on a $1,000 state-issued bond purchased in 1865. The Wilsons bought the bond in 1992 from a widow who had inherited it from her husband. They calculated the amount they claim they are owed by compounding interest at an annual rate of 24 percent for 130 years. The state of Nevada successfully maintained that time had run out for redeeming the bond.

In 1996 the U.S. Congress passed legislation which would have limited punitive damage claims in civil suits brought in federal and state courts to a maximum of $250,000, or three times the plaintiff's economic damages from such things as lost income and medical expenses—whichever would have been greater. Under this legislation, known as the Civil

Class-Action Suit to Target N.J. Police

Kevin Keenan, seated, acting executive director of the American Civil Liberties Union of New Jersey, responds to reporters' questions about the resignation of New Jersey State Police Superintendent Colonel Carl Williams during a news conference in Newark, New Jersey. Williams was forced to resign after his department became embroiled in a "racial profiling" flap, and he made remarks that appeared to support the policy. Other ACLU officials look on.
Mike Derer, AP/Wide World Photos.

TRENTON, N.J.—The American Civil Liberties Union of New Jersey said today it's putting together a class-action lawsuit on behalf of minority motorists who claim to have been unfairly subjected to traffic stops as a result of their race.

The group is amending a joint civil suit filed in a state Superior Court in 1997 and adding more minority motorists who believe they were victims of "racial profiling," an alleged practice of discrimination in which blacks and Latinos are pulled over more often than whites.

"We know that more people of color are having their cars pulled over for no other reason than because of their color," Lenora Lapidus, attorney for the ACLU-NJ, told APBNews.com. "We've been working with attorneys and trying to get the word out to see if there are

more victims out there. We expect to name many additional plaintiffs to the suit in coming months."

The Black Ministers Council of New Jersey has set up a hot line for potential victims, said its executive director, the Rev. Reginald Jackson.

New Jersey State Police refused to comment. The state attorney general's office did not return numerous calls seeking comment.

Top Cop Forced to Resign

Two weeks ago, the state released documents that revealed minorities accounted for 75 percent of motorists arrested on the New Jersey Turnpike over a two-month stretch in 1997. The ACLU said that number was disproportionately high because minorities make up less than 20 percent of the population.

"The statistics show that these races

are being unfairly targeted," Lapidus said.

The controversy came to a head Sunday when state police Superintendent Col. Carl Williams, a 35-year police veteran, was forced to resign after he was quoted in *The Star-Ledger* of Newark as saying that minorities were more likely to be involved in drug crimes.

His resignation came less than two weeks after Gov. Christine Todd Whitman backed him when minority groups demanded he be held responsible for the racial profiling controversy.

Policies Being Reviewed

The racial profiling controversy flared last April when two state troopers fired 11 shots into a van carrying four minority men on the New Jersey Turnpike, authorities said.

Accusations later surfaced that troopers are coaxed by their superiors to target minorities to attain their ticket quotas.

State police have vehemently denied that accusation.

Earlier this year, New Jersey Attorney General Peter Verniero ordered his office to review state police policies to determine if troopers engage in "racial profiling." But state officials said the U.S. Justice Department's Civil Rights Division already had been investigating New Jersey State Police practices for two years.

Today, the New Jersey Legislative Black and Latino Caucus announced at a news conference at the Statehouse in Trenton that members will conduct their own investigation into possible racial profiling by the state police.

Claim Verbal and Physical Assault

In the original civil suit lodged against New Jersey, the New Jersey Turnpike Authority, the New Jersey State

(Continued)

CRIME IN THE NEWS

Class-Action Suit to Target N.J. Police

Police and two of its state troopers, the plaintiffs claim to have been pulled over on the turnpike on Jan. 16, 1996, and verbally and physically assaulted.

Felix Morka and Laila Maher, two prominent minority attorneys, said they were also ridiculed by troopers Scott Jiras and Leonard Nerbetski and were urged by a police sergeant not to

pursue a civil suit. They filed one more than a year later.

"The actions of the State Police terrorize people of color and have a disparate impact on the rights of the people of color to utilize the turnpike, turnpike facilities and accommodations, and facilities and accommodations accessible via the turnpike," the lawsuit reads.

In addition to monetary damages

for pain, suffering and loss of wages, the lawsuit requests that the state police keep detailed records on the race of drivers pulled over for traffic violations and set up a warning system to spot police officers who show racist or violent tendencies.

Source: Michelle Gotthelf, *"Class-Action Suit to Target N.J. Police,"* APB News, March 2, 1999.

Justice Fairness Act, compensatory damages would have been awarded only for the amount of damages the plaintiff could prove were actually incurred.[15] The Act, however, was vetoed by then-President Clinton, and an attempted override of the presidential veto failed. Opponents of the congressional initiative argued that limits on punitive damages are inherently unfair and claimed that federal restrictions on suits filed in state courts illegally preempt state authority over such matters.

A short time later, however, the U.S. Supreme Court ruled that the U.S. Constitution does not permit "grossly excessive" damage awards in civil suits. The 1996 case[16] involved Dr. Ira Gore, Jr., who sued Bavarian Motor Works after learning that a new BMW he had bought in 1990 had been repainted before he took delivery of the car. Dr. Gore's vehicle had been damaged by acid rain during shipment to the United States from a manufacturing facility in Germany, and BMW repainted portions of the car when it arrived in the United States—without telling Dr. Gore that it had done so before selling the vehicle to him. When Gore sued, a state jury awarded him $4,000 in compensatory damages and $4 million in punitive damages. The state's supreme court reduced the award to $2 million. In overturning the huge award, the U.S. Supreme Court ruled that "the due process (fair hearing) clause of the 14th Amendment prohibits a state from imposing a 'grossly excessive' punishment on a [civil wrongdoer]." The wrongdoing in this case, said the Court, "involved a decision by a national distributor of automobiles [BMW] not to advise its dealers, and hence their customers, of predelivery damage to new cars when the cost of repair amounted to less than 3 percent of the car's suggested retail price." In wording that may hold considerable significance for future civil suits seeking large punitive damages, the Court's majority wrote: "Elementary notions of fairness enshrined in our constitutional jurisprudence dictate that a person receive fair notice not only of the conduct that will subject him to punishment but also of the severity of the penalty that a state may impose." Since the amount of punitive damages awarded in the Gore case was hundreds of times the amount of the actual damage done to the vehicle, the Court reasoned, BMW could never have anticipated having to pay such massive damages for such a relatively minor transgression. The case was sent back to the Alabama Supreme Court for a new hearing and concluded in 1997 when that court ordered BMW to pay Dr. Gore $50,000.[17]

Administrative Law

Administrative law refers to the body of *regulations* which have been created by governments to control the activities of industry, business, and individuals. Tax laws, health codes, restrictions on pollution and waste disposal, vehicle registration, building codes, and the like are examples of administrative law.

Other administrative laws cover practices in the areas of customs (imports/exports), immigration, agriculture, product safety, and most areas of manufacturing. Modern individualists claim that overregulation characterizes the American way of life, although they are in turn criticized for failing to adequately recognize the complexity of modern society. Overregulation has also been used on occasion as a rallying cry for political hopefuls who believe that many Americans wish to return to an earlier and simpler form of free enterprise.

Although the criminal law is, for the most part, separate from administrative regulations, the two may overlap. For instance, the rise in organized criminal activity in the area of toxic waste disposal—an area covered by many administrative regulations—has led to criminal prosecutions in several states. The intentional and systematic denial of civil rights in areas generally thought to be administrative in nature, such as hiring, employment, job compensation, and so forth, may also lead to criminal sanctions through the federal system of laws.

Administrative agencies will sometimes arrange settlements which fall short of court action but that are considered binding on individuals or groups who have not lived up to the intent of federal or state regulations. Education, environmental protection, and discriminatory hiring practices are all areas in which such settlements have been employed.

Case Law

Precedent

A legal principle that operates to ensure that previous judicial decisions are authoritatively considered and incorporated into future cases.

Case law (which comes from judicial decisions) is also referred to as the law of **precedent**. It represents the accumulated wisdom of trial and appellate courts (those which hear appeals) in criminal, civil, and administrative law cases over the years. Once a court decision is rendered, it is written down. At the appellate level, the reasoning behind the decision is recorded as well. Under the rule of precedent, this reasoning should then be taken into consideration by other courts in settling future cases.

Appellate courts have considerable power to influence new court decisions at the trial level. The court with the greatest influence, of course, is the U.S. Supreme Court. The precedents it establishes are incorporated as guidelines into the process of legal reasoning by which lower courts reach conclusions.

Jonathan Schmitz (center) looks toward his friend Donna Riley (left) as he is hugged by Scott Amendure in this image taken from video shown to jurors in Schmitz's first-degree murder trial in Pontiac, Michigan, in 1996. Schmitz was convicted of killing Amendure after Amendure revealed during a taping of the Jenny Jones show that he had a crush on Schmitz. The segment, which never aired, was titled "Same-Sex Secret Crushes." In 1999 Schmitz was sentenced to 25 to 50 years in prison for the murder.
Court TV, AP/Wide World Photos.

CAREERS IN JUSTICE

Working for the U.S. Park Police

TYPICAL POSITIONS:

U.S. Park Police provide enforcement services in the nation's national parks. They also serve the nation's capitol and grounds, including federal areas within the District of Columbia. Branches include the Horse-Mounted Unit, the Criminal Investigations Branch, the Traffic Safety Unit, the Special Equipment and Tactics Team, the Motor Unit (which employs motorcycles), the Canine Unit, the Marine Unit, and the Aviation Unit.

EMPLOYMENT REQUIREMENTS:

Applicant must (1) be at least 21 years of age and have not reached his or her 31st birthday by the time of appoint-ment, (2) be a U.S. citizen, (3) possess a high school diploma or equivalent, (4) have 20/60 vision or better that is correctable to 20/20, and (5) have had two years of progressively responsible experience.

OTHER REQUIREMENTS:

Applicant must (1) successfully complete 18 weeks of intensive training at the Federal Law Enforcement Training Center (Glynco, Georgia) and (2) perform satisfactorily on periodic written tests.

SALARY:

Agents are typically hired at federal pay grade GS-5 or GS-7, depending on education and prior work history.

BENEFITS:

Benefits include (1) participation in the Federal Employee's Retirement System, (2) paid annual leave, (3) paid sick leave, (4) overtime that is compensated at the rate of time and one-half of regular pay, and (5) all uniforms and equipment, which are provided.

DIRECT INQUIRIES TO:

U.S. Park Police, Personnel Office, 1100 Ohio Drive SW, Washington, DC 20242. Phone: (202) 619-7056. Web site: www.doi.gov/u.s.park.police

---

The principle of recognizing previous decisions as precedents to guide future deliberations is called **stare decisis** and forms the basis for our modern law of precedent. Lief H. Carter has pointed out how precedent operates along two dimensions.[18] He calls them the vertical and the horizontal. A vertical rule requires that decisions made by a higher court be taken into consideration by lower courts in their deliberations. Under this rule, state appellate courts, for example, should be expected to follow the spirit of decisions rendered by their state supreme courts.

The horizontal dimension means that courts on the same level should be consistent in their interpretation of the law. The U.S. Supreme Court, operating under the horizontal rule, for example, should not be expected to change its ruling in cases similar to those it has already decided.

Stare decisis makes for predictability in the law. Defendants walking into a modern courtroom will have the opportunity to be represented by lawyers who are trained in legal precedents as well as procedure. As a consequence, they will have a good idea of what to expect about the manner in which their trial will proceed.

Stare Decisis

The legal principle which requires that courts be bound by their own earlier decisions and by those of higher courts having jurisdiction over them regarding subsequent cases on similar issues of law and fact. The term literally means "standing by decided matters."

Procedural Law

Procedural law is another kind of statutory law. It is a body of rules which regulates the processing of an offender by the criminal justice system. **Procedural law,** for example, specifies in most jurisdictions that the testimony of one party to certain "victimless crimes" cannot be used as the sole evidence against the other party. General rules of evidence, search and seizure, procedures to be followed in an arrest, and other specified processes by which the justice system operates are also contained in procedural law.

As a great jurist once said, however, the law is like a living thing. It changes and evolves over time. Legislatures enact new statutory laws, and justices set new precedents, sometimes overruling established ones. Many jurisdictions today, for example, because of the changed role of women in society, now allow wives to bring charges of rape against their husbands—

Procedural Law

That aspect of the law that specifies the methods to be used in enforcing substantive law.

something not permitted under the laws of most states as little as a decade or two ago. Similarly, under newly written laws in many states, wives may testify against their husbands in certain cases, even though such action is contrary to years of previously acknowledged precedent.

General Categories of Crime

Violations of the criminal law can be of many different types and vary in severity. Five categories of violation will be discussed in the pages which follow. They are as follows:

- Felonies
- Misdemeanors
- Offenses
- Treason
- Inchoate offenses

Felonies

Felony

A criminal offense punishable by death or by incarceration in a prison facility for at least a year.

Violations of the criminal law can be more or less serious. **Felonies** are serious crimes. The felony category includes crimes such as murder, rape, aggravated assault, robbery, burglary, arson, and so on. Under common law, felons could be sentenced to death and/or have their property confiscated. Today, many felons receive prison sentences, although the potential range of penalties can include anything from probation and a fine to capital punishment in many jurisdictions. Following common law tradition, people who are today convicted of felonies usually lose certain privileges. Some states, for example, make conviction of a felony and incarceration grounds for uncontested divorce. Others prohibit offenders from running for public office or owning a firearm and exclude them from some professions such as medicine, law, and police work.

The federal government and many states have moved to a scheme of classifying felonies, from most to least serious, using a number or letter designation. The federal system,[19] for example, for purposes of criminal sentencing, assigns a score of 43 to first-degree murder, while the crime of theft is only rated a "base offense level" of 4. Attendant circumstances and the criminal history of the offender are also taken into consideration in sentencing decisions.

Because of differences among the states, a crime classified as a felony in one part of the country may be a misdemeanor in another, while in still other areas it may not even be a crime at all! This is especially true of some drug law violations and of certain other social order offenses such as homosexuality, prostitution, and gambling—which, in a number of jurisdictions, are perfectly legal (although such activity may still be subject to certain administrative regulations).

Misdemeanors

Misdemeanor

An offense punishable by incarceration, usually in a local confinement facility, for a period of which the upper limit is prescribed by statute in a given jurisdiction, typically limited to a year or less.

Misdemeanors are relatively minor crimes, consisting of offenses such as petty theft (the theft of items of little worth), simple assault (in which the victim suffers no serious injury, and in which none was intended), breaking and entering, the possession of burglary tools, disorderly conduct, disturbing the peace, filing a false crime report, and writing bad checks (although the amount for which the check is written may determine the classification of this offense).

In general, misdemeanors can be thought of as any crime punishable by a year or less in prison. In fact, most misdemeanants receive suspended sentences involving a fine and supervised probation. If an "active sentence" is received for a misdemeanor violation of the law, it probably will involve time to be spent in a local jail, perhaps on weekends, rather than imprisonment in a long-term confinement facility. Alternatively, some misdemeanants are sentenced to community service activities, requiring them to do such things as wash school buses, paint local government buildings, or clean parks and other public areas.

Normally, a police officer cannot arrest a person for a misdemeanor, unless the crime was committed in the officer's presence. If the in-presence requirement is missing, the officer will need to seek an arrest warrant from a magistrate or other judicial officer. Once a warrant has been issued, the officer may then proceed with the arrest.

Offenses

A third category of crime is the offense. Although, strictly speaking, all violations of the law can be called "criminal offenses," the term **offense** is sometimes used to specifically refer to minor violations of the law which are less serious than misdemeanors. When the term is used in that sense, it refers to such things as jaywalking, spitting on the sidewalk, littering, and certain traffic violations, including the failure to wear a seat belt. Another word used to describe such minor law violations is **infraction.** People committing infractions are typically ticketed and released, usually upon a promise to later appear in court. Court appearances may often be waived through payment of a small fine, which is often mailed in.

Treason

Felonies, misdemeanors, offenses, and the people who commit them constitute the daily work of the justice system. Special categories of crime, however, exist and should be recognized. They include treason and espionage. **Treason** has been defined as "the act of a U.S. citizen's helping a foreign government to overthrow, make war against, or seriously injure the United States."[20] Treason is also a crime under the laws of most states. Hence, treason can be more generally defined as the attempt to overthrow the government of the society of which one is a member. Some states, such as California, have legislatively created the crime of treason, while in others the crime is constitutionally defined. Florida's constitution, for example, which mirrors wording in the U.S. Constitution, says that "treason against the state shall consist only in levying war against it, adhering to its enemies, or giving them aid and comfort, and no person shall be convicted of treason except on the testimony of two witnesses to the same overt act or on confession in open court."[21]

Espionage, an offense akin to treason, refers to the "gathering, transmitting, or losing"[22] of information related to the national defense in such a manner that the information becomes available to enemies of the United States and may be used to their advantage. Espionage against the United States did not end with the Cold War. In 1994, for example, CIA agent Aldrich Hazen Ames and his wife, Rosario, were arrested and charged with conspiracy to commit espionage in a plot to sell U.S. government secrets to the Russian KGB.[23] The Ameses apparently told their Russian handlers of CIA operatives within the former Soviet Union and revealed the extent of American knowledge of KGB plans. Their activities had gone undetected for nearly a decade. Following arrest, the Ameses pleaded guilty to charges of espionage and tax fraud. Aldrich Ames was sentenced to life in prison; his wife received a five-year term.

Two years later, in 1996, CIA station chief Harold Nicholson was arrested as he was preparing to leave Washington's Dulles Airport—allegedly on his way to meet his Russian handlers. Nicholson is the highest-ranking CIA employee to ever be charged with espionage. Also in 1996, 43-year-old Earl Edwin Pitts, a 13-year FBI veteran, was taken into custody at the FBI academy in Quantico, Virginia, and arraigned on charges of attempted espionage and conspiracy.[24] Pitts was charged with spying for the Russians and is said to have turned over lists of Russian agents within the United States who had been compromised. Nicholson and Pitts pled guilty to espionage charges in early 1997,[25] and both were sentenced to lengthy prison terms.

Treason and espionage may be committed for personal gain or for ideological reasons, or both. The Ameses received millions of dollars from the Russians for secrets they sold, Nicholson allegedly received $180,000 or more, and Pitts was charged with accepting more than $224,000 over a five-year period. Both treason and espionage are often regarded as the most serious of felonies.

In 1999, one of the most significant espionage cases ever came to light. It involved the theft of highly classified American nuclear weapons secrets by spies working for the People's

---

Offense

(1) A violation of the criminal law, or, in some jurisdictions, (2) a minor crime, such as jaywalking, sometimes described as "ticketable."

Infraction

A minor violation of state statute or local ordinance punishable by a fine or other penalty, but not by incarceration, or by a specified, usually limited term of incarceration.

Treason

"[A] U.S. citizen's actions to help a foreign government overthrow, make war against, or seriously injure the United States." Source: *Daniel Oran,* Oran's Dictionary of the Law *(St. Paul, MN: West, 1983), p. 306. Also, the attempt to overthrow the government of the society of which one is a member.*

Espionage

The "gathering, transmitting, or losing" of information related to the national defense in such a manner that the information becomes available to enemies of the United States and may be used to their advantage. Source: *Henry Campbell Black, Joseph R. Nolan, and Jacqueline M. Nolan-Haley,* Black's Law Dictionary, *6th ed. (St. Paul, MN: West, 1990), p. 24.*

Republic of China. Over at least three decades, beginning in the 1960s, Chinese spies apparently stole enough weapons-related information to advance China's nuclear weapons program into the modern era. Were it not for the missile and bomb information gathered by the spies, congressional officials said, China's nuclear weapons technology might still be where America's was in the 1950s. See WebExtra! 3-2 at CJToday.com for additional information on this very serious incident.

Inchoate Offenses

Inchoate Offense

One not yet completed. Also, an offense which consists of an action or conduct which is a step toward the intended commission of another offense.

Another special category of crime is called inchoate. The word *inchoate* means incomplete or partial, and **inchoate offenses** are those which have not yet been fully carried out. Conspiracies are an example. When a person conspires to commit a crime, any action undertaken in furtherance of the conspiracy is generally regarded as a sufficient basis for arrest and prosecution. For instance, a woman who intends to kill her husband may make a phone call to find a "hit man" to carry out her plan. The call itself is evidence of her intent and can result in her imprisonment for conspiring to murder.

Another type of inchoate offense is the attempt. Sometimes an offender is not able to complete the crime. Homeowners may arrive just as a burglar is beginning to enter their residence. The burglar may drop his tools and run. Even so, in most jurisdictions, this frustrated burglar can be arrested and charged with attempted burglary.

General Features of Crime

Jurisprudence

The philosophy of law; the science and study of the law.

From the perspective of Western **jurisprudence,** all crimes can be said to share certain features, and the notion of crime itself can be said to rest upon such general principles. Taken together, these features, which are described in the paragraphs that follow, comprise the legal essence of the concept of crime. Conventional legal wisdom holds that the essence of crime consists of three conjoined elements: (1) the criminal act (which, in legal parlance is termed the *actus reus*), (2) a culpable mental state (*mens rea*), and (3) a concurrence of the two. Hence, as we shall see in the following few pages, the essence of criminal conduct consists of a concurrence of a criminal act with a culpable mental state.

The Criminal Act (*Actus Reus*)

Actus Reus

An act in violation of the law; a guilty act.

A necessary first feature of any crime is some act in violation of the law. Such an act is termed the **actus reus** of a crime. The term means a "guilty act." Generally, a person must commit some voluntary act before he or she is subject to criminal sanctions. Someone who admits (perhaps on a TV talk show) that he or she is a drug user, for example, cannot be arrested on that basis. To *be something* is not a crime—to *do something* may be. In the case of the admitted drug user, police who heard the admission might begin gathering evidence to prove some specific law violation in that person's past, or perhaps they might watch that individual for future behavior in violation of the law. An arrest might then occur. If it did, it would be based upon a specific action in violation of the law pertaining to controlled substances.

Vagrancy laws, popular in the early part of the twentieth century, have generally been invalidated by the courts because they did not specify what act violated the law. In fact, the *less* a person did, the more vagrant they were.

An *omission to act,* however, may be criminal when the person in question is required by law to do something. Child-neglect laws, for example, focus on parents and child guardians who do not live up to their responsibilities for caring for their children.

Threatening to act can itself be a criminal offense. Telling someone, "I'm going to kill you," might result in an arrest based upon the offense of "communicating threats." Threatening the president of the United States is taken seriously by the Secret Service, and individuals are regularly arrested for boasting about planned violence to be directed at the president.

Attempted criminal activity is also illegal. An attempt to murder or rape, for example, is a serious crime, even though the planned act was not accomplished.

"No State shall make or enforce any law which shall abridge the privileges or immunities of citizens of the United States; nor shall any State deprive any person of life, liberty, or property, without due process of law; nor deny to any person within its jurisdiction the equal protection of the laws."

—Fourteenth Amendment to the U.S. Constitution

Conspiracy statutes were mentioned earlier in this chapter. When a conspiracy unfolds, the ultimate act that it aims to bring about does not have to occur for the parties to the conspiracy to be arrested. When people plan to bomb a public building, for example, they can be legally stopped before the bombing. As soon as they take steps to "further" their plan, they have met the requirement for an act. Buying explosives, telephoning one another, or drawing plans of the building may all be actions in "furtherance of the conspiracy."

Not all conspiracy statutes require actions in furtherance of the "target crime" before an arrest can be made. Technically speaking, crimes of conspiracy can be seen as entirely distinct from the crimes which are contemplated by the conspiracy. So, for example, in 1994[26] the U.S. Supreme Court upheld the drug-related conviction of Reshat Shabani when it ruled that in the case of certain antidrug laws[27] "it is presumed that Congress intended to adopt the common law definition of conspiracy, which does not make the doing of any act other than the act of conspiring a condition of liability. . . ." Hence, according to the Court, "the criminal agreement itself," even in the absence of actions directed toward realizing the target crime, can be grounds for arrest and prosecution.

Similar to conspiracy statutes are many newly enacted antistalking laws. Antistalking statutes are intended to prevent harassment and intimidation, even when no physical harm occurs. According to the U.S. Senate's Judiciary Committee, "there are 200,000 people in the United States who are currently 'stalking' someone. . . ."[28] It is estimated that half of those being stalked are celebrities. Stalkers often strike after their victims have unsuccessfully complained to authorities about stalking-related activities such as harassing phone calls and letters. Antistalking statutes, however, still face a constitutional hurdle of attempting to prevent people not otherwise involved in criminal activity from walking and standing where they wish and from speaking freely. Ultimately, the U.S. Supreme Court will probably have to decide the legitimacy of such statutes.

A Guilty Mind (*Mens Rea*)

Mens Rea

The state of mind which accompanies a criminal act. Also, guilty mind.

Mens rea is the second general component of crime. The term literally means "guilty mind" and refers to the specific mental state operative in the defendant at the time the behavior in question was being enacted. The importance of *mens rea* as a component of crime cannot be overemphasized and can be seen in the fact that some courts have held that "[a]ll crime exists primarily in the mind."[29] The extent to which a person can be held criminally responsible for his or her actions generally depends upon the nature of the mental state under which he or she was laboring at the time of the offense.

Four levels, or types, of *mens rea* can be distinguished: (1) purposeful (or intentional), (2) knowing, (3) reckless, and (4) negligent. *Mens rea* is most clearly present when a person acts purposefully and knowingly, but *mens rea* sufficient for criminal prosecution may also result from reckless or negligent behavior. Pure accident, however, which involves no recklessness or negligence cannot serve as the basis for either criminal or civil liability. "Even a dog," once wrote the famous Supreme Court Justice Oliver Wendell Holmes, "distinguishes between being stumbled over and being kicked."[30]

Criminal Negligence

Behavior in which a person fails to reasonably perceive substantial and unjustifiable risks of dangerous consequences.

Nonetheless, *mens rea* is said to be present when a person *should have known better,* even if the person did not directly intend the consequences of his or her action. A person who acts negligently, and thereby endangers others, may be found guilty of **criminal negligence** when harm occurs, even though no negative consequences were intended. For example, a mother who left her 12-month-old child alone in the tub can later be prosecuted for negligent homicide if the child drowns.[31] It should be emphasized, however, that negligence in and of itself is not a crime. Negligent conduct can be evidence of crime only when it falls below some acceptable standard of care. That standard is today applied in criminal courts through the fictional creation of a *reasonable person*. The question to be asked in a given case is whether a reasonable person, in the same situation, would have known better and acted differently than the defendant. The reasonable person criterion provides a yardstick for juries faced with thorny issues of guilt or innocence.

Purposeful or intentional action, in contrast to negligent action, is that which is undertaken to achieve some goal. Sometimes the harm that results from intentional action may be quite unintended—and yet fail to reduce criminal liability. The doctrine of transferred intent, for example, which operates in all U.S. jurisdictions, would hold a person guilty of murder even if that person took aim and shot at an intended victim but missed, killing another person instead. The philosophical notion behind the concept of transferred intent is that the killer's intent to kill, which existed at the time of the crime, transferred from the intended victim to the person who was struck by the bullet and died.

Knowing behavior is action undertaken with awareness. Hence, a person who acts purposefully always acts knowingly, although a person may act in a knowingly criminal way but for another purpose. An airline captain, for example, who allows a flight attendant to transport cocaine aboard an airplane may do so in order to gain sexual favors from the attendant—but without having the purpose of drug smuggling in mind. Knowing behavior involves near certainty. Hence, if the flight attendant in this example carries cocaine aboard the airplane, it *will* be transported; and if an HIV-infected individual has unprotected sexual intercourse with another person, his or her partner *will* be exposed to the virus.

Reckless Behavior

Activity which increases the risk of harm.

Reckless behavior, in contrast, is activity which increases the risk of harm. Although knowledge may be a part of such behavior, it exists more in the form of probability than certainty. So, for example, an old Elton John song about Marilyn Monroe says "you lived your life like a candle in the wind." The wind is, of course, a risky place to keep a lighted candle—and doing so increases the likelihood that its flame will be extinguished. But there is no certainty that the flame will be blown out, or, if so, when it might happen. As a practical example, reckless driving is a frequent charge in many jurisdictions and is generally brought when a driver engages in risky activity which endangers others.

Mens rea is a thorny concept. Not only is it philosophically and legally complex, but a person's state of mind during the commission of an offense can rarely be known directly, unless the person confesses. Hence, *mens rea* must generally be inferred from a person's actions and from all the circumstances which surround those actions. It is also important to note that *mens rea,* even in the sense of intent, is not the same thing as motive. A **motive** refers to a person's reason for committing a crime. While evidence of motive may be admissible during a criminal trial in order to help prove a crime, motive itself is not an essential element of a crime. As a result we cannot say that a bad or immoral motive makes an act a crime.

Motive

A person's reason for committing a crime.

Strict Liability and *Mens Rea*

Strict Liability

Liability without fault or intention. Strict liability offenses do not require mens rea.

A special category of crimes, called **strict liability** offenses, requires no culpable mental state and presents a significant exception to the principle that all crimes require a conjunction of *actus reus* and *mens rea.* Strict liability offenses (also called absolute liability offenses) make it a crime simply to *do* something, even if the offender has no intention of violating the law. Strict liability is philosophically based upon the presumption that causing harm is in itself blameworthy, regardless of the actor's intent.

Routine traffic offenses are generally considered "strict liability" offenses, which do not require intent and may be committed by someone who is unaware of what he or she is doing. A driver commits minor violations of his or her state motor vehicle code simply by doing that which is forbidden. Hence, driving 65 miles per hour in a 55-miles-per-hour zone is a violation of the law, even though the driver may be listening to music, thinking, or simply going with the flow of traffic—entirely unaware that his or her vehicle is exceeding the posted speed limit.

Statutory rape provides another example of the concept of strict liability.[32] The crime of statutory rape generally occurs between two consenting individuals and requires only that the offender have sexual intercourse with a person under the age of legal consent. Statutes describing the crime routinely avoid any mention of a culpable mental state. In many jurisdictions it matters little in the crime of statutory rape that the "perpetrator" knew the exact age of the "victim" or that the "victim" lied about his or her age or may have given consent, since such laws are "an attempt to prevent the sexual exploitation of persons deemed legally incapable of giving consent."[33]

Concurrence

The concurrence of an unlawful act and a culpable mental state provides the third basic component of crime. **Concurrence** requires that the act and the mental state occur together in order for a crime to take place. If one precedes the other, the requirements of the criminal law will not have been met. A person may intend to kill a rival, for example. As she drives to the intended victim's house, gun in hand, fantasizing about how she will commit the murder, the victim may be crossing the street on the way home from grocery shopping. If the two accidentally collide, and the intended victim dies, there has been no concurrence of act and intent.

Some scholars contend that the three features of crime which we have just outlined— *actus reus, mens rea,* and concurrence—are sufficient to constitute the essence of the legal concept of crime. Other scholars, however, see modern Western law as more complex. They argue that recognition of five additional principles is necessary to fully appreciate contemporary understandings of crime. These five principles are (1) causation, (2) a resulting harm, (3) the principle of legality, (4) the principle of punishment, and (5) necessary attendant circumstances. We will now discuss each of these additional features in turn.

> **Concurrence**
>
> *The coexistence of an act in violation of the law and a culpable mental state.*

Causation

Causation refers to the fact that the concurrence of a guilty mind and a criminal act may produce or *cause* harm. While some statutes criminalize only conduct, others subsume the notion of concurrence under causality and specify that a causality relationship is a necessary element of a given crime. Such laws require that the offender *cause* a particular result before criminal liability can be incurred. Sometimes, however, a causal link is anything but clear. A classic example of this principle involves assault with a deadly weapon with intent to kill. If a person shoots another, but the victim is seriously injured and not killed, the victim might survive for a long time in a hospital. Death may occur, perhaps a year or more later, because pneumonia sets in or because blood clots form in the injured person from lack of activity. In such cases, defense attorneys will likely argue that the defendant did not cause the death, but rather the death occurred because of disease. If a jury agrees with the defense's claim, the shooter may go free or be found guilty of a lesser charge, such as assault.

To clarify the issue of causation, the American Law Institute suggests use of the term **legal cause** in order to emphasize the notion of a legally recognizable cause and to preclude any assumption that such a cause must be close in time and space to the result it produces. Legal causes can be distinguished from those causes which may have produced the result in question, but which may not provide the basis for a criminal prosecution because they are too complex, too indistinguishable from other causes, not knowable, or not provable in a court of law.

> **Legal Cause**
>
> *A legally recognizable cause. The type of cause that is required to be demonstrated in court in order to hold an individual criminally liable for causing harm.*

Harm

A harm occurs in any crime, although not all harms are crimes. When a person is murdered or raped, harm can clearly be identified. Some crimes, however, have come to be called "victimless." Perpetrators maintain that they are not harming anyone in committing such crimes. Rather, they say, the crime is pleasurable. Prostitution, gambling, "crimes against nature" (sexual deviance), and drug use are but a few crimes classified as victimless. People involved in such crimes will argue that, if anyone is being hurt, it is only they. What these offenders fail to recognize, say legal theorists, is the social harm caused by their behavior. Areas afflicted with chronic prostitution, drug use, sexual deviance, and illegal gambling usually will find property values falling, family life disintegrating, and other, more traditional crimes increasing as money is sought to support the victimless activities and law-abiding citizens flee the area.

In a criminal prosecution, however, it is rarely necessary to prove harm as a separate element of a crime, since it is subsumed under the notion of a guilty act. In the crime of murder, for example, the "killing of a human being" brings about a harm, but is, properly speaking, an act. When done with the requisite *mens rea* it becomes a crime. A similar type of reasoning applies to the criminalization of attempts, and some writers have used the example of throwing rocks at blind people to illustrate that behavior need not actually produce harm for it to be criminal. One could imagine a scenario in which vandals decide to throw rocks at visually impaired individuals but, because of bad aim, the rocks never hit anyone and the intended targets remain blissfully unaware that anyone is trying to harm them. In such a case, shouldn't throwing rocks provide a basis for criminal liability? As one authority on the subject observes, "[c]riticism of the principle of harm has . . . been based on the view that the harm actually caused may be a matter of sheer accident and that the rational thing to do is to base the punishment on the *mens rea,* and the action, disregarding any actual harm or lack of harm or its degree."[34] This observation also shows why we have said that the essence of crime consists only of three things: (1) an *actus reus,* (2) *mens rea,* and (3) a concurrence of an illegal act and a culpable mental state.

Legality

The principle of legality is concerned with the fact that a behavior cannot be criminal if no law exists which defines it as such. It is all right to drink beer if you are of "drinking age" because there is no statute "on the books" prohibiting it. During prohibition times, of course, the situation was quite different. (In fact, some parts of the United States are still "dry," and the purchase or public consumption of alcohol can be a law violation regardless of age.) The principle of legality also includes the notion that a law cannot be created tomorrow which will hold a person legally responsible for something he or she does today. These are called *ex post facto* laws. Laws are binding only from the date of their creation or from some future date at which they are specified as taking effect.[35]

Punishment

The principle of punishment says that no crime can be said to occur where punishment has not been specified in the law. Larceny, for example, would not be a crime if the law simply said, "It is illegal to steal." Punishment needs to be specified so that if a person is found guilty of violating the law, sanctions can be lawfully imposed.

Necessary Attendant Circumstances

Attendant Circumstances

The facts surrounding an event.

Finally, statutes defining some crimes specify that additional elements, called **attendant circumstances,** be present in order for a conviction to be obtained. Attendant circumstances refer to the "facts surrounding an event"[36] and include such things as time and place. Attendant circumstances, specified by law as necessary elements of an offense, are sometimes referred to as necessary attendant circumstances to indicate the fact that the existence of such circumstances is necessary, along with the other elements included in the relevant statute for all of the elements of a crime to be met.

Florida law, for example, makes it a crime to "knowingly commit any lewd or lascivious act in the presence of any child under the age of 16 years. . . ."[37] In this case, the behavior in question might not be a crime if committed in the presence of persons older than 16. Also, curfew violations are being increasingly criminalized by states shifting liability for a minor's behavior to his or her parents. In order to violate a curfew, it is necessary that a juvenile be in a public place between specified times (such as 11 P.M. or midnight, and 5 or 6 A.M.). In those states which hold parents liable for the behavior of their children, parents can be jailed or fined when such violations occur.

Sometimes attendant circumstances increase the degree, or level of seriousness, of an offense. Under Texas law, for example, the crime of burglary has two degrees, defined by state law as follows: burglary is a "(1) state jail felony if committed in a building other than a habitation; or (2) felony of the second degree [i.e., a more serious crime] if committed in a habitation." Hence, the degree of the offense of burglary changes depending upon the nature of the place burglarized.

Circumstances surrounding a crime can also be classified as aggravating or mitigating and may, by law, lessen or increase the penalty that can be imposed upon a convicted offender.

Aggravating and mitigating circumstances are not elements of an offense, since they are primarily relevant at the sentencing stage of a criminal prosecution and will therefore be discussed in a later chapter.

Elements of a Specific Criminal Offense

While we have just identified the principles which constitute the *general* notion of crime, we can also examine individual statutes in order to see what particular statutory **elements** comprise a *specific* crime. Written laws specify exactly what conditions are necessary for a person to be charged in a given instance of criminal activity, and they do so for every particular offense. Hence, elements of a crime are specific legal aspects of a criminal offense which must be proven by the prosecution in order to obtain a conviction. The crime of first-degree murder, for example, in almost every jurisdiction in the United States involves four quite distinct elements:

1. An unlawful killing
2. Of a human being
3. Intentionally
4. With planning (or "malice aforethought")

Elements of a Crime

The basic components of crime. In a specific crime, the essential features of that crime as specified by law or statute.

O. J. Simpson reacts as not guilty verdicts are announced at the conclusion of his 1995 double-murder trial. All of the elements of a crime must be proven beyond a reasonable doubt in order for a defendant in a criminal case to be convicted.
Corbis/Sygma.

The elements of any specific crime are the statutory minimum without which that crime cannot be said to have occurred. In any case that goes to trial, the task of the prosecution is to prove that all the elements were indeed present and that the accused was ultimately responsible for producing them. Since statutes differ between jurisdictions, the specific elements of a particular crime, such as murder, may vary. In order to convict a defendant of a particular crime, prosecutors must prove to a judge or jury that all the required statutory elements are present.[38] If even one element of an offense cannot be established beyond a reasonable doubt, criminal liability will not have been demonstrated, and the defendant will be found not guilty.

The Example of Murder

Every statutory element in a given instance of crime serves some purpose and is necessary. As mentioned, the crime of first-degree murder includes *an unlawful killing* as one of its required elements. Even if all the other elements of first-degree murder are present, the act will still not be first-degree murder if the initial element has not been met. In a wartime situation, for instance, killings of human beings occur. They are committed with planning and sometimes with malice. They are certainly intentional. Yet killing in war is not unlawful, so long as the belligerents wage war according to international conventions.

The second element of first-degree murder specifies that the killing must be of a *human being.* People kill all the time. They kill animals for meat, they hunt, and they practice euthanasia upon aged and injured pets. Even if the killing of an animal is planned and involves malice (perhaps a vendetta against a neighborhood dog that wrecks trash cans), it does not constitute first-degree murder. Such a killing, however, may violate statutes pertaining to cruelty to animals.

The third element of first-degree murder, *intentionality,* is the basis for the defense of accident. An unintentional or nonpurposeful killing is not first-degree murder, although it may violate some other statute.

Finally, murder has not been committed unless *malice* is involved. There are different kinds of malice. Second-degree murder involves malice in the sense of hatred or spite. A more extreme form of malice is necessary for a finding of first-degree murder. Sometimes the phrase used to describe this type of feeling is *malice aforethought.* This extreme kind of malice can be demonstrated by showing that planning was involved in the commission of the murder. Often, first-degree murder is described as "lying in wait," a practice which shows that thought and planning went into the illegal killing.

Whether any particular behavior meets the specific statutory minimums to qualify as a crime may be open to debate. A few years ago, for example, Adam Brown, 30, of Roseburg, Oregon, was charged with attempted first-degree murder for having knowingly exposed five children to the AIDS virus when he allegedly had unprotected sex with them. Mr. Brown, a lay minister, was informed that he had tested positive for the AIDS virus more than a year prior to the incidents. Brown was also charged with sodomy, rape, sexual penetration with a foreign object, and reckless endangerment.[39]

A charge of second-degree murder in most jurisdictions would necessitate proving that a voluntary (or intentional) killing of a human being took place—although a "crime of passion" may have been committed without the degree of malice necessary for it to be classified as first degree. Third-degree murder, or manslaughter, can be defined simply as the unlawful killing of a human being. Not only is malice lacking in third-degree murder cases, but the killer may not have even intended that any harm come to the victim. Third-degree murder statutes, however, frequently necessitate some degree of negligence on the part of the killer, and charges such as negligent homicide may result from automobile accidents resulting in death in which the driver did not exercise due care. When legally defined "gross negligence" (involving a wanton disregard for human life) is present, however, some jurisdictions permit the offender to be charged with a more serious count of murder.

A few years ago, for example, in the case of Karin Smith, a grand jury returned a homicide indictment against a laboratory doctor and technician for a fatal misdiagnosis.[40] The laboratory workers had misread a Pap smear performed on Smith, returning a clean bill of health to the doctor in charge of her care. Smith died on March 8, 1995, at age 29 from cervical cancer that had spread throughout her body. Experts testifying before a grand jury said that evidence of the presence of cancer was "unequivocal" in slides from Pap smears done on Smith in 1988 and 1989, but that the laboratory which received the sample tissue had misread the test results. The prosecutor in the case claimed that laboratory personnel had demonstrated a wanton disregard for human life when they "failed to install random controls to check the quality of the Pap smear analysis; [a]nd showed indifference toward professional standards and the need for continuing education."[41]

Although most people think that homicide charges are brought primarily against those who intend to kill, the recent trend in charging negligent medical personnel with murder is evidence that the machinery of the criminal justice system is being increasingly applied outside its traditional sphere. About the time of the Smith case, for example, Denver anesthesiologist Dr. Joseph J. Verbrugge, Sr., was charged with manslaughter in the death of an eight-year-old boy undergoing ear surgery.[42] Police investigators said the doctor had fallen asleep during the surgery, allowing the boy to receive a lethal dose of anesthetic. In a similar case, Dr. Gerald Einaugler of New York was ordered to spend 52 weekends in jail for causing the death of a nursing home patient when he mistook a dialysis tube for a feeding tube and pumped food into the patient's kidneys;[43] and New York Dr. David Benjamin faced a possible life prison sentence after being convicted of murder in the death of a woman who went to him for an abortion. Upon his August 8, 1995, conviction, Dr. Benjamin became the first doctor in New York state to be found guilty of murder for the medical mistreatment of a patient.[44] The patient, Guadalupe Negron, bled to death following a bungled abortion in the doctor's storefront clinic.

Finally, the 1997 manslaughter convictions of three youths in Tampa, Florida, who pulled up stop signs at rural intersections near Lithia, Florida, provides another clear example that criminal liability in such crimes does not require an intent to cause death. Defendants Christopher Cole, 20, Nissa Baillie, 21, and Thomas Miller, 20, were each sentenced to 30 years in prison for causing the deaths of three 18-year-olds who were returning home from an evening of bowling. The victims were killed by an eight-ton truck hauling fertilizer as they crossed through an intersection where a stop sign had been removed. At sentencing Florida Circuit Judge Bob Mitchum told the defendants, "I don't believe for one minute that you . . . pulled these signs up with the intent of causing the death of anyone. . . ."[45] Cole, Baillie, and Miller will be eligible for parole after 13 years.[46]

The *Corpus Delicti* of a Crime

The term **corpus delicti** literally means "body of crime." The term is often confused with the statutory elements of a crime. Sometimes the concept is mistakenly thought to mean the body of a murder victim or some other physical result of criminal activity. It actually means something quite different.

One way to understand the concept of *corpus delicti* is to realize that a person cannot be tried for a crime unless it can first be shown that the offense has, in fact, occurred. In other words, to establish the *corpus delicti* of a crime, the state has to demonstrate that a criminal law has been violated and that someone violated it. Hence, there are only two aspects to the *corpus delicti* of an offense: (1) that a certain result has been produced and (2) that a person is criminally responsible for its production. As one court said, "[c]orpus delicti consists of a showing of (1) the occurrence of the specific kind of injury and (2) someone's criminal act as the cause of the injury."[47] So, for example, the crime of larceny requires proof that the property of another has been stolen—that is, unlawfully taken by someone whose intent it was to permanently deprive the owner of its possession.[48] Hence, evidence offered to prove the *corpus delicti* in a trial for larceny is insufficient where the evidence fails to prove that any property has been stolen or where property found in a defendant's possession cannot be identified as having been stolen. Similarly, "[i]n an arson case, the *corpus delicti* consists of (1) a burned building or other property, and (2) some criminal agency which caused the burning . . . In other words, the *corpus delicti* includes not only the fact of burning, but it must also appear that the burning was by the willful act of some person, and not as a result of a natural or accidental cause. . . ."[49]

Corpus Delicti

The "body of crime." Facts which show that a crime has occurred.

*Evidence and arguments
offered by a defendant and
his or her attorney(s) to
show why that person
should not be held liable for
a criminal charge.*

Alibi

*A statement or contention
by an individual charged
with a crime that he or she
was so distant when the
crime was committed, or so
engaged in other provable
activities, that participation
in commission of that crime
was impossible.*

Justifications

*A category of legal
defenses in which the
defendant admits
committing the act in
question but claims it was
necessary in order to avoid
some greater evil.*

Excuses

*A category of legal
defenses in which the
defendant claims that some
personal condition or
circumstance at the time of
the act was such that he or
she should not be held
accountable under the
criminal law.*

Procedural Defense

*A defense which claims that
the defendant was in some
significant way discriminated
against in the justice process
or that some important
aspect of official procedure
was not properly followed in
the investigation or
prosecution of the crime
charged.*

We might add to the requirement to establish the *corpus delicti* of a crime before a successful prosecution can occur, the observation that the identity of the perpetrator is not an element of the *corpus delicti* of an offense. Hence, the fact that a crime has occurred can be established without having any idea who committed it or even why it was committed. This principle was clearly enunciated in a Montana case when the state's supreme court held that "the identity of the perpetrator is not an element of the *corpus delicti*." In *State* v. *Kindle* (1924),[50] the court continued, "we stated that '[i]n a prosecution for murder, proof of the *corpus delicti* does not necessarily carry with it the identity of the slain nor of the slayer' . . . The essential elements of the *corpus delicti* are . . . establishing the death and the fact that the death was caused by a criminal agency, nothing more." *Black's Law Dictionary* puts it another way: "[t]he *corpus delicti* [of a crime] is the fact of its having been actually committed."[51]

Types of Defenses to a Criminal Charge

When a person is charged with a crime, he or she typically offers some defense. A **defense** consists of evidence and arguments offered by a defendant and his or her attorneys to show why that person should not be held liable for a criminal charge. Our legal system generally recognizes four broad categories of defenses: (1) **alibi;** (2) **justifications;** (3) **excuses;** and (4) **procedural defenses.** An alibi, if shown to be valid, means that the defendant could not have committed the crime in question because he or she was somewhere else (and generally with someone else) at the time of the crime. When a defendant offers a justification as a defense, he or she admits committing the act in question, but claims that it was necessary in order to avoid some greater evil. A defendant who offers an excuse as a defense, on the other hand, claims that some personal condition or circumstance at the time of the act was such that he or she should not be held accountable under the criminal law. Procedural defenses make the claim that the defendant was in some significant way discriminated against in the justice process or that some important aspect of official procedure was not properly followed in the investigation or prosecution of the crime charged. Finally, a number of innovative defense strategies have emerged in recent years and will be discussed as a fifth category—although, technically speaking, each of the innovative defenses we shall discuss could be classified as a justification or as an excuse. Table 3-1 lists the types of defenses which fall into our five categories. Each will be discussed in the pages that follow.

Alibi

A current reference book for criminal trial lawyers says, "Alibi is different from all of the other defenses . . . because . . . it is based upon the premise that the defendant is truly innocent. . . ."[52] The defense of alibi denies that the defendant committed the act in question. All of the other defenses we are about to discuss grant that the defendant committed the act, but they deny that he or she should be held criminally responsible. While justifications and excuses may produce findings of not guilty, the defense of alibi claims outright innocence.

Alibi is best supported by witnesses and documentation. A person charged with a crime can use the defense of alibi to show that he or she was not present at the scene when the crime was alleged to have occurred. Hotel receipts, eyewitness identification, and participation in social events have all been used to prove alibis.

Justifications

As defenses, justifications claim a kind of moral high ground. Justifications may be offered by people who find themselves facing a choice between a "lesser of two evils." Generally speaking, conduct which a person believes is necessary in order to avoid a harm or evil to him- or herself or to avoid harm to another is justifiable if the harm or evil to be avoided is greater than that which the law defining the offense seeks to avoid. So, for example, a fireman might set a controlled fire in order to create a firebreak to head off a conflagration threatening a community. While intentionally setting a fire may constitute arson, doing so in order to

TABLE 3-1 ■ Types of Defenses

ALIBI	JUSTIFICATIONS	EXCUSES	PROCEDURAL	INNOVATIVE
A claim of alibi	Self-defense	Duress	Entrapment	Abuse defense
	Defense of others	Age	Double jeopardy	Premenstrual stress syndrome
	Defense of home and property	Mistake	*Collateral estoppel*	
		Involuntary intoxication	Selective prosecution	Other biological defenses
	Necessity	Unconsciousness	Denial of a speedy trial	
	Consent	Provocation	Prosecutorial misconduct	Black rage
	Accident	Insanity	Police fraud	Urban survival syndrome
	Resisting unlawful arrest	Diminished responsibility		

save a town may be justifiable behavior in the eyes of the community *and* in the eyes of the law. Included under the broad category of "justifications" are (1) self-defense, (2) the defense of others, (3) defense of home and property, (4) necessity, (5) consent, and (6) resisting unlawful arrest.

Self-Defense

Self-defense is probably the best known of the justifications. This defense strategy makes the claim that it was necessary to inflict some harm on another in order to ensure one's own safety in the face of near-certain injury or death. A person who harms an attacker can generally use this defense. However, the courts have held that where a "path of retreat" exists for a person being attacked, it should be taken. In other words, the safest use of self-defense is only when "cornered," with no path of escape.

The amount of defensive force used must be proportionate to the amount of force or perceived degree of threat that one is seeking to defend against. Hence, **reasonable force** is that degree of force that is appropriate in a given situation and is not excessive. Reasonable force can also be thought of as the minimum degree of force necessary to protect oneself, one's property, a third party, or the property of another in the face of a substantial threat. **Deadly force,** the highest degree of force, is considered reasonable only when used to counter an immediate threat of death or great bodily harm. Deadly force cannot be used against non-deadly force.

Force, as the term is used within the context of self-defense, means physical force and does not extend to emotional, psychological, economic, psychic, or other forms of coercion. A person who turns the tables on a robber and assaults him during a robbery attempt, for example, may be able to claim self-defense, while the businessperson who physically assaults a financial rival to prevent a hostile takeover of her company will have no such recourse.

Self-defense has been used recently in a spate of killings, by wives, of their abusive spouses. Killings which occur while the physical abuse is in process, especially when a history of such abuse can be shown, are likely to be accepted by juries as justified. On the other hand, wives who suffer repeated abuse but coldly plan the killing of their husbands have not fared well in court.

Defense of Others

The use of force to defend oneself has generally been extended to permit the use of reasonable force to defend others who are or appear to be in imminent danger. The defense of others, however, sometimes called "defense of a third person," is circumscribed in some jurisdictions by the **alter ego rule.** The alter ego rule holds that a person can only defend a third party under circumstances and only to the degree that the third party could act. In other words, a person who aids a person whom he sees being accosted may become criminally liable if that person initiated the attack or if the assault is a lawful one—for example, if

Self-Defense

The protection of oneself or one's property from unlawful injury or the immediate risk of unlawful injury; the justification that the person who committed an act which would otherwise constitute an offense reasonably believed that the act was necessary to protect self or property from immediate danger.

Reasonable Force

A degree of force that is appropriate in a given situation and is not excessive. The minimum degree of force necessary to protect oneself, one's property, a third party, or the property of another in the face of a substantial threat.

Deadly Force

Force likely to cause death or great bodily harm.

Alter Ego Rule

A rule of law that, in some jurisdictions, holds that a person can only defend a third party under circumstances and only to the degree that the third party could act on his or her own behalf.

the seeming "attack" is being made by a law enforcement officer conducting a lawful arrest of a person who is resisting. A few jurisdictions, however, do not recognize the alter ego rule and allow a person to act in defense of another if the actor reasonably believes that his intervention is immediately necessary to protect the third person.

Defense of others cannot be claimed by an individual who joins an illegal fight merely in order to assist a friend or family member. Likewise, one who intentionally aids an offender in an assault, even though the tables have "turned" and the offender is losing the battle, cannot claim "defense of others." Under the law, defense of third persons always requires that the defender be free from fault and that he or she act to aid an innocent person who is in the process of being victimized. Also, the same restrictions that apply to self-defense also apply to the defense of a third party. Hence, a defender must only act in the face of an immediate threat to another person, cannot use deadly force against nondeadly force, and must only act to the extent and use only the degree of force needed to repel the attack.

Defense of Home and Property

In most jurisdictions the owner of property can justifiably use reasonable, *nondeadly* force to prevent others from unlawfully taking or damaging it. As a general rule, however, the preservation of human life outweighs protection of property and the use of deadly force to protect property is not justified unless the perpetrator of the illegal act may intend to commit, or is in the act of committing, a violent act against another human being. A person who shoots an unarmed trespasser, for example, could not claim "defense of property" in order to avoid criminal liability. However, one who shoots and kills an armed robber while being robbed can. The difference is that a person facing an armed robber has a right to protect his or her property but is also in danger of death or serious bodily harm. An unarmed trespasser represents no such serious threat.[53]

The use of mechanical devices to protect property is a special area of law. Since, generally speaking, deadly force is not permitted in defense of property, the setting of booby traps such as spring-loaded shotguns, electrified grates, explosive devices, and the like, is generally not permitted to protect property which is unattended and unoccupied. If an individual is injured as a result of a mechanical device intended to cause death or injury in the protection of property, criminal charges may be brought against the person who set the device.

On the other hand, acts which would otherwise be criminal may carry no criminal liability if undertaken to protect one's home. For purposes of the law, one's "home" is one's dwelling, whether owned, rented, or merely "borrowed." Hotel rooms, rooms on board vessels, and rented rooms in houses belonging to others are all considered, for purposes of the law, one's "dwelling." The retreat rule, referred to earlier, which requires a person under attack to retreat when possible before resorting to deadly force, is subject to what some call the castle exception. The castle exception can be traced to the writings of the sixteenth-century English jurist Sir Edward Coke, who said, "A man's house is his castle—for where shall a man be safe if it be not in his house?"[54] The castle exception generally recognizes that a person has a fundamental right to be in his or her home and also recognizes the home as a final and inviolable place of retreat (that is, the home offers a place of retreat from which a person can be expected to retreat no further). Hence, it is not necessary for one to retreat from one's home in the face of an immediate threat, even when such retreat is possible, before resorting to deadly force in protection of the home. A number of court decisions have extended the castle exception to include one's place of business, such as a store or office.

Necessity

Necessity, or the claim that some illegal action was needed to prevent an even greater harm, is a useful defense in cases which do not involve serious bodily harm. One of the most famous uses of this defense occurred in *Crown* v. *Dudly & Stephens* in the late 1800s.[55] The case involved a shipwreck in which three sailors and a cabin boy were set adrift in a lifeboat. After a number of days at sea without rations, two of the sailors decided to kill and eat the cabin boy. At their trial, they argued that it was necessary to do so, or none of them would have survived. The court, however, reasoned that the cabin boy was not a direct threat to the survival of the men and rejected this defense. Convicted of murder, they were sentenced to death, although they were spared the gallows by royal intervention.

Although cannibalism is usually against the law, courts have sometimes recognized the necessity of consuming human flesh where survival was at issue. Those cases, however, involved only "victims" who had already died of natural causes.

Consent

The defense of consent claims that whatever harm was done occurred only after the injured person gave his or her permission for the behavior in question. A 1980s trial, for example, saw Robert Chambers plead guilty to first-degree manslaughter in the killing of 18-year-old Jennifer Levin. In what was dubbed "the Preppy Murder Case,"[56] Chambers had claimed Levin died as a result of "rough sex" during which she had tied his hands behind his back and injured his testicles. Other cases, some involving sexual asphyxia (partial suffocation designed to heighten erotic pleasures) and bondage, culminated in a headline in *Time* heralding the era of "The Rough-Sex Defense."[57] The article suggested that such a defense works best with a good-looking defendant who appears remorseful; "[a] hardened type of character . . . ,"[58] said the story, could not effectively use the defense.

In the "condom rapist" case, Joel Valdez was found guilty of rape in 1993 after a jury in Austin, Texas, rejected his claim that the act became consensual once he complied with his victim's request to use a condom. Valdez, who was drunk and armed with a knife at the time of the offense, claimed that his victim's request was a consent to sex. After that, he said, "we were making love."[59]

Resisting Unlawful Arrest

All jurisdictions consider resistance in the face of an unlawful arrest justifiable. Some have statutory provisions detailing the limits imposed on such resistance and the conditions under which it can be used. Such laws generally state that a person may use a reasonable amount of force, other than deadly force, to resist an unlawful arrest or an unlawful search by a law enforcement officer if the officer uses or attempts to use greater force than necessary to make the arrest or search. Such laws are inapplicable in cases in which the defendant is the first to resort to force. Deadly force to resist arrest is not justified unless the law enforcement officer resorts to deadly force when it is not called for.

Excuses

An excuse, in contrast to a justification, does not claim that the conduct in question is justified by the situation nor that it is moral. An excuse claims, rather, that the actor who engaged in the unlawful behavior was, at the time, not legally responsible for his or her actions and should not be held accountable under the law. So, for example, a person who assaults a police officer thinking that the officer is really a disguised "space alien" who has come to abduct him may be found not guilty of the charge of assault and battery by reason of insanity. Actions for which excuses are offered do not morally outweigh the wrong committed, but criminal liability may still be negated on the basis of some personal disability of the actor or because of some special circumstances that characterize the situation. Excuses recognized by the law include: (1) duress, (2) age, (3) mistake, (4) involuntary intoxication, (5) unconsciousness, (6) provocation, (7) insanity, and (8) diminished responsibility.

Duress

Duress is another of the defenses which depends upon an understanding of the situation. *Duress* has been defined as "any unlawful threat or coercion used by a person to induce another to act (or to refrain from acting) in a manner he or she otherwise would not (or would)."[60] A person may act under duress if, for example, he or she steals an employer's payroll in order to meet a ransom demand for kidnappers holding the person's children. Should the person later be arrested for larceny or embezzlement, the person can claim that he or she felt compelled to commit the crime to help ensure the safety of the children. The defense of duress is sometimes also called coercion. Duress is generally not a useful defense when the crime committed involves serious physical harm, since the harm committed may outweigh the coercive influence in the minds of jurors and judges.

Age

Age offers another kind of excuse in the face of a criminal charge, and the defense of "infancy"—as it is sometimes known in legal jargon—has its roots in the ancient belief that children cannot reason logically until around the age of seven. Early doctrine in the Christian church sanctioned that belief by declaring that rationality develops around the age of seven. As a consequence, only children past that age could be held responsible for their crimes.

The defense of infancy today has been expanded to include people well beyond the age of seven. Many states set the sixteenth birthday as the age at which a person becomes an adult for purposes of criminal prosecution. Others use the age of 17 and still others 18. When a person below the age required for adult prosecution commits a "crime," it is termed a *juvenile offense.* He or she is not guilty of a criminal violation of the law by virtue of youth.

In most jurisdictions, children below the age of seven cannot be charged even with juvenile offenses, no matter how serious their actions may appear to others. However, in a rather amazing 1994 case, prosecutors in Cincinnati, Ohio, charged a 12-year-old girl with murder after she confessed to drowning her toddler cousin 10 years previously. The cousin, 13-month-old Lamar Howell, drowned in 1984 in a bucket of bleach mixed with water. Howell's drowning had been ruled an accidental death until his cousin came forward. In discussing the charges with the media, Hamilton (Ohio) County prosecutor Joe Deters admitted that the girl could not be prosecuted. "Frankly," he said, "anything under seven cannot be an age where you form criminal intent. . . ."[61] The prosecution's goal, claimed one of Deters's associates, was simply to "make sure she gets the counseling she needs."

Mistake

Two types of mistake may serve as a defense. One is mistake of law, and the other is mistake of fact. Rarely is the defense of mistake of law acceptable. Most people realize that it is their responsibility to know the law as it applies to them. "Ignorance of the law is no excuse" is an old dictum still heard today. On occasion, however, humorous cases do arise in which such a defense is accepted by authorities—for example, the instance of the elderly woman who raised marijuana plants because they could be used to make a tea which relieved her arthritis. When her garden was discovered she was not arrested, but advised as to how the law applied to her.

Mistake of fact is a much more useful form of the "mistake" defense. In 1987, Jerry Hall, fashion model and girlfriend of Mick Jagger, a well-known rock star, was arrested in Barbados as she attempted to leave a public airport baggage claim area after picking up a suitcase.[62] The bag contained 20 pounds of marijuana and was under surveillance by officials who were waiting for just such a pickup. Ms. Hall defended herself by arguing that she had mistaken the bag for her own, which looked similar. She was released after a night in jail.

Involuntary Intoxication

The claim of involuntary intoxication may form the basis for another excuse defense. Either drugs or alcohol may produce intoxication. Voluntary intoxication itself is rarely a defense to a criminal charge because it is a self-induced condition. It is widely recognized in our legal tradition that an altered mental condition which is the product of voluntary activity cannot be used to exonerate guilty actions which follow from it. Some state statutes formalize this general principle of law and specifically state that voluntary intoxication cannot be offered as a defense to a charge of criminal behavior.[63]

Involuntary intoxication, however, is another matter. On occasion a person may be tricked into consuming an intoxicating substance. Secretly "spiked" punch, popular aphrodisiacs, or LSD-laced desserts all might be ingested unknowingly. A few years ago, for example, the Drug Enforcement Administration reported that a powerful sedative manufactured by Hoffmann-LaRoche Pharmaceuticals and sold under the brand name Rohypnol had become popular with college students and with "young men [who] put doses of Rohypnol in women's drinks without their consent in order to lower their inhibitions."[64] What other behavioral effects the pills, known variously as "roples," "roche," "ruffles," "roofies," and "rophies" on the street, might have is unknown. But a woman secretly drugged with Rohypnol might be able to offer the defense of involuntary intoxication were she to commit a crime while under the influence of the drug.

Because the effects and taste of alcohol are so widely known in our society, the defense of involuntary intoxication due to alcohol consumption can be difficult to demonstrate. A more unusual situation results from a disease caused by the yeast *Candida albicans,* occasionally found living in human intestines. A Japanese physician was the first to identify this disease, in which a person's digestive processes ferment the food they eat. Fermentation turns a portion of the food into alcohol, and people with this condition become intoxicated whenever they eat. First recognized about 10 years ago, the disease has not yet been used successfully in this country to support the defense of involuntary intoxication.

Unconsciousness

A very rarely used excuse is that of unconsciousness. An individual cannot be held responsible for anything he or she does while unconscious. Because unconscious people rarely do anything at all, this defense is almost never seen in the courts. However, cases of sleepwalking, epileptic seizure, and neurological dysfunction may result in injurious, although unintentional, actions by people so afflicted. Under such circumstances a defense of unconsciousness might be argued with success.

Provocation

Provocation recognizes that a person can be emotionally enraged by another who intends to elicit just such a reaction. Should that person then strike out at his or her tormentor, some courts have held, he or she may not be guilty of criminality, or may be guilty of a lesser degree of criminality than might otherwise be the case. The defense of provocation is commonly used in barroom brawls where a person's parentage may have been called into question, although most states don't look favorably upon verbal provocation alone. It has also been used in some recent spectacular cases where wives have killed their husbands, or children their fathers, citing years of verbal and physical abuse. In these latter instances, perhaps because the degree of physical harm inflicted appears to be out of proportion to the claimed provocation, the defense of provocation has not been as readily accepted by the courts. As a rule, the defense of provocation is generally more acceptable in minor offenses than in serious violations of the law.

Insanity

The defense of insanity has received much attention from the broadcast media, where movies and shows highlighting this defense are commonplace. In practice, however, the defense of insanity is rarely raised. According to a recent eight-state study, which was funded by the National Institute of Mental Health and reported in the *Bulletin of the American Academy of Psychiatry and the Law,*[65] the insanity defense was used in less than 1 percent of the cases that came before county-level courts. The study showed that only 26 percent of all insanity pleas were argued successfully and further found that 90 percent of those who employed the defense had been previously diagnosed with a mental illness. As the American Bar Association says, "[t]he best evidence suggests that the mental nonresponsibility defense is raised in less than one percent of all felony cases in the United States and is successful in about a fourth of these."[66]

It is important to realize that, for purposes of the criminal law, insanity is a legal definition and not a psychiatric one. Legal definitions of insanity often have very little to do with psychological or psychiatric understandings of mental illness. Legal insanity is a concept developed over time to meet the needs of the judicial system in assigning guilt or innocence to particular defendants. It is not primarily concerned with understanding the origins of mental pathology or with its treatment, as is the idea of mental illness in psychiatry. As a consequence, medical conceptions of mental illness do not always fit well into the legal categories created by courts and legislators to deal with the phenomenon. The differences between psychiatric and legal conceptualizations of insanity often lead to disagreements among expert witnesses who, in criminal court, may appear to provide conflicting testimony as to the sanity of a defendant.

Insanity Defense

A legal defense based on claims of mental illness or mental incapacity.

M'Naghten Rule

A rule for determining insanity which asks whether the defendant knew what he or she was doing or whether the defendant knew that what he or she was doing was wrong.

The M'Naghten Rule. Prior to the nineteenth century the **insanity defense,** as we know it today, was nonexistent. Insane people who committed crimes were punished in the same way as other law violators. It was **Daniel M'Naghten** (sometimes also spelled McNaughten or M'Naughten), a woodworker from Glasgow, Scotland, who, in 1844, became the first person to be found not guilty of a crime by reason of insanity. M'Naghten had tried to assassinate Sir Robert Peel, the British prime minister. He mistook Edward Drummond, Peel's secretary, for Peel himself, and killed Drummond instead. At his trial, defense attorneys argued that M'Naghten suffered from vague delusions centered on the idea that the Tories, a British political party, were persecuting him. Medical testimony at the trial agreed with the assertion of M'Naghten's lawyers that he didn't know what he was doing at the time of the shooting. The jury accepted M'Naghten's claim, and the insanity defense was born. The **M'Naghten rule,** as it has come to be called, was not so much a product of the *M'Naghten* trial, however, as it was of a later convocation of English judges assembled by the leadership of the House of Lords in order to define the criteria necessary for a finding of insanity.

The M'Naghten rule holds that *people are not guilty of a crime if, at the time of the crime, they either didn't know what they were doing, or didn't know that what they were doing was wrong.* The inability to distinguish right from wrong must be the result of some mental defect or disability. The M'Naghten rule is still followed in many U.S. jurisdictions today. However, in most states, the burden of proving insanity falls upon the defendant. Just as defendants are assumed innocent, they are also assumed to be sane at the outset of any criminal trial.

Irresistible Impulse. The M'Naghten rule worked well for a time. Eventually, however, some cases arose in which defendants clearly knew what they were doing, and they knew it was wrong. Even so, they argued in their defense that they couldn't help themselves. They couldn't stop doing that which was wrong. Such people are said to suffer from an irresistible impulse and may be found not guilty by reason of that particular brand of insanity in 18 of the United States. Some states which do not use the irresistible impulse test in determining insanity may still allow the successful demonstration of such an impulse to be considered in sentencing decisions.

In a spectacular 1994 Virginia trial, Lorena Bobbitt successfully employed the irresistible impulse defense against charges of malicious wounding stemming from an incident in which she cut off her husband's penis with a kitchen knife as he slept. The case, which made headlines around the world, found Bobbitt's defense attorney telling the jury, "What we have is Lorena Bobbitt's life juxtaposed against John Wayne Bobbitt's penis. The evidence will show that in her mind it was his penis from which she could not escape, that caused her the most pain, the most fear, the most humiliation."[67] The impulse to sever the organ, said the lawyer, became irresistible.

The irresistible impulse test has been criticized on a number of grounds. Primary among them is the belief that all of us suffer from compulsions. Most of us, however, learn to control them. Should we give in to a compulsion, the critique goes, then why not just say it was unavoidable so as to escape any legal consequences?

The Durham Rule. A third rule for gauging insanity is called the Durham rule. It was originally created in 1871 by a New Hampshire court and later adopted by Judge David Bazelon in 1954 as he decided the case of *Durham* v. *United States* for the Court of Appeals in the District of Columbia. The Durham rule states that *persons are not criminally responsible for their behavior if their illegal actions were the result of some mental disease or defect.*

Courts which follow the Durham rule will typically hear from an array of psychiatric specialists as to the mental state of the defendant. Their testimony will inevitably be clouded by the need to address the question of cause. A successful defense under the Durham rule necessitates that jurors be able to see the criminal activity in question as the *product* of mental deficiencies harbored by the defendant. And, yet, many people who suffer from mental diseases or defects never commit crimes. In fact, low IQ, mental retardation, or lack of general mental capacity are not allowable as excuses for criminal behavior. Because the Durham rule is especially vague, it provides fertile grounds for conflicting claims.

The Substantial Capacity Test. Nineteen states follow another guideline—the Substantial Capacity Test—as found in the Model Penal Code of the American Law Institute.[68] Also called the ALI rule or the MPC rule, it suggests that insanity should be defined as the lack of a substantial capacity to control one's behavior. This test requires a judgment to the effect that the defendant either had, or lacked, "the mental capacity needed to understand the wrongfulness of his act or to conform his behavior to the requirements of the law."[69] The Substantial Capacity Test is a blending of the M'Naghten rule with the irresistible impulse standard. "Substantial capacity" does not require total mental incompetence, nor does the rule require the behavior in question to live up to the criterion of total irresistibility. The problem, however, of establishing just what constitutes "substantial mental capacity" has plagued this rule from its conception.

The Brawner Rule. Judge Bazelon, apparently dissatisfied with the application of the Durham rule, created a new criterion for gauging insanity in the 1972 case of *U.S.* v. *Brawner*. The Brawner rule, as it has come to be called, places responsibility for deciding insanity squarely with the jury. Bazelon suggested that the jury should be concerned with whether the defendant could be *justly* held responsible for the criminal act in the face of any claims of insanity. Under this proposal, juries are left with few rules to guide them other than their own sense of fairness.

Insanity and Social Reality. The insanity defense originated as a means of recognizing the social reality of mental disease. Unfortunately, the history of this defense has been rife with change, contradiction, and uncertainty. Psychiatric testimony is expensive, sometimes costing thousands of dollars per day for one medical specialist. Still worse is the fact that each "expert" is commonly contradicted by another.

Public dissatisfaction with the jumble of rules defining legal insanity peaked in 1982, when John Hinckley was acquitted of trying to assassinate then-President Reagan. At his trial, Hinckley's lawyers claimed that a series of delusions brought about by a history of schizophrenia left him unable to control his behavior. Government prosecutors were unable to counter defense contentions of insanity. The resulting acquittal shocked the nation and resulted in calls for a review of the insanity defense.

One response has been to ban the insanity defense from use at trial. A ruling by the U.S. Supreme Court in support of a Montana law allows states to prohibit defendants from claiming that they were insane at the time they committed their crimes. In 1994, without comment, the high court let stand a Montana Supreme Court ruling which held that eliminating the insanity defense does not violate the U.S. Constitution. Currently, only three states—Montana, Idaho, and Utah—bar use of the insanity defense.[70]

Guilty But Insane. In 1997 Pennsylvania multimillionaire John E. du Pont was found **guilty but mentally ill** (GBMI) in the shooting death of former Olympic gold medalist David Schultz during a delusional episode. Although defense attorneys were able to show that du Pont sometimes saw Nazis in his trees, heard the walls talking, and had cut off pieces of his skin to remove bugs from outer space, he was held criminally liable for Schultz's death and sentenced to 13 to 30 years in confinement.

The guilty but mentally ill verdict (in a few states the finding is guilty but insane) is now possible in at least 11 states. It is one form of response to public frustration with the insanity issue. A GBMI verdict means that a person can be held responsible for a specific criminal act even though a degree of mental incompetence may be present in his or her personality. In most GBMI jurisdictions, a jury must return a finding of "guilty but mentally ill" if (1) every element necessary for a conviction has been proven beyond a reasonable doubt, (2) the defendant is found to have been *mentally ill* at the time the crime was committed, and (3) the

Guilty But Mentally Ill (GBMI)

Equivalent to a finding of "guilty," a GBMI verdict establishes that the defendant, although mentally ill, was in sufficient possession of his or her faculties to be morally blameworthy for his or her acts.

defendant was *not* found to have been *legally insane* at the time the crime was committed. The difference between mental illness and legal insanity is a crucial one, since a defendant can be mentally ill by standards of the medical profession but sane for purposes of the law.

Upon return of a GBMI verdict, a judge may impose any sentence possible under the law for the crime in question. Mandated psychiatric treatment, however, will often be part of the commitment order. The offender, once cured, will usually be placed in the general prison population to serve any remaining sentence.

As some authors have observed, the legal possibility of a guilty but mentally ill finding has three purposes: "[F]irst, to protect society; second, to hold some offenders who were mentally ill accountable for their criminal acts; (and) third, to make treatment available to convicted offenders suffering from some form of mental illness."[71]

In 1975 Michigan became the first state to pass a guilty but mentally ill statute, permitting a GBMI finding[72]—and the movement toward GBMI verdicts continues today among state legislatures. The U.S. Supreme Court case of *Ford* v. *Wainwright,* however, recognized an issue of a different sort.[73] The 1986 decision specified that prisoners who become insane while incarcerated cannot be executed. Hence, although insanity may not always be a successful defense to criminal prosecution, it can later become a block to the ultimate punishment.

Temporary Insanity. Temporary insanity is another possible defense against a criminal charge. Widely used in the 1940s and 1950s, temporary insanity meant that the offender claimed to be insane only at the time of the commission of the offense. If a jury agreed, the defendant virtually went free. The suspect was not guilty of the criminal action by virtue of having been insane and could not be ordered to undergo psychiatric counseling or treatment because the insanity was no longer present. This type of plea has become less popular as legislatures have regulated the circumstances under which it can be made.

The Insanity Defense Under Federal Law. In 1984 the U.S. Congress passed the federal Insanity Defense Reform Act (IDRA). The act created major revisions in the federal insanity defense. Insanity under the law is now defined as a condition in which the defendant can be shown to have been suffering under a "severe mental disease or defect" and, as a result, "was unable to appreciate the nature and quality or the wrongfulness of his acts."[74] This definition of insanity comes close to that set forth in the old M'Naghten rule.

Lorena Bobbitt, acquitted in 1994 of charges of malicious wounding, after she admittedly cut off her husband's penis with a razor-sharp kitchen knife as he slept. Ms. Bobbitt's attorneys successfully employed the irresistible impulse defense.
Stephen Jaffe/Reuters, Corbis.

Multimillionaire eccentric John E. du Pont being taken into custody by SWAT team members at his Newtown Square, Pennsylvania, estate in 1996. Du Pont shot and killed former Olympic gold medalist David Schultz during a delusional episode, and insanity became an issue at his 1997 murder trial. Although defense attorneys were able to show that du Pont sometimes saw Nazis in his trees, heard the walls talking, and had cut off pieces of his skin to remove bugs from outer space, he was found guilty but mentally ill, and sentenced to serve 13 to 30 years in confinement. **Jim Graham, AP/Wide World Photos.**

The act also places the burden of proving the insanity defense squarely on the defendant—a provision which has been challenged a number of times since the act was passed. Such a requirement was supported by the Supreme Court prior to the act's passage. In 1983, in the case of *Jones* v. *U.S.* (1983),[75] the Court ruled that defendants can be required to prove their insanity when it becomes an issue in their defense. Shortly after the act became law, the Court, in *Ake* v. *Oklahoma* (1985),[76] held that the government must assure access to a competent psychiatrist whenever a defendant indicates that insanity will be an issue at trial.

Consequences of an Insanity Ruling. The insanity defense today is not an "easy way out" of criminal prosecution, as some have assumed. Once a verdict of "not guilty by reason of insanity" is returned, the judge may order the defendant to undergo psychiatric treatment until cured. Because psychiatrists are reluctant to declare any potential criminal "cured," such a sentence may result in more time spent in an institution than would have resulted from a prison sentence. In *Foucha* v. *Louisiana*, 504 U.S. 71 (1992),[77] however, the U.S. Supreme Court held that a defendant found not guilty by reason of insanity in a criminal trial could not thereafter be institutionalized indefinitely without a showing that he or she was either dangerous or mentally ill.

Diminished Capacity

The defense of **diminished capacity,** also called diminished responsibility, is available in some jurisdictions. However, "the terms 'diminished responsibility' and 'diminished capacity' do not have a clearly accepted meaning in the courts."[78] Some defendants who offer diminished capacity defenses do so in recognition of the fact that such claims may be based on a mental condition which would not qualify as mental disease or mental defect nor be sufficient to support the defense of insanity—but which might still lower criminal culpability. According to Peter Arenella, "the defense [of diminished responsibility] was first recognized by Scottish common law courts to reduce the punishment of the 'partially insane' from murder to culpable homicide, a noncapital offense."[79]

The diminished capacity defense is similar to the defense of insanity in that it depends upon a showing that the defendant's mental state was impaired at the time of the crime. As a defense, diminished capacity is most useful when it can be shown that, because of some defect of reason or mental shortcoming, the defendant's capacity to form the *mens rea* required by a specific crime was impaired. Unlike an insanity defense, however, which can

Diminished Capacity (also Diminished Responsibility)

A defense based upon claims of a mental condition which may be insufficient to exonerate a defendant of guilt but that may be relevant to specific mental elements of certain crimes or degrees of crime.

result in a finding of not guilty, a diminished capacity defense is built upon the recognition that "[m]ental condition, though insufficient to exonerate, may be relevant to specific mental elements of certain crimes or degrees of crime."[80] So, for example, defendants might present evidence of mental abnormality in an effort to reduce first-degree murder to second-degree murder or second-degree murder to manslaughter when a killing occurs under extreme emotional disturbance. Similarly, in some jurisdictions very low intelligence will, if proved, serve to reduce first-degree murder to manslaughter.[81]

As is the case with the insanity defense, some jurisdictions have entirely eliminated the diminished capacity defense. The California Penal Code, for example, provides: "The defense of diminished capacity is hereby abolished . . . ,"[82] and adds that "[a]s a matter of public policy there shall be no defense of diminished capacity, diminished responsibility, or irresistible impulse in a criminal action or juvenile adjudication hearing."[83]

Procedural Defenses

Procedural defenses make the claim that defendants were in some manner discriminated against in the justice process or that some important aspect of official procedure was not properly followed and that, as a result, they should be released from any criminal liability. The procedural defenses we shall discuss here are (1) entrapment, (2) double jeopardy, (3) *collateral estoppel,* (4) selective prosecution, (5) denial of a speedy trial, (6) prosecutorial misconduct, and (7) police fraud.

Entrapment

Entrapment

An improper or illegal inducement to crime by agents of enforcement. Also, a defense that may be raised when such inducements occur.

Entrapment, which can be defined as an improper or illegal inducement to crime by agents of enforcement, is a defense which limits the enthusiasm with which police officers may enforce the law. Entrapment defenses argue that enforcement agents effectively create a crime where there would otherwise have been none. For entrapment to have occurred, the idea for the criminal activity must have originated with official agents of the criminal justice system. Entrapment can also result when overzealous undercover police officers convince a defendant that the contemplated law-violating behavior is not a crime. In order to avoid claims of entrapment, officers must not engage in activity that would cause a person to commit a crime that he or she would not otherwise commit. Merely providing an opportunity for a willing offender to commit a crime, however, is *not* entrapment.

Entrapment was claimed in the still-famous case of automaker John DeLorean. DeLorean was arrested on October 19, 1982, by federal agents near the Los Angeles airport.[84] An FBI videotape, secretly made at the scene, showed him allegedly "dealing" with undercover agents and holding packets of cocaine, which he said were "better than gold." DeLorean was charged with narcotics smuggling violations involving a large amount of drugs.

At his 1984 trial, DeLorean claimed that he had been "set up" by the police to commit a crime which he would not have been involved in were it not for their urging. DeLorean's auto company had fallen upon hard times, and he was facing heavy debts. Federal agents, acting undercover, proposed to DeLorean a plan whereby he could make a great deal of money through drugs. Because the idea originated with the police, not with DeLorean, and because DeLorean was able to demonstrate successfully that he was repeatedly threatened not to "pull out" of the deal by a police informant, the jury returned a not guilty verdict.

The concept of entrapment is well summarized in a statement made by DeLorean's defense attorney to *Time* before the trial: "This is a fictitious crime. Without the Government there would be no crime. This is one of the most insidious and misguided law-enforcement operations in history."[85]

Double Jeopardy

The Fifth Amendment to the U.S. Constitution makes it clear that no person may be tried twice for the same offense. People who have been acquitted or found innocent may not be again put in "jeopardy of life or limb" for the same crime. The same is true of those who have been convicted: They cannot be tried again for the same offense. Cases that are dismissed for a lack of evidence also come under the double jeopardy rule and cannot result in a new trial. The U.S. Supreme Court has ruled that "the Double Jeopardy Clause protects against three distinct abuses: a second prosecution for the same offense after acquittal; a second prosecution for the same offense after conviction; and multiple punishments for the same offense."[86]

Double jeopardy does not apply in cases of trial error. Hence, convictions which are set aside because of some error in proceedings at a lower court level (for example, inappropriate instructions to the jury by the trial court judge) will permit a retrial on the same charges. Similarly, when a defendant's motion for a mistrial is successful, or members of the jury cannot agree upon a verdict (resulting in a "hung jury"), a second trial may be held.

Defendants, however, may be tried in both federal and state courts without necessarily violating the principle of double jeopardy. For example, 33-year-old Rufina Canedo pleaded guilty to possession of 50 kilograms of cocaine in 1991 and received a six-year prison sentence in a California court.[87] Federal prosecutors, however, indicted her again—this time under a federal law—for the same offense. They offered her a deal—testify against her husband or face federal prosecution and the possibility of 20 years in a federal prison. Because state and federal statutes emanate from different jurisdictions, this kind of dual prosecution has been held constitutional by the U.S. Supreme Court. To prevent abuse, the U.S. Justice Department acted in 1960 to restrict federal prosecution in such cases to situations involving a "compelling federal interest"—such as civil rights violations. However, in recent years, in the face of soaring drug law violations, the restriction has been relaxed.

In 1992, in another drug case, the U.S. Supreme Court ruled that the double jeopardy clause of the U.S. Constitution "only prevents duplicative prosecution for the same offense," but that "a substantive offense and a conspiracy to commit that offense are not the same offense for double jeopardy purposes." In that case, *U.S. v. Felix* (1992),[88] a Missouri man was convicted in that state of manufacturing methamphetamine and then convicted again in Oklahoma of the "separate crime" of conspiracy to manufacture a controlled substance—in part based upon his activities in Missouri.

Generally, because civil and criminal law differ as to purpose, it is possible to try someone in civil court to collect damages for a possible violation of civil law even though that person has been found not guilty in criminal court, without violating the principle of double jeopardy. The well-known 1996–1997 California civil trial of O. J. Simpson on grounds of wrongful death resulted in widespread publicity of just such a possibility. In cases where civil penalties, however, are "so punitive in form and effect as to render them criminal,"[89] a person sanctioned by a court in a civil case may not be tried in criminal court.

> **Double Jeopardy**
>
> *A common law and constitutional prohibition against a second trial for the same offense.*

> "No person shall be . . . twice put in jeopardy of life or limb. . . ."
>
> —*The Fifth Amendment to the U.S. Constitution*

Collateral Estoppel

Collateral estoppel is similar to double jeopardy and applies to facts that have been determined by a "valid and final judgment."[90] Such facts cannot become the object of new litigation. Where a defendant, for example, has been acquitted of a multiple murder charge by virtue of an alibi, it would not be permissible to try that person again for the murder of a second person killed along with the first.

Selective Prosecution

The procedural defense of selective prosecution is based upon the Fourteenth Amendment's guarantee of equal protection of the laws. The defense may be available where two or more individuals are suspected of criminal involvement, but not all are actively prosecuted. Selective prosecution based fairly upon the strength of available evidence is not the object of this defense. But when prosecution proceeds unfairly on the basis of some arbitrary and discriminatory attribute, such as race, sex, friendship, age, or religious preference, protection may be feasible under it. In 1996, however, in a case that reaffirmed reasonable limits on claims of selective prosecution, the U.S. Supreme Court ruled that for a defendant to successfully "claim that he was singled out for prosecution on the basis of his race, he must make a . . . showing that the Government declined to prosecute similarly situated suspects of other races."[91]

Denial of Speedy Trial

The Sixth Amendment to the Constitution guarantees a right to a speedy trial. The purpose of the guarantee is to prevent unconvicted and potentially innocent people from languishing in jail. The federal government[92] and most states have laws (generally referred to as "speedy trial acts") that define the time limit necessary for a trial to be "speedy" and generally set a reasonable period, such as 90 or 120 days following arrest. Excluded from the counting procedure are delays which result from requests by the defense to prepare its case. If the limit set by law is exceeded, the defendant must be set free and no trial can occur.

Some legal experts expect speedy trial claims to be raised by defense attorneys in the case of Byron De La Beckwith, the unrepentant 75-year-old white supremacist who was recently convicted of the murder of black civil rights leader Medgar Evers in Mississippi in 1963. More than 30 years after the killing, Beckwith was sentenced to life in prison, but only after two previous trials ended in hung juries.

Prosecutorial Misconduct

Another procedural defense may be found in prosecutorial misconduct. Generally speaking, *prosecutorial misconduct* is a term used by legal scholars to describe actions undertaken by prosecutors which give the government an unfair advantage or that prejudice the rights of a defendant or witness. Prosecutors are expected to uphold the highest ethical standards in the performance of their roles. When they knowingly permit false testimony, when they hide information that would clearly help the defense, or when they make unduly biased statements to the jury in closing arguments, the defense of prosecutorial misconduct may be available to the defendant.

The most famous instance of prosecutorial misconduct in recent history may have occurred during a convoluted 17-year-long federal case against former Cleveland autoworker John Demjanjuk. Demjanjuk, who was accused of committing war crimes as the notorious Nazi guard "Ivan the Terrible," was extradited in 1986 by the federal government to Israel to face charges there. In late 1993, however, the 6th U.S. Circuit Court of Appeals in Cincinnati, Ohio, ruled that federal prosecutors, working under what the court called a "win-at-any-cost" attitude, had intentionally withheld evidence which might have exonerated Demjanjuk (who was stripped of his U.S. citizenship when extradited, but later returned to the United States after the Supreme Court of Israel overturned his sentence there).[93]

Police Fraud

During the 1995 double-murder trial of O. J. Simpson, defense attorneys suggested the possibility that evidence against Simpson may have been concocted and even planted by police officers with a personal dislike of the defendant. In particular, defense attorneys pointed the finger at Los Angeles Police Department detective Mark Fuhrman, suggesting that he may have planted a bloody glove at the Simpson estate and tampered with blood stain evidence taken from the infamous white Ford Bronco Simpson was known to drive. To support allegations that Fuhrman was motivated by racist leanings, defense attorneys subpoenaed tapes Fuhrman made over a 10-year period with a North Carolina screenwriter who had been documenting life within the LAPD.

As one observer put it, however, the defense of police fraud builds upon extreme paranoia about the government and police agencies. This type of defense, said Francis Fukuyama, carries "to extremes a distrust of government and the belief that public authorities are in a vast conspiracy to violate the rights of individuals."[94] It can also be extremely unfair to innocent people, for a strategy of this sort subjects what may otherwise be well-meaning public servants to intense public scrutiny, effectively shifting attention away from criminal defendants and onto them—sometimes with disastrous personal results. Anthony Pellicano, a private investigator hired by Fuhrman's lawyers, put it this way: "His life right now is in the toilet. He has no job, no future. People think he's a racist. He can't do anything to help himself. He's been ordered not to talk. His family and friends, he's told them not to get involved. . . . Mark Fuhrman's life is ruined. For what? Because he found a key piece of evidence."[95] The 43-year-old Furhman retired from police work before the Simpson trial concluded.

Innovative Defenses

In recent years some innovative defense strategies have been employed, with varying degrees of success, in criminal cases—and it is to these that we now turn our attention. Technically speaking, the defenses listed here can be properly subsumed under the broader categories of justifications or excuses. They are discussed as a separate group, however, because each is virtually new and relatively untried. The unique and emerging character of these novel defenses, however, makes discussing them worthwhile. The innovative defenses discussed in the next few pages include: (1) the abuse defense, (2) premenstrual stress syndrome, (3) other biological defenses, (4) black rage, and (5) urban survival syndrome.

The Abuse Defense

One innovative defense which seems to be gaining in popularity with defense attorneys today, especially in murder cases, is that of abuse. Actually, the abuse defense is not new, having evolved from domestic abuse cases in the 1970s, which emphasized the inability of some battered women to escape from the demeaning situations surrounding them. **Battered woman's syndrome** (BWS), involving long-term abuse, was said to effectively prevent women from seeking divorce and, in some cases, to drive women temporarily insane—turning them into killers of their abusive spouses. BWS, sometimes also referred to as "battered spouse syndrome" or "battered person's syndrome," entered contemporary awareness with the 1979 publication of Lenore Walker's book, *The Battered Woman*.[96] Defense attorneys were quick to use Walker's slogan of "learned helplessness" to explain why battered women were unable to leave abusive situations and why they sometimes found it necessary to resort to violence in order to free themselves from it. Early versions of the abuse defense depended upon its link to the more traditional defenses of insanity and self-defense. As judges and juries increasingly accepted such defenses, however, "attorneys began to use similar arguments to defend not only wives, but also homosexual lovers, and then children, husbands, and a slew of other accused criminals."[97]

> **Battered Woman's Syndrome (BWS)**
>
> *A series of common characteristics that appear in women who are abused physically and psychologically over an extended period of time by the dominant male figure in their lives; a pattern of psychological symptoms that develop after somebody has lived in a battering relationship; or a pattern of responses and perceptions presumed to be characteristic of women who have been subjected to continuous physical abuse by their mates.*

The abuse defense attempts to turn the tables on criminal prosecutors by claiming that chronic abuse sufferers may have to defend themselves at times when their abusers are most vulnerable—such as when they are asleep or otherwise distracted. This kind of argument is more frequently offered when the "victim" is weaker than the abuser, as in the case of women and children said to be abused by men.

Aspects of the abuse defense could be seen in the trials of Lorena Bobbitt, discussed earlier in this chapter, who was acquitted on charges of malicious wounding after admitting she severed her husband's penis with a kitchen knife, and Lyle and Erik Menendez, brothers whose first trial on charges of murdering their parents ended in hung juries after their attorneys claimed the boys' actions were the results of a lifetime of sexual abuse at the hands of their father. In 1996, in a second trial, however, the Menendez brothers were convicted of the murders of their parents and sentenced to life imprisonment without parole.[98]

Some observers of the American scene say that jurors in today's society are especially sympathetic to abuse victims who act out their frustrations through crime. New York attorney Ronald L. Kuby says, for example, "One of the salutary effects of the pop psychology boom of the 1970s is that people increasingly ask, 'How did I end up like this and what can I do about it.' "[99] Popular television talk shows have probably also played a part in sensitizing people to the role of personal and family tragedies in people's lives. As a consequence, people everywhere may be ready to excuse criminal culpability if they can be shown its roots in a given situation. Southwestern University Law School professor Robert Pugsley puts it this way: "We are entering the age of the empathetic or sympathetic jury that is willing to turn the courtroom into the Oprah [Winfrey] or Phil [Donahue] show."[100]

Not everyone is enamored with the willingness of juries to consider the abuse defense, however. Los Angeles Deputy District Attorney Kathleen Cady, for example, recently saw Moosa Hanoukai convicted of voluntary manslaughter rather than first-degree murder as Cady had hoped. Hanoukai had beaten his wife to death with a wrench, but attorneys claimed he killed her because she made him sleep on the floor, called him names, and paid him a small allowance for work he did around the house. Jurors were told that Hanoukai, whose Jewish background prevented divorce, had been psychologically emasculated by his overbearing wife.

But, as Cady puts it, "Every single murderer has a reason why they killed someone. . . . I think it sends a very frightening message to the rest of society that all you have to do is come up with some kind of excuse when you commit a crime."[101] Even a history of abuse, others say, should not be a license to kill.

Even so, the long-term trend may favor those with an abuse defense available to them. James Blatt, the attorney who defended Hanoukai, says, "I think the trend is, if you can show legitimate psychological abuse over a prolonged period of time, then be prepared for a jury's reaction to that. . . . Whether a lot of people like it or not, it may become an inherent part of American jurisprudence."[102]

Premenstrual Stress Syndrome

The use of premenstrual stress syndrome (PMS) as a defense against criminal charges is very new and demonstrates how changing social conceptions and advancing technology may modify the way in which courts view illegal behavior. In 1980 British courts heard the case of Christine English, who killed her live-in lover when he threatened to leave her. An expert witness at the trial testified that English had been the victim of PMS for more than a decade. The witness, Dr. Katharina Dalton, advanced the claim that PMS had rendered Ms. English "irritable, aggressive . . . and confused, with loss of self-control."[103] The jury, apparently accepting the claim, returned a verdict of not guilty.

PMS is not an officially acceptable defense in American criminal courts. However, in 1991 a Fairfax, Virginia, judge dismissed drunk-driving charges against a woman who cited the role PMS played in her behavior.[104] The woman, an orthopedic surgeon named Dr. Geraldine Richter, admitted to drinking four glasses of wine and allegedly kicked and cursed a state trooper who stopped her car because it was weaving down the road. A Breathalyzer test showed a blood-alcohol level of 0.13 percent—higher than the 0.10 percent needed to meet the requirement for drunk driving under Virginia law. But a gynecologist who testified on Dr. Richter's behalf said that the behavior she exhibited is characteristic of PMS. "I guess this is a new trend," said the state's attorney in commenting on the judge's ruling.

Other Biological Defenses

Modern nutritional science appears to be on the verge of establishing a new category of defense related to "chemical imbalances" in the human body produced by eating habits. Vitamins, food allergies, the consumption of stimulants (including coffee and nicotine), and the excessive ingestion of sugar all will probably soon be advanced by attorneys in defense of their clients.

The case of Dan White provides an example of this new direction in the development of innovative defenses.[105] In 1978, White, a former San Francisco police officer, walked into the office of Mayor Moscone and shot both the mayor and City Councilman Harvey Milk to death. It was established at the trial that White had spent the night before the murders drinking Coca-Cola and eating Twinkies, a packaged pastry. Expert witnesses testified that the huge amounts of sugar consumed by White prior to the crime substantially altered his judgment and ability to control his behavior. The jury, influenced by the expert testimony, convicted White of a lesser charge, and he served a short prison sentence.

The strategy used by White's lawyers came to be known as the "Twinkie defense." It may well have set the tone for many of the innovative defense strategies now being used in cases across the nation.

Black Rage

The defense of "black rage" originated with the multiple-murder trial of Colin Ferguson, who was charged with killing six passengers and wounding 19 others in what authorities described as "a racially motivated attack" on the Long Island Rail Road in December 1993. In preparation for trial Ferguson's original attorneys, William Kunstler and Ronald Kuby, had planned to argue that Ferguson, who is black, was overcome by rage resulting from society-wide mistreatment of blacks by whites. (All the victims in the shooting spree initiated by Ferguson were either white or Asian.)

Kunstler suggested that the "black rage" defense is fundamentally a claim of insanity. "We are mounting a traditional insanity defense, long recognized in our law, with 'black rage' triggering last December's massacre,"[106] Kunstler and Kuby wrote in a letter to the *New York Times*. "Without a psychiatric defense, Colin has no defense," Kunstler was quoted as saying.[107] "There was no doubt that he was there, that he fired the weapon, that he would have fired it more if he had not been wrestled to the ground. There is no doubt that Colin Ferguson, if sane, was guilty," said Kunstler.

Ferguson eventually rejected the recommendation of Kuby and Kunstler that he plead not guilty by reason of insanity caused by "black rage" at racial injustice. After conducting his own defense, in what some called a mockery of an accused's right to act as his own attorney, Ferguson was convicted of all the charges against him. Ferguson had maintained his innocence throughout the trial, despite the fact he was identified by more than a dozen eyewitnesses, including some he had shot.

Urban Survival Syndrome

A few years ago, in a Fort Worth, Texas, murder case, a mistrial was declared after jurors deadlocked over lawyers' claims that their client, 18-year-old Daimion Osby, had killed two men because he suffered from "urban survival syndrome." Although Osby admitted to shooting both unarmed men in the head in a downtown parking lot, his attorneys told jurors that he had simply staged a preemptive strike against vicious people who had been threatening him for a year.

Jurors in Osby's trial heard defense attorneys argue that urban survival syndrome is a predilection to engage in violence in order to prevent oneself from being victimized—a kind of "shoot first, ask questions later" response to the growing violence now so characteristic of many American inner cities. Lawyers described the syndrome as "a sort of mind fix that comes over a young black male living in an urban neighborhood when he's been threatened with deadly force by another black male."[108] "For young blacks to take into account what they see happening in their own neighborhoods is not being racist," said David Bays, one of Osby's lawyers. "It's being realistic." Osby, said his lawyers, had been scared into a state of "hypervigilance," convinced that he had no alternative but to kill in order to ensure his own survival. Recently, however, Osby was tried again. This time jurors rejected urban survival syndrome as a defense. Osby was convicted and sentenced to life in prison.[109]

As one commentator on the new defense put it, "I certainly don't like the idea of using some syndrome to get someone off a murder beef. But I've met enough people who use bathtubs as bulletproof beds to know that urban survival syndrome is real. How long can people live in fear before they snap?"[110]

A similar defense, that of "urban fear syndrome," was used in the 1995 murder trial of Nathaniel Hurt. Hurt, 62, fired a .357 Magnum revolver at teenagers, killing a 13-year-old, after young people had repeatedly trashed his yard and thrown rocks at his car. His attorneys claimed that Hurt snapped under the strain of constant harassment from inner-city thugs and that his murderous reaction was excusable because he lived in constant fear. Hurt was convicted of lesser charges after the judge in the case limited application of the defense by ruling that the syndrome claimed by Hurt's lawyers was not "medically recognized."[111]

The Future of Innovative Defenses

Future years will no doubt hold many surprises for students of the criminal law as defense attorneys become ever more willing to experiment with innovative tactics. As David Rosenhan, a professor of law and psychology at Stanford University, explains it: "We're getting to see some very, very interesting things, and obviously some long shots. . . . There are a terrific number of them."[112] To make his case, Rosenhan points to a number of situations in which people who didn't file income taxes escaped IRS prosecution by arguing that traumatic life experiences gave them an aversion to forms—a condition their legal counselors termed "failure to file syndrome." Some defenses to even very serious charges seem to border on the ludicrous. In 1995, for example, the state of Texas executed John Fearance, Jr., 40, for stabbing a man 19 times during a burglary, killing him while the man's spouse watched. In his defense, Fearance had claimed that he was temporarily insane at the time of the burglary-murder, saying his "wife had baked a meat casserole" for dinner on the night of the crimes and he "likes his meat served separately."[113]

The number of new and innovative defenses being tried on juries and judges today is staggering. Some attribute the phenomenon to what they call "creative lawyering." Others, such as Kent Scheidegger of the Criminal Justice Legal Foundation, calls most such defenses "outrageous." They're the tactics of lawyers "who have nothing left to argue," Scheidegger says.[114] He includes such defenses as those of 37-year-old Michael Ricksgers, a Pennsylvania man who argued that sleep apnea (a disorder that causes irregular breathing during sleep) led him to pick up a .357-caliber Magnum and kill his wife; and Edward Kelly, who says he's not guilty of rape because the crime was committed by one of his 30 personalities and not by him. Ricksgers was convicted of first-degree murder, while Kelly's case is still pending.

In an insightful article,[115] Stephen J. Morse, an expert in psychiatry and the law, says that American criminal justice is now caught in the grips of a "new syndrome excuse syndrome"— meaning that new excuses are being offered on an almost daily basis for criminal activity. Many of these "excuses" are documented in the psychiatric literature as "syndromes" or conditions, and include antisocial personality disorder, posttraumatic stress disorder, intermittent explosive disorder, kleptomania, pathological gambling, postconcussional disorder, caffeine withdrawal, and premenstrual dysphoric disorder (discussed earlier as premenstrual stress syndrome). All these conditions are listed in the American Psychiatric Association's authoritative *Diagnostic and Statistical Manual of Mental Disorders*.[116] Emerging defenses, says Morse, include battered women's syndrome, Vietnam syndrome, child sexual abuse syndrome, Holocaust survivor syndrome, urban survival syndrome, rotten social background syndrome, and adopted child syndrome. "Courts," says Morse, "are increasingly inundated with claims that syndromes old and new, validated and unvalidated, should be the basis for two types of legal change:" (1) the creation of new defenses to a criminal charge and (2) "the expansion of old defenses: for example, loosening objective standards for justifications such as self-defense." Morse says that the new syndromes tend to work as defenses because they describe personal abnormalities, and most people are willing to accept abnormalities as "excusing conditions that bear on the accused's responsibility." The mistake, says Morse, is to think "that if we identify a cause for conduct, including mental or physical disorders, then the conduct is necessarily excused." "Causation," he cautions, "is not an excuse," only an explanation for the behavior.

Even so, attempts to offer novel defenses which are intended to convince jurors that even admitted criminal offenders should not be held responsible for their actions are becoming increasingly characteristic of the American way of justice. Whether such strategies will ultimately provide effective defenses may depend more upon finding juries sympathetic to them than it will upon the inherent quality of the defenses themselves.

Summary

Laws regulate relationships between people and also between parties. Hence, one of the primary functions of law is the maintenance of social order. Generally speaking, laws reflect the values held by the society of which they are a part, and legal systems throughout the world reflect the experiences of the societies which created them. The emphasis placed by any law upon individual rights, personal property, and criminal reformation and punishment can tell us much about the cultural and philosophical basis of the society of which it is a part. Islamic law, for example, which provides the basis for many Middle Eastern systems of criminal justice, has a strong religious component and requires judicial decisions in keeping with the Muslim Koran.

Western criminal law generally distinguishes between serious crimes (felonies) and those which are less grave (misdemeanors). Guilt can be demonstrated, and criminal offenders convicted, only if all of the statutory elements of a particular crime can be proven in court.

Our legal system recognizes a number of defenses to a criminal charge. Primary among them are justifications and excuses. One form of excuse, the insanity defense, has recently met with considerable criticism, and efforts to reduce its application have been underway for more than a decade. Even as limits are placed on some traditional defenses, however, new and innovative defenses are emerging.

Discussion Questions

1. What kinds of concerns have influenced the development of the criminal law? How are social values and power arrangements in society represented in today's laws?
2. What is meant by the *corpus delicti* of a crime? How does the *corpus delicti* of a crime differ from the statutory elements that must be proven in order to convict a particular defendant of committing that crime?
3. Does the insanity defense serve a useful function today? If you could create your own rules for determining insanity in criminal trials, what would they be? How would they differ from existing rules?
4. Near the end of this chapter Stephen J. Morse describes many emerging defenses, saying that an explanation for behavior is not the same thing as an excuse. What does Morse mean? Might an explanation be an excuse under some circumstances? If so, when?

Web Quest!

Use the Cybrary to locate Web sites containing state criminal codes. Choose a state (it may be your home state, if your state's statutes are available via the Web) and locate that state's statutes pertaining to the FBI's eight major crimes. (Remember that the terminology may be different. Whereas the FBI may use the term *rape,* for example, the state you've selected may say *sexual assault.*) After studying the statutes, describe the *corpus delicti* of each major offense. That is, list the elements of each offense that must be proven by a prosecutor in a court in order for a conviction to be obtained.

Now choose a second state—preferably from a different geographic region of the country. Again, list the elements of each major offense. Compare the way in which those elements are described with the terminology used by the first state you chose. What differences, if any, exist? Submit your findings to your instructor if requested to do so.

Library Extras!

The Library Extras! listed here complement the WebExtras! found throughout this chapter. Library Extras! may be accessed on the Web at CJToday.com.

Library Extra! 3-1. The *"Cox Report"* on Chinese spying (U.S. Congress, 1999).
Library Extra! 3-2. *The National Institute of Justice Journal* (current issue).
Library Extra! 3-3. *The National Institute of Justice Journal* (prior issue).
Library Extra! 3-4. *Tort Cases in Large Counties* (BJS, 1995).

References

1. Henry Campbell Black, Joseph R. Nolan, and Jacqueline M. Nolan-Haley, *Black's Law Dictionary,* 6th ed. (St. Paul, MN: West, 1990), p. 884.
2. Ibid.
3. American Bar Association Section of International and Comparative Law, *The Rule of Law in the United States* (Chicago, IL: ABA, 1958).
4. "Jury Finds 'Jenny Jones Show' Negligent," APB News, May 7, 1999. Web posted at www.apbnews.com/newscenter/breakingnews/1999/05/07/jones0507_01.html. Accessed January 10, 2000.

5. Black, Nolan, and Nolan-Harley, *Black's Law Dictionary,* 6th ed.
6. Carrie Dowling, "Jury Awards $150 Million in Blazer Crash," *USA Today,* June 4, 1996, p. 3A.
7. "Jury Awards $4.9 Billion in Suit against GM," *USA Today* Online, July 7, 1999. Web posted at www.usatoday.com/hlead.htm. Accessed July 9, 1999.
8. *Facts on File, 1988* (New York: Facts on File, 1988), p. 175.
9. "Man Who Spent 6½ Years in Jail Is Awarded $1.9 Million by Judge," *Fayetteville Observer-*

Times (North Carolina), October 20, 1989, p. 7A.

10. While the state supreme court ruled in favor of Ms. Kitchen on the general issue of liability for gun sales, it agreed with a lower court that the case should be retried because of a procedural error.

11. Robert Davis and Tony Mauro, "Judge OKs Suit Against Gun Maker," *USA Today*, April 12, 1995, p. 3A.

12. Paul Shepard, "NAACP to Sue Gun Industry," Associated Press wire services, July 11, 1999. Web posted at http://search.washingtonpost.com/wpsrv/WAPO/19990711/V000281-071199-idx.html. Accessed July 13, 1999.

13. "Jury Says Halcion Led to Murder, Awards $2.15 Million," *Fayetteville Observer-Times* (North Carolina), November 13, 1992, p. 4A.

14. "Part-Time Carpenter Seeks $657 Trillion Payment," Reuters wire services, June 13, 1994.

15. See Liz Spayd, "America, the Plaintiff; In Seeking Perfect Equity, We've Made a Legal Lottery," *Washington Post* wire services, March 5, 1995.

16. *BMW of North America, Inc. v. Gore,* 116 S.Ct. 1589 (1996).

17. Phillip Rawls, "BMW Paint-Liability," Associated Press wire services, May 9, 1997.

18. Lief H. Carter, *Reason in Law,* 2nd ed. (Boston: Little, Brown, 1984).

19. United States Sentencing Commission, *Federal Sentencing Guidelines Manual* (St. Paul, MN: West, 1987).

20. Daniel Oran, *Oran's Dictionary of the Law* (St. Paul, MN: West, 1983).

21. Florida Constitution, Section 20.

22. Black, Nolan, and Nolan-Harley, *Black's Law Dictionary,* 6th ed.

23. The KGB is now defunct. It was broken up into the SVR (*Sluzhba Vneshney Razvedki,* or Federal Counterintelligence Service), the FSK (*Federal'naya sluzhba kontr-razvedky*), and a number of other agencies.

24. Steven Komarow, "FBI Agent Is Accused of Spying for Russians," *USA Today*, December 19, 1996, p. 1A.

25. "Ex-CIA Officer Pleads Guilty to Spying," Reuters wire services, March 4, 1997.

26. *United States v. Shabani,* 115 S. Ct. 382.

27. Specifically, 21 U.S.C. 846.

28. "Senate Begins to Consider Anti-Stalking Legislation," *Criminal Justice Newsletter,* March 2, 1993, p. 2.

29. *Gordon v. State,* 52 Ala. 3008, 23 Am. Rep. 575 (1875).

30. Oliver Wendell Holmes, *The Common Law,* vol. 3 (1881).

31. But not for more serious degrees of homicide, since leaving a young child alone in a tub of water, even if intentional, does not necessarily mean that the person who so acts intends the child to drown.

32. There is some disagreement, however, among jurists as to whether the crime of statutory rape is a strict liability offense. Some jurisdictions treat it as such and will not accept a reasonable mistake about the victim's age. Others, however, do accept such a mistake as a defense.

33. *State v. Stiffler,* 763 P.2d. 308 (Idaho App. 1988).

34. John S. Baker, Jr., et al., *Hall's Criminal Law,* 5th ed. (Charlottesville, VA: Michie, 1993), p. 138.

35. The same is not true for procedures within the criminal justice system, which can be modified even after a person has been sentenced and, hence, become retroactive. See, for example, the U.S. Supreme Court case of *California Department of Corrections v. Morales,* 514 U.S. 499 (1995), which approved of changes in the length of time between parole hearings, even though those changes applied to offenders already sentenced.

36. Black, Nolan, and Nolan-Harley, *Black's Law Dictionary,* p. 127.

37. The statute also says, "A mother's breastfeeding of her baby does not under any circumstance violate this section."

38. Common law crimes, of course, are not based upon statutory elements.

39. "Murder Attempt Charged in AIDS Exposure Case," *Fayetteville Observer-Times* (North Carolina), November 16, 1992, p. 11A.

40. James A. Carlson, "Cancer Inquest," The Associated Press wire services, April 10, 1995.

41. Ibid.

42. Ibid.

43. Ibid.

44. Lynette Holloway, "Doctor Found Guilty of Murder in Botched Abortion," *New York Times* News Service, August 8, 1995.

45. "Three Get 15 Years in Prison," The Associated Press, June 21, 1997; Deborah Sharp, "Missing Stop Sign, Lost Lives," *USA Today,* June 19, 1997, p. 3A.

46. The judge suspended half of each 30-year sentence, resulting in a 13-year parole eligibility date.

47. *Willoughby v. State* (1990), Ind., 552 N.E.2d 462, 466.

48. See *Maughs v. Commonwealth,* 181 Va. 117, 120, 23 S.E.2d 784, 786 (1943).

49. See *State v. Stephenson,* Opinion No. 24403 (South Carolina, 1996), and *State v. Blocker,* 205 S.C. 303, 31 S.E.2d 908 (1944).

50. *State v. Kindle* (1924), 71 Mont. 58, 64, 227.

51. Black, Nolan, and Nolan-Harley, *Black's Law Dictionary,* 6th ed., p. 343.

52. Patrick L. McCloskey and Ronald L. Schoenberg, *Criminal Law Deskbook* (New York: Matthew Bender, 1988), Section 20.03[13].

53. The exception, of course, is that of a trespasser who trespasses in order to commit a more serious crime.

54. Sir Edward Coke, 3 *Institute,* 162.

55. *The Crown v. Dudly & Stephens,* 14 Q.B.D. 273, 286, 15 Cox C. C. 624, 636 (1884).

56. "The Rough-Sex Defense," *Time,* May 23, 1988, p. 55.

57. Ibid.

58. "The Preppie Killer Cops a Plea," *Time,* April 4, 1988, p. 22.

59. "Jury Convicts Condom Rapist," *USA Today,* May 14, 1993, p. 3A.

60. Black, Nolan, and Nolan-Harley, *Black's Law Dictionary,* 6th ed., p. 504.

61. "Girl Charged," The Associated Press wire services, northern edition, February 28, 1994.

62. *Facts on File, 1987* (New York: Facts on File, 1988).

63. See, for example, *Montana* v. *Egelhoff,* 116 S.Ct. 2013, 135 L. Ed. 2d 361 (1996).

64. " 'Rophies' Reported Spreading Quickly Throughout the South," *Drug Enforcement Report,* June 23, 1995, pp. 1–5.

65. *Bulletin of the American Academy of Psychiatry and the Law,* vol. 19, no. 4, 1991.

66. American Bar Association Standing Committee on Association Standards for Criminal Justice, *Proposed Criminal Justice Mental Health Standards* (Chicago: ABA, 1984).

67. "Mrs. Bobbitt's Defense 'Life Worth More than Penis,' " Reuters world wire services, January 10, 1994.

68. American Law Institute, *Model Penal Code: Official Draft and Explanatory Notes* (Philadelphia: The Institute, 1985).

69. Ibid.

70. See Joan Biskupic, "Insanity Defense: Not a Right; In Montana Case, Justices Give States Option to Prohibit Claim," *Washington Post* wire services, March 29, 1994.

71. Ibid.

72. John Klofas and Ralph Weischeit, "Guilty but Mentally Ill: Reform of the Insanity Defense in Illinois," *Justice Quarterly,* vol. 4, no. 1 (March 1987), pp. 40–50.

73. *Ford* v. *Wainright,* 477 U.S. 399, 106 S.Ct. 2595, 91 L. Ed. 2d 335 (1986).

74. 18 United States Code, §401.

75. *Jones* v. *U.S.,* U.S. Sup. Ct. (1983), 33 CrL 3233.

76. *Ake* v. *Oklahoma,* 470 U.S. 68, 105 S.Ct. 1087, 84 L. Ed. 2d 53.

77. *Foucha* v. *Louisiana,* 504 U.S. 71 (1992).

78. *U.S.* v. *Pohlot,* 827 F.2d 889 (1987).

79. Peter Arenella, "The Diminished Capacity and Diminished Responsibility Defenses: Two Children of a Doomed Marriage," *Columbia Law Review,* vol. 77 (1977), p. 830.

80. *U.S.* v. *Brawner,* 471 F.2d 969 (1972).

81. Black, Nolan, and Nolan-Harley, *Black's Law Dictionary,* p. 458.

82. California Penal Code, Section 25 (a).

83. California Penal Code, Section 28 (b).

84. *Time,* March 19, 1984, p. 26.

85. Ibid.

86. *U.S.* v. *Halper,* 490 U.S. 435 (1989).

87. "Dual Prosecution Can Give One Crime Two Punishments," *USA Today,* March 29, 1993, p. 10A.

88. *U.S.* v. *Felix,* 112 S.Ct. 1377 (1992).

89. See, for example, *Hudson* v. *U.S.,* 522 U.S. 93 (1997); and *United States* v. *Ursery,* 518 U.S. 267 (1996).

90. McCloskey and Schoenberg, *Criminal Law Deskbook,* Section 20.02[4].

91. *U.S.* v. *Armstrong,* 116 S.Ct. 1480, 134 L. Ed. 2d 687 (1996).

92. Speedy Trial Act, 18 U.S.C. §3161. Significant cases involving the U.S. Speedy Trial Act are those of *U.S.* v. *Carter,* 476 U.S. 1138, 106 S.Ct. 2241, 90 L. Ed. 2d 688 (1986), and *Henderson* v. *U.S.,* 476 U.S. 321, 106 S.Ct. 1871, 90 L. Ed. 2d 299 (1986).

93. See Jim McGee, "Judges Increasingly Question U.S. Prosecutors' Conduct," *Washington Post* wire services, November 23, 1993.

94. Francis Fukuyama, "Extreme Paranoia About Government Abounds," *USA Today,* August 24, 1995, p. 17A.

95. Lorraine Adams, "Simpson Trial Focus Shifts to Detective with Troubling Past," *Washington Post* wire services, August 22, 1995.

96. Lenore E. Walker, *The Battered Woman* (New York: Harper Collins, 1980).

97. Niko Price, "Abuse Defenses," The Associated Press wire services, May 29, 1994.

98. "Menendez Brothers Get Life Without Parole," *CNN,* Web posted July 2, 1996.

99. "Abuse Defenses," The Associated Press wire services, May 29, 1994.

100. "In S.C. Case, Reports of Abuse," *USA Today,* April 12, 1995, p. 3A.

101. "Abuse Defenses," May 29, 1994.

102. Ibid.

103. As reported in Arnold Binder, *Juvenile Delinquency: Historical, Cultural, Legal Perspectives* (New York: Macmillan, 1988), p. 494.

104. "Drunk Driving Charge Dismissed: PMS Cited," *Fayetteville Observer-Times* (North Carolina), June 7, 1991, p. 3A.

105. *Facts on File, 1978* (New York: Facts on File, 1979).

106. Niko Price, "Abuse Defenses," The Associated Press wire services, May 29, 1994.

107. "Train Shooting," The Associated Press wire services, August 12, 1994.

108. Courtland Milloy, "Self-Defense Goes Insane in the City," *Washington Post* wire services, May 18, 1994.

109. Robert Davis, "We Live in Age of Exotic Defenses," *USA Today,* November 22, 1994, p. 1A.

110. Ibid.

111. "Murder Acquittal in 'Urban Fear' Trial," *USA Today,* April 12, 1995, p. 3A.

112. Ibid.

113. "Nationline: Execution," *USA Today,* June 21, 1995, p. 3A.

114. Robert Davis, "We Live in Age of Exotic Defenses."

115. Stephen J. Morse, "The 'New Syndrome Excuse Syndrome,' " *Criminal Justice Ethics,* Winter-Spring, 1995, pp. 3–15.

116. American Psychiatric Association, *Diagnostic and Statistical Manual of Mental Disorders,* 4th ed. (Washington, D.C.: APA, 1994).

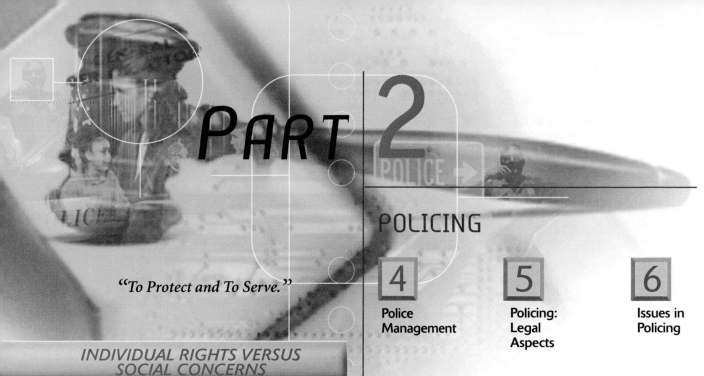

PART 2

POLICING

4 — Police Management

5 — Policing: Legal Aspects

6 — Issues in Policing

"To Protect and To Serve."

INDIVIDUAL RIGHTS VERSUS SOCIAL CONCERNS

THE RIGHTS OF THE ACCUSED UNDER INVESTIGATION

Common law, constitutional, statutory, and humanitarian rights of the accused:

- A Right Against Unreasonable Searches
- A Right Against Unreasonable Arrest
- A Right Against Unreasonable Seizures of Property
- A Right to Fair Questioning by Authorities
- A Right to Protection from Personal Harm

The individual rights listed must be effectively balanced against these community concerns:

- The Efficient Apprehension of Offenders
- The Prevention of Crimes

How does our system of justice work toward balance?

*F*amed police administrator and former New York City police commissioner Patrick V. Murphy once said, "It is a privilege to be a police officer in a democratic society." While Murphy's words still ring true, many of today's law enforcement officers might hear in them only the echo of a long-dead ideal, unrealistic for today's times.

America's police officers form the front line in the unending battle against crime—a battle which seems to get more sinister and demanding with each passing day. It is the police who are called when a crime is in progress or when one has been committed. The police are expected to objectively and impartially investigate law violations, gather evidence, solve crimes, and make arrests resulting in the successful prosecution of suspects—all the while adhering to strict due process standards set forth in the Constitution and enforced by the courts. The chapters in this section of *Criminal Justice: A Brief Introduction* provide an overview of the historical development of policing; describe law enforcement agencies at the federal, state, and local levels; and discuss the due process and legal environments surrounding police activity.

As you will see, while the police are ultimately charged with protecting the public, they often feel that members of the public do not accord them the respect they deserve, and the distance between the police and the public is not easily bridged. Recently, however, a new image of policing has emerged which may do much to heal that divide. This new viewpoint, known as "community policing," goes well beyond traditional conceptions of the police as mere law enforcers and encompasses the idea that police agencies should take counsel from the communities they serve. Under this new model they are expected to prevent crime as well as to solve it and to help members of the community deal with other pressing social issues.

Police

Courts

Correction

CHAPTER 4

Police Management

"There is more law at the end of the policeman's nightstick than in all the decisions of the Supreme Court."
—Alexander "Clubber" Williams, Turn of the Century NYPD Officer

"I liken the Los Angeles police to a business. We have 3½ million customers. . . ."
—Willie Williams, Former Los Angeles Chief of Police[1]

"The single most striking fact about the attitudes of citizens, black and white, toward the police is that in general those attitudes are positive, not negative."
—James Q. Wilson[2]

CHAPTER OUTLINE

◆ Contemporary Policing: The Administrative Perspective

◆ Scientific Police Management

◆ Contemporary Policing: The Individual Officer

—Bonnie Sue, Photo Researchers, Inc.

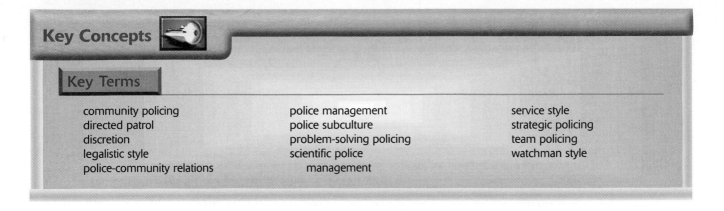

AUDIO
EXTRA!

Hear the author discuss this chapter at *cjtoday.com*

Contemporary Policing: The Administrative Perspective

A few years ago, a Stanislaus County police SWAT team wearing ski masks and acting on a tip that an illegal methamphetamine lab was in operation, kicked down the doors of the Oakdale, California, home of Marian and William Hauselmann.[3] Once inside they handcuffed Mrs. Hauselmann, put a pillowcase over her head, and wrestled her to the floor. Her 64-year-old husband, who suffers from a heart condition, was shouted into silence. His face was cut and officers stepped on his back after throwing him down. No illegal drugs were found. Police soon realized that they had been misled by their informant and apologized to the Hauselmanns. Then they borrowed a knife from the couple's kitchen to cut the plastic handcuffs from their wrists. The county sheriff offered to pay for the broken doors. Following the incident the Hauselmanns reported being unable to sleep.

A few months prior to the Hauselmanns' ordeal, multimillionaire rancher Donald Scott was fatally shot during a drug raid gone terribly wrong. His Malibu, California, property, the target of a police attack, yielded no drugs, and Scott appears to have been trying to protect himself from what he thought were intruders when he was shot.

Both these cases highlight the potentially disastrous consequences of improper police action. Effective **police management,** through which laws are enforced while the rights of suspects and of innocent people are protected, may be the single most important emerging issue facing the criminal justice system in the twenty-first century. As Dorothy Ehrlich of northern California's ACLU says, efficient enforcement of the laws is necessary, "[b]ut terrorizing innocent people is a price no one should have to pay."[4]

Styles of Policing

Police management refers to the administrative activities of controlling, directing, and coordinating police personnel, resources, and activities in the service of crime prevention, the apprehension of criminals, the recovery of stolen property, and the performance of a variety of regulatory and helping services.[5] Police managers include any "sworn" law enforcement personnel with administrative authority, from the rank of sergeant to captain, chief or sheriff, and civilian personnel such as police commissioners, attorneys general, state secretaries of crime control, public safety directors, and so on.

In a recent symposium, members of Harvard University's Kennedy School of Government divided the history of American policing into three different eras.[6] Each era was distinguished from the others by the apparent dominance of a particular administrative approach to police operations. The first period, the political era, was characterized by close ties between police and public officials. It began in the 1840s and ended around 1930. Throughout the period American police agencies tended to serve the interests of powerful politicians and their cronies, while providing community order maintenance services almost as an afterthought. The second period, the reform era, began in the 1930s and lasted until the 1970s. The reform era was char-

Police Management

The administrative activities of controlling, directing, and coordinating police personnel, resources, and activities in the service of crime prevention; the apprehension of criminals and the recovery of stolen property; and the performance of a variety of regulatory and helping services.

Key Concepts

Key Terms

community policing
directed patrol
discretion
legalistic style
police-community relations

police management
police subculture
problem-solving policing
scientific police
   management

service style
strategic policing
team policing
watchman style

acterized by pride in professional crime fighting. Police departments during this period focused most of their resources on solving "traditional" crimes such as murder, rape, and burglary and on capturing offenders. The final era—one which is just beginning—is the era of community problem solving. The problem-solving approach to police work stresses the service role of police officers and envisions a partnership between police agencies and their communities.

The influence of each historical phase identified by the Harvard team survives today in what James Q. Wilson calls policing styles.[7] Simply put, a style of policing describes how a particular police agency sees its purpose and the methods and techniques it undertakes to fulfill that purpose. Wilson's three types of policing—which he did not identify with a particular historical era—are (1) the watchman style (characteristic of the Harvard symposium's political era), (2) the legalistic style (professional crime fighting), and (3) the service style (which is becoming more commonplace today). These three styles, taken together, characterize nearly all municipal law enforcement agencies now operating in this country—although some departments are a mixture of two or more styles.

The Watchman Style of Policing

Police departments marked by the **watchman style** of policing are primarily concerned with achieving a goal that Wilson calls "order maintenance." They see their job as one of controlling illegal and disruptive behavior. The watchman style, however, as opposed to the legalistic, makes considerable use of discretion. Order in watchman-style communities may be arrived at through informal police intervention, including persuasion and threats, or even by "roughing up" a few disruptive people from time to time. Some authors have condemned this style of policing, suggesting that it is unfairly found in lower-class or lower-middle-class communities, especially where interpersonal relations may include a fair amount of violence or physical abuse.

The watchman style of policing appears to have been operative in Los Angeles, California, at the time of the well-known Rodney King beating (see Chapter 5 for details). Following the riots that ensued, the Independent Commission on the Los Angeles Police Department (the Christopher Commission) determined that the Los Angeles "[p]olice placed greater emphasis on crime control over crime prevention, a policy that distanced cops from the people they serve."

"Crime is a community problem and stands today as one of the most serious challenges of our generation. Our citizens must . . . recognize their responsibilities in its suppression."
—*O. W. Wilson*

Watchman Style

A style of policing marked by a concern for order maintenance. This style of policing is characteristic of lower-class communities where informal police intervention into the lives of residents is employed in the service of keeping the peace.

The maintenance of social order is a police function closely akin to strict law enforcement. Here, Austin, Texas, police officers remove protesters at an antiabortion sit-in.
Bob Daemmrich, Stock Boston.

The Legalistic Style of Policing

Departments operating under the **legalistic model** are committed to enforcing the "letter of the law." Years ago, for example, when the speed limit on I-95 running north and south through North Carolina was dropped to 55 MPH, a state highway patrol official was quoted by newspapers as saying that troopers would issue tickets at 56 MPH. The law was the law, he said, and it would be enforced.

Conversely, legalistically oriented departments can be expected to routinely avoid involvement in community disputes arising from violations of social norms which do not break the law. Gary Sykes calls this enforcement style "laissez-faire policing," in recognition of its "hands-off" approach to behaviors which are simply bothersome or inconsiderate of community principles.

The Service Style of Policing

Departments which stress the goal of service reflect the felt needs of the community. In service-oriented departments, the police see themselves more as helpers than as embattled participants in a war against crime. Such departments work hand in hand with social service and other agencies to provide counseling for minor offenders and to assist community groups in preventing crimes and solving problems. Prosecutors may support the **service style** of policing by agreeing not to prosecute law violators who seek psychiatric help, or who voluntarily participate in such programs as Alcoholics Anonymous, family counseling, drug treatment, and the like. The service style of policing is commonly found in wealthy neighborhoods, where the police are well paid and well educated. The service style is supported in part by citizen attitudes which seek to avoid the personal embarrassment which might result from a public airing of personal problems. Such attitudes reduce the number of criminal complaints filed, especially in minor disputes.

Evolving Styles of Policing

Historically, American police work has involved a fair amount of order maintenance activity. The United States a few decades ago consisted of a large number of immigrant communities, socially separated from one another by custom and language. Immigrant workers were often poorly educated, and some were prone toward displays of "manhood," which challenged police authority in the cities. Reports of police in "pitched battles" with bar-hopping laborers out for Saturday night "good times" were not uncommon. Arrests were infrequent, but "street justice" was often imposed through the use of the "billy stick" and blackjack. In these historical settings, the watchman style of policing must have seemed especially appropriate to both the police and many members of the citizenry.

As times changed, so too have American communities. Even today, however, it is probably fair to say that the style of policing which characterizes a community tends to flow, at least to some degree, from the lifestyles of those who live there. Rough-and-tumble lifestyles encourage an oppressive form of policing; refined styles produce a service emphasis with stress on working together.

Police-Community Relations

In the 1960s, the legalistic style of policing, so common in America until then, began to yield to the newer service-oriented style of policing. The decade of the 1960s was one of unrest, fraught with riots and student activism. The war in Vietnam, civil rights concerns, and other burgeoning social movements produced large demonstrations and marches. The police, who were generally inexperienced in crowd control, all too often found themselves embroiled in tumultuous encounters with citizen groups. The police came to be seen by many as agents of "the establishment," and pitched battles between the police and the citizenry sometimes occurred.

As social disorganization increased, police departments across the nation sought ways to understand and deal better with the problems they faced. Significant outgrowths of this effort were the police-community relations (PCR) programs, which many departments created. Some authors have traced the development of the police-community relations concept to an annual conference begun in 1955.[8] Entitled the "National Institute of Police and Community Relations," the meetings were sponsored jointly by the National Conference of Christians and Jews and the Michigan State University Department of Police Administration and Public Safety. The emphasis on police community relations also benefited substantially from the 1967 report by the President's Commission on Law Enforcement and the Administration of Justice,[9] which found that police agencies were often socially isolated from the communities they served.

PCR represented a movement away from an exclusive police emphasis on the apprehension of law violators and meant increasing the level of positive police-citizen interaction. At the height of the PCR movement city police departments across the country opened storefront centers where citizens could air complaints and easily interact with police representatives. As Egon Bittner recognized,[10] for PCR programs to be truly effective, they need to reach to "the grassroots of discontent," where citizen dissatisfaction with the police exists.

Many contemporary PCR programs involve public-relations officers appointed to provide an array of services to the community. "Neighborhood Watch" programs, drug awareness workshops, "Project ID"—which uses police equipment and expertise to mark valuables for identification in the event of theft—and police-sponsored victim's assistance programs are all examples of services embodying the spirit of PCR. Modern PCR programs, however, often fail to achieve their goal of increased community satisfaction with police services because they focus on providing services to groups who already are well satisfied with the police. On the other hand, PCR initiatives which do reach disaffected community groups are difficult to manage and may even alienate participating officers. Thus, as Bittner says, "while the first approach fails because it leaves out those groups to which the program is primarily directed, the second fails because it leaves out the police department."[11]

"The police in the United States are not separate from the people. They draw their authority from the will and consent of the people, and they recruit their officers from them. The police are the instrument of the people to achieve and maintain order; their efforts are founded on principles of public service and ultimate responsibility to the public."

—The National Advisory Commission on Criminal Justice Standards and Goals

Contemporary police work involves a lot more than enforcing the law.
Courtesy of New York Police Department Photo Unit.

Team Policing

During the 1960s and 1970s a number of communities began to experiment with the concept of **team policing.** An idea thought to have originated in Aberdeen, Scotland,[12] team policing, which in its heyday was defined as the reorganization of conventional patrol strategies into "an integrated and versatile police team assigned to a fixed district,"[13] rapidly became an extension of the PCR movement. Some authors have called team policing a "technique to deliver total police services to a neighborhood."[14] Others, however, have dismissed it as "little more than an attempt to return to the style of policing that was prevalent in the United States over a century ago."[15]

Team policing assigned officers on a semipermanent basis to particular neighborhoods, where it was expected they would become familiar with the inhabitants and with their problems and concerns. Patrol officers were given considerable authority in processing complaints from receipt through to resolution. Crimes were investigated and solved at the local level, with specialists called in only if the resources needed to continue an investigation were not locally available.

Community Policing

In recent years the police-community relations concept has undergone a substantial shift in emphasis. The old PCR model was built around the unfortunate self-image held by many police administrators of themselves as enforcers of the law who were isolated from, and often in opposition to, the communities they policed. Under such jaded administrators, PCR easily became a shallowly disguised and insecure effort to overcome public suspicion and community hostility.

In contrast, an increasing number of enlightened law enforcement administrators today are embracing the role of service provider. Modern police departments are frequently called upon to help citizens resolve a vast array of personal problems—many of which involve no law-breaking activity. Such requests may involve help for a sick child or the need to calm a distraught person, open a car with the keys locked inside, organize a community crime-prevention effort, investigate a domestic dispute, regulate traffic, or give a talk to a class of young people on the dangers of drug abuse. Calls for service today far exceed the number of calls received by the police which directly relate to law violations. As a consequence, the referral function of the police is crucial in producing effective law enforcement. Officers may

Police officers serve food during an anticrime rally to encourage citizen involvement in crime fighting. Activities such as this help foster the community-policing ideal—through which law enforcement officers and members of the public become partners in controlling crime and keeping communities safe. Dale Stockton.

make referrals, rather than arrests, for interpersonal problems to agencies as diverse as Alcoholics Anonymous, departments of social service, domestic violence centers, drug rehabilitation programs, and psychiatric clinics.

In contemporary America, according to Harvard University's Executive Session on Policing, police departments function a lot like business corporations. According to the Session, three generic kinds of "corporate strategies" guide American policing.[16] They are (1) strategic policing, (2) problem-solving policing, and (3) community policing.

The first, strategic policing, is something of a holdover from the reform era of the mid-1900s. **Strategic policing** "emphasizes an increased capacity to deal with crimes that are not well controlled by traditional methods."[17] Strategic policing retains the traditional police goal of professional crime fighting, but enlarges the enforcement target to include nontraditional kinds of criminals such as serial offenders, gangs and criminal associations, drug distribution networks, and sophisticated white-collar and computer criminals. To meet its goals, strategic policing generally makes use of innovative enforcement techniques, including intelligence operations, undercover stings, electronic surveillance, and sophisticated forensic methods.

The other two strategies give greater cognizance to the service style described by Wilson. **Problem-solving** (or problem-oriented) **policing** takes the view that many crimes are caused by existing social conditions in the communities served by the police. To control crime, problem-oriented police managers attempt to uncover and effectively address underlying social problems. Problem-solving policing makes thorough use of other community resources such as counseling centers, welfare programs, and job-training facilities. It also attempts to involve citizens in the job of crime prevention through education, negotiation, and conflict management. Residents of poorly maintained housing areas, for example, might be asked to clean up litter, install better lighting, and provide security devices for their homes and apartments, in the belief that clean, secure, and well-lighted areas are a deterrent to criminal activity.

The third, and newest, police strategy goes a step beyond the other two. **Community policing** (sometimes called "community-oriented policing") can be defined as "a collaborative effort between the police and the community that identifies problems of crime and disorder and involves all elements of the community in the search for solutions to these problems."[18] It has also been described as "a philosophy based on forging a partnership between the police and the community, so that they can work together on solving problems of crime, [and] fear of crime and disorder, thereby enhancing the overall quality of life in their neighborhoods."[19]

Community policing is a concept which evolved out of the early work of Robert C. Trojanowicz and George L. Kelling, who conducted studies of foot patrol programs in Newark, New Jersey,[20] and Flint, Michigan,[21] showing that "police could develop more positive attitudes toward community members and could promote positive attitudes toward police if they spent time on foot in their neighborhoods."[22] The definitive work in the area is said by many to be Trojanowicz's book *Community Policing*,[23] published in 1990.

Community policing attempts to actively involve the community with the police in the task of crime control by creating an effective working partnership between the community and the police.[24] As a consequence, community policing permits members of the community to participate more fully than ever before in defining the police role. In the words of Jerome Skolnick, community policing is "grounded on the notion that, together, police and public are more effective and more humane coproducers of safety and public order than are the police alone."[25] According to Skolnick, community policing involves at least one of four elements: (1) community-based crime prevention, (2) the reorientation of patrol activities to emphasize the importance of nonemergency services, (3) increased police accountability to the public, and (4) a decentralization of command, including a greater use of civilians at all levels of police decision making.[26] As one writer explains it, "Community policing seeks to integrate what was traditionally seen as the different law enforcement, order maintenance and social service roles of the police. Central to the integration of these roles is a working partnership with the community in determining what neighborhood problems are to be addressed, and how."[27] Table 4-1 highlights the differences between traditional and community policing.

Strategic Policing

A style of policing that retains the traditional police goal of professional crime fighting, but enlarges the enforcement target to include nontraditional kinds of criminals such as serial offenders, gangs and criminal associations, drug distribution networks, and sophisticated white-collar and computer criminals. Strategic policing generally makes use of innovative enforcement techniques, including intelligence operations, undercover stings, electronic surveillance, and sophisticated forensic methods.

Problem-Solving Policing (also called Problem-Oriented Policing)

A style of policing that assumes that many crimes are caused by existing social conditions within the community and that crimes can be controlled by uncovering and effectively addressing underlying social problems. Problem-solving policing makes use of other community resources such as counseling centers, welfare programs, and job-training facilities. It also attempts to involve citizens in the job of crime prevention through education, negotiation, and conflict management.

Community Policing

A collaborative effort between the police and the community that identifies problems of crime and disorder and involves all elements of the community in the search for solutions to these problems.

TABLE 4-1 ■ Traditional versus Community Policing

QUESTION	TRADITIONAL	COMMUNITY POLICING
Who are the police?	A government agency principally responsible for law enforcement	Police are the public and the public are the police: The police officers are those who are paid to give full-time attention to the duties of every citizen.
What is the relationship of the police force to other publicservice departments?	Priorities often conflict	The police are one department among many responsible for improving the quality of life.
What is the role of the police?	Focusing on solving crimes	A broader problem-solving approach.
How is police efficiency measured?	By detection and arrest rates	By the absence of crime and disorder.
What are the highest priorities?	Crimes that are high value (e.g., bank robberies) and those involving violence	Whatever problems disturb the community most.
What, specifically, do police deal with?	Incidents	Citizens' problems and concerns.
What determines the effectiveness of police?	Response times	Public cooperation.
What view do police take of service calls?	Deal with them only if there is no real police work to do	Vital function and great opportunity.
What is police professionalism?	Swift effective response to serious crime	Keeping close to the community.
What kind of intelligence is most important?	Crime intelligence (study of particular crimes or series of crimes)	Criminal intelligence (information about the activities of individuals or groups).
What is the essential nature of police accountability?	Highly centralized; governed by rules, regulations, and policy directives; accountable to the law	Emphasis on local accountability to community needs.
What is the role of headquarters?	To provide the necessary rules	To preach organizational valuesand policy directives.
What is the role of the press liaison department?	To keep the "heat" off operational officers so they can get on with the job	To coordinate an essential channel of communication with the community.
How do the police regard prosecutions?	As an important goal	As one tool among many.

Source: Malcolm K. Sparrow, Implementing Community Policing (National Institute of Justice, Washington, DC: U.S. Department of Justice, 1988), pp. 8–9.

Community policing is a two-way street. It not only requires the police to be aware of community needs, it also mandates both involvement and crime-fighting action on the part of citizens themselves. As Detective Tracie Harrison of the Denver, Colorado, police department explains it, "When the neighborhood takes stock in their community and they're serious they don't want crime, then you start to see crime go down. . . . They're basically fed up and know the police can't do it alone."[28]

Creative approaches to policing have produced a number of innovative programs in recent years. In the early 1980s, for example, Houston's DART (Directed Area Responsibility Teams) Program emphasized problem-oriented policing; the Baltimore County, Maryland, police department began project COPE (Citizen Oriented Police Enforcement) in 1982; and Denver, Colorado, initiated its Community Service Bureau—one of the first major community-policing programs. By the late 1980s, Jerome H. Skolnick and David Bayley's study of six American cities, entitled *The New Blue Line: Police Innovation in Six American Cities*,[29] documented the growing strength of community-police cooperation throughout the nation, giving further credence to the continuing evolution of service-oriented styles of policing.

Police departments throughout the country continue to join the community-policing bandwagon. In April 1993, the city of Chicago launched a new comprehensive community-policing program called CAPS (Chicago's Alternative Policing Strategy). The Chicago plan uses rapid response teams composed of roving officers to handle emergencies, while many other officers have been put on permanent beats where they are highly visible throughout the city, with the avowed goal of maintaining and heightening citizens' perceptions of a police presence in their neighborhoods. Central to the CAPS program are monthly "beat meetings" between patrol officers and members of local neighborhoods. District Neighborhood Relations Offices provide an additional channel for communications between the police department and members of the public. CAPS actively brings other city agencies into the process of community-order maintenance, tearing down deserted buildings, towing away abandoned cars, erasing graffiti, improving street lighting, and removing pay phones frequented by drug dealers. "Most of all," says Chicago Mayor Richard M. Daley, "we've enlisted the active participation of the people of Chicago. We have formed citizen advisory councils to track court cases and address other community issues that contribute to crime. . . . CAPS only works when people get involved."[30]

The CAPS program also makes innovative use of cutting-edge technology. At the start of the program, citywide cellular service providers Ameritech and Cellular One developed a plan to equip Chicago police officers and selected community members with cellular phones and voice mail to facilitate communication, and Chicago's high-tech Emergency Communications Center improved the department's response to emergency calls for police service. As Matt L. Rodriguez, who was superintendent of police for the city of Chicago at the time CAPS was initiated, explained it: "When most people think of community policing, they tend to focus on the interpersonal aspects of this new strategy—beat officers working with individual residents to address neighborhood problems. This type of personal partnership is certainly critical to CAPS. . . . In Chicago, however, we have also invested heavily in the technological aspects of community policing. We are using technology to strengthen the partnership between police and community and to help us work together on identifying and solving crime problems in our neighborhoods."[31]

Evaluations of CAPS conducted in 1995 and 1996[32] found that the program had "improved the lives of residents in virtually every area."[33] Survey-based measures showed crime-related problems declining after CAPS implementation, and official crime statistics continue to show a steady decline in major crimes committed in Chicago.[34] Residents also report that street drug dealing, shootings, violence by gangs, and robbery victimization have all declined since CAPS has been implemented, although it is difficult to conclude from the evaluations that the decline has been entirely due to CAPS. The study did report conclusively, however, that city residents have experienced a significant increase in optimism about police services since CAPS began, especially in the area of police responsiveness to neighborhood concerns. Learn more about CAPS via **WebExtra!** 4-1 at CJToday.com.

In 1994, in another example of the continuing move toward community policing, the Los Angeles Police Department began helping residents focus on problems that provide a breeding ground for crime. Throughout the city, LAPD officers began to help find jobs for

teenagers, assist tenants in getting landlords to repair run-down rental property, and accompany citizen patrols in high-drug areas. The department also developed a "Community Enhancement Request" form that "enables an officer to request specific services from city agencies to handle conditions that may result in crime or community decay."[35] Their efforts appear to be paying off. FBI crime statistics released a year after the program began showed that major crimes in Los Angeles fell by 12 percent. Major crimes in Los Angeles, as in most other American cities, continue to decline steadily into the present day.[36] Today, the LAPD fields 18 Community-Police Advisory Boards (CPABs), serving the various geographic areas in which the department operates. A CPAB is comprised of members from residential and business communities who live or work in a particular geographic area. CPABs serve to provide advice to LAPD commanding officers in their respective areas, and to provide community members with a voice in the policing of their communities.[37]

Although community-policing programs began in the nation's metropolitan areas, the spirit of such programs, which centers on "community engagement and problem solving," has since spread to rural areas. Sheriff's departments that operate community-policing programs sometimes refer to them as "neighborhood-oriented policing" in recognition of the decentralized nature of rural communities. A report on neighborhood-oriented policing by the Bureau of Justice Assistance says that "[t]he stereotypical view is that police officers in rural areas naturally work more closely with the public than do officers in metropolitan areas."[38] Such a view, warns BJA, may not be entirely accurate, and rural departments would do well "to recognize that considerable diversity exists among rural communities and rural law enforcement agencies." Hence, as in metropolitan areas, effective community policing requires involvement of all members of the community in problem identification and problem solving.

The emphasis on community policing continues to grow. Title I of the Violent Crime Control and Law Enforcement Act of 1994, known as the Public Safety Partnership and Community Policing Act of 1994, highlighted the role of community policing in combating crime nationwide and made funding available for (among other things) "increas[ing] the number of law enforcement officers involved in activities that are focused on interaction with members of the community on proactive crime control and prevention by redeploying officers to such activities." The avowed purposes of the Community Policing Act were to (1) substantially increase the number of law enforcement officers interacting directly with members of the community (through a funded program known as "cops on the beat"); (2) provide additional and more effective training to law enforcement officers in order to enhance their problem-solving, service, and other skills needed in interacting with members of the community; (3) encourage the development and implementation of innovative programs to permit members of the community to assist local law enforcement agencies in the prevention of crime in the community; and (4) encourage the development of new technologies to assist local law enforcement agencies in reorienting the emphasis of their activities from reacting to crime to preventing crime.

In response to the 1994 law, the U.S. Department of Justice created the Office of Community Oriented Policing Services (COPS). The COPS Office administers funds necessary to add 100,000 community-policing officers to our nation's streets—the number originally targeted by law. On May 12, 1999, the U.S. Department of Justice and COPS reached an important milestone by funding the 100,000th officer ahead of schedule and under budget. Although the Community Policing Act provided COPS funding only through 2000, Congress has continued to fund COPS—making another $500 million available for the hiring of an additional 50,000 officers.[39]

About the same time the Violent Crime Control and Law Enforcement Act was passed, the Community Policing Consortium, based in Washington, D.C., began operations. The Consortium, which is administered and funded by the U.S. Department of Justice's Bureau of Justice Assistance, provides a forum for training and information exchange in the area of community policing. Members of the Consortium include the International Association of Chiefs of Police (IACP), the National Sheriff's Association (NSA), the Police Executive Research Forum (PERF), the Police Foundation, and the National Organization of Black Law Enforcement Executives (NOBLE). Visit the Community Policing Consortium via WebExtra! 4-2 at CJToday.com.

Critique of Community Policing

Unfortunately, problems remain in the community-policing area.[40] For one thing, there is evidence that not all police officers or police managers are ready to accept nontraditional images of police work. Many are loathe to take on new responsibilities as service providers whose role is increasingly defined by community needs and less by strict interpretation of the law. As one writer, a police sergeant with a Ph.D. in sociology, puts it, "It is an unrealistic leap of faith to presume that the police institution has the resources or capability to carry on all that its newly defined function will demand of it. . . . There is no valid reason for the police to take on all of these responsibilities other than what appears to be a tacit argument that the agency of last resort is the only one that can be held strictly accountable to the public."[41] In this writer's view, the police, once their role is broadly defined by community needs, become a kind of catchall agency, or "agency of last resort," required to deal with problems ranging from handling the homeless to "worrying about the small mountains of trash on the all-too-many empty lots that once housed people and businesses."

A New York City police officer offers yet another criticism: "If we make the goals of community policing impossible to achieve, we doom the undertaking to failure. If we overwhelm police administrators with the enormity and vagueness of their proposed function, they will resist all attempts at reform."[42] He adds, "The notion of allowing the 'community' to participate in defining the police role is ill-conceived, and the most potentially explosive idea associated with community policing. . . . If we follow the proposal that the police function is now anything the community defines it to be, it will become virtually impossible for police departments to accomplish any goals."[43]

Some authors have warned that the **police subculture** is so committed to a traditional view of police work, which is focused almost exclusively on crime fighting, that efforts to promote community policing can demoralize an entire department, rendering it ineffective at its basic tasks.[44] As the Independent Commission on the Los Angeles Police Department (the Christopher Commission) found following the "Rodney King riots," "[t]oo many . . . patrol officers view citizens with resentment and hostility; too many treat the public with rudeness and disrespect."[45] Some analysts warn that only when the formal values espoused by today's innovative police administrators begin to match those of rank and file officers can any police organization begin to be high performing in terms of the goals espoused by community police reformers.[46]

Nor are all public officials ready to accept community policing. Recently, for example, New York City Mayor Rudolph W. Giuliani criticized the NYPD Community Police Officer Program (CPOP), saying that it "has resulted in officers doing too much social work and making too few arrests."[47] Similarly, many citizens are not ready to accept a greater involvement of the police in their personal lives. Although the turbulent protest-prone years of the 1960s and early 1970s are but a memory, some groups remain suspicious of the police. No matter how inclusive community-policing programs become, it is doubtful that the gap between the police and the public will ever be entirely bridged. The police role of restraining behavior which violates the law will always produce friction between police departments and some segments of the community.

Interestingly, as American police departments have outwardly embraced the community-policing model, they have also steadily increased their paramilitary capabilities. While only about 59 percent of police departments had SWAT (Special Weapons and Tactics) teams in 1982, for example, approximately 90 percent had such units by 1995. Moreover, a 1997 survey of police departments nationwide showed that 20 percent of departments without such a unit said they are planning to establish one. Hence, as the survey authors observe, "[t]hese findings reflect the aggressive turn many law enforcement agencies are assuming behind the rhetoric of community and problem-oriented policing reforms."[48]

If police agencies are to retain their relevance, however, it is likely that they will need to embrace community-policing principles. In an intriguing 1997 article,[49] William F. Walsh, director of the Southern Police Institute at the University of Louisville, "posits that policing has reached an important crossroads with organizational managers dividing their support between traditional [and] community/problem solving operational models." In order for the police to remain valuable within the society they serve, says Walsh, they must adapt their

Police Subculture

A particular set of values, beliefs, and acceptable forms of behavior characteristic of American police and with which the police profession strives to imbue new recruits.

"The ability of the police to fulfill their sacred trust will improve as a lucid sense of ethical standards is developed."

—*Patrick V. Murphy, former Commissioner of the NYPD*

methods and their strategies to the political, social, and economic trends of emerging postindustrial society. "Community policing," Walsh writes, "requires the empowerment of patrol officers and operational supervisors who are being charged with the responsibility of developing solutions to community problems." Hence, community policing represents a shift in organizational power; that is, a movement away from centralized command and control. Walsh conceives of this shift in power as one leading to the creation of what he calls "learning organizations" staffed with "knowledge workers"—terms derived from organizational theory. "In an increasingly dynamic and unpredictable world," says Walsh, "learning organizations with the flexibility and responsiveness to adapt will be the ones most able to effectively fulfill their purpose." Information gathering and processing will emerge as the core technologies of modern police departments. As gatherers and users of information, police officers will become knowledge workers. In short, says Walsh, "the problems of the present and future call for fundamental rethinking of operational strategies if the police are to survive as a viable institution." As a result, predicts Walsh, police training and resource development in the next century "will differ drastically from what we are experiencing now." Others agree. Captain Andrew J. Harvey of the Covina, California, Police Department suggests that "in order to deal with the rapidly changing environment in the twenty-first century, law enforcement's paramilitary hierarchy, with rigid controls and strict chains of command, must give way to a structure that emphasizes network-type communication and flexibility. The traditional organizational pyramid, with the chief at the top and line officers at the bottom, must become inverted."[50] Instead, says Harvey, "the community must sit at the top of the pyramid, followed by line officers, then supervisors, and finally the chief." Effective police administrators of the future, says Harvey, "will be consensus builders and agents of change." These leaders will look to the future, "anticipating trends while they perform day-to-day tasks."

Scientific Police Management

In 1969, with passage of the Omnibus Crime Control and Safe Streets Act, the U.S. Congress created the Law Enforcement Assistance Administration. LEAA was charged with combating crime via the expenditure of huge amounts of money in support of crime prevention and crime reduction programs. Some have compared the philosophy establishing LEAA to that which supported the American space program's goal of landing people on the moon: "Put enough money into whatever problem there is, and it will be solved!" Unfortunately, the crime problem was more difficult to address than the challenge of a moon landing; even after the expenditure of nearly $8 billion, LEAA had not come close to its goal. In 1982 LEAA expired when Congress refused it further funding.

The legacy of LEAA is an important one for police managers, however. The research-rich years of 1969 to 1982, supported largely through LEAA funding, have left a plethora of scientific findings of relevance to police administration and, more importantly, have established a tradition of program evaluation within police management circles. This tradition, which is known as **scientific police management,** is a natural outgrowth of LEAA's insistence that any funded program had to contain a plan for its evaluation. Scientific police management means the application of social scientific techniques to the study of police administration for the purpose of increased effectiveness, reduced frequency of citizen complaints, and enhancing the efficient use of available resources. The heyday of scientific police management occurred in the 1970s, when federal monies were far more readily available to support such studies than they are today.

LEAA was not alone in funding police research during the 1970s. On July 1, 1970, the Ford Foundation announced the start of a Police Development Fund totaling $30 million, to be spent over the next five years on police departments to support major crime-fighting strategies. This funding led to the establishment of the Police Foundation, which continues to exist today with the mission of "foster[ing] improvement and innovation in American policing."[51] Police Foundation-sponsored studies over the past 20 years have added to the growing body of scientific knowledge which concerns itself with policing.

Federal support for criminal justice research and evaluation continues today under the National Institute of Justice (NIJ) and the Bureau of Justice Statistics (BJS), both a part of

Scientific Police Management

The application of social scientific techniques to the study of police administration for the purpose of increasing effectiveness, reducing the frequency of citizen complaints, and enhancing the efficient use of available resources.

CRIME IN THE NEWS

Study: Blacks Distrust Police

WASHINGTON (APBNews.com)—Blacks across the country are more likely to be dissatisfied with the police in their cities than white residents, according to a study released today by the U.S. Department of Justice.

Overall, 24 percent of blacks polled in 12 cities across the country expressed dissatisfaction with police, while only 10 percent of white residents polled said they were dissatisfied.

While the numbers ranged from city to city, blacks in some places were three to four times more likely than their white neighbors to express dissatisfaction.

In Knoxville, Tenn., 37 percent of blacks expressed dissatisfaction with the police, compared to 9 percent of whites. In Chicago, 31 percent of blacks expressed dissatisfaction, compared to 11 percent of whites.

Using Study to Improve Training

Titled "Criminal Victimization and Perceptions of Community Safety in 12 Cities, 1998," the study polled 800 people in each city from February to May 1998. The Department of Justice's Community Oriented Policing Services, an office that helps local police departments set up crime prevention and local patrol programs, commissioned the study.

"We certainly are looking at the study as one of many tools to improve the training and resources we offer law enforcement agencies and community-oriented policing programs," said Dan Pfeiffer, a spokesman for the Community Oriented Policing Services office.

The study focused on residents of Chicago; Kansas City, Mo.; Knoxville, Tenn.; Los Angeles; Madison, Wis.; New York; San Diego; Savannah, Ga.; Spokane, Wash.; Springfield, Ma.; Tucson, Ariz.; and Washington.

Lawsuits Claim Racial Profiling

The study comes at a time when relations between police and minorities have been strained amid allegations that departments across the county unfairly target minorities. After several unarmed black motorists sued the New Jersey State Police for shooting at their van, the state admitted to racial profiling, or pulling over drivers based on race. Lawsuits in Maryland, Oklahoma and Illinois make the same claim against police there.

In New York City, two incidents of alleged police brutality led to outrage in black and Latino communities, massive protests and an investigation into the Police Department by the U.S. Commission on Civil Rights.

In August 1997, four police officers allegedly sexually assaulted Haitian immigrant Abner Louima, in a police station bathroom. In February earlier this year, four officers shot and killed Amadou Diallo, an unarmed African immigrant, in a barrage of 41 bullets.

Study Underestimates, Say Critics

In this atmosphere of distrust, some said the study greatly underestimated the dissatisfaction blacks feel toward police.

By focusing the study on incidents of crime, which have become less frequent, the study glossed over the resentment created by racial profiling and police misconduct, said Norman Siegel, the director of the New York Civil Liberties Union and a frequent critic of the New York Police Department.

"I think that the numbers from the Justice Department are not credible and the only thing I can think of is that the questionnaire was geared toward the reduction in crime in America and the methodology and questioning was focused on that aspect of the job performance of the police," Siegel said.

In a poll released Wednesday by Connecticut's Quinnipiac College on the subject of police fairness, 62 percent of blacks in New York state said they disapproved of the job done by police, compared to 15 percent of whites. Eighty-three percent of blacks said the police treated blacks more harshly, while 44 percent of whites held the same opinion.

'Public Perception of Police Response'

One police official said such studies only reflect a mistaken perception of poor police work.

"Everybody sees things through their own particular set of circumstances," said Dick Cottam, a spokesman for the Police Department in Spokane, Wash., one of the cities covered in today's study. "It's not necessarily indicative of police response. It's indicative of public perception of police response."

Source: Hans H. Chen, "Study: Blacks Distrust Police," APB News (www.apbnews.com), June 3, 1999. Reprinted with permission.

the Office of Justice Assistance, Research, and Statistics (OJARS). OJARS was created by Congress in 1980 and functions primarily as a clearinghouse for criminal justice statistics and information. The National Criminal Justice Reference Service (NCJRS), a part of NIJ, is available to assist researchers nationwide in locating information applicable to their research projects. "Custom searches" of the NCJRS computer database can be done online and can yield voluminous information in most criminal justice subject areas. NIJ also publishes a series of informative reports, on a monthly basis (*NIJ Reports*), which serve to keep criminal justice practitioners and researchers informed about recent findings.

Exemplary Projects

Beginning in 1973 LEAA established the Exemplary Projects Program designed to recognize outstanding innovative efforts to combat crime and provide assistance to crime victims, so that such initiatives might serve as models for the nation. One project which won exemplary status early in the program was the Street Crimes Unit of the New York City Police Department. The SCU used officers disguised as potential mugging victims and put them in areas where they were most likely to be attacked. In its first year, the SCU made nearly 4,000 arrests and averaged a successful conviction rate of around 80 percent. Perhaps the most telling statistic was the "average officer days per arrest." The SCU invested only 8.2 days in each arrest, whereas the department average for all uniformed officers was 167 days.[52]

Many other programs were supported and evaluated. The Hidden Cameras Project in Seattle, Washington, was one of those. The project utilized cameras hidden in convenience stores, which were triggered when a "trip" bill located in the cash register drawer was removed. Clearance rates for robberies of businesses with hidden cameras were twice that of other similar businesses. Conviction rates for photographed robbers were shown to be over twice those of suspects arrested for robbing non-camera-equipped stores. Commercial robbery in Seattle decreased by 38 percent in the year following the start of the project.

The Kansas City Experiment

By far the most famous application of social research principles to police management was the Kansas City Preventive Patrol Experiment.[53] Sponsored by the Police Foundation, the results of this year-long study were published in 1974. The study divided the southern part of Kansas City into 15 areas. Five of these beats were patrolled in the usual fashion. Another five beats experienced a doubling of patrol activities and had twice the normal number of patrol officers assigned to them. The final third of the beats received a novel "treatment" indeed—no patrols were assigned to them and no uniformed officers entered that part of the city unless they were called. The program was kept something of a secret, and citizens were unaware of the difference between the patrolled and "unpatrolled" parts of the city.

The results of the Kansas City experiment were surprising. Records of "preventable crimes," those toward which the activities of patrol were oriented—such as burglary, robbery, auto theft, larceny, and vandalism—showed no significant differences in rate of occurrence among the three experimental beats. Similarly, citizens didn't seem to notice the change in patrol patterns in the two areas where patrol frequency was changed. Surveys conducted at the conclusion of the experiment showed no difference among citizens in the three areas as to their fear of crime before and after the study.

The 1974 study can be summed up in the words of the author of the final report: "The whole idea of riding around in cars to create a feeling of omnipresence just hasn't worked. . . . Good people with good intentions tried something that logically should have worked, but didn't."[54]

A second Kansas City study focused on "response time."[55] It found that even consistently fast police response to citizen reports of crime had little effect on either citizen satisfaction with the police or on the arrest of suspects. The study uncovered the fact that most reports made to the police came only after a considerable amount of time had passed. Hence, the police were initially handicapped by the timing of the report, and even the fastest police response was not especially effective.

"Effective police work in the emerging society will depend less on the holster and more on the head."

—Alvin Toffler

TABLE 4-2 ■ Scientific Studies in Law Enforcement

YEAR	STUDY NAME	FOCUS
1999	National Evaluation of Weed and Seed Programs	A study of "weed and seed" programs in eight states showed that those based on participatory decision-making approaches worked best.
1998	Community Policing in Action (Indianapolis)	Cooperation between police and citizens created a feeling of neighborhood security.
1994	The Kansas City Gun Experiment	Supplemental police patrol to reduce gun crime.
1992	The New York City Police Department's Cadet Corps Study	Level of education among officers and hiring of minority officers.
1992	Metro-Dade Spouse Abuse Experiment Replication	Replication of the 1984 Minneapolis study (but conducted in Florida).
1991	Quality Policing in Madison, Wisconsin management.	Community policing and participatory police
1990	Minneapolis "Hot Spot" Patrolling	Intensive patrol of problem areas.
1987	Newport News (Virginia) Problem-Oriented Policing	Police solutions to community crime problems.
1986	Crime Stoppers: A National Evaluation	Media crime reduction programs.
1986	Reducing Fear of Crime in Houston and Newark	Strategies for fear reduction among urban populations.
1984	Minneapolis Domestic Violence Experiment	Effective police action in domestic violence situations.
1981	Newark Foot Patrol Experiment	Costs versus benefits of foot patrol.
1977	Cincinnati Team Policing Experiment	Team versus traditional policing.
1977	Patrol Staffing in San Diego	One- versus two-officer units.
1976	Police Response Time (Kansas City)	Citizen satisfaction with police response.
1976	The Police and Interpersonal Conflict	Police intervention in domestic and other disputes.
1976	Managing Investigations	Detective/patrol officer teams.
1976	Kansas City Peer Review Panel	Improving police behavior.
1974	Kansas City Patrol Study	Effectiveness of police patrol.

The Kansas City study has been credited with beginning the now established tradition of scientific police evaluation. Patrick V. Murphy, former police commissioner in New York City and past president of the Police Foundation, said the Kansas City study "ranks among the very few *major* social experiments ever to be completed."[56] It, and other scientific studies of special significance to law enforcement, are summarized in Table 4-2.

Effects of the Kansas City Study on Patrol

The Kansas City studies greatly impacted managerial assumptions about the role of preventive patrol and traditional strategies for responding to citizen calls for assistance. As Joseph Lewis, then director of evaluation at the Police Foundation, said, "I think that now almost everyone would agree that almost anything you do is better than random patrol. . . ."[57]

While some basic assumptions about patrol were called into question by the Kansas City studies, patrol remains the backbone of police work. New patrol strategies for the effective utilization of human resources have led to various kinds of **directed patrol** activities. One form of directed patrol varies the number of officers involved in patrolling according to time of day or on the basis of frequency of reported crimes within areas. The idea is to put the most officers where and when crime is most prevalent.

Other cities have prioritized calls for service,[58] ordering a quick police response only when crimes are in progress or where serious crimes have occurred. Less-significant offenses, such as minor larcenies or certain citizen complaints, are handled through the mail or by having citizens come to the police station to make a report. Wilmington, Delaware, was one of the first cities to make use of split-force patrol, in which only a part of the patrol force performed routine patrol.[59] The remainder were assigned the duty of responding to calls for service, taking reports, and conducting investigations.

Recent Studies

Early scientific studies of policing, such as the Kansas City Patrol experiment, were designed to identify and probe some of the basic, and often taken for granted, assumptions that guided police work throughout the twentieth century. The initial response to many such studies was, "Why should we study that? Everybody knows the answer already!" As in the case of the Kansas City study, however, it soon became obvious that conventional wisdom was not always correct. The value of applying evaluative techniques to police work can also be seen in the following, more recent, examples:

- The 1999 National Evaluation of Weed and Seed programs focused on programs in eight states. It found that effectiveness of the Weed and Seed philosophy (a community-based anticrime approach that links intensified geographically targeted law enforcement efforts by police and prosecutors with local neighborhood improvement initiatives and human service programs) varied considerably. Programs that worked best were those that relied on bottom-up, participatory decision-making approaches, especially when combined with efforts to build capacity and partnerships among local organizations.[60]

- The 1994 Kansas City "gun experiment" was designed to "learn whether vigorous enforcement of existing gun laws could reduce gun crime." The Kansas City Police Department's "weed and seed" program targeted areas designated as "hot spots" within the city. These were locations identified by computer analysis as having the most gun-related crimes within the metropolitan area. A special gun detection unit was assigned to the area, and guns were removed from citizens following searches incident to arrest for other (non-gun-related) crimes, traffic stops, and as the result of other legal stop-and-frisk activities. While the program was in operation, gun crimes declined by 49 percent in the target area, while they increased slightly in a comparison area. Drive-by shootings, which dropped from seven (in the six months prior to the program) to only one (following implementation of the program), were particularly affected.[61]

- The 1984 Minneapolis domestic violence experiment was the first scientifically engineered social experiment to test the impact of the use of arrest (versus alternative forms of disposition) upon crime.[62] In this case, the crime in focus was violence in the home environment. Investigators found that offenders who were arrested were less likely to commit repeat offenses than those who were handled in some other fashion. A Police Foundation—sponsored 1992 study of domestic violence in the Metro-Dade (Florida) area reinforced the Minneapolis findings, but found that the positive effect of arrest applied almost solely to those who were employed.

- A fifth example of modern scientific police management comes from Newport News, Virginia.[63] In the late 1980s, the police in Newport News decided to test traditional incident-driven policing against a new approach called problem-oriented policing. Incident-driven policing mobilizes police forces to respond to citizen complaints and offenses reported by citizens. It is what the Newport News police called "the standard method for delivering police services." Problem-oriented polic-ing, on the other hand, was developed in Newport News to identify critical crime problems in the community and to address effectively the underlying causes of crime. For example, one identified problem involved thefts from vehicles parked in the Newport News shipbuilding yard. As many as 36,000 cars were parked in those lots during the day. Applying the principles of problem-oriented policing, Newport News officers sought to explore the dimensions of the problem. After identifying theft-prone lots and a small group of frequent offenders, officers arrested one sus-pect in the act of breaking into a vehicle. That suspect provided the information police were seeking: It turned out that drugs were the real target of the car thieves. "Muscle cars," rock music bumper stickers, and other indicators were used by the thieves as clues to which cars had the highest potential for yielding drugs. The police learned that what seemed to be a simple problem of thefts from automobiles was really a search for drugs by a small group of hard-core offenders. Strategies to address the problem were developed, including wider efforts to reduce illicit drug use throughout the city.

These and other studies have established a new basis for the use of scientific evaluation in police work today. The accumulated wisdom of police management studies can be summed up in the words of Patrick Murphy, who, near retirement as director of the Police Founda-tion, stated five tenets for guiding American policing into the next century:[64]

1. Neighborhood policing programs of all kinds need to be developed, improved, and expanded.
2. More police officers need college- and graduate-level education.
3. There should be more civilianization of police departments. Civilian specialists can add to department operations and release sworn officers for police duties.
4. Departments must continue to become more representative of the communities they serve by recruiting more women and minorities.
5. Restraint in the use of force, especially deadly force, must be increased.

Contemporary Policing: The Individual Officer

Regardless of the official policing style espoused by a department, individual officers retain considerable **discretion** in what they do. Police discretion refers to the exercise of choice by law enforcement officers in the decision to investigate or apprehend, the disposition of sus-pects, the carrying out of official duties, and in the application of sanctions. As one author has observed, "police authority can be, at once, highly specific and exceedingly vague."[65] The determination to stop and question suspects, the choice to arrest, and many other police practices are undertaken solely by individual officers acting in a decision-making capacity. Kenneth Culp Davis says, "The police make policy about what law to enforce, how much to enforce it, against whom, and on what occasions."[66] The discretionary authority exercised by individual law enforcement officers is of potentially greater significance to the individual who has contact with the police than are all department manuals and official policy state-ments combined.

Patrolling officers will often decide against a strict enforcement of the law, preferring instead to handle situations informally. Minor law violations, crimes committed out of the officer's presence for which the victim refuses to file a complaint, and certain violations of the criminal law in which the officer suspects sufficient evidence to guarantee a conviction is lacking may all lead to discretionary action short of arrest. Although the widest exercise of discretion is more likely in routine situations involving relatively less-serious violations of the law, serious and clear-cut criminal behavior may occasionally result in discretionary decisions to avoid an arrest. Drunk driving, possession of controlled substances, and assault are but a few examples of crimes in which on-the-scene officers may decide warnings or referrals are more appropriate than arrest.

Discretion

The exercise of choice by law enforcement agents in the disposition of suspects, in the carrying out of official duties, and in the application of sanctions.

"Pressures—from the community, from peers, from the circumstances in which police find themselves—are intense."
—*James Q. Wilson,* former chairman of the board, the Police Foundation

21st Century CJ

Cybercops

THE TERM *cybercop* was first used in 1997 by the Software Engineering Institute at Carnegie Mellon University in its *Report to the President's Commission on Critical Infrastructure Protection.* "Cybercops," said the report, "are law enforcement personnel whose beat is cyberspace." The day-to-day work of some front-line cybercops is described in the article that follows.

When police "net" a crook these days, cops may be referring to the Internet. There was no escaping the World Wide Web for fugitive Les Rogge, a 56-year-old Seattle bank robber hiding in Guatemala. Or for Catherine Suh, a 27-year-old Chicago murderer on the lam in Hawaii from a 100-year prison sentence. Both were captured this year after tipsters spotted their mugs on "Most Wanted" electronic posters on the Internet.

From Scotland Yard to Edmonds, police have gone online to take a byte out of crime. On the Internet, citizens anonymously report drug dealers to the cyberpolice, check out crime in their neighborhoods, calculate their risk of being murdered and communicate directly with the chief of police.

Police say the Internet is a powerful and versatile law-enforcement tool: communication is immediate and crosses jurisdictional boundaries, information is just a keystroke away and the cost is commonly less than hiring a police officer. "I think it's the most effective money you can spend to prevent crime," said Bill Taylor, crime analyst for the Sacramento Police Department, which has developed one of the nation's most sophisticated Internet police sites. More than 2,000 law-enforcement agencies have gone online, extending the long reach of the law to millions of Internet users, said Ken Reeves, a Microsoft man-

ager who recently established a Web site promoting new technology in law enforcement. "They're creating virtual police," he said.

But even in the land of Microsoft, authorities are struggling to keep up with the technology. Seattle and Bellevue police are just starting to look at going online. King County (Washington) police offer a primitive Internet site that resembles an electronic copy of a police brochure. "Some may say we're being dragged into the 21st century, technologically speaking," said King County police spokesman Jerrell Wills, who readily acknowledges that his Web page lacks content and style. "I'm a police officer, not an artist."

Many small- and medium-sized police departments are taking the lead in Internet technology. Edmonds police offer an electronic site where citizens can look up crime statistics, hiring information, minutes of police–community meetings and tips on crime prevention. Ironically, the information is beyond the reach of the department's own officers, since none of the Edmonds police computers has Internet access. In the border town of Blaine, population 3,150, the police department's crime logs are reported each day on the Internet. A recent cybercrime log included a woman's report of being followed, the citation of an unlicensed driver at the Peace Arch and complaints of in-line skaters obstructing traffic.

It is that kind of timely, detailed information that police have found especially well-suited for the Internet. In Virginia's Roanoke County, for example, citizens can click on a map to find out about the latest crime in their communities. "People in Roanoke County have the right to know what kind of crimes are occur-

ring and where they are occurring so they can take steps to prevent them from happening to them," said Officer Tom Kincaid, who created his department's Web site.

Consultant Kevin Wirth also offers "Crime Online Around the Sound," a Web page that provides detailed maps and charts of major crimes in Seattle and King County.

Some police agencies have expanded their search for fugitives to the World Wide Web. The Internet was credited for helping capture Rogge, the Seattle bank robber discovered in Guatemala, after a 14-year-old neighbor spotted the fugitive's photograph on the FBI's "10 Most Wanted" Web site. A net tipster also led authorities to Hawaii, where convicted Chicago killer Suh was living the high life under the name Tiffani Escada, a police spokeswoman said.

The Internet also has become a popular tool for police to communicate among themselves. Thousands of police officers subscribe to electronic mailing lists and read electronic bulletin boards where they can discuss ethical issues in private and exchange information about firearms, narcotics and other sensitive topics. "These are things you don't want to make public, but you need other professionals to bounce off ideas," said Ira Wilsker, a former police officer who is leading a series of U.S. Department of Justice seminars on law enforcement and the Internet. Run for and by police officers, the computer exchanges often offer information that cannot be found elsewhere, Wilsker said. For example, police raised the alarm on the Internet about illegal use of Rohypnol, the notorious "date rape" sedative, more than a year before warnings about the drug were issued

(Continued)

Cybercops

through official channels, he said. On the philosophy of know thy enemy, Wilsker said police also turn to the Internet as an intelligence source, monitoring online chatter by hate groups, drug users and others who discuss their views on computer news groups. The news groups, though commonly thought of as private communications, are open to public view. The Internet also can be an effective people finder, he said.

For example, more than 90 million people and their telephone numbers and addresses can be found at the Internet site www.switchboard.com, making a nationwide search sometimes as simple as keying in a name, he said. The service is free.

With an address in hand, Wilsker advises police to turn to www.mapquest.com, which in seconds can pinpoint on a map the location of a suspect's home. "We use it for serving warrants where we don't know the area," he said.

Police officers increasingly carry portable computers in their patrol cars, providing quick access to information that could save lives, said Reeves, marketing manager for Microsoft's Justice and Public Safety division. "It's another protective device, just like the bulletproof vest," he said of computer access.

President Clinton also has been promoting the use of computers to

track criminal activity. In June, Clinton called for a national computer register of sexual offenders. Last month, he announced the creation of a federal computer system to trace the illegal sale of guns to youths. "I've been in law enforcement for 25 years, and this is the most powerful law-enforcement tool I have ever seen," Joe Vince, chief of the firearms division of the federal Bureau of Alcohol, Tobacco and Firearms, said of the new gun-tracking system.

These computer networks likely will be off-limits to the public, but most law-enforcement Internet efforts are aimed at opening communications with the public. In Northern California, Placer County citizens are invited to file complaints (or commendations) on the sheriff's department's Internet site. The Web page includes Sheriff Edward Bonner's e-mail address. The department also accepts online crime reports. The 2-year-old Web page, one of the nation's oldest police sites, was introduced to promote community policing, said Sgt. Bill Langton, who designed the Web site. "To make our world a whole lot safer, we have to do it as a community. We can't do it ourselves," he said. Its popularity has exceeded expectations. The Web page last month logged its 20,000th visitor.

While most law-enforcement sites are as dull as a police blotter,

some departments have spiced up their Internet connections with entertaining interactive fare. In Maryland, Baltimore County police offer sound clips of the Heat, the department's all-cop rock 'n' roll band. Nashville police invite users of its Web site to calculate their odds of being raped, robbed, stabbed, beaten or murdered. Scotland Yard provides a historic tour of the world-famous detective agency.

Still, the response to serious attempts at online policing at times has been disappointing. The vast majority of people prefer to deal directly with police than go online to report a crime. Chicago's effort to elicit information about drug dealing over the Internet has drawn only a smattering of responses. Some departments have dropped their most-wanted postings on the Internet because they brought in so few tips.

Despite these shortcomings, police on the Web remain the envy of those just getting started. "I'm going to do my best to copy and plagiarize other people's ideas," said Wills, who views his development of King County's Web page as a long-term investment. "I don't see this as a fad, like the mood ring."

Source: Scott Maier, "Long Arm of Law Is Going Online: Internet Helps Police Do Their Job," Seattle Post-Intelligencer, *August 6, 1996. Reprinted courtesy of* Seattle Post-Intelligencer.

A summation of various studies of police discretion tells us that a number of factors influence the discretionary decisions of individual officers. Some of these factors are as follows:

▪ *Background of the officer.* Law enforcement officers bring to their job all of life's previous experiences. Values shaped through early socialization in family environments, as well as attitudes acquired from ongoing socialization, impact the decisions an officer will make. If the officer has learned prejudice against certain ethnic groups, it is likely that such prejudices will manifest themselves in enforcement decisions. Officers who place a high value on the nuclear family may handle spouse abuse, child abuse, and other forms of domestic disputes in predetermined ways.

☐ *Characteristics of the suspect.* Some officers may treat men and women differently. A police friend of the author's has voiced the belief that women "are not generally bad . . . but when they do go bad, they go very bad." His official treatment of women has been tempered by this belief. Very rarely will this officer arrest a woman, but when he does, he spares no effort to see her incarcerated. Other characteristics of the suspect which may influence police decisions include demeanor, style of dress, and grooming. Belligerent suspects are often seen as "asking for it" and as challenging police authority. Well-dressed suspects are likely to be treated with deference, but poorly groomed suspects can expect less exacting treatment. Suspects sporting personal styles with a message—biker's attire, unkempt beards, outlandish haircuts, and other nonconformist styles—are more likely to be arrested than are others.

☐ *Department policy.* Discretion, while not entirely subject to control by official policy, can be influenced by it. If a department has targeted certain kinds of offenses, or if especially close control of dispatches and communications is held by supervisors who adhere to strict enforcement guidelines, discretionary release of suspects will be quite rare.

☐ *Community interest.* Public attitudes toward certain crimes will increase the likelihood of arrest for suspected offenders. Contemporary attitudes toward crimes involving children—including child sex abuse, the sale of drugs to minors, domestic violence involving children, and child pornography—have all led to increased and strict enforcement of laws governing such offenses across the nation. Communities may identify particular problems affecting them and ask law enforcement to respond. Fayetteville, North Carolina, adjacent to a major military base, was plagued a few years ago by a downtown area notorious for prostitution and massage parlors. Once the community voiced its concern over the problem and clarified its economic impact on the city, the police responded with a series of highly effective arrests, which eliminated massage parlors within the city limits. Departments which require officers to live in the areas they police are operating in recognition of the fact that community interests impact citizens and officers alike.

☐ *Pressures from victims.* Victims who refuse to file a complaint are commonly associated with certain crimes such as spouse abuse, the "robbery" of drug merchants, and assaults on customers of prostitutes. When victims refuse to cooperate with the police, there is often little that can be done. On the other hand, some victims are very vocal in insisting that their victimization be recognized and dealt with. Modern victim's assistance groups, including People Assisting Victims, the Victim's Assistance Network, and others, have sought to keep pressure on police departments and individual investigators to ensure the arrest and prosecution of suspects.

☐ *Disagreement with the law.* Some laws lack a popular consensus. Among them are many victimless offenses, such as homosexuality, lesbianism, drug use, gambling, pornography, and some crimes involving alcohol. Not all of these behaviors are even crimes in certain jurisdictions. Gambling is legal in Atlantic City, New Jersey, on board cruise ships, and in parts of Nevada. Many states have now legalized homosexuality and lesbianism and most forms of sexual behavior between consenting adults. Prostitution is officially sanctioned in portions of Nevada, and some drug offenses have been decriminalized, with offenders being ticketed rather than arrested. Unpopular laws are not likely to bring much attention from law enforcement officers. Sometimes such crimes are regarded as just "part of the landscape" or as the consequence of laws which have not kept pace with a changing society. When arrests do occur, it may be because individuals investigated for more serious offenses were caught in the act of violating an unpopular statute. Drug offenders, for example, arrested in the middle of the night, may be "caught in the act" of an illegal sexual performance when the police break in. Charges may then include "crime against nature," as well as possession or sale of drugs.

■ On the other hand, certain behaviors which are not law violations and which may even be protected by guarantees of free speech may be annoying, offensive, or disruptive according to the normative standards of a community or the personal standards of an officer. When the law has been violated, and the guilty party is known to the officer, the evidence necessary for a conviction in court may be "tainted" or in other ways not usable. Sykes, in recognizing these possibilities, says, "One of the major ambiguities of the police task is that officers are caught between two profoundly compelling moral systems: justice as due process . . . and conversely, justice as righting a wrong as part of defining and maintaining community norms."[67] In such cases, discretionary police activity may take the form of street justice and approach vigilantism.

■ *Available alternatives.* Police discretion can be impacted by the officer's awareness of alternatives to arrest. Community treatment programs, including outpatient drug and alcohol counseling, psychiatric or psychological services, domestic dis-

---

CAREERS IN JUSTICE

Working for the U.S. Secret Service

TYPICAL POSITIONS:

Special agent, Uniformed Division police officers, and special officer. Clerical and administrative positions are also available.

EMPLOYMENT REQUIREMENTS:

Requirements for appointment at GS-5 level include (1) successful completion of the Treasury Enforcement Agent examination; (2) a bachelor's degree from an accredited college or university; (3) excellent physical condition, including at least 20/40 vision in each eye, correctable to 20/20; and (4) successful completion of a thorough background investigation. Appointment at the GS-7 level also requires (1) one additional year of specialized experience, (2) a bachelor's degree with superior academic achievement, or (3) one year of graduate study in a related field (police science, police administration, criminology, law, law enforcement, business administration, accounting, economics, finance, or other directly related fields).

"Superior academic achievement" is defined as meeting one or more of

the following criteria: (1) a B average (3.0 on a 4.0 scale) for all courses completed at time of application or for all courses during the last two years of the undergraduate curriculum, (2) a B+ average (3.5 on a 4.0 scale) for all courses in the major field of study or all courses in the major during the last two years of the undergraduate curriculum, (3) rank in the upper third of the undergraduate class or major subdivision (i.e., school of liberal arts), and (4) membership in an honorary scholastic society that meets the requirements of the Association of College Honor Societies.

Specialized experience is defined as responsible criminal investigative or comparable experience that required (1) the exercise of tact, resourcefulness, and judgment in collecting, assembling, and developing facts, evidence, and other pertinent data through investigative techniques that include personal interviews; (2) the ability to make oral and written reports and presentations of personally conducted or personally directed investigations; and (3) the ability to analyze and evaluate evidence and arrive at sound conclusions.

OTHER REQUIREMENTS:

Valid driver's license, urinalysis test for the presence of illegal drugs prior to appointment, and the ability to qualify for top-secret security clearance.

SALARY:

Special agents are appointed at the GS-5 or GS-7 level, depending on qualifications. A high-cost area supplement ranging from 4 to 16 percent is paid in specified geographic areas.

BENEFITS:

Benefits include (1) 13 days of sick leave annually, (2) 2½ to 5 weeks of annual paid vacation and 10 paid federal holidays each year, (3) federal health and life insurance, and (4) a comprehensive retirement program.

DIRECT INQUIRIES TO:

Chief of Staffing, U.S. Secret Service, Suite 912, 950 H Street, Washington, DC 20001. Phone: (202) 406-5800. Applications are not accepted earlier than nine months prior to graduation. Web site: www.treas.gov/uss.

Source: U.S. Office of Personnel Management.

pute resolution centers, and other options may all be kept in mind by officers looking for a way out of official action.

■ *Personal practices of the officer.* Some officers, because of actions undertaken in their personal lives, view potential law violations more or less seriously than other officers. The police officer who has an occasional marijuana cigarette with friends at a party may be inclined to deal less harshly with minor drug offenders than nonuser officers. The officer who routinely exceeds speed limits while driving the family car may be prone toward lenient action toward speeders encountered while on duty.

Summary

"A successful community policing program also requires officers to be well versed in cultural diversity and competent to perform tasks needed to accomplish their duties. This, obviously, requires considerable training for officers at all levels of the department."
—*Samuel D. Pratcher,*
Chief of Police, Wilmington, Delaware

Contemporary police management has become increasingly scientific, applying the principles and techniques of the social sciences to police organization and administration. At the same time, a strong emphasis on service has led U.S. law enforcement agencies at the local level toward a greater sensitivity to community needs and expectations. Community policing, a concept that has emerged over the past two decades and is now a primary model for police agencies everywhere, stresses the need for an integration of law enforcement activities and local priorities. Community policing is built on the principle that police departments and the communities they serve can work together effectively as partners in the fight against crime.

Not to be forgotten in the idealism surrounding community policing, however, is the huge amount of discretion available to individual officers engaged in the daily work of law enforcement. Such discretion can easily circumvent the best intentions of police administrators and community leaders, or it can embody and uphold the highest principles of both.

Discussion Questions

1. What is community policing? Do you think that community policing offers an important opportunity to improve policing services in the United States? Why or why not?
2. Do you think police officers exercise too much discretion in the performance of their duties? Why or why not? If it is desirable to limit discretion, how would you do it?
3. Describe scientific police management. What scientific studies of the police would you like to see undertaken? Why?

Web Quest!

Visit the National Criminal Justice Reference Service (NCJRS) at www.ncjrs.org. Click on the "Keyword Search" option, then on "help text" in order to view tips on performing effective searches, modifying search queries, and interpreting search results. Write a description of the search techniques available under "Keyword Search," including wildcard and proximity searching, concept, Boolean, and pattern searching. What does the help text suggest you do if you find too much in your search? If you find too little?

Return to the "Keyword Search" page and click "Advanced search." What kinds of advanced searches are available? How can you search for a phrase (as distinguished from a single word)?

Revisit the NCJRS home page and click on "Abstracts Database." What is the Abstracts Database? How does the Abstracts Database differ from the NCJRS full-text collection?

After you have familiarized yourself with searching techniques, put your skills to use by conducting a search of the NCJRS site in order to identify documents on community policing. (*Note:* You may have to develop your own search strategy using other keywords in combination with *community policing* in order to narrow down the results of your search.) What kinds of documents did you find? What conclusions, if any, did you come to about community policing after reading these documents? Would you recommend that every law enforcement agency should have a community-policing program? Why or why not?

Library Extras

The Library Extras! listed here complement the WebExtras! found throughout this chapter. Library Extras! may be accessed on the Web at CJToday.com.

Library Extra! 4-1. *Americans' Views on Crime and Law Enforcement: Survey Findings* (NIJ, 1997).

Library Extra! 4-2. *Community Policing in Action: Lessons from an Observational Study* (NIJ, 1998).

Library Extra! 4-3. "Community Policing: Chicago's Experience," *The National Institute of Justice Journal* (NIJ, April 1999).

Library Extra! 4-4. *Measuring What Matters: Developing Measures of What the Police Do* (NIJ, November 1997).

References

1. "L.A. Police Chief: Treat People Like Customers," *USA Today,* March 29, 1993, p. 13A.
2. James Q. Wilson, *Thinking About Crime* (New York: Basic Books, 1975), p. 99.
3. "Bust 180 Degrees Wrong," *USA Today,* December 1, 1992, p. 3A.
4. Ibid.
5. The elements of this definition draw upon the now-classic work by O. W. Wilson, *Police Administration* (New York: McGraw-Hill, 1950), pp. 2–3.
6. Francis X. Hartmann, "Debating the Evolution of American Policing," *Perspectives on Policing,* no. 5 (Washington, D.C.: National Institute of Justice, November 1988).
7. James Q. Wilson, *Varieties of Police Behavior: The Management of Law and Order in Eight Communities* (Cambridge, MA: Harvard University Press, 1968).
8. Louis A. Radelet, *The Police and the Community* (Encino, CA: Glencoe, 1980).
9. President's Commission on Law Enforcement and Administration of Justice, *The Challenge of Crime in a Free Society* (Washington, D.C.: U.S. Government Printing Office, 1967).
10. Egon Bittner, "Community Relations," in Alvin W. Cohn and Emilio C. Viano, eds., *Police Community Relations: Images, Roles, Realities* (Philadelphia: J. B. Lippincott, 1976), pp. 77–82.
11. Ibid.
12. Charles Hale, *Police Patrol: Operations and Management* (New York: John Wiley, 1981), p. 112.
13. Sam Souryal, *Police Administration and Management* (St. Paul, MN: West, 1977), p. 261.
14. Paul B. Weston, *Police Organization and Management* (Pacific Palisades, CA: Goodyear, 1976), p. 159.
15. Hale, *Police Patrol.*
16. Mark H. Moore and Robert C. Trojanowicz, "Corporate Strategies for Policing," *Perspectives on Policing,* no. 6 (Washington, D.C.: National Institute of Justice, November 1988).
17. Ibid., p. 6.
18. The Community Policing Consortium, "What Is Community Policing," 1995.
19. The Community Policing Consortium, "Community Policing Is Alive and Well," 1995, p. 1.
20. George L. Kelling, *The Newark Foot Patrol Experiment* (Washington, D.C.: Police Foundation, 1981).
21. Robert C. Trojanowicz, "An Evaluation of a Neighborhood Foot Patrol Program," *Journal of Police Science and Administration,* vol. 11 (1983).
22. Bureau of Justice Assistance, *Understanding Community Policing: A Framework for Action* (Washington, D.C.: Bureau of Justice Statistics, 1994), p. 10.
23. Robert C. Trojanowicz and Bonnie Bucqueroux, *Community Policing* (Cincinnati, OH: Anderson, 1990).
24. Moore and Trojanowicz, *Perspectives on Policing,* p. 8.
25. See Jerome H. Skolnick and David H. Bayley, *Community Policing: Issues and Practices Around the World* (Washington, D.C.: National Institute of Justice, 1988), and Jerome H. Skolnick and David H. Bayley, "Theme and Variation in Community Policing," in Norval Morris and Michael Tonry, eds., *Crime and Justice: An Annual Review of Research,* vol. 10 (Chicago: University of Chicago Press, 1988), pp. 1–37.
26. Ibid.
27. William L. Goodbody, "What Do We Expect New-Age Cops to Do?" *Law Enforcement News,* (April 30, 1995), pp. 14, 18.
28. Sam Vincent Meddis and Desda Moss, "Many 'Fed-Up' Communities Cornering Crime," *USA Today,* (May 22, 1995), p. 8A.
29. Jerome H. Skolnick and David H. Bayley, *The New Blue Line: Police Innovation in Six American Cities* (New York: The Free Press, 1986).
30. Richard M. Daley, "A Message from the Mayor," Chicago Police Department's World Wide Web home page, June 9, 1995.
31. Matt L. Rodriguez, "A Message from the Superintendent of Police," Chicago Police Department's World Wide Web home page, June 9, 1995.
32. The Chicago Community Policing Evaluation Consortium, *Community Policing in Chicago: Year Three Evaluation* (Chicago: Illinois Criminal Justice Information Authority, December 1996).
33. The Chicago Community Policing Evaluation Consortium, *Community Policing in Chicago, Year Two: An Interim Report* (Chicago: Illinois Criminal Justice Information Authority, June 1995).
34. For the latest statistics, visit the CAPS program on the World Wide Web at www.ci.chi.il.us/CommunityPolicing. Accessed May 20, 2000.

35. Edwin Meese III, "Community Policing and the Police Officer," *Perspectives on Policing* (Washington, D.C.: National Institute of Justice, January 1993), p. 8.

36. FBI, *Uniform Crime Reports* (Washington, D.C.: U.S. Government Printing Office, various years). See also LAPD crime statistics at www.lapdonline.org/general_information/crime_statistics/crime_statistics_main.htm. Accessed May 20, 2000.

37. To learn more about CPABs, visit the LAPD Community Policing Opportunities Web page at www.lapdonline.org/get_involved/community_policing/community_policing_main.htm. Accessed May 20, 2000.

38. Bureau of Justice Assistance, *Neighborhood-Oriented Policing in Rural Communities: A Program Planning Guide* (Washington, D.C.: BJA, 1994), p. 4.

39. See the COPS Office Web site at www.usdoj.gov/cops. Information in this section comes from www.usdoj.gov/cops/news_info/default.htm. Accessed January 22, 2000.

40. For a good critique of community policing and of the current state of American policing in general, see Malcolm K. Sparrow, Mark H. Moore, and David M. Kennedy, *Beyond 911: A New Era for Policing* (New York: Basic Books, 1990).

41. Goodbody, "What Do We Expect New-Age Cops to Do?"

42. Ibid.

43. Ibid.

44. Malcolm K. Sparrow, "Implementing Community Policing," *Perspectives on Policing,* no. 9 (Washington, D.C.: National Institute of Justice, 1988).

45. "L.A. Police Chief: Treat People Like Customers," *USA Today,* March 29, 1993, p. 13A.

46. Robert Wasserman and Mark H. Moore, "Values in Policing," *Perspectives in Policing,* no. 8 (Washington, D.C.: National Institute of Justice, November 1988), p. 7.

47. "New York City Mayor Sparks Debate on Community Policing," *Criminal Justice Newsletter,* vol. 25, no. 2 (January 18, 1994), p. 1.

48. Peter B. Kraska and Victor E. Kappeler, "Militarizing American Police: The Rise and Normalization of Paramilitary Units," *Social Problems,* vol. 44, no. 1 (February 1997), pp. 1–18.

49. William F. Walsh, "Policing at the Crossroads: Changing Directions for the New Millennium," paper presented at the Academy of Criminal Justice Sciences annual meeting, Louisville, Kentucky, March 1997.

50. Andrew J. Harvey, "Building an Organizational Foundation for the Future," *FBI Law Enforcement Bulletin* (November 1996), pp. 12–17.

51. Thomas J. Deaken, "The Police Foundation: A Special Report," *FBI Law Enforcement Bulletin* (November 1986), p. 2.

52. National Institute of Justice, *The Exemplary Projects Program* (Washington, D.C.: U.S. Government Printing Office, 1982), p. 11.

53. George L. Kelling et al., *The Kansas City Patrol Experiment* (Washington, D.C.: Police Foundation, 1974).

54. Kevin Krajick, "Does Patrol Prevent Crime?" *Police Magazine* (September 1978), quoting Dr. George Kelling.

55. William Bieck and David Kessler, *Response Time Analysis* (Kansas City, MO: Board of Police Commissioners, 1977). See also J. Thomas McEwen et al., *Evaluation of the Differential Police Response Field Test: Executive Summary* (Alexandria, VA: Research Management Associates, 1984), and Lawrence Sherman, "Policing Communities: What Works?" in Michael Tonry and Norval Morris, eds., *Crime and Justice: An Annual Review of Research,* vol. 8 (Chicago: University of Chicago Press, 1986).

56. Ibid., p. 8.

57. Krajick, "Does Patrol Prevent Crime?"

58. Ibid.

59. Ibid.

60. Terence Dunworth and Gregory Mills, "National Evaluation of Weed and Seed" (Washington, D.C.: National Institute of Justice, June 1999).

61. Lawrence W. Sherman, Dennis P. Rogan, and James W. Shaw, "The Kansas City Gun Experiment—NIJ Update," *Research in Brief* (Washington, D.C.: NIJ, November 1994).

62. Lawrence W. Sherman and Richard A. Berk, *Minneapolis Domestic Violence Experiment,* Police Foundation Report #1 (Washington, D.C.: Police Foundation, April 1984).

63. National Institute of Justice, *Newport News Tests Problem-Oriented Policing,* National Institute of Justice Reports (Washington, D.C.: U.S. Government Printing Office, January–February 1987).

64. Adapted from Deakin, "The Police Foundation."

65. Howard Cohen, "Overstepping Police Authority," *Criminal Justice Ethics* (Summer/Fall 1987), pp. 52–60.

66. Kenneth Culp Davis, *Police Discretion* (St. Paul, MN: West, 1975).

67. Gary Sykes, "Street Justice: A Moral Defense of Order Maintenance Policing," *Justice Quarterly,* vol. 3 (1986), pp. 497–512.

CHAPTER 5

Policing: Legal Aspects

"Yeah," the detective mumbled. "Fifteen guys. You might want to think about that. Only two of us." . . . "On the other hand . . ." He shook his head. "Sneaking a bunch of cops into a neighborhood like this is going to be like trying to sneak the sun past a rooster." . . . As he started up the stairs, Angelo reached not for his gun but for his wallet. He took out a Chase Manhattan calendar printed on a supple but firm slip of plastic. He flicked the card at Rand. "I'll open the door with this. You step in and freeze them."

"Jesus Christ, Angelo," the agent almost gasped. "We can't do that. We haven't got a warrant."

"Don't worry about it, kid," Angelo said, drawing up to the second door on the right on the second floor. "It ain't a perfect world."

—Larry Collins and Dominique Lapierre, The Fifth Horseman [1]

CHAPTER OUTLINE

- The Abuse of Police Power
- Individual Rights
- Search and Seizure
- Arrest
- The Intelligence Function

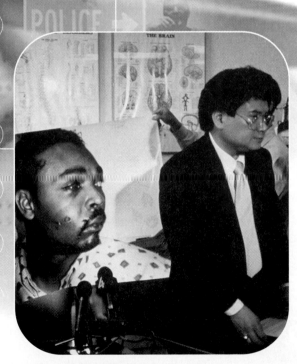

—Venegez, SIPA Press.

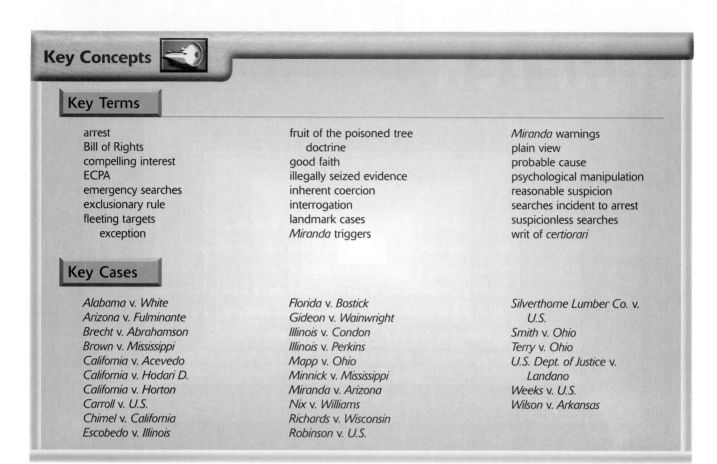

Key Concepts

Key Terms

arrest
Bill of Rights
compelling interest
ECPA
emergency searches
exclusionary rule
fleeting targets
    exception

fruit of the poisoned tree
    doctrine
good faith
illegally seized evidence
inherent coercion
interrogation
landmark cases
Miranda triggers

Miranda warnings
plain view
probable cause
psychological manipulation
reasonable suspicion
searches incident to arrest
suspicionless searches
writ of *certiorari*

Key Cases

Alabama v. *White*
Arizona v. *Fulminante*
Brecht v. *Abrahamson*
Brown v. *Mississippi*
California v. *Acevedo*
California v. *Hodari D.*
California v. *Horton*
Carroll v. *U.S.*
Chimel v. *California*
Escobedo v. *Illinois*

Florida v. *Bostick*
Gideon v. *Wainwright*
Illinois v. *Condon*
Illinois v. *Perkins*
Mapp v. *Ohio*
Minnick v. *Mississippi*
Miranda v. *Arizona*
Nix v. *Williams*
Richards v. *Wisconsin*
Robinson v. *U.S.*

Silverthorne Lumber Co. v.
    U.S.
Smith v. *Ohio*
Terry v. *Ohio*
U.S. Dept. of Justice v.
    Landano
Weeks v. *U.S.*
Wilson v. *Arkansas*

The Abuse of Police Power

Hear the author discuss this chapter at **cjtoday.com**

What some people believe was a hate crime committed by New York City police officers made national headlines in 1999. During the incident, four white officers unleashed a barrage of 41 gunshots at Amadou Diallo, a 22-year-old West African immigrant.[2] Diallo, who was black, was struck by 19 of the 41 bullets and died at the scene. The incident began when officers of a special NYPD street crimes unit were searching for a rape suspect in a Bronx neighborhood. They came across Diallo standing in the doorway of his apartment building. Although accounts of what happened next vary, attorneys for the officers told reporters that Diallo resembled the suspect they were looking for. When the officers yelled "freeze" Diallo apparently did not comply, but instead reached into his pocket. The officers later indicated that they fired because they thought he was reaching for a gun. Diallo's shocked friends, however, later said that he spoke little English, and may have been reaching for identification. The seemingly excessive use of firepower resulted in charges of second-degree murder being brought against the officers involved. In February 2000 a state jury found the officers innocent of any criminal wrongdoing. Read more about the Diallo case at WebExtra! 5-1 at CJToday.com

The Diallo incident was the latest in a series of alleged abuses committed by NYPD officers. Earlier, in August 1997, a storm of protest swirled around NYPD police officers serving Brooklyn's 70th Precinct. In the midst of the storm stood four officers accused of savagely beating and sexually assaulting Abner Louima, a 30-year-old Haitian immigrant, in a station house bathroom. Louima, a black man who worked as a security guard, had been arrested on charges of assaulting a police officer following an early morning scuffle outside a city nightclub. He claimed that after his arrival at the station house a white officer, Justin Volpe, beat him nearly senseless, then sodomized him with the handle of a toilet plunger, while another white officer, Charles Schwarz, held him down. Louima underwent surgery to repair a torn rectum and gall bladder and was hospitalized for weeks following the incident.[3] In 1999 Volpe, the lead defendant in the case, pleaded guilty to charges stemming from the beating. Schwarz was convicted separately in a federal trial of violating Louima's civil rights. Three other NYPD officers were acquitted in the racially charged case.[4]

While the activities of Volpe and Schwarz were despicable, national publicity surrounding the incident was considerably less intense than that which centered on the videotaped 1991 beating of black motorist Rodney King by Los Angeles police officers. King, an unemployed 25-year-old black man, was stopped by LAPD officers for an alleged violation of motor vehicle laws. Police said King had been speeding and refused to stop for a pursuing patrol car. Officers claimed to have clocked King's 1988 Hyundai at 115 MPH on suburban Los Angeles' Foothill Freeway—even though the car's manufacturer later said the vehicle was not capable of speeds over 100 MPH and recordings of police radio communications surrounding the incident never mentioned excessive speed.

Eventually King did stop, but then officers of the Los Angeles Police Department attacked him—shocking him twice with electronic stun guns and striking him with nightsticks and fists. Kicked in the stomach, face, and back, he was left with 11 skull fractures, missing teeth, a crushed cheekbone, and a broken ankle. A witness told reporters she heard King begging officers to stop the beating, but that they "were all laughing, like they just had a party."[5] King eventually underwent surgery for brain injuries.

Twenty-five police officers—21 from the LAPD, 2 California Highway Patrol officers, and 2 school district officers—were involved in the incident. Four of them, who were later indicted, beat King as the other 21 watched. Los Angeles County District Attorney Ira Reiner called the behavior of the officers who watched "irresponsible and offensive," but not criminal.[6]

There are two important differences between the King incident and the other crime stories related in this textbook: (1) this time the criminals wore police uniforms, and (2) the entire incident was captured on videotape by an amateur photographer from a nearby balcony who was trying out his new night-sensitive video camera. The two-minute videotape

"The calculus of reasonableness must embody allowance for the fact that police officers are often forced to make split-second judgments—in circumstances that are tense, uncertain, and rapidly evolving—about the amount of force that is necessary in a particular situation."

—**Graham v. Connor,** *490 U.S. 386, 396–397 (1989).*

Amadou Diallo, the 22-year-old West African immigrant who died in a hail of police gunfire in New York City in 1999. Four white officers fired 41 gunshots at Diallo, apparently believing that he was wanted in a rape case. Diallo, who was unarmed, was struck 19 times and died at the scene. Charges of second-degree murder were filed against the officers.
AP/Wide World Photos.

was repeatedly broadcast over national television and picked up by hundreds of local TV stations. The furor that erupted over the tape led to the ouster of LAPD Chief Daryl Gates and initiated a Justice Department review of law enforcement practices across the country.[7] Some defended the police, citing the "war zone" mentality of today's inner-city crime fighters as fostering a violent mind-set. Officers involved in the beating claimed that King, at 6 feet 3 inches and 225 pounds, appeared strung out on PCP and that he and his two companions made officers feel threatened.[8]

"[The police] are not perfect; we don't sign them up on some far-off planet and bring them into police service. They are products of society, and let me tell you, the human product today often is pretty weak."

—*Former LAPD Chief Daryl Gates*

In 1992 a California jury found the four police defendants not guilty—a verdict that resulted in days of rioting across Los Angeles. A year later, however, in the spring of 1993 two of the officers, Sergeant Stacey Koon and Officer Laurence Powell, were found guilty by a jury in federal court of denying King his constitutional right "not to be deprived of liberty without due process of law, including the right to be . . . free from the intentional use of unreasonable force."[9] Later that year both were sentenced to two and one-half years in prison, far less than might have been expected under federal sentencing guidelines. They were released from prison in December of 1995, and a three-year-long court battle over whether federal sentencing guideline provisions were violated during sentencing was resolved in the officers' favor in 1996. Officers Theodore Briseno and Timothy Wind were exonerated at the federal level.

In 1994 King settled a civil suit against the city of Los Angeles for a reported $3.8 million. Observers later concluded that King himself was not a model citizen. At the time of the beating he was on parole after having served time in prison for robbery. Following the beating he came under investigation for another robbery and was arrested again three months after his release from the hospital for allegedly picking up a male prostitute dressed as a woman and for trying to run over police who confronted him.[10] He was sentenced in 1996 to 90 days in jail on charges of assault with a deadly weapon for trying to run over his wife during a domestic dispute,[11] and a month later was fined $1,436 and ordered to serve 30 days on a highway cleanup crew for violating probation on a drunk-driving conviction.[12] Regardless of King's personal life, however, the King incident, more than seven years after it occurred, continues to serve as a rallying point for individual rights activists concerned with ensuring that citizens remain protected from the abuse of police power in an increasingly conservative society.

This chapter shows how the police, like everyone else, are not above the law. It describes the legal environment surrounding police activities—from search and seizure through arrest and the interrogation of suspects. As we shall see throughout, it is democratically inspired legal restraints upon the police which help ensure individual freedoms in our society and

The beating of Rodney King by Los Angeles police officers, captured here by a man trying out a new video camera. The 1991 incident raised many questions about police integrity, while simultaneously highlighting the power of new technology to uncover police abuses.
Photo courtesy of Corbis/Sygma

which prevent the development of a police state in America. Like anything else, however, the rules by which the police are expected to operate are in constant flux, and their continuing development forms the meat of this chapter.

A Changing Legal Climate

The Constitution of the United States is designed—especially in the **Bill of Rights**—to protect citizens against abuses of police power (see Table 5-1). However, the legal environment surrounding the police in modern America is much more complex than it was just 30 years ago. Up until that time, the Bill of Rights was largely given only lip service in criminal justice proceedings around the country. In practice, law enforcement, especially on the state and local level, revolved around tried and true methods of search, arrest, and interrogation, which sometimes left little room for recognition of individual rights. Police operations during that period were often far more informal than they are today, and investigating officers frequently assumed that they could come and go as they pleased, even to the extent of invading someone's personal space without the need for a search warrant. Interrogations could quickly turn violent, and the infamous rubber hose, which was reputed to leave few marks on the body, was probably more widely used during the questioning of suspects than many would like to believe. Similarly, "doing things by the book" could mean the use of thick telephone books for beating suspects, since the books spread out the force of blows and left few visible bruises. Although such abuses were not necessarily day-to-day practices in all police agencies, and while they probably did not characterize more than a relatively small proportion of all officers, such conduct pointed to the need for greater control over police activities so that even the potential for abuse might be curtailed.

It was during the 1960s that the U.S. Supreme Court, under the direction of Chief Justice Earl Warren, accelerated the process of guaranteeing individual rights in the face of criminal prosecution. Warren court rulings bound the police to strict procedural requirements in the areas of investigation, arrest, and interrogation. Later rulings scrutinized trial court procedure and enforced humanitarian standards in sentencing and punishment. The Warren court also seized upon the Fourteenth Amendment and made it a basis for judicial mandates requiring that both state and federal criminal justice agencies adhere to the Court's interpretation of the Constitution. The apex of the individual rights emphasis in Supreme Court

Bill of Rights

The first 10 amendments to the U.S. Constitution, considered especially important in the processing of criminal defendants.

TABLE 5-1 ■ Constitutional Amendments of Special Significance to the American System of Justice, from the Bill of Rights

THIS RIGHT IS GUARANTEED	BY THIS AMENDMENT
The Right Against Unreasonable Searches and Seizures	Fourth
No Arrest Without Probable Cause	Fourth
The Right Against Self-Incrimination	Fifth
The Right Against "Double Jeopardy"	Fifth
The Right to Due Process of Law	Fifth, Fourteenth
The Right to a Speedy Trial	Sixth
The Right to a Jury Trial	Sixth
The Right to Know the Charges	Sixth
The Right to Cross-Examine Witnesses	Sixth
The Right to a Lawyer	Sixth
The Right to Compel Witnesses on One's Behalf	Sixth
The Right to Reasonable Bail	Eighth
The Right Against Excessive Fines	Eighth
The Right Against Cruel and Unusual Punishments	Eighth
The Applicability of Constitutional Rights to All Citizens, Regardless of State Law or Procedure (not part of the Bill of Rights)	Fourteenth

decisions was reached in the 1966 case of *Miranda* v. *Arizona*,[13] which established the famous requirement of a police rights advisement of suspects. In wielding its brand of idealism, the Warren court (which held sway from 1953 until 1969) accepted the fact that a few guilty people would go free in order that the rights of the majority of Americans would be protected.

Supreme Court decisions of the last decade or so—the product of a new conservative Court philosophy—have begun what some call a "reversal" of Warren-era advances in the area of individual rights. By creating exceptions to some of the Warren court's rules and restraints, and in allowing for the emergency questioning of suspects before they are read their rights, a changed Supreme Court has recognized the realities attending day-to-day police work and the need to ensure public safety. This practical approach to justice, which came into vogue during the Reagan-Bush political era and is still with us, is all the more interesting for the fact that it must struggle to emerge from within the confines of earlier Supreme Court decisions.

Individual Rights

The Constitution of the United States provides for a system of checks and balances among the legislative, judicial, and executive (presidential) branches of government. By this we mean that one branch of government is always held accountable to the other branches. The system is designed to ensure that no *one* individual or agency can become powerful enough to usurp the rights and freedoms guaranteed under the Constitution. Without accountability, it is possible to imagine a police state in which the power of law enforcement is absolute and related to political considerations and personal vendettas more than to objective considerations of guilt or innocence.

Under our system of government, courts become the arena for dispute resolution, not just between individuals but between citizens and the agencies of government themselves. After handling by the justice system, people who feel they have not received the respect and dignity due them under the law can appeal to the courts for redress. Such appeals are usually based upon procedural issues and are independent of more narrow considerations of guilt or innocence.

In this chapter, we spend a great deal of time on cases that are important because they are famous for having clarified constitutional guarantees concerning individual liberties within the criminal justice arena. They involve issues which have come to be called *rights* by most of us. It is common to hear arrestees today say: "You can't do that! I know my rights!" Rights are concerned with procedure, that is, with how police and other actors in the criminal justice system handle each part of the process of dealing with suspects. Rights violations have often become the basis for the dismissal of charges, acquittal of defendants, or the release of convicted offenders after an appeal to a higher court.

Due Process Requirements

As you may recall from Chapter 1, due process is a requirement of the Fifth, Sixth, and Fourteenth Amendments to the U.S. Constitution which mandates that justice-system officials respect the rights of accused individuals throughout the criminal justice process. Most due process requirements of relevance to the police pertain to three major areas: (1) evidence and investigation (often called "search and seizure"), (2) arrest, and (3) interrogation. Each of these areas has been addressed by a plethora of landmark U.S. Supreme Court decisions. **Landmark cases** are recognizable by the fact that they produce substantial changes in both the understanding of the requirements of due process and in the practical day-to-day operations of the justice system. Another way to think of landmark decisions is that they help significantly in clarifying the rules of the game—the procedural guidelines by which the police and the rest of the justice system must abide.

The three areas we are about to discuss have been well defined by decades of court precedent. Keep in mind, however, that judicial interpretations of the constitutional requirement of due process are constantly evolving. As new decisions are rendered, and as the composition of the Court itself changes, additional refinements (and even major changes) may occur.

Landmark Cases

Precedent-setting court decisions, often recognizable by the fact that they produce substantial changes in both the understanding of the requirements of due process and in the practical day-to-day operations of the justice system.

Search and Seizure

The U.S. Constitution declares that people must be secure in their homes and in their persons against unreasonable searches and seizures. This right is asserted by the Fourth Amendment, which reads: "The right of the people to be secure in their persons, houses, papers, and effects, against unreasonable searches and seizures shall not be violated, and no warrants shall issue but upon probable cause, supported by oath or affirmation, and particularly describing the place to be searched, and the persons or things to be seized." This amendment, a part of the Bill of Rights, was adopted by Congress and became effective on December 15, 1791.

The language of the Fourth Amendment is familiar to all of us. *Warrants, probable cause,* and other phrases from the amendment are frequently cited in editorials, TV news shows, and daily conversation. It is the interpretation of these phrases over time by the U.S. Supreme Court, however, which has given them the impact they have on the justice system today.

"In terms that apply equally to seizures of property and to seizures of persons, the Fourth Amendment has drawn a firm line at the entrance to the house. Absent exigent circumstances, that threshold may not reasonably be crossed without a warrant."

—Payton v. New York, *445 U.S. 573, 590 (1980).*

The Exclusionary Rule

The first landmark case concerning search and seizure was that of *Weeks* v. *U.S.* (1914).[14] Freemont Weeks was suspected of using the U.S. mail to sell lottery tickets, a federal crime. Weeks was arrested and federal agents went to his home to conduct a search. They had no search warrant, since at the time investigators did not routinely use warrants. They confiscated many incriminating items of evidence, as well as personal possessions of the defendant, including clothes, papers, books, and even candy.

Prior to trial, Weeks's attorney asked that the personal items be returned, claiming that they had been illegally seized under Fourth Amendment guarantees. A judge agreed and ordered the **illegally seized evidence** returned. On the basis of the evidence that was retained, however, Weeks was convicted in federal court and sentenced to prison. He appealed his conviction through other courts and eventually reached the U.S. Supreme Court. There, his lawyer reasoned that if some of his client's belongings had been illegally seized, then the remainder of them were also taken improperly. The Supreme Court agreed and overturned Weeks's earlier conviction.

Illegally Seized Evidence

Evidence seized in opposition to the principles of due process as described by the Bill of Rights. Most illegally seized evidence is the result of police searches conducted without a proper warrant or of improperly conducted interrogations.

Exclusionary Rule

The understanding, based on Supreme Court precedent, that incriminating information must be seized according to constitutional specifications of due process, or it will not be allowed as evidence in criminal trials.

"The right of the people to be secure in their persons, houses, papers, and effects, against unreasonable searches and seizures, shall not be violated, and no warrants shall issue but upon probable cause, supported by oath or affirmation, and particularly describing the place to be searched, and the persons or things to be seized."

—*Fourth Amendment to the U.S. Constitution*

The *Weeks* case forms the basis of what is now called the **exclusionary rule.** The exclusionary rule means that evidence illegally seized by the police cannot be used in a trial. The rule acts as a control over police behavior and specifically focuses upon the failure of officers to obtain warrants authorizing them to either conduct searches or to effect arrests (especially when arrest may lead to the acquisition of incriminating statements or to the seizure of physical evidence).

It is important to note, incidentally, that Freemont Weeks could have been retried on the original charges following the Supreme Court decision in his case. He would not have faced double jeopardy because he was in fact not *finally convicted* on the earlier charges. His conviction was nullified on appeal, resulting in neither a conviction nor an acquittal. Double jeopardy becomes an issue only when a defendant faces retrial on the same charges following acquittal at his or her original trial or when the defendant is retried after having been convicted.

It is also important to recognize that the decision of the Supreme Court in the Weeks case was binding, at the time, only upon federal officers, because it was federal agents who were involved in the illegal seizure. Read the *Weeks* decision in its entirety in **WebExtra!** 5-2 at CJToday.com.

Problems with Precedent

The *Weeks* case demonstrates the power of the Supreme Court in enforcing what we have called the "rules of the game." It also lays bare the much more significant role that the Court plays in rule creation. Until the *Weeks* case was decided, federal law enforcement officers had little reason to think they were acting in violation of due process. Common practice had not required that they obtain a warrant before conducting searches. The rule which resulted from *Weeks* was new, and it would forever alter the enforcement activities of federal officers. Yet the *Weeks* case was also retroactive, in the sense that it was applied to Weeks himself.

There is a problem in the way in which our system generates and applies principles of due process, which may be obvious from our discussion of the *Weeks* case. The problem is that the present appeals system, focusing as it does upon the rules of the game, presents a ready-made channel for the guilty to go free. There can be little doubt but that Freemont Weeks had violated federal law. A jury had convicted him. Yet he escaped punishment because of the illegal behavior of the police—behavior which, until the Court ruled, had not been regarded as anything but legitimate.

Even if the police knowingly violate the principles of due process, which they sometimes do, our sense of justice is compromised when the guilty go free. Famed Supreme Court Justice Benjamin Cardozo (1870–1938) once complained, "The criminal is to go free because the constable has blundered."

Students of criminal justice have long considered three possible solutions to this problem. The first solution suggests that rules of due process, especially when newly articulated by the courts, should be applied only to future cases, not to the initial case in which they are stated. The justices in the *Weeks* case, for example, might have said, "We are creating the 'exclusionary rule,' based upon our realization in this case. Law enforcement officers are obligated to use it as a guide in all future searches. However, insofar as the guilt of Mr. Weeks was decided by a jury under rules of evidence existing at the time, we will let that decision stand."

A second solution would punish police officers or other actors in the criminal justice system who act illegally, but would not allow the guilty defendant to escape punishment. This solution would be useful in applying established precedent where officers and officials had the benefit of clearly articulated rules and should have known better. Under this arrangement, any officer today who intentionally violates due process guarantees might be suspended, reduced in rank, lose pay, or be fired. Some authors have suggested that "decertification" might serve as "an alternative to traditional remedies for police misconduct."[15] Departments which employed the decertification process would punish violators by removing their certification as police officers. Because officers in every state except Hawaii[16] must meet the certification requirements of state boards (usually called Training and Standards Commissions or Peace Officer Standards and Training Boards) in order to hold employment, some authors[17] argue that decertification would have a much more personal (and therefore more effective) impact on individual officers than the exclusionary rule ever could.

A third possibility would allow the Supreme Court to address theoretical questions involving issues of due process. Concerned supervisors and officials could ask how the Court would rule "if. . . ." As things now work, the Court can only address real cases and does so on a **writ of** *certiorari,* in which the Court orders the record of a lower court case to be prepared for review.

The obvious difficulty with these solutions, however, is that they would substantially reduce the potential benefits available to defendants through the appeals process and, hence, would effectively eliminate the process itself.

Writ of *Certiorari*

An order, by an appellate court, specifying whether that court will review the judgment of a lower court.

The Fruit of the Poisoned Tree Doctrine

The Court further built upon the rules concerning evidence with its ruling in *Silverthorne Lumber Co. v. U.S.*[18] In 1918 Frederick Silverthorne and his sons operated a lumber company and were accused of avoiding payment of federal taxes. When asked to turn over the company's books to federal investigators, the Silverthornes refused, citing their Fifth Amendment privilege against self-incrimination.

Shortly thereafter, federal agents, without a search warrant, descended on the lumber company and seized the wanted books. The Silverthornes' lawyer appeared in court and asked that the materials be returned, citing the need for a search warrant as had been established in the *Weeks* case. The prosecutor agreed, and the books were returned to the Silverthornes.

The Silverthornes came to trial thinking they would be acquitted because the evidence against them was no longer in the hands of prosecutors. In a surprise move, however, the prosecution introduced photocopies of incriminating evidence which they had made from the returned books. The Silverthornes were convicted in federal court. Their appeal eventually reached the Supreme Court of the United States. The Court ruled that just as illegally seized evidence cannot be used in a trial, neither can evidence be used which *derives* from an illegal seizure.[19] The conviction of the Silverthornes was overturned, and they were set free.

The *Silverthorne* case articulated a new principle of due process which we today call the **fruit of the poisoned tree doctrine.** This doctrine is potentially far reaching. Complex cases developed after years of police investigative effort may be ruined if defense attorneys are able to demonstrate that the prosecution's case, no matter how complex, was originally based upon a search or seizure which violated due process. In such cases, it is likely that all evidence will be declared "tainted" and become useless.

Still, prior to the Warren court era, most U.S. Supreme Court decisions were regarded as applicable only to federal law enforcement agencies. You can read the full text of the Court's opinion in the *Silverthorne* case in **WebExtra!** 5-3 at CJToday.com.

Fruit of the Poisoned Tree Doctrine

A legal principle which excludes from introduction at trial any evidence later developed as a result of an originally illegal search or seizure.

The Warren Court Era (1953–1969)

Before the 1960s, the U.S. Supreme Court intruded only infrequently upon the overall operation of the criminal justice system at the state and local level. As some authors have observed, however, the 1960s provided a time of youthful idealism, and "without the distraction of a depression or world war, individual liberties were examined at all levels of society."[20] Hence, while the exclusionary rule became an overriding consideration in federal law enforcement from the time that it was first defined by the Supreme Court in the *Weeks* case in 1914, it was not until 1961 that the Warren court, under Chief Justice Earl Warren, decided a case that was to change the face of American law enforcement forever. That case, *Mapp v. Ohio* (1961),[21] made the exclusionary rule applicable to criminal prosecutions at the state level.[22] Beginning with the now-famous *Mapp* case, the Warren court set out to chart a course which would guarantee nationwide recognition of individual rights, as it understood them, by agencies at all levels of the criminal justice system.

The Warren Court Applies the Exclusionary Rule to the States

The *Mapp* case began like many others during the protest-prone 1960s. Dolree Mapp was suspected of harboring a fugitive wanted in a bombing. When Ohio police officers arrived at her house, she refused to admit them. Eventually, they forced their way in. During the search which ensued, pornographic materials, including photographs, were uncovered. Mapp was arrested, and eventually convicted, under a state law which made possession of such materials illegal.

Prior decisions by the U.S. Supreme Court, including *Wolf* v. *Colorado*,[23] had led officers to expect that the exclusionary rule did not apply to agents of state and local law enforcement. Nonetheless, in a wide-reaching and precedent-setting decision, Mapp's conviction was overturned upon appeal by a majority of Warren court justices who decided that the U.S. Constitution, under the Fourteenth Amendment's due process guarantee, mandates that state and local law enforcement officers must be held to the same standards of accountability as federal officers. There could be little doubt, said the justices, that the evidence against Mapp had been illegally obtained and therefore could not be used against her in any court of law in the United States. The precedent established in *Mapp* v. *Ohio* firmly applied the principles developed in *Weeks* and *Silverthorne* to trials in state courts, making police officers at all levels accountable to the rule of law, which, as embodied in the words of the Fourteenth Amendment, reads: "nor shall any State deprive any person of life, liberty, or property, without due process of law; nor deny to any person within its jurisdiction the equal protection of the laws." The full text of the Court's opinion in *Mapp* v. *Ohio* is available at CJToday.com in **WebExtra!** 5-4.

Another important Warren-era case, that of *Chimel* v. *California* (1969),[24] involved both arrest as well as search activities by local law enforcement officers. Ted Chimel was convicted of the burglary of a coin shop, based upon evidence gathered at the scene of his arrest—his home. Officers, armed with an arrest warrant but not a search warrant, had taken Chimel into custody when they arrived at his residence and proceeded with a search of his entire three-bedroom house, including the attic, a small workshop, and the garage. Although officers realized that the search might be challenged in court, they justified it by claiming that it was conducted not so much to uncover evidence, but as part of the arrest process. Searches which are conducted incidental to arrest, they argued, are necessary for the officers' protection and should not require a search warrant. Coins taken from the burglarized coin shop were found at various places in Chimel's residence, including the garage, and provided the evidence used against him at trial.

Chimel's appeal eventually reached the U.S. Supreme Court, which ruled that the search of Chimel's residence, although incidental to arrest, became invalid when it went beyond the person arrested and the area subject to that person's "immediate control." The thrust of the Court's decision was that searches during arrest can be made to protect arresting officers, but that, without a search warrant, their scope must be strongly circumscribed. Legal implications of *Chimel* v. *California* are summarized in Table 5-2.

The decision in the case of Ted Chimel was predicated upon earlier reasoning by the Court in the case of *U.S.* v. *Rabinowitz* (1950).[25] Rabinowitz, a stamp collector, had been arrested and charged by federal agents with selling altered postage stamps in order to defraud other collectors. Employing a valid arrest warrant, officers arrested Rabinowitz at his place of employment and then proceeded to search his desk, file cabinets, and safe. They did not have a search warrant, but his office was small—only one room—and the officers conducted the search with a specific object in mind, the illegal stamps. Eventually, 573 altered postage stamps were seized in the search, and Rabinowitz was convicted in federal court of charges related to selling altered stamps.

Rabinowitz's appeal to the U.S. Supreme Court, based upon the claim that the warrantless search of his business was illegal, was denied. The Court ruled that the Fourth Amendment provides protection against *unreasonable* searches, but that the search, in this case, followed legally from the arrest of the suspect. In the language used by the Court, "It is not disputed that there may be reasonable searches, incident to arrest, without a search warrant. Upon acceptance of this established rule that some authority to search follows from lawfully taking the person into custody, it becomes apparent that such searches turn upon the reasonable-

TABLE 5-2 ■ Implications of *Chimel* v. *California*

What Arresting Officers May Search

• The defendant
• The physical area within easy reach of the defendant

Valid Reasons for Conducting a Search

• To protect the arresting officers
• To prevent evidence from being destroyed
• To keep the defendant from escaping

When a Search Becomes Illegal

• When it goes beyond the defendant and the area within the defendant's immediate control
• When it is conducted for other than a valid reason

ness under all the circumstances and not upon the practicability of procuring a search warrant, for the warrant is not required."

Since the early days of the exclusionary rule, other court decisions have highlighted the fact that "the Fourth Amendment protects people, not places."[26] In other words, although the commonly heard claim that "a person's home is his or her castle" has a great deal of validity within the context of constitutional law, persons can have a reasonable expectation to privacy in "homes" of many descriptions. Apartments, duplex dwellings, motel rooms—even the cardboard boxes or makeshift tents of the homeless—can all become protected places under the Fourth Amendment. In *Minnesota* v. *Olson* (1990),[27] for example, the U.S. Supreme Court extended the protection against warrantless searches to overnight guests residing in the home of another. The capacity to claim the protection of the Fourth Amendment, said the Court, depends upon whether the *person* who makes that claim has a legitimate expectation of privacy in the place searched.

Finally, in 1998, in the case of *Minnesota* v. *Carter,*[28] the Court held that in order for a defendant to be entitled to Fourth Amendment protection, "he must demonstrate that he personally has an expectation of privacy in the place searched, and that his expectation is

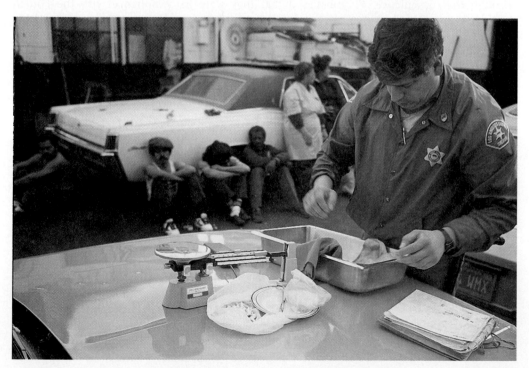

A California police officer spot checks a seized substance suspected of being cocaine. The exclusionary rule means that illegally gathered evidence cannot be used later in court, requiring that police officers pay close attention to the way in which they gather and handle evidence.
Mark Richards.

reasonable." The Court noted that "the extent to which the Amendment protects people may depend upon where those people are. While an overnight guest may have a legitimate expectation of privacy in someone else's home . . . one who is merely present with the consent of the householder may not."

The Burger (1969–1986) and Rehnquist (1986–Present) Courts

The swing toward conservatism which our country experienced during the 1980s and early 1990s gave rise to "yuppies," the X-generation, designer clothes, and a renewed concern with protecting the financial and other interests of those who live within the law. The Reagan-Bush years, and the popularity of two presidents in whom many saw the embodiment of old-fashioned values, reflected the tenor of a nation seeking a return to simpler times.

Throughout the late 1980s, the U.S. Supreme Court mirrored the nation's conservative tenor by distancing itself from certain earlier decisions of the Warren court. The underlying theme of the new Court, the Burger court (which held sway from 1969 until 1986), was its adherence to the principle that criminal defendants, in claiming violations of their due process rights, need to bear the bulk of responsibility in showing that police went beyond the law in the performance of their duties. That trend continues into the present day under the Rehnquist Court (1986–present), led by Chief Justice William H. Rehnquist.

Good Faith Exceptions to the Exclusionary Rule

The Burger court, led by Chief Justice Warren E. Burger, began a chipping away at the strict application of the exclusionary rule originally set forth in the *Weeks* and *Silverthorne* cases. In the case of *Illinois* v. *Gates* (1983),[29] the Court was asked to modify the exclusionary rule to permit the use of evidence in court which had been seized in "reasonable good faith" by officers, even though the search was later ruled illegal. The Court, however, chose not to address the issue at that time.

But only a year later, in the 1984 case of *U.S.* v. *Leon*,[30] the Court recognized what has come to be called the "**good faith** exception to the exclusionary rule." The *Leon* case involved the Burbank, California, Police Department and its investigation of a drug-trafficking suspect. The suspect, Leon, was placed under surveillance following a tip from a confidential informant. Investigators applied for a search warrant based upon information gleaned through the surveillance. They believed that they were in compliance with the Fourth Amendment requirement that "no warrants shall issue but upon probable cause." **Probable cause,** a tricky but important concept, can be defined as "a legal criterion residing in a set of facts and circumstances which would cause a reasonable person to believe that a particular other person has committed a specific crime." Probable cause must be satisfactorily demonstrated by police officers in a written affidavit to a magistrate before a search warrant can be issued. Magistrates[31] are low-level judges and, under our system of checks and balances, act to ensure that the police have established the probable cause needed for warrants to be obtained.

In *U.S.* v. *Leon*, the affidavit submitted by police to a magistrate requesting a search warrant was reviewed by numerous deputy district attorneys, and the magistrate decided to issue the warrant. A search of Leon's three residences yielded a large amount of drugs and other evidence. Although Leon was convicted of drug trafficking, a later ruling in a federal district court resulted in the suppression of evidence against him on the basis that the original affidavit prepared by the police had not, in the opinion of the Court, been sufficient to establish probable cause.

The government petitioned the U.S. Supreme Court to consider whether evidence gathered by officers acting in good faith as to the validity of a warrant, should fairly be excluded at trial. The impending modification of the exclusionary rule was intoned in the first sentence of that Court's written decision: "This case presents the question whether the Fourth Amendment exclusionary rule should be modified so as not to bar the use in the prosecution's case-in-chief of evidence obtained by officers acting in reasonable reliance on a search warrant issued by a detached and neutral magistrate but ultimately found to be unsupported

---

Good Faith

A possible legal basis for an exception to the exclusionary rule. Law enforcement officers who conduct a search, or seize evidence, on the basis of good faith (that is, where they believe they are operating according to the dictates of the law) and who later discover that a mistake was made (perhaps in the format of the application for a search warrant) may still use, in court, evidence seized as the result of such activities.

Probable Cause. (Also discussed in Chapter 1.)

Refers to that necessary level of belief which would allow for police seizures (arrests) of individuals and searches of dwellings, vehicles, and possessions. Probable cause can generally be found in a set of facts and circumstances which would cause a reasonable person to believe that a particular individual has committed a specific crime. Upon a demonstration of probable cause, magistrates will issue warrants authorizing law enforcement officers to effect arrests and conduct searches.

by probable cause." The Court continued: "When law enforcement officers have acted in objective good faith or their transgressions have been minor, the magnitude of the benefit conferred on such guilty defendants offends basic concepts of the criminal justice system." Reflecting the renewed conservatism of the Burger court, the justices found for the government and reinstated the conviction of Leon.

In that same year the Supreme Court case of *Massachusetts* v. *Sheppard* (1984)[32] further reinforced the concept of good faith. In the *Sheppard* case, officers executed a search warrant which failed to describe accurately the property to be seized. Although they were aware of the error, they had been assured by a magistrate that the warrant was valid. After the seizure was complete and a conviction had been obtained, the Massachusetts Supreme Judicial Court reversed the finding of the trial court. Upon appeal the U.S. Supreme Court reiterated the good-faith exception and let the original conviction stand.

While the cases of *Leon* and *Sheppard* represented a clear reversal of Warren court philosophy, the trend continued with the 1987 case of *Illinois* v. *Krull*.[33] In *Krull*, the Court, now under the leadership of Chief Justice William H. Rehnquist, held that the good-faith exception applied to a warrantless search supported by state law even when the state statute was later found to violate the Fourth Amendment. Similarly, another 1987 Supreme Court case, *Maryland* v. *Garrison*,[34] supported the use of evidence obtained with a search warrant which was inaccurate in its specifics. In *Garrison*, officers had procured a warrant to search an apartment believing it was the only dwelling on a building's third floor. After searching the entire floor, they discovered that it housed more than one apartment. Even so, evidence acquired in the search was held to be admissible based upon the reasonable mistake of the officers.

The 1990 case of *Illinois* v. *Rodriguez*[35] further diminished the scope of the exclusionary rule. In *Rodriguez*, a badly beaten woman named Gail Fischer complained to police that she had been assaulted in a Chicago apartment. Fischer led police to the apartment—which she indicated she shared with the defendant—produced a key, and opened the door to the dwelling. Inside, investigators found the defendant, Edward Rodriguez, asleep on a bed, with drug paraphernalia and cocaine spread around him. Rodriguez was arrested and charged with assault and possession of a controlled substance.

Upon appeal, Rodriguez demonstrated that Fischer had not lived with him for at least a month—and argued that she could no longer be said to have legal control over the apartment. Hence, the defense claimed, Fischer had no authority to provide investigators with access to the dwelling. According to arguments made by the defense, the evidence, which had been obtained without a warrant, had not been properly seized. The Supreme Court disagreed, ruling that "even if Fischer did not possess common authority over the premises, there was no Fourth Amendment violation if the police *reasonably believed* at the time of their entry that Fischer possessed the authority to consent."

Legal scholars have suggested that the exclusionary rule may undergo even further modification in the near future. One analyst of the contemporary scene points to the fact that "the [Rehnquist] Court's majority is [now] clearly committed to the idea that the exclusionary rule is not directly part of the Fourth Amendment (and Fourteenth Amendment due process), but instead is an evidentiary device instituted by the Court to effectuate it."[36] In other words, if the Court should be persuaded that the rule is no longer effective, or that some other strategy could better achieve the aim of protecting individual rights, the rule could be abandoned entirely. A general listing of established exceptions to the exclusionary rule is provided in Table 5-3, including three which we will now discuss.

The Plain-View Doctrine

Police officers have the opportunity to begin investigations or confiscate evidence, without the need for a warrant, based upon what they find in **plain view** and open to public inspection. The plain-view doctrine was first stated in the Supreme Court case of *Harris* v. *U.S.* (1968)[37] in which a police officer inventorying an impounded vehicle discovered evidence of a robbery. In the *Harris* case, the Court ruled that "objects falling in the plain view of an officer who has a right to be in the position to have that view are subject to seizure and may be introduced in evidence."[38] Read the full text of the *Harris* opinion in **WebExtra!** 5-5 at CJToday.com.

Plain View

A legal term describing the ready visibility of objects which might be seized as evidence during a search by police in the absence of a search warrant specifying the seizure of those objects. In order for evidence in plain view to be lawfully seized, officers must have a legal right to be in the viewing area and must have cause to believe that the evidence is somehow associated with criminal activity.

Common situations in which the plain-view doctrine is applicable include emergencies such as crimes in progress, fires, and accidents. A police officer responding to a call for assistance, for example, might enter a residence intending to provide aid to an injured person and find drugs or other contraband in plain view. If so, he or she would be within his or her legitimate authority to confiscate the materials and effect an arrest if the owner of the substance could be identified.

The plain-view doctrine applies only to sightings by the police under legal circumstances—that is, in places where the police have a legitimate right to be and, typically, only if the sighting was coincidental. Similarly, the incriminating nature of the evidence seized must have been "immediately apparent" to the officers making the seizure.[39] If officers conspired to avoid the necessity for a search warrant by helping to create a plain-view situation through surveillance, duplicity, or other means, the doctrine likely would not apply.

The plain-view doctrine, however, has been restricted by more recent federal court decisions. In the 1982 case of *U.S.* v. *Irizarry*[40] the First Circuit Court of Appeals held that officers could not move objects to gain a view of evidence otherwise hidden from view. Agents had arrested a number of men in a motel room in Isla Verde, Puerto Rico. A valid arrest warrant formed the legal basis for the arrest, and some quantities of plainly visible drugs were seized from the room. An agent, looking through a window into the room prior to the arrest,

TABLE 5-3 ■ Established Exceptions to the Exclusionary Rule

POLICE POWERS	SUPPORTED BY
Stop and frisk	*Terry* v. *Ohio* (1968)
Warrantless searches incident to a lawful arrest	*U.S.* v. *Rabinowitz* (1950)
Seizure of evidence in "good faith," even in the face of some exclusionary rule violations	*U.S.* v. *Leon* (1984) *Illinois* v. *Krull* (1987)
Warrantless vehicle searches where probable cause exists to believe that the vehicle contains contraband and/or the occupants have been lawfully arrested	*Carroll* v. *U.S.* (1925) *New York* v. *Belton* (1981) *U.S.* v. *Ross* (1982) *California* v. *Carney* (1985) *California* v. *Acevedo* (1991) *Ornelas* v. *U.S.* (1996)
Gathering of incriminating evidence during interrogation in noncustodial circumstances	*Beckwith* v. *United States* (1976)
Authority to search incidental to arrest and/or to conduct a protective sweep in conjunction with an in-home arrest	*Chimel* v. *California* (1969) *U.S.* v. *Edwards* (1974) *Maryland* v. *Buie* (1990)
Authority to enter and/or search an "open field" without a warrant	*Hester* v. *U.S.* (1924) *Oliver* v. *U.S.* (1984) *U.S.* v. *Dunn* (1987)
Permissibility of warrantless naked-eye aerial observation of open areas and/or greenhouses	*California* v. *Ciraolo* (1986) *Florida* v. *Riley* (1989)
Warrantless seizure of abandoned materials and refuse	*California* v. *Greenwood* (1988)
Prompt action in the face of threats to public or personal safety	*Warden* v. *Hayden* (1967) *New York* v. *Quarles* (1984) *Borchardt* v. *U.S.* (1987)
Evidence in "plain view" may be seized	*Harris* v. *New York* (1968) *Coolidge* v. *New Hampshire* (1971) *Horton* v. *California* (1990)
Use of police informants in jail cells	*Kuhlman* v. *Wilson* (1986) *Illinois* v. *Perkins* (1990) *Arizona* v. *Fulminante* (1991)
Lawfulness of arrests based upon computer errors made by clerks	*Arizona* v. *Evans* (1995)

had seen one of the defendants with a gun. After the arrest was complete, and no gun had been found on the suspects, another officer noticed a bathroom ceiling panel out of place. The logical conclusion was that a weapon had been secreted there. Upon inspection, a substantial quantity of cocaine and various firearms were found hidden in the ceiling. The Court, however, refused to allow these weapons and drugs to be used as evidence because, it said, "the items of evidence found above the ceiling panel were not plainly visible to the agents standing in the room."[41]

In the Supreme Court case of *Arizona* v. *Hicks* (1987),[42] the requirement that evidence be in plain view, without the need for officers to move or dislodge evidence, was reiterated. In the *Hicks* case, officers responded to a shooting in an apartment. A bullet had been fired in a second-floor apartment and had gone through the floor, injuring a man in the apartment below. The quarters of James Hicks were found to be in considerable disarray when entered by investigating officers. As officers looked for the person who might have fired the weapon, they discovered and confiscated a number of guns and a stocking mask, such as might be used in robberies. In one corner, however, officers noticed two expensive stereo sets. One of the officers, suspecting that the sets were stolen, went over to the equipment and was able to read the serial numbers of one of the components from where it rested. Some of the serial numbers, however, were not clearly visible, and the investigating officer moved some of the components in order to read the numbers. When he called the numbers into headquarters, he was told that the equipment indeed had been stolen. The stereo components were seized, and James Hicks was arrested. Hicks was eventually convicted on a charge of armed robbery, based upon the evidence seized.

Upon appeal, the *Hicks* case reached the U.S. Supreme Court, which ruled that the officer's behavior had become illegal when he moved the stereo equipment to record serial numbers. The Court held that persons have a "reasonable expectation to privacy,"[43] which means that officers lacking a search warrant, even when invited into a residence, must act more like guests than inquisitors.

Most evidence seized under the plain-view doctrine is discovered "inadvertently"—that is, by accident.[44] However, in 1990, the U.S. Supreme Court, in the case of *Horton* v. *California*,[45] ruled that "even though inadvertence *is* a characteristic of most legitimate 'plain view' seizures, it *is not* a necessary condition."[46] In the *Horton* case, a warrant was issued authorizing the search of a defendant's home for stolen jewelry. The affidavit, completed by the officer who requested the warrant, alluded to an Uzi submachine gun and a stun gun—weapons purportedly used in the jewel robbery. It did not request that those weapons be listed on the search warrant. Officers searched the defendant's home, but did not find the stolen jewelry. They did, however, seize a number of weapons—among them the Uzi, two stun guns, and a .38-caliber revolver. Horton was convicted of robbery in a trial where the seized weapons were introduced into evidence. He appealed his conviction, claiming that officers had reason to believe that the weapons were in his home at the time of the search and were therefore not seized inadvertently. His appeal was rejected by the Court. As a result of the *Horton* case, "inadvertence" is no longer considered a condition necessary to ensure the legitimacy of a seizure which results when evidence other than that listed in a search warrant is discovered.

> "While every person is entitled to stand silent, it is more virtuous for the wrongdoer to admit his offense and accept the punishment he deserves. . . . It is wrong, and subtly corrosive of our criminal justice system, to regard an honest confession as a mistake."
>
> —*Justice Antonin Scalia,* dissenting in Minnick v. Mississippi, *498 U.S. 146 (1990).*

Emergency Searches of Property

Certain emergencies may justify a police officer in searching a premise, even without a warrant. Recent decisions by U.S. Appeals Courts have resulted in such activities being termed exigent circumstances searches. According to the Legal Counsel Division of the FBI, there are three threats which "provide justification for emergency warrantless action."[47] They are clear dangers (1) to life, (2) of escape, and (3) of the removal or destruction of evidence. Any one of these situations may create an exception to the Fourth Amendment's requirement of a search warrant. Where emergencies necessitate a quick search of premises, however, law enforcement officers are responsible for demonstrating that a dire situation existed which justified their actions. Failure to do so successfully in court will, of course, taint any seized evidence and make it unusable.

The need for **emergency searches** was first recognized by the U.S. Supreme Court in 1967 in the case of *Warden* v. *Hayden*.[48] There, the Court approved the search of a residence con-

Emergency Searches

Those searches conducted by the police without a warrant, which are justified on the basis of some immediate and overriding need—such as public safety, the likely escape of a dangerous suspect, or the removal or destruction of evidence.

Although the concept of plain view is difficult to define, Latasha Smith (shown here sitting on a curb) provides a personal example of the concept. After Dallas narcotics officers searched the house behind her for crack cocaine, they turned their attention to Latasha, who was arrested for failing to appear in court for a previous misdemeanor violation.
Pat Sullivan, AP/Wide World Photos.

"Our police officers are high-school graduates; they are not lawyers; they are not judges."

—*U.S. Representative Chuck Douglas (R-N.H.)*

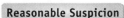

Reasonable Suspicion

(1) That level of suspicion which would justify an officer in making further inquiry or in conducting further investigation. Reasonable suspicion may permit stopping a person for the purpose of questioning, or a simple "pat-down" search. (2) A belief, based upon a consideration of the facts at hand and upon reasonable inferences drawn from those facts, which would induce an ordinarily prudent and cautious person under the same circumstances to generally conclude that criminal activity is taking place or that criminal activity has recently occurred. Reasonable suspicion is a general and reasonable belief that a crime is in progress or has occurred, whereas probable cause is a reasonable belief that a particular person has committed a specific crime.

ducted without a warrant which followed reports that an armed robber had fled into the building. In *Mincey* v. *Arizona* (1978),[49] the Supreme Court held that "the Fourth Amendment does not require police officers to delay in the course of an investigation if to do so would gravely endanger their lives or the lives of others."[50]

A 1990 decision, rendered in the case of *Maryland* v. *Buie*,[51] extended the authority of police to search locations in a house where a potentially dangerous person could hide, while an arrest warrant is being served. The *Buie* decision was meant primarily to protect investigators from potential danger and can apply even when officers lack a warrant, probable cause, or even **reasonable suspicion.**

In 1995, in the case of *Wilson* v. *Arkansas*,[52] the U.S. Supreme Court ruled that police officers generally must knock and announce their identity before entering a dwelling or other premises—even when armed with a search warrant. Under certain emergency circumstances, however, exceptions may be made, and officers may not need to knock or identify themselves prior to entering.[53] In *Wilson,* the Court added that Fourth Amendment requirements that searches be reasonable "should not be read to mandate a rigid rule of announcement that ignores countervailing law enforcement interests." Hence, officers need not announce themselves, the Court said, when suspects may be in the process of destroying evidence, officers are pursuing a recently escaped arrestee, or when officers' lives may be endangered by such an announcement. Because the *Wilson* case involved an appeal from a drug dealer, who was in fact apprehended by police officers who entered her unlocked house while she was flushing marijuana down a toilet, some say that it establishes a "drug law exception" to the knock and announce requirement.

In 1997, however, in *Richards* v. *Wisconsin*,[54] the Supreme Court clarified its position on "no knock" exceptions, saying that individual courts have the duty in each case to "determine whether the facts and circumstances of the particular entry justified dispensing with the requirement." The Court went on to say that "[a] 'no knock' entry is justified when the police have a reasonable suspicion that knocking and announcing their presence, under the particular circumstances, would be dangerous or futile, or that it would inhibit the effective investigation of the crime. This standard strikes the appropriate balance," said the Court, "between the legitimate law enforcement concerns at issue in the execution of search warrants and the individual privacy interests affected by no knock entries."[55]

Arrest

Officers seize not only property, but persons as well—a process we refer to as *arrest*. Most people think of arrest in terms of what they see on popular TV crime shows. The suspect is chased, subdued, and cuffed after committing some loathsome act in view of the camera. Some arrests do occur that way. In reality, however, most instances of arrest are far more mundane.

In technical terms, an **arrest** occurs whenever a law enforcement officer restricts a person's freedom to leave. There may be no yelling "*You're under arrest!*" no *Miranda* warnings may be offered, and, in fact, the suspect may not even consider himself or herself to be in custody. Such arrests, and the decision to enforce them, evolve as the situation between the officer and suspect develops. They usually begin with polite conversation and a request by the officer for information. Only when the suspect tries to leave, and tests the limits of the police response, may he or she discover that he or she is really in custody. In the 1980 case of *U.S.* v. *Mendenhall*,[56] Justice Stewart set forth the "free to leave" test for determining whether a person has been arrested. Stewart wrote: "A person has been 'seized' within the meaning of the Fourth Amendment only if in view of all the circumstances surrounding the incident, a reasonable person would have believed that he was not free to leave." The free to leave test "has been repeatedly adopted by the Court as the test for a seizure."[57] In 1994, in the case of *Stansbury* v. *California*,[58] the Court once again used such a test in determining the point at which an arrest had been made. In *Stansbury*, where the focus was on the interrogation of a suspected child molester and murderer, the Court ruled, "In determining whether an individual was in custody, a court must examine all of the circumstances surrounding the interrogation, but the ultimate inquiry is simply whether there [was] a formal arrest or restraint on freedom of movement of the degree associated with a formal arrest."

Arrests which follow the questioning of a suspect are probably the most common type. When the decision to arrest is reached, the officer has come to the conclusion that a crime has been committed and that the suspect is probably the one who committed it. The presence of these mental elements constitutes the probable cause needed for an arrest. Probable cause is the basic minimum necessary for an arrest under any circumstances.

Arrests may also occur when the officer comes upon a crime in progress. Such situations often require apprehension of the offender to ensure the safety of the public. Most arrests made during crimes in progress, however, are for misdemeanors rather than felonies. In fact, many states do not allow arrest for a misdemeanor unless it is committed in the presence of an officer. In any event, crimes in progress clearly provide the probable cause necessary for an arrest.

Most jurisdictions allow arrest for a felony without a warrant when a crime is not in progress, as long as probable cause can be established.[59] Some, however, require a warrant. In the case of *Payton* v. *New York* (1980), the U.S. Supreme Court ruled that, unless the suspect gives consent or an emergency exists, an arrest warrant is necessary if an arrest requires entry into a suspect's private residence.[60] Arrest warrants are issued by magistrates when police officers can demonstrate probable cause. Magistrates will usually require that the officers seeking an arrest warrant submit a written affidavit outlining their reason for the arrest.

Searches Incident to Arrest

The U.S. Supreme Court has established a clear rule that police officers have the right to conduct a search of a person being arrested and to search the area under the immediate control of that person in order to protect themselves from attack. This is true even if the officer and the arrestee are of different sexes.

This rule of the game was created in the *Rabinowitz* and *Chimel* cases cited earlier. It became firmly established in other cases involving personal searches, such as the 1973 case of

"In this case, we hold that this common-law "knock and announce" principle forms a part of the reasonableness inquiry under the Fourth Amendment."

—*Majority opinion in* **Wilson** v. **Arkansas,** *514 U.S. 927 (1995).*

Arrest

Taking an adult or juvenile into physical custody by authority of law for the purpose of charging the person with a criminal offense or a delinquent act or status offense, terminating with the recording of a specific offense. Technically, an arrest occurs whenever a person's freedom to leave is curtailed by a law enforcement officer.

Searches Incident to an Arrest

Those warrantless searches of arrested individuals which are conducted to ensure the safety of the arresting officer(s). Because individuals placed under arrest may be in the possession of weapons, courts have recognized the need for arresting officers to protect themselves by conducting an immediate and warrantless search of arrested individuals without the need for a warrant.

Robinson v. *U.S.*[61] Robinson was stopped for a traffic violation when it was learned that his driver's license was expired. He was arrested for operating a vehicle without a valid license. Officers subsequently searched the defendant to be sure he wasn't carrying a weapon and discovered a substance which later proved to be heroin. He was convicted of drug possession, but appealed. When Robinson's appeal reached the U.S. Supreme Court, the Court upheld the officers' right to conduct a search without a warrant for purposes of personal protection and to use the fruits of such a search when it turns up other contraband. In the words of the Court, "A custodial arrest of a suspect based upon probable cause is a reasonable intrusion under the Fourth Amendment; that intrusion being lawful, a search incident to the arrest requires no additional jurisdiction."[62]

The Court's decision in *Robinson* reinforced an earlier ruling involving a seasoned officer who conducted a "pat down" search of two men whom he suspected were "casing" a store, about to commit a robbery.[63] The officer in the case was a 39-year veteran of police work who testified that the men "did not look right." When he approached them, he suspected they might be armed. Fearing for his life, he quickly spun the men around, put them up against a wall, patted down their clothing, and found a gun on one of the men. The man, Terry, was later convicted in Ohio courts of carrying a concealed weapon.

Terry's appeal was based upon the argument that the suspicious officer had no probable cause to arrest him and therefore no cause to search him. The search, he argued, was illegal, and the evidence obtained should not have been used against him. The Supreme Court disagreed, saying: "In view of these facts, we cannot blind ourselves to the need for law enforcement officers to protect themselves and other prospective victims of violence in situations where they may lack probable cause for an arrest."[64]

The *Terry* case set the standard for brief stops and frisks based upon reasonable suspicion. Attorneys also refer to such brief encounters as "Terry-type" stops. Reasonable suspicion can be defined as a belief, based upon a consideration of the facts at hand and upon reasonable

21st Century CJ

The Computer Errors Exception to the Exclusionary Rule

Over the past few decades, criminal justice agencies have become increasingly dependent upon computer technology for records management and other purposes. As we enter the twenty-first century, the use of such technology will continue to grow, further impacting the daily activities of criminal justice agencies and bringing with it the increased likelihood of computer-generated or computer-based mistakes.

In 1995, in the case of *Arizona* v. *Evans*,[1] the U.S. Supreme Court created a "computer errors exception" to the exclusionary rule, by holding that a traffic stop which led to the seizure of marijuana was legal even though officers conducted the stop based upon an arrest warrant improperly stored in their computer. The case began in 1991 when Isaac Evans was stopped in

Phoenix, Arizona, for driving the wrong way on a one-way street in front of a police station. A routine computer check reported an outstanding arrest warrant for Evans, and he was taken into custody. Police found marijuana in the car Evans had been driving, and he was eventually convicted on charges of possessing a controlled substance. After his arrest, however, police learned that the arrest warrant reported to them by their computer had actually been quashed a few weeks earlier but, through the clerical oversight of a court employee, had never been removed from the computer.

In upholding Evans's conviction, the high court reasoned that officers could not be held responsible for a clerical error made by a court worker and concluded that the arresting officers were acting in good faith based upon the

information available to them at the time of the arrest. In addition, the majority opinion said that "the rule excluding evidence obtained without a warrant was intended to deter police misconduct, not mistakes by court employees."

In what may have been a warning to police administrators not to depend upon the excuse of computer error, however, Justice Sandra Day O'Connor, in a concurring opinion, wrote: "The police, of course, are entitled to enjoy the substantial advantages [computer] technology confers.... They may not, however, rely on it blindly. With the benefits of more efficient law enforcement mechanisms comes the burden of corresponding constitutional responsibilities."

[1]*Arizona* v. Isaac Evans, *115 S.Ct. 1185, 131 L. Ed. 2d 34 (1995).*

inferences drawn from those facts, which would induce an ordinarily prudent and cautious person under the same circumstances to generally conclude that criminal activity is taking place or that criminal activity has recently occurred. It is also the level of suspicion needed to justify an officer in making further inquiry or in conducting further investigation. Reasonable suspicion, which is a *general* and reasonable belief that a crime is in progress or has occurred, should be differentiated from probable cause. Probable cause is a reasonable belief that a *particular* person has committed a *specific* crime. It is important to note that the *Terry* case, for all the authority it conferred on officers, also made it clear that officers must have reasonable grounds for any stop or frisk that they conduct. Read the full text of the Court's opinion in *Terry* at **WebExtra!** 5-6 at CJToday.com.

In 1989, the Supreme Court, in the case of *U.S. v. Sokolow*,[65] clarified the basis upon which law enforcement officers, lacking probable cause to believe that a crime has occurred, may stop and briefly detain a person for investigative purposes. In *Sokolow*, the Court ruled that the legitimacy of such a stop must be evaluated according to a "totality of circumstances" criteria—in which all aspects of the defendant's behavior, taken in concert, may provide the basis for a legitimate stop based upon reasonable suspicion. In this case, the defendant, Sokolow, appeared suspicious to police because, while traveling under an alias from Honolulu, he had paid $2,100 in $20 bills (from a large roll of money) for two airplane tickets after spending a surprisingly small amount of time in Miami. In addition, the defendant was obviously nervous and checked no luggage. A warrantless airport investigation by DEA agents uncovered more than 1,000 grams of cocaine in the defendant's belongings. The Court, in upholding Sokolow's conviction, ruled that, although no single activity was proof of illegal activity, taken together they created circumstances under which suspicion of illegal activity was justified.

In 1993, however, in the case of *Minnesota* v. *Dickerson*,[66] the U.S. Supreme Court placed new limits on an officer's ability to seize evidence discovered during a pat down search conducted for protective reasons when the search itself was based merely upon suspicion and failed to immediately reveal the presence of a weapon. In this case, Timothy Dickerson, who was observed leaving a building known for cocaine trafficking, was stopped by Minneapolis police officers after they noticed him acting suspiciously. The officers decided to investigate further and ordered Dickerson to submit to a pat down search. The search revealed no weapons, but the officer conducting it testified that he felt a small lump in Dickerson's jacket pocket, believed it to be a lump of crack cocaine upon examining it with his fingers, and then reached into Dickerson's pocket and retrieved a small bag of cocaine. Dickerson was arrested, tried, and convicted of possession of a controlled substance. His appeal, which claimed that the pat down search had been illegal, eventually made its way to the U.S. Supreme Court. The high court ruled that "if an officer lawfully pats down a suspect's outer clothing and feels an object whose contour or mass makes its identity immediately apparent, there has been no invasion of the suspect's privacy beyond that already authorized by the officer's search for weapons." However, in *Dickerson*, the Justices ruled, "the officer never thought that the lump was a weapon, but did not immediately recognize it as cocaine." The lump was determined to be cocaine only after the officer "squeezed, slid, and otherwise manipulated the pocket's contents." Hence, the Court held, the officer's actions in this case did not qualify under what might be called a "plain feel" exception. In any case, said the Court, the search in *Dickerson* went far beyond what is permissible under *Terry*—in which officer safety was the crucial issue. The Court summed up its ruling in *Dickerson* this way: "While *Terry* entitled [the officer] to place his hands on respondent's jacket and to feel the lump in the pocket, his continued exploration of the pocket after he concluded that it contained no weapon was unrelated to the sole justification for the search under Terry" and was therefore illegal.

Just as arrest must be based upon probable cause, officers may not stop and question an unwilling citizen whom they have no reason to suspect of a crime. In the case of *Brown* v. *Texas* (1979),[67] two Texas law enforcement officers stopped the defendant and asked for identification. Brown, they later testified, had not been acting suspiciously nor did they think he might have a weapon. The stop was made simply because officers wanted to know who he was. Brown was arrested under a Texas statue which required a person to identify himself properly and accurately when requested to do so by peace officers. Eventually, his appeal reached the U.S. Supreme Court which ruled that, under circumstances found in the *Brown* case, a person "may not be punished for refusing to identify himself."

In *Smith* v. *Ohio* (1990),[68] the Court held that an individual has the right to protect his or her belongings from unwarranted police inspection. In *Smith,* the defendant was approached by two officers in plain clothes who observed that he was carrying a brown paper bag. The officers asked him to "come here a minute" and, when he kept walking, identified themselves as police officers. The defendant threw the bag onto the hood of his car and attempted to protect it from the officers' intrusion. Marijuana was found inside the bag, and the defendant was arrested. Since there was little reason to stop the suspect in this case, and because control over the bag was not thought necessary for the officer's protection, the Court found that the Fourth Amendment protects both "the traveler who carries a toothbrush and a few articles of clothing in a paper bag" and "the sophisticated executive with the locked attaché case."[69]

The following year, however, in what some Court observers saw as a turnabout, the U.S. Supreme Court ruled in *California* v. *Hodari D.* (1991)[70] that suspects who flee from the police and throw away evidence as they retreat may later be arrested based upon the incriminating nature of the abandoned evidence. The case, which began in Oakland, California, centered on the behavior of a group of juveniles who had been standing around a parked car. Two city police officers, driving an unmarked car but with the word *Police* emblazoned in large letters on their jackets, approached the youths. As they came close, the juveniles apparently panicked and fled. One of them tossed away a "rock" of crack cocaine, which was retrieved by the officers. The juvenile was later arrested and convicted of the possession of a controlled substance, but the California Court of Appeals reversed his conviction, reasoning that the officers did not have sufficient reasonable suspicion to make a "Terry-type stop." The Supreme Court, in reversing the finding of the California court, found that reasonable suspicion was not needed, since no "stop" was made. The suspects had not been "seized" by the police, the Court ruled. Therefore, the evidence taken was not the result of an illegal seizure within the meaning of the Fourth Amendment. The significance of *Hodari* for future police action was highlighted by California prosecutors who pointed out that cases like *Hodari* occur "almost everyday in this nation's urban areas."[71]

Emergency Searches of Persons

It is possible to imagine emergency situations in which officers may have to search people based upon quick decisions: a person who matches the description of an armed robber, a woman who is found lying unconscious, a man who has what appears to be blood on his shoes. Such searches can save lives by disarming fleeing felons or by uncovering a medical reason for an emergency situation. They may also prevent criminals from escaping or destroying evidence.

Emergency searches of persons, like those of premises, fall under the exigent circumstances exception to the warrant requirement of the Fourth Amendment. The Supreme

Plain-View Requirements

Following the opinion of the U.S. Supreme Court in the case of *Horton* v. *California* (1990), items seized under the plain-view doctrine may be admissible as evidence in a court of law if the officer who seized the evidence

1. Was lawfully in the viewing area, and

2. Had probable cause to believe the evidence was somehow associated with criminal activity.

Court, in the 1979 case of *Arkansas* v. *Sanders*,[72] recognized the need for such searches "where the societal costs of obtaining a warrant, such as danger to law officers or the risk of loss or destruction of evidence, outweigh the reasons for prior recourse to a neutral magistrate."[73]

The 1987 case of *Borchardt* v. *U.S.*,[74] decided by the Fifth Circuit Court of Appeals, held that Borchardt could be prosecuted for heroin uncovered during medical treatment, even though the defendant had objected to the treatment. Borchardt was a federal inmate at the time he was discovered unconscious in his cell. He was taken to a hospital where tests revealed heroin in his blood. His heart stopped, and he was revived using CPR. Borchardt was given three doses of Narcan, a drug used to counteract the effects of heroin, and he improved, regaining consciousness. The patient refused requests to pump his stomach, but began to become lethargic, indicating the need for additional Narcan. Eventually, he vomited nine plastic bags full of heroin, along with two bags which had burst. The heroin was turned over to federal officers, and Borchardt was eventually convicted of heroin possession. Attempts to exclude the heroin from evidence were unsuccessful, and the appeals court ruled that the necessity of the emergency situation overruled the defendant's objections to search his person.

The Legal Counsel Division of the FBI provides the following guidelines in conducting emergency warrantless searches of individuals, where the possible destruction of evidence is at issue (keep in mind that there may be no probable cause to *arrest* the individual being searched). All four conditions must apply:[75]

1. There was probable cause to believe at the time of the search that there was evidence concealed on the person searched.
2. There was probable cause to believe an emergency threat of destruction of evidence existed at the time of the search.
3. The officer had no prior opportunity to obtain a warrant authorizing the search.
4. The action was no greater than necessary to eliminate the threat of destruction of evidence.

> "The public safety exception was intended to protect the police, as well as the public, from danger."
>
> —**U.S.** *v.* **Brady,** *819 F2d 884 (1987).*

Vehicle Searches

Vehicles present a special law enforcement problem. They are highly movable, and, when an arrest of a driver or an occupant occurs, the need to search them may be immediate.

The first significant Supreme Court case involving an automobile was that of *Carroll* v. *U.S.*,[76] in 1925. In the *Carroll* case a divided Court ruled that a warrantless search of an automobile or other vehicle is valid if it is based upon a reasonable belief that contraband is present. In 1964, however, in the case of *Preston* v. *U.S.*,[77] the limits of warrantless vehicle searches were defined. Preston was arrested for vagrancy and taken to jail. His vehicle was impounded, towed to the police garage, and later searched. Two revolvers were uncovered in the glove compartment, and more incriminating evidence was found in the trunk. Preston was convicted on weapons possession and other charges and eventually appealed to the U.S. Supreme Court. The Court held that the warrantless search of Preston's vehicle had occurred while the automobile was in secure custody and had been, therefore, illegal. Time and circumstances would have permitted, the Court reasoned, acquisition of a warrant to conduct the search.

When the search of a vehicle occurs after it has been impounded, however, that search may be legitimate if it is undertaken for routine and reasonable purposes. In the case of *South Dakota* v. *Opperman* (1976),[78] for example, the Court held that a warrantless search undertaken for purposes of the inventorying and safekeeping of personal possessions of the car's owner was not illegal, even though it turned up marijuana. The intent of the search had not been to discover contraband, but to secure the owner's belongings from possible theft. Again, in *Colorado* v. *Bertine* (1987), the Court reinforced the idea that officers may open closed containers found in a vehicle while conducting a routine search for inventorying purposes. In the words of the Court, such searches are "now a well-defined exception in the warrant requirement. . . ."[79] In 1990, however, in the precedent-setting case of *Florida* v. *Wells*,[80] the Court agreed with a lower court's suppression of marijuana discovered in a locked suitcase in the trunk of a defendant's impounded vehicle. In *Wells*, the Court held that standardized criteria authorizing the search of a vehicle for inventorying purposes were necessary before such a discovery could be legitimate. Standardized criteria, said the Court, might take the form of department policies, written general orders, or established routines.

Generally speaking, where vehicles are concerned, an investigatory stop is permissible under the Fourth Amendment if supported by reasonable suspicion,[81] and a warrantless search of a stopped car is valid if it is based on probable cause.[82] Reasonable suspicion can expand into probable cause when the facts in a given situation so warrant. In the 1996 case of *Ornelas* v. *U.S.*,[83] for example, two experienced police officers stopped a car driven by two men whom a computer check revealed to be known or suspected drug traffickers. One of the officers noticed a loose panel above an armrest in the vehicle's backseat, and then searched the car. A package of cocaine was found beneath the panel. Following conviction, the defendants appealed to the U.S. Supreme Court, claiming that no probable cause to search the car existed at the time of the stop. The majority opinion, however, noted that in the view of the court which originally heard the case, "the model, age, and source-State origin of the car, and the fact that two men traveling together checked into a motel at 4 o'clock in the morning without reservations, formed a drug-courier profile and . . . this profile together with the [computer] reports gave rise to a reasonable suspicion of drug-trafficking activity. . . . [I]n the court's view, reasonable suspicion became probable cause when Deputy Luedke found the loose panel."[84] Probable cause permits a warrantless search of a vehicle under what has been called the **fleeting targets exception** to the exclusionary rule.[85]

Fleeting Targets Exception

An exception to the exclusionary rule that permits law enforcement officers to search a motor vehicle based upon probable cause but without a warrant. The fleeting targets exception is predicated upon the fact that vehicles can quickly leave the jurisdiction of a law enforcement agency.

Warrantless vehicle searches may extend to any area of the vehicle, and may include sealed containers, the trunk area, and the glove compartment if officers have probable cause to conduct a purposeful search or if officers have been given permission to search the vehicle. In the 1991 case of *Florida* v. *Jimeno*,[86] arresting officers stopped a motorist who gave them permission to search his car. The defendant was later convicted on a drug charge when a bag on the floor of the car was found to contain cocaine. Upon appeal to the Supreme Court, however, he argued that the permission given to search his car did not extend to bags and other items within the car. In a decision which may have implications beyond vehicle searches, the Court held that "[a] criminal suspect's Fourth Amendment right to be free from unreasonable searches is not violated when, after he gives police permission to search his car, they open a closed container found within the car that might reasonably hold the object of the search. The amendment is satisfied when, under the circumstances, it is objectively reasonable for the police to believe that the scope of the suspect's consent permitted them to open the particular container."[87]

In *United States* v. *Ross* (1982),[88] the Court found that officers had not exceeded their authority in opening a bag in the defendant's trunk which was found to contain heroin. The search was held to be justifiable on the basis of information developed from a search of the passenger compartment. The Court said, "If probable cause justifies the search of a lawfully stopped vehicle, it justifies the search of every part of the vehicle and its contents that may conceal the object of the search."[89] Moreover, according to the 1996 U.S. Supreme Court decision of *Whren* v. *U.S.*,[90] officers may stop a vehicle being driven suspiciously and then search it once probable cause has developed, even though their primary assignment centers on duties other than traffic enforcement *or* "if a reasonable officer would not have stopped the motorist absent some additional law enforcement objective" (which, in the case of *Whren,* was drug enforcement). Motorists[91] and their passengers may be ordered out of stopped vehicles in the interest of officer safety, and any evidence developed as a result of such a procedure may be used in court. In 1997, for example, in the case of *Maryland* v. *Wilson*,[92] the U.S. Supreme Court overturned a decision by a Maryland court which held that crack cocaine found during a traffic stop was seized illegally when it fell from the lap of a passenger ordered out of a stopped vehicle by a Maryland state trooper. The Maryland court reasoned that the police should not have authority to order seemingly innocent passengers out of vehicles—even those which have been stopped for legitimate reasons. The Supreme Court cited concerns for officer safety in overturning the Maryland's courts ruling and held that the activities of passengers are subject to police control.

In 1998, however, the U.S. Supreme Court placed clear limits on warrantless vehicle searches. In the case of *Knowles* v. *Iowa*,[93] an Iowa policeman stopped Patrick Knowles for speeding and issued him a citation, but did not make a custodial arrest. The officer then conducted a full search of his car without either Knowles' consent or probable cause. Marijuana was found and Knowles was arrested. At the time, Iowa state law gave officers authority to conduct full-blown automobile searches when issuing only a citation. The Supreme Court found, however, that while concern for officer safety during a routine traffic stop may justify the minimal intrusion of ordering a driver and passengers out of a car, it does not by itself justify what it called "the considerably greater intrusion attending a full field-type search." Hence, while a search incident to arrest may be justifiable in the eyes of the Court, a search incident to citation clearly is not.

Finally, in 1999, in the case of *Wyoming* v. *Houghton*,[94] the Court ruled that police officers with probable cause to search a car may inspect passengers' belongings found in the car that are capable of concealing the object of the search.

Watercraft and Motor Homes

The 1983 case of *U.S.* v. *Villamonte-Marquez*[95] widened the *Carroll* decision (discussed earlier) to include watercraft. The case involved an anchored sailboat occupied by Villamonte-Marquez which was searched by a U.S. Customs officer after one of the crew members appeared unresponsive to being hailed. The officer thought he smelled burning marijuana after boarding the vessel and saw burlap bales through an open hatch which he suspected might be contraband. A search proved him correct, and the ship's occupants were arrested. Their conviction was overturned upon appeal, but the U.S. Supreme Court reversed the appeals court. The Court reasoned that a vehicle on the water can easily leave the jurisdiction of enforcement officials, just as a car or truck can.

In *California* v. *Carney* (1985),[96] the Court extended police authority to conduct warrantless searches of vehicles to include motor homes. Earlier arguments had been advanced that a motor home, because it is more like a permanent residence, should not be considered a vehicle in the same sense of an automobile for purposes of search and seizure. The Court, in a 6-to-3 decision, rejected those arguments, reasoning that a vehicle's appointments and size do not alter its basic function of providing transportation.

Houseboats were brought under the automobile exception to the Fourth Amendment warrant requirement in the 1988 Tenth Circuit Court case of *U.S.* v. *Hill*.[97] In the *Hill* case, DEA agents developed evidence which led them to believe that methamphetamine was being manufactured on board a houseboat traversing Lake Texoma in Oklahoma. Because a storm warning had been issued for the area, agents decided to board and search the boat prior to obtaining a warrant. During the search, an operating amphetamine laboratory was discovered, and the boat was seized. In an appeal, the defendants argued that the houseboat search had been illegal because agents lacked a warrant to search their home. The appellate court, however, in rejecting the claims of the defendants, ruled that a houseboat, because it is readily mobile, may be searched without a warrant where probable cause exists to believe that a crime has been or is being committed.

Suspicionless Searches

In two 1989 decisions, the U.S. Supreme Court ruled for the first time in its history that there may be instances when the need to ensure public safety provides a **compelling interest** which negates the rights of any individual to privacy, permitting searches even when a person is not suspected of a crime. In the case of *National Treasury Employees Union* v. *Von Raab* (1989),[98] the Court, by a 5-to-4 vote, upheld a program of the U.S. Customs Service which required mandatory drug testing for all workers seeking promotions or job transfers involving drug interdiction and the carrying of firearms. The Court's majority opinion read: "We think the government's need to conduct the suspicionless searches required by the Customs program outweighs the privacy interest of employees engaged directly in drug interdiction, and of those who otherwise are required to carry firearms."

The second case, *Skinner* v. *Railway Labor Executives' Association* (1989),[99] was decided on the same day. In *Skinner*, the justices voted 7 to 2 to permit the mandatory testing of railway crews for the presence of drugs or alcohol following serious train accidents. The *Skinner* case involved evidence of drugs in a 1987 train wreck outside of Baltimore, Maryland, in which 16 people were killed and hundreds injured.

Suspicionless Searches

Those searches conducted by law enforcement personnel without a warrant and without suspicion. Suspicionless searches are only permissible if based upon an overriding concern for public safety.

Compelling Interest

A legal concept which provides a basis for suspicionless searches (urinalysis tests of train engineers, for example) when public safety is at issue. It is the concept upon which the Supreme Court cases of Skinner v. Railway Labor Executives' Association *(1989) and* National Treasury Employees Union v. Von Raab *(1989) turned. In those cases the Court held that public safety may provide a sufficiently compelling interest such that an individual's right to privacy can be limited under certain circumstances.*

The 1991 Supreme Court case of *Florida* v. *Bostick,*[100] which permitted warrantless "sweeps" of intercity buses, moved the Court deeply into conservative territory. The *Bostick* case came to the attention of the Court as a result of the Broward County (Florida) Sheriff Department's routine practice of boarding buses at scheduled stops and asking passengers for permission to search their bags. Terrance Bostick, a passenger on one of the buses, gave police permission to search his luggage, which was found to contain cocaine. Bostick was arrested and eventually pleaded guilty to charges of drug trafficking. The Florida Supreme Court, however, found merit in Bostick's appeal, which was based upon a Fourth Amendment claim that the search of his luggage had been unreasonable. The Florida court held that "a reasonable passenger in [Bostick's] situation would not have felt free to leave the bus to avoid questioning by the police" and overturned the conviction.

The state appealed to the U.S. Supreme Court, which held that the Florida Supreme Court erred in interpreting Bostick's *feelings* that he was not free to leave the bus. In the words of the Court, "Bostick was a passenger on a bus that was scheduled to depart. He would not have felt free to leave the bus even if the police had not been present. Bostick's movements were 'confined' in a sense, but this was the natural result of his decision to take the bus." In other words, Bostick was constrained not so much by police action as by his own feelings that he might miss the bus were he to get off. Following this line of reasoning, the Court concluded that police warrantless, suspicionless "sweeps" of buses, "trains, planes, and city streets" are permissible so long as officers (1) ask individual passengers for permission before searching their possessions, (2) do not coerce passengers to consent to a search, and (3) do not convey the message that citizen compliance with the search request is mandatory. Passenger compliance with police searches must be voluntary for the searches to be legal.

In contrast to the tone of Court decisions more than two decades earlier, the justices did not require officers to inform passengers that they were free to leave nor that they had the right to deny officers the opportunity to search (although Bostick himself was so advised by Florida officers). Any reasonable person, the Court ruled, should feel free to deny the police

21st Century CJ

Search Warrants by Fax

The government of Ontario recently announced the availability of search warrants by fax. The program, which began on an experimental basis in early 1997, now allows police officers across the province to use a fax machine to apply for a search warrant from a justice of the peace or local magistrate. The new service, called telewarrants, is available 24 hours per day, seven days a week. Other Canadian provinces, including Alberta, British Columbia, Manitoba, New Brunswick, Quebec, and the Yukon, all use some form of telewarrant services.

According to Ontario's Attorney General Charles Harnick, the telewarrant service is part of an ongoing effort to build a swifter, more effective justice system. "Often the success of a criminal investigation hinges on timely police access to a justice of the peace to apply for a search warrant," said Harnick. "No longer will police investigations be at risk because of difficulty accessing a justice of the peace," he added. "By adopting modern technology in the justice system, we will help police crack down on criminals."

Ontario's newly established telewarrant center makes a justice of the peace available to police investigators via fax at any time. Officers fax their request for a search warrant to the center, where the justice of the peace on duty reviews the application, and faxes an approval or denial of the request back to the officers.

The telewarrant service is available to all municipal and regional police services, as well as to the Ontario Provincial Police, the Royal Canadian Mounted Police, and peace officers working for the province's ministries of transportation, natural resources, and environment and energy.

According to Trevor McCagherty, president of the Ontario Association of Chiefs of Police, "The time saved by our police officers in using the telewarrant service will translate into increased public safety for every citizen.... The new telewarrant service is one more very important weapon in our arsenal against criminal activity."

Source: Press release, Office of the Ontario Attorney General, Ontario, Toronto, Canada, November 7, 1996.

request. In the words of the Court, "[t]he appropriate test is whether, taking into account all of the circumstances surrounding the encounter, a reasonable passenger would feel free to decline the officers' requests or otherwise terminate the encounter." The Court continued: "[R]ejected, however, is Bostick's argument that he must have been seized because no reasonable person would freely consent to a search of luggage containing drugs, since the 'reasonable person' test presumes an innocent person."

Critics of the decision saw it as creating new "Gestapo-like" police powers in the face of which citizens on public transportation will feel compelled to comply with police requests for search authority. Dissenting Justices Blackmun, Stevens, and Marshall held that "the bus sweep at issue in this case violates the core values of the Fourth Amendment." However, in words which may presage a significant change of direction for other Fourth Amendment issues, the Court's majority defended its ruling by writing: "[T]he Fourth Amendment proscribes unreasonable searches and seizures; it does not proscribe voluntary cooperation."

The Intelligence Function

The police role includes the need to gather information through the questioning of both suspects and informants. Even more often, the need for information leads police investigators to question potentially knowledgeable citizens who may have been witnesses or victims. Data gathering is a crucial form of intelligence, without which enforcement agencies would be virtually powerless to plan and effect arrests.

The importance of gathering information in police work cannot be overstressed. Studies have found that the one factor most likely to lead to arrest in serious crimes is the presence of a witness who can provide information to the police. Undercover operations, neighborhood watch programs, "crime stopper" groups, and organized detective work all contribute information to the police.

Informants

Information gathering is a complex process, and many ethical questions have been raised about the techniques police use to gather information. Police use of paid informants, for example, is an area of concern to ethicists who believe that informants are often paid to get away with crimes. The police practice (endorsed by some prosecutors) of agreeing not to charge one offender out of a group if he or she will "talk," and testify against others, is another concern of students of justice ethics.

As we have seen, probable cause is an important aspect of both police searches and legal arrests. The Fourth Amendment specifies, "No warrants shall issue, but upon probable cause." As a consequence, the successful use of informants in supporting requests for a warrant depends upon the demonstrable reliability of their information. The case of *Aguilar* v. *Texas* (1964)[101] clarified the use of informants and established a two-pronged test to the effect that informant information could establish probable cause if *both* of the following criteria are met:

- ■ The source of the informant's information is made clear.
- ■ The police officer has a reasonable belief that the informant is reliable.

The two-pronged test of *Aguilar* v. *Texas* was intended to prevent the issuance of warrants on the basis of false or fabricated information. Two later cases provided exceptions to the two-pronged test. *Harris* v. *United States* (1971)[102] recognized the fact that when an informant provided information that was damaging to him or her, it was probably true. In *Harris* an informant told police that he had purchased nontax-paid whiskey from another person. Since the information also implicated the informant in a crime, it was held to be accurate, even though it could not meet the second prong of the *Aguilar* test. The 1969 Supreme Court case of *Spinelli* v. *United States*[103] created an exception to the requirements of the first prong. In *Spinelli,* the Court held that some information can be so highly specific that it must be accurate, even if its source is not revealed. In 1983, in the case of *Illinois* v. *Gates,*[104] the Court adopted a totality of circumstances approach, which held that sufficient probable cause for issuing a warrant exists where an informer can be reasonably believed on the basis of everything that is known by the police. The *Gates* case involved an anonymous informant who provided incriminating information about another person through a letter to the police. Although the source of the information was not stated, and the police were unable to say whether the informant was reliable, the overall sense of things, given what was already known to police, was that the information supplied was probably valid.

In the 1990 case of *Alabama* v. *White*,[105] the Supreme Court ruled that an anonymous tip, even in the absence of other, corroborating information about a suspect, could form the basis for an investigatory stop where the informant accurately predicts the *future* behavior of the suspect. The Court reasoned that the ability to predict a suspect's behavior demonstrates a significant degree of familiarity with the suspect's affairs. In the words of the Court, "Because only a small number of people are generally privy to an individual's itinerary, it is reasonable for the police to believe that a person with access to such information is likely to also have access to reliable information about that individual's illegal activities."[106]

The identity of informants may be kept secret if sources have been explicitly assured of confidentiality by investigating officers or if a reasonably implied assurance of confidentiality has been made. In *U.S. Department of Justice* v. *Landano* (1993),[107] the U.S. Supreme Court required that an informant's identity be revealed through a request made under the federal Freedom of Information Act. In that case, the FBI had not specifically assured an informant of confidentiality, and the Court ruled that "the government is not entitled to a presumption that all sources supplying information to the FBI in the course of a criminal investigation are confidential sources. . . ."

Police Interrogation

A few years ago Richard Jewell, a former campus security guard, became the primary suspect in the pipe-bombing attack that took place in Atlanta's Centennial Park during the 1996 Olympics. FBI investigators were apparently convinced that Jewell was guilty and, according to Jewell, used a ruse to try and trick him into confessing.[108] Jewell claimed that agents asked him to sign a waiver of his *Miranda* rights, even before he knew he was a suspect, by telling him that the waiver document was a prop in a training film. Agents told Jewell that they were making a film about how to interrogate suspects and that Jewell was chosen for the star role because of his heroic activities at the time of the bombing. Later, when authorities dropped their investigation of Jewell, he sued CNN, the Atlanta *Journal-Constitution,* and his former college employer for libel and character defamation—and threatened suit against the FBI. FBI Director Louis Freeh later admitted that agents had made a "major error in judgment" when they tried to trick Jewell.[109] As the Jewell investigation was to show, police interrogators must remember that not all suspects are guilty and that everyone is entitled to constitutional rights during investigation and interrogation.

Interrogation has been defined by the U.S. Supreme Court as any behaviors by the police "that the police should know are reasonably likely to elicit an incriminating response from the suspect." Hence, **interrogation** may involve activities which go well beyond mere verbal questioning, and the Court has held that interrogation may include "staged lineups, reverse lineups, positing guilt, minimizing the moral seriousness of crime, and casting blame on the victim or society." It is noteworthy that the Court has also held that "police words or actions normally attendant to arrest and custody do not constitute interrogation,"[110] unless they involve pointed or directed questions. Hence, an arresting officer may instruct a suspect on what to do and may chit-chat with the offender without engaging in interrogation within the meaning of the law. Once police officers make inquiries intended to elicit information about the crime in question, however, interrogation has begun. The interrogation of suspects, like other areas of police activity, is subject to constitutional limits as interpreted by the courts, and a series of landmark decisions by the U.S. Supreme Court has focused on police interrogation.

> **Interrogation**
>
> *The information-gathering activities of police officers which involve the direct questioning of suspects.*

Physical Abuse

The first in a series of significant cases was that of *Brown* v. *Mississippi*,[111] decided in 1936. The *Brown* case began with the robbery of a white store owner in Mississippi in 1934. During the robbery, the victim was killed. A posse formed and went to the home of a local black man rumored to have been one of the perpetrators. They dragged the suspect from his home, put a rope around his neck, and hoisted him into a tree. They repeated this process a number of times, hoping to get a confession from the man, but failing. The posse was headed by a deputy sheriff who then arrested other suspects in the case and laid them over chairs in the local jail and whipped them with belts and buckles until they "confessed." These confessions were used in the trial which followed, and all three defendants were convicted of murder. Their convictions were upheld by the Mississippi Supreme Court. In 1936, however, the case was reviewed by the U.S. Supreme Court, which overturned all of the convictions, saying that it was difficult to imagine techniques of interrogation more "revolting" to the sense of justice than those used in this case. Read the full text of the Court's opinion in *Brown* v. *Mississippi* at **WebExtra!** 5-7 on CJToday.com.

Inherent Coercion

Interrogation need not involve physical abuse for it to be contrary to constitutional principles. In the case of *Ashcraft* v. *Tennessee*,[112] the Court found that inherently coercive interrogation was not acceptable. Ashcraft had been charged with the murder of his wife, Zelma. He was arrested on a Saturday night and interrogated by relays of skilled interrogators until Monday morning, when he purportedly made a statement implicating him in the murder. During questioning he had been faced by a blinding light, but not physically mistreated. Investigators later testified that when the suspect requested cigarettes, food, or water, they "kindly" provided them. The Supreme Court's ruling, which reversed Ashcraft's conviction, made it plain that the Fifth Amendment guarantee against self-incrimination excludes *any* form of official coercion or pressure during interrogation.

A similar case, involving four black defendants, occurred in Florida in 1940.[113] The four men, including one whose name was Chambers, were arrested without warrants as suspects in a robbery and murder of an aged white man. After several days of questioning in a hostile atmosphere, the men confessed to the murder. The confessions were used as the primary evidence against them at a trial which ensued, and all four were sentenced to die. Upon appeal to the Supreme Court, the Court held that "the very circumstances surrounding their confinement and their questioning without any formal charges having been brought, were such as to fill petitioners with terror and frightful misgivings."[114]

Psychological Manipulation

Interrogation must not only be free of coercion and hostility, but it also cannot involve sophisticated trickery designed to ferret out a confession. While interrogators do not necessarily have to be scrupulously honest in confronting suspects, and while the expert opinions of medical and psychiatric practitioners may be sought in investigations, the use of professionals skilled in **psychological manipulation** to gain confessions was banned by the Court in the case of *Leyra* v. *Denno*[115] in 1954.

The early 1950s were the "heyday" of psychiatric perspectives on criminal behavior. In the Leyra case, detectives employed a psychiatrist to question Leyra, who had been charged with the hammer slayings of his parents. Leyra had been led to believe that the medical doctor to whom he was introduced in an interrogation room had actually been sent to help him with a sinus problem. Following a period of questioning, including subtle suggestions by the psychiatrist that he would feel better if he confessed to the murders, Leyra did indeed confess.

The Supreme Court, on appeal, ruled that the defendant had been effectively, and improperly, duped by the police. In the words of the Court, "Instead of giving petitioner the medical advice and treatment he expected, the psychiatrist by subtle and suggestive questions simply continued the police effort of the past days and nights to induce petitioner to admit his guilt. For an hour and a half or more the techniques of a highly trained psychiatrist were used to break petitioner's will in order to get him to say he had murdered his parents."[116] After a series of three trials which ended in convictions, each with less and less evidence permitted into the courtroom by appeals courts, Leyra was finally set free by a state appeals court which found insufficient evidence for the final conviction.

In 1991 the Supreme Court, in the case of *Arizona* v. *Fulminante*[117] threw an even more dampening blanket of uncertainty over the use of sophisticated techniques to gain a confession. Oreste Fulminante was an inmate in a federal prison when he was approached secretly

Inherent Coercion

Those tactics used by police interviewers which fall short of physical abuse but which, nonetheless, pressure suspects to divulge information.

Psychological Manipulation

Manipulative actions by police interviewers designed to pressure suspects to divulge information, which are based upon subtle forms of intimidation and control.

by a fellow inmate who was an FBI informant. The informant told Fulminante that other inmates were plotting to kill him because of a rumor that he had killed a child. He offered to protect Fulminante if he was told the details of the crime. Fulminante then described his role in the murder of his 11-year-old stepdaughter. Fulminante was arrested for that murder, tried, and convicted. Upon appeal to the U.S. Supreme Court, his lawyers argued that Fulminante's confession had been coerced because of the threat of violence communicated by the informant. The Court agreed that the confession had been coerced and ordered a new trial at which the confession could not be admitted into evidence. Simultaneously, however, the Court found that the admission of a coerced confession should be considered a harmless "trial error" which need not necessarily result in reversal of a conviction if other evidence still proves guilt. The decision was especially significant because it partially reversed the Court's earlier ruling, in *Chapman* v. *California*,[118] where it was held that forced confessions were such a basic form of constitutional error that they could never be used, and automatically invalidated any conviction to which they related.

Theory Into Practice

Individual Rights versus Group Interests—The Fourth Amendment and Sobriety Checkpoints

The Fourth and Fourteenth Amendments to the U.S. Constitution guarantee liberty and personal security to all persons residing within the United States. Lacking probable cause to believe that a crime has been committed, the courts have generally held that police officers have no legitimate authority to detain or arrest people who are going about their business in a peaceful manner. The U.S. Supreme Court has, however, in a number of cases, decided that community interests may necessitate a temporary suspension of personal liberty, even where probable cause is lacking. One such case is that of *Michigan Department of State Police* v. *Sitz* (1990),[1] which involved the legality of highway sobriety checkpoints—even those at which nonsuspicious drivers are subjected to scrutiny.

The Court had previously established that traffic stops, including those at checkpoints along a highway, are "seizures" within the meaning of the Fourth Amendment.[2] In *Michigan Department of State Police* v. *Sitz*, however, a Court that was on its way to becoming increasingly conservative ruled that such seizures are reasonable insofar as they are essential to the welfare of the community as a whole. That

the Court reached its conclusion based upon pragmatic social interests is clear from the words used by Chief Justice Rehnquist:

> No one can seriously dispute the magnitude of the drunken driving problem or the States' interest in eradicating it. Media reports of alcohol-related death and mutilation on the Nation's roads are legion. Drunk drivers cause an annual death toll of over 25,000 and in the same time span cause nearly one million personal injuries and more than five billion dollars in property damage.... [t]he balance of the State's interest in preventing drunken driving, the extent to which this system can reasonably be said to advance that interest, and the degree of intrusion upon individual motorists who are briefly stopped, weighs in favor of the state program.

But, critics say, how far should the Court go in allowing officers to act without probable cause? Figures on domestic violence (child and spouse abuse, murder, incest, and other forms of victimization in the home), if compared to traffic statistics, are probably far more shocking. Using the same

kind of reasoning as in *Michigan Department of State Police* v. *Sitz*, one could imagine the chief justice writing, "the balance of the State's interest in preventing domestic violence, the extent to which preventive programs briefly inconvenience individual citizens, and the relatively small degree of intrusion upon law-abiding citizens which such a program represents, weighs in favor of random home incursions by well-intentioned police officers."

❓ QUESTIONS FOR DISCUSSION

1. Do you agree with the assertion that "community interests may necessitate a temporary suspension of personal liberty, even where probable cause is lacking"? Why or why not? If so, under what circumstances might liberties be suspended?

2. Would you, as this box suggests, be willing to "take intrusion upon law-abiding citizens" further? If so, what areas would you consider?

[1]Michigan Department of State Police *v.* Sitz, *110 S.Ct. 2481 (1990).*

[2]U.S. *v.* Martinea-Fuerte, *428 U.S. 543, 96 S.Ct. 3074 (1976), and* Brower *v.* County of Inyo, *109 S.Ct. 1378 (1989).*

The Right to a Lawyer at Interrogation

In 1964, in the case of *Escobedo* v. *Illinois,*[119] the right to have legal counsel present during police interrogation was recognized. Danny Escobedo was arrested without a warrant for the murder of his brother-in-law, made no statement during his interrogation, and was released the same day. A few weeks later another person identified Escobedo as the killer. Escobedo was rearrested and taken back to the police station. During the interrogation which followed, officers told him that they "had him cold" and that he should confess. Escobedo asked to see his lawyer, but was told that an interrogation was in progress and that he couldn't just go out and see his lawyer. Soon the lawyer arrived and asked to see Escobedo. Police told him that his client was being questioned and could be seen after questioning concluded. Escobedo later claimed that while he repeatedly asked for his lawyer, he was told, "Your lawyer doesn't want to see you."

Eventually, Escobedo confessed and was convicted at trial on the basis of his confession. Upon appeal to the U.S. Supreme Court, the Court overturned Escobedo's conviction, ruling that counsel is necessary at police interrogations to protect the rights of the defendant and should be provided when the defendant desires.

In 1981, the case of *Edwards* v. *Arizona*[120] established a "bright-line rule" for investigators to use in interpreting a suspect's right to counsel. In *Edwards,* the Supreme Court reiterated its *Miranda* concern that once a suspect, who is in custody and who is being questioned, has requested the assistance of counsel, all questioning must cease until an attorney is present. In 1990 the Court refined the rule in *Minnick* v. *Mississippi,* when it held that interrogation may *not* resume after the suspect has had an opportunity to consult his or her lawyer, when the lawyer is no longer present. Similarly, according to *Arizona* v. *Roberson* (1988),[121] the police may not avoid the defendant's request for a lawyer by beginning a new line of questioning, even if it is about an unrelated offense. In 1994, however, the Court, in the case of *Davis* v. *United States,*[122] "put the burden on custodial suspects to make unequivocal invocations of the right to counsel." In the Davis case, a man being interrogated in the death of a sailor waived his *Miranda* rights, but later said: "Maybe I should talk to a lawyer." Investigators asked the defendant clarifying questions, and he responded, "No, I don't want a lawyer." Upon conviction he appealed, claiming that interrogation should have ceased when he mentioned a lawyer. The Court, in affirming the conviction, stated that "it will often be good police practice for the interviewing officers to clarify whether or not (the defendant) actually wants an attorney."

Suspect Rights: The *Miranda* Decision

In the area of suspect rights, no case is as famous as that of *Miranda* v. *Arizona,*[123] which was decided in 1966. Many people regard *Miranda* as the centerpiece of Warren Court due process rulings.

The case involved Ernesto Miranda, who was arrested in Phoenix, Arizona, and accused of having kidnapped and raped a young woman. At police headquarters he was identified by the victim. After being interrogated for two hours, Miranda signed a confession which formed the basis of his later conviction on the charges.

Upon eventual appeal to the U.S. Supreme Court, the Court rendered what some regard as the most far-reaching opinion to have impacted criminal justice in the last few decades. The Court ruled that Miranda's conviction was unconstitutional because "[t]he entire aura and atmosphere of police interrogation without notification of rights and an offer of assistance of counsel tends to subjugate the individual to the will of his examiner."

The Court continued, saying that the defendant "must be warned prior to any questioning that he has the right to remain silent, that anything he says can be used against him in a court of law, that he has the right to the presence of an attorney, and that if he cannot afford an attorney one will be appointed for him prior to any questioning if he so desires. Opportunity to exercise these rights must be afforded to him throughout the interrogation. After such warnings have been given, and such opportunity afforded him, the individual may knowingly and intelligently waive these rights and agree to answer the questions or make a statement. But unless and until such warnings and waiver are demonstrated by the prosecution at the trial, no evidence obtained as a result of interrogation can be used against him."[124]

To ensure that proper advice is given to suspects at the time of their arrest, the now-famous *Miranda* rights are read before any questioning begins. These rights, as they appear on a *Miranda* warning card commonly used by police agencies, appear in a "Theory into Practice" box in this chapter.

Once suspects have been advised of their *Miranda* rights, they are commonly asked to sign a paper which lists each right, in order to confirm that they were advised of their rights, and that they understand each right. Questioning may then begin, but only if suspects waive their rights not to talk or to have a lawyer present during interrogation.

When the *Miranda* decision was handed down, some hailed it as one which ensured the protection of individual rights guaranteed under the Constitution. To guarantee those rights, they suggested, what better agency is available than the police themselves, since the police are present at the initial stages of the criminal justice process? Critics of *Miranda*, however, argued that the decision put police agencies in the uncomfortable and contradictory position of not only enforcing the law, but also of having to offer defendants advice on how potentially to circumvent conviction and punishment. Under *Miranda* the police partially assume the role of legal advisor to the accused.

During the last years of the Reagan administration, then-Attorney General Edwin Meese called the *Miranda* decision the antithesis of "law and order." He pledged the resources of his office to an assault upon the *Miranda* rules in order to eliminate what he saw as the frequent release of guilty parties on the basis of "technicalities." Meese was unsuccessful, and later administrations vigorously defended the *Miranda* decision.

In 1999, however, the Fourth Circuit U.S. Court of Appeals, in the case of *U.S.* v. *Dickerson*,[125] upheld an almost-forgotten law that Congress had passed in 1968 with the intention of overturning *Miranda*. That law, Section 3501 of Chapter 223, Part II of Title 18 of the U.S. Code, says that "a confession . . . shall be admissible in evidence if it is voluntarily given." In determining the voluntariness of the confession, the trial judge is to "take into consideration all the circumstances surrounding the giving of the confession, including 1. the time elapsing between arrest and arraignment of the defendant making the confession, if it was made after arrest and before arraignment, 2. whether such defendant knew the nature of the offense with which he was charged or of which he was suspected at the time of making the confession, 3. whether or not such defendant was advised or knew that he was not required to make any statement and that any such statement could be used against him, 4. whether or not such defendant had been advised prior to questioning of his right to the assistance of counsel, and 5. whether or not such defendant was without the assistance of counsel when questioned and when giving such confession."

Upon appeal, the U.S. Supreme Court did not side with the Fourth Circuit Court, and upheld *Miranda*. Read the full text of the original *Miranda* decision, the text of Section 3501, the Fourth Circuit Court's 1999 opinion in *Dickerson*, and the final decision by the U.S. Supreme Court at **WebExtra!** 5-8 on CJToday.com.

Waiver of *Miranda* Rights by Suspects

Suspects in police custody may legally waive their *Miranda* rights through a *voluntary* "knowing and intelligent" waiver. A *knowing waiver* can only be made if a suspect has been advised of his or her rights and was in a condition to understand the advisement. A rights advisement made in English, for example, to a Spanish-speaking defendant, cannot produce a knowing waiver. Likewise, an *intelligent waiver* of rights requires that the defendant be able to understand the consequences of not invoking the *Miranda* rights. In the case of *Moran* v. *Burbine* (1986),[126] the Supreme Court defined an intelligent and knowing waiver as one "made with a full awareness both of the nature of the right being abandoned and the consequences of the decision to abandon it."[127] Similarly, in *Colorado* v. *Spring* (1987),[128] the court held that an intelligent and knowing waiver can be made even though a suspect has not been informed of all the alleged offenses about which he or she is about to be questioned.

In 1992 *Miranda* rights were effectively extended to illegal immigrants living in the United States. In a settlement of a class-action lawsuit reached in Los Angeles with the Immigration and Naturalization Service, U.S. District Court Judge William Byrne, Jr., approved

CRIME IN THE NEWS

Miranda Decision Sparks Debate

Does Ruling Safeguard Liberties or Favor Criminals?

June 26, 2000

By Amy Worden

WASHINGTON—Civil liberties advocates and defendants' rights groups are claiming victory today following the Supreme Court's decision to uphold the *Miranda* warning, but prosecutors and police organizations are warning the decision may mean more criminals will go free.

In its 7–2 decision, the court found that the 34-year-old *Miranda* warning, which notifies suspects of their right to remain silent and have a lawyer present when questioned, may not be overruled by an act of Congress.

"It's an important victory for individual liberties given the inherently coercive nature of interrogation while in custody," said Deanne Maynard, a Washington attorney and author of the friend-of-the-court brief filed by the National Association of Criminal Defense Lawyers.

Maynard and others said they feared that essential due process rights were at risk had the court ruled differently.

"Even if someone knows their rights, being reminded of them and knowing that they will be honored is important," she said.

Capitalizing on Technicalities?

Prosecutors and police groups said they were disappointed with the ruling, arguing that guilty people are set free every day on technicalities relating not to *Miranda* itself, but how and when it is administered.

"The court did not even address the more limited argument we tried to make, that the existing [congressional] statute didn't overrule *Miranda*, it just

gave alternatives," said Richard Samp, chief counsel for the Washington Legal Foundation, a conservative public interest law firm, which challenged the *Miranda* decision in a friend-of-the-court brief.

Paul Cassell, a University of Utah professor and *Miranda* critic who filed the friend-of-the-court brief in the case of *Charles Dickerson* v. *U.S.* that propelled the case before the Supreme Court, said hundreds of thousands of crimes are going unsolved each year because of *Miranda* procedures.

"For too long defense attorneys have been able to capitalize on technical issues surrounding *Miranda*," he wrote in the *Los Angeles Times* last year.

Prosecutor: Times Have Changed

Josh Marquis, the district attorney for Clatsop County, Ore., and spokesman for the National District Attorneys Association, said he is prosecuting an aggravated murder case in which the defendant's attorney is arguing that his 18-year-old client did not understand the warning that was given to him.

"Our concern is that [*Miranda*] shouldn't have this talismanic significance—if you drop a pronoun someone is let go. That doesn't happen often, but often enough for us to be concerned," he said.

Marquis said the 1966 *Miranda* decision was the result of bad police practices that are no longer tolerated.

"[We're] not trying to tear down [the] *Miranda* decision, but we're saying, 'Haven't we gone a long way in 50 years from a time when police routinely abused suspects?' " he said.

'Rigid Application'

Police groups said the court's ruling establishes a "rigid application" of *Miranda* that will exclude voluntary

confessions, even when there is no evidence of police wrongdoing.

"If an officer makes just one misstep, not giving a suspect a *Miranda* warning because he in good faith believes that the suspect is not yet in custody, the incriminating statement is thrown out and the suspect goes free, if the court disagrees," said Robert Scully, executive director of the National Association of Police Organizations.

"Interrogation of criminal suspects is essential, yet this decision makes police officers proceed at their own risk," he said.

Rights Can Be Eroded

Officials with the American Civil Liberties Union (ACLU), which filed a friend-of-the-court brief in the *Dickerson* case, said cases of police misconduct throughout the country prove that *Miranda* remains a vital component of the justice system today.

"There were several cases where we represented plaintiffs last year in Los Angeles where police were trying to get around *Miranda*," said Emily Whitfield, a spokeswoman for the ACLU. "These rights can be eroded in the extreme like beating confessions out of people, or in more subtle but also coercive ways."

Another Case Coming

Despite today's ruling, the debate over *Miranda* is far from over. This fall the Supreme Court will consider another case, *Texas* v. *Cobb,* which involves a *Miranda* rights issue.

"That they agreed to hear this case says they don't want to have [*Dickerson*] as the last decision on *Miranda*," said Samp of the Washington Legal Foundation.

the printing of millions of notices in several languages to be given to those arrested. The approximately 1.5 million illegal aliens arrested each year must be told they may (1) talk with a lawyer, (2) make a phone call, (3) request a list of available legal services, (4) seek a hearing before an immigration judge, (5) possibly obtain release on bond, and (6) contact a diplomatic officer representing their country. This kind of thing was "long overdue," said Roberto Martinez of the American Friends Service Committee's Mexico–U.S. border program. "Up to now, we've had total mistreatment of civil rights of undocumented people."[129]

Inevitable Discovery Exception to *Miranda*

A good example of the change in Supreme Court philosophy, alluded to earlier in this chapter as a movement away from an individual rights and toward a social order perspective, can be had in the case of Robert Anthony Williams. The *Williams* case epitomizes what some have called a "nibbling away" at the advances in defendant rights which reached their apex in *Miranda.* The case had its beginnings in 1969, at the close of the Warren court era, when Williams was convicted of murdering a 10-year-old girl, Pamela Powers, around Christmastime. Although Williams had been advised of his rights, detectives searching for the girl's body were riding in a car with the defendant when one of them made what has since come to be known as the "Christian burial speech." The detective told Williams that, since Christmas was almost upon them, it would be "the Christian thing to do" to see to it that Pamela could have a decent burial rather than having to lie in a field somewhere. Williams relented and led detectives to the body. However, because Williams had not been reminded of his right to have a lawyer present during his conversation with the detective, the Supreme Court in *Brewer* v. *Williams* (1977)[130] overturned Williams's conviction, saying that the detective's remarks were "a deliberate eliciting of incriminating evidence from an accused in the absence of his lawyer."

In 1977 Williams was retried for the murder, but his remarks in leading detectives to the

A suspect being read his Miranda *rights immediately after arrest. Officers often read* Miranda *rights from a card to preclude the possibility of mistake.*
Bob Daemmrich, Stock Boston.

body were not entered into evidence. The discovery of the body was itself used, however, prompting another appeal to the Supreme Court based upon the argument that the body should not have been used as evidence since it was discovered due to the illegally gathered statements. This time, in *Nix* v. *Williams* (1984),[131] the Supreme Court affirmed Williams's second conviction, holding that the body would have been found anyway, since detectives were searching in the direction where it lay when Williams revealed its location. That ruling came during the heyday of the Burger court, and clearly demonstrates a tilt by the Court away from suspect's rights and an accommodation with the imperfect world of police procedure. The *Williams* case, as it was finally resolved, is said to have created the "inevitable discovery exception" to the *Miranda* requirements.

Public Safety Exceptions to *Miranda*

In 1984 the U.S. Supreme Court also established what has come to be known as the public safety exception to the *Miranda* rule. The case *New York* v. *Quarles*[132] centered upon an alleged rape in which the victim told police her assailant had fled, with a gun, into a nearby A&P supermarket. Two police officers entered the store and apprehended the suspect. One officer immediately noticed that the man was wearing an empty shoulder holster and, apparently fearing that a child might find the discarded weapon, quickly asked, "Where's the gun?"

Quarles was convicted of rape, but appealed his conviction, requesting that the weapon be suppressed as evidence because officers had not advised him of his *Miranda* rights before asking him about it. The Supreme Court disagreed, stating that considerations of public safety were overriding and negated the need for rights advisement prior to limited questioning which focused on the need to prevent further harm.

Where the police have not been coercive, and have issued **Miranda warnings,** the Supreme Court has held that even a later demonstration that a person may have been suffering from mental problems will not necessarily negate a confession. *Colorado* v. *Connelly* (1986)[133] involved a man who approached a Denver police officer and said he wanted to confess to the

Miranda Warnings

The advisement of rights due criminal suspects by the police prior to the beginning of questioning. Miranda warnings were first set forth by the Court in the 1966 case of Miranda v. Arizona.

Theory Into Practice

Adult Rights Warning

Persons 18 years old or older who are in custody must be given this advice of rights before any questioning.

1. You have the right to remain silent.
2. Anything you say can be used against you in a court of law.
3. You have the right to talk to a lawyer and to have a lawyer present while you are being questioned.
4. If you want a lawyer before or during questioning but cannot afford to hire a lawyer, one will be appointed to represent you at no cost before any questioning.
5. If you answer questions now without a lawyer here, you still have the right to stop answering questions at any time.

Waiver of Rights

After reading and explaining the rights of a person in custody, an officer must also ask for a waiver of those rights before any questioning. The following waiver questions must be answered affirmatively, either by express answer or by clear implication. Silence alone is not a waiver.

1. Do you understand each of these rights I have explained to you? (Answer must be YES.)
2. Having these rights in mind, do you now wish to answer questions? (Answer must be YES.)

3. Do you now wish to answer questions without a lawyer present? (Answer must be YES.)

For juveniles age 14, 15, 16, and 17, the following question must be asked:

4. Do you now wish to answer questions without your parents, guardians, or custodians present? (Answer must be YES.)

? QUESTIONS FOR DISCUSSION

1. Are there any other "rights" that you would add to those listed here? If so, which ones?
2. Are there any "rights" that you would remove from those listed here? If so, which ones?

Source: N.C. Justice Academy. Reprinted with permission.

murder of a young girl. The officer immediately informed him of his *Miranda* rights, but the man waived them and continued to talk. When a detective arrived, the man was again advised of his rights and again waived them. After being taken to the local jail the man began to hear "voices" and later claimed that it was these voices which had made him confess. At the trial the defense moved to have the earlier confession negated on the basis that it was not voluntarily or freely given because of the defendant's mental condition. Upon appeal, the Supreme Court disagreed, saying that "no coercive government conduct occurred in this case."[134] Hence, "self-coercion," be it through the agency of a guilty conscience or faulty thought processes, does not appear to bar prosecution based on information revealed willingly by the defendant.

In a final refinement of *Miranda,* the lawful ability of a police informant placed in a jail cell along with a defendant to gather information for later use at trial was upheld in the 1986 case of *Kuhlmann* v. *Wilson.*[135] The passive gathering of information was judged to be acceptable, provided that the informant did not make attempts to elicit information.

In the case of *Illinois* v. *Perkins* (1990),[136] the Court expanded its position to say that, under appropriate circumstances, even the active questioning of a suspect by an undercover officer posing as a fellow inmate does not require *Miranda* warnings. In *Perkins,* the Court found that, lacking other forms of coercion, the fact that the suspect was not aware of the questioner's identity as a law enforcement officer ensured that his statements were freely given. In the words of the Court, "[t]he essential ingredients of a 'police-dominated atmosphere' and compulsion are not present when an incarcerated person speaks freely to someone that he believes to be a fellow inmate."

Miranda and the Meaning of Interrogation

Modern interpretations of the applicability of *Miranda* warnings turn upon an understanding of *interrogation.* The *Miranda* decision, as originally rendered, specifically recognized the necessity for police investigators to make inquiries at crime scenes in order to determine facts or establish identities. So long as the individual questioned is not yet in custody, and so long as probable cause is lacking in the investigator's mind, such questioning can proceed without the need for *Miranda* warnings. In such cases, interrogation, within the meaning of *Miranda,* has not yet begun.

The case of *Rock* v. *Zimmerman* (1982)[137] provides a different sort of example—one in which a suspect willingly made statements to the police before interrogation began. The suspect had burned his own house and shot and killed a neighbor. When the fire department arrived, he began shooting again and killed the fire chief. Cornered later in a field, the defendant, gun in hand, spontaneously shouted at police, "How many people did I kill, how many people are dead?"[138] This spontaneous statement was held to be admissible evidence at the suspect's trial.

It is also important to recognize that the Supreme Court, in the *Miranda* decision, required that officers provide warnings only in those situations involving *both* arrest and custodial interrogation. In other words, it is generally permissible for officers to take a suspect into custody and listen without asking questions while he or she tells a story. Similarly, they may ask questions without providing a *Miranda* warning, even within the confines of a police station house, as long as the person questioned is not a suspect and is not under arrest.[139] Warnings are required only when officers begin actively to solicit responses from the defendant. Recognizing this fact, the FBI, in some of its training literature, has referred to custodial interrogation as the **Miranda trigger.**

Officers were found to have acted properly in the case of *South Dakota* v. *Neville* (1983)[140] in informing a DWI suspect, without reading him his rights, that he would stand to lose his driver's license if he did not submit to a Breathalyzer test. When the driver responded, "I'm too drunk. I won't pass the test," his answer became evidence of his condition and was permitted at trial.

A third-party conversation recorded by the police after a suspect has invoked the *Miranda* right to remain silent may be used as evidence, according to a 1987 ruling in *Arizona* v. *Mauro.*[141] In *Mauro,* a man who willingly conversed with his wife in the presence of a police tape recorder, even after invoking his right to keep silent, was held to have effectively abandoned that right.

Miranda Triggers

The dual principles of custody and interrogation, both of which are necessary before an advisement of rights is required.

Theory Into Practice

The *Miranda* Triggers[1]

◆ Custody ◆ Interrogation

[1]*Custodial interrogation triggers the need for* Miranda *warnings.*

When a waiver is not made, however, in-court references to a defendant's silence following the issuing of *Miranda* warnings is unconstitutional. In 1976 (*Doyle* v. *Ohio*),[142] the U.S. Supreme Court definitively ruled that "a suspect's [post-*Miranda*] silence will not be used against him." Even so, according to the Court in *Brecht* v. *Abrahamson* (1993),[143] prosecution efforts to use such silence against a defendant may not invalidate a finding of guilt by a jury unless such "error had substantial and injurious effect or influence in determining the jury's verdict."[144]

Gathering Special Kinds of Nontestimonial Evidence

The police environment is complicated by the fact that suspects are often privy to special evidence of a nontestimonial sort. Nontestimonial evidence is generally physical evidence, and most physical evidence is subject to normal procedures of search and seizure. A special category of nontestimonial evidence, however, includes very personal items, which may be within or part of a person's body, such as ingested drugs, blood cells, foreign objects, medical implants, and human DNA. Also included in this category might be fingerprints and other kinds of biological residue. The gathering of such special kinds of nontestimonial evidence is a complex area rich in precedent. The Fourth Amendment guarantee that persons be secure in their homes and in their persons has been interpreted by the courts to generally mean that the improper seizure of physical evidence of any kind is illegal and will result in exclusion of that evidence at trial. When very personal kinds of nontestimonial evidence are considered, however, the issue becomes more complicated still.

The Right to Privacy

Two 1985 cases, *Hayes* v. *Florida*[145] and *Winston* v. *Lee*,[146] are examples of limits the courts have placed upon the seizure of very personal forms of nontestimonial evidence. The *Hayes* case established the right of suspects to refuse to be fingerprinted when probable cause necessary to effect an arrest does not exist. *Winston* demonstrated the inviolability of the body against surgical and other substantially invasive techniques which might be ordered by authorities against a suspect's will.

In the *Winston* case, Rudolph Lee, Jr., was found a few blocks from a store robbery with a gunshot wound in his chest. The robbery had involved an exchange of gunshots by the store owner and the robber, with the owner noting that the robber had apparently been hit by a bullet. At the hospital, the store owner identified Lee as the robber. The prosecution sought to have Lee submit to surgery to remove the bullet in his chest, arguing that the bullet would provide physical evidence linking him to the crime. Lee refused the surgery, and the Supreme Court in *Winston* v. *Lee* ruled that Lee could not be ordered to undergo surgery because such a magnitude of intrusion into his body was unacceptable under the right to privacy guaranteed by the Fourth Amendment. The *Winston* case was based upon precedent established in *Schmerber* v. *California* (1966).[147] The *Schmerber* case turned upon the extraction of a blood sample to be measured for alcohol content against the defendant's will. In *Schmerber* the Court ruled that warrants must be obtained for bodily intrusions unless fast action is necessary to prevent the destruction of evidence by natural physiological processes.

High-Technology Searches

The burgeoning use of high technology to investigate crime and to uncover what might otherwise remain undiscovered violations of the criminal law is forcing courts throughout the nation to evaluate the applicability of constitutional guarantees in light of high-tech searches and seizures. The 1996 California appellate court decision, *People* v. *Deutsch,*[1] presages the kinds of issues likely to be encountered as the American justice system enters the twenty-first century. Excerpts from the decision are reproduced as follows:

This case presents the question of whether a warrantless scan made with a thermal imaging device of a private dwelling constitutes an unreasonable search within the meaning of the Fourth Amendment to the United States Constitution. We hold that it does.

Defendant, Dorian Deutsch, pleaded no contest to a single count of furnishing a room in a building for the cultivation of marijuana (Health & Safety Code, section 11366.5). On appeal she contends that the trial court erred in denying her motion to suppress evidence which was seized in a search made with a warrant issued in part upon the basis of the thermal imager scan of her home (Penal Code, section 1538.5.). That evidence included some 200 cannabis plants which were being cultivated hydroponically under high wattage lights in two walled-off portions of the home's garage.

According to the police officer's affidavit offered in support of the search warrant, a confidential informant gave a friend a ride to defendant's home. When they arrived defendant gave the informant a small amount of dried marijuana as a thank you. The informant did not report seeing any growing cannabis plants inside the home, but did note that two doors in the living room were "blocked off with bedsheets." The officer obtained a search warrant for utility records which showed "an unusually high electrical usage" which he concluded was "extremely consistent with the indoor cultivation of cannabis." Some four days later, without having obtained a warrant, the officer drove by the residence at 1:30 in the morning and scanned it with a thermal imager.

As described in the officer's affidavit a thermal imaging device is "a passive, nonintrusive system which detects differences in temperature at surface levels." Such devices measure radiant energy in the thermal portion of the electromagnetic spectrum[2] and display their readings showing areas which are relatively cold as nearly black, warmer areas in shades of gray and hot areas as white.... With the imager the officer "observed high heat level readings, showing excessive heat release" from the "west side, north face, of the residence, which appeared to be the garage area."

Discussion

Defendant maintains that use of the thermal imager on her residence was a warrantless search conducted in violation of the right, under the Fourth Amendment to the United States Constitution "of the people to be secure in their persons, houses, papers and effects, against unreasonable searches...." In *Katz* v. *United States* (1967) 389 U.S. 347 the Supreme Court rejected the notion that every impermissible governmental intrusion must involve a physical invasion or trespass. Instead, it read the protections of the amendment to foreclose a warrantless electronic interception of telephone calls made from a glass enclosed public phone booth. As articulated in Justice Harlan's concurrence the appropriate test for Fourth Amendment purposes is twofold: first, the person must demonstrate an actual, subjective expectation of privacy in that which is searched and second, that expectation must be one our society recognizes to be reasonable...More recently the Supreme Court has restated the particular deference accorded the home characterizing as a basic "Fourth Amendment principle" the notion that "private residences are places in which the individual normally expects privacy free of governmental intrusion not authorized by a warrant, and that expectation is plainly one that society is prepared to recognize as justifiable." (*United States* v. *Karo* [1984], 468 U.S. 705, 714.)

Information or activities which are exposed to public view cannot be characterized as something in which a person has a subjective expectation of privacy, nor can they fulfill the second prong of *Katz*—as being that which society reasonably expects will remain private. A common theme of public disclosure which defeats privacy runs through many cases in which no search was found to have occurred: such as a mechanically recorded list of phone numbers dialed kept by the phone company which has been held to be as publicly disclosed as if the calls had been made through an operator (*Smith* v. *Maryland* [1979] 442 U.S. 735, 743–744), or high resolution photographs of structures in an industrial building complex viewed from the air which are as available to government inspection as to that of any airborne passerby (*Dow Chemical Co.* v. *United States* [1986] 476 U.S. 227, 237, fn. 4, 239.) Accordingly, a warrantless thermal scan of an outbuilding located some 200–300 yards from a

(Continued)

21st Century CJ

High-Technology Searches

home has been upheld because the structure was in an "open field." (*U.S.* v. *Ishmael* [5th Cir. 1995] 48 F.3d 850, 857.)

One who discards garbage by setting it out on the public street has renounced any expectation of privacy in the contents of his garbage bin (*California* v. *Greenwood* [1988] 486 U.S. 35, 40.) Analogizing to the discarded garbage of *Greenwood* certain thermal imaging opinions have characterized the heat signatures registered by the device as "heat waste" ... The analogy is neither good law nor good physics. As a recent decision from the Tenth Circuit points out, the thermal imager does not simply measure the waste heat radiating from a structure, but it measures all temperature differentials across the exterior surface of the structure (*U.S.* v. *Cusumano* [10th Cir. 1995] 67 F.3d 1497). Therefore, the function of the device is to paint an infrared picture of the heat sources which permits inferences about the heat generating activities occurring within the residence. (Id. at p. 1501.) Moreover, as the *Cusumano* court notes, the thermal imager is no more directed to measuring waste heat than the electronic bug affixed to the phone booth in Katz was directed to collecting waste sound waves.

The principle that nondisclosed activities within the home are those in which society accepts a reasonable expectation of privacy and therefore activities which require a warrant for government intrusion is clearly set out in two Supreme Court beeper cases. In *United States* v. *Karo,* supra, 468 U.S. 705, drug enforcement agents arranged for a beeper to be inserted in a can of ether the agents believed was being obtained for the purpose of extracting cocaine from drug-impregnated clothing. (Id. at p. 708.) Using the signals from the beeper the agents located the can in the course of its movements to a private residence, to two different storage facilities, and then to a second residence. (Id. at pp. 708–709.) The court concluded that the monitoring of the beeper when it was inside a private residence was an unreasonable search because "[t]he beeper tells the agent that a particular article is actually located at a particular time in the private residence and is in the possession of the person or persons whose residence is being watched." (Id. at p. 715.) While the court noted that the monitoring of the beeper was less intrusive than a full-scale search would be, nonetheless the beeper revealed information to the government which would not other-

wise have been obtained without a search warrant... Like the beeper signal being monitored inside the residence in *Karo* the thermal imaging scan of defendant's residence told the police something about activities within the house which they could not otherwise have learned without obtaining a warrant to search it. ...

Defendant demonstrated a subjective expectation of privacy in the activities she conducted inside her home. The grow rooms found in her garage were walled off, and the view by visitors into the rest of her house from the living room was blocked by bedsheets hung over the doorways. We find that society recognizes as reasonable an expectation that the heat generated from within a private residence may not be measured by the government without a warrant permitting such a search. In this instance the warrantless thermal scan of defendant's home was an unreasonable search prohibited by the Fourth Amendment. ...

[1]People v. Dorian Odette Deutsch, *96 C.D.O.S. 2827 (1996).*

[2]*The thermal imager differs from infrared devices (such as night vision goggles) in that the latter amplify the infrared spectrum of light whereas the thermal imager registers solely that portion of the infrared spectrum that we call heat.*

Body Cavity Searches

Body cavity searches are among the most problematic for police today. "Strip" searches of convicts in prisons, including the search of body cavities, have generally been held permissible. The 1985 Supreme Court case of *U.S.* v. *Montoya de Hernandez*[148] focused on the issue of "alimentary canal smuggling," in which the suspect typically swallows condoms filled with cocaine or heroin and waits for nature to take its course to recover the substance.

In the *Montoya* case, a woman known to be a "balloon swallower" arrived in the United States on a flight from Colombia. She was detained by customs officials and given a "pat down" search by a female agent. The agent reported that the woman's abdomen was firm and suggested that X rays be taken. The suspect refused and was given the choice of submitting to further tests or taking the next flight back to Colombia. No flight was immediately available, however, and the suspect was placed in a room for 16 hours, where she refused all food and drink. Finally, a court order for an X ray was obtained. The procedure revealed "balloons," and the woman was detained another four days, during which time she passed numerous cocaine-filled plastic condoms. The Court ruled that the woman's confinement was not unreasonable, based as it was upon the supportable suspicion that she was "body-packing" cocaine. Any discomfort she experienced, the court ruled, "resulted solely from the method that she chose to smuggle illicit drugs."[149]

Electronic Eavesdropping

Modern technology makes possible increasingly complex forms of communication. From fiber-optic phone lines, microwave and cellular transmissions, and fax machines to computer communications involving modems and databases, today's global village is a close-knit weave of flowing information.

One of the first and best known of the Supreme Court decisions in the area of electronic communications was the 1928 case of *Olmstead* v. *U.S.*[150] In *Olmstead*, bootleggers used their personal telephones to discuss and transact business. Agents had tapped the lines and based their investigation and ensuing arrests upon conversations they had overheard. The defendants were convicted and eventually appealed to the high court, arguing that the agents had in effect seized information illegally without a search warrant in violation of their Fourth Amendment right to be secure in their homes. The Court ruled, however, that telephone lines were not an extension of the defendant's homes and therefore were not protected by the constitutional guarantee of security. Subsequent federal statutes (discussed shortly) have substantially modified the significance of *Olmstead*.

Recording devices carried on the body of an undercover agent or an informant were ruled to produce admissible evidence in *On Lee* v. *U.S.* (1952)[151] and *Lopez* v. *U.S.* (1963).[152] The 1967 case of *Berger* v. *New York*[153] permitted wiretaps and "bugs" in instances where state law provided for the use of such devices and where officers obtained a warrant based upon probable cause.

The Court appeared to undertake a significant change of direction in the area of electronic eavesdropping when, in 1967, it decided the case of *Katz* v. *U.S.*[154] Federal agents had monitored a number of Katz's telephone calls from a public phone using a device separate from the phone lines and attached to the glass of the phone booth. The Court, in this case, stated that what a person makes an effort to keep private, even in a public place, requires a judicial decision, in the form of a warrant issued upon probable cause, to unveil. In the words of the Court, "The government's activities in electronically listening to and recording the petitioner's words violated the privacy upon which he justifiably relied while using the telephone booth and thus constituted a 'search and seizure' within the meaning of the Fourth Amendment."

In 1968, with the case of *Lee* v. *Florida*,[155] the Court applied the Federal Communications Act[156] to telephone conversations which may be the object of police investigation and held that evidence obtained without a warrant could not be used in state proceedings if it resulted from a wiretap. The only person who has the authority to permit eavesdropping, according to that act, is the sender of the message.

The Federal Communications Act was originally passed in 1934 but did not specifically mention the potential interest of law enforcement agencies in monitoring communications. Title III of the Omnibus Crime Control and Safe Streets Act of 1968, however, mostly prohibits wiretaps but does allow officers to listen to electronic communications where (1) the officer is one of the parties involved in the communication, (2) one of the parties is not the officer, but willingly decides to share the communication with the officer, or (3) officers obtain a warrant based upon probable cause. In the 1971 case of *U.S.* v. *White*,[157] the Court held that law enforcement officers may intercept electronic information when one of the parties involved in the communication gives his or her consent, even without a warrant.

In 1984 the Supreme Court decided the case of *U.S.* v. *Karo*,[158] in which DEA agents had arrested James Karo for cocaine importation. Officers had placed a radio transmitter inside a 50-gallon drum of ether purchased by Karo for use in processing the cocaine. The transmitter was placed inside the drum with the consent of the seller of the ether but without a search warrant. The shipment of ether was followed to the Karo house, and Karo was arrested and convicted of cocaine-trafficking charges. Karo appealed to the Supreme Court, claiming that the radio beeper had violated his reasonable expectation of privacy inside his premises and that, without a warrant, the evidence it produced was tainted. The Court agreed and overturned his conviction.

Minimization Requirements in Electronic Surveillance

The Supreme Court established a minimization requirement pertinent to electronic surveillance in the 1978 case of *United States* v. *Scott.*[159] *Minimization* means that officers must make every reasonable effort to monitor only those conversations, through the use of phone taps, body bugs, and the like, which are specifically related to criminal activity under investigation. As soon as it becomes obvious that a conversation is innocent, then the monitoring personnel are required to cease their invasion of privacy. Problems arise if the conversation occurs in a foreign language, if it is "coded," or if it is ambiguous. It has been suggested that investigators involved in electronic surveillance maintain log books of their activities which specifically show monitored conversations, as well as efforts made at minimization.[160]

The Electronic Communications Privacy Act of 1986

Passed by Congress in 1986, the Electronic Communications Privacy Act (**ECPA**)[161] has brought major changes in the requirements law enforcement officers must meet when using wiretaps. The ECPA deals specifically with three areas of communication: (1) wiretaps and bugs, (2) pen registers (which record the numbers dialed from a telephone), and (3) tracing devices which determine the number from which a call emanates. The act also addresses the procedures to be followed by officers in obtaining records relating to communications services, and it establishes requirements for gaining access to stored electronic communications and records of those communications.

ECPA

An acronym for the Electronic Communications Privacy Act.

The ECPA basically requires that investigating officers must obtain wiretap-type court orders to eavesdrop on *ongoing communications*. The use of pen registers and recording devices, however, are specifically excluded by the law from court order requirements. *Stored communications,* such as computer files made from telephonic sources, fax reproductions, digitally stored information, electronic bulletin boards, and other physical and electronic records of communications which have already occurred, are categorized by the act according to the length of time they have been stored. Messages stored for fewer than 180 days are protected in the same manner as the contents of U.S. mail, and a search warrant issued upon probable cause is required to access them.[162] Information which has been on file in excess of 180 days, however, can be accessed with a court order based upon a simple showing that the information sought is relevant to an ongoing criminal investigation. Such a "showing" is less demanding than a demonstration of probable cause, which includes the claim that the information in question will provide evidence of a law violation.

A related measure, the Communications Assistance for Law Enforcement Act of 1994,[163] called for spending $500 million to modify the United States' phone network to allow for continued wiretapping by law enforcement agencies. The law also specifies a standard-setting process for the redesign of existing equipment which would permit effective wiretapping in the face of coming technological advances. In the words of the FBI's Telecommunications Industry Liaison Unit (TILU), "This law requires telecommunications carriers, as defined in the Act, to ensure law enforcement's ability, pursuant to court order or other lawful authorization, to intercept communications notwithstanding advanced telecommunications technologies."[164]

The Telecommunications Act of 1996

Title V of the Telecommunications Act of 1996,[165] signed into law by President Clinton on February 8 of that year, made it a federal offense for anyone engaged in interstate or international communications to knowingly use a telecommunications device "to create, solicit, or initiate the transmission of any comment, request, suggestion, proposal, image, or other communication which is obscene, lewd, lascivious, filthy, or indecent, with intent to annoy, abuse, threaten, or harass another person." The law also provided special penalties for anyone who "makes a telephone call . . . without disclosing his identity and with intent to annoy, abuse, threaten, or harass any person at the called number or who receives the communication . . . ," or "makes or causes the telephone of another repeatedly or continuously to ring, with intent to harass any person at the called number; or makes repeated telephone calls" for the purpose of harassing a person at the called number.

A section of the law, known as the Communications Decency Act[166] (CDA), criminalized the transmission to minors of "patently offensive" obscene materials over the Internet or other telecommunications services via computer. Portions of the CDA were invalidated by the U.S. Supreme Court in the case of *Reno* v. *ACLU* (1997).[167]

Summary

"Police work is the only profession that gives you the test first, then the lesson."

—Anonymous

This chapter describes the legal environment surrounding police activities—from search and seizure through arrest and the interrogation of suspects. It is important to realize that democratically inspired legal restraints upon the police help ensure individual freedoms in our society and prevent the development of a "police state" in America. In police work and elsewhere, the principles of individual liberty and social justice are cornerstones upon which the American way of life rests. For police action to be "just," it must recognize the rights of individuals while simultaneously holding them accountable to the social obligations defined by law.

Ideally, the work of the criminal justice system is to ensure justice while guarding liberty. The liberty/justice issue is the dual thread which weaves the tapestry of the justice system together—from the simplest daily activities of police on the beat to the often complex and lengthy renderings of the U.S. Supreme Court.

For the criminal justice system as a whole, the question becomes "How can individual liberties be maintained in the face of the need for official action, including arrest, interrogation, incarceration, and the like?" The answer is far from simple, but it begins with recognition of the fact that "liberty" is a double-edged sword, entailing obligations as well as rights.

Discussion Questions

1. Which Supreme Court decisions discussed in this chapter do you see as most important? Why? Are there any Supreme Court decisions discussed in this chapter with which you disagree? If so, which ones? Why do you disagree?
2. Do you agree with the theme of this chapter's summary that "for police action to be just, it must recognize the rights of individuals, while holding citizens to the social obligations defined by law"? What is the basis for your agreement or disagreement?
3. What does the *due process environment* mean to you? How can we ensure due process in our legal system?
4. Justice Benjamin Cardozo once complained, "The criminal is to go free because the constable has blundered." Can we afford to let some guilty people go free in order to ensure that the rights of the rest of us are protected? Is there some other (better) way to achieve the same goal?

Web Quest!

Create a list of every U.S. Supreme Court decision discussed in this chapter. Group the cases by subject matter area (i.e., vehicle searches, searches following arrest, interrogation, and so on) and list them in order by year of decision. Use the Web to collect full-text opinions from the Court for as many of these cases as you can find. (Hint: Visit the Legal Information Institute at Cornell University at www.law.cornell.edu for some of the best Supreme Court information available anywhere.) Submit the materials you create to your instructor if asked to do so.

Note: This is a large project, and your instructor may ask that you work with just one area (such as vehicle searches), or may assign the entire project to your class—asking individual students or groups of students to be responsible for separate subject matter areas.

Library Extras!

The Library Extras! listed here complement the WebExtras! found throughout this chapter. Library Extras! may be accessed on the Web at CJToday.com.

Library Extra! 5-1. *FBI Law Enforcement Bulletin,* May 2001 (Vol. 70, No. 5).

Library Extra! 5-2. *FBI Law Enforcement Bulletin,* April 2001 (Vol. 70, No. 4).

Library Extra! 5-3. *FBI Law Enforcement Bulletin,* March 2001 (Vol. 70, No. 3).

Library Extra! 5-4. *FBI Law Enforcement Bulletin,* February 2001 (Vol. 70, No. 2).

Library Extra! 5-5. *FBI Law Enforcement Bulletin,* January 2001 (Vol. 70, No. 1).

Library Extra! 5-6. *Police Integrity: Public Service with Honor* (NIJ, 1997).

References

1. Larry Collins and Dominique Lapierre, *The Fifth Horseman* (New York: Simon & Schuster, 1980).
2. Michelle Gotthelf, "41 Shots Heard Around the World," APB Online. Web posted at www.apbonline.com/majorcases/diallo/background.html.
3. "One Cop Convicted in NYC Torture Case," APB Online. Web posted at www.apbonline.com/911/1999/06/08/louima0608_01.html. Accessed January 10, 2000.
4. Ibid.
5. "Police Brutality!" *Time,* March 25, 1991, p. 18.
6. "L.A. Officers Not Indicted," *Fayetteville Observer-Times* (North Carolina), May 11, 1991, p. 10C.
7. "Police Brutality!" pp. 16–19.
8. "Police Charged in Beating Case Say They Feared for Their Lives," *Boston Globe,* May 22, 1991, p. 22.
9. "Cries of Relief," *Time,* April 26, 1993, p. 18.
10. "Rodney King's Run-ins," *USA Today,* May 30, 1991, p. 2A.
11. "Rodney King Gets Jail Time," *The Island Packet,* August 22, 1996, p. 4A.
12. "Rodney King to Clean Streets," *The Island Packet,* September 15, 1996, p. 5A.
13. *Miranda* v. *Arizona,* 384 U.S. 436 (1966).
14. *Weeks* v. *U.S.,* 232 U.S. 383 (1914).
15. Roger Goldman and Steven Puro, "Decertification of Police: An Alternative to Traditional Remedies for Police Misconduct," *Hastings Constitutional Law Quarterly,* vol. 15 (1988), pp. 45–80.
16. Hawaii police departments set their own training requirements. The Honolulu Police Department, for example, requires 6½ months of student officer training, and another 14 weeks of post-graduation field training. See the Honolulu Police Department's home page at www.honolulupd.org/main/index.html. Accessed March 27, 2000.
17. Ibid.
18. *Silverthorne Lumber Co.* v. *U.S.,* 251 U.S. 385 (1920).
19. Ibid.
20. Clemmens Bartollas, *American Criminal Justice* (New York: Macmillan, 1988), p. 186.
21. *Mapp* v. *Ohio,* 367 U.S. 643 (1961).
22. Ibid.
23. *Wolf* v. *Colorado,* 338 U.S. 25 (1949).
24. *Chimel* v. *California,* 395 U.S. 752 (1969).
25. *U.S.* v. *Rabinowitz,* 339 U.S. 56 (1950).
26. *Katz* v. *U.S.,* 389 U.S. 347, 88 S.Ct. 507 (1967).
27. *Minnesota* v. *Olson,* 110 S.Ct. 1684 (1990).
28. *Minnesota* v. *Carter,* No. 97-1147 (1998).
29. *Illinois* v. *Gates,* 426 U.S. 318 (1982).
30. *U.S.* v. *Leon,* 468 U.S. 897, 104 S.Ct. 3405, 82 L. Ed. 2d 677, 52 U.S.L.W. 5155 (1984).
31. Judicial titles vary between jurisdictions. Many lower-level state judicial officers are referred to as *magistrates.* Federal magistrates, however, are generally regarded as functioning at a significantly higher level of judicial authority.
32. *Massachusetts* v. *Sheppard,* 104 S.Ct. 3424 (1984).
33. *Illinois* v. *Krull,* 107 S.Ct. 1160 (1987).
34. *Maryland* v. *Garrison,* 107 S.Ct. 1013 (1987).
35. *Illinois* v. *Rodriguez,* 110 S.Ct. 2793 (1990).
36. William H. Erickson, William D. Neighbors, and B. J. George, Jr., *United States Supreme Court Cases and Comments* (New York: Matthew Bender, 1987), Section 1.13 [7].
37. *Harris* v. *U.S.,* 390 U.S. 234 (1968).
38. As cited in Kimberly A. Kingston, "Look But Don't Touch: The Plain View Doctrine," *FBI Law Enforcement Bulletin* (December 1987), p. 18.
39. *Horton* v. *California,* 110 S.Ct. 2301, 47 CrL. 2135 (1990).
40. *U.S.* v. *Irizarry* (1982).
41. *FBI Law Enforcement Bulletin* (December 1987), p. 20.
42. *Arizona* v. *Hicks,* 107 S.Ct. 1149 (1987).
43. See *Criminal Justice Today,* North Carolina Justice Academy (Fall 1987), p. 24.
44. "Inadvertency" as a requirement of legitimate plain-view seizures was first cited in the U.S. Supreme Court case of *Coolidge* v. *New Hampshire,* 403 U.S. 443, 91 S.Ct. 2022 (1971).
45. *Horton* v. *California,* 110 S.Ct. 2301, 47 CrL. 2135 (1990).
46. Ibid.
47. John Gales Sauls, "Emergency Searches of Premises," Part 1, *FBI Law Enforcement Bulletin* (March 1987), p. 23.
48. *Warden* v. *Hayden,* 387 U.S. 294 (1967).
49. *Mincey* v. *Arizona,* 437 U.S. 385, 392 (1978).

50. Sauls, "Emergency Searches of Premises," p. 25.
51. *Maryland* v. *Buie,* 110 S.Ct. 1093 (1990).
52. *Wilson* v. *Arkansas,* 115 S.Ct. 1914 (1995).
53. For additional information, see Michael J. Bulzomi, "Knock and Announce: A Fourth Amendment Standard," *FBI Law Enforcement Bulletin,* vol. 66, no. 5 (May 1997), pp. 27–31.
54. *Richards* v. *Wisconsin,* 117 S.Ct. 1416 (1997), syllabus.
55. Ibid.
56. *U.S.* v. *Mendenhall,* 446 U.S. 544 (1980).
57. A Louis DiPietro, "Voluntary Encounters or Fourth Amendment Seizures," *FBI Law Enforcement Bulletin,* January 1992, pp. 28–32 at note 6.
58. *Stansbury* v. *California,* 114 S.Ct. 1526, 1529, 128 L. Ed. 2d 293 (1994).
59. In 1976, in the case of *Watson* v. *U.S.* (432 U.S. 411), the U.S. Supreme Court refused to impose a warrant requirement for felony arrests that occur in public places.
60. In 1981, in the case of *U.S.* v. *Steagald* (451 U.S. 204), the Court ruled that a search warrant is also necessary when the planned arrest involves entry into a third party's premises.
61. *Robinson* v. *U.S.,* 414 U.S. 218 (1973).
62. Ibid.
63. *Terry* v. *Ohio,* 392 U.S. 1 (1968).
64. Ibid.
65. *U.S.* v. *Sokolow,* 109 S.Ct. 1581 (1989).
66. *Minnesota* v. *Dickerson,* 113 S.Ct. 2130, 124 L.Ed. 2d 334 (1993).
67. *Brown* v. *Texas,* 443 U.S. 47 (1979).
68. *Smith* v. *Ohio,* 110 S.Ct. 1288 (1990).
69. Ibid., at 1289.
70. *California* v. *Hodari D.,* 111 S.Ct. 1547 (1991).
71. *Criminal Justice Newsletter,* May 1, 1991, p. 2.
72. *Arkansas* v. *Sanders,* 442 U.S. 753 (1979).
73. Ibid.
74. *Borchardt* v. *U.S.,* 809 F.2d 1115 (5th Cir. 1987).
75. *FBI Law Enforcement Bulletin,* January 1988, p. 28.
76. *Carroll* v. *U.S.,* 267 U.S. 132 (1925).
77. *Preston* v. *U.S.,* 376 U.S. 364 (1964).
78. *South Dakota* v. *Opperman,* 428 U.S. 364 (1976).
79. *Colorado* v. *Bertine,* 479 U.S. 367, 107 S.Ct. 741 (1987).
80. *Florida* v. *Wells,* 110 S.Ct. 1632 (1990).
81. *Terry* v. *Ohio,* 392 U.S. 1 (1968).
82. *California* v. *Acevedo,* 500 U.S. 565 (1991).
83. *Ornelas* v. *U.S.,* 116 S.Ct. 1657 L. Ed. 2d 911 (1996).
84. Ibid.
85. The phrase is usually attributed to the 1991 U.S. Supreme Court case of *California* v. *Acevedo.* See Devallis Rutledge, "Taking an Inventory," *Police,* (November 1995), pp. 8–9.
86. *Florida* v. *Jimeno,* 111 S.Ct. 1801 (1991).
87. *Jimeno,* online syllabus.
88. *United States* v. *Ross,* 456 U.S. 798 (1982).
89. Ibid.
90. *Whren* v. *U.S.,* 116 S.Ct. 1769, 135 L. Ed. 2d (1996).
91. See *Pennsylvania* v. *Mimms,* 434 U.S. 106 (1977).
92. *Maryland* v. *Wilson,* 117 S.Ct. 882 (1997).
93. *Knowles* v. *Iowa,* No. 97-7597 (1998).
94. *Wyoming* v. *Houghton,* No. 98-184 (1999).
95. *U.S.* v. *Villamonte-Marquez,* 462 U.S. 579 (1983).
96. *California* v. *Carney,* 471 U.S. 386, 105 S.Ct. 2066, 85 L. Ed. 2d 406, 53 U.S.L.W. 4521 (1985).
97. *U.S.* v. *Hill,* 855 F.2d 664 (10th Cir. 1988).
98. *National Treasury Employees Union* v. *Von Raab,* 489 U.S. 656 (1989).
99. *Skinner* v. *Railway Labor Executives' Association,* 489 U.S. 602 (1989).
100. *Florida* v. *Bostick,* 111 S.Ct. 2382 (1991).
101. *Aguilar* v. *Texas,* 378 U.S. 108 (1964).
102. *Harris* v. *United States,* 403 U.S. 573 (1971).
103. *Spinelli* v. *United States,* 393 U.S. 410 (1969).
104. *Illinois* v. *Gates,* 426 U.S. 318 (1982).
105. *Alabama* v. *White,* 110 S.Ct. 2412 (1990).
106. Ibid., at 2417.
107. *U.S. Dept. of Justice* v. *Landano,* 113 S.Ct. 2014, 124 L. Ed. 2d 84 (1993).
108. Kevin Johnson and Gary Fields, "Jewell Investigation Unmasks FBI 'Tricks,' " *USA Today,* November 8, 1996, p. 13A.
109. Gary Fields, "FBI Admits Mistake in Jewell Case," *USA Today,* April 9, 1997, p. 2A.
110. *South Dakota* v. *Neville,* 103 S.Ct. 916 (1983).
111. *Brown* v. *Mississippi,* 297 U.S. 278 (1936).
112. *Ashcraft* v. *Tennessee,* 322 U.S. 143 (1944).
113. *Chambers* v. *Florida,* 309 U.S. 227 (1940).
114. Ibid.
115. *Leyra* v. *Denno,* 347 U.S. 556 (1954).
116. Ibid.
117. *Arizona* v. *Fulminante,* 111 S.Ct. 1246 (1991).
118. *Chapman* v. *California,* 386 U.S. 18 (1967).
119. *Escobedo* v. *Illinois,* 378 U.S. 478 (1964).
120. *Edwards* v. *Arizona,* 451 U.S. 477, 101 S.Ct. 1880, 68 L. Ed. 2d 378, (1981).
121. *Arizona* v. *Roberson,* 486 U.S. 675, 108 S.Ct. 2093 (1988).
122. *Davis* v. *United States,* 114 S.Ct. 2350 (1994).
123. *Miranda* v. *Arizona,* 384 U.S. 436 (1966).
124. Ibid.
125. *Dickerson* v. *U.S.,* No. 97-4750 (4th Cir. 1999).
126. *Moran* v. *Burbine,* 475 U.S. 412, 421 (1986).
127. Ibid.
128. *Colorado* v. *Spring,* 479 U.S. 564, 107 S.Ct. 851 (1987).
129. "Immigrants Get Civil Rights," *USA Today,* June 11, 1992, p. 1A.
130. *Brewer* v. *Williams,* 430 U.S. 387.
131. *Nix* v. *Williams,* 104 S.Ct. 2501 (1984).
132. *New York* v. *Quarles,* 104 S.Ct. 2626, 81 L. Ed. 2d 550 (1984).
133. *Colorado* v. *Connelly,* 107 S.Ct. 515, 93 L. Ed. 2d 473 (1986).
134. Ibid.
135. *Kuhlmann* v. *Wilson,* 477 U.S., 106 S.Ct. 2616 (1986).
136. *Illinois* v. *Perkins,* 495 U.S. 292 (1990).
137. *Rock* v. *Zimmerman,* 543 F. Supp. 179 (M.D. Pa. 1982).
138. Ibid.
139. See *Oregon* v. *Mathiason,* 429 U.S. 492, 97 S.Ct. 711 (1977).
140. *South Dakota* v. *Neville,* 103 S.Ct. 916 (1983).
141. *Arizona* v. *Mauro,* 107 S.Ct. 1931, 95 L. Ed. 2d 458 (1987).
142. *Doyle* v. *Ohio,* 426 U.S. 610 (1976).
143. *Brecht* v. *Abrahamson,* 113 S.Ct. 1710, 123 L. Ed. 2d 353 (1993).
144. *Citing Kotteakos* v. *United States,* 328 U.S. 750 (1946).

145. *Hayes* v. *Florida,* 470 U.S.811, 105 S.Ct. 1643 (1985).

146. *Winston* v. *Lee,* 470 U.S.753, 105 S.Ct. 1611 (1985).

147. *Schmerber* v. *California,* 384 U.S. 757 (1966).

148. *U.S.* v. *Montoya de Hernandez,* 473 U.S. 531, 105 S.Ct. 3304 (1985).

149. Ibid.

150. *Olmstead* v. *U.S.,* 277 U.S. 438 (1928).

151. *On Lee* v. *U.S.,* 343 U.S. 747 (1952).

152. *Lopez* v. *U.S.,* 373 U.S. 427 (1963).

153. *Berger* v. *New York,* 388 U.S. 41 (1967).

154. *Katz* v. *U.S.,* 389 U.S. 347 (1967).

155. *Lee* v. *Florida,* 392 U.S. 378 (1968).

156. Federal Communications Act, 1934.

157. *U.S.* v. *White,* 401 U.S. 745 (1971).

158. Ibid.

159. *United States* v. *Scott,* 436 U.S. 128 (1978).

160. For more information, see *FBI Law Enforcement Bulletin* (June 1987), p. 25.

161. The Electronic Communications Privacy Act, 1986.

162. For more information on the ECPA, see Robert A. Fiatal, "The Electronic Communications Privacy Act: Addressing Today's Technology," *FBI Law Enforcement Bulletin* (April 1988), pp. 24–30.

163. Pub. L. 103–414.

164. Federal Bureau of Investigation, "Notice: Implementation of The Communications Assistance for Law Enforcement Act," February 23, 1995.

165. Public Law 104, 110 Statute 56.

166. Title 47, U.S.C.A., Section 223(a)(1)(B)(ii) (Supp. 1997).

167. *Reno* v. *ACLU* (1997), 117 S.Ct. 2329 (1997).

CHAPTER 6

Issues in Policing

"The police in the United States are not separate from the people. They draw their authority from the will and consent of the people, and they recruit their officers from them. The police are the instrument of the people to achieve and maintain order; their efforts are founded on principles of public service and ultimate responsibility to the public."
—The National Advisory Commission on Criminal Justice Standards and Goals

"The ability of the police to fulfill their sacred trust will improve as a lucid sense of ethical standards is developed."
—Patrick V. Murphy, Former Commissioner of the NYC Police Department

"Effective police work in the emerging society will depend less on the holster and more on the head."

—Alvin Toffler

CHAPTER OUTLINE

◆ Contemporary Policing: Issues and Challenges

◆ Professionalism and Ethics

◆ Private Protective Services

—Photo by Peter Marlow, Magnum Photos, Inc.

188

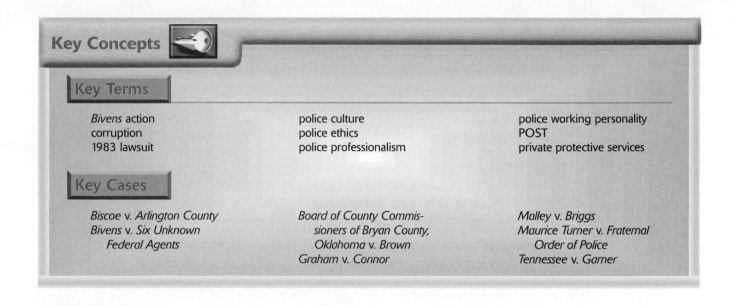

Key Concepts

Key Terms

Bivens action	police culture	police working personality
corruption	police ethics	POST
1983 lawsuit	police professionalism	private protective services

Key Cases

Biscoe v. *Arlington County*	*Board of County Commissioners of Bryan County, Oklahoma* v. *Brown*	*Malley* v. *Briggs*
Bivens v. *Six Unknown Federal Agents*		*Maurice Turner* v. *Fraternal Order of Police*
	Graham v. *Connor*	*Tennessee* v. *Garner*

Contemporary Policing: Issues and Challenges

A number of issues hold special interest for today's police administrators and officers. Some concerns, such as police stress, danger, and the use of deadly force, derive from the very nature of police work. Others have arisen over the years due to commonplace practice, characteristic police values, and public expectations surrounding the enforcement of laws. Included here are such negatives as the potential for corruption, as well as positive efforts which focus on ethics and recruitment strategies to increase professionalism.

Police Personality and Culture

Some years ago Jerome Skolnick described what he called the "working personality" of police officers.[1] Skolnick's description was consistent with William Westley's classic study[2] of the Gary, Indiana, police department, in which he found a **police culture** with its own "customs, laws, and morality," and with Niederhoffer's observation that cynicism was pervasive among officers in New York City.[3] More recent authors[4] have claimed that the "big curtain of secrecy" surrounding much of police work shields knowledge of the nature of the police personality from outsiders.

Skolnick found that a process of informal socialization, through which officers learn what is appropriate police behavior, occurs when new officers begin to work with seasoned veterans. Such informal socialization is often far more important than formal police academy training in determining how rookies will see police work. In everyday life, formal socialization occurs through schooling, church activities, job training, and so on. Informal socialization is acquired primarily from one's peers in less-institutionalized settings and provides an introduction to value-laden subcultures. The information that passes between officers in the locker room, in a squad car, over a cup of coffee, or in many other relatively private moments produces a shared view of the world that can be best described as "streetwise." The streetwise cop may know what official department policy is, but he or she also knows the most efficient way to get a job done. By the time they become streetwise, rookie officers will know just how acceptable various informal means of accomplishing the job will be to other officers. The police subculture creates few real mavericks, but it also produces few officers who view their job exclusively in terms of public mandates and official dictums.

Hear the author discuss this chapter at cjtoday.com

Police Culture (also Subculture)

A particular set of values, beliefs, and acceptable forms of behavior characteristic of American police and with which the police profession strives to imbue new recruits. Socialization into the police subculture commences with recruit training and is ongoing thereafter.

"Good cops always seem to be able to identify causes of problems and to come up with the least troublesome ways of solving them."

—*Jerome Skolnick*

Skolnick says that the **police working personality** has at least six recognizable characteristics. Additional writers[5] have identified others. Taken in concert, they create the picture of the police personality shown in Table 6-1.

Some components of the police working personality are essential for survival and effectiveness. Officers are exposed daily to situations which are charged with emotions and can be potentially threatening. The need to gain control quickly over belligerent people leads to the development of authoritarian strategies for handling people. Eventually, such strategies become second nature, and the cornerstone of the police personality is firmly set. Cynicism evolves from a constant flow of experiences which demonstrate that people and events are not always what they seem to be. The natural tendency of most suspects, even when they are clearly guilty in the eyes of the police, is denial. Repeated attempts to mislead the police in the performance of their duty creates an air of suspicion and cynicism in the minds of most officers.

The police personality has at least two sources. On the one hand, some aspects of the world view which comprise that personality can be attributed to the socialization which occurs when rookie officers are inducted into police ranks. On the other, it may be that some of the components of the police personality already exist in some individuals and lead them into police work.[6] Supporting the latter view are studies which indicate that police officers who come from conservative backgrounds continue to view themselves as defenders of middle-class morality.[7]

Police methods and the police culture are not static, however. Lawrence Sherman, for example, has reported on the modification of police tactics surrounding the use of weapons which characterized the period from 1970 to the 1980s.[8] Firearms, Sherman tells us, were routinely brought into play 25 years ago. Although not often fired, they would be frequently drawn and pointed at suspects. Few departmental restrictions were placed on the use of weapons, and officers employed them almost as they would their badge in the performance of duties. Today, the situation has changed. It is a rare officer who will discharge a weapon during police work, and those who do know that only the gravest of situations can justify the public use of firearms.

Some authors attribute this shift in thinking about firearms to increased training and the growth of restrictive policies.[9] Changes in training, however, are probably more a response to a revolution in social understandings about the kind of respect due citizens. For example, the widespread change in social consciousness regarding the worth of individuals, which has taken place over the past few decades, appears to have had considerable impact upon police subculture itself.

Corruption

The police role carries considerable authority, and officers are expected to exercise a well-informed discretion in all of their activities. The combination of authority and discretion, however, produces great potential for abuse.

Police deviance has been a problem in American society since the early days of policing. It is probably an ancient and natural tendency of human beings to attempt to placate or "win over" those in positions of authority over them. This tendency is complicated in today's materialistic society by greed and by the personal and financial benefits to be derived from

TABLE 6-1 ■ The Police Personality	
Authoritarian	Individualistic
Conservative	Insecure
Cynical	Loyal
Efficient	Prejudiced
Honorable	Secret
Hostile	Suspicious

evading the law. Hence, the temptations toward illegality offered to police range all the way from a free cup of coffee given by a small restaurant owner in the thought that one day it may be necessary to call upon the goodwill of the officer, perhaps for something as simple as a traffic ticket, to huge monetary bribes arranged by drug dealers to guarantee the police will look the other way as an important shipment of contraband arrives.

Exactly what constitutes corruption is not always clear. In recognition of what some have called corruption's "slippery slope,"[10] even the acceptance of minor gratuities is now explicitly prohibited by most police departments. The slippery slope perspective holds that even small "thank you's" which are accepted from members of the public can lead to a more ready acceptance of larger bribes. An officer who begins to accept, and then expect, gratuities may soon find that his or her practice of policing becomes influenced by such gifts and that larger ones soon follow. At that point the officer may easily slide to the bottom of the moral slope, one made slippery by previous small concessions.

Ethicists say that police corruption ranges from minor offenses to those which are themselves serious violations of the law. Another useful distinction is made by Barker and Carter, who distinguish between *occupational deviance* and *abuse of authority*.[11] Occupational deviance, they say, is motivated by the desire for personal benefit. Abuse of authority, however, occurs most often in order to further the organizational goals of law enforcement—including arrest, ticketing, and the successful conviction of suspects.

Examples of police deviance, ranked in what this author judges to be an increasing level of severity, are shown in Figure 6-1. Not everyone, however, would agree with this ranking. A recent survey[12] of 6,982 New York City police officers found that 65 percent did not classify excessive force as corrupt behavior. Likewise, 71.4 percent of responding officers said that accepting a free meal is not a corrupt practice. Another 15 percent said that the use of illegal drugs should not be considered corruption.

Years ago, Frank Serpico made headlines as he testified before the Knapp Commission on police corruption in New York City.[13] Serpico, an undercover operative within the police department, revealed a complex web of corruption in which money and services routinely changed hands in "protection rackets" created by unethical officers. The Knapp Commission report distinguished between two types of corrupt officers, which they termed grass eaters and meat eaters.[14] "Grass eating," the most common form of police deviance, was described as illegitimate activity which occurs from time to time in the normal course of police work. It involves mostly small bribes or relatively minor services offered by citizens seeking to avoid arrest and prosecution. "Meat eating" is a much more serious form of corruption,

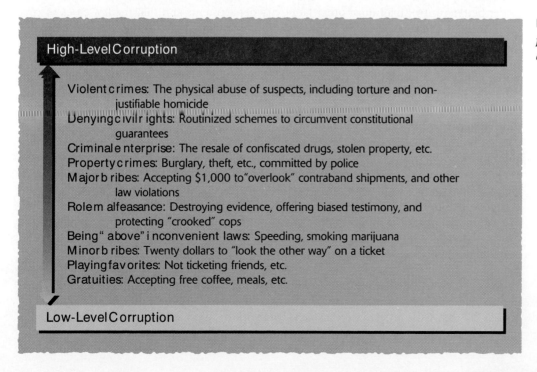

FIGURE 6-1 ■ *Types of police deviance by category and example.*

High-Level Corruption

Violent crimes: The physical abuse of suspects, including torture and non-justifiable homicide

Denying civil rights: Routinized schemes to circumvent constitutional guarantees

Criminal enterprise: The resale of confiscated drugs, stolen property, etc.

Property crimes: Burglary, theft, etc., committed by police

Major bribes: Accepting $1,000 to "overlook" contraband shipments, and other law violations

Role malfeasance: Destroying evidence, offering biased testimony, and protecting "crooked" cops

Being "above" inconvenient laws: Speeding, smoking marijuana

Minor bribes: Twenty dollars to "look the other way" on a ticket

Playing favorites: Not ticketing friends, etc.

Gratuities: Accepting free coffee, meals, etc.

Low-Level Corruption

involving as it does the active seeking of illicit money-making opportunities by officers. Meat eaters solicit bribes through threat or intimidation, whereas grass eaters make the simpler mistake of not refusing those which are offered.

Popular books often tell the story of police misbehavior. A few years ago, Robert Daley's best-seller *Prince of the City*[15] detailed the adventures of New York City detective Robert Leuci who walked among corrupt cops with a tape recorder hidden on his body. The more recent best-seller, *Buddy Boys*[16] by Mike McAlary is subtitled *When Good Cops Turn Bad.* McAlary, an investigative reporter with *New York Newsday,* began his efforts to uncover police corruption with a list of 13 names of officers who had been suspended in New York's 77th precinct. His book describes organized criminal activity among police in the Big Apple, involving holdups of drug dealers, organized burglaries, fencing operations, and numerous other illegal activities conducted from behind the shield. McAlary says New York's criminal officers saw themselves as a kind of "elite" within the department and applied the name "Buddy Boys" to their gang.[17]

In 1993, during 11 days of corruption hearings reminiscent of the Knapp Commission era, a parade of crooked New York police officers testified before the Mollen Commission, headed by former judge and deputy mayor Milton Mollen. Among the many revelations, officers spoke of dealing drugs, stealing confiscated drug funds, stifling investigations, and beating innocent people. Officer Michael Dowd, for example, told the commission that he had run a cocaine ring out of his station house in Brooklyn and bought three homes on Long Island and a Corvette with the money he made. Most shocking of all, however, were allegations that high-level police officials attempted to hide embarrassing incidents in a "phantom file" and that many such officials may have condoned unprofessional and even criminal practices by law enforcement officers under their command. Honest officers, including internal affairs investigators, reported on how their efforts to end corruption among their fellows had been defused and resisted by higher authorities.

Spectacular as they were, however, many doubt that the Mollen hearings will have much long-term impact on policing in New York City. "The Knapp Commission exposed a form of corruption that was systemic and pervasive," said Daniel Guido, a professor at John Jay College of Criminal Justice in New York. "It involved not only the working levels of the force and plainclothes men but their supervisors. It was part of the culture of the force. . . . What we're seeing [with the Mollen Hearings] is not systemic, and it involves only police officers in the main. It's all been sensational and revolting, but it's important not to overgeneralize the extent to which this is going on."

Some experts say that the New York City Police Department actually has corruption under better control than most other large-city departments and that the few cases of corruption identified by the Mollen Commission were trivial relative to the size of the department. Even so, the hearings do seem to show that corruption is nearly impossible to completely stamp out and that it reemerges with each new generation of officers.

Corruption, of course, is not unique to New York. In 1992 Detroit Police Chief William Hart was sentenced to a maximum of 10 years in federal prison for embezzling $2.6 million from a secret police department fund and for tax evasion. The fund, which was to be used for undercover drug buys and to pay informants, had secretly paid out nearly $10 million since its creation in 1980. Hart, who was 68 years old at the time of sentencing, had been police chief in Detroit since 1976. He resigned from office the day after his conviction, following a pension board ruling that he is entitled to receive a $53,000 annual pension despite the conviction. Hart's arrest had come on the heels of other problems for Detroit police. Two years earlier a city police officer was arrested for allegedly committing five robberies in one evening, and eight other officers were arrested for breaking and entering and assault. At the time, the *Detroit News,* a major newspaper in the city, conducted a study in which it found that Detroit police are "accused of committing crimes more often than officers in any other major U.S. city."[18] There are plenty of signs that corruption in Detroit continues. In 1999, for example, six Detroit police officers were indicted on charges of beating and robbing city residents, and hoarding money, guns, and drugs taken in illegal searches of suspected drug houses. Three of the officers were also charged with drug possession, conspiracy to distribute controlled substances, and with taking money to protect drug dealers.[19]

In 1997, although not charged with corruption, Chicago Police Superintendent Matt Rodriguez resigned after a report[20] by the *Chicago Tribune* that he had violated department rules forbidding fraternization with convicted criminals. Rodriguez admitted having a long-standing friendship with Frank Milito, a former gas station owner who had served nine months in prison after pleading guilty in 1986 to charges of mail fraud. Milito was also convicted of having failed to pay $250,000 in taxes on gasoline sold by his station.

In mid-2000, the Los Angeles Police Department became embroiled in a far-reaching corruption scandal involving fabricated evidence and a drug ring run by department members. In late 2000, following months of negotiations between LAPD officials, federal investigators, and Los Angeles city council members, the LAPD was put under federal oversight. Following the terms of a consent decree, the department will have to meet standards set for it by the U.S. Department of Justice. Former LAPD officer Rafael Perez, a central figure in the scandal, warned young officers as he was sentenced to prison that "he who chases monsters must see that he has not become a monster himself."

Money—The Root of Police Evil?

The police personality provides fertile ground for the growth of corrupt practices. Police "cynicism" develops out of continued association with criminals and problem-laden people. The cop who is "streetwise" is also ripe for corrupt influences to take root. Years ago, Edwin Sutherland applied the concept of differential association to deviant behavior.[21] You may recall from our discussion in Chapter 3 in connection with causes of crime that Sutherland suggested that continued association with one type of person, more frequently than with any other, would make the associates similar.

Sutherland was talking about criminals, not police officers. Consider, however, the dilemma of the average officer: A typical day is spent running down petty thieves, issuing traffic citations to citizens who try to talk their way out of the situation, dealing with prostitutes who feel "hassled" by the police presence, and arresting drug users who think it should be their right to do what they want as long as it "doesn't hurt anyone." The officer encounters personal hostility and experiences a constant, and often quite vocal, rejection of society's formalized norms. Bring into this environment low pay and the resulting sense that police work is not really valued, and it is easy to understand how an officer might develop a jaded attitude about the double standards of the civilization he or she is sworn to protect.

In fact, low pay may be a critical ingredient of the corruption mix. Salaries paid to police officers in this country have been notoriously low when compared to other professions involving personal dedication, extensive training, high stress, and the risk of bodily harm. As police professionalism increases, many police administrators hope that salaries will rise. No matter how much police pay grows, however, it will never be able to compete with the staggering amounts of money to be made though dealing in contraband. In *The Underground Empire: Where Crime and Governments Embrace*, James Mills[22] tells the story of a man he calls a "young American entrepreneur," whom, he writes, has "criminal operations on four continents and a daily income greater than U.S. Steel's."[23] Mills's book is about "Centac," a semisecret arm of the Drug Enforcement Administration, which coordinates the operations of various agencies in the ongoing battle against illicit drugs. Although international drug trafficking is the focus of *The Underground Empire*, the book contains details of international police corruption fostered via the vast resources available to the trade.

Working hand in hand with monetary pressures toward corruption are the moral dilemmas produced by unenforceable laws which provide the basis for criminal profit. During the Prohibition Era the Wickersham Commission warned of the potential for official corruption inherent in the legislative taboos on alcohol. The demand for drink, immense as it was, called into question the wisdom of the law, while simultaneously providing vast resources designed to circumvent the law. Today's drug scene bears some similarities to the Prohibition Era. As long as substantial segments of the population are willing to make large financial and other sacrifices to feed the drug trade, the pressures on the police to embrace corruption will remain substantial.

Combating Corruption

High moral standards, embedded into the principles of the police profession and effectively communicated to individual officers through formal training and peer group socialization, are undoubtedly the most effective way to combat corruption in police work. There are, of course, many officers of great personal integrity who hold to the highest of professional ideals. There is evidence that law enforcement training programs are becoming increasingly concerned with instruction designed to reinforce the high ideals many recruits bring to police work. As a recent FBI article puts it, "Ethics training must become an integral part of academy and in-service training for new and experienced officers alike."[24]

Recently, a "reframing" strategy targeting police corruption has emphasized *integrity* rather than *corruption*. In 1997, for example, the National Institute of Justice released a report entitled *Police Integrity: Public Service With Honor.*[25] The report built upon recommendations made by participants in the National Symposium on Police Integrity, which was held a year earlier in Washington, D.C. Symposium participants included police chiefs, sheriffs, police researchers, police officers, members of other professional disciplines, community leaders, and members of other federal agencies from throughout the country. Following the lead of symposium participants, the NIJ report included many recommendations for enhancing police integrity, such as (1) integrating ethics training into the programs offered by newly funded Regional Community Policing Institutes throughout the country, (2) broadening research activities in the area of ethics through NIJ-awarded grants for research on police integrity, and (3) conducting case studies of departments that have an excellent track record in the area of police integrity.

On the practical side, most large law enforcement agencies have their own Internal Affairs Divisions, which are empowered to investigate charges of wrongdoing made against officers. Where necessary, state police agencies may be called upon to examine reported incidents. Federal agencies, including the FBI and the DEA, involve themselves when corruption goes far enough to violate federal statutes. The U.S. Department of Justice, through various investigative offices, has the authority to examine possible violations of civil rights which may result from the misuse of police authority and is often supported by the American Civil Liberties Union, the NAACP, and other "watchdog" groups in such endeavors.

> "Every society gets the kind of criminal it deserves. What is equally true is that every community gets the kind of law enforcement it insists on."
>
> —*Robert Kennedy*

Drug Testing of Police Employees

In 1997 a federal grand jury charged seven Chicago police tactical officers, considered to be among the city's finest frontline troops in the war on drugs, with plotting to arrest undercover agents posing as drug dealers and to steal their drugs. Prosecutors accused one of the indicted officers of being both a police officer and a street-gang leader. "Edward Lee Jackson," said prosecutors, "is a high-ranking leader of the Conservative Vice Lords street gang." The Jackson indictment led many to conclude that the 13,500-member Chicago Police Department had been deeply penetrated by members or associates of the city's drug gangs.[26]

On a wider scale, the widespread potential for police corruption created by illicit drugs has led to focused efforts to combat drug use by officers. Drug testing programs at the department level are an example of such efforts. When concern was at its highest, the National Institute of Justice conducted a telephone survey of 33 large police departments across the nation to determine what measures were being taken to identify officers and civilian employees who were using drugs.[27] NIJ learned that almost all departments had written procedures to test employees who were reasonably suspected of drug abuse. Applicants for police positions were being tested by 73 percent of the departments surveyed, and 21 percent of the departments were actively considering testing all officers. In what some people found a surprisingly low figure, 21 percent reported that they might offer treatment to identified violators rather than dismiss them, depending upon their personal circumstances.

The International Association of Chiefs of Police makes available to today's police managers a "Model Drug Testing Policy." The policy is directed toward the needs of local departments and suggests the following:[28]

- Testing all applicants and recruits for drug or narcotics use
- Testing current employees when performance difficulties or documentation indicate a potential drug problem

- Testing current employees when they are involved in the use of excessive force or suffer or cause on-duty injury

- Routine testing of all employees assigned to special "high-risk" areas such as narcotics and vice

Drug testing based upon a reasonable suspicion that drug abuse has been or is occurring has been supported by the courts (*Maurice Turner* v. *Fraternal Order of Police,* 1985),[29] although random testing of officers was banned by the New York State Supreme Court in the case of *Philip Caruso, President of P.B.A.* v. *Benjamin Ward, Police Commissioner* (1986).[30] Citing overriding public interests, a 1989 decision by the U.S. Supreme Court upheld the testing of U.S. Customs personnel applying for transfer into positions involving drug law enforcement or carrying a firearm.[31] Many legal issues surrounding employee drug testing, however, remain to be resolved in court.

Complicating the situation is the fact that drug and alcohol addiction are "handicaps" protected by the Federal Rehabilitation Act of 1973. As such, federal law enforcement employees, as well as those working for agencies with federal contracts, are entitled to counseling and treatment before action toward termination can be taken.

The issue of employee drug testing in police departments, as in many other agencies, is a sensitive one. Some claim that existing tests for drug use are inaccurate, yielding a significant number of "false positives." Repeated testing and high "threshold" levels for narcotic substances in the blood may eliminate many of these concerns. Less easy to address, however, is the belief that drug testing intrudes upon the personal rights and professional dignity of individual employees.

The Dangers of Police Work

On October 15, 1991, the National Law Enforcement Officers' Memorial was unveiled in Washington, D.C. Initially, the memorial contained the names of 12,561 law enforcement officers killed in the line of duty, including that of U.S. Marshals Service Officer Robert Forsyth, who, in 1794 became the nation's first law enforcement officer ever killed. Nearly 2,300 names have been added since opening day.[32] At the memorial, an interactive video system provides visitors with a brief biography and photograph of officers who have died. Video clips of the monument's milestone events, such as dedication and groundbreaking ceremonies, are also available. You can take a tour of the memorial by visiting WebExtra! 6-1 at CJToday.com.

An LAPD officer walks past the body of an armed robbery suspect that lies covered in front of his getaway vehicle after being gunned down by police following a bank robbery attempt in North Hollywood, California. Two suspects were killed, eight officers and three civilians were wounded during the day-long drama northwest of Los Angeles.
Sam Mircovich, Archive Photos.

As the memorial shows, police work is, by its very nature, dangerous. While most officers throughout their careers never fire their weapons in the line of duty, it is also plain that some officers meet death while performing their jobs. On-the-job police deaths occur from stress, training accidents, and auto crashes. However, it is violent death at the hands of criminal offenders that police officers and their families fear most.

Violence in the Line of Duty

On February 28, 1997, two heavily armed men bungled a daylight bank robbery attempt in North Hollywood, California. The men were wearing full body armor and carried automatic weapons.

LAPD Lt. Greg Meyer described the scene this way: "Imagine yourself working uniformed patrol at 9:15 A.M. on a warm sunny day and you suddenly find yourself in Beirut, Bosnia, or back in the Mekong Delta. You go from thinking about where you'll stop for that next cup of coffee, to having your black-and-white shot up with full-automatic AK-47 rounds. Within the next few minutes, officers and civilians all about you are shot down in the street by bank robbers who look like Ninja Turtles dressed to kill. And unlike the usual 'gunbattle' that lasts a few seconds, this time the shooting just keeps going, and going, and going. . . ."[33]

> "At one time my only wish was to be a police official. . . . Later I realized that it was good that I did not become one. . . ."
>
> —*Søren Kierkegaard*

The robbers didn't run when police arrived, instead standing their ground and firing bursts of armor-piercing rounds from 100-clip magazines. Covered from head to toe in bulletproof armor, the men took numerous hits from police small arms fire without seeming to notice. Detective Gordon Hagge, one of the first officers on the scene of the shootout later told reporters for the *Los Angeles Times* that he started thinking, "I'm in the wrong place with the wrong gun."[34] Then reality set in, said Lt. Meyer, and officers soon realized that they had "brought cap guns to World War III."[35]

Courageous officers succeeded in blocking the robbers' escape route long enough for the LAPD SWAT team's armored personnel carrier to arrive. Both would-be robbers, Larry Eugene Philips, Jr., and Emil Mataasarenanu, were finally killed in the massive exchange of gunfire that ensued. The firefight lasted nearly 20 minutes and was televised by a KTLA-TV helicopter hovering over the scene. By the time the incident ended, 18 civilians and officers had been injured.[36]

A few weeks later, in a move to give police officers heavier firepower, the Los Angeles Police Commission voted to authorize the city's officers to carry .45-caliber semiautomatic pistols in place of the 9 mm and .38-caliber revolvers that they had been using. In addition, 550 police supervisors throughout the city were given easy access to M-16 assault rifles,[37] along with "slug" ammunition (that has greater "knockdown" power when fired against suspects wearing body armor) for their shotguns.[38]

Although running gun battles are a rarity in police work, they appear to be occurring with greater regularity. Unlike the North Hollywood "incident," however, most officers are killed by lone suspects armed with a single weapon. In the early morning hours of September 30, 1992, for example, Oregon State Police Trooper Bret Clodfelter[39] stopped an intoxicated driver near Klamath Falls, Oregon. The driver was accompanied by two companions. Trooper Clodfelter arrested the car's operator, handcuffed him, and placed him in the rear of his patrol car. Since the offender's companions did not have a ride, Trooper Clodfelter offered to take them into town. After patting the men down for weapons he placed them in the rear of his patrol car, along with the arrestee. As the officer started to take the men home, one of the passengers told the killer several times (in Spanish) to shoot the trooper. Trooper Clodfelter, who did not speak Spanish, was unaware of what was being said. The killer, Francisco Mando-Hernandez, pulled out a .38 caliber handgun and shot Trooper Clodfelter four times in the back of the head. The weapon had been concealed in a coat pocket, but had not been discovered during the pat down search. All suspects fled the scene but were captured a few days later after an intensive manhunt.

Trooper Clodfelter had been married only 33 days before he died and left behind a new bride and two young children from a previous marriage. Thirteen months after his murder, Trooper Clodfelter's wife, devastated by the loss, took her own life. In 1995 Mando-Hernandez was found guilty of first-degree murder and sentenced to prison.

In 1999, 142 American law enforcement officers were killed in the line of duty.[40] Figure 6-2 shows the number of officers killed by circumstances. A recent study by the FBI found that slain

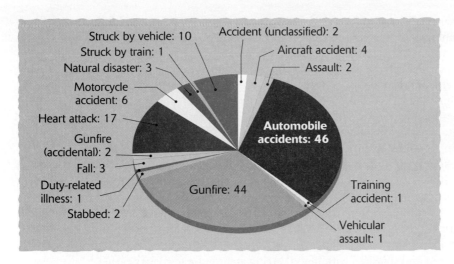

FIGURE 6-2 ■ *U.S. law enforcement officers killed in the line of duty—number by type of incident, 1999.*
Source: *Officer Down Memorial Page on the World Wide Web, http://odmp.org.*

officers appeared to be good natured and conservative in the use of physical force, "as compared to other law enforcement officers in similar situations. They were also perceived as being well-liked by the community and the department, friendly to everyone, laid back, and easy going."[41] Finally, the study also found, officers who were killed failed to wear protective vests.

For statistics on police killings to have meaning beyond the personal tragedy they entail, however, it is necessary to place them within a larger framework. There are approximately 800,000 state and local police employees in this country, and another 70,000 federal agents nationwide. Such numbers demonstrate that the rate of violent death among law enforcement officers in the line of duty is small indeed.

Risk of Disease and Infected Evidence

Not all the dangers facing law enforcement officers are as direct as outright violence and assault. The increasing incidence of serious diseases capable of being transmitted by blood and other bodily fluids, combined with the fact that crime and accident scenes are inherently

21st Century CJ

"Smart Guns" and Line-of-Duty Deaths

Statistics show that, of all officers killed feloniously in the line of duty, 16 percent, or one in six, are killed by a suspect with their own or another officer's service weapon. In an effort to reduce the number of such line-of-duty deaths, the National Institute of Justice recently funded a research project with Sandia National Laboratory intended to develop "smart gun" technology. *Smart gun* is a term used to describe a firearm that "recognizes" the user and can be fired only by an authorized user.

A variety of smart gun enabling mechanisms are being tested by San-dia, including those with esoteric names such as surface acoustic wave tagging, passive radio frequency coding, touch memory, magnetic encoding, capacitive sensors/encoding, and remote radio frequency disablement. It is expected that, as a result of tests that are now ongoing, mechanical or electromechanical safing mechanisms that can be activated or deactivated by the weapon's legitimate user will soon be incorporated during the manufacturing process into firearms carried by law enforcement personnel. Working models are already available. Colt Manufacturing Company, one of the manufacturers collaborating on smart gun technology, demonstrated the first working prototype of a smart gun at a Capitol Hill press conference in late 1996.

In addition to reducing line-of-duty deaths, smart gun technology holds the potential to substantially reduce the number of children and adolescents who die each year from the accidental discharge of firearms and to reduce the likelihood that stolen weapons will be used in criminal activities.

Source: *Sandia National Laboratories, World Wide Web site.*

dangerous, has made *caution* a necessary byword among investigators and first-on-the-scene officers. Potential for minor cuts and abrasions abounds in the broken glass and torn metal of a wrecked car, in the sharp edges of weapons remaining at the scene of an assault or murder, and in drug implements such as razor blades and hypodermic needles secreted in vehicles, apartments, and in pockets. Such minor injuries, previously shrugged off by many police personnel, have become a focal point for warnings about the dangers of AIDS (acquired immune deficiency syndrome), hepatitis B, tuberculosis, and other diseases spread through contact with infected blood.

In 1988 in Sonoma County, California, Sheriff Dick Michaelson became the first law enforcement supervisor to announce a clear-cut case of AIDS infection in an officer caused by interaction with a suspect. A deputy in Michaelson's department apparently contracted AIDS a few years earlier when he was pricked by a hypodermic needle during a pat down search.[42]

In 1992 a 46-year-old San Francisco police officer won $50,547 in disability pay and AIDS medical treatment expenses[43] and a possible $25,000-per-year permanent retirement benefit. Inspector Thomas Cady became infected with the HIV (human immunodeficiency virus) after being bitten and splashed with blood during an arrest a few years earlier.

Understandably, there is much concern among officers as to how to deal with the threat of AIDS and other bloodborne diseases. However, as a manual of the New York City Police Department reminds its officers, "Police officers have a professional responsibility to render assistance to those who are in need of our services. We cannot refuse to help. Persons with infectious diseases must be treated with the care and dignity we show all citizens."[44]

The FBI has also become concerned with the use of breath alcohol instruments on infected persons, the handling of evidence of all types, seemingly innocuous implements such as staples, the emergency delivery of babies in squad cars, and with the risk of attack (especially bites) by infected individuals who are being questioned or who are in custody. The following are among the 16 recommendations made by the FBI as "defenses against exposure" to infectious substances (others are listed in Table 6-2):[45]

1. The first line of defense against infection at the crime scene is protecting the hands and keeping them away from the eyes, mouth, and nose.
2. Any person with a cut, abrasion, or any other break in the skin on the hands should never handle blood or other body fluids without protection.
3. Use gloves and replace them whenever you leave the crime scene. Wash hands thoroughly.
4. No one at the crime scene should be allowed to smoke, eat, drink, or apply makeup.
5. Use the utmost care when handling knives, razors, broken glass, nails, and the like to prevent a puncture of the skin.
6. If a puncture of the skin does occur, cleanse it thoroughly with rubbing alcohol and wash with soap and water. Then seek immediate medical assistance.
7. When possible, use disposable items at the crime scene, such as pencils, gloves, and throw-away masks. These items should be incinerated after use.
8. Nondisposable items, such as cameras, notebooks, and so on, should be decontaminated using bleach mixed with water.

The National Institute of Justice adds to this list the recommendations that suspects should be asked to empty their own pockets, where possible, and that puncture wounds should be "milked" as in the case of snakebites in order to help flush infectious agents from the wound.[46]

In order to better combat the threat of infectious diseases among health care professionals and public safety employees, the federal Bloodborne Pathogens Act of 1991[47] requires that police officers receive proper training in how to prevent contamination by bloodborne infectious agents. The act also requires that police officers undergo an annual refresher course on the topic.

Police departments will face an increasing number of legal challenges in the years to come in cases involving infectious diseases such as AIDS. Some predictable areas of concern will involve (1) the need to educate officers and other police employees relative to AIDS and other serious infectious diseases, (2) the responsibility of police departments to prevent the spread of AIDS in police lockups, and (3) the necessity of effective and nondiscriminatory

TABLE 6-2 ■ Responses to AIDS-Related Law Enforcement Concerns

ISSUE/CONCERN	EDUCATIONAL AND ACTION MESSAGES
Human bites	Person who bites usually receives the victim's blood; viral transmission through saliva is highly unlikely. If bitten by anyone, milk wound to make it bleed; wash the area thoroughly, and seek medical attention.
Spitting	Viral transmission through saliva is highly unlikely.
Urine/feces	Virus isolated in only very low concentrations in urine; not at all in feces; no cases of AIDS or AIDS virus infection associated with either urine or feces.
Cuts/puncture wounds	Use caution in handling sharp objects and searching areas hidden from view; needle stick studies show risk of infection is very low.
CPR/first aid	To eliminate the already minimal risk associated with CPR, use masks/airways; avoid blood-to-blood contact by keeping open wounds covered and wearing gloves when in contact with bleeding wounds.
Body removal	Observe crime scene rules: Do not touch anything. Those who must come into contact with blood or other bodily fluids should wear gloves.
Casual contact	No cases of AIDS or AIDS virus infection attributed to casual contact.
Any contact with blood or body fluids	Wear gloves if contact with blood or body fluids is considered likely. If contact occurs, wash thoroughly with soap and water; clean up spills with one part water to nine parts household bleach.
Contact with dried blood or body fluids	No cases of infection have been traced to exposure to dried blood. The drying process itself appears to inactivate the virus. Despite low risk, however, caution dictates wearing gloves, a mask, and protective shoe coverings if exposure to dried blood particles is likely (for example, crime scene investigation).

Source: National Institute of Justice, Report No. 206 (November/December 1987), p. 6.

enforcement activities and life-saving measures by police officers in AIDS environments. With regard to nondiscriminatory activities, the National Institute of Justice has suggested that legal claims in support of an officer's refusal to render assistance to people with AIDS would probably not be effective in court.[48] The reason is twofold: The officer has a basic duty to render assistance to individuals in need of it, and the possibility of AIDS transmission by casual contact has been scientifically established as extremely remote. A final issue of growing concern involves activities by police officers infected with the AIDS virus. A recent issue of *Law Enforcement News* reports, "Faced with one of the nation's largest populations of AIDS sufferers—and perhaps one of the largest cadres of AIDS-infected officers—the New York City Police Department has debuted its own AIDS awareness effort."[49] Few statistics are currently available on the number of officers with AIDS, but public reaction to those officers may be a developing problem area, which police managers will soon need to address.

Stress among Police Officers

Perhaps the most insidious and least visible of all threats facing law enforcement personnel today is debilitating stress. While some degree of stress can be a positive motivator, serious stress, over long periods of time, is generally regarded as destructive, even life threatening.

Police detectives, for example, who worked around the clock in 1994 searching for two missing South Carolina boys whose mother first reported them as kidnapped but later confessed to drowning them, found the case especially stressful since it brought to mind many emotions. "I feel like I aged 10 years in 10 days,"[50] said Union County Sheriff Howard Wells, after Susan Smith confessed to her sons' murders.

Stress is a natural component of police work.[51] The American Institute of Stress, based in Yonkers, New York, ranks policing among the top 10 stress-producing jobs in the country.[52] Danger, frustration, paperwork, the daily demands of the job, and a lack of understanding from family members and friends contribute to the negative stresses officers experience.

Joseph Victor has identified four sources of police stress:[53] (1) external stress, which results from "real dangers," such as responding to calls involving armed suspects; (2) organizational stress, generated by the demands of police organizations themselves, such as scheduling, paperwork, training requirements, and so on; (3) personal stress, produced by interpersonal relationships among officers themselves; and (4) operational stress, which Victor defines as "the total effect of the need to combat daily the tragedies of urban life."

Some of the stressors in police work are particularly destructive. One is frustration brought on by the inability to be effective, regardless of the amount of personal effort expended. From the point of view of the individual officer, the police mandate is to bring about some change in society for the better. The crux of police work involves making arrests based upon thorough investigations which lead to convictions and the removal of individuals who are damaging to the social fabric of the community—all under the umbrella of the criminal law. Unfortunately, reality is often far from the ideal. Arrests may not lead to convictions. Evidence which is available to the officer may not be allowed in court. Sentences which are imposed may seem too "light" to the arresting officer. The feelings of powerlessness and frustration which come from seeing repeat offenders back on the streets and from experiencing numerous injustices worked upon seemingly innocent victims, may greatly stress police officers and cause them to question the purpose of their professional lives. It may also lead to desperate attempts to find relief. As Kevin Barrett observes, "The suicide rate of police officers is more than twice that of the general population."[54]

Another source of stress—that of living with constant danger—is incomprehensible to most of us, even to the family members of many officers. As one officer says, "I kick in a door and I've gotta talk some guy into putting a gun down. . . . And I go home, and my wife's upset because the lawn isn't cut and the kids have been bad. Now, to her that's a real problem."[55]

Stress is not unique to the police profession, but because of the "macho" attitude that has traditionally been associated with police work, denial of the stress experience may be found more often among police officers than in other occupational groups. Certain types of individuals are probably more susceptible to the negative effects of stress than are others. The Type A personality was popularized a few years ago as the category of person more likely to perceive life in terms of pressure and performance. Type B personalities were said to be more "laid back" and less likely to suffer from the negative effects of stress. Police ranks, drawn as they are from the general population, are filled with both stress-sensitive and stress-resistant personalities.

Stress Reduction. It is natural to try to reduce and control stress.[56] Humor helps, even if it's somewhat cynical. Health care professionals, for example, have long been noted for their ability to joke around patients who may be seriously ill or even dying. Police officers may similarly use humor to defuse their reactions to dark or threatening situations. Keeping an emotional distance from stressful events is another way of coping with them, although such distance is not always easy to maintain. Police officers who have had to deal with serious cases of physical child abuse have often reported on the emotional turmoil they experienced as a consequence of what they saw.

The support of family and friends can be crucial in developing other strategies to handle stress. Exercise, meditation, abdominal breathing, biofeedback, self-hypnosis, guided imaging, induced relaxation, subliminal conditioning, music, prayer, and diet have all been cited as techniques which can be useful in stress reduction. Devices to measure stress levels are available in the form of hand-held heart-rate monitors, blood pressure devices, "biodots" (which change color according to the amount of blood flow in the extremities), and psychological inventories.

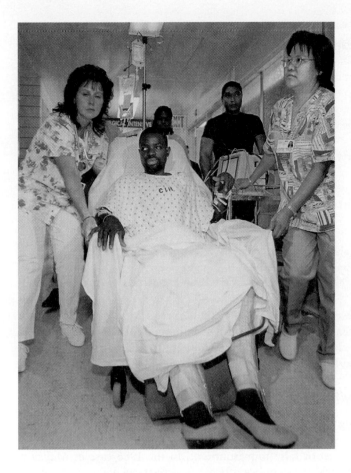

Abner Louima, the 30-year-old Haitian immigrant around whom a storm of protest swirled in late 1997 after a small group of NYPD officers serving Brooklyn's 70th Precinct savagely beat and sexually assaulted him in a stationhouse bathroom, forcing the handle of a toilet plunger up his rectum.
Todd Plitt, AP/Wide World Photos.

Along with stress, fatigue can affect police officer performance. As Bryan Vila points out: "Tired, urban street cops are a national icon. Weary from overtime assignments, shift work, night school, endless hours spent waiting to testify, and the emotional and physical demands of the job, not to mention trying to patch together a family and social life during irregular islands of off-duty time, they fend off fatigue with coffee and hard-bitten humor."[57] As Vila notes, few departments set work-hour standards, and fatigue associated with the pattern and length of work hours may be expected to contribute to police accidents, injuries, and misconduct. Vila suggests controlling the work hours of police officers "just as we control the working hours of many other occupational groups."[58]

Police Civil Liability

In 1996 51-year-old Richard Kelley filed suit in federal court against the Massachusetts State Police and the Weymouth (Massachusetts) police department.[59] The suit resulted from an incident during which Kelley alleged that state troopers and Weymouth police officers treated him as a drunk, rather than recognizing the fact that he had just suffered a stroke while driving. According to Kelley, following a minor traffic accident caused by the stroke, officers pulled him from his car, handcuffed him, dragged him along the ground, and ignored his pleas for help—forcing him to stay at a state police barracks for seven hours before taking him for medical treatment. Drunk-driving charges against Kelley were dropped after medical tests failed to reveal the presence of any intoxicating substances in his body.

As the Kelley case demonstrates, police officers may become involved in a variety of situations which create the potential for civil suits against the officers, their superiors, and their departments. Major sources of police civil liability are listed in Table 6-3. Swanson says that the most common source of lawsuits against the police involve "assault, battery, false imprisonment, and malicious prosecution."[60]

Civil suits brought against law enforcement personnel are of two types: state or federal.

"Nothing's so sacred as honor...."

—Wyatt Earp's headstone

TABLE 6-3 ■ Major Sources of Police Civil Liability

Failure to protect property in police custody
Negligence in the care of persons in police custody
Failure to render proper emergency medical assistance
Failure to prevent a foreseeable crime
Failure to aid private citizens
Lack of due regard for the safety of others
False arrest
False imprisonment
Inappropriate use of deadly force
Unnecessary assault or battery
Malicious prosecution
Violations of constitutional rights

Suits brought in state courts have generally been the most common form of civil litigation involving police officers. In recent years, however, an increasing number of suits are being brought in federal courts on the basis of the legal rationale that the civil rights of the plaintiff, as guaranteed by federal law, have been denied.

Common Sources of Civil Suits

Of all complaints brought against the police, assault charges are the best known, being, as they are, subject to high media visibility. Less visible, but not uncommon, are civil suits charging the police with false arrest or false imprisonment. In the 1986 case of *Malley* v. *Briggs*,[61] the U.S. Supreme Court held that a police officer who effects an arrest or conducts a search on the basis of an improperly issued warrant may be liable for monetary damages when a reasonably well trained officer, under the same circumstances "would have known that his affidavit failed to establish probable cause and that he should not have applied for the warrant." Significantly, the Court, in *Malley,* also ruled that an officer "cannot excuse his own default by pointing to the greater incompetence of the magistrate."[62] That is, the officer, rather than the judge who issued the warrant, is ultimately responsible for establishing the basis for pursuing the arrest or search.

When an officer makes an arrest without just cause, or simply impedes an individual's right to leave the scene without good reason, he or she may also be liable for the charge of false arrest. Officers who enjoy "throwing their weight around" are especially subject to this type of suit, grounded as it is on the abuse of police authority. Because employers may generally be sued for the negligent or malicious actions of their employees, many police departments are finding themselves named as co-defendants in lawsuits today.

Negligent actions by officers may also provide the basis for suits. High-speed chases are especially dangerous because of the potential they entail for injury to innocent bystanders. Flashing blue or red lights (the color of police vehicle lights varies by state) legally only *request* the right-of-way on a highway; they do not demand it. Officers who drive in such a way as to place others in danger may find themselves the subject of suits. In the case of *Biscoe* v. *Arlington County* (1984),[63] for example, Alvin Biscoe was awarded $5 million after he lost both legs as a consequence of a high-speed chase while he was waiting to cross the street. Biscoe was an innocent bystander and was struck by a police car which had gone out of control. The officer driving the car apparently had not been thoroughly trained in department policies prohibiting high-speed chases. Departments may protect themselves to some degree through proper training and regulations limiting the authority of their personnel. In a 1985 case, for example, a Louisiana police department was exonerated in an accident which occurred during a high-speed chase because of its policy limiting emergency driving to no more than 20 miles over the posted speed limit, and because it had trained its officers in that policy. The officer, however, who drove 75 mph in a 40-mph zone was found to be negligent and held liable for damages.[64]

Law enforcement supervisors may find themselves the object of lawsuits by virtue of the fact that they are responsible for the actions of their officers. Where it can be shown that supervisors were negligent in hiring (as when someone with a history of alcoholism, mental problems, sexual deviance, or drug abuse is employed), or if supervisors failed in their responsibility to properly train officers before they armed and deployed them, they may be found liable for damages.

In the 1989 case of the *City of Canton, Ohio* v. *Harris*,[65] the U.S. Supreme Court ruled that a "failure to train" can become the basis for legal liability on the part of a municipality where the "failure to train amounts to deliberate indifference to the rights of persons with whom the police come in contact."[66] In that case, Geraldine Harris was arrested and taken to the Canton, Ohio, police station. While at the station she slumped to the floor several times. Officers finally decided to leave her on the floor and never called for qualified medical assistance. Upon release, Ms. Harris was taken by family members to a local hospital. She was hospitalized for a week and received follow-up outpatient treatment for the next year. The Court ruled that although municipalities could not justifiably be held liable for limited instances of unsatisfactory training, they could be held accountable when the failure to train results from a deliberate or conscious choice.

In 1997, however, the Supreme Court, in the case of *Board of the County Commissioners of Bryan County, Oklahoma* v. *Brown*,[67] ruled that to establish liability plaintiffs must show that "the municipal action in question was not simply negligent, but was taken with 'deliberate indifference' as to its known or obvious consequences." In *Brown*, a deputy named Burns was hired by the sheriff of Bryan County, Oklahoma. Burns later used excessive force in arresting a woman, and the woman sued the county for damages, claiming that Deputy Burns had been hired in spite of his having a criminal record. In fact, some years earlier Burns had pleaded guilty to various driving infractions and other misdemeanors, including assault and battery—a charge which resulted from a college fight. At trial, a spokesperson for the sheriff's department admitted to receiving Burns' driving and criminal records, but said he had not reviewed either in detail before the decision to hire Burns was made. Nonetheless, the Supreme Court held that deliberate indifference on the part of the county had not been established because it had not been demonstrated by the plaintiffs that "Burns' background made his use of excessive force in making an arrest a plainly obvious consequence of the hiring decision." According to the Court, "[o]nly where adequate scrutiny of the applicant's background would lead a reasonable policymaker to conclude that the plainly obvious consequence of the decision to hire the applicant would be the deprivation of a third party's federally protected right can the official's failure to adequately scrutinize the applicant's background constitute 'deliberate indifference.' " In other words, according to this decision, a municipality (in this case, a county) may not be held liable solely because it employs a person with an arrest record.

Federal Lawsuits

Federal suits are often called **1983 lawsuits** because they are based upon Section 1983 of Title 42 of the United States Code—an act passed by Congress in 1871 to ensure the civil rights of men and women of all races. That act requires due process of law before any person can be deprived of life, liberty, or property and specifically provides redress for the denial of these constitutional rights by officials acting under color of state law. For example, a 1983 suit may be brought against officers who shoot suspects under questionable circumstances—thereby denying them of their right to life without due process. The 1981 case of *Prior* v. *Woods*[68] resulted in a $5.7 million judgment against the Detroit Police Department after David Prior—who was mistaken for a burglar—was shot and killed in front of his home.

Another type of liability action, this one directed specifically at federal officials or enforcement agents, is called a Bivens suit. The case of *Bivens* v. *Six Unknown Federal Agents* (1971)[69] established a path for legal action against agents enforcing federal laws, which is similar to that found in a 1983 suit. **Bivens actions** may be addressed against individuals, but not the United States or its agencies.[70] Federal officers have generally been granted a court-created qualified immunity and have been protected from suits where they were found to have acted in the belief that their action was consistent with federal law.[71]

1983 Lawsuits

Civil suits brought under Title 42, Section 1983, of the United States Code, against anyone denying others of their constitutional rights to life, liberty, or property without due process of law.

Bivens Action

The name given to civil suits, based on the case of Bivens v. Six Unknown Named Defendants, brought against federal government officials for denial of the constitutional rights of others.

Theory Into Practice

An Example of Police Civil Liability— The Case of Bernard McCummings

A 1993 U.S. Supreme Court decision in a civil suit that drew wide outrage saw convicted subway mugger Bernard McCummings awarded $4.3 million in a suit he had brought against the city of New York. McCummings was shot twice in the back in 1984 by Transit Authority officer Manuel Rodriguez as McCummings attempted to flee a subway platform after beating and robbing a 71-year-old man. At the time of the crime, McCummings had just gotten out of prison for robbery. Since the shooting, McCummings, who was 23 years old when he was injured, has remained paralyzed from the chest down. After pleading guilty to the mugging, he was sentenced to prison, where he served two years. When McCummings brought suit against the city, however, a jury and appeals court found that officers had used excessive force. Before paying the award, the city appealed to the Supreme Court. In upholding the cash award to McCummings, the Supreme Court reiterated earlier rulings that police officers cannot use deadly force against unarmed fleeing suspects who pose no apparent threat to officers or to the public.

McCummings's victim, Jerome Sandusky, who was carrying less than $30 at the time he was attacked, decried the ruling, saying, "It's justice turned upside down . . . and it sends a terrible message . . . that crime *does* pay." Sandusky added, "Ordinarily I would be sorry for anyone that was made a cripple. But he was made a cripple because of his own action." Gerald Arenberg, of the National Association of Chiefs of Police, sided with Sandusky. "The criminal is very well protected by the Supreme Court," Arenberg said in a national interview. Lawyers for the city were disappointed. One lawyer said that, when faced with a fleeing suspect, "the message is, it's probably wiser for a police officer to do nothing, in terms of civil liability."

Opinions on the case, however, were varied. "It was the right decision," said David Breibart, McCummings's lawyer. "It gives me great faith in the system." A *Washington Post* editorial, on the other hand, suggested that police should not be bound by the rules of fair play when criminals are not. "What if felons knew that cops could shoot them if they fled?" the editorial asked. "More of them would likely freeze and put up their hands. . . . [C]riminal behavior should not be treated as if it were some sort of quasi-legitimate enterprise, gov-

erned by the laws of negligence." The writer continued, "McCummings was as much a victim of his own criminality as he was of a violation of the rules regarding the use of deadly force. Once he chose to break the law he wasn't entitled to be compensated by it." McCummings's victim agreed. Recently, Sandusky filed suit against McCummings, seeking to get the $4.3 million award. Sandusky brought suit under New York's modified "Son of Sam" law, which is intended to prevent criminals from profiting from their crimes.

? QUESTIONS FOR DISCUSSION

1. Do you feel McCummings should have been compensated for his injuries? Why or why not?
2. Do you agree with the assertion in this box that "cops should not be bound by the rules of fair play when criminals are not?" Why or why not?

Source: "Mugger Shot by Cop to Keep $4.3 million," USA Today, November 30, 1993, p. 1A; "Mugging Lawsuit," Associated Press wire services, December 15, 1993; "Compensation for a Criminal," Washington Post wire services, December 2, 1993; and "Scotus-Excessive Force," Associated Press wire services, November 30, 1993.

In times past, the doctrine of sovereign immunity barred legal actions against state and local governments. Sovereign immunity was a legal theory which held that a governing body could not be sued because it made the law and therefore could not be bound by it. Immunity is a much more complex issue today. Some states have officially abandoned any pretext of immunity through legislative action. New York State, for example, has declared that public agencies are equally as liable as private agencies for violations of constitutional rights. Other states, such as California, have enacted statutory provisions which define and place limits on governmental liability.[72] A number of state immunity statutes have been struck down by court decision. In general, states are moving in the direction of setting dollar limits on liability and adopting federal immunity principles to protect individual officers, including "good faith" and "reasonable belief" rules.

At the federal level, the concept of sovereign immunity is embodied in the Federal Tort Claims Act (FTCA),[73] which grants broad immunity to federal government agencies engaged in discretionary activities. When a federal employee is sued for a wrongful or negligent act, the Federal Employees Liability Reform and Tort Compensation Act of 1988, commonly known as the Westfall Act, empowers the attorney general to certify that the employee was acting within the scope of his or her office or employment at the time of the incident out of which the claim arose. Upon certification, the employee is dismissed from the action and the United States is substituted as defendant. The case then falls under the governance of the FTCA.

In 1995, in a case involving the FTCA, a Miami federal judge ordered the federal government to pay out more than $1 million to five crew members and a passenger on board an airplane from Belize (a small Latin American country), which was scheduled to stop in Miami after taking on additional passengers in Honduras. Testimony revealed that DEA agents had planted cocaine on the plane at its point of origin and had planned to arrest Miami dealers when they retrieved the drugs. Unfortunately, the agents had failed to notify Honduran authorities of the planted drugs, and when the plane landed in Honduras it was searched. Honduran police then arrested the six men—beating them with rubber hoses and kicking them down stairs in an effort to get confessions.[74] The judge hearing the suit against the government ruled that although the FTCA gives broad immunity to government agencies whose officials exercise discretion in everyday activities, it was not the intent of Congress to extend immunity to government agencies when the actions of their officials fail to comply with established regulations. In effect, the judge said, the failure by DEA agents to notify Honduran police of the "sting" in progress constituted a failure to perform an official duty.

For its part, the U.S. Supreme Court has supported a type of "qualified immunity" for individual officers (as opposed to the agencies for which they work) which "shields law enforcement officers from constitutional lawsuits if reasonable officers believe their actions to be lawful in light of clearly established law and the information the officers possess." The Supreme Court has also described qualified immunity as a defense "which shields public officials from actions for damages unless their conduct was unreasonable in light of clearly established law."[75] According to the Court, "the qualified immunity doctrine's central objective is to protect public officials from undue interference with their duties and from potentially disabling threats of liability. . . ."[76] In the context of a warrantless arrest, the Court said, in *Hunter* v. *Bryant* (1991),[77] "even law enforcement officials who reasonably but mistakenly conclude that probable cause is present are entitled to immunity."[78] Most departments carry liability insurance to protect them against the severe financial damage which can result from the loss of a large suit. Some officers make it a point to acquire private policies which provide coverage in the event they are named as individuals in such suits. Both types of insurance policies generally provide for a certain amount of legal fees to be paid by the police for defense against the suit, regardless of the outcome of the case. Police departments who face civil prosecution because of the actions of an officer, however, may find that legal and financial liability extend to supervisors, city managers, and the community itself. Where insurance coverage does not exist, or is inadequate, city coffers may be nearly drained to meet the damages awarded.[79]

Theory Into Practice

Title 42, United States Code, Section 1983

Every person who, under color of any statute, ordinance, regulation, custom, or usage, of any State or Territory, subjects, or causes to be subjected, any citizen of the United States or other person within the jurisdiction thereof to the deprivation of any rights, privileges, or immunities secured by the Constitution and laws, shall be liable to the party injured in an action at law, suit in equity, or other proper proceeding for redress.

In a recent five-year period, for example, the city of Los Angeles, California, paid out $23 million to people who brought suits against the LAPD for civil rights violations.[80] Former Los Angeles Chief of Police Daryl Gates, in commenting on the prevalence of lawsuits against police officers today, has observed that although California cities are allowed to pay damage awards for individual officers, they do not have to. Gates continued: "Think about the chilling factor in that. [It says] 'Hey, Chief, you're on your own. We're not gonna pay anything.' Think what that does. It says, 'Hey, Chief, don't open your mouth—Don't tell the public anything. Don't let them know what the real facts are in this case. Don't tell the truth.' And what does it tell the police officers? 'Don't do your work, because you're liable to wind up in court, being sued.' That, to me, is probably the most frightening thing that's happening in the United States today."[81]

Police Use of Deadly Force

The use of deadly force by police officers is one area of potential civil liability which has received considerable attention in recent years. Historically, the fleeing felon rule applied to most U.S. jurisdictions. It held that officers could use deadly force to prevent the escape of a suspected felon, even when that person represented no immediate threat to the officer or to the public. The fleeing felon rule probably stemmed from early common-law punishments, which specified death for a large number of crimes. Today, however, the death penalty is far less frequent in application, and the fleeing felon rule has been called into question in a number of courts.

The 1985 Supreme Court case of *Tennessee* v. *Garner*[82] specified the conditions under which deadly force could be used in the apprehension of suspected felons. Edward Garner, a 15-year-old suspected burglar, was shot to death by Memphis police after he refused their order to halt and attempted to climb over a chain-link fence. In an action initiated by Garner's father, who claimed that his son's constitutional rights had been violated, the Court held that the use of deadly force by the police to prevent the escape of a fleeing felon could be justified only when the suspect could reasonably be thought to represent a significant threat of serious injury or death to the public or to the officer *and* where deadly force is necessary to effect the arrest. In reaching its decision, the Court declared, "The use of deadly force to prevent the escape of *all* felony suspects, whatever the circumstances, is constitutionally unreasonable."[83]

In 1989 the Court, in the case of *Graham* v. *Connor*,[84] established the standard of "objective reasonableness" under which an officer's use of deadly force could be assessed in terms of "reasonableness at the moment." In other words, whether deadly force has been used appropriately or not should be judged, the Court said, from the perspective of a reasonable officer on the scene and not with the benefit of "20/20 hindsight." "The calculus of reasonableness," wrote the Justices, "must embody allowance for the fact that police officers are often forced to make split-second judgments—in circumstances that are tense, uncertain, and rapidly evolving—about the amount of force that is necessary in a particular situation."

In 1995, following investigations into the actions of federal agents at the deadly siege of the Branch Davidian compound at Waco, Texas, and the tragic deaths associated with a 1992 FBI assault on antigovernment separatists in Ruby Ridge, Idaho, the federal government announced that it was adopting an "imminent danger" standard for the use of deadly force by federal agents. The federal "imminent danger" standard restricts the use of deadly force to only those situations in which the lives of agents or others are in danger. As the new standard was announced, federal agencies were criticized for taking so long to adopt it. Morton Feldman, executive vice president of the National Association of Chiefs of Police, said the federal government was finally catching up with policies adopted by state and local law enforcement agencies 17 years previously. "It is totally irresponsible and reprehensible that it took the federal government so long to catch up," said Feldman. "How many hundreds of lives of officers and civilians may have been senselessly lost during the last 17 years because of this reckless, unjustifiable disregard for having an appropriate policy in place?"[85] The federal use of deadly force policy, as adopted by the FBI, is partially reproduced in a box in this section.

Studies of killings by the police have often focused on claims of discrimination, that is, that black and minority suspects are more likely to be shot than whites. Research in the area, however, has not provided solid support for such claims. While individuals shot by police are more likely to be minorities, an early study by James Fyfe[86] found that police officers will generally respond with deadly force when mortally threatened and that minorities are considerably more likely to use weapons in assaults on officers than are whites. Complicating the picture further were Fyfe's data showing that minority officers are involved in the shooting of suspects more often than other officers, a finding that may be due to the assignment of such officers to inner-city and ghetto areas. However, a more recent study by Fyfe,[87] which analyzed police shootings in Memphis, Tennessee, found that black property offenders were twice as likely as whites to be shot by police.

Although relatively few police officers will ever feel the need to fire their weapons during the course of their careers, those who do may find themselves embroiled in a web of social, legal, and personal complications. It is estimated that an average year sees 600 suspects killed by gunfire from public police in America, while another 1,200 are shot and wounded, and 1,800 individuals are shot at and missed.[88]

The personal side of police shootings is well summarized in the title of an article which appeared in *Police Magazine.* The article, "I've Killed That Man Ten Thousand Times,"[89] demonstrated how police officers who have to use their weapons may be haunted by years of depression and despair. Not long ago, according to Anne Cohen, author of the article, all departments did to help officers who had shot someone was to "give him enough bullets to reload his gun." The stress and trauma which result from shootings by officers in defense of themselves or others are only now beginning to be realized, and most departments have yet to develop mechanisms for adequately dealing with such reactions.[90]

Especially difficult to deal with are instances of "suicide by cop," in which individuals bent on dying engage in behavior that causes responding officers to resort to deadly force. In 1997, for example, 19-year-old Moshe "Moe" Pergament, a well-mannered college student, was shot to death by Nassau County (New York) police officers after he pulled a $1.79 toy revolver from his waistband and pointed it at the officers during a traffic stop. Pergament apparently wanted to be shot by law enforcement personnel, and had planned his death. In a note found after his death and addressed to "the officer who shot me," Pergament apologized for what he had planned. "Officer," the note read, "It was a plan. I'm sorry to get you involved. I just needed to die."[91] Pergament had also written goodbye messages to friends and family members. He was apparently depressed over a $6,000 gambling debt. A 1998 study of fatal Los Angeles shootings by police officers found that an astonishingly large number— over 10 percent—could be classified as "suicide by cop."[92]

A South Carolina SWAT team prepares for action during an inmate uprising at the Broad River Correctional Institution near Columbia. Deadly force can be used only in situations involving extreme and imminent danger.
Jamie Francis, Pool, AP/Wide World Photos.

Theory Into Practice

The FBI's Policy on the Use of Deadly Force

A. **Defense of Life:** Agents may use deadly force only when necessary, that is, when the agents have probable cause to believe that the subject of such force poses an imminent danger of death or serious physical injury to the agents or other persons.

B. **Fleeing Subject:** Deadly force may be used to prevent the escape of a fleeing subject if there is probable cause to believe (1) the subject has committed a felony involving the infliction or threatened infliction of serious physical injury or death, and (2) the subject's escape would pose an imminent danger of death or serious physical injury to the agents or other persons.

C. **Verbal Warnings:** If feasible, and if to do so would not increase the danger to the agent or others, a verbal warning to submit to the authority of the agent shall be given prior to the use of deadly force.

D. **Warning Shots:** No warning shots are to be fired by agents.

E. **Vehicles:** Weapons may not be fired solely to disable moving vehicles. Weapons may be fired at the driver or other occupant of a moving motor vehicle only when the agents have probable cause to believe that the subject poses an imminent danger of death or serious physical injury to the agents or others, and the use of deadly force does not create a danger to the public that outweighs the likely benefits of its use.

Source: John C. Hall, "FBI Training on the New Federal Deadly Force Policy," FBI Law Enforcement Bulletin, April 1996, pp. 25–32.

A few years ago the National Institute of Justice reported on efforts begun in 1987 to develop "less than lethal weapons" for use by law enforcement officers. Questions to be answered include (1) "Can an officer stop a fleeing felon without use of deadly force?" (2) "Are there devices and substances that would rapidly subdue assailants before they could open fire or otherwise harm their hostages?" and (3) "Can technology provide devices to incapacitate assailants without also harming nearby innocent hostages and bystanders?" Chemical agents, knockout gases, stunning explosives, tranquilizing darts, and remote-delivery electronic shocks are all being studied by the agency. NIJ says it is "moving forward with research development and evaluation of devices for use by line patrol officers under a wide variety of circumstances. . . . [T]he goal is to give line officers effective and safe alternatives to lethal force."[93]

> **Police Professionalism**
>
> *The increasing formalization of police work and the rise in public acceptance of the police that accompanies it. Any profession is characterized by a specialized body of knowledge and a set of internal guidelines that hold members of the profession accountable for their actions. A well-focused code of ethics, equitable recruitment and selection practices, and informed promotional strategies among many agencies contribute to a growing level of professionalism among American police agencies today.*

Professionalism and Ethics

Police administrators have responded in a variety of ways to issues of danger, liability, and the potential for corruption. Among the most significant responses have been calls for increased professionalism at all levels of policing. A profession is characterized by a body of specialized knowledge, acquired through extensive education,[94] and by a well-considered set of internal standards and ethical guidelines which hold members of the profession accountable to one another and to society. Associations of like-minded practitioners generally serve to create and disseminate standards for the profession as a whole.

Contemporary policing evidences many of the attributes of a profession. Specialized knowledge in policing includes a close familiarity with criminal law, laws of procedure, constitutional guarantees and relevant Supreme Court decisions, a working knowledge of weapons and hand-to-hand tactics, driving skills and vehicle maintenance, a knowledge of radio communications, report-writing abilities, interviewing techniques, and media and human-relations skills. Other specialized knowledge may include Breathalyzer operation, special weapons firing, polygraph operation, conflict resolution, and hostage negotiation skills. Supervisory personnel require an even wider range of skills, including administrative knowledge, management techniques, personnel administration, and department strategies for optimum utilization of officers and physical resources.

> **Police Ethics**
>
> *The special responsibility for adherence to moral duty and obligation inherent in police work.*

Basic law enforcement training requirements were begun in the 1950s by the state of New

York and through a voluntary system of Peace Officer Standards and Training (**POST**) in California. Additional information on California's POST standards can be accessed via *WebExtra!* 6-2 at CJToday.com. Today, POST-like requirements are mandated by law in every state in the nation, although they vary considerably from region to region. Modern police education generally involves training in subject areas as diverse as human relations, firearms and weapons, communications, legal aspects of policing, patrol, criminal investigations, administration, report writing, and criminal justice systems. According to a 1999 Bureau of Justice Statistics report,[95] the median number of hours of classroom training required of new officers is highest in state police agencies (823), and lowest in sheriffs' departments (448). The requirements for county and municipal police are 760 and 640 hours, respectively.

Federal law enforcement agents receive schooling at the Federal Law Enforcement Training Center (FLETC) at Glynco, Georgia. The Center provides training for about 60 federal law enforcement agencies (excluding the FBI and DEA, which have their own training academies at Quantico, Virginia) and has begun offering advanced training to state and local police organizations (through the National Center for State and Local Law Enforcement Training, located on the FLETC campus), where such training is not available under other auspices. Specialized schools, such as Northwestern University's Traffic Institute, have also been credited with raising the level of police practice from purely operational concerns to a more professional level.

Police work is guided by an ethical code originated in 1956 by the Peace Officer's Research Association of California (PORAC), in conjunction with Dr. Douglas M. Kelley of Berkeley's School of Criminology.[96] *The Law Enforcement Code of Ethics* is reproduced in a box in this chapter. Ethics training is still not well integrated into most basic law enforcement training programs, but a movement in that direction has begun and calls for expanded training in ethics are on the increase.

Professional associations abound in police work. The Fraternal Order of Police (FOP) is one of the best-known organizations of public service workers in the United States. The International Association of Chiefs of Police (IACP) has done much to raise professional standards in policing and continually strives for improvements in law enforcement nationwide.

Accreditation provides another channel toward police professionalism. The Commission on Accreditation for Law Enforcement Agencies (CALEA) was formed in 1979. Police departments wishing to apply for accreditation through the Commission must meet hundreds of standards relating to areas as diverse as day-to-day operations, administration, review of incidents involving the use of a weapon by officers, and evaluation and promotion of personnel. To date, relatively few police agencies are accredited, although a number are currently undergoing the accreditation process. Although accreditation makes possible the identification of high-quality police departments, it is often undervalued because it carries few incentives. Accreditation is still only "icing on the cake" and does not guarantee a department any rewards beyond that of peer recognition. As of January 1, 2000, nearly 470 U.S. law enforcement agencies were accredited by CALEA—although that number represents only 2.5 percent of the nation's 18,769 police agencies.[97] You can visit CALEA online via *WebExtra!* 6-3 at CJToday.com.

Educational Requirements

As the concern for quality policing builds, increasing emphasis is being placed on the education of police officers. As early as 1931, the National Commission of Law Observance and Enforcement (the Wickersham Commission) highlighted the importance of a well-educated police force by calling for "educationally sound" officers.[98] In 1967 the President's Commission on Law Enforcement and the Administration of Justice voiced the belief that "[t]he ultimate aim of all police departments should be that all personnel with general enforcement powers have baccalaureate degrees." At the time, the average educational level of police officers in the United States was 12.4 years—slightly beyond a high-school degree. In 1973 the National Advisory Commission on Criminal Justice Standards and Goals made the following rather specific recommendation:[99] Every police agency should, no later than 1982, require as

POST

An acronym for Peace Officer Standards and Training.

"You can't measure what a patrolman standing on a corner has prevented. There is no product at the end of a policeman's day."
—*Charles McCarthy*

"There is more to being a professional than just looking like one."
—*Rob Edwards*

a condition of initial employment the completion of at least four years of education . . . at an accredited college or university."[100]

Recommendations, of course, do not always translate into practice. A 1999 Bureau of Justice Statistics Report[101] found that 16 percent of state police agencies require a two-year college degree, and 4 percent require a four-year degree. County police are the next most likely to require either a two-year (13 percent) or four-year (3 percent) degree. Among large municipal police agencies, 9 percent have a degree requirement, with 2 percent requiring a four-year degree. Among sheriffs' departments, 6 percent require a degree, including 1 percent with a four-year-degree requirement.

A survey of 699 police departments by The Police Executive Research Forum (PERF) found that the average level of educational achievement among both black and white officers was 14 years of schooling, nearly the equivalent of an associate's degree from a two-year or community college.[102] Female officers (with an average level of educational achievement of 14.6 years) tend to be better educated than their male counterparts (who report an average attainment level of 13.6 years). Only 3.3 percent of male officers hold graduate degrees, while almost one-third (30.2 percent) of women officers hold such degrees. On the downside, 34.8 percent of male officers have no college experience, and 24.1 percent of female officers have none. The PERF report explained the difference between male and female educational achievement by saying that "[w]omen tend to rely on higher education more than men as a springboard for a law enforcement career . . . [and] [p]olice departments may utilize higher standards—consciously or unconsciously—for selecting women officers."[103]

The report also stressed the need for educated police officers, citing the following benefits which accrue to police agencies from the hiring of educated officers:[104] (1) better written reports, (2) enhanced communications with the public, (3) more effective job performance, (4) fewer citizens' complaints, (5) greater initiative, (6) a wiser use of discretion, (7) a heightened sensitivity to racial and ethnic issues, and (8) fewer disciplinary problems. On the other hand, a greater likelihood that educated officers will leave police work, and their tendency to question orders and request reassignment with relative frequency, are some education-related drawbacks.

A recent Bureau of Justice Statistics report[105] found that 12 percent of all local police departments required that rookie officers have at least some college coursework, while 1 percent required new officers to have a four-year college degree, and 7 percent required a two-year degree. An even greater number of agencies now require the completion of at least some college-level work for officers seeking promotion. The San Diego Police Department, for example, requires two years of college work for promotion to the rank of sergeant.[106] A decade ago the Sacramento, California, police department set completion of a four-year college degree as a requirement for promotion to lieutenant, and, in 1988, the New York City Police Department announced a requirement of at least 64 college credits for promotion to supervisory ranks. At the state level, a variety of plans exist for integrating college work into police careers. Minnesota now requires a college degree for new candidates taking the state's Peace Office Standards and Training Board's licensing examination. Successful completion of all POST requirements permits employment as a fully certified law enforcement officer in the state of Minnesota. In 1991 the state of New York set 60 semester hours of college-level work as a mandated minimum for hiring into the New York State Police. Finally, many federal agencies require college degrees for entry-level positions. Among them are the FBI, DEA, ATF, Secret Service, the U.S. Customs Service, and the Immigration and Naturalization Service.

Recruitment and Selection

Any profession needs informed, dedicated, and competent personnel. When the National Advisory Commission on Criminal Justice Standards and Goals issued its 1973 report on the police, it bemoaned the fact that "many college students are unaware of the varied, interesting, and challenging assignments and career opportunities that exist within the police service."[107] In the intervening years, the efforts made by police departments to correct such misconceptions have had a considerable effect. Today, police organizations actively recruit new officers from college campuses, professional organizations, and two-year junior colleges and technical institutes. Education is an important criterion in selecting today's police

Theory Into Practice

The Law Enforcement Code of Ethics

As a Law Enforcement Officer, my fundamental duty is to serve mankind; to safeguard lives and property; to protect the innocent against deception, the weak against oppression or intimidation, and the peaceful against violence or disorder; and to respect the Constitutional rights of all men to liberty, equality and justice.

I will keep my private life unsullied as an example to all; maintain courageous calm in the face of danger, scorn, or ridicule; develop self-restraint; and be constantly mindful of the welfare of others. Honest in thought and deed in both my personal and official life, I will be exemplary in obeying the laws of the land and the regulations of my department. Whatever I see or hear of a confidential nature or that is confided to me in my official capacity will be kept secret unless revelation is necessary in the performance of my duty.

I will never act officiously or permit personal feelings, prejudices, animosities or friendships to influence my decisions. With no compromise for crime and with relentless prosecution of criminals, I will enforce the law courteously and appropriately without fear or favor, malice or ill will, never employing unnecessary force or violence and never accepting gratuities.

I recognize the badge of my office as a symbol of public faith, and I accept it as a public trust to be held so long as I am true to the ethics of the police service. I will constantly strive to achieve these objectives and ideals, dedicating myself before God to my chosen profession . . . law enforcement.

Source: International Association of Chiefs of Police. Reprinted with permission.

recruits. As mentioned earlier, some departments require a minimum number of college credits for entry-level work. A policy of the Dallas, Texas, Police Department[108] requiring a minimum of 45 semester hours of successful college-level study for new recruits was upheld in 1985 by the U.S. Fifth Circuit Court of Appeals in the case of *Davis* v. *Dallas*.[109]

The National Commission report stressed the setting of high standards for police recruits and recommended a strong emphasis on minority recruitment, an elimination of residence requirements (which required officers to live in the area they were hired to serve) for new officers, a decentralized application and testing procedure, and various recruiting incentives. The commission also suggested that a four-year college degree should soon become a reasonable expectation for police recruits. The survey also found that 62 percent of responding agencies had at least one formal policy in support of officers pursuing higher education.[110]

Effective policing, however, may depend more upon personal qualities than it does upon educational attainment. O. W. Wilson once enumerated some of the "desirable personal qualities of patrol officers."[111] They include (1) initiative; (2) the capacity for responsibility; (3) the ability to deal alone with emergencies; (4) the capacity to communicate effectively with persons of diverse social, cultural, and ethnic backgrounds; (5) the ability to learn a variety of tasks quickly; (6) the attitude and ability necessary to adapt to technological changes; (7) the desire to help people in need; (8) an understanding of others; (9) emotional maturity; and (10) sufficient physical strength and endurance.

Standard procedures employed by modern departments in selecting trainees usually include basic skills tests, physical agility measurements, interviews, physical examinations, eye tests, psychological evaluations, and background investigations into the personal character of applicants. After training, successful applicants are typically placed on a period of probation approximately one year in length. The probationary period in police work has been called the "first true job-related test . . . in the selection procedure,"[112] providing as it does the opportunity for supervisors to gauge the new officer's response to real-life situations.

> "A good cop stays a rookie at heart, excited by every shift."
>
> *—A Nashville, Tennessee, policeman*

Ethnic and Racial Minorities and Women

In 1967 the National Advisory Commission on Civil Disorders conducted a survey of supervisory personnel in police departments.[113] It found a marked disparity between the number of black and white officers in leadership positions. One of every 26 black police officers had

Women in uniform have become a common sight throughout the nation. Here, a female police officer directs an intoxicated man awaiting further processing in Austin, Texas.
Bob Daemmrich, The Image Works.

been promoted to the rank of sergeant, while the ratio among whites was 1 in 12. Only 1 of every 114 black officers had become a lieutenant, while among whites the ratio was 1 out of 26. At the level of captain the disparity was even greater—1 out of every 235 black officers had achieved the rank of captain, while 1 of every 53 whites had climbed to that rank.

Since then, the emphasis placed upon minority recruitment by task forces, civil rights groups, courts, and society in general, has done much to rectify the situation. In 1979, for example, one of the first affirmative action disputes involving a police department was settled out of court. The settlement required the San Francisco Police Department to ensure that over the next 10 years minorities would receive 50 percent of all promotions and that 20 percent of all new officers hired would be women.[114]

Today, the situation is changing. Many departments, through dedicated recruitment efforts, have dramatically increased their complement of officers from underrepresented groups. The Metropolitan Detroit Police Department, for example, now has a force that is more than 30 percent black. According to a recent report by the Bureau of Justice Statistics,[115] blacks comprise 11.3 percent of sworn officers nationwide, while other ethnic minorities constitute 7.7 percent of sworn personnel.

Unfortunately, although ethnic minorities have moved into policing in substantial numbers (see Figure 6-3), females are still significantly underrepresented. A study by the Police Foundation[116] found that women accounted for nearly 9 percent of all officers in municipal departments serving populations of 50,000 or more but that they comprised only 3 percent of all supervisors in city agencies, and 1 percent of supervisors in state police agencies. Female officers made up 10.1 percent of the total number of officers in departments which were functioning under court order to increase their proportion of women officers, while women constituted 8.3 percent of officers in agencies with voluntary affirmative action programs, and only 6.1 percent of officers in departments without such programs. A recent BJS report found that, overall, females comprise 8.8 percent of full-time sworn personnel in local police departments nationwide.[117]

A report[118] on women police officers in Massachusetts found that female officers (1) are "extremely devoted to their work," (2) "see themselves as women first, and then police officers," and (3) were more satisfied when working in nonuniformed capacities. Two groups of

"We must strive to eliminate any racial, ethnic, or cultural bias that may exist among our ranks."
—*Sherman Block,* Los Angeles County Sheriff

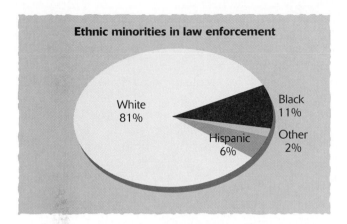

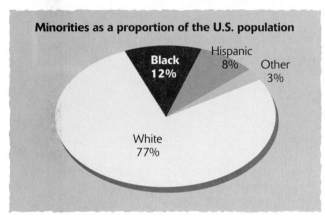

FIGURE 6-3 ■ *Ethnic minorities as a proportion of sworn state law enforcement officers, and as a proportion of the U.S. population.*
Source: *Adapted from Kathleen Maguire and Ann L. Pastore, Sourcebook of Criminal Justice Statistics 1999 (Washington, D.C.: Bureau of Justice Statistics, 2000).*

women officers were identified: (1) those who felt themselves to be well integrated into their departments and were confident in their jobs, and (2) those who experienced strain and on-the-job isolation. The officers' children were cited as a significant influence on their self-perceptions and on the way in which they viewed their jobs. The demands which attend child rearing in contemporary society were found to be major factors contributing to the resigna-

A female police officer comforts a victim of a pit bull attack. Women and minorities, while still underrepresented in the criminal justice profession, have many opportunities for employment throughout the system.
Jodi Cobb, National Geographic Society.

tion of female officers. The study also found that the longer women officers stayed on the job, the greater stress and frustration they tended to experience—primarily as a consequence of the noncooperative attitudes of male officers. Some of the female officers interviewed identified networking as a potential solution to the stresses encountered by female officers, but also said that when women get together to solve problems they are seen as "crybabies" rather than professionals. Said one of the women in the study, "[W]e've lost a lot of good women who never should have left the job. If we had helped each other maybe they wouldn't have left."[119]

Networking is a concept that is quickly taking root among the nation's women police officers, as attested to by the growth of such organizations as the International Association of Women Police, based in New York City. Mentoring, another method for introducing women to police work, has been suggested by some authors.[120] Mentoring would create semiformal

21st Century CJ

Police

In a recent speech before several civic groups, Pueblo County (Colorado) sheriff's department commander Dave Pettinari predicted that law enforcement agencies of the twenty-first century will

◆ Become more, rather than less, specialized.

◆ Become better trained to deal with emerging threats, including blood-borne pathogens, domestic violence, increasingly sophisticated firepower available to "bad guys," and the resurgence of militias and survivalist groups.

◆ Become part of a communications revolution. "Our agencies will be individually wired into the World Wide Web," said Pettinari, "and each of us will have a mobile data terminal and a cellular phone in our police cars."

◆ Make use of identification by means of electronic telecommunications, with fingerprints, facial ratios, retinal patterns, and so on becoming part of worldwide policing. "In a world in which a person wanted in Moscow can be in New York in less than 8 hours, and fraud in Los Angeles can be committed by someone sitting at a terminal in Sao Paulo," said Pettinari, "traditional jurisdictional lines will blur."

◆ Become fully involved in the revolutionary changes now sweeping the workplace. "We're looking at not only privatizing jails," said Pettinari, "but perhaps contracting out law enforcement as a whole to private concerns—rent-a-cops or temp-cops to cover shifts or even whole jurisdictions."

According to Pettinari, who is also past president of the Society of Police Futurists International, "Law enforcement's technical knowledge and skills need to be honed to deal with future crimes; and we should not wait for these types of crimes to become rampant before we start preparing our officers. Not only is computer knowledge vital, but it is expected that a bachelor's degree from a university—not just a high-school diploma—will be the mandatory qualifier for a law enforcement career in the near future."

Pettinari attributed many of his views to an oft-cited study conducted a decade ago by police futurist Bill Tafoya,[1] and noted that twenty-first-century law enforcement agencies "must begin to learn to deal with hacking, phreaking, piggybacking, data diddling, superzapping, scavenging, trapdoors, Trojan horses, logic bombs, and a whole host of other computer threats propounded not only by professionals, but also by pre-

cocious but naive youngsters. To deal with such threats, law enforcement needs not only computer-literate officers, civilians, and managers, but a new sophistication."

"On another computer-related topic," noted Pettinari, "predictions are that we will see an upswing in successful lawsuits charging invasion of privacy due to inadequacies of and inaccuracies in police computerized files. . . . Community involvement and self-help by citizens (community oriented policing) will become a common practice in much of the nation. . . . Even so, policing in the future may, in large part, be contracted out to private security firms." Pettinari added, "Finally, most police executives will have to adopt a non-traditional (proactive/goal-oriented rather than top-down) leadership style."

"All in all," says Pettinari, "it's going to be a constantly changing, ever evolving dance between us and the criminals—well into the 21st century and beyond!"

[1]William L. Tafoya, "The Future of Law Enforcement? A Chronology of Events," *Criminal Justice International* (May/June 1991), p. 4.

Source: Pueblo County Sheriff's Department World Wide Web site (www.co.pueblo.co.us/sheriff). Quoted selections reprinted with permission of the author.

relationships between experienced women officers and rookies entering the profession. Through such relationships, problems could be addressed as they arose, and the experienced officer could serve to guide her junior partner through the maze of formal and informal expectations which surround the job of policing.

Other studies, like those already discussed, have found that female officers are often underutilized and that many departments are hesitant to assign women to patrol and other potentially dangerous field activities. As a consequence, some women in police work experience frustrations and a lack of satisfaction with their jobs.[121] A recent analysis of the genderization of the criminal justice workplace by Susan Ehrlich Martin and Nancy C. Jurik,[122] for example, points out that gender inequality is part of an historical pattern of entrenched forms of gender interaction relating to the division of labor, power, and culture. According to Martin and Jurik, women working the justice system are viewed in terms of such historically developed filters, causing them to be judged and treated according to normative standards developed for men rather than for women. As a consequence, formal and informal social controls continue to disenfranchise women who wish to work in the system and make it difficult to recognize the gender-specific contributions that they make as women.

Barriers, however, continue to fall. In 1979, San Francisco became the first city in the world to actively recruit homosexuals for its police force. That action resulted in a reduced fear of reporting crimes among many city homosexuals, who for years had been victims of organized assaults by bikers and street gangs. Recently, Attorney General Janet Reno ordered all Justice Department agencies to end hiring discrimination based on sexual orientation. Other barriers are falling as women have begun to enter the ranks of police administration. The 2,000-member International Association of Women Police estimates, for example, that there are more than 100 female chiefs of police throughout the country. A newly formed but growing organization, the Women's Police Chief Association, seeks to offer networking opportunities to women seeking and holding high rank within police departments nationwide.[123] Another organization, the National Center for Women and Policing, which is a project of the Feminist Majority Foundation, provides a nationwide resource for law enforcement agencies, community leaders, and public officials seeking to increase the numbers of women police in their communities.

In a continuing effort to increase the representation of women and ethnic minorities in police work, the Police Foundation recommends (1) involving underrepresented groups in affirmative action and long-term planning programs which are undertaken by police departments, (2) encouraging the development of an open system of promotions whereby women can feel free to apply for promotion and in which qualified individuals of any race or gender will face equity in the promotion process, and (3) using periodic audits to ensure that women officers are not being underutilized by being ineffectively tracked into clerical and support positions.[124]

Private Protective Services

Private police constitute a fourth level of enforcement activity in the United States today. *Private security* has been defined as "those self-employed individuals and privately funded business entities and organizations providing security-related services to specific clientele for a fee, for the individual or entity that retains or employs them, or for themselves, in order to protect their persons, private property, or interests from various hazards."[125] Public police are employed by the government and enforce public laws. Private security personnel work for corporate employers and secure private interests. The 1996 Olympics, for example, provided employment for 30,000 private security personnel—or three security officers for every one athlete that attended the Atlanta games.[126]

According to the Hallcrest Report II,[127] a major government-sponsored analysis of the private security industry, more people are employed in private security than in all local, state, and federal police agencies combined. Estimates report that 1.9 million people are working in private security today, while slightly less than half that number are engaged in public law enforcement activities.[128] Employment in the field of private security is antici-

Private Protective Services

Independent or proprietary commercial organizations that provide protective services to employers on a contractual basis. Private security agencies, which already employ about twice as many people as public law enforcement, are expected to experience substantial growth over the next few decades.

TABLE 6-4 ■ American Policing: Private Police Agencies

Private Security Services

Company guards	Store/mall security	Automated teller machine services
Airport security	School security	Railroad detectives
Bank guards	Nuclear facility security	Loss prevention specialists
Executive protection	Hospital security	Computer/information security

The Largest Private Security Agencies in the United States

Advance Security, Inc.	Burns International Security	Pinkerton's, Inc.
Allied Security, Inc.	Services	Security Bureau, Inc.
American Protective	Globe Security	The Wackenhut Corp.
Services	Guardsmark, Inc.	Wells Fargo Guard Services

Source: The Hallcrest Report II *(McLean, VA: Hallcrest Systems, 1990).*

pated to continue to expand by around 4 percent per year, while public police agencies are expected to grow by only 2.8 percent per year for the foreseeable future. Still faster growth is predicted in private security industry revenues—anticipated to increase at around 7 percent per year, a growth rate almost three times greater than that projected for the nation's GNP. Table 6-4 lists the 10 largest private security agencies in business today. It also lists some of the types of services they offer.

Private agencies provide tailored policing funded by the guarded organization rather than through the expenditure of public monies. Experts estimate that private security services cost American industries an astounding $64.5 billion in 1993, while monies spent on public policing totaled only $40 billion.[129] Contributing to this vast expenditure is the federal government, which is itself a major employer of private security personnel, contracting for services which range from guards to highly specialized electronic snooping and countermeasures at military installations and embassies throughout the world.

Major reasons for the quick growth of the American proprietary security sector include "(1) an increase in crimes in the workplace, (2) an increase in fear (real or perceived) of crime, (3) the fiscal crises of the states, [which have] limited public protection, and (4) an increased public and business awareness and use of . . . more cost-effective private security products and services."[130]

The Development of Private Policing

Private policing in America has a long and rich history. The first security firms began operation in the mid-1800s, hired mostly by the railroad companies which were laying tracks to support the burgeoning westward expansion of our nation. Company shipments of supplies, guns, and money, as well as engineers and company officials, all needed protection from Indians, outlaws, and assorted desperadoes.

Allan Pinkerton opened his Pinkerton National Detective Agency in 1851 with the motto "We Never Sleep."[131] Pinkerton's agency specialized in railroad security and would protect shipments as well as hunt down thieves who had made a getaway. The Pinkerton service emblazoned an open eye, to signify constant vigilance, on its office doors and stationery. The term *private eye* is thought to have developed out of the use of this logo. Henry Wells and William Fargo built their still-famous Wells Fargo Company in 1852 and supplied detective and protective services to areas west of Missouri. Anyone willing to pay their fee could have a force of private guards and investigators working for them.

The early days of private security services led quickly to abuses by untrained and poorly disciplined agents. No licensing standards applied to the private security field, and security personnel sometimes became private "goons," catering only to the wishes of their employers. To cope with the situation, Pinkerton developed an elaborate code of ethics for his employees. Pinkerton's code prohibited his men and women from accepting rewards, from working for one political party against another, or from handling divorce cases (which are a primary source of revenue for private detectives today).

Another firm, the Brinks Company, began as a general package delivery service in 1859 and grew to a fleet of 85 armored wagons by 1900. The year 1859 was a busy one for private security, for in that year Edwin Holmes began the first electronic burglar alarm firm in Boston, Massachusetts. Former law enforcement administrators began to get into the private security field in 1909 when a former director of the Bureau of Investigation formed the William J. Burns International Detective Agency. In 1954 George R. Wackenhut formed the Wackenhut Security Corporation, which has become one of the largest private security firms today.

Much has changed since the early days of private policing. Security firms today provide services for hospitals, manufacturing plants, communications industries, retirement homes, hotels, casinos, exclusive communities and clubs, nuclear storage facilities and reactors, and many other types of businesses. Physical security, loss prevention, information security, and the protection of personnel are all service areas for private security organizations.

Private security agencies have been praised for their ability to adapt to new situations and technology. While most security personnel are poorly paid and perform typical "watchmen" roles, the security industry is able to contract with experts in almost any area. Specially assembled teams, hired on a subcontractual basis, have allowed some firms to move successfully into information and technology security. As financial opportunities continue to build in high-tech security, the industry is seeing the creation of a well-educated and highly specialized cadre of workers able to meet the most exacting needs of today's large and multinational corporations. The ability of private agents to work across state lines, and even international boundaries, is an added benefit of private security to many employers.

Security personnel sometimes work undercover, blending with company employees to learn who is pilfering inventories or selling business secrets to competitors. According to the Society of Competitor Intelligence Professionals, over 80 percent of the *Fortune* 1000 companies have regular in-house "snoops" on the payroll.[132] Interestingly, a corporate backlash is now occurring, which has led to the hiring of even more security specialists by private industry—companies everywhere are becoming concerned with "spookproofing" their files and corporate secrets.[133]

Bodyguards, another area of private security activity, are commonplace among wealthy business executives, media stars, and successful musicians. One of the most respected executive protection programs in the world is offered by Executive Security International (ESI) in Aspen, Colorado. ESI was incorporated in 1981, and its founder, Bob Duggan, built terrorist simulation exercises into most course sequences.[134] A few years ago another firm, the Richard W. Kobetz Company, began an executive protection training program at its North Mountain Pines Training Center in Berryville, Virginia.[135] Training at Kobetz includes "offensive and escort driving techniques," threat assessment education, searches, alarms, weapons, communications, protocol, legal issues, and firearms and defensive techniques. Activities focus on "low profile" protection utilizing limited personnel and resources, in contrast to the use of very expensive "high-profile" security as a deterrent technique, which such agencies as the Secret Service are able to use.[136] The Kobetz Company offers "certification" as a personal protection specialist (PPS) following successful completion of its training.

The Private System of Justice

Security agencies work for paying clients, while law enforcement agencies are government entities. Differences between the role of private and public agencies were recently revealed in a National Institute of Justice-sponsored survey,[137] which showed that security executives order their managerial priorities as follows: (1) the protection of lives and property, (2) crime prevention, (3) loss prevention, (4) fire prevention, and (5) access control. In contrast, public law enforcement officials list a somewhat different set of priorities: (1) the protection of lives and property, (2) the arrest and prosecution of suspects, (3) the investigation of criminal incidents, (4) the maintenance of public order, and (5) crime prevention.

This difference in priorities, combined with the fact that hired security operatives serve the interest of corporate employers rather than the public, has led to charges that a private justice system operates next to the official government-sponsored system of criminal justice in America. The private system may see behavior which public police agencies would interpret as a violation of the criminal law, as merely misguided employee activity. Within the private justice system conflict resolution, economic sanctions, and retraining can supplant criminal prosecution as the most efficacious system for dealing with offending parties. According to a survey[138] published by the National Institute of Justice, "security managers in all sectors . . . report that the most frequently investigated crime is employee theft, and nearly half of them resolve such incidents within their own organizations."

One reason why white-collar and business crimes may be substantially underreported in official crime statistics is that unofficial resolutions, based upon investigations by proprietary security forces, may be the most frequent method of handling such offenses. As some writers have observed, the public justice system may find itself increasingly bypassed by proprietary security operations who generally find in the courts "an unsympathetic attitude . . . concerning business losses due to crime."[139] The *Hallcrest* report points out that not only has a "fundamental shift in protection resources . . . occurred from public policing to the private sector," but "this shift has also been accompanied by a shift in the character of social control."[140] According to the report, "private security defines deviance in instrumental rather than moral terms: protecting corporate interests becomes more important than fighting crime, and sanctions are applied more often against those who *create* opportunities for loss rather than those who *capitalize* on the opportunity—the traditional offenders."[141]

Hallcrest II identified the growth of the private justice system as a major source of friction between private security and public law enforcement. According to the report, "[l]aw enforcement agencies have enjoyed a dominant position in providing protective services to their communities but now foresee an erosion of their 'turf' to private security."[142] Other sources of friction between the two include (1) "moonlighting" for private agencies by pub-

---

CAREERS IN JUSTICE

Working in Proprietary Nuclear Security

TYPICAL POSITIONS:

Armed guard, threat-response team member, midlevel management.

EMPLOYMENT REQUIREMENTS:

Basic requirements for armed private security personnel in the nuclear area are specified by Part 73 of the Code of Federal Regulations, which mandates (1) a high school education or equivalent, (2) an age of 21 years or older, (3) successful completion of comprehensive psychological and physical examinations, (4) corrected vision of 20/40, (5) good hearing, (6) no history of drug addiction or potentially disabling diabetes or epilepsy, and (7) a thorough background investigation. A bachelor's degree is preferred by companies hir-

ing armed personnel in the nuclear security sector. Lateral-entry midlevel managers may be exempted from a number of the specified physical requirements, but are expected to have a substantially higher level of education (B.A. or M.A. degree) and/or experience in private security, law enforcement, or a related field.

OTHER REQUIREMENTS:

New officers undergo intensive training in as many as 78 subject matter areas specified by the federal code.

SALARY:

Armed guards earned hourly wages ranging from $8.50 to $15.00 per hour, depending on geographic location, in

mid-1998, with incomes ranging to $36,000. Threat-response team (also called *reactionary force team*) members earned $11.50 to $18.00 per hour, depending on employer. Midlevel managers typically earned salaries in the $30,000 to $40,000 range, although contractual commissions paid to such personnel can push salaries to six figures.

DIRECT INQUIRIES TO:

Proprietary nuclear security providers, including Burns International Security Services, 387 Shuman Boulevard, Suite 120 W. Naperville, IL 60563. Phone: (800) 934-6577. Web site: www.burnsinternational.com.

lic officers, (2) the fact that "[c]ases brought by private security are usually well developed, putting the law enforcement agency in the thankless position of being an information processor for the prosecutor's office,"[143] and (3) the fact that many cases developed by private security agencies are disposed of through "plea bargaining, which police officers may not understand or support, but which may suit the purposes of a company interested in [deterrence]."[144] Moonlighting by public officers is a source of conflict because, under such circumstances, (1) police authority may be seen as used for personal gain, (2) officers who moonlight long hours may not be fit for their official duties due to exhaustion, and (3) public police departments may be legally liable for the actions of their uniformed officers even though they are temporarily working for private employers.

The Professionalization of Private Security

An issue facing lawmakers across the country today is the extent of authority and the degree of force that can be legitimately used by security guards. Courts have generally held that private security personnel derive their legitimacy from the same basic authority that an employer would have in protecting his or her own property. In other words, if I have the legal right to use force to protect my home or business, then so do guards whom I have hired to act in my place. According to some courts, private security personnel, because their authority is simply an extension of private rights, are not directly bound by the legal strictures which govern the use of force, the gathering of evidence, and so on by sworn police officers.

Other courts, however, have ruled that private security personnel should be bound by the same procedural rules as sworn officers, because they are *perceived* by the public as wielding the authority of public law enforcement officers.[145] The situation is complicated by the fact that, as previously discussed, many police officers "moonlight" as private guards when they are off duty.

In order to ensure at least a minimal degree of competence among private security personnel, a number of states have moved to a licensing process for officers, although a few still require little other than an application and a small fee.[146] Twenty-three states mandate training if the security officer is to be armed, but only 14 require any training for unarmed guards.[147] Most training which does occur is relatively simplistic. Topics typically covered include (1) fire prevention, (2) first aid, (3) building safety, (4) equipment use, (5) report writing, and (6) the legal powers of private security personnel.[148] Reflecting on training and licensing requirements, one specialist has warned, "We have a vast private police force largely untrained, with few restraints, with the power to use force to take liberty and life."[149]

Most private security firms today depend upon their own training programs to prevent actionable mistakes by employees. Training in private security operations is also available from a number of schools and agencies. One is the International Foundation for Protection Officers, with offices in Cochrane, Alberta (Canada), and Midvale, Utah. Following a home-study course, successful students are accorded the status of certified protection officer (CPO). In an effort to increase the professional status of the private security industry, the 32,000-member American Society for Industrial Security (ASIS), established in 1955, administers a comprehensive examination periodically in various locations across the country. Applicants who pass the examination win the coveted title of certified protection professional (CPP). CPP examinations are thorough and usually require a combination of experience and study to earn a passing grade. Examination subject areas include[150] (1) security management, (2) physical security, (3) loss prevention, (4) investigations, (5) internal/external relations, (6) protection of sensitive information, (7) personnel security, (8) emergency planning, (9) legal aspects of security, and (10) substance abuse. In addition, candidates are allowed to select from a group of specialized topic areas (such as nuclear power security, public utility security, retail security, computer security, etc.), which pertain to the fields in which they plan to work.

ASIS also functions as a professional association, with yearly meetings held to address the latest in security techniques and equipment. ASIS Online, sponsored by ASIS, provides sub-

scribers with daily security news, up-to-date international travel briefings, and a searchable security news database. In its efforts to heighten professionalism throughout the industry, ASIS has developed a private security code of ethics for its members which is reproduced in a "Theory Into Practice" box in this chapter. Visit ASIS Online via **WebExtra!** 6-4 at CJToday.com.

An additional sign of the increasing professionalization of private security is the ever growing number of publications offered in the area. The *Journal of Security Administration,* published in Miami, Florida, ASIS's *Security Management* magazine, and the *Security Management Newsletter* published semimonthly by the National Foremen's Institute in Waterford, Connecticut, along with the older journal *Security World,* serve the field as major sources of up-to-date information.

Integrating Public and Private Security

As the private security field grows, its relationship to public law enforcement continues to evolve. Although competition between the sectors remains, many experts now recognize that each can help the other. A government-sponsored report[151] makes the following policy recommendations designed to maximize the cooperative crime-fighting potential of existing private and public security resources:

1. The resources of proprietary and contract security should be brought to bear in cooperative, community-based crime prevention and security awareness programs.
2. An assessment should be made of (1) the basic police services the public is willing to support financially, (2) the types of police services most acceptable to police administrators and the public for transfer to the private sector, and (3) which services might be performed for a lower unit cost by the private sector with the same level of community satisfaction.
3. With special police powers, security personnel could resolve many or most minor criminal incidents prior to police involvement. State statutes providing such powers could also provide for standardized training and certification requirements, thus assuring uniformity and precluding abuses. . . . Ideally, licensing and regulatory requirements would be the same for all states, with reciprocity for firms licensed elsewhere.
4. Law enforcement agencies should be included in the crisis-management planning of private organizations. . . . Similarly, private security should be consulted when law enforcement agencies are developing SWAT and hostage-negotiation teams. The federal government should provide channels of communication with private security with respect to terrorist activities and threats.

Theory Into Practice

Ethics in Private Security

American Society for Industrial Security Code of Ethics

I. A member shall perform professional duties in accordance with the law and the highest moral principles.

II. A member shall observe the precepts of truthfulness, honesty, and integrity.

III. A member shall be faithful and diligent in discharging professional responsibilities.

IV. A member shall be competent in discharging professional responsibilities.

V. A member shall safeguard confidential information and exercise due care to prevent its improper disclosure.

VI. A member shall not maliciously injure the professional reputation or practice of colleagues, clients, or employers.

Source: Courtesy of the American Society for Industrial Security.

5. States should enact legislation permitting private security firms access to criminal history records in order to improve the selection process for security personnel and also to enable businesses to assess the integrity of key employees.

6. Research should . . . attempt to delineate the characteristics of the private justice system; identify the crimes most frequently resolved; assess the types and amount of unreported crime in organizations; quantify the redirection of [the] public criminal justice workload . . . and examine [the] . . . relationships between private security and . . . components of the criminal justice system.

7. A federal tax credit for security expenditures, similar to the energy tax credit, might be a cost-effective way to reduce police workloads.

Summary

Police work today is characterized by the opportunity for individual officers to exercise considerable discretion, by a powerful subculture that communicates select values in support of a "police personality," and by the very real possibility of corruption and deviance. Opposed to the illegitimate use of police authority, however, are increased calls for integrity and ethical awareness in police work and for continuing growth of the professionalism ideal. Professionalism, with its emphasis on education, training, high ethical values, and personal accountability, should soon lead to greater public recognition of the significance of police work and to higher salaries for career police personnel. Increased salaries and a clear public appreciation for the work done by police officers and other police department employees should, in turn, do much to decrease corruption and deviance in law enforcement ranks.

Given the tendencies that exist today, we can expect that police departments of the twenty-first century, while they will continue to fill many traditional law enforcement roles, will be highly professional organizations that emphasize ethical enforcement of the criminal law and limit the discretionary activities of their members. Similarly, as American police forces continue to evolve, the role of underrepresented groups in police work—including women and ethnic and racial minorities—will face continued examination.

Discussion Questions

1. What are the central features of the police "working personality"? How does the police working personality develop? What programs might be initiated to shape the police personality in a more desirable way?

2. What themes run through the findings of the Knapp Commission and the Wickersham Commission? What innovative steps might police departments take to reduce or eliminate corruption among their officers?

3. Is police work a profession? Why do you think it is, or why do you think it is not? What advantages are there to viewing policing as a profession? How do you think most police officers today see their work—as a "profession" or as just a "job"?

4. Reread the Law Enforcement Code of Ethics found in this chapter. Do you think most police officers make conscious efforts to apply the code in the performance of their duties? How might ethics training in police departments be improved?

Web Quest!

Choose two of the Library Extras! from the list in this chapter. Download your selections from CJToday.com, and write summaries of the documents. Search the Cybrary (at talkjustice.com/cybrary.asp) to locate Web sites dealing with issues similar to those discussed in your choice of documents. List the URLs for such sites in your written summaries, and submit the material to your instructor if requested to do so.

Library Extras!

Library Extra! 6-1. *Understanding the Use of Force by and Against the Police* (NIJ, 1996).
Library Extra! 6-2. "Noble Cause Corruption and the Police Ethic," *FBI Law Enforcement Bulletin* (August, 1999).
Library Extra! 6-3. *Use of Force by Police: Overview of National and Local Data* (BJS, 1999).
Library Extra! 6-4. *"Broken Windows" and Police Discretion* (NIJ, 1999).

References

1. Jerome H. Skolnick, *Justice Without Trial: Law Enforcement in a Democratic Society* (New York: John Wiley, 1966).
2. William A. Westley, *Violence and the Police: A Sociological Study of Law, Custom, and Morality* (Cambridge, MA: MIT Press, 1970), and William A. Westley "Violence and the Police," *American Journal of Sociology,* vol. 49 (1953), pp. 34–41.
3. Arthur Niederhoffer, *Behind the Shield: The Police in Urban Society* (Garden City, NY: Anchor Press, 1967).
4. Thomas Barker and David L. Carter, *Police Deviance* (Cincinnati, OH: Anderson, 1986).
5. See, for example, Michael Brown, *Working the Street: Police Discretion and the Dilemmas of Reform* (New York: Russell Sage Foundation, 1981).
6. Richard Bennett and Theodore Greenstein, "The Police Personality: A Test of the Predispositional Model," *Journal of Police Science and Administration,* vol 3. (1975), pp. 439–445.
7. James Teevan and Bernard Dolnick, "The Values of the Police: A Reconsideration and Interpretation," *Journal of Police Science and Administration* (1973) pp. 366–369.
8. Lawrence Sherman and Robert Langworthy, "Measuring Homicide by Police Officers," *Journal of Criminal Law and Criminology,* vol. 4 (1979), pp. 546–560, and Lawrence W. Sherman et al., *Citizens Killed by Big City Police, 1970–1984* (Washington, D.C.: Crime Control Institute, 1986).
9. Joel Samaha, *Criminal Justice* (St. Paul, MN: West, 1988), p. 235.
10. Tim Prenzler and Peta Mackay, "Police Gratuities: What the Public Thinks," *Criminal Justice Ethics,* Winter–Spring 1995, pp. 15–25.
11. Barker and Carter, *Police Deviance.*
12. "Nationline: NYC Cops—Excess Force Not Corruption," *USA Today,* June 16, 1995, p. 3A.
13. *Knapp Commission Report on Police Corruption* (New York: George Braziller, 1973).
14. Ibid.
15. Robert Daley, *Prince of the City: The Story of a Cop Who Knew Too Much* (Boston: Houghton Mifflin, 1978).
16. Mike McAlary, *Buddy Boys: When Good Cops Turn Bad* (New York: G. P. Putnam's Sons, 1987).
17. Ibid.
18. "Ex-Detroit Police Chief Sentenced," *Fayetteville Observer-Times* (North Carolina), August 28, 1992, p. 5A.
19. "Police Officers Indicted," Associated Press, August 14, 1999.
20. Pam Belluck, "Chicago Police Superintendent Steps Down After Report of Tie With Felon," *New York Times* News Service, Nov. 5, 1997.
21. Edwin H. Sutherland and Donald Cressey, *Principles of Criminology,* 8th ed. (Philadelphia: J. B. Lippincott, 1970).
22. James Mills, *The Underground Empire: Where Crime and Governments Embrace* (New York: Dell, 1986), p. 15.
23. Ibid.
24. Tim R. Jones, Compton Owens, and Melissa A. Smith, "Police Ethics Training: A Three-Tiered Approach," *FBI Law Enforcement Bulletin,* June, 1995, pp. 22–26.
25. Stephen J. Gaffigan and Phyllis P. McDonald, *Police Integrity: Public Service With Honor* (Washington, D.C.: National Institute of Justice, 1997).
26. Mike Robinson, "Gangbanger Cops?" The Associated Press wire services, February 10, 1997.
27. See National Institute of Justice, "Employee Drug Testing Policies in Police Departments," *National Institute of Justice Research in Brief* (Washington, D.C.: U.S. Department of Justice, 1986).
28. Ibid.
29. *Maurice Turner* v. *Fraternal Order of Police,* 500 A.2d 1005 (D.C. 1985).
30. *Philip Caruso, President of P.B.A.* v. *Benjamin Ward, Police Commissioner,* New York State Supreme Court, Pat. 37, Index no. 12632-86, 1986.
31. *National Treasury Employees Union* v. *Von Raab,* 489 U.S. 656, 659 (1989).
32. The National Law Enforcement Officers' Memorial Fund on the World Wide Web at www.nleomf.com. Accessed January 20, 2000.
33. Greg Meyer, "LAPD Faces Urban Warfare in North Hollywood Bank Shoot-Out," *Police,* April 1997, pp. 20–23.
34. Ibid.
35. Ibid.
36. Nine police officers and two civilians were wounded by gunfire. Seven other people were injured, including a police officer and a civilian involved in a car crash. For a definitive accounting of injuries in the incident, see Lt. Greg Meyer, "40 Minutes in North Hollywood," *Police,* June 1997, p. 27–37.
37. The M-16s were military surplus. See Steve Marshall, "L.A. Cops Get 600 M-16s to Help

Even Odds on Street," *USA Today,* September 17, 1997, p. 4A.

38. "Police Commission Beefs Up LAPD Firepower," CNN Interactive on the World Wide Web, March 19, 1997.

39. The incident described here comes from the World Wide Web page of the Constable Public Safety Memorial Foundation, Inc., of Bend, Oregon, from which some of the wording is taken. www.survival-spanish.com/foundation.htm. Accessed May 20, 2000.

40. Officer Down Memorial Home Page on the World Wide Web, http://odmp.org. Accessed January 20, 2001.

41. Anthony J. Pinizzotto and Edward F. Davis, "Cop Killers and Their Victims," *FBI Law Enforcement Bulletin,* December 1992, p. 10.

42. As reported by The Headline News Network, April 26, 1988.

43. "Homosexual Officer Wins AIDS Ruling," *Fayetteville Observer-Times* (North Carolina), June 8, 1992, p. 5A.

44. New York City Police Department pamphlet, "AIDS and Our Workplace" (November 1987).

45. "Collecting and Handling Evidence Infected with Human Disease-Causing Organisms," *FBI Law Enforcement Bulletin* (July 1987).

46. Theodore M. Hammett, "Precautionary Measures and Protective Equipment: Developing a Reasonable Response," *National Institute of Justice Bulletin* (Washington, D.C.: U.S. Government Printing Office, 1988).

47. See, Occupational Safety and Health Administration, OSHA Bloodborne Pathogens Act of 1991 (29 CFR 1910.1030).

48. *National Institute of Justice Reports,* no. 206 (November/December 1987).

49. "Taking Aim at a Virus: NYPD Tackles AIDS on the Job and in the Ranks," *Law Enforcement News,* March 15, 1988, p. 1.

50. "Drowned Boys Case Takes Toll on Officers, Clergy," *Florida Times-Union* (Jacksonville), November 10, 1994, p. A6.

51. See Kevin Barrett, "More EAPs Needed in Police Departments to Quash Officers' Superhuman Self-Image," *EA Professional Report,* January 1994, p. 3.

52. "Stress on the Job," *Newsweek,* April 25, 1988, p. 43.

53. Joseph Victor, "Police Stress: Is Anybody Out There Listening," *New York Law Enforcement Journal* (June 1986), pp. 19–20.

54. Kevin Barrett, "Police Suicide: Is Anyone Listening?" *Journal of Safe Management of Disruptive and Assaultive Behavior,* Spring 1997, pp. 6–9.

55. Ibid.

56. For an excellent review of coping strategies among police officers, see Robin N. Haarr and Merry Morash, "Gender, Race, and Strategies of Coping with Occupational Stress in Policing," *Justice Quarterly,* vol. 16, no. 2 (June 1999), pp. 303–336.

57. Bryan Vila, "Tired Cops: Probable Connections Between Fatigue and the Performance, Health, and Safety of Patrol Officers," *American Journal of Police,* vol. 15, no. 2 (1996), pp. 51–92.

58. Bryan Vila and Erik Y. Taiji, "Fatigue and Police Officer Performance," paper presented at the annual meeting of the American Society of Criminology, Chicago, 1996.

59. "Stroke Victim Sues State Over Arrest," The Associated Press, April 24, 1996.

60. Charles R. Swanson, Leonard Territo, and Robert W. Taylor, *Police Administration: Structures, Processes, and Behavior,* 2nd ed. (New York: Macmillan, 1988).

61. *Malley* v. *Briggs,* 475 U.S. 335, 106 S.Ct. 1092 (1986).

62. Ibid., *Malley* at 4246.

63. *Biscoe* v. *Arlington County,* 238 U.S. App. D.C. 206, 738 F.2d 1352, 1362 (1984).

64. *Kaplan* v. *Lloyd's Insurance Co.,* 479 So. 2d 961 (La. App. 1985).

65. *City of Canton, Ohio* v. *Harris,* U.S. 109 S.Ct. 1197 (1989).

66. Ibid., at 1204.

67. No. 95-1100. Argued November 5, 1996—Decided April 28, 1997.

68. *Prior* v. *Woods* (1981), *National Law Journal,* November 2, 1981.

69. *Bivens* v. *Six Unknown Federal Agents,* 403 U.S. 388 (1971).

70. See *F.D.I.C.* v. *Meyer,* 510 U.S. 471 (1994), in which the U.S. Supreme Court reiterated its ruling under *Bivens,* stating that only government employees and not government agencies can be sued.

71. *Wyler* v. *U.S.,* 725 F.2d 157 (2d Cir. 1983).

72. California Government Code, §818.

73. Federal Tort Claims Act, 28 U.S.C. 1346(b), 2671–2680.

74. "Victims of Failed DEA Sting Win More than $1 Million Judgment," *Drug Enforcement Report,* March 23, 1995, pp. 1–2.

75. *Elder* v. *Holloway,* 114 S.Ct. 1019, 127 L. Ed. 2d 344 (1994).

76. Ibid.

77. *Hunter* v. *Bryant,* 112 S.Ct. 534 (1991).

78. William U. McCormack, "Supreme Court Cases: 1991–1992 Term," *FBI Law Enforcement Bulletin,* November 1992, p. 30.

79. For more information on police liability, see Daniel L. Schofield, "Legal Issues of Pursuit Driving," *FBI Law Enforcement Bulletin* (May 1988), pp. 23–29.

80. "Playboy Interview: Daryl Gates," *Playboy,* August 1991, p. 60.

81. Ibid., p. 63.

82. *Tennessee* v. *Garner,* 471 U.S. 1 (1985).

83. Ibid.

84. *Graham* v. *Connor,* 490 U.S. 386, 396–397 (1989).

85. "NACOP Questions Delay in Federal Use of 'Imminent Danger' Standards for Deadly Force," National Association of Chiefs of Police press release, October 19, 1995.

86. James Fyfe, *Shots Fired: An Examination of New York City Police Firearms Discharges* (Ann Arbor, MI: University Microfilms, 1978).

87. James Fyfe, "Blind Justice? Police Shootings in Memphis," paper presented at the annual meeting of the Academy of Criminal Justice Sciences, Philadelphia, March 1981.

88. It is estimated that American police shoot at approximately 3,600 people every year. See William Geller "Deadly Force" study guide

Crime File Series (Washington, D.C.: National Institute of Justice, no date).

89. Anne Cohen: "I've Killed That Man Ten Thousand Times," *Police Magazine* (July 1980).

90. For more information, see Joe Auten, "When Police Shoot," *North Carolina Criminal Justice Today,* vol. 4, no. 4 (Summer 1986), pp. 9–14.

91. "Man Attracts Police Gunfire to Commit Suicide," Associated Press, Nov. 17, 1997.

92. "10% of Police Shootings Found to be 'Suicide by Cop,'" Criminal Justice Newsletter, vol. 29, no. 17 (September 1, 1998), p. 1–2.

93. David W. Hayeslip and Alan Preszler, "NIJ Initiative on Less-than-Lethal Weapons," *NIJ Research in Brief* (Washington, D.C.: National Institute of Justice, 1993).

94. As quoted by Michael Siegfried, "Notes on the Professionalization of Private Security," *The Justice Professional* (Spring 1989).

95. Brian A. Reaves and Andrew L. Goldberg, "Law Enforcement Management and Administrative Statistics, 1997: Data for Individual State and Local Law Enforcement Agencies with 100 or More Officers," (Washington, D.C.: Bureau of Justice Statistics, 1999).

96. See Edward A. Farris "Five Decades of American Policing, 1932–1982: The Path to Professionalism," *The Police Chief* (November 1982), p. 34.

97. The Commission on Accreditation for Law Enforcement Agencies (CALEA) World Wide Web site, www.calea.org. Accessed January 10, 2000. Agency estimates are from: Brian A. Reaves and Andrew L. Goldberg, "Census of State and Local Law Enforcement Agencies, 1996," (Washington, D.C.: Bureau of Justice Statistics, 1998).

98. National Commission on Law Observance and Enforcement, *Report on Police* (Washington, D.C.: U.S. Government Printing Office, 1931).

99. National Advisory Commission on Criminal Justice Standards and Goals, *Report on the Police* (Washington, D.C.: U.S. Government Printing Office, 1973).

100. Ibid.

101. Reaves and Goldberg, "Law Enforcement Management and Administrative Statistics, 1997."

102. David L. Carter, Allen D. Sapp, and Darrel W. Stephens, *The State of Police Education: Policy Direction for the 21st Century* (Washington, D.C.: Police Executive Research Forum, 1989).

103. Ibid., p. xiv.

104. Ibid., pp. xxii–xxiii.

105. Brian A. Reaves, "Local Police Departments, 1993," (Washington, D.C.: Bureau of Justice Statistics, April 1996).

106. Ibid., p. 84.

107. National Advisory Commission on Criminal Justice Standards and Goals, *Police* (Washington, D.C.: U.S. Government Printing Office, 1973), p. 238.

108. "Dallas PD College Rule Gets Final OK," *Law Enforcement News,* July 7, 1986, pp. 1, 13.

109. *Davis v. Dallas,* 777 F.2d 205 (5th Cir. 1985).

110. David L. Carter and Allen Sapp, *The State of Police Education: Critical Findings* (Washington, D.C.: Police Executive Research Forum, no date).

111. O. W. Wilson and Roy Clinton McLaren, *Police Administration,* 4th ed. (New York: McGraw-Hill, 1977), p. 259.

112. Ibid., p. 270.

113. Report of the National Advisory Commission on Civil Disorders, p. 332.

114. As reported in Charles Swanson and Leonard Territo, *Police Administration: Structures, Processes, and Behavior* (New York: Macmillan, 1983), p. 203, from *Affirmative Action Monthly* (February 1979), p. 22.

115. Brian A. Reaves, "Local Police Departments, 1993," (Washington, D.C.: Bureau of Justice Statistics, April 1996).

116. The Police Foundation, *On the Move: The Status of Women in Policing* (Washington, D.C.: The Foundation, 1990).

117. Reaves, "Local Police Departments, 1993."

118. C. Lee Bennett, *Interviews with Female Police Officers in Western Massachusetts,* paper presented at the annual meeting of the Academy of Criminal Justice Sciences, Nashville, Tennessee, March 1991.

119. Ibid., p. 9.

120. See, for example, Pearl Jacobs, "Suggestions for the Greater Integration of Women into Policing," paper presented at the annual meeting of the Academy of Criminal Justice Sciences, Nashville, Tennessee, March 1991, and Cynthia Fuchs Epstein, *Deceptive Distinctions: Sex, Gender, and the Social Order* (New Haven, CT: Yale University Press, 1988).

121. Carole G. Garrison, Nancy K. Grant, and Kenneth L. J. McCormick, "Utilization of Police Women," unpublished manuscript.

122. Susan Ehrlich Martin and Nancy C. Jurik, *Doing Justice, Doing Gender: Women in Law and Criminal Justice Occupations* (Thousand Oaks, CA: Sage, 1996).

123. See Sara Roen, "The Longest Climb," *Police,* October 1996, pp. 44–46, 66.

124. The Police Foundation, *On the Move.*

125. *Private Security: Report of the Task Force on Private Security* (Washington, D.C.: U.S. Government Printing Office, 1976), p. 4.

126. See The Atlanta Committee for the Olympic Games, *Securing the Safest Games Ever* (Atlanta: ACOG, no date).

127. William C. Cunningham, John J. Strauchs, and Clifford W. Van Meter, *The Hallcrest Report II: Private Security Trends 1970–2000* (McLean, VA: Hallcrest Systems, 1990).

128. Includes full-time employees working for local police, sheriffs' departments, special police, and state police. See Brian A. Reaves and Andrew L. Goldberg, *Census of State and Local Law Enforcement Agencies, 1996* (Washington, D.C.: Bureau of Justice Statistics, 1998).

129. The Security Industry Association World Wide Web site, www.siaonline.org/wp_size.html. Accessed January 20, 2000.

130. *Hallcrest II,* p. 236.

131. Dae H. Chang and James A. Fagin, eds., *Introduction to Criminal Justice: Theory and Application,* 2nd ed. (Geneva, IL: Paladin House, 1985), pp. 275–277.

132. "George Smiley Joins the Firm," *Newsweek,* May 2, 1988, pp. 46–47.

133. Ibid.

134. For more information on ESI, see E. Duane Davis, "Executive Protection: An Emerging Trend in Criminal Justice Education and Training," *The Justice Professional,* vol. 3, no. 2 (Fall 1988).

135. "More than a Bodyguard," *Security Management,* February 10, 1986.

136. "A School for Guards of Rich, Powerful," *Akron Beacon Journal* (Ohio), April 21, 1986.

137. National Institute of Justice, *Crime and Protection in America: A Study of Private Security and Law Enforcement Resources and Relationships,* Executive Summary (Washington, D.C.: U.S. Department of Justice, 1985), p. 42.

138. Ibid., p. 60.

139. *Hallcrest II,* p. 299.

140. Ibid., p. 301.

141. Ibid. (italics added).

142. Ibid., p. 117.

143. National Institute of Justice, *Crime and Protection in America,* p. 12.

144. Ibid.

145. *People* v. *Zelinski,* 594 P.2d 1000 (1979).

146. For additional information, see Joseph G. Deegan, "Mandated Training for Private Security," *FBI Law Enforcement Bulletin,* March 1987, pp. 6–8.

147. *Hallcrest II,* p. 147.

148. National Institute of Justice, *Crime and Protection in America,* p. 37.

149. Richter Moore, "Private Police: The Use of Force and State Regulation," unpublished manuscript.

150. "The Mark of Professionalism," *Security Management,* 35th Anniversary Supplement, 1990, pp. 97–104.

151. National Institute of Justice, *Crime and Protection in America,* pp. 59–72.

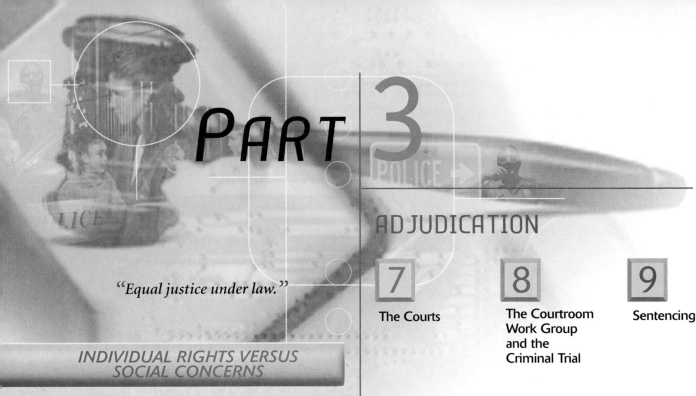

PART 3

ADJUDICATION

"Equal justice under law."

INDIVIDUAL RIGHTS VERSUS SOCIAL CONCERNS

THE RIGHTS OF THE ACCUSED BEFORE THE COURT

Common law, constitutional, statutory, and humanitarian rights of the accused:

- The Right to a Speedy Trial
- The Right to Legal Counsel
- The Right Against Self-Incrimination
- The Right Not to Be Tried Twice for the Same Offense
- The Right to Know the Charges
- The Right to Cross-Examine Witnesses
- The Right to Speak and Present Witnesses
- The Right Against Excessive Bail

The individual rights listed must be effectively balanced against these community concerns:

- Conviction of the Guilty
- Exoneration of the Innocent
- The Imposition of Appropriate Punishment
- Protection of Society
- Efficient and Cost-Effective Procedures
- Seeing Justice Done

How does our system of justice work toward balance?

*T*he well-known British philosopher and statesman Benjamin Disraeli (1804–1881) once defined justice as "truth in action." The study of criminal case processing by courts at all levels provides perhaps the best opportunity available to us from within the criminal justice system to observe what should ideally be "truth in action." The courtroom search for truth, which is characteristic of criminal trials, pits the resources of the accused against those of the state. The ultimate outcome of such procedures, say advocates of our adversarial-based system of trial practice, should be both truth and justice.

Others are not so sure. British novelist William McIlvanney (1936–) once wrote: "Who thinks the law has anything to do with justice? It's what we have because we can't have justice." Indeed, many critics of the present system claim that courts at all levels have become so concerned with procedure and with sets of formalized rules that they have lost sight of truth.

The chapters which comprise this section of *Criminal Justice: A Brief Introduction* provide an overview of American courts, including their history and present structure, and examine the multifaceted roles played by both professional and lay courtroom participants. Sentencing—the practice whereby juries recommend and judges impose sanctions on convicted offenders—is covered in the concluding chapter of this section. Whether American courts routinely uncover truth and therefore dispense justice or whether they are merely locked into a pattern of hollow procedure which does little other than mock the justice ideal will be for you to decide.

Police

Courts

Corrections

CHAPTER | 7

The Courts

"There is no such thing as justice—in or out of court."
—Clarence Darrow (1857–1938)

"No person shall be held to answer for a capital or otherwise infamous crime, unless on a present-ment or indictment of a grand jury . . . nor shall any person be subject for the same offense to be twice put in jeopardy of life or limb; nor shall be compelled in any criminal case to be a witness against himself, nor be deprived of life, liberty, or property, without due process of law. . . ."
—Fifth Amendment to the U.S. Constitution

CHAPTER OUTLINE

—Robert Shafer, Stone.

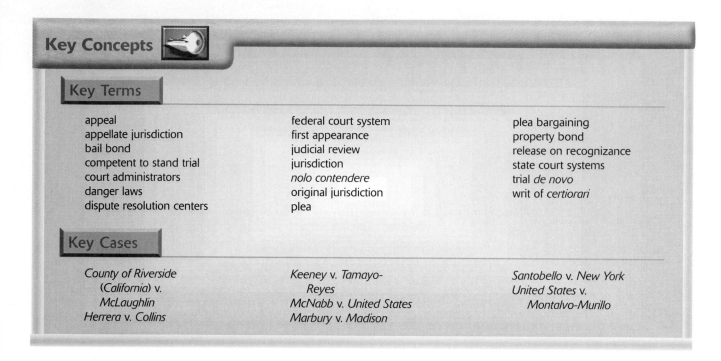

Key Concepts

Key Terms

appeal
appellate jurisdiction
bail bond
competent to stand trial
court administrators
danger laws
dispute resolution centers

federal court system
first appearance
judicial review
jurisdiction
nolo contendere
original jurisdiction
plea

plea bargaining
property bond
release on recognizance
state court systems
trial *de novo*
writ of *certiorari*

Key Cases

County of Riverside (California) v. McLaughlin
Herrera v. Collins

Keeney v. Tamayo-Reyes
McNabb v. United States
Marbury v. Madison

Santobello v. New York
United States v. Montalvo-Murillo

Hear the author discuss this chapter at **cjtoday.com**

Introduction

In January of 1997 two dynamite bombs exploded in downtown Vallejo, California, a small city of slightly more than 100,000 people located at the mouth of the Napa River in Solano County. One bomb damaged automatic teller machines at a Wells Fargo bank, while the other blew a hole in the side of the Solano County courthouse. About the same time, authorities found 30 sticks of dynamite in a backpack lying against the wall of a public library where some police evidence was kept. A few days later police arrested Kevin Lee Robinson, 29, an ex-convict who was scheduled to soon be tried on drug-related charges and accused him and five other men of the bombings. According to investigators, Robinson planned the bombings in order to derail the county's criminal justice system. Bombing the courthouse, said detectives, was an attempt by Robinson to prevent his being tried under the state's three-strikes-and-you're-out law—which could have meant a sentence of life in prison for the already twice-convicted Robinson.[1] Following the arrest, police confiscated 500 pounds of dynamite.

Robinson's alleged plan highlights the central role played by our nation's courts in the criminal justice process. Without courts to decide issues of guilt or innocence and to impose sentence on those convicted of crimes, the activities of law enforcement officials would become meaningless, and the nation's correctional facilities would serve little purpose.

There are many different kinds of courts in the United States. But courts at all levels dispense justice on a daily basis and work to ensure that all official actors in the justice system carry out their duties in recognition of the rule of law. At many points in this volume we take a close look at court precedents which have defined the legality of enforcement efforts and correctional action. In Chapter 3, Criminal Law, we explored the lawmaking function of courts. This chapter, in order to provide readers with a picture of how courts work, will describe the American court system at both the state and federal levels. Then in Chapter 8 we will look at the roles of courtroom actors—from attorneys to victims and from jurors to judges—and examine each of the steps in a criminal trial.

Federal Court System

The three-tiered structure of federal courts, involving U.S. district courts, U.S. courts of appeal, and the U.S. Supreme Court.

State Court Systems

State judicial structures. Most states have at least three court levels, generally referred to as trial courts, appellate courts, and a state supreme court.

American Court History

Two types of courts function within the American criminal justice system: (1) state courts and (2) federal courts. Figure 7-1 outlines the structure of today's **federal court system,** while Figure 7-2 diagrams a typical **state court system.** This dual-court system is the result

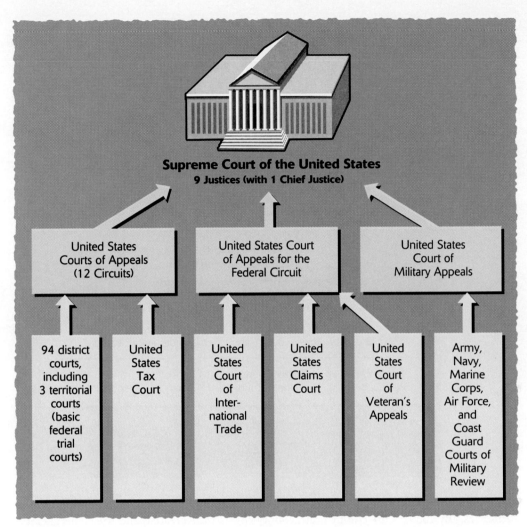

Supreme Court of the United States
9 Justices (with 1 Chief Justice)

United States Courts of Appeals (12 Circuits)

United States Court of Appeals for the Federal Circuit

United States Court of Military Appeals

94 district courts, including 3 territorial courts (basic federal trial courts)

United States Tax Court

United States Court of International Trade

United States Claims Court

United States Court of Veteran's Appeals

Army, Navy, Marine Corps, Air Force, and Coast Guard Courts of Military Review

FIGURE 7-1 ■ *The structure of federal courts.*

"Oyez, oyez, oyez! All persons having business before the honorable, the Supreme Court of the United States, are admonished to draw near and give their attention, for the court is now sitting. God save the United States and this honorable Court."

—*Marshal's cry at the opening of public sessions of the U.S. Supreme Court*

of general agreement among the nation's founders about the need for individual states to retain significant legislative authority and judicial autonomy separate from federal control. Under this concept, the United States developed as a relatively loose federation of semi-independent provinces. New states joining the union were assured of limited federal intervention into local affairs. Under this arrangement, state legislatures were free to create laws, and state court systems were needed to hear cases in which violations of those laws occurred. The last 200 years have been a slow ebbing of states' rights relative to the power of the federal government. Even today, however, state courts do not hear cases involving alleged violations of federal law nor do federal courts involve themselves in deciding issues of state law, unless there is a conflict between local or state statutes and federal constitutional guarantees. When that happens, however, claimed violations of federal due process guarantees—especially those found in the Bill of Rights—can provide the basis for appeals made to federal courts by offenders convicted in state court systems.

This chapter describes both federal and state court systems in terms of their historical development, **jurisdiction,** and current structure. Because it is within state courts that the large majority of criminal cases originate, we turn our attention first to them.

State Court Development

Each of the original American colonies had its own court system for resolving disputes, both civil and criminal. As early as 1629 the Massachusetts Bay Colony had created a "General Court," composed of the governor, his deputy, 18 assistants, and 118 elected officials. The General Court was a combined legislature/court that made laws, held trials, and imposed

Jurisdiction

The territory, subject matter, or persons over which lawful authority may be exercised by a court or other justice agency, as determined by statute or constitution.

FIGURE 7-2 ■ *A typical state court system.*

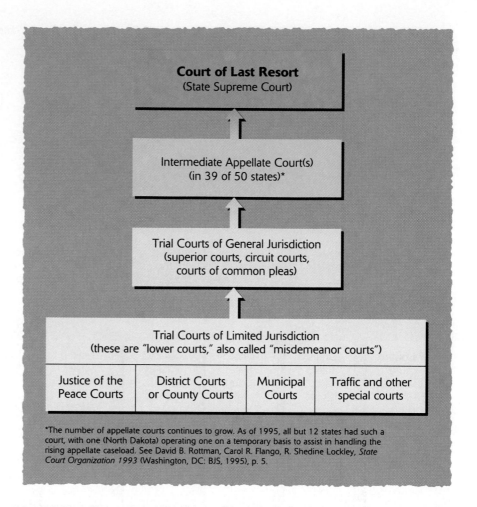

*The number of appellate courts continues to grow. As of 1995, all but 12 states had such a court, with one (North Dakota) operating one on a temporary basis to assist in handling the rising appellate caseload. See David B. Rottman, Carol R. Flango, R. Shedine Lockley, *State Court Organization 1993* (Washington, DC: BJS, 1995), p. 5.

sentences.[2] By 1639, as the colony grew, county courts were created, and the General Court took on as its primary job—the hearing of appeals—retaining original jurisdiction only in cases involving "tryalls of life, limm, or banishment . . ." (and divorce).[3]

Pennsylvania began its colonial existence with the belief that "every man could serve as his own lawyer."[4] The Pennsylvania system utilized "common peacemakers" who served as referees in disputes. Parties to a dispute, including criminal suspects, could plead their case before a common peacemaker they had chosen. The decision of the peacemaker was binding upon the parties. Although the Pennsylvania referee system ended in 1766, lower-level judges, called magistrates in many other jurisdictions, are still referred to as "justices of the peace" in Pennsylvania and a few other states.

Prior to 1776 all American colonies had established fully functioning court systems. The practice of law, however, was substantially inhibited by a lack of trained lawyers. A number of the early colonies even displayed a strong reluctance to recognize the practice of law as a profession. A Virginia statute, for example, enacted in 1645, provided for the removal of "mercenary attorneys" from office and prohibited the practice of law for a fee. Most other colonies retained strict control over the number of authorized barristers (another name for lawyers) by requiring formal training in English law schools and appointment by the governor. New York, which provided for the appointment of "counselors at law," permitted a total of only 41 lawyers to practice law between 1695 and 1769[5]—in large part due to the distrust of formally trained attorneys which was then widespread.

The tenuous status of lawyers in the colonies was highlighted by the 1735 New York trial of John Zenger. Zenger was editor of the *New York Journal,* a newspaper, and was accused of slandering then-Governor Cosby. When Cosby threatened to disbar any lawyer who defended Zenger, he hired Pennsylvania lawyer Andrew Hamilton who was immune from the governor's threats because he was from out of state.[6]

Following the American Revolution, colonial courts provided the organizational basis for the growth of fledgling state court systems. Since there had been considerable diversity in the structure of colonial courts, state courts were anything but uniform. Initially, most states made no distinction between **original jurisdiction** (which can be defined as the lawful authority of a court to hear cases which arise within a specified geographic area or which involve particular kinds of law violations) and **appellate jurisdiction** (that is, the lawful authority of a court to review a decision made by a lower court). Many, in fact, had no provisions for appeal. Delaware, for example, did not allow for appeals in criminal cases until 1897. States that did permit appeals often lacked any established appellate courts and sometimes used state legislatures for that purpose.

By the late 1800s a dramatic increase in population, growing urbanization, the settlement of the West, and other far-reaching changes in the American way of life led to a tremendous increase in civil litigation and criminal arrests. Legislatures tried to keep pace with the rising tide of suits. They created a multiplicity of courts at the trial, appellate, and supreme court levels, calling them by a diversity of names and assigning them functions which sometimes bore little resemblance to like-sounding courts in neighboring states. City courts, which were limited in their jurisdiction by community boundaries, arose to handle the special problems of urban life, such as disorderly conduct, property disputes, and the enforcement of restrictive and regulatory ordinances. Other tribunals, such as juvenile courts, developed to handle special kinds of problems or special clients. Some, like magistrates' or small claims courts, handled only petty disputes and minor law violations. Still others, like traffic courts, were very narrow in focus. The result was a patchwork quilt of hearing bodies, some only vaguely resembling modern notions of a trial court.

State court systems did, however, have several models to follow during their development. One was the New York State Field Code of 1848, which was eventually copied by most other states. The Field Code clarified jurisdictional claims and specified matters of court procedure, but was later amended so extensively that its usefulness as a model dissolved. Another court system model was provided by the federal Judiciary Act of 1789 and later by the federal Reorganization Act of 1801. States which followed the federal model developed a three-tiered structure of (1) trial courts of limited jurisdiction, (2) trial courts of general jurisdiction, and (3) appellate courts.

State Court Systems Today

The three-tiered federal model was far from a panacea, however. Within the structure it provided, many local and specialized courts proliferated. Traffic courts, magistrates' courts, municipal courts, recorders' courts, probate courts, and courts held by justices of the peace were but a few which functioned at the lower levels. A movement toward simplification of state court structures, led primarily by the American Bar Association and the American Judicature Society, began in the early 1900s. Proponents of state court reform sought to unify redundant courts, which held overlapping jurisdiction. Most reform-minded thinkers suggested a uniform model for states everywhere which would build upon (1) a centralized court structure composed of a clear hierarchy of trial and appellate courts, (2) the consolidation of numerous lower-level courts holding overlapping jurisdiction, and (3) a centralized state court authority which would be responsible for budgeting, financing, and management of all courts within a state.

The court reform movement is still ongoing today. Although it has made a substantial number of inroads in many states, there are still many differences between and among state court systems. Reform states, which early on embraced the reform movement, are now characterized by streamlined judicial systems consisting of precisely conceived trial courts of limited and general jurisdiction, supplemented by one or two appellate court levels. Nonreform, or traditional, states retain judicial systems which are a conglomeration of multilevel and sometimes redundant courts with poorly defined jurisdiction. Even in nonreform states, however, most criminal courts can be classified within the three-story structure of two trial court echelons and an appellate tier.

Original Jurisdiction

The authority of a given court over a specific geographic area or over particular types of cases. We say that a case falls "within the jurisdiction" of the court.

Appellate Jurisdiction

The lawful authority of a court to review a decision made by a lower court.

A criminal trial in progress. Courts have often been called "the fulcrum of the criminal justice system."
Michael Heron, Woodfin Camp & Associates.

State Trial Courts

"I have tried to minimize what I feel is one of the less desirable aspects of the job, one Justice (Arthur) Goldberg felt strongly about—that judges can become isolated from the people whose lives their decisions affect."

—U.S. Supreme Court Justice Stephen Breyer

Trial courts are where criminal cases begin. The trial court conducts arraignments, sets bail, takes pleas, and conducts trials. (We will discuss each of these separate functions in more depth later in the chapter.) If the defendant is found guilty (or pleads guilty), the trial court imposes sentence. Trial courts of limited or special jurisdiction are also called lower courts. Lower courts are authorized to hear only less-serious criminal cases, usually involving misdemeanors, or to hear special types of cases, such as traffic violations, family disputes, small claims, and so on. Courts of limited jurisdiction, which are depicted in TV shows such as *Night Court* and *Family Court,* rarely hold jury trials, depending instead on the hearing judge to make determinations of both fact and law. At the lower-court level a detailed record of the proceedings is not maintained. Case files will only include information on the charge, the plea, the finding of the court, and the sentence. All but six states make use of trial courts of limited jurisdiction.[7]

Lower courts are much less formal than are courts of general jurisdiction. In an intriguing analysis of court characteristics, Thomas Henderson[8] found that misdemeanor courts process cases according to what he called a "decisional model." The decisional model, said Henderson, is informal, personal, and decisive. It depends upon the quick resolution of relatively uncomplicated issues of law and fact.

Trial courts of general jurisdiction, called variously high courts, circuit courts, or superior courts, are authorized to hear any criminal case. In many states they also provide the first appellate level for courts of limited jurisdiction. In most cases, superior courts offer defendants whose cases originated in lower courts the chance for a new trial instead of a review of the record of the earlier hearing. When a new trial is held, it is referred to as **trial de novo.**

| **Trial *de Novo*** |

Literally, a new trial. The term is applied to cases which are retried on appeal, as opposed to those which are simply reviewed on the record.

Henderson[9] describes courts of general jurisdiction according to a procedural model. Such courts, he says, make full use of juries, prosecutors, defense attorneys, witnesses, and all the other actors we usually associate with American courtrooms. The procedural model, which is far more formal than the decisional model, is fraught with numerous court appearances to ensure that all of a defendant's due process rights are protected. The procedural model makes for a long, expensive, relatively impersonal, and highly formal series of legal maneuvers involving many professional participants—a fact clearly seen in the widely televised 1995 double-murder trial of famed athlete and television personality O. J. Simpson.

Trial courts of general jurisdiction operate within a fact-finding framework called the adversarial process. That process pits the interests of the state, represented by prosecutors, against the professional skills and abilities of defense attorneys. The adversarial process is not a free-for-all, but is, rather, constrained by procedural rules specified in law and sustained through tradition.

State Appellate Courts

Most states today have an appellate division, consisting of an intermediate appellate court (often called the Court of Appeals) and a high-level appellate court (generally termed the state supreme court). High-level appellate courts are referred to as courts of last resort, to indicate that no other appellate route remains to a defendant within the state court system once the high court rules on a case. All states have supreme courts, although only 39 have intermediate appellate courts.[10]

An **appeal** by a convicted defendant asks that a higher court review the actions of a lower one. Courts within the appellate division, once they accept an appeal, do not conduct a new trial. Instead they provide a review of the case on the record. In other words, appellate courts examine the written transcript of lower-court hearings to ensure that those proceedings were carried out fairly and in accordance with proper procedure and state law. They may also allow brief oral arguments to be made by attorneys for both sides and will generally consider other briefs or information filed by the appellant (the party initiating the appeal) or appellee (the side opposed to the appeal). State statutes generally require that sentences of death or life imprisonment be automatically reviewed by the state supreme court.

> **Appeal**
>
> *Generally, the request that a court with appellate jurisdiction review the judgment, decision, or order of a lower court and set it aside (reverse it) or modify it.*

Most convictions are affirmed upon appeal. Occasionally, however, an appellate court will determine that the trial court erred in allowing certain kinds of evidence to be heard or that it failed to interpret properly the significance of a relevant statute. When that happens, the verdict of the trial court will be reversed, and the case may be remanded, or sent back for a new trial. Where a conviction is overturned by an appellate court because of constitutional issues, or where a statute is determined to be invalid, the state usually has recourse to the state supreme court, or the U.S. Supreme Court (when an issue of federal law is involved, as when a state court has ruled a federal law unconstitutional).

Defendants who are not satisfied with the resolution of their case within a state court system may attempt an appeal to the U.S. Supreme Court. For such an appeal to have any chance of being heard, it must be based upon claimed violations of the defendant's rights as guaranteed under federal law or the U.S. Constitution. Under certain circumstances federal district courts may also provide a path of relief for state defendants who can show that their federal constitutional rights have been violated. However, in the 1993 case of *Keeney* v. *Tamayo-Reyes*,[11] the U.S. Supreme Court ruled that a "respondent is entitled to a federal evidentiary hearing [only] if he can show cause for his failure to develop the facts in the state-court proceedings and actual prejudice resulting from that failure, or if he can show that a fundamental miscarriage of justice would result from failure to hold such a hearing." Justice Byron White, writing for the Court, said "[I]t is hardly a good use of scarce judicial resources to duplicate fact-finding in federal court merely because a petitioner has negligently failed to take advantage of opportunities in state court proceedings." Likewise, in *Herrera* v. *Collins* (1993),[12] the Court ruled that new evidence of innocence is no reason for a federal court to order a new state trial if constitutional grounds are lacking. In *Herrera*, where the defendant was under a Texas death sentence for the murder of two police officers, the Court said: "[w]here a defendant has been afforded a fair trial and convicted of the offense for which he was charged, the constitutional presumption of innocence disappears. . . . Thus, claims of actual innocence based on newly discovered evidence have never been held [to be] grounds for relief, absent an independent constitutional violation occurring in the course of the underlying state criminal proceedings. To allow a federal court to grant relief . . . would in effect require a new trial 10 years after the first trial, not because of any constitutional violation at the first trial, but simply because of a belief that in light of his new found evidence a jury might find him not guilty at a second trial." The *Keeney* and *Herrera* decisions have had the effect of severely limiting access by state defendants to federal courts.

The Florida Court System: An Example

Florida provides an example of a reform state which has streamlined the structure of its courts. Prior to a 1973 reorganization, Florida had more different kinds of trial courts than any state except New York.[13] Today the Florida system, which is diagrammed in Figure 7-3, consists of one state supreme court, five district courts of appeal, trial courts of general jurisdiction called "circuit courts," and county courts of limited jurisdiction which hear cases involving petty offenses and civil disputes involving $15,000 or less. County courts are often called "people's courts" in Florida.

Florida's supreme court, headquartered in the Supreme Court Building in Tallahassee, is composed of seven justices, at least four of whom must agree on a decision in each case. By a majority vote of the justices, one of the justices is elected to serve as chief justice (an office which is rotated every two years). The supreme court must review final orders imposing death sentences, district court decisions declaring a state statute or provisions of the state constitution invalid, and actions of statewide agencies relating to public utilities. At its discretion, the court may also review any decision of a district court of appeal that declares invalid a state statute, interprets a provision of the state or federal constitution, affects a class of state officers, or directly conflicts with a decision of another district court or of the state supreme court on a question of law.

The bulk of trial court decisions which are appealed are never heard by the supreme court. Rather, they are reviewed by three-judge panels of the district courts of appeal. Florida's constitution provides that the legislature shall divide the state into appellate court districts and that there shall be a district court of appeal (DCA) serving each district. There are five such districts, which are headquartered in Tallahassee, Lakeland, Miami, West Palm Beach, and Daytona Beach. Fifteen judges serve in the first DCA, 14 in the sec-

FIGURE 7-3 ■ *The court system of the state of Florida.*

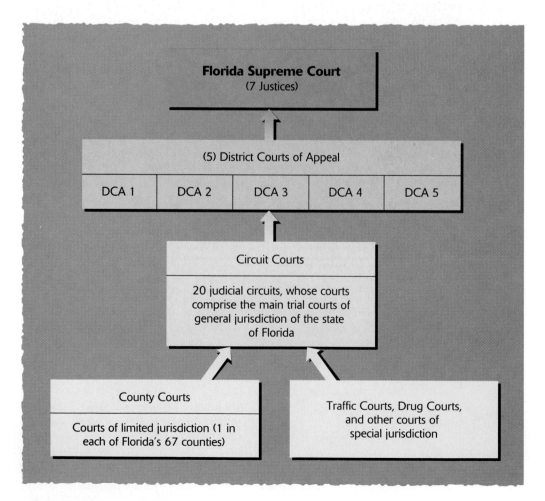

ond, 11 in the third, 12 in the fourth, and 9 in the fifth. Like supreme court justices, district court judges serve terms of six years and are eligible for successive terms under a merit retention vote of the electors in their districts. In each district court, a chief judge, who is selected by other district court judges, is responsible for the administrative duties of the court.

The jurisdiction of the district courts of appeal extends to appeals from judgments or orders of trial courts and to the review of certain nonfinal orders. By law, district courts in Florida have been granted the power to review most actions taken by state agencies. As a general rule, decisions of the district courts of appeal represent the final appellate review of litigated cases. A person who is displeased with a district court's express decision may ask for review in the Florida supreme court or in the United States Supreme Court, but neither tribunal is required to accept the case for further hearing.

The majority of jury trials in Florida take place before one judge sitting as judge of a circuit court. The circuit courts are sometimes referred to as courts of general jurisdiction, in recognition of the fact that most criminal and civil cases originate at this level. Florida's constitution provides that a circuit court shall be established to serve each judicial circuit established by the legislature, of which there are 20. Within each circuit, there may be any number of judges, depending upon the population and caseload of the particular area. At present, the most judges sit in the Eleventh Judicial Circuit, and the fewest judges sit in the Sixteenth Judicial Circuit. To be eligible for the office of circuit judge, a person must be a resident elector of Florida and must have been admitted to the practice of law in the state for the preceding five years. Circuit court judges are elected by the voters of the various circuits. Circuit court judges serve six-year terms and are subject to the same disciplinary standards and procedures as supreme court justices and district court judges. A chief judge is chosen from among the circuit judges in each judicial circuit to carry out administrative responsibilities for all trial courts (both circuit and county courts) within the circuit.

Circuit courts have general trial jurisdiction over matters not assigned by statute to the county courts and also hear appeals from county court cases. Thus, circuit courts are simultaneously the highest trial courts and the lowest appellate courts in Florida's judicial system. The trial jurisdiction of circuit courts includes, among other matters, original jurisdiction over civil disputes involving more than $15,000; controversies involving the estates of decedents, minors, and persons adjudicated to be incompetent; cases relating to juveniles; criminal prosecutions for all felonies; tax disputes; and actions to determine the title and boundaries of real property.

County courts represent the lowest trial court level in Florida. State constitution establishes a county court in each of Florida's 67 counties. The number of judges in each county court varies with the population and caseload of the county. To be eligible for the office of county judge, a person must be a resident of the county and must have been a member of the Florida Bar for five years; in counties with a population of 40,000 or less, a person must only be a member of the Florida Bar. County judges serve four-year terms, and they are subject to the same disciplinary standards as all other judicial officers. The trial jurisdiction of county courts is established by statute. The jurisdiction of county courts extends to civil disputes involving $15,000 or less. The majority of nonjury trials in Florida take place before one judge sitting as a judge of the county court. The county courts are sometimes referred to as "the people's courts," probably because a large part of the court's work involves high-volume citizen disputes, such as traffic offenses, less-serious criminal matters (misdemeanors), and relatively small monetary disputes.

Other, special-purpose courts do exist in the state. In 1989, for example, the Florida legislature authorized the establishment of a Civil Traffic Infraction Hearing Officer Program to free up county judges for other county court work and for circuit court assignments. Initially, participation in the program was limited to those counties with a civil traffic infraction caseload of 20,000 hearings, but the threshold was subsequently lowered to 15,000. The 1990–1991 legislature expanded the magistrate's jurisdiction to include accidents resulting in property damage (not bodily injury). At the end of the year-long pilot project, the Florida supreme court recommended, and the legislature approved, the program for continuation on a local option basis.

"The judicial Power of the United States shall be vested in one supreme Court, and in such inferior Courts as the Congress may from time to time ordain and establish."

—*Article III, U.S. Constitution*

State Court Administration

To function efficiently, courts require uninterrupted funding, adequate staffing, trained support personnel, a well-managed case flow, and coordination between levels and among jurisdictions. To oversee these and other aspects of judicial management, every state today has its own mechanism for court administration. Most make use of state **court administrators** who manage these operational functions.

The first state court administrator was appointed in New Jersey in 1948.[14] Although other states were initially slow to follow the New Jersey lead, increased federal funding for criminal justice administration during the 1970s and a growing realization that some form of coordinated management was necessary for effective court operation eventually led most states to create similar administrative offices.

Florida, discussed earlier, created its Office of the State Courts Administrator (OSCA) on July 1, 1972. Florida's OSCA is divided into three sections with a deputy state courts administrator heading each one. The Information Systems and Program Support section includes Research; Planning and Court Services; Alternative Dispute Resolution; and Information Systems Services. The Administrative Services section includes Finance and Accounting, Budget, Personnel Services, and General Services. The Legal Affairs and Education section includes Legal Affairs, Judiciary Education Services, and various commissions and committees authorized by the legislature and the court. As in many other states, the state court administrator in Florida serves as the liaison between the court system and the legislative branch, the executive branch, the auxiliary agencies of the court, and national court research and planning agencies.

The following tasks are typical of state court administrators across the country today:[15]

1. The preparation, presentation, and monitoring of a budget for the state court system
2. The analysis of case flows and backlogs to determine where additional resources such as judges, prosecutors, and other court personnel are needed
3. The collection and publication of statistics describing the operation of state courts
4. Efforts to streamline the flow of cases through individual courts and the system as a whole
5. Service as a liaison between state legislatures and the court system
6. The development and/or coordination of requests for federal and other outside funding
7. The management of state court personnel, including promotions for support staff and the handling of retirement and other benefits packages for court employees
8. The creation and the coordination of plans for the training of judges and other court personnel (in conjunction with local chief judges and supreme court justices)
9. The assignment of judges to judicial districts (especially in states that use rotating judgeships)
10. The administrative review of payments to legal counsel for indigent defendants

State court administrators can receive assistance from the National Center for State Courts (NCSC) in Williamsburg, Virginia. NCSC is an independent, nonprofit organization dedicated to the improvement of the American court system. It was founded in 1971 at the behest of then-Chief Justice Warren E. Burger. NCSC provides services to state courts, which include helping to

- ▣ Develop policies to enhance state courts
- ▣ Advance state courts' interests within the federal government
- ▣ Secure sufficient resources for state courts
- ▣ Strengthen state court leadership
- ▣ Facilitate state court collaboration
- ▣ Provide a model for organizational administration

You can visit the National Center for State Courts via WebExtra! 7-1 at CJToday.com.

At the federal level, the federal court system is administered by the Administrative Office of the United State Courts (AO), located in Washington, D.C. The AO was created by Congress in 1939 and prepares the budget and legislative agenda for federal courts. It also per-forms audits of court accounts, manages funds for the operation of federal courts, compiles and publishes statistics on the volume and type of business conducted by the courts, and rec-ommends plans and strategies to efficiently manage court business. You can visit the Admin-istrative Office of the United State Courts via **WebExtra!** 7-2 at CJToday.com.

Dispute Resolution Centers

Some communities have begun to recognize that it is possible to resolve at least minor dis-putes without the need for formal court hearings. **Dispute resolution centers,** which func-tion to hear victim's claims of minor wrongs, such as passing bad checks, trespassing, shoplifting, and petty theft, function today in over 200 locations throughout the country.[16] Frequently staffed by volunteer mediators, such programs work to resolve disagreements (in which minor criminal offenses might otherwise be charged) without the need to assign blame. Dispute resolution programs began in the early 1970s, with the earliest being the Community Assistance Project in Chester, Pennsylvania; the Columbus, Ohio, Night Prose-cutor Program; and the Arbitration as an Alternative Program in Rochester, New York. Fol-lowing the lead of these programs, the U.S. Department of Justice helped promote the development of three experimental "Neighborhood Justice Centers" in Los Angeles, Kansas City, and Atlanta. Each center accepted both minor civil and criminal cases.

Mediation centers are often closely integrated with the formal criminal justice process and may substantially reduce the caseload of lower-level courts. Some centers are, in fact, run by the courts and work only with court-ordered referrals. Others are semiautonomous but may be dependent upon courts for endorsement of their decisions; others function with complete autonomy. Rarely, however, do dispute resolution programs entirely supplant the formal crim-inal justice mechanism, and defendants who appear before a community mediator may also later be charged with a crime. Community mediation programs have become a central feature of today's restorative justice movement and are discussed in more detail later in this book.

Mediation centers have been criticized for the fact that they typically work only with minor offenses, thereby denying the opportunity for mediation to victims and offenders in more serious cases, and for the fact that they may be seen by defendants as just another form of criminal sanction, rather than as a true alternative to criminal justice system processing.[17] Other critiques claim that community dispute resolution centers do little other than provide a forum for shouting matches between the parties involved.

Dispute Resolution Centers

Informal hearing infrastructures designed to mediate interpersonal disputes without need for the more formal arrangements of criminal trial courts.

The Rise of the Federal Courts

As we have seen, state courts had their origins in early colonial arrangements. Federal courts, however, were created by the U.S. Constitution. Section 1 of Article III of the Constitution provides for the establishment of "one supreme Court, and . . . such inferior Courts as the Congress may from time to time ordain and establish." Article III, Section 2, specifies that such courts are to have jurisdiction over cases arising under the Constitution, federal laws, and treaties. Federal courts are also to settle disputes between states and to have jurisdiction in cases where one of the parties is a state.

Today's federal court system represents the culmination of a series of congressional man-dates which have expanded the federal judicial infrastructure so that it can continue to carry out the duties envisioned by the Constitution. Notable federal statutes which have con-tributed to the present structure of the federal court system include the Judiciary Act of 1789, the Judiciary Act of 1925, and the Magistrate's Act of 1968.

As a result of constitutional mandates, congressional action, and other historical develop-ments, today's federal judiciary consists of three levels: (1) U.S. district courts, (2) U.S. courts of appeals, and (3) the U.S. Supreme Court. Each is described in turn in the following sections.

Federal District Courts

The lowest level of the federal court system consists of 94 district courts located in the 50 states (except for the District of Wyoming, which includes the Montana and Idaho portions of Yellowstone National Park); Puerto Rico; the District of Columbia; and the U.S. territories of Guam, the Virgin Islands, and the Northern Mariana Islands. District courts are the trial courts of the federal judicial system. They have original jurisdiction over all cases involving alleged violations of federal statutes. Each state has at least one U.S. district court, and some, such as New York and California, have as many as four. A district may itself be divided into divisions and may have several places where the court hears cases. As just discussed, district courts were first authorized by Congress through the 1789 Judiciary Act, which allocated one federal court to each state. Because of population increases over the years, new courts have been added in a number of states.

Nearly 650 district court judges staff federal district courts. District court judges are appointed by the president, confirmed by the Senate, and serve for life. An additional 369 full-time and 110 part-time magistrate judges (referred to as "U.S. magistrates" prior to 1990) serve the district court system and assist federal judges. Magistrate judges have the power to conduct arraignments and may set bail, issue warrants, and try minor offenders.

U.S. district courts handle thousands of criminal cases per year. In 1999, for example, 59,923 criminal cases and 260,271 civil cases were filed in U.S. district courts.[18] Because some courts are much busier than others, the number of district court judges varies from a low of two in some jurisdictions to a high of 27 in others. During the past 20 years the number of cases handled by the entire federal district court system has grown exponentially. The hiring of new judges has not kept pace with the increase in caseload, and questions persist as to the quality of justice that can be delivered by overworked judges.

One of the most pressing issues facing district court judges is the fact that their pay, which at $133,600 in late 1998[19] placed them in the top 1 percent of income-earning Americans, is small compared to what most could earn in private practice. Many federal judges, however, made substantial amounts of money from private practice before assuming the bench, while others had income from investments or held family fortunes.

U.S. Courts of Appeals

The intermediate appellate courts in the federal judicial system are the courts of appeals.[20] Twelve of these courts have jurisdiction over cases from certain geographic areas. The Court of Appeals for the Federal Circuit has national jurisdiction over specific types of cases.

The U.S. Court of Appeals for the Federal Circuit and the 12 regional courts of appeals are often referred to as circuit courts. That is because early in the nation's history, the judges of the first courts of appeals visited each of the courts in one region in a particular sequence, traveling by horseback and riding "circuit." These courts of appeals review matters from the district courts of their geographical regions, the U.S. Tax Court, and from certain federal administrative agencies. A disappointed party in a district court usually has the right to have the case reviewed in the court of appeals for the circuit. Appeals court judges are appointed for life by the president with the advice and consent of the Senate. The First through Eleventh Circuits each include three or more states, as illustrated by Figure 7-4.

Each court of appeals consists of six or more judges, depending on the caseload of the courts. The judge who has served on the court the longest and who is under 65 years of age is designated as the chief judge and performs administrative duties in addition to hearing cases. The chief judge serves for a maximum term of seven years. Each court of appeals judge is appointed for life. There are 167 judges on the 12 regional courts of appeals.

The U.S. Court of Appeals for the District of Columbia, which is often called the Twelfth Circuit, hears cases arising in the District of Columbia and has appellate jurisdiction assigned by Congress in legislation concerning many departments of the federal government. The U.S. Court of Appeals for the Federal Circuit (in effect, the thirteenth circuit) was created in 1982 by the merging of the U.S. Court of Claims and the U.S. Court of Customs and Patent Appeals. The court hears appeals in cases from the U.S. Court of Federal Claims, the U.S. Court of International Trade, the U.S. Court of Veterans Appeals, the International Trade Commission, the Board of Contract Appeals, the Patent and Trademark Office, and the Merit Systems Protection Board. The Federal Circuit also hears appeals from certain decisions of the secretaries of the Department of Agriculture and the Department of Commerce and cases from district courts involving patents and minor claims against the federal government.

"When we have examined in detail the organization of the Supreme Court, and the entire prerogatives which it exercises, we shall readily admit that a more imposing judicial power was never constituted by any people."

—*Alexis de Tocqueville,* Democracy in America *(1835)*

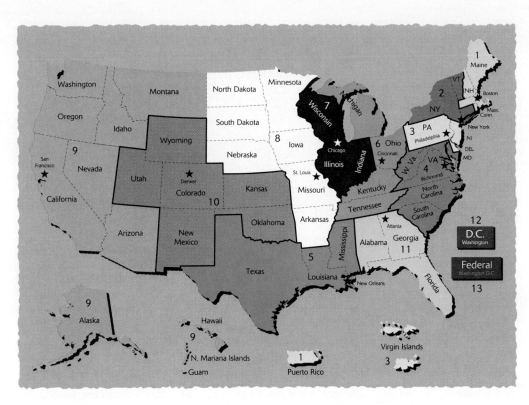

FIGURE 7-4 ■ *The 13 federal judicial circuits.*

Federal appellate courts have mandatory jurisdiction over the decisions of district courts within their circuits. Mandatory jurisdiction means that U.S. courts of appeals are required to hear the cases brought to them. Criminal appeals from federal district courts are usually heard by panels of three judges sitting on a court of appeals rather than by all the judges of each circuit.

Federal appellate courts operate under the *Federal Rules of Appellate Procedure,* although each has also created its own separate Local Rules. Local Rules may mean that one circuit, such as the Second, will depend heavily upon oral arguments, while others may substitute written summary depositions in their place. Appeals generally fall into one of three categories:[21] (1) frivolous appeals, which have little substance, raise no significant new issues, and are generally quickly disposed of; (2) ritualistic appeals, which are brought primarily because of the demands of litigants, even though the probability of reversal is negligible; and (3) nonconsensual appeals, which entail major questions of law and policy and on which there is considerable professional disagreement among the courts and within the legal profession. The probability of reversal is, of course, highest in the case of nonconsensual appeals.

Because the Constitution guarantees a right to an appeal, federal circuit courts have found themselves facing an ever increasing workload. Almost all appeals from federal district courts go to the court of appeals serving the circuit in which the case was first heard. A defendant's right to appeal, however, has been interpreted to mean the right to one appeal. Hence, the U.S. Supreme Court need not necessarily hear the appeals of defendants who are dissatisfied with the decision of a federal appeals court.

> "...Out of the 106 people who served on the Supreme Court, only 58 of them actually attended law school. Law schools didn't come into being or become very popular until after the Civil War."
>
> —**The Honorable Joseph F. Baca,** *Justice, New Mexico supreme court*

The Supreme Court of the United States

At the apex of the federal court system stands the U.S. Supreme Court. The Supreme Court is located in Washington, D.C., across the street from the U.S. Capitol Building. The Court consists of nine justices, eight of whom are referred to as associate justices. The ninth presides over the Court as the chief justice of the United States. (See Table 7-1.) Supreme Court justices are nominated by the president, confirmed by the Senate, and serve for life. Lengthy terms of service are a tradition among justices. One of the earliest chief justices, John Marshall, served the Court for 34 years, from 1801 to 1835. The same was true of Justice Stephen J.

TABLE 7-1 ■ Justices of the U.S. Supreme Court as of June 2001

JUSTICE	ENTERED DUTY	VIEWS
CHIEF JUSTICE		
William H. Rehnquist*	January 1972	Very conservative
ASSOCIATE JUSTICES		
John Paul Stevens	December 1975	Moderate to liberal
Sandra Day O'Connor	September 1981	Moderate to conservative
Antonin Scalia	September 1986	Very conservative
Anthony M. Kennedy	February 1988	Conservative
David H. Souter	October 1990	Conservative
Clarence Thomas	October 1991	Conservative
Ruth Bader Ginsburg	August 1993	Moderate
Stephen G. Breyer	August 1994	Moderate

* Appointed Chief Justice September 1986.

Judicial Review

The power of a court to review actions and decisions made by other agencies of government.

Field who sat on the bench for 34 years, between 1863 and 1897. Justice Hugo Black passed the 34-year milestone, serving an additional month, before he retired in 1971. Justice William O. Douglas set a record for longevity on the bench, retiring in 1975 after 36 years and 6 months of service. You may view the biographies of today's Supreme Justices via WebExtra! 7-3 at CJToday.com.

The Supreme Court of the United States wields immense power. The Court's greatest authority lies in its capacity for **judicial review** of lower-court decisions and state and federal statute. By exercising its power of judicial review, the Court decides what laws and lower-court decisions are in keeping with the intent of the U.S. Constitution. The power of judicial review is not explicit in the Constitution, but was anticipated by its framers. In the *Federalist Papers,* which urged adoption of the Constitution, Alexander Hamilton wrote that, through the practice of judicial review, the Court would ensure that "the will of the whole people," as grounded in the Constitution, would be supreme over the "will of the legislature . . . ," which might be subject to temporary whims.[22]

It was not until 1803, however, that the Court forcefully asserted its power of judicial review. In an opinion written for the case of *Marbury* v. *Madison* (1803),[23] Chief Justice John Marshall established the Court's authority as final interpreter of the U.S. Constitution, declaring that "It is emphatically the province of the judicial department to say what the law is. . . ."

Increasing Complexity and the Supreme Court. The evolution of the U.S. Supreme Court provides one of the most dramatic examples of institutional development in American history. Sparsely described in the Constitution, the Court has grown from a handful of circuit-riding justices into a modern organization that wields tremendous legal power over all aspects of American life. Much of the Court's growth has been due to its increasing willingness to mediate fundamental issues of law and to act as a resort from arbitrary and capricious processing by the justice systems of the states and national government.

The *Marbury* decision established the Court as a mighty force in federal government by virtue of the power of judicial review. As we have discussed in Chapter 5, the Court began to apply that power during the 1960s to issues of crime and justice at the state and local levels. You may recall that the Court signaled its change in orientation in 1961 with the case of *Mapp* v. *Ohio,*[24] which extended the exclusionary rule to the states. Such extension, combined with the near-simultaneous end of the hands-off doctrine which had previously exempted state prison systems from Court scrutiny, placed the authority of the Court squarely over the activities of state criminal justice systems. From that time forward, the Court's workload became increasingly heavy and even today shows few signs of abatement.

The Supreme Court Today. The Supreme Court has limited original jurisdiction and does not conduct trials except in disputes between states and some cases of attorney disbarment.

Chambers of the United States Supreme Court in Washington, D.C.
Doug Mills, AP/Wide World Photos.

The Court, rather, reviews the decisions of lower courts and may accept cases from both U.S. courts of appeals and state supreme courts. For a case to be heard, at least four justices must vote in favor of a hearing. When the Court agrees to hear a case, it will issue a **writ of *certiorari*** to a lower court, ordering it to send the records of the case forward for review. Once having granted *certiorari,* the justices can revoke the decision. In such cases a writ is dismissed by ruling it improvidently granted.

The U.S. Supreme Court may review any decision appealed to it which it decides is worthy of review. In fact, however, the Court elects to review only cases which involve a substantial federal question. Of approximately 5,000 requests for review received by the Court yearly, only about 200 are actually heard.

A term of the Supreme Court begins, by statute, on the first Monday in October and lasts until early July. The term is divided among sittings, when cases will be heard, and time for the writing and delivering of opinions. Between 22 and 24 cases will be heard at each sitting, with each side allotted 30 minutes for arguments before the justices. Intervening recesses allow justices time to study arguments and supporting documentation and to work on their opinions.

Decisions rendered by the Supreme Court are rarely unanimous. Instead, opinions that a majority of the Court's justices agree upon become the judgment of the Court. Justices who agree with the Court's judgment, but for a different reason or because they feel that they have come new light to shed on a particular legal issue involved in the case, write concurring opin-

Writ of *Certiorari*

A writ issued by an appellate court for the purpose of obtaining from a lower court the record of its proceedings in a particular case. In some states this writ is the mechanism for discretionary reviews. A request for review is made by petitioning for a writ of certiorari and granting of review is indicated by issuance of the writ.

Thurgood Marshall (1909–1993), the nation's first black U.S. Supreme Court justice.
John Ficara, Woodfin Camp & Associates.

ions. Justices who do not agree with the decision of the Court write dissenting opinions. Those dissenting opinions may offer new possibilities for successful appeals made at a later date.

Ideas for Change. Increasing caseloads at the federal appellate court level, combined with the many requests for Supreme Court review, have led to proposals to restructure the federal appellate court system. In 1973, a study group appointed by then-Chief Justice Burger suggested the creation of a National Court of Appeals, which would serve as a kind of "mini-Supreme Court."[25] Under the proposal, the National Court of Appeals would be staffed on a rotating basis by judges who now serve the various circuit courts of appeal. The purpose of the new court was suggested to include a review of cases awaiting hearings before the Supreme Court so that the High Court's workload might be reduced.

A similar National Court of Appeals was proposed in 1975 by the Congressional Commission on Revision of the Federal Court Appellate System. The National Court proposed by the Commission would have heard cases sent to it via transfer jurisdiction, from lower appellate courts, and through reference jurisdiction—when the Supreme Court decided to forward cases to it. The most recent version of a mini-Supreme Court was proposed by the Senate Judiciary Committee in 1986, when it called for the creation of an Intercircuit Tribunal of the U.S. courts of appeals. To date, however, no legislation to establish such a court has passed both houses of Congress. Visit the U.S. Supreme Court via WebExtra! 7-4.

Pretrial Activities

In the next chapter we will discuss typical stages in a criminal trial, as well as describe the many roles assumed by courtroom participants including judges, prosecutors, defense attorneys, victims, and suspects. A number of court-related pretrial activities, however, routinely take place before trial can begin. Although such activities (as well as the names given to them) vary between jurisdictions, they are generally described in the pages which follow.

First Appearance

First Appearance (also Initial Appearance)

An appearance before a magistrate which entails the process whereby the legality of a defendant's arrest is initially assessed, and he or she is informed of the charges on which he or she is being held. At this stage in the criminal justice process, bail may be set or pretrial release arranged.

Following arrest, most defendants do not come into contact with an officer of the court until their **first appearance** before a magistrate, or lower-court judge.[26] A first appearance, sometimes called an initial appearance or magistrate's review, occurs when defendants are brought before a judge to be (1) given formal notice of the charges against them, (2) advised of their rights, (3) given the opportunity to retain a lawyer or to have one appointed to represent them, and (possibly) (4) afforded the opportunity for bail.

According to the procedural rules of all jurisdictions, defendants who have been taken into custody must be offered an in-court appearance before a magistrate "without unnecessary delay." The 1943 Supreme Court case of *McNabb* v. *U.S.*[27] established that any unreasonable delay in an initial court appearance would make confessions inadmissible if interrogating officers obtained them during the delay. Based upon the *McNabb* decision, 48 hours following arrest became the rule of thumb for reckoning the maximum time by which a first appearance should have been held.

The first appearance may also involve a probable cause hearing, although such hearings may be held separately (or may be combined, in some jurisdictions, with the preliminary hearing) since they do not require the defendant's presence. Probable cause hearings are necessary when arrests are made without a warrant, because such arrests do not require a prior judicial determination of probable cause. Such hearings ensure that probable cause for arrest and continued detention exist. During a probable cause hearing, also called a probable cause determination, a judicial officer will review police documents and reports to ensure that probable cause supported the arrest. The review of the arrest proceeds in a relatively informal fashion, with the judge seeking to decide whether, at the time of apprehension, the arresting officer had reason to believe both (1) that a crime had been or was being committed and (2) that the defendant was the person who committed it. Most of the evidence presented to the judge comes either from the arresting officer or from the victim. If probable cause is not found to exist, the suspect will be released.

In 1991, the U.S. Supreme Court, in a class-action suit entitled *County of Riverside (California)* v. *McLaughlin*,[28] imposed a promptness requirement upon probable cause determinations for in-custody arrestees. The Court held that "a jurisdiction that provides judicial determinations of probable cause within 48 hours of arrest will, as a general matter, comply with the promptness requirement. . . ." The Court specified, however, that weekends and holidays could not be excluded from the 48-hour requirement (as they had been in Riverside County) and that, depending upon the specifics of the case, delays of fewer than two days may still be unreasonable.

During a first appearance, the suspect is not given an opportunity to present evidence, although the U.S. Supreme Court has held that defendants are entitled to representation by counsel at their first appearance.[29] Following a reading of the charges and a rights advisement, indigent defendants may have counsel appointed to represent them, and proceedings may be adjourned until counsel can be obtained.

In cases where suspects are unruly, intoxicated, or uncooperative, judicial review may occur in their absence. Some states waive a first appearance and proceed directly to arraignment (discussed following), especially when the defendant has been arrested on a warrant. In states which move directly to arraignment, the procedures undertaken to obtain a warrant are regarded as sufficient to demonstrate a basis for detention prior to arraignment.

Bail

A highly significant aspect of the first appearance hearing is consideration of bail or pretrial release. Defendants charged with very serious crimes, or those thought likely to escape or injure others, will usually be held in jail until trial. Such a practice is called pretrial detention.

The majority of defendants, however, will be afforded the opportunity for release. However, since it is important to make sure that a released defendant will return for further court processing, he or she is asked to "post bail." Bail serves two purposes: (1) it helps ensure reappearance of the accused, and (2) it prevents unconvicted persons from suffering imprisonment unnecessarily.

Bail involves the posting of a bond as a pledge that the accused will return for further hearings. **Bail bonds** are usually cash deposits but may consist of property or other valuables. A fully secured bond requires the defendant to post the full amount of bail set by the court. The usual practice, however, is for a defendant to seek privately secured bail through the services of a professional bail bondsman. The bondsman will assess a percentage (usually 10–15 percent) of the required bond as a fee, which the defendant will have to pay up front. Those who "skip bail" by hiding or fleeing will sometimes find their bond ordered forfeit by

Bail Bond

An agreement guaranteeing the required appearance of a defendant in court, which records a pledge of money or property to be paid to the court if he or she does not appear and which is signed by the person to be released and any other persons acting in his or her behalf.

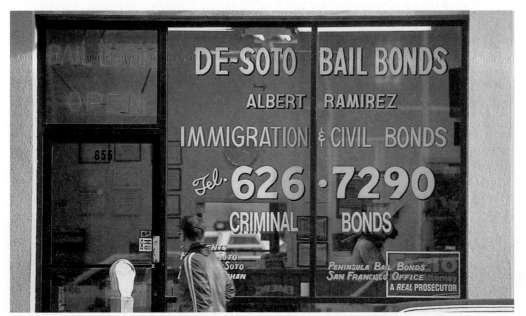

A typical bail bond office. Bail bond offices such as this one are usually found near courthouses where criminal trials are held.
Mark Richards.

the court. Forfeiture hearings must be held before a bond can be taken, and most courts will not order bail forfeit unless it appears that the defendant intends permanently to avoid prosecution. Bail forfeiture will often be reversed where the defendant later willingly appears to stand trial.

In many states bondsmen are empowered to hunt down and bring back defendants who have fled. In some jurisdictions bondsmen hold virtually unlimited powers and have been permitted by courts to pursue, arrest, and forcibly extradite their charges from foreign jurisdiction without concern for the due process considerations or statutory limitations which apply to law enforcement officers.[30] Recently, however, a number of states have enacted laws which eliminate for-profit bail bond businesses, replacing them instead with state-operated pretrial service agencies. Visit the Professional Bail Agents of the United States Web site via **WebExtra!** 7-5 in order to learn more about the job of bail bondsman and to view the group's code of ethics.

Alternatives to Bail

The Eighth Amendment to the U.S. Constitution, while it does not guarantee the opportunity for bail, does state that "Excessive bail shall not be required. . . ." Some studies, however, have found that many defendants who are offered the opportunity for bail are unable to raise the needed money. Years ago, a report by the National Advisory Commission on Criminal Justice Standards and Goals found that as many as 93 percent of felony defendants in some jurisdictions were unable to make bail.[31]

To extend the opportunity for pretrial release to a greater proportion of nondangerous arrestees, a number of states and the federal government now make available various alternatives to the cash bond system. Alternatives include (1) release on recognizance, (2) property bond, (3) deposit bail, (4) conditional release, (5) third-party custody, (6) unsecured or signature bond, and (7) attorney affidavit.

Release on recognizance (ROR) involves no cash bond, requiring as a guarantee only that the defendant agree in writing to return for further hearings as specified by the court. As an alternative to cash bond, release on recognizance was tested during the 1960s in a social experiment called the Manhattan Bail Project.[32] In the experiment not all defendants were eligible for release on their own recognizance. Those arrested for serious crimes, including murder, rape, and robbery, and defendants with extensive prior criminal records, were excluded from participating in the project. The rest of the defendants were scored and categorized according to a number of "ideal" criteria used as indicators of both dangerousness and the likelihood of pretrial flight. Criteria included (1) no previous convictions, (2) residential stability, and (3) a good employment record. Those likely to flee were not released.

Studies of the bail project revealed that it released four times as many defendants prior to trial as had been freed under the traditional cash bond system.[33] Even more surprising was the finding that only 1 percent of those released fled from prosecution—a figure which was the same as for those set free on cash bond.[34] Later studies, however, were unclear as to the effectiveness of release on recognizance, with some finding a no-show rate as high as 12 percent.[35]

Property bonds substitute other items of value in place of cash. Land, houses, automobiles, stocks, and so on may be consigned to the court as collateral against pretrial flight.

An alternative form of cash bond available in some jurisdictions is deposit bail. *Deposit bail* places the court in the role of the bondsman, allowing the defendant to post a percentage of the full bail with the court. Unlike private bail bondsmen, court-run deposit bail programs usually return the amount of the deposit except for a small (perhaps 1 percent) administrative fee. If the defendant fails to appear for court, the entire amount of court-ordered bail is forfeited.

Conditional release imposes a set of requirements upon the defendant. Requirements might include attendance at drug-treatment programs; staying away from specified others, such as potential witnesses; and regular job attendance. Release under supervision is similar to conditional release but adds the stipulation that defendants report to an officer of the court or a police officer at designated times.

Third-party custody is a bail bond alternative that assigns custody of the defendant to an

Release on Recognizance (ROR)

Refers to the pretrial release of criminal defendants on their written promise to appear. No cash or property bond is required.

Property Bond

The setting of bail in the form of land, houses, stocks, or other tangible property. In the event the defendant absconds prior to trial, the bond becomes the property of the court.

individual or agency which promises to assure his or her later appearance in court.[36] Some pretrial release programs allow attorneys to assume responsibility for their clients in this fashion. If clients fail to appear, however, the attorney's privilege to participate in the program may be ended.

An *unsecured bond* is based upon a court-determined dollar amount of bail. Like a credit contract, it requires no monetary deposit with the court. The defendant agrees in writing that failure to appear will result in forfeiture of the entire amount of the bond, which might then be taken in seizures of land, personal property, bank accounts, and so on.

A *signature bond* allows release based upon the defendant's written promise to appear. Signature bonds involve no particular assessment of the defendant's dangerousness or likelihood of later appearance in court. They are used only in cases of minor offenses such as traffic law violations and some petty drug law violations. Signature bonds may be issued by the arresting officer acting on behalf of the court.

Pretrial release is common practice. Approximately 85 percent of all state-level criminal defendants[37] and 82 percent of all federal criminal defendants[38] are released prior to trial. Sixty-three percent of all state-level *felony* defendants[39] and 64 percent of federal felony defendants[40] are similarly released (see Figure 7-5). A growing movement, however, stresses the fact that defendants released prior to trial may be dangerous to themselves or others and seeks to reduce the number of defendants released under any conditions. This conservative policy has been promoted by an increasing concern for public safety in the face of a number of studies documenting crimes committed by defendants released on bond. One such study found that 16 percent of defendants released before trial were rearrested, and, of those, 30 percent were arrested more than once.[41] Another determined that as many as 41 percent of those released prior to trial for serious crimes, such as rape and robbery, were rearrested before their trial date.[42] Not surprisingly, such studies generally find that the longer the time spent on bail prior to trial, the greater the likelihood of misconduct.

In response to claims like these, some states have enacted **danger laws,** which limit the right to bail for certain kinds of offenders.[43] Others, including Arizona, California, Colorado, Florida, and Illinois, have approved constitutional amendments restricting the use of bail.[44] Most such provisions exclude persons charged with certain crimes from being eligible for bail and demand that other defendants being considered for bail meet stringent conditions. Some states combine these strictures with tough release conditions designed to keep close control over defendants prior to trial.

The 1984 federal Bail Reform Act allows federal judges to assess the danger represented by an accused to the community and to deny bail to persons who are thought dangerous. In the words of the act, a suspect held in pretrial custody on federal criminal charges is required to be detained if, "after a hearing . . . he is found to pose a risk of flight and a danger to others or the community and if no condition of release can give reasonable assurances against these

Danger Laws

Those intended to prevent the pretrial release of criminal defendants judged to represent a danger to others in the community.

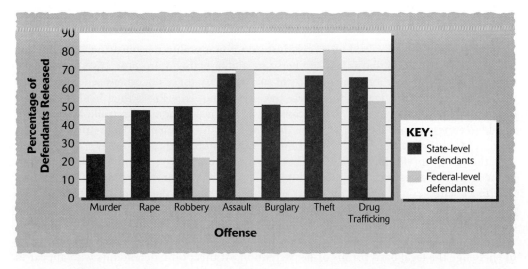

FIGURE 7-5 ■ *Proportion of state and federal felony defendants released prior to trial.*

Sources: Brian A. Reaves, Felony Defendants in Large Urban Counties, 1994: State Court Processing Statistics *(Washington, D.C.: Bureau of Justice Statistics, 1998); Brian A. Reaves and Jacob Perez, Pretrial Release of Felony Defendants, 1992 (Washington, D.C.: Bureau of Justice Statistics, November 1994); and John Scalia, Federal Pretrial Release and Detention, 1996 (Washington, D.C.: Bureau of Justice Statistics, February 1999).*
Note: *Federal pretrial release statistics are not available for the crimes of rape and burglary.*

contingencies."[45] Defendants seeking bail are faced with the necessity of demonstrating a high likelihood of later court appearance. The act also requires that a defendant is entitled to a speedy first appearance and, if he or she is to be detained, that a detention hearing must be held together with the initial appearance.

In the 1990 case of *U.S.* v. *Montalvo-Murillo*,[46] however, a defendant who was not provided with a detention hearing at the time of his first appearance, and was subsequently released by an appeals court, was found to have no "right" to freedom because of this "minor" statutory violation. The Supreme Court held that "unless it has a substantial influence on the outcome of the proceedings . . . failure to comply with the Act's prompt hearing provision does not require release of a person who should otherwise be detained" because, "[a]utomatic release contravenes the statutory purpose of providing fair bail procedures while protecting the public's safety and assuring a defendant's appearance at trial."[47]

Court challenges to the constitutionality of pretrial detention legislation have not met with much success. The U.S. Supreme Court case of *U.S.* v. *Hazzard* (1984),[48] decided only a few months after enactment of federal bail reform, held that Congress was justified in providing for denial of bail to offenders who represent a danger to the community. Later cases have supported the presumption of flight, which federal law presupposes for certain types of defendants.[49]

The Grand Jury

The federal government and about half of the states use grand juries as part of the pretrial process. Grand juries are composed of private citizens (often 23 in number) who hear evidence presented by the prosecution. Grand juries serve primarily as filters to eliminate from further processing cases for which there is not sufficient evidence.

In early times grand juries served a far different purpose. The grand jury system began in England in 1166 as a way of identifying law violators. Lacking a law enforcement agency with investigative authority, the government looked to the grand jury as a source of information on criminal activity in the community. Even today, grand juries in most jurisdictions may initiate prosecution independently of the prosecutor, although they rarely do.

Grand jury hearings are held in secret, and the defendant is not afforded the opportunity to appear before the grand jury.[50] Similarly, the opportunity to cross-examine prosecution witnesses is absent. Grand juries have the power to subpoena witnesses and to mandate a review of books, records, and other documents crucial to their investigations.

After hearing the evidence, the grand jury votes on the indictment presented to it by the prosecution. The indictment is a formal listing of proposed charges. If the majority of grand jury members agree to forward the indictment to the trial court, it becomes a "true bill" upon which further prosecution will turn.

The Preliminary Hearing

States which do not use grand juries rely instead upon a preliminary hearing "for charging defendants in a fashion that is less cumbersome and arguably more protective of the innocent."[51] In these jurisdictions, the prosecutor files an accusatorial document called an "information," or complaint, against the accused. A preliminary hearing is then held in order to determine whether there is probable cause to hold the defendant for trial. A few states, notably Tennessee and Georgia, use both the grand jury mechanism and a preliminary hearing as a "double check against the possibility of unwarranted prosecution."[52]

Although the preliminary hearing is not nearly as elaborate as a criminal trial, it has many of the same characteristics. The defendant is taken before a lower-court judge who will summarize the charges and review the rights to which all criminal defendants are entitled. The prosecution may present witnesses and will offer evidence in support of the complaint. The defendant will be afforded the right to testify and may also call witnesses.

The primary purpose of the preliminary hearing is to give the defendant an opportunity to challenge the legal basis for his or her detention. At this point, defendants who appear or claim to be mentally incompetent may be ordered to undergo further evaluation to determine their competency to stand trial. **Competency to stand trial** may become an issue when a defendant appears to be incapable of understanding the proceedings against him or her or is unable to assist in his or her own defense due to mental disease or defect. In 1996, for example, lawyers for multimillionaire chemical heir John E. du Pont successfully argued at a pretrial hearing that their client was psychotic and unable to work effectively with lawyers in preparing a defense to murder charges. Du Pont had been accused of shooting and killing David Schultz, an Olympic wrestler and 1984 gold medalist who had trained on du Pont's estate near Philadelphia. At the hearing, du Pont was declared schizophrenic, and his delusions of being the Dalai Lama, Jesus, and "heir to the Third Reich" were publicized in national media.[53]

Barring a finding of mental incompetence, all that is required for the wheels of justice to grind forward is a demonstration "sufficient to justify a prudent man's belief that the suspect has committed or was committing an offense"[54] within the jurisdiction of the court. If the magistrate finds enough evidence to justify a trial, the defendant is bound over to the grand jury—or sent directly to the trial court in those states which do not require grand jury review. If the complaint against the defendant cannot be substantiated, the defendant is released. A release is not a bar to further prosecution, and the defendant may be rearrested if further evidence comes to light.

Arraignment and the Plea

Once an indictment has been returned, or an information filed, the accused will be formally arraigned. Arraignment is "the first appearance of the defendant before the court that has the authority to conduct a trial."[55] Arraignment is generally a brief process with two purposes: (1) to once again inform the defendant of the specific charges against him or her and (2) to allow the defendant to enter a **plea.** The Federal Rules of Criminal Procedure allow for one of three types of pleas to be entered: guilty, not guilty, and *nolo contendere* (no contest). A no contest (**nolo contendere**) plea is much the same as a plea of guilty. A defendant who pleads no contest is immediately convicted and may be sentenced just as though he or she had entered a plea of guilty. A no contest plea, however, is no admission of guilt and provides one major advantage to defendants: It may not be used as a later basis for civil proceedings which seek monetary or other damages against the defendant.

Some defendants refuse to enter any plea and are said to "stand mute." Standing mute is a defense strategy that is rarely employed by an accused. Defendants who choose this alternative simply do not answer the request for a plea. However, for procedural purposes, a defendant who stands mute is considered to have entered a plea of not guilty.

Plea Bargaining

Guilty pleas often are not as straightforward as they might seem and are typically arrived at only after complex negotiations known as **plea bargaining.** Plea bargaining is a process of negotiation which usually involves the defendant, prosecutor, and defense counsel. It is founded upon the mutual interests of all involved. Defense attorneys and their clients will agree to a plea of guilty when they are unsure of their ability to win acquittal at trial. Prosecutors may be willing to bargain because the evidence they have against the defendant is weaker than they would like it to be. From the prosecutorial perspective, plea bargaining results in a quick conviction without the need to commit the time and resources necessary for trial. Benefits to the accused include the possibility of reduced or combined charges, lessened defense costs, and a lower sentence than might have otherwise been anticipated.

The U.S. Supreme Court has held that a guilty plea constitutes conviction.[56] In order to validate the conviction, negotiated pleas require judicial consent. Judges are often likely to accept pleas which are the result of a bargaining process because such pleas reduce the workload of the court. Although few judges are willing to guarantee a sentence before a plea is entered, most prosecutors and criminal trial lawyers know what sentences to expect from typical pleas.

In the past, plea bargaining, though apparently common, had often been veiled in secrecy. Judicial thinking held that, for pleas to be valid, they had to be freely given. Pleas struck as

---

Competent to Stand Trial

A finding by a court, when the defendant's sanity at the time of trial is at issue, that a defendant has sufficient present ability to consult with his or her lawyer with a reasonable degree of rational understanding and that he or she has a rational as well as factual understanding of the proceedings against him or her.

Plea

In criminal proceedings, a defendant's formal answer in court to the charge contained in a complaint, information, or indictment that he or she is guilty of the offense charged, not guilty of the offense charged, or does not contest the charge.

Nolo Contendere

A plea of "no contest." A no contest plea may be used where the defendant does not wish to contest conviction. Because the plea does not admit guilt, however, it cannot provide the basis for later civil suits, which might follow upon the heels of a criminal conviction.

Plea Bargaining

The negotiated agreement among defendant, prosecutor, and the court as to what an appropriate plea and associated sentence should be in a given case. Plea bargaining circumvents the trial process and dramatically reduces the time required for the resolution of a criminal case.

the result of bargains seemed to depend upon the state's coercive power to encourage the defendant's cooperation. The 1973 National Advisory Commission on Criminal Justice Standards and Goals recommended abolishing the practice of plea negotiation.[57] That recommendation came in the midst of a national debate over the virtues of trading pleas for reductions in sentences. However, in 1970, even before the Commission's recommendation, the U.S. Supreme Court had given its consent to the informal decision-making processes of bargained pleas. In the case of *Brady* v. *U.S.*,[58] the court reasoned that such pleas were acceptable if voluntarily and knowingly made. A year later, in *Santobello* v. *New York* (1971),[59] the high court forcefully ruled that plea bargaining is an important and necessary component of the American system of justice. In the words of the Court, "The disposition of criminal charges by agreement between the prosecutor and the accused, sometimes loosely called 'plea bargaining,' is an essential component of the administration of justice. Properly administered, it is to be encouraged. If every criminal charge were subjected to a full-scale trial, the States and the Federal Government would need to multiply by many times the number of judges and court facilities."[60]

Today, bargained pleas are commonplace. Some surveys have found that 90 percent of all criminal cases prepared for trial are eventually resolved through a negotiated plea.[61] In a study of 37 big-city prosecutors,[62] the Bureau of Justice Statistics found that for every 100 adults arrested on a felony charge, half were eventually convicted of either a felony or a misdemeanor. Of all convictions, fully 94 percent were the result of a plea. Only 6 percent of convictions were the result of a criminal trial.

After a guilty plea has been entered, it may be withdrawn with the consent of the court. In the case of *Henderson* v. *Morgan* (1976),[63] for example, the U.S. Supreme Court permitted a defendant to withdraw a plea of guilty nine years after it had been given. In *Henderson* the defendant had originally entered a plea of guilty to second-degree murder but attempted to withdraw it before trial. Reasons for wanting to withdraw the plea included the defendant's belief that he had not been completely advised as to the nature of the charge or the sentence he might receive as a result of the plea.

Recent Supreme Court decisions, however, have enhanced the prosecutor's authority in the bargaining process by declaring that negotiated pleas cannot be capriciously withdrawn by defendants.[64] Other rulings have supported discretionary actions by prosecutors in which sentencing recommendations were retracted even after bargains had been struck.[65] Some lower-court cases have upheld the government's authority to withdraw from a negotiated plea where the defendant fails to live up to certain conditions.[66] Conditions may include requiring the defendant to provide information on other criminal involvement, criminal cartels, the activities of smugglers, and so on.

Because it is a process of negotiation involving many interests, plea bargaining may have unintended consequences. For example, while it is generally agreed that bargained pleas should relate in some way to the original charge, actual practice may not adhere to such expectations. Many plea negotiations turn on the acceptability of the anticipated sentence rather than on a close relationship between the charge and the plea. Entered pleas may be chosen for the punishments likely to be associated with them rather than for their accuracy in describing the criminal offense in which the defendant was involved.[67] This is especially true where the defendant is concerned with minimizing the socially stigmatizing impact of the offense. A charge of "indecent liberties," for example, in which the defendant is accused of sexual misconduct, may be pled out as assault. Such a plea, which takes advantage of the fact that "indecent liberties" can be thought of as a form of sexual assault, would effectively disguise the true nature of the offense.

Even though plea bargaining has been endorsed by the Supreme Court, the public continues to view it suspiciously. "Law and order" advocates, who generally favor harsh punishments and long jail terms, claim that plea bargaining results in unjustifiably light sentences. As a consequence, prosecutors who regularly engage in the practice rarely advertise it. Often unrealized is the fact that plea bargaining can be a powerful prosecutorial tool.

Power carries with it, however, the potential for misuse. Plea bargains, because they circumvent the trial process, hold the possibility of abuse by prosecutors and defense attorneys who are more interested in a speedy resolution of cases than they are in seeing justice done. Carried to the extreme, plea bargaining may result in defendants being convicted of crimes they did not commit. Although it probably happens only rarely, it is conceivable that innocent defendants (especially those with prior criminal records) who—for whatever reason—think a jury will convict them, may plead guilty to lessened charges in order to avoid a trial. In an effort to protect defendants against hastily arranged pleas, the Federal Rules of Criminal Procedure require judges to (1) inform the defendant of the various rights he or she is surrendering by pleading guilty, (2) determine that the plea is voluntary, (3) require disclosure of any plea agreements, and (4) make sufficient inquiry to ensure there is a factual basis for the plea.[68]

Bargained pleas can take many forms and be quite inventive. The case of Jeffrey Morse is illustrative of an unusual attempt at a bargained plea. In 1998, Morse, a convicted sex offender, petitioned courts in Illinois for permission to leave jail prior to sentencing for sexual assaults on two young girls so that he could undergo surgical castration. A judge agreed, and he was surgically castrated in a 45-minute outpatient procedure. Morse's mother noted that the surgery was done in an effort to avoid a long prison sentence. "He will cut whatever bodily part he has to be able to reduce his sentence," she said.[69] Two months later, however, Kane County Judge Donald C. Hudson refused to show leniency for Morse. Instead, Hudson sentenced Morse to 26 years in prison, saying that he wouldn't "place a seal of approval on trading body parts for a lesser sentence."[70]

Summary

Throughout the United States there are two judicial systems. One consists of state and local courts established under the authority of state governments. The other is the federal court system, created by Congress under the authority of the Constitution of the United States.

State courts have virtually unlimited power to decide nearly every type of case, subject only to the limitations of the U.S. Constitution, their own state constitutions, and state law. State and local courts are located in almost every town and county across the nation and are the courts with which citizens usually have contact. These courts handle most criminal matters and the great bulk of legal business concerning wills and inheritance, estates, marital disputes, real estate and land dealings, commercial and personal contracts, and other day-to-day matters.

State criminal courts present an intriguing contrast. On the one hand, they exude an aura of highly formalized judicial procedure, while on the other they demonstrate a surprising lack of organizational uniformity. Courts in one jurisdiction may bear little resemblance to those in another state. Court reform, because it has not equally impacted all areas of the country, has in some instances exacerbated the differences between court systems.

Federal courts have power to decide only those cases over which the Constitution gives them authority. These courts are located principally in larger cities. Only carefully selected types of cases may be heard in federal courts. The highest federal court, the U.S. Supreme Court, is located in Washington, D.C., and hears cases only on appeal from lower courts.

This chapter also described pretrial practices in preparation for a detailed consideration of trial-related activities which are described in the next chapter. Prior to trial, courts often act to shield the accused from the punitive power of the state through the use of pretrial release. In doing so, they must balance the rights of the unconvicted defendant against the potential for future harm which that person may represent. A significant issue facing pretrial decision makers is how to ensure that all defendants, rich or poor, black or white, male or female, are afforded the same degree of protection.

Discussion Questions

1. What is the "dual court system"? Why do we have a dual court system in America? Could the drive toward court unification eventually lead to a monolithic court system? Would such a system be effective?

2. This chapter says that 90 percent of all criminal cases carried beyond the initial stages are finally resolved through bargained pleas. What are some of the problems associated

with plea bargaining? Given those problems, do you believe that plea bargaining is an acceptable practice in today's criminal justice system? Give reasons for your answer.

3. People who are accused of crimes are often granted pretrial release. Do you think all defendants accused of crimes should be so released? If not, what types of defendants might you keep in jail? Why?

4. What inequities exist in today's system of pretrial release? How might the system be improved?

Web Quest!

Visit the Federal Judiciary home page run by the Administrative Office of the United States Courts at www.uscourts.gov. After visiting the site, describe the purpose and history of the Administrative Office, the courts it serves, and the nature of the services it provides.

Also visit the National Center for State Courts (NCSC) at http://ncsc.dni.us. What is the mission of the NCSC? What are the divisions of the NCSC? What does each division do?

What "affiliated associations" are listed on the NCSC home page? What is the purpose of each of these associations?

Write down and submit what you have learned to your instructor if asked to do so.

Library Extras!

The Library Extras! listed here complement the WebExtras! found throughout this chapter. Library Extras! may be accessed on the Web at CJToday.com.

Library Extra! 7-1. *Federal Habeas Corpus Review: Challenging State Court Criminal Convictions* (USDOJ, 1995).

Library Extra! 7-2. *Prisoner Petitions in the Federal Courts,* 1980–96 (BJS, October 1997).

Library Extra! 7-3. *Survey of Judicial Salaries* (NCSC).

Library Extra! 7-4. "Therapeutic Jurisprudence and the Emergence of Problem-Solving Courts," *The National Institute of Justice Journal* (NIJ, July 1999).

References

1. Debbie Howlett and Gary Fields, "Cluster of Bombings Touches Off Concerns," *USA Today,* February 4, 1997, p. 3A.

2. Law Enforcement Assistance Administration, *Two Hundred Years of American Criminal Justice* (Washington, D.C.: U.S. Government Printing Office, 1976), p. 31.

3. Ibid.

4. Ibid.

5. Ibid., p. 32.

6. Ibid.

7. David B. Rottman, Carol R. Flango, and R. She-dine Lockley, *State Court Organization 1993* (Washington, D.C.: Bureau of Justice Statistics, 1995), p. 11.

8. Thomas A. Henderson, Cornelium M. Kerwin, Randall Guynes, Carl Baar, Neal Miller, Hildy Saizow, and Robert Grieser, *The Significance of Judicial Structure: The Effects of Unification on Trial Court Operations* (Washington, D.C.: National Institute of Justice, 1984).

9. Ibid.

10. In 1957 only 13 states had permanent intermediate appellate courts. Now, all but 12 states have such a court, and North Dakota is operating one on a temporary basis to assist in handling the ris-ing appellate caseload in that state. See Rottman, Flango, and Lockley, *State Court Organization, 1993,* p. 5.

11. *Keeney, Superintendent, Oregon State Penitentiary* v. *Tamayo-Reyes,* 113 S.Ct. 853, 122 L. Ed. 2d 203 (1993).

12. *Herrera* v. *Collins,* 113 S.Ct. 853, 122 L. Ed. 2d 203 (1993).

13. Some of the wording in this section is taken from "Overview of the Florida State Courts System," on *Joshua,* the Florida court's World Wide Web page on the Internet, August 26, 1997.

14. H. Ted Rubin, *The Courts: Fulcrum of the Justice System* (Pacific Palisades, CA: Goodyear, 1976), p. 200.

15. Ibid., p. 198.

16. Martin Wright, *Justice for Victims and Offenders* (Bristol, PA: Open University Press, 1991), p. 56.

17. Ibid., pp. 104 and 106.

18. Administrative Office of the United States Courts, World Wide Web site, November 2, 2000.

19. Ibid.

20. Some of the materials in this section are adapted from the Administrative Office of the United States Courts, "Courts of Appeals," and "U.S. Court of Appeals for the Federal Circuit," Admin-

istrative Office of the United States Courts, World Wide Web site, July 27, 1995.

21. Stephen L. Wasby, *The Supreme Court in the Federal Judicial System,* 3d ed. (Chicago: Nelson-Hall, 1988), p. 58.

22. *The Supreme Court of the United States* (Washington, D.C.: U.S. Government Printing Office, no date), p. 4.

23. 1 Cranch 137 (1803).

24. *Mapp v. Ohio,* 367 U.S. 643 (1961).

25. Wasby, *The Supreme Court,* pp. 58–59.

26. *Arraignment* is also a term used to describe an initial appearance, although we will reserve use of that word to describe a later court appearance following the defendant's indictment by a grand jury or the filing of an information by the prosecutor.

27. *McNabb v. United States,* 318 U.S. 332 (1943).

28. *County of Riverside v. McLaughlin,* 111 S.Ct. 1661 (1991).

29. *White v. Maryland,* 373 U.S. 59 (1963).

30. *Taylor v. Taintor,* 83 U.S. 66 (1873).

31. National Advisory Commission on Criminal Justice Standards and Goals, *The Courts* (Washington, D.C.: U.S. Government Printing Office, 1973), p. 37.

32. C. Ares, A. Rankin, and H. Sturz, "The Manhattan Bail Project: An Interim Report on the Use of Pre-Trial Parole," *New York University Law Review,* vol. 38 (January 1963), pp. 68–95.

33. H. Zeisel, "Bail Revisited," *American Bar Foundation Research Journal,* vol. 4 (1979), pp. 769–789.

34. Ibid.

35. "12% of Those Freed on Low Bail Fail to Appear," *New York Times,* December 2, 1983, p. 1.

36. Bureau of Justice Statistics, *Report to the Nation on Crime and Justice,* 2nd ed. (Washington, D.C.: U.S. Department of Justice, 1988) p. 76.

37. See Brian A. Reaves, *Felony Defendants in Large Urban Counties, 1994: State Court Processing Statistics* (Washington, D.C.: Bureau of Justice Statistics, 1998); and M. A. Toborg, *Pretrial Release: A National Evaluation of Practice and Outcomes* (McLean, VA: Lazar Institute, 1981).

38. Bureau of Justice Statistics, *Report to the Nation on Crime and Justice,* 2nd ed., p. 77.

39. John Scalia, *Federal Pretrial Release and Detention, 1996* (Washington, D.C.: Bureau of Justice Statistics, 1999).

40. Ibid.

41. Donald E. Pryor and Walter F. Smith, "Significant Research Findings Concerning Pretrial Release," *Pretrial Issues,* vol. 4, no. 1 (Washington, D.C.: Pretrial Services Resource Center, February 1982). See also the Pretrial Services Resource Center on the Web at www.pretrial.org/mainpage.htm. Accessed January 24, 2000.

42. Bureau of Justice Statistics, *Report to the Nation on Crime and Justice,* 2nd ed., p. 77.

43. According to Joseph B. Vaughn and Victor E. Kappeler, the first such legislation was the 1970 District of Columbia Court Reform and Criminal Procedure Act. See: Vaughn and Kappeler, "The Denial of Bail: Pre-Trial Preventive Dention," *Criminal Justice Research Bulletin,* vol. 3, no. 6 (Huntsville, TX: Sam Houston State University, 1987), p. 1.

44. Ibid.

45. Bail Reform Act of 1984, 18 U.S.C. 3142(e).

46. *U.S. v. Montalvo-Murillo,* 495 U.S. 711 (1990).

47. *U.S. v. Montalvo-Murillo* (1990), syllabus.

48. *U.S. v. Hazzard,* 35 CrL 2217 (1984).

49. See, for example, *U.S. v. Motamedi,* 37 CrL 2394, CA 9 (1985).

50. A few states now have laws that permit the defendant to appear before the grand jury.

51. John M. Scheb and John M. Scheb II, *American Criminal Law* (St. Paul, MN: West, 1996), p. 31.

52. Ibid., p. 31.

53. In February 1997, following six months of treatment with antipsychotic drugs, du Pont was found guilty of third-degree murder in the killing of Schultz and sentenced to 13 to 30 years in confinement.

54. *Federal Rules of Criminal Procedure* 5.1(a).

55. John M. Scheb and John M. Scheb II, *American Criminal Law* (St. Paul, MN: West, 1996), p. 32.

56. *Kercheval v. U.S.,* 274 U.S. 220, 223, 47 S.Ct. 582, 583 (1927); *Boykin v. Alabama,* 395 U.S. 238 (1969); and *Dickerson v. New Banner Institute, Inc.,* 460 U.S. 103 (1983).

57. The National Advisory Commission on Criminal Justice Standards and Goals, *Courts* (Washington, D.C.: U.S. Government Printing Office, 1973), p. 46.

58. *Brady v. United States,* 397 U.S. 742 (1970).

59. *Santobello v. New York,* 404 U.S. 257 (1971).

60. Ibid.

61. U.S. Department of Justice, Bureau of Justice Statistics, *The Prosecution of Felony Arrests* (Washington, D.C.: U.S. Government Printing Office, 1983).

62. Barbara Boland, Wayne Logan, Ronald Sones, and William Martin, *The Prosecution of Felony Arrests, 1982* (Washington, D.C.: U.S. Government Printing Office, May 1988).

63. *Henderson v. Morgan,* 426 U.S. 637 (1976).

64. *Santobello v. New York.*

65. *Mabry v. Johnson,* 467 U.S. 504 (1984).

66. *U.S. v. Baldacchino,* 762 F.2d 170 (1st Cir. 1985); *U.S. v. Reardon,* 787 F.2d 512 (10th Cir. 1986); and *U.S. v. Donahey,* 529 F.2d 831 (11th Cir. 1976).

67. For a now classic discussion of such considerations, see David Sudnow, "Normal Crimes: Sociological Features of the Penal Code in a Public Defender Office," *Social Problems,* vol. 12 (1965), p. 255.

68. *Federal Rules of Criminal Procedure,* No. 11.

69. "A Desperate Act," *Prime Time Live,* ABC-News.com, January 28, 1998. Web posted at http://archive.abcnews.go.com/onair/PTL/html_files/transcripts/pt10128c.html. Accessed on July 21, 1999.

70. Dan Rozek, "Castration Doesn't Gain Leniency for Pedophile," *Chicago Sun-Times,* March 4, 1998, News Section.

CHAPTER 8

The Courtroom Work Group and the Criminal Trial

"To hear patiently, to weigh deliberately and dispassionately, and to decide impartially; these are the chief duties of a judge."

—*Albert Pike (1809–1891)*

"A jury consists of 12 persons chosen to decide who has the better lawyer."

—*Robert Frost*

CHAPTER OUTLINE

- Introduction
- The Courtroom Work Group: Professional Courtroom Actors
- Outsiders: Nonprofessional Courtroom Participants
- The Criminal Trial
- Improving the Adjudication Process

—*PictureQuest Vienna.*

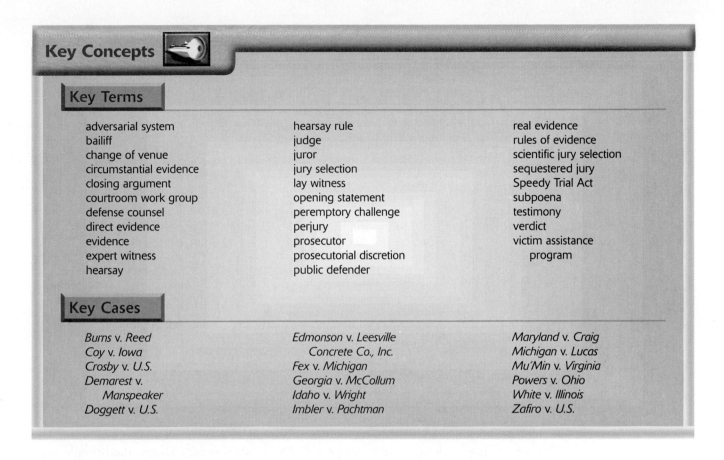

Key Concepts

Key Terms

adversarial system
bailiff
change of venue
circumstantial evidence
closing argument
courtroom work group
defense counsel
direct evidence
evidence
expert witness
hearsay

hearsay rule
judge
juror
jury selection
lay witness
opening statement
peremptory challenge
perjury
prosecutor
prosecutorial discretion
public defender

real evidence
rules of evidence
scientific jury selection
sequestered jury
Speedy Trial Act
subpoena
testimony
verdict
victim assistance
program

Key Cases

Burns v. *Reed*
Coy v. *Iowa*
Crosby v. *U.S.*
Demarest v.
  Manspeaker
Doggett v. *U.S.*

Edmonson v. *Leesville*
  Concrete Co., Inc.
Fex v. *Michigan*
Georgia v. *McCollum*
Idaho v. *Wright*
Imbler v. *Pachtman*

Maryland v. *Craig*
Michigan v. *Lucas*
Mu'Min v. *Virginia*
Powers v. *Ohio*
White v. *Illinois*
Zafiro v. *U.S.*

Introduction

"Every day, as he ambles through the cobwebbed halls of the New Orleans criminal court building, public defender Richard Tessier feels he violates his clients' constitutional rights"[1] to legal counsel. Tessier, an attorney who is paid just $18,500 per year by the state of Louisiana, has so many clients and so few resources he believes that he can't possibly do them all justice. A few years ago, in an effort to bring his plight before the public, Tessier filed suit against his own office. A local judge agreed, finding Louisiana's system of indigent defense unconstitutional. Former Louisiana Governor Edwin Edwards, commenting on the ruling, said that underfunding of public defenders is not limited to New Orleans but is "a state problem and a national problem."[2]

Were it not for people like Richard Tessier, few would be aware of the problems facing our nation's courts. To the public eye, criminal trials generally appear to be well managed and even dramatic events. Like plays on a stage, they involve many participants playing many different roles. Parties to the event can be divided into two categories: "professionals" and "outsiders." The professional category includes official courtroom actors, well versed in criminal trial practice, who set the stage for and conduct the business of the court. Judges, prosecuting attorneys, defense attorneys, public defenders, and others who earn a living serving the court fall into this category. Professional courtroom actors are also called the **courtroom work group.** Some writers[3] have pointed out that, aside from statutory requirements and ethical considerations, courtroom interaction among professionals involves an implicit recognition of informal rules of civility, cooperation, and shared goals. Hence, even within the adversarial framework of a criminal trial, the courtroom work group is dedicated to bringing the procedure to a successful close.[4]

In contrast, outsiders are generally unfamiliar with courtroom organization and trial procedure. Most outsiders visit the court temporarily to provide information or to serve as members of the jury. Similarly, because of their temporary involvement with the court, defendant and victim are also outsiders, even though they may have more of a personal investment in the outcome of the trial than anyone else.

Hear the author discuss this chapter at *cjtoday.com*

Courtroom Work Group

Professional courtroom actors, including judges, prosecuting attorneys, defense attorneys, public defenders, and others who earn a living serving the court.

This chapter continues to examine trial court activities, building upon the pretrial process described in the last chapter. In order to place the trial process within its human context, however, the various roles of the many participants in a criminal trial are first discussed.

The Courtroom Work Group: Professional Courtroom Actors

The Judge

Judge

An elected or appointed public official who presides over a court of law and who is authorized to hear and sometimes to decide cases and to conduct trials.

Role of the Judge

The trial judge is probably the figure most closely associated with a criminal trial. The judge has the primary duty of ensuring justice. The American Bar Association's *Standards for Criminal Justice* describe the duties of a trial judge as follows: "The trial judge has the responsibility for safeguarding both the rights of the accused and the interests of the public in the administration of criminal justice. . . . The only purpose of a criminal trial is to determine whether the prosecution has established the guilt of the accused as required by law, and the trial judge should not allow the proceedings to be used for any other purpose."[5]

In the courtroom, the judge holds ultimate authority, ruling on matters of law, weighing objections from either side, deciding on the admissibility of evidence, and disciplining anyone who challenges the order of the court. In most jurisdictions, judges also sentence offenders after a verdict has been returned, and in some states judges serve to decide guilt or innocence for defendants who waive a jury trial.

Each state jurisdiction normally has a chief judge who, besides serving on the bench as a trial judge, must also manage the court system. Management includes hiring staff, scheduling sessions of court, ensuring the adequate training of subordinate judges, and coordinating activities with other courtroom actors. Chief judges usually assume their positions by virtue of seniority and rarely have any formal training in management. Hence, the managerial effectiveness of a chief judge is often a matter of personality and dedication more than anything else.

"I don't know if I ever want to try another case. I don't know if I ever want to practice law again."

—Christopher Darden, L.A. County assistant prosecutor, expressing frustration over the O. J. Simpson case

Judicial Selection

As we discussed in Chapter 7, judges at the federal level are nominated by the president of the United States and take their place on the bench only after confirmation by the Senate. At the state level, things work somewhat differently. Depending upon the jurisdiction, state judgeships are won either through popular election or political (usually gubernatorial) appointment. The processes involved in judicial selection at the state level are set by law.

Both judicial election and appointment have been criticized for the fact that each system allows politics to enter the judicial arena—although in somewhat different ways. Under the appointment system, judicial hopefuls must be in favor with incumbent politicians in order to receive appointments. Under the elective system, judicial candidates must receive the endorsement of their parties, generate contributions, and manage an effective campaign. Because partisan politics plays a role in both systems, critics have claimed that sitting judges can rarely be as neutral as they should be. They carry to the bench with them campaign promises, personal indebtedness, and possible political agendas.

To counter some of these problems, a number of states have adopted what has come to be called the Missouri Plan[6] (or the "Missouri Bar Plan") for judicial selection. The Missouri Plan combines elements of both election and appointment. It requires judicial vacancies to undergo screening by a nonpartisan state judicial nominating committee. Candidates selected by the committee are reviewed by an arm of the governor's office, which selects a final list of names for appointment. Incumbent judges must face the electorate after a specified term in office. They then run unopposed, in nonpartisan elections, in which only their records may be considered. Voters have the choice of allowing a judge to continue in office or asking that another be appointed to take his or her place. Because the Missouri Plan provides for periodic public review of judicial performance, it is also called the merit plan of judicial selection.

Qualifications of Judges

A few decades ago many states did not require any special training, education, or other qualifications for judges. Anyone (even someone without a law degree) who won election or was appointed could assume a judgeship. Today, however, almost all states require that judges in appellate and general jurisdiction courts hold a law degree, be licensed attorneys, and be members of their state bar associations. Many states also require newly elected judges to attend state-sponsored training sessions dealing with subjects such as courtroom procedure, evidence, dispute resolution, judicial writing, administrative record keeping, and ethics.

While most states provide instruction to meet the needs of trial judges, other organizations also provide specialized training. The National Judicial College, located on the campus of the University of Nevada at Reno, is one such institution. The National Judicial College was established in 1963 by the Joint Committee for the Effective Administration of Justice, chaired by Justice Tom C. Clark of the U.S. Supreme Court.[7] Courses offered by the college have enrolled over 32,000 judges since the College began operation.[8] Visit the National Judicial College via WebExtra! 8-1 at CJToday.com

Lower-court judges, such as justices of the peace, local magistrates, and "district" court judges in some parts of the United States, may still be elected without educational and other professional requirements. Today, in 43 states some 1,300 nonlawyer judges are serving in mostly rural courts of limited jurisdiction.[9] In New York, for example, of the 3,300 judges in the state's unified court system, approximately 65 percent are part-time town or village justices. Approximately 80 percent of town and village justices, comprising about 55 percent of all judges in the state's court system, are not lawyers.[10] The majority of cases which come before New York lay judges involve alleged traffic violations, although they may also include misdemeanors, small claims actions, and some civil cases (of up to $3,000).

Some authors have defended lay judges as being closer to the citizenry in their understanding of justice.[11] Even so, in most jurisdictions the number of lay judges appears to be declining. States which continue to use lay judges in lower courts do require that candidates for judgeships not have criminal records and that most attend special training sessions, if elected.

Illinois Supreme Court Justice James D. Heiple, shown here being "mugged" by the Pekin, Illinois, Police Department, was forced to resign his position as Chief Justice after admitting that he used his office in attempts to evade traffic tickets. Most judges are highly respected members of the criminal justice system. Some, however, overstep the boundaries of judicial propriety, and can be disciplined.
AP/Wide World Photos.

Judicial Misconduct

A June 1997 West Virginia bond hearing took a turn for the worse when Pleasant County Circuit Judge Joseph Troisi allegedly bit defendant Bill Whittens on the nose.[12] The bite, said Whittens, was inflicted after he directed a derogatory remark at the judge. Whittens' nose required medical treatment at a local hospital. Judge Troisi had no comment, and the FBI was called in to investigate.

While most judges are highly professional, in and out of the courtroom, some judges occasionally overstep the limits of their authority. Poor judgment may result from bad taste or archaic attitudes, as in the case of a lower-court judge who repeatedly told a female defense counselor that she was too pretty to be a lawyer and should be at home having children. Other sexist comments resulted in calls for that judge's dismissal. Sexist behavior hasn't been confined to male judges. In 1996, for example, Cleveland Judge Shirley Strickland Saffold caused an outcry among Ohio voters when she told a woman being sentenced for misusing a credit card to "dump your boyfriend, show your legs, and marry a doctor." The judge, who is herself married to a physician, continued, "You can go sit in the bus stop, put on a short skirt, cross your legs, and pick up 25 [men]. Ten of them will give you their money."[13]

All states provide mechanisms for administratively dealing with complaints about judicial conduct. In 1995, for example, Pennsylvania district justice Bradford C. Timbers was suspended by the state's Judicial Conduct Board after being charged with "trying to fix a friend's speeding ticket, slapping a female co-worker's buttocks, and drinking alcohol on the job."[14] In 1997, the chief justice of the Alaska Supreme Court, Allen T. Compton, 59, stepped down from his position after being admonished for sexual harassment. He remains on the court but no longer serves as chief justice. Compton resigned his post as chief justice after receiving a private rebuke from the Alaska Commission on Judicial Conduct, which said that his conduct on two occasions in 1995 and 1996, with two different female court employees, constituted sexual harassment.[15] Also in 1997, 62-year-old Illinois Supreme Court Justice James D. Heiple was forced to resign his position as chief justice after admitting that he used his office in attempts to evade traffic tickets.[16] Although he remains on the court, the Illinois Courts Commission officially censured Heiple for "conduct that is prejudicial to the administration of justice and conduct that brings the judicial office into disrepute."

At the federal level, the Judicial Councils Reform and Judicial Conduct and Disability Act, passed by Congress in 1980, specifies the procedures necessary to register complaints against federal judges and, in serious cases, to begin the process of impeachment—or forced removal from the bench. In 1987, in a rare display of its authority, Walter L. Nixon, Jr., a chief judge of the U.S. District Court for the Southern District of Mississippi, was convicted under the law on two counts of making false statements before a federal grand jury and sentenced to prison.[17] His 1993 appeal to the U.S. Supreme Court was denied.[18]

The Prosecuting Attorney

Prosecutor (also District Attorney)

*An elected or appointed public official, licensed to practice law, whose job it is to conduct criminal proceedings on behalf of the state or the people against an accused person. Also called a **state's attorney**.*

The prosecuting attorney—called variously the "solicitor," "district attorney," "state's attorney," "county attorney," "commonwealth attorney," and so on—is responsible for presenting the state's case against the defendant. Technically speaking, the prosecuting attorney is the primary representative of the people by virtue of the belief that violations of the criminal law are an affront to the public. Except for federal prosecutors (called U.S. attorneys) and solicitors in five states, **prosecutors** are elected and generally serve four-year terms with the possibility of continuing reelection.[19] Widespread criminal conspiracies, whether they involve government officials or private citizens, may require the services of a special prosecutor whose office can spend the time and resources needed for efficient prosecution.[20]

In many jurisdictions, because the job of prosecutor entails too many duties for one person to handle, most prosecutors supervise a staff of assistant district attorneys who do most in-court work. Assistants are trained attorneys, usually hired directly by the chief prosecutor and licensed to practice law in the states where they work. Approximately 2,343 chief prosecutors, assisted by 24,000 deputy attorneys, serve the nation's counties and independent cities.[21]

Another prosecutorial role has traditionally been that of quasi-legal advisor to local police departments. Because prosecutors are sensitive to the kinds of information needed for conviction, they may help guide police investigations and will exhort detectives to identify usable witnesses, uncover additional evidence, and the like. This role is limited, however. Police departments are independent of the administrative authority of the prosecutor and cooperation between them, although based on the common goal of conviction, is purely voluntary.[22]

Once trial begins, the job of the prosecutor is to vigorously present the state's case against the defendant. Prosecutors introduce evidence against the accused, steer the testimony of witnesses "for the people," and argue in favor of conviction. Since defendants are presumed innocent until proven guilty, the burden of demonstrating guilt beyond a reasonable doubt rests with the prosecutor.

Prosecutorial Discretion

Prosecutors occupy a unique position in the nation's criminal justice system by virtue of the considerable discretion they exercise. As Justice Robert H. Jackson noted in 1940, "[T]he prosecutor has more control over life, liberty, and reputation than any other person in America."[23] Before a case comes to trial, prosecutors may decide to accept a plea bargain, divert suspects to a public or private social-service agency, or dismiss the case entirely for lack of evidence or for a variety of other reasons. Various studies have found that from one-third to one-half of all felony cases are dismissed by the prosecution prior to trial or before a plea bargain is made.[24] Prosecutors also play a significant role before grand juries. States which use the grand jury system depend upon prosecutors to bring evidence before the grand jury and to be effective in seeing indictments returned against suspects.

In preparation for trial, the prosecutor decides what charges are to be brought against the defendant, examines the strength of incriminating evidence, and decides what witnesses to call. Two important Supreme Court decisions have held that it is the duty of prosecutors to, in effect, assist the defense in building its case by making available any evidence in their possession. The first case, that of *Brady* v. *Maryland*,[25] was decided in 1963. In *Brady*, the Court held that the prosecution is required to disclose to the defense exculpatory evidence that directly relates to claims of either guilt or innocence. A second, and more recent, case is that of *U.S.* v. *Bagley*,[26] decided in 1985. In *Bagley* the Court ruled that the prosecution must disclose any evidence that the defense requests. The Court reasoned that to withhold evidence, even when it does not relate directly to issues of guilt or innocence, may mislead the defense into thinking that such evidence does not exist.

One special decision the prosecutor makes concerns the filing of separate or multiple charges. The decision to try a defendant simultaneously on multiple charges can allow for the presentation of a considerable amount of evidence and permit an in-court demonstration of a complete sequence of criminal events. Such a strategy has a practical side as well; it saves time and money by substituting one trial for what might otherwise be any number of trials if each charge were to be brought separately before the court. From the prosecutor's point of view, however, trying the charges one at a time carries the advantage of allowing for another trial on a new charge if a not guilty verdict is returned the first time.

The activities of the prosecutor do not end with a finding of guilt or innocence. Following conviction, prosecutors usually are allowed to make sentencing recommendations to the judge. They can be expected to argue that aggravating factors (which we will discuss in Chapter 9, on sentencing), prior criminal record, or especially heinous qualities of the offense in question call for strict punishment. When convicted defendants appeal, prosecutors may need to defend their own actions and to argue, in briefs filed with appellate courts, that convictions were properly obtained. Most jurisdictions also allow prosecutors to make recommendations when defendants they have convicted are being considered for parole or early release from prison.

Until relatively recently, it has generally been held that prosecutors enjoyed much the same kind of immunity against liability in the exercise of their official duties that judges do. The 1976 Supreme Court case of *Imbler* v. *Pachtman*[27] provided the basis for such thinking with its ruling that "state prosecutors are absolutely immune from liability . . . for their con-

"From the moment you walk into the courtroom, you are the defendant's only friend."

—Austin, Texas, defense attorney Michael E. Tigar

Prosecutorial Discretion

The decision-making power of prosecutors, based upon the wide range of choices available to them, in the handling of criminal defendants, the scheduling of cases for trial, the acceptance of bargained pleas, and so on. The most important form of prosecutorial discretion lies in the power to charge, or not to charge, a person with an offense.

CRIME IN THE NEWS

Prosecutor Becomes Abused Girl's Angel

TOWSON, Md.—Prosecutor James Gentry Jr. promised a severely abused teenage girl before he helped send her only close relatives to prison last year that he would never forget her. And he hasn't.

Gentry has set up a trust fund for the girl, 17-year-old Georgia Fisher, whose 9-year-old sister, Rita, died in what Gentry calls the worst abuse case he has seen in his 15 years as an assistant state's attorney and nine years as a Baltimore County police officer.

Georgia barely survived the abuse and was the star witness last year at the trial of her mother, sister and her sister's boyfriend. All three were convicted of murdering Georgia's sister.

Money Will Cover Basic Needs

Gentry, who is the trustee of the fund, said he developed an affinity with Georgia while helping prepare her for the trial.

"She was the kind of little girl that needed a lot of support," Gentry told APBNews.com today. "I told her early on when I was having a difficult time getting her prepared that I would never forget her. I refer to myself as her friend. That's how I see my role. I realize my limitations as far as taking care of her, but, at the very least, I think I can make her life a little better. Maybe with the help of the trust fund she can live a more normal and happy life."

Gentry established the trust fund to help pay for Georgia's medical, educational and housing needs once the county Department of Social Services no longer is responsible for her care.

Remains in Psychiatric Hospital

Georgia is in a locked ward at a Baltimore psychiatric hospital, where she receives treatment and vocational training, but she may be moved to a group home once she turns 18 on Aug. 26, Gentry said. Georgia, who

has learning disabilities, could be in the custody of social services until she turns 21, he said.

"She's done very well," Gentry said. "She's become much happier, much more hopeful, but she still is emotionally scarred and will remain that way the rest of her life."

Georgia has come a long way, though, from the condition she was in when police found her and her younger sister near death on June 27, 1997, in the home in the Baltimore suburb of Woodlawn where the girls lived with their mother, Mary Utley, sister, Rose Fisher, and her boyfriend, Frank Scarpola.

Someone in the family called for an ambulance because Georgia's sister, Rita, was unconscious after supposedly falling down the stairs and hitting her head. The girl was taken to Johns Hopkins Hospital in Baltimore, where she died that day.

"Covered With Bruises"

"The police went to the hospital and they saw the condition of the body and they knew instantly this was not the result of a fall," Gentry said. "Her body was literally—and I say literally—covered with bruises."

Investigators found more than 70 injuries on the 9-year-old girl's body, including bruises, broken ribs and brain injuries, he said. She weighed 47 pounds at the time of her death, which an autopsy showed was caused by starvation and dehydration, Gentry said.

"The photographs we introduced at trial were the most incredible photographs you would ever want to see," Gentry said.

Georgia, who was 15 at the time, was not far from death herself, he said. She weighed 82 pounds and was malnourished, emaciated and bruised. She was in a catatonic state and lay in a fetal position in the hospital.

"The people at the hospital couldn't even talk to her, that's how devastated she was," Gentry said.

Girls Locked in "The Hole"

Months of therapy brought Georgia back to life and allowed her to recount the horrific abuse she and her sister suffered, he said.

Georgia talked about how she and her sister were locked in a basement room the family called "The Hole" for three to five days at a time with no food or water. There was a toilet in the room, and they each would get one cup of water a day.

She talked about her sister's boyfriend, Scarpola, blindfolding and gagging her and telling her afterward it was because she was a bad girl. She told of how Scarpola would take her and her sister into the basement and make them stand at attention while he put on martial-arts gloves and beat them until they fell down. He would then make them get up and beat them some more.

"The family said the reason they did this was they were bad little girls and had to be punished," Gentry said.

Sisters Were Raped, Kicked, Molested

Georgia, who was raped and sexually molested, is particularly haunted by guilt from her sister's death, he said.

The night before Rita died, Scarpola took their toys out of their bedroom and destroyed them because, he told them, they wouldn't need the toys where they were going, Gentry said. He then kicked Rita, causing a large gash on her chin.

He returned several hours later and found the 9-year-old girl picking at the wound. He tied her up, binding her arms to the dresser and her legs to the bed, and told Georgia to sit up all night and watch her younger sister to

(Continued)

CRIME IN THE NEWS

Prosecutor Becomes Abused Girl's Angel

make sure she didn't get loose, Gentry said.

The next morning, Rita was near death. The family placed her in a tub of cold water, but that failed to bring her around.

Scarpola then hit Georgia and told her this was her fault because she was supposed to be watching over her sister.

"The last thing Georgia said to Rita was, 'I love you,'" Gentry said. "That was the last time Georgia ever saw her."

Testimony Led to Murder Conviction

Georgia's testimony was a major factor in the second-degree murder conviction of her mother, sister and sister's

boyfriend in April 1998. Scarpola, 23, is serving 95 years in state prison; her mother, who is in her 50s, is serving 75 years; and her 22-year-old sister is serving 30.

Gentry remains moved by the case.

"This is as bad as it gets, as bad as I've ever seen," said the 48-year-old prosecutor, who is the father of a 22-year-old son. "It probably affected me more than any case I've ever had."

Gentry's supervisor, Deputy State's Attorney Sue Schenning, has high praise for the emotional support he has given Georgia as what Schenning calls a "surrogate parent."

"I think what he's done is amazing," Schenning said. "Hopefully it will mean that her life will be saved and that she'll be able to lead a productive and stable

life and hopefully be able to give love to other people."

Actions Praised

Attorney Michael Smith, who is assisting Gentry with the trust fund, likewise has plaudits for the prosecutor.

"What he's doing is above and beyond the call of duty," Smith said. "He always, from my perspective, takes a strong interest in doing well for the community as a prosecutor, but this is more as a citizen of the community. It's a shame none of us stepped to the plate before him."

Source: *Richard Zitrin, "Prosecutor Becomes Abused Girl's Angel," APB News, May 30, 1999. Reprinted with permission.*

duct in initiating a prosecution and in presenting the State's case." However, the Court, in the 1991 case of *Burns* v. *Reed*,[28] held that "[a] state prosecuting attorney is absolutely immune from liability for damages . . . for participating in a probable cause hearing, but not for giving legal advice to the police." The *Burns* case involved Cathy Burns of Muncie, Indiana, who allegedly shot her sleeping sons while laboring under a multiple-personality disorder. In order to explore the possibility of multiple personality further, the police asked the prosecuting attorney if it would be appropriate for them to hypnotize the defendant. The prosecutor agreed that hypnosis would be a permissible avenue for investigation, and the suspect confessed to the murders while hypnotized. She later alleged in her complaint to the Supreme Court "that [the prosecuting attorney] knew or should have known that hypnotically induced testimony was inadmissible"[29] at trial.

The Abuse of Discretion

Because of the large amount of discretion prosecutors wield, there is considerable potential for them to abuse it. Discretionary decisions not to prosecute friends or political cronies or to accept guilty pleas to drastically reduced charges for personal considerations are always inappropriate and potentially dangerous possibilities. On the other hand, overzealous prosecution by district attorneys seeking heightened visibility in order to support grand political ambitions can be another source of abuse. Administrative decisions, such as case scheduling, which can wreak havoc with the personal lives of defendants and the professional lives of defense attorneys, can also be used by prosecutors to harass defendants into pleading guilty. Some forms of abuse may be unconscious. At least one study suggests that some prosecutors may have a built-in tendency toward leniency where female defendants are concerned, but tend to discriminate against minorities in deciding whether or not to prosecute.[30]

Although the electorate are the final authority to which prosecutors must answer, gross misconduct by prosecutors may be addressed by the state supreme court or by the state attorney general's office. Short of criminal misconduct, however, most of the options available to either the court or the attorney general are limited.

The Prosecutor's Professional Responsibility

As members of the legal profession, prosecutors are subject to the American Bar Association's (ABA) Code of Professional Responsibility. Serious violations of the code may result in a prosecutor being disbarred from the practice of law. The ABA Standard for Criminal Justice 3-1.1 describes the prosecutor's duty this way: "The duty of the prosecutor is to seek justice, not merely to convict." Hence, a prosecutor is barred by the standards of the legal profession from advocating any fact or position which he or she knows is untrue. Prosecutors have a voice in influencing public policy affecting the safety of America's communities through the National District Attorneys Association (NDAA). Visit NDAA via WebExtra! 8-2 at CJToday.com.

Defense Counsel

Role of the Defense Attorney

The defense counsel is a trained lawyer who may specialize in the practice of criminal law. The task of the defense attorney is to represent the accused as soon as possible after arrest and to ensure that the civil rights of the defendant are not violated through processing by the criminal justice system. Other duties of the defense counsel include testing the strength of the prosecution's case, being involved in plea negotiations, and preparing an adequate defense to be used at trial. In the preparation of a defense, criminal lawyers may enlist private detectives, experts, witnesses to the crime, and character witnesses. Some will perform aspects of the role of private detective or of investigator themselves. They will also review relevant court precedents in order to determine what the best defense strategy might be.

Defense preparation may involve intense communications between lawyer and defendant. Such discussions are recognized as privileged communications, which are protected under the umbrella of lawyer-client confidentiality. In other words, lawyers cannot be compelled to reveal information that their clients have confided to them.[31]

If their clients are found guilty, defense attorneys will be involved in arguments at sentencing, may be asked to file an appeal, and will probably counsel the defendants and the defendants' families as to what civil matters (payment of debts, release from contractual obligations, etc.) may need to be arranged after sentence is imposed. Hence, the role of defense attorney encompasses many aspects, including attorney, negotiator, confidant, family and personal counselor, social worker, investigator, and, as we shall see, bill collector.

The Criminal Lawyer

Three major categories of defense attorneys assist criminal defendants in the United States: (1) private attorneys, usually referred to as criminal lawyers; (2) court-appointed counsel; and (3) public defenders.

Private attorneys (also called "retained counsel") either have their own legal practices or work for law firms in which they may be partners or employees. As those who have had to hire defense attorneys know, the fees of private attorneys can be high. Most privately retained criminal lawyers charge in the range of $100 to $200 per hour. Included in their bill is the time it takes to prepare for a case, as well as time spent in the courtroom. High-powered criminal defense attorneys who have established a regional or national reputation for successfully defending their clients can be far more expensive. A few such attorneys, such as Alan Dershowitz, Robert Shapiro, F. Lee Bailey, Johnnie Cochran (who was catapulted to fame during the O. J. Simpson criminal trial), the now-deceased civil-rights attorney William Kunstler, and Stephen Jones (who defended Timothy McVeigh), have become household names by virtue of their association with famous defendants and well-publicized trials. Fees charged by famous criminal defense attorneys can run into the hundreds of thousands of dollars—and sometimes exceed $1 million—for handling just one case!

Defense Counsel (also Defense Attorney)

A licensed trial lawyer hired or appointed to conduct the legal defense of an individual accused of a crime and to represent him or her before a court of law.

"In all criminal prosecutions the accused shall enjoy the right to a speedy and public trial, by an impartial jury . . . and to be informed of the nature and cause of the accusation; to be confronted with the witnesses against him; to have compulsory process for obtaining witnesses in his favor; and to have the assistance of counsel for his defense."

—Sixth Amendment to the U.S. Constitution

No less an authority than Chief Justice of the U.S. Supreme Court, William H. Rehnquist, has complained that the profit motive has turned the practice of law into a business, leaving many lawyers dissatisfied and perhaps less trusted by their clients than was true in the past. At a speech some years ago to Catholic University's graduating law students, Rehnquist noted that "market capitalism has come to dominate the legal profession in a way that it did not a generation ago. . . . Today, the profit margin seems to be writ large in a way that it was not in the past." "[T]he practice of law is today a business where once it was a profession . . . ," said Rehnquist.[32] Even so, the Chief Justice concluded, practicing law is still "the most satisfying way of making a living that I know of."

Although there are many high-priced criminal defense attorneys in the country, Rehnquist's comments were meant to apply mostly to civil attorneys who take a large portion of monetary awards they win for their clients. Few law students actually choose to specialize in criminal law, even though the job of a criminal lawyer may appear glamorous. Those who do often begin their careers immediately following law school, while others seek to gain experience working as assistant district attorneys or assistant public defenders for a number of years before going into private practice. In contrast to criminal lawyers whose names are household words, the collection of fees can be a significant source of difficulty for other defense attorneys. Most defendants are poor. Those who aren't are often reluctant to pay what may seem to them to be an exorbitant fee, and woe be it to the defense attorney whose client is convicted before the fee has been paid! Visit the National Association of Criminal Defense Lawyers (NACDL) via WebExtra! 8-3 at CJToday.com, and the Association of Federal Defense Attorneys (AFDA is at WebExtra! 8-4) to learn more about the practice of criminal law.

Criminal Defense of the Poor. Over 80 percent of all defendants in felony cases depend upon court-appointed attorneys or **public defenders** to represent them.[33] A series of U.S. Supreme Court decisions have guaranteed that defendants unable to pay for private criminal defense attorneys will receive adequate representation at all stages of criminal justice processing.

In *Powell* v. *Alabama* (1932),[34] the Court held that the Fourteenth Amendment required state courts to appoint counsel for defendants in capital cases who were unable to afford their own. In 1938, in *Johnson* v. *Zerbst*,[35] the Court established the right of indigent defendants to receive the assistance of appointed counsel in all criminal proceedings in federal courts. The 1963 case of *Gideon* v. *Wainwright*[36] extended the right to appointed counsel in state courts to all indigent defendants charged with a felony. *Argersinger* v. *Hamlin* (1972)[37] saw the Court require adequate legal representation for anyone facing a potential sentence of imprisonment. Juveniles charged with delinquent acts were granted the right to appointed counsel in the case of *In re Gault* (1967).[38]

States have responded to the federal mandate for indigent defense in a number of ways. Most now use one of three systems to deliver legal services to criminal defendants who are unable to afford their own: (1) court-assigned counsel, (2) public defenders, and (3) contractual arrangements. Most such systems are administered at the county level, although funding arrangements may involve state, county, and municipal monies.

Court-appointed defense attorneys, whose fees are paid at a rate set by the state or local government, comprise the most widely used system of indigent defense. Such defenders, also called "assigned counsel," are usually drawn from a roster of all practicing criminal attorneys within the jurisdiction of the trial court.

One problem with assigned counsel concerns degree of effort. Although most attorneys assigned by the court to indigent defense probably take their jobs seriously, some feel only a loose commitment to their clients. Paying clients, in their eyes, deserve better service and are apt to get it. The most recently available nationwide study of indigent defense systems found that the average cost per case for indigent defense was $223, although the figure varied from a low of $63 in Arkansas to a high of $540 in New Jersey.[39]

The second type of indigent defense, the public defender program (such as the one described in the opening paragraph of this chapter), depends upon full-time salaried staff. Staff members include defense attorneys, defense investigators, and office personnel. Defense investigators gather information in support of the defense effort. They may interview friends, family members, and employers of the accused, with an eye toward effective

Public Defender

An attorney employed by a government agency or subagency, or by a private organization under contract to a unit of government, for the purpose of providing defense services to indigents.

"O Lord, look down upon these the multitudes, and spread strife and dissension, so that this, Thy servant, might prosper."

—*The Lawyer's Prayer (anonymous)*

defense. Public defender programs have become popular in recent years, with approximately 64 percent of counties nationwide now funding them.[40] A 1996 BJS report found that a public defender system is the primary method used to provide indigent counsel for criminal defendants and that 28 percent of state jurisdictions nationwide use public defender programs *exclusively* to provide indigent defense.[41] Critics charge that public defenders, because they are government employees, are not sufficiently independent from prosecutors and judges. For the same reason, clients may be suspicious of public defenders, viewing them as state functionaries. Finally, the huge caseloads typical of public defenders' offices create pressures toward an excessive use of plea bargaining.

A third type of indigent defense, contract attorney programs, arranges with local criminal lawyers to provide for indigent defense on a contractual basis. Individual attorneys, local bar associations, and multipartner law firms may all be used to provide for such arranged services. Contract defense programs are the least widely used form of indigent defense at present, although their numbers are growing.

Critics of the current system of indigent defense point out that the system is woefully underfunded. "In 1990," for example, "states spent $1.3 billion to prosecute individuals, but only $548 million on indigent defense; local governments spent $2.7 billion versus only $788 million; and the federal government $1.6 billion versus $408 million."[42] Overall, only 2.3 percent of monies spent on criminal justice activities goes to pay for indigent defense—an amount many consider too small.[43] As a consequence of such limited funding, many public defender's offices employ what critics call a "plead-'em-and-speed-'em through" strategy, often involving a heavy use of plea bargaining and initial meetings with clients in courtrooms as trials are about to begin. Mary Broderick of the National Legal Aid and Defender Association says, "We aren't being given the same weapons. . . . It's like trying to deal with smart bombs when all you've got is a couple of cap pistols."[44] Proposed enhancements to indigent defense systems are offered by the National Legal Aid and Defender Association (NLADA). You can visit NLADA via WebExtra! 8-5 at CJToday.com.

A heated exchange between prosecutor Marcia Clark and defense attorney F. Lee Bailey during the O. J. Simpson trial. "I do not appreciate being called a liar in any court!" Bailey told the judge. The Simpson trial gave the public a bird's-eye view of the adversarial nature of our criminal justice system.
AFP/Agence France-Presse.

Of course, defendants need not accept any assigned counsel. Defendants who elect to do so may waive their right to an attorney and undertake their own defense—a right held to be inherent in the Sixth Amendment to the U.S. Constitution by the U.S. Supreme Court in the 1975 case of *Faretta* v. *California*.[45] Self-representation is uncommon, however, and only 1 percent of federal inmates and 3 percent of state inmates report having represented themselves.[46] Two famous and relatively recent instances of self-representation can be found in the 1995 trial of Long Island Rail Road commuter train shooter Colin Ferguson (which is discussed later in this chapter), and the trial of Dr. Jack Kevorkian.

Defendants who are not pleased with the lawyer appointed to defend them are in a somewhat different situation. They may request, through the court, that a new lawyer be assigned to represent them (as Timothy McVeigh did following his conviction and death sentence in the Oklahoma bombing case). However, unless there is clear reason for reassignment, such as an obvious personality conflict between defendant and attorney, few judges are likely to honor a request of this sort. Short of obvious difficulties, most judges will trust in the professionalism of appointed counselors.

The Ethics of Defense

As we have discussed, the job of defense counsel at trial is to prepare and offer a vigorous defense on behalf of the accused. A proper defense often involves the presentation of evidence and the examination of witnesses, all of which requires careful thought and planning. Good attorneys, like quality craftspeople everywhere, may find themselves emotionally committed to the outcome of trials in which they are involved. Beyond the immediacy of a given trial, attorneys also realize that their reputations can be influenced by lay perceptions of their performance and that their careers and personal financial success depend upon consistently "winning" in the courtroom.

Theory Into Practice

Gideon v. *Wainwright* and Indigent Defense

Today about three-fourths of state-level criminal defendants and one-half of federal defendants are represented in court by publicly funded counsel.[1] As little as 30 years ago, however, the practice of publicly funded indigent defense was uncommon. That changed in 1963 when, in the case of *Gideon* v. *Wainwright*, the U.S. Supreme Court extended the right to legal counsel to indigent defendants charged with a criminal offense. The reasoning of the Court is well summarized in this excerpt from the majority opinion written by Justice Hugo Black:

> ...Governments, both state and federal, quite properly spend vast sums of money to establish machinery to try defendants accused of crime. Lawyers to prosecute are everywhere deemed essential to protect the public's interest in an orderly society. Similarly, there are few defendants charged with crime, few indeed, who fail to hire the best lawyers they can get to prepare and present their defenses. That government hires lawyers to prosecute and defendants who have the money hire lawyers to defend are the strongest indications of the widespread belief that lawyers in criminal courts are necessities, not luxuries. The right of one charged with crime to counsel may not be deemed fundamental and essential to fair trials in some countries, but it is in ours. From the very beginning, our state and national constitutions and laws have laid great emphasis on procedural and substantive safeguards designed to assure fair trials before impartial tribunals in which every defendant stands equal before the law. This noble ideal cannot be realized if the poor man charged with crime has to face his accusers without a lawyer to assist him.

? QUESTIONS FOR DISCUSSION

1. Do you agree with the Court that all indigent defendants should have the opportunity to have counsel appointed to represent them? Why or why not?

2. What would our system of criminal justice be like if court-appointed attorneys were not available to poor defendants?

[1]Steven K. Smith and Carol J. DeFrances, *Indigent Defense* (Washington, D.C.: Bureau of Justice Statistics, February 1996).

The nature of the adversarial process, fed by the emotions of the participants, conspires with the often privileged and extensive knowledge that defense attorneys have about a case to tempt the professional ethics of some counselors. Because the defense counsel may often know more about the guilt or innocence of the defendant than anyone else prior to trial, the defense role is one which is carefully prescribed by ethical and procedural considerations. Attorneys violate both law and the standards of their own profession if they knowingly misrepresent themselves or their clients.

To help attorneys know what is expected of them, ethical standards abound. Four main groups of standards, each drafted by the American Bar Association, (which you can visit via **WebExtra!** 8-6 at CJToday.com) are especially applicable to defense attorneys:

- ■ *Canons of Professional Ethics*
- ■ *Model Code of Professional Responsibility*
- ■ *Model Rules of Professional Conduct*
- ■ *Standards for Criminal Justice*

Each set of standards is revised periodically. The ABA Standard for Criminal Justice, Number 4-1.2, reads in part:

(e) Defense counsel, in common with all members of the bar, is subject to standards of conduct stated in statutes, rules, decisions of courts, and codes, canons, or other standards of professional conduct. Defense counsel has no duty to execute any directive of the accused which does not comport with law or such standards. Defense counsel is the professional representative of the accused, not the accused's alter ego.

(f) Defense counsel should not intentionally misrepresent matters of fact or law to the court.

(g) Defense counsel should disclose [information] to the tribunal legal authority in the controlling jurisdiction known to defense counsel to be directly adverse to the position of the accused and not disclosed by the prosecutor.

(h) It is the duty of every lawyer to know and be guided by the standards of professional conduct as defined in codes and canons of the legal profession applicable in defense counsel's jurisdiction. Once representation has been undertaken, the functions and duties of defense counsel are the same whether defense counsel is assigned, privately retained, or serving in a legal aid or defender program.

Even with these directives, however, defense attorneys are under no obligation to reveal information obtained from a client without the client's permission. Sometimes, however, they may go too far. In 1992, Minneapolis multimillionaire Russell Lund, Jr., was arrested and charged with the murder of his estranged wife and her boyfriend—a former Iowa state senator. Following the murder, attention shifted to the activities of Lund's attorneys who, police claim, waited until the day after the killings before reporting the shooting, hired a private detective who may have destroyed some evidence, and checked Mr. Lund into a private psychiatric facility under a different name without telling police where he was—all activities which may have been both unethical and illegal.[47]

In 1986, the Supreme Court case of *Nix* v. *Whiteside*[48] clarified the duty of lawyers to reveal known instances of client perjury. The *Nix* case came to the Court upon the complaint of the defendant, Whiteside, who claimed that he was deprived of the assistance of effective counsel during a murder trial because his lawyer would not allow him to testify untruthfully. Whiteside wanted to testify that he had seen a gun or something metallic in his victim's hand before killing him. Before trial, however, Whiteside admitted to his lawyer that he had actually seen no weapon, but he believed that to testify to the truth would result in his conviction. The lawyer told Whiteside that, as a professional counselor, he would be forced to challenge Whiteside's false testimony if it occurred and to explain to the court the facts as he knew them. On the stand, Whiteside said only that he thought the victim was reaching for a gun, but did not claim to have seen one. He was found guilty of second-degree murder and appealed to the Supreme Court, on the claim of inadequate representation.

The Court, recounting the development of ethical codes in the legal profession, held that a lawyer's duty to a client "is limited to legitimate, lawful conduct compatible with the very nature of a trial as a search for truth. . . . Counsel is precluded from taking steps or in any way assisting the client in presenting false evidence or otherwise violating the law."[49]

The Bailiff

Also called a court officer, the **bailiff,** another member of the professional courtroom work group, is usually an armed law enforcement officer. The job of the bailiff is to ensure order in the courtroom, announce the judge's entry into the courtroom, call witnesses, and prevent the escape of the accused (if the accused has not been released on bond). The bailiff also supervises the jury when it is sequestered and controls public and media access to the jury. Bailiffs in federal courtrooms are deputy U.S. marshals.

Courtrooms can be dangerous places. In 1993, George Lott was sentenced to die for a courtroom shooting in Tarrant County, Texas, which left two lawyers dead and three other people injured.[50] Lott said he had been frustrated by the court's handling of his divorce and by child molestation charges filed against him by his ex-wife. In a similar case, on May 5, 1992, a man opened fire with two pistols in a St. Louis courtroom during divorce proceedings, killing his wife and wounding her two lawyers and a security officer. The same day a presiding judge in Grand Forks, North Dakota, was shot to death by a man accused of failing to pay child support.[51] In 1997 a hooded man walked into an Urbana, Illinois, courtroom and lobbed a fire-bomb at a judge. The gas-filled bottle bounced off the judge's head and burst against a wall, setting the courtroom on fire. Three people were injured, and the judge suffered a cut on his head. "There's no court security in our building," explained Champaign County (Illinois) Sheriff Dave Madigan.[52] Following such incidents, most courts initiated the use of metal detectors, and many now require visitors to leave packages, cellular phones, and other objects that might conceal weapons in lockers or to check them with personnel before entering the courtroom.

Local Court Administrators

Many states now employ trial court administrators whose job it is to facilitate the smooth functioning of courts in particular judicial districts or areas. A major impetus toward the hiring of local court administrators came from the 1967 President's Commission on Law Enforcement and Administration of Justice. Examining state courts, the report found: "A system that treats defendants who are charged with minor offenses with less dignity and con-

Bailiff

The court officer whose duties are to keep order in the courtroom and to maintain physical custody of the jury.

Defense attorney Stephen Jones (right), *appointed by the court to defend suspected Oklahoma City bomber Timothy McVeigh* (center). **Stephen Jones, AP/Wide World** Photos.

sideration than it treats those who are charged with serious crimes."[53] A few years later, the National Advisory Commission on Criminal Justice Standards and Goals recommended that all courts with five or more judges should create the position of trial court administrator.[54]

Court administrators provide uniform court management, assuming many of the duties previously performed by chief judges, prosecutors, and court clerks. Where court administrators operate, the ultimate authority for running the court still rests with the chief judge. Administrators, however, are able to relieve the judge of many routine and repetitive tasks, such as record keeping, scheduling, case flow analysis, personnel administration, space utilization, facilities planning, and budget management. They may also serve to take minutes at meetings of judges and their committees.

Juror management is another area in which trial court administrators are becoming increasingly involved. Juror utilization studies can identify such problems as the overselection of citizens for the jury pool and the reasons for what may be excessive requests to be excluded from jury service. They can also reduce the amount of wasted time jurors spend waiting to be called or empanelled.

Effective court administrators are able to track lengthy cases and identify bottlenecks in court processing. They then suggest strategies to make the administration of justice increasingly efficient for courtroom professionals and more humane for lay participants.

The Court Recorder

Also called the court stenographer or court reporter, the role of the recorder is to create a record of all that occurs during trial. Accurate records are very important in criminal trial courts because appeals may be based entirely upon what went on in the courtroom. Especially significant are all verbal comments made in the courtroom, including testimony, objections, the rulings of the judge, the judge's instructions to the jury, arguments made by attorneys, and the results of conferences between the attorneys and the judge. Occasionally, the judge will rule that a statement should be "stricken from the record" because it is inappropriate or unfounded. The official trial record, often taken on a stenotype machine or audio recorder, may later be transcribed in manuscript form and will become the basis for

---

Theory Into Practice

American Bar Association Standards of Professional Responsibility

The intense effort of defense advocacy results, for most criminal trial lawyers, in an emotional and personal investment in the outcome of a case. To strike a balance between zealous and effective advocacy, on the one hand, and just professional conduct within the bounds of the law on the other, the American Bar Association has developed a Code of Professional Responsibility which reads in part:

In his representation of a client, a lawyer shall not:

◆ File a suit, assert a position, conduct a defense, delay a trial, or take other action on behalf of his client when he knows or when it is obvious that such action would serve merely to harass or maliciously injure another.

◆ Knowingly advance a claim or defense that is unwarranted under existing law . . .

◆ Conceal or knowingly fail to disclose that which he is required by law to reveal.

◆ Knowingly use perjured testimony or false evidence.

◆ Knowingly make a false statement of law or fact.

◆ Participate in the creation or preservation of evidence when he knows or it is obvious that the evidence is false.

◆ Counsel or assist his client in conduct that the lawyer knows to be illegal or fraudulent.

Source: *Excerpted from American Bar Association,* Code of Professional Responsibility, *Disciplinary Rule 7-102. Reprinted by permission. All rights reserved. Copies of this publication are available from Service Center, ABA, 750 N. Lakeshore Dr., Chicago, IL 60611.*

any appellate review of the trial. Today's court stenographers often employ computer-aided transcription software (CAT), which translates typed stenographic shorthand into complete and readable transcripts. Court reporters may be members of the National Court Reporters Association, the United States Court Reporters Association, and the Association of Legal Administrators—all of which support the activities of these professionals. You may visit the National Court Reporters Association via **WebExtra!** 8-7 at CJToday.com.

Clerk of Court

The duties of the clerk of court (also known as the county clerk) extend beyond the courtroom. The clerk maintains all records of criminal cases, including all pleas and motions made both before and after the actual trial. The clerk also prepares a jury pool and issues jury summonses and subpoenas witnesses for both the prosecution and defense. During the trial, the clerk (or an assistant) marks physical evidence for identification as instructed by the judge and maintains custody of such evidence. The clerk also swears in witnesses and performs other functions as the judge directs.

Some states allow the clerk limited judicial duties such as the power to issue warrants and to serve as judge of probate—overseeing wills and the administration of estates and handling certain matters relating to persons declared mentally incompetent.[55]

The Expert Witness

Most of the "insiders" we've talked about so far are either employees of the state or have ongoing professional relationships with the court (as in the case of defense counsel). Expert witnesses, however, may or may not have that kind of status, although some do. Expert witnesses are recognized for specialized skills and knowledge in an established profession or technical area. They must demonstrate their expertise through education, work experience, publications, and awards. By testifying at a trial they provide an effective way of introducing scientific evidence in such areas as medicine, psychology, ballistics, crime scene analysis, photography, and many other disciplines. An expert witness, like the other courtroom actors described in this chapter, is generally a paid professional. And, like all other witnesses, they are subject to cross-examination. Unlike other (lay) witnesses, they are allowed to express opinions and draw conclusions, but only within their particular area of expertise. Expert witnesses may be veterans of many trials. Some well-known expert witnesses traverse the country and earn very high fees by testifying at one trial after another.

Expert witnesses have played significant roles in many well-known cases. The 1995 criminal trial of O. J. Simpson, for example, became a stage for a battle between experts in the analysis of human DNA, while expert testimony in the trial of John Hinckley resulted in a finding of "not guilty by reason of insanity" for the man accused of shooting then-President Reagan. Similarly, the highly publicized trial of Susan Smith, the South Carolina mother who confessed to the murder by drowning of her two young children, relied heavily upon the testimony of psychiatric experts and social workers. An important U.S. Supreme Court case addressing the admissibility of expert witness testimony is *Daubert* v. *Merrell Dow Pharmaceuticals* (1993).[56]

One of the difficulties with expert testimony is that it can be confusing to the jury. Sometimes the trouble is due to the nature of the subject matter and sometimes to disagreements between the experts themselves. Often, however, it arises from the strict interpretation given to expert testimony by procedural requirements. The difference between medical and legal definitions of insanity, for example, points to a divergence in both history and purpose between the law and science. Courts which attempt to apply criteria, such as the M'Naghten rule (discussed earlier), in deciding claims of insanity often find themselves faced with the testimony of psychiatric experts who refuse even to recognize the word. Such experts may prefer, instead, to speak in terms of *psychosis* and *neurosis*—words which have no place in judicial jargon. Legal requirements, because of the uncertainties they create, may pit experts against one another and confuse the jury.

Even so, most authorities agree that expert testimony is usually interpreted by jurors as more trustworthy than other forms of evidence. In a study of scientific evidence, one prose-

Expert Witness

A person who has special knowledge and skills recognized by the court as relevant to the determination of guilt or innocence. Expert witnesses may express opinions or draw conclusions in their testimony—unlike lay witnesses.

"If O.J. is so innocent, why are they trying to suppress all the evidence?"

—**Denise Brown**, *Nicole Brown Simpson's sister, commenting on defense efforts to exclude evidence at the murder trial of O. J. Simpson*

cutor commented that if he had to choose between presenting a fingerprint or an eyewitness at trial, he would always go with the fingerprint.[57] As a consequence of the effectiveness of scientific evidence, the National Institute of Justice recommends that "prosecutors consider the potential utility of such information in all cases where such evidence is available."[58] Some authors have called attention to the difficulties surrounding expert testimony. Procedural limitations often severely curtail the kinds of information which experts can provide.

Expert witnesses can earn substantial fees. DNA specialist John Gerdes, for example, was paid $100 per hour for his work in support of the defense in the O. J. Simpson criminal trial, and New York forensic pathologist Michael Baden charged $1,500 per day for time spent working for Simpson in Los Angeles. Baden billed Simpson more than $100,000, and the laboratory for which Gerdes worked received more than $30,000 from Simpson's defense attorneys.[59]

Outsiders: Nonprofessional Courtroom Participants

A number of people find themselves either unwilling or unwitting participants in criminal trials. Into this category fall defendants, victims, and most witnesses. Although they are "outsiders" who lack the status of paid professional participants, these are precisely the people who provide the grist for the judicial mill. Without them, trials could not occur, and the professional roles described earlier would be rendered meaningless.

Lay Witnesses

Lay Witness

An eyewitness, character witness, or any other person called upon to testify who is not considered an expert. Lay witnesses must testify to facts alone and may not draw conclusions or express opinions.

Nonexpert witnesses, otherwise known as lay witnesses, may be called by either the prosecution or defense. Lay witnesses may be eyewitnesses who saw the crime being committed or who came upon the crime scene shortly after the crime had occurred. Another type of lay witness is the character witness, who provides information about the personality, family life, business acumen, and so on of the defendant in an effort to show that this is not the kind of person who would commit the crime he or she is charged with. Of course, the victim may also be a witness, providing detailed and sometimes lengthy testimony about the defendant and the event in question.

Subpoena

An order issued by a court of law requiring an individual to appear in court and to give testimony. Some subpoenas mandate that books, papers, and other items be surrendered to the court.

Witnesses are officially notified that they are to appear in court to testify by a written document called a **subpoena.** Subpoenas are generally "served" by an officer of the court or by a police officer, though they sometimes are mailed. Both sides in a criminal case may subpoena witnesses and might ask that persons called to testify bring with them books, papers, photographs, videotapes, or other forms of physical evidence. Witnesses who fail to appear when summoned may face contempt of court charges.

The job of a witness is to provide accurate testimony concerning only those things of which he or she has direct knowledge. Normally, witnesses will not be allowed to repeat things told to them by others unless it is necessary to do so in order to account for certain actions of their own. Since few witnesses are familiar with courtroom procedure, the task of testifying is fraught with uncertainty and can be traumatizing.

Anyone who testifies in a criminal trial must do so under oath, in which some reference to God is made, or after affirmation,[60] where a pledge to tell the truth is used by those who find either "swearing" or a reference to God objectionable. All witnesses are subject to cross-examination, a process that will be discussed in detail later in this chapter. Lay witnesses may be surprised to find that cross-examination can force them to defend their personal and moral integrity. A cross-examiner may question a witness about past vicious, criminal, or immoral acts, even where such matters have never been the subject of a criminal proceeding.[61] As long as the intent of such questions is to demonstrate to the jury that the witness may not be a person who is worthy of belief, they will normally be permitted by the judge.

Witnesses have traditionally been shortchanged by the judicial process. Subpoenaed to attend court, they have often suffered from frequent and unannounced changes in trial dates. A witness who promptly responds to a summons to appear may find that legal maneuvering has resulted in unanticipated delays. Strategic changes by either side may make the testimony of some witnesses entirely unnecessary, and people who have prepared themselves for the psychological rigors of testifying often experience an emotional letdown.

In order to compensate witnesses for their time, and to make up for lost income, many states pay witnesses for each day that they spend in court. Payments range from $5 to $30 per day,[62] although some states pay nothing at all. In the case of *Demarest* v. *Manspeaker* (1991),[63] the U.S. Supreme Court held that federal prisoners, subpoenaed to testify, are entitled to witness fees just as nonincarcerated witnesses would be.

In another move to make the job of witnesses less onerous, 39 states and the federal government have laws or guidelines requiring that witnesses be notified of scheduling changes and cancellations in criminal proceedings.[64] In 1982 Congress passed the Victim and Witness Protection Act, which required the U.S. attorney general to develop guidelines to assist victims and witnesses in meeting the demands placed upon them by the justice system. A number of **victim assistance programs** (also called victim/witness assistance programs), described shortly, have also taken up a call for the rights of witnesses and are working to make the courtroom experience more manageable.

Jurors

Article III of the U.S. Constitution requires that "[t]he trial of all crimes . . . shall be by jury. . . ." States have the authority to determine the size of criminal trial juries. Most states use juries composed of 12 persons and one or two alternates designated to fill in for jurors who are unable to continue due to accident, illness, or personal emergency. Some states allow for juries smaller than 12, and juries with as few as six members have survived Supreme Court scrutiny.[65]

Jury duty is regarded as a responsibility of citizenship. Other than juveniles and certain job occupants such as police personnel, physicians, members of the armed services on active duty, and emergency services workers, persons called for jury duty must serve unless they can convince a judge that they should be excused for overriding reasons. Aliens, those convicted of a felony, and citizens who have served on a jury within the past two years are excluded from jury service in most jurisdictions.

The names of prospective jurors are often gathered from the tax register, DMV records, or voter registration rolls of a county or municipality. Minimum qualifications for jury service include adulthood, a basic command of spoken English, citizenship, "ordinary intelligence," and local residency. Jurors are also expected to possess their "natural faculties," meaning that they should be able to hear, speak, see, move, and so forth. Some jurisdictions have recently allowed handicapped persons to serve as jurors, although the nature of the evidence to be presented in a case may preclude persons with certain kinds of handicaps from serving.

Ideally, the jury is to be a microcosm of society, reflecting the values, rationality, and common sense of the average person. The U.S. Supreme Court has held that criminal defendants have a right to have their cases heard before a jury of their peers.[66] Ideally, peer juries are those composed of a representative cross section of the community in which the alleged crime has occurred and where the trial is to be held. The idea of a peer jury stems from the Magna Carta's original guarantee of jury trials for "freemen." "Freemen" in England during the thirteenth century, however, were more likely to be of similar mind than is a cross section of Americans today. Hence, although the duty of the jury is to deliberate upon the evidence and, ultimately, determine guilt or innocence, social dynamics may play just as great a role in jury verdicts as do the facts of a case.

In a 1945 case, *Thiel* v. *Southern Pacific Company*,[67] the Supreme Court clarified the concept of a "jury of one's peers" by noting that while it is not necessary for every jury to contain representatives of every conceivable racial, ethnic, religious, gender, and economic group in the community, court officials may not systematically and intentionally exclude any juror solely because of his or her social characteristics.

The Role of the Victim in a Criminal Trial

Not all crimes have clearly identifiable victims. Some, such as murder, do not have victims who survive. Where there is an identifiable surviving victim, however, he or she is often one of the most forgotten people in the courtroom. Although the victim may have been pro-

---

Victim Assistance Program

An organized program which offers services to victims of crime in the areas of crisis intervention and follow-up counseling and which helps victims secure their rights under the law.

Juror

*A member of a jury, selected for jury duty, and required to serve as an arbiter of the facts in a court of law. Jurors are expected to render verdicts of guilt or innocence as to the charges brought against an accused, although they may sometimes fail to do so (as in the case of a **hung jury**).*

"The beauty of the jury is their morality. Tap into it."

—San Francisco defense attorney Tony Serra

The defendant's role can be crucial to the outcome of any trial, especially if he or she takes the stand. Shown here is 19-year-old Louise Woodward, the British "nanny" convicted of second-degree murder in the death of Matthew Eappen, an 8-month-old Massachusetts infant in her care. Although originally sentenced to 15 years in prison after a jury did not believe her testimony, Judge Hiller Zobel ordered her conviction reduced to involuntary manslaughter and resentenced her to the time she had already served in jail.
Jim Bourg, Liaison Agency, Inc.

"I do not know whether the jury is useful to those who are in litigation; but I am certain it is highly beneficial to those who decide the litigation; and I look upon it as one of the most efficacious means for the education of the people which society can employ."

—Alexis de Tocqueville (1835)

foundly affected by the crime itself, and is often emotionally committed to the proceedings and trial outcome, he or she may not even be permitted to participate directly in the trial process. Although a powerful movement to recognize the interests of victims is in full swing in this country (and is discussed in detail in the next chapter), it is still not unusual for crime victims to be totally unaware of the final outcome of a case which intimately concerns them.[68]

Hundreds of years ago the situation surrounding victims was far different. During the early Middle Ages in much of Europe, victims, or their survivors, routinely played a central role in trial proceedings and in sentencing decisions. They testified, examined witnesses, challenged defense contentions, and pleaded with the judge or jury for justice, honor, and often revenge. Sometimes they were even expected to carry out the sentence of the court, by flogging the offender or by releasing the trapdoor used for hangings. This "golden age" of the victim ended with the consolidation of power into the hands of monarchs who declared that vengeance was theirs alone.

Today, victims, like witnesses, experience many hardships as they participate in the criminal court process. Some of the rigors they endure are as follows:

1. Uncertainties as to their role in the criminal justice process
2. A general lack of knowledge about the criminal justice system, courtroom procedure, and legal issues
3. Trial delays which result in frequent travel, missed work, and wasted time
4. Fear of the defendant or of retaliation from the defendant's associates
5. The trauma of testifying and of cross-examination

The trial process itself can make for a bitter experience. If victims take the stand, defense attorneys may test their memory, challenge their veracity, or even suggest that they were somehow responsible for their own victimization. After enduring cross-examination, some victims report feeling as though they, and not the offender, have been portrayed as the criminal to the jury. The difficulties encountered by victims have been compared to a second victimization at the hands of the criminal justice system. Additional information on victims and victim's issues, including victim's assistance programs, is provided in the next chapter.

The Role of the Defendant in a Criminal Trial

Generally, defendants must be present at their trials. Similar to state rules, federal rules of criminal procedure require that a defendant "must be present at every stage of a trial . . . [except that a defendant who] is initially present may . . . be voluntarily absent after the trial has commenced." In *Crosby* v. *U.S.* (1993),[69] the U.S. Supreme Court held that a defendant may not be tried in absentia even if he or she was present at the beginning of a trial where his or her absence is due to escape or failure to appear. In a related issue, *Zafiro* v. *U.S.* (1993)[70] held that, at least in federal courts, defendants charged with similar or related offenses may be tried together—even when their defenses differ substantially.

The majority of criminal defendants are poor, uneducated, and often alienated from the philosophy which undergirds the American justice system. A common view of the defendant in a criminal trial is that of a relatively powerless person at the mercy of judicial mechanisms. Many defendants are just that. However, such an image is often far from the truth. Defendants, especially those who seek an active role in their own defense, choreograph many courtroom activities. Experienced defendants, notably those who are career offenders, may be well versed in courtroom demeanor.

Defendants in criminal trials have a right to represent themselves and need not retain counsel nor accept the assistance of court-appointed attorneys. Such a choice, however, may not be in their best interests. The most famous instance of self-representation in recent years was probably the 1995 trial of Long Island Rail Road commuter train shooter, Colin Ferguson. Ferguson, who rejected both legal advice and in-court assistance from defense attorneys and chose to represent himself during trial, was convicted of killing six passengers and wounding 19 others during a racially motivated shooting rampage in December 1993. Some observers said that Ferguson's performance as defendant turned defense attorney "distressed his court-appointed lawyer-advisers, exacerbated the pain of the victims' family members and turned the courtroom of Nassau County Judge Donald E. Belfi into a theater of the bizarre."[71] Others called it a "sham" and a "circus," but astute observers noted that it set up the possibility for a successful appeal. Following conviction, Ferguson reportedly[72] asked famed defense attorney William M. Kunstler, one of his original lawyers, to file an appeal, focusing on whether Ferguson was mentally fit to represent himself and whether the judge erred in allowing him to do so.

Even without self-representation, every defendant who chooses to do so can substantially influence events in the courtroom. Defendants exercise choice in (1) deciding whether to testify personally, (2) selecting and retaining counsel, (3) planning a defense strategy in coordination with their attorney, (4) deciding what information to provide to (or withhold from) the defense team, (5) deciding what plea to enter, and (6) determining whether to file an appeal, if convicted.

Nevertheless, even the most active defendants suffer from a number of disadvantages. One is the tendency of others to assume that anyone on trial must be guilty. Although a person is "innocent until proven guilty," the very fact that he or she is accused of an offense casts a shadow of suspicion that may foster biases in the minds of jurors and other courtroom actors. Another disadvantage lies in the often-substantial social and cultural differences which separate the offender from the professional courtroom staff. While lawyers and judges tend to identify with upper-middle-class values and lifestyles, few offenders do. The consequences of such a gap between defendant and courtroom staff may be insidious and far reaching.

> "It is the very hardest cases that truly test the system, and this is certainly one of them."
>
> *—American Bar Association President Roberta Cooper Ramo,* commenting on the Oklahoma City bombing case

The Press in the Courtroom

Often overlooked, because they do not have an official role in courtroom proceedings, are spectators and the press. At any given trial both spectators and media representatives may be present in large numbers. Spectators include members of the families of both victim and defendant, friends of either side, and curious onlookers—some of whom are avocational court watchers.

Newswriters, TV reporters, and other members of the press are apt to be present at "spectacular" trials (those involving some especially gruesome aspect or famous personality) and at those in which there is a great deal of community interest. The right of reporters and spectators to be present at a criminal trial is supported by the Sixth Amendment's insistence upon a public trial.

Press reports at all stages of a criminal investigation and trial often create problems for the justice system. Significant pretrial publicity about a case may make it difficult to find jurors who have not already formed an opinion as to the guilt or innocence of the defendant. News reports from the courtroom may influence or confuse nonsequestered jurors who hear them, especially when they contain information brought to the bench, but not heard by the jury.

In the 1976 case of *Nebraska Press Association* v. *Stuart*,[73] the U.S. Supreme Court ruled that trial court judges could not legitimately issue gag orders, preventing the pretrial publication of information about a criminal case, as long as the defendant's right to a fair trial and an impartial jury could be ensured by traditional means.[74] These means include (1) a change of venue, whereby the trial is moved to another jurisdiction less likely to have been exposed to the publicity; (2) trial postponement, which would allow for memories to fade and emotions to cool; and (3) jury selection and screening to eliminate biased persons from the jury pool. In 1986 the Court extended press access to preliminary hearings, which, it said, are "sufficiently like a trial to require public access."[75] In 1993, in the case of *Caribbean International News Corporation* v. *Puerto Rico*,[76] the Court effectively applied that requirement to territories under U.S. control.

Today, members of the press as well as video, television, and still cameras are allowed into most state courtrooms. Thirty-three states allow cameras at most trials,[77] while 15 states substantially restrict the use of cameras. Two states (Mississippi and South Dakota) and the District of Columbia completely prohibit cameras at trial and appellate hearings.[78]

The U.S. Supreme Court has been far less favorably disposed to television coverage than have most state courts. In 1981, a Florida defendant appealed his burglary conviction to the Supreme Court,[79] arguing that the presence of TV cameras at his trial had turned the court into a circus for attorneys and made the proceedings more a sideshow than a trial. The Supreme Court, recognizing that television cameras have an untoward effect upon many people, agreed. In the words of the Court, "Trial courts must be especially vigilant to guard against any impairment of the defendant's right to a verdict based solely upon the evidence and the relevant law."[80]

The Judicial Conference of the United States, the primary policy-making arm of the federal courts, seems to agree with the Justices. A three-year pilot project which allowed television cameras into six U.S. District Courts and two appeals courts on an experimental basis closed on December 31, 1994, when the Conference voted to end the project. The Conference terminated the experiment, ruling that neither still nor video cameras would be allowed into federal courtrooms in the future. Conference members expressed concerns that cameras were a distracting influence and were having a "negative impact on jurors [and] witnesses"[81] by exposing them to possible harm by revealing their identities. Hence, under current policy, television and radio coverage of federal criminal and civil proceedings at both the trial and appellate level is effectively banned. Changes, however, may soon be in the offing. In 1998, the House of Representatives passed legislation that would end the ban on television cameras and microphones in federal courts. The proposed legislation, known as the Sunshine in the Courtroom Act, is part of the Judicial Reform Act which is awaiting further consideration by Congress as this book goes to press.[82]

The Criminal Trial

From arrest through sentencing, the criminal justice process is carefully choreographed. Arresting officers must follow proper procedure in the gathering of evidence and in the arrest and questioning of suspects. Magistrates, prosecutors, jailers, and prison officials are all subject to similar strictures. Nowhere, however, is the criminal justice process more closely circumscribed than at the stage of the criminal trial.

Rules of Evidence

Rules of court which govern the admissibility of evidence at a criminal hearing and trial.

Procedures in a modern courtroom are highly formalized. **Rules of evidence,** which govern the admissibility of evidence, and other procedural guidelines determine the course of a criminal hearing and trial. Rules of evidence are partially based upon tradition. All U.S. jurisdictions, however, have formalized rules of evidence in written form. Criminal trials at the federal level generally adhere to the requirements of *Federal Rules of Evidence.*

Trials are also circumscribed by informal rules and professional expectations. An important component of law school education is the teaching of rules which structure and define appropriate courtroom demeanor. In addition to statutory rules, law students are thoroughly exposed to the ethical standards of their profession as found in American Bar Association standards and other writings.

In the next few pages we will describe the chronology of a criminal trial and comment on some of the widely accepted rules of criminal procedure. Before we begin the description, however, it is good to keep two points in mind. One is that the primary purpose of any criminal trial is the determination of the defendant's guilt or innocence. In this regard it is important to recognize the crucial distinction that scholars make between legal guilt and factual guilt. *Factual guilt* deals with the issue of whether the defendant is actually responsible for the crime of which he or she stands accused. If the defendant "did it," then he or she is, in fact, guilty. Legal guilt is not so clear. *Legal guilt* is established only when the prosecutor presents evidence which is sufficient to convince the judge (where the judge determines the verdict) or jury that the defendant is guilty as charged. The distinction between legal guilt and factual guilt is crucial because it points to the fact that the burden of proof rests with the prosecution, and it indicates the possibility that guilty defendants may, nonetheless, be found not guilty.

The second point to remember is that criminal trials under our system of justice are built around an adversarial system and that central to such a system is the advocacy model. Participating in the adversarial system are advocates for the state (the prosecution or district attorney) and for the defendant (defense counsel, public defender, etc.). The philosophy behind the adversarial system holds that the greatest number of just resolutions in all foreseeable criminal trials will occur when both sides are allowed to argue their cases effectively and vociferously before a fair and impartial jury. The system requires that advocates for both sides do their utmost, within the boundaries set by law and professional ethics, to protect and advance the interests of their clients (that is, the defendant and the state). The advocacy model makes clear that it is not the job of the defense attorney or the prosecution to judge the guilt of any defendant. Hence, even defense attorneys who are convinced that their client is guilty are still exhorted to offer the best possible defense and to counsel their client as effectively as possible.

The **adversarial system** has been criticized by some thinkers who point to fundamental differences between law and science in the way the search for truth is conducted.[83] While proponents of traditional legal procedure accept the belief that truth can best be uncovered through an adversarial process, scientists adhere to a painstaking process of research and replication to acquire knowledge. Most of us would agree that scientific advances in recent years may have made factual issues less difficult to ascertain. For example, some of the new scientific techniques in evidence gathering, such as DNA fingerprinting, are now able to unequivocally link suspects to criminal activity. Whether scientific findings should continue to serve a subservient role to the adversarial process itself is a question now being raised. The ultimate answer will probably be couched in terms of the results either process is able to produce. If the adversarial model results in the acquittal of too many demonstrably guilty people because of legal "technicalities," or the scientific approach inaccurately identifies too many suspects, either could be restricted.

We turn now to a discussion of the steps in a criminal trial. As Figure 8-1 shows, trial chronology consists of eight stages:

Trial initiation

Jury selection

Opening statements

Presentation of evidence

Closing arguments

The judge's charge to the jury

Jury deliberations

The verdict

For purposes of brevity, jury deliberations and the verdict will be discussed jointly. If the defendant is found guilty, a sentence will be imposed by the judge at the conclusion of the trial. Sentencing is discussed in the next chapter.

Adversarial System

The two-sided structure under which American criminal trial courts operate, which pits the prosecution against the defense. In theory, justice is done when the most effective adversary is able to convince the judge or jury that his or her perspective on the case is the correct one.

"From what I see in my courtroom every day, many American juries might as well be using Ouija boards."

—*Judge Harold J. Rothwax*

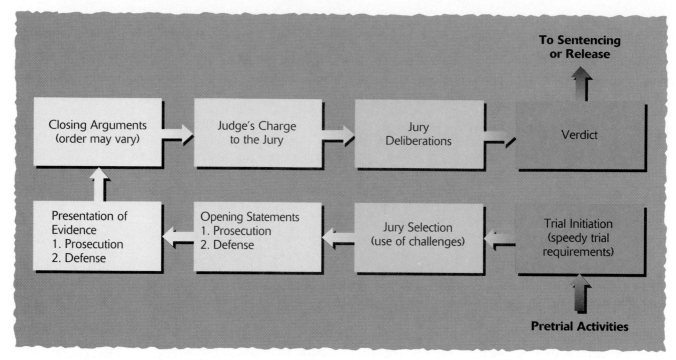

FIGURE 8-1 ■ *Stages in a criminal trial.*

Trial Initiation: The Speedy Trial Act

Speedy Trial Act

A 1974 federal law requiring that proceedings in a criminal case against a defendant begin before passage of a specified period of time, such as 70 working days after indictment. Many states also have speedy trial requirements.

As we mentioned in Chapter 7, the Sixth Amendment to the U.S. Constitution guarantees that "[i]n all criminal prosecutions, the accused shall enjoy the right to a speedy and public trial." Clogged court calendars, limited judicial resources, and general inefficiency, however, often combine to produce what appears to many to be unreasonable delays in trial initiation. The attention of the Supreme Court was brought to bear on trial delays in three precedent-setting cases: *Klopfer* v. *North Carolina* (1967),[84] *Baker* v. *Wingo* (1972),[85] and *Strunk* v. *United States* (1973).[86] The *Klopfer* case involved a Duke University professor and focused on civil disobedience in a protest against segregated facilities. In Klopfer's long-delayed trial, the Court asserted that the right to a speedy trial is a fundamental guarantee of the Constitution. In the *Baker* case, the Court held that Sixth Amendment guarantees to a quick trial could be illegally violated even in cases where the accused did not explicitly object to delays. In *Strunk,* it found that denial of a speedy trial should result in a dismissal of all charges.

In 1974, against the advice of the Justice Department, the U.S. Congress passed the federal Speedy Trial Act.[87] The act, which was phased in gradually and became fully effective in 1980, allows for the dismissal of federal criminal charges in cases where the prosecution does not seek an indictment or information within 30 days of arrest (a 30-day extension is granted when the grand jury is not in session) or where a trial does not begin within 70 working days after indictment for defendants who plead not guilty. If a defendant is not available for trial, or witnesses cannot be called within the 70-day limit, the period may be extended to 180 days. Delays brought about by the defendant, through requests for a continuance or because of escape, are not counted in the specified time periods. The Speedy Trial Act has been condemned by some as shortsighted. One federal judge, for example, wrote: "The ability of the criminal justice system to operate effectively and efficiently has been severely impeded by the Speedy Trial Act. Resources are misdirected, unnecessary severances required, cases proceed to trial inadequately prepared, and in some indeterminate number of cases, indictments against guilty persons are dismissed."[88]

In an important 1988 decision, *U.S.* v. *Taylor,*[89] the U.S. Supreme Court applied the requirements of the Speedy Trial Act to the case of a drug defendant who had escaped following arrest. The Court made it clear that trial delays, when they derive from the willful actions of the defendant, do not apply to the 70-day period. The Court also held that trial delays, even when they result from government action, do not necessarily provide grounds for dismissal if they occur "without prejudice." Delays without prejudice are those which are due to circumstances beyond the control of criminal justice agencies.

In 1993, an Indiana prisoner, William Fex, appealed a Michigan conviction on armed robbery and attempted murder charges, claiming that he had to wait 196 days after submitting a request to Indiana prison authorities for his Michigan trial to commence. In *Fex* v. *Michigan* (1993),[90] the U.S. Supreme Court ruled that "commonsense compel[s] the conclusion that the 180-day period does not commence until the prisoner's disposition request has actually been delivered to the court and prosecutor of the jurisdiction that lodged the detainer against him." In Fex's case, Indiana authorities had taken 22 days to forward his request to Michigan.

However, in a 1992 case, *Doggett* v. *U.S.*,[91] the Court held that a delay of eight and one-half years violated speedy trial provisions because it resulted from government negligence. In *Doggett,* the defendant was indicted on a drug charge in 1980, but left the country for Panama, where he lived until 1982 when he reentered the United States. He lived openly in the United States until 1988 when a credit check revealed him to authorities. He was arrested, tried, and convicted of federal drug charges stemming from his 1980 indictment. In overturning his conviction, the U.S. Supreme Court ruled: ". . . even delay occasioned by the Government's negligence creates prejudice that compounds over time, and at some point, as here, becomes intolerable."[92]

The federal Speedy Trial Act is applicable only to federal courts. However, the *Klopfer* case (just discussed) effectively made constitutional guarantees of a speedy trial applicable to state courts. In keeping with the trend toward reduced delays, many states have since enacted their own speedy trial legislation. Typical state legislation sets limits of 120 or 90 days as a reasonable period of time for a trial to commence.

Jury Selection

As we mentioned in our discussion of the role of the jury in a criminal trial, the Sixth Amendment also guarantees the right to an impartial jury. An impartial jury is not necessarily an ignorant one. In other words, jurors will not always be excused from service on a jury if they have some knowledge of the case which is before them.[93] Jurors, however, who have already formed an opinion as to the guilt or innocence of a defendant are likely to be excused.

Anyone who has ever been called as a juror knows that some prospective jurors try to get excused and others who would like to serve are excused because they are not judged to be suitable. Prosecution and defense attorneys use challenges to ensure the impartiality of the jury which is being empanelled. Three types of challenges are recognized in criminal courts: (1) challenges to the array, (2) challenges for cause, and (3) **peremptory challenges.**

Challenges to the array signify the belief, generally by the defense attorney, that the pool from which potential jurors are to be selected is not representative of the community or is biased in some significant way. A challenge to the array is argued before the hearing judge before jury selection begins.

During the jury selection process, both prosecution and defense attorneys question potential jurors in a process known as *voir dire* examination. Jurors are expected to be unbiased and free of preconceived notions of guilt or innocence. Challenges for cause, which may arise during *voir dire* examination, make the claim that an individual juror cannot be fair or impartial. One special issue of juror objectivity has concerned the Supreme Court. It is whether jurors with philosophical opposition to the death penalty should be excluded from juries whose decisions might result in the imposition of capital punishment. In the case of *Witherspoon* v. *Illinois* (1968),[94] the Court ruled that a juror opposed to the death penalty could be excluded from such juries if it were shown that (1) the juror would automatically vote against conviction without regard to the evidence or (2) the juror's philosophical orientation would prevent an objective consideration of the evidence. The *Witherspoon* case has left unresolved a number of issues, among them the concern that it is difficult to demonstrate how a juror would automatically vote, a fact which may not even be known to the juror before trial begins.

"In suits at common law . . . the right of trial by jury shall be preserved, and no fact tried by a jury shall be otherwise reexamined in any court of the United States, than according to the rules of the common law."

—Seventh Amendment to the U.S. Constitution

Jury Selection

The process whereby, according to law and precedent, members of a particular trial jury are chosen.

Peremptory Challenge

A means of removing unwanted potential jurors without the need to show cause for their removal. Prosecutors and defense attorneys routinely use peremptory challenges in order to eliminate from juries individuals who, although they express no obvious bias, may be thought to hold the potential to sway the jury in an undesirable direction.

Another area of concern which has been addressed by the Supreme Court involves the potential that jurors may be biased because of being exposed to stories about a case in the news media that appear before the start of trial. Such concerns provided an especially tricky issue for Judge Lance Ito during the double-murder trial of O. J. Simpson as Ito supervised the process of jury selection. A similar, but far less well known case which has been reviewed by the Court is that of *Mu'Min* v. *Virginia* (1991).[95] Mu'Min was a Virginia inmate who was serving time for first-degree murder. While accompanying a work detail outside of the institution, he committed another murder. At the ensuing trial, 8 of the 12 jurors who were seated admitted that they had heard or read something about the case, although none indicated that he or she had formed an opinion in advance as to Mu'Min's guilt or innocence. Following his conviction, Mu'Min appealed to the Supreme Court, claiming that his right to a fair trial had been denied due to pretrial publicity. The Court disagreed and upheld his conviction, citing the admittedly unbiased nature of the jurors.

The third kind of challenge, the peremptory challenge, effectively removes potential jurors without the need to give a reason. Peremptory challenges, used by both the prosecution and defense, are limited in number. Federal courts allow each side up to 20 peremptory challenges in capital cases and as few as three in minor criminal cases.[96] States vary as to the number of peremptory challenges they permit.

A developing field, which seeks to take advantage of peremptory challenges, is scientific jury selection. **Scientific jury selection** uses correlational techniques from the social sciences to gauge the likelihood that potential jurors will vote for conviction or acquittal. It makes predictions based on the economic, ethnic, and other personal and social characteristics of each member of the juror pool. Intentional jury selection techniques appeared to play a significant role in the outcome of the trial of Larry Davis. Davis, who is black, was charged with the 1986 shooting of seven white New York City police officers as they attempted to arrest the heavily armed defendant for the alleged murder of four drug dealers.[97] None of the officers died, and Davis was later apprehended. At the trial, defense attorney William Kunstler assembled a jury of 10 blacks and two Hispanics. On two occasions Judge Bernard Fried had dismissed previous juries before the trial could begin, saying that Kunstler was packing the panel with blacks.[98] Although many of the wounded officers testified against Davis, and no one seriously disputed the contention that Davis was the triggerman in the shooting of the officers, the jury found him innocent. The finding prompted one of the injured policemen to claim, "It was a racist verdict."[99] Explaining the jury's decision another way, a spokesperson for the NAACP Legal Defense Fund said after the trial, "The experience of blacks in the criminal justice system may make them less prone to accept the word of a police officer."[100]

Criticisms of jury selection techniques have focused on the end result of the process. Such techniques generally remove potential jurors who have any knowledge or opinions about the case to be tried. Also removed are persons trained in the law or in criminal justice. Anyone working for a criminal justice agency or anyone who has a family member working for such an agency or for a defense attorney will likely be dismissed through peremptory challenges on the chance that they may be biased in favor of one side or the other. Scientific jury selection techniques may result in the additional dismissal of educated or professionally successful individuals, to eliminate the possibility of such individuals exercising undue control over jury deliberations. The end result of the jury selection process may be to produce a jury composed of people who are uneducated, uninformed, and generally inexperienced at making any type of well-considered decision. Some of the jurors may not understand the charges against the defendant or comprehend what is required for a finding of guilt or innocence. Likewise, some selected jurors may not even possess the span of attention needed to hear all the testimony that will be offered in a case. As a consequence, decisions rendered by such a jury may be based more upon emotion than upon findings of fact.

Jury Selection and Race

Juries intentionally selected so that they are racially unbalanced may soon be a thing of the past. As long ago as 1880, the U.S. Supreme Court held that "a statute barring blacks from service on grand or petit juries denied equal protection of the laws to a black man convicted of murder by an all-white jury."[101] Even so, peremptory challenges continued to tend to lead

---

Scientific Jury Selection

The use of correlational techniques from the social sciences to gauge the likelihood that potential jurors will vote for conviction or acquittal.

to racial imbalance. In 1965, for example, a black defendant in Alabama was convicted of rape by an all-white jury. The local prosecutor had used his peremptory challenges to exclude blacks from the jury. The case eventually reached the Supreme Court, where the conviction was upheld.[102] At that time, the Court refused to limit the practice of peremptory challenges, reasoning that to do so would place them under the same judicial scrutiny as challenges for cause.

However, in 1986, following what many claimed were widespread abuses of peremptory challenges by prosecution and defense alike, the Supreme Court was forced to overrule its earlier decision. It did so in the case of *Batson* v. *Kentucky.*[103] Batson, a black man, had been convicted of second-degree burglary and other offenses by an all-white jury. The prosecutor had used his peremptory challenges to remove all blacks from jury service at the trial. The Court agreed that the use of peremptory challenges for apparently purposeful discrimination constitutes a violation of the defendant's right to an impartial jury.

The *Batson* decision laid out the requirements that defendants seeking to establish the discriminatory use of peremptory challenges must prove. They include the need to prove that the defendant is a member of a recognized racial group which has been intentionally excluded from the jury and the need to raise a reasonable suspicion that the prosecutor used peremptory challenges in a discriminatory manner. Justice Thurgood Marshall, writing a concurring opinion in *Batson,* presaged what was to come: "The inherent potential of peremptory challenges to destroy the jury process," he wrote, "by permitting the exclusion of jurors on racial grounds should ideally lead the Court to ban them entirely from the criminal justice system."

A few years later, in *Ford* v. *Georgia* (1991),[104] the Court moved much closer to Justice Marshall's position when it remanded a case for a new trial based upon the fact that the prosecutor had used peremptory challenges to remove potential minority jurors. Nine of the 10 peremptory challenges available to the prosecutor under Georgia law had been used to eliminate prospective black jurors. Following his conviction on charges of kidnapping, raping, and murdering a white woman, the black defendant, James Ford, argued that the prosecutor had demonstrated a systematic and historical racial bias in other cases as well as his own. Specifically, Ford argued that his Sixth Amendment right to an impartial jury had been violated by the prosecutor's racially based method of jury selection. His defense attorney's written appeal to the Supreme Court made the claim, "The exclusion of members of the black race in the jury when a black accused is being tried is done in order that the accused will receive excessive punishment if found guilty, or to inject racial prejudice into the fact finding process of the jury."[105] While the Court did not find a basis for such a Sixth Amendment claim, it did determine that the civil rights of the jurors themselves were violated under the Fourteenth Amendment due to a pattern of discrimination based on race.

In another 1991 case, *Powers* v. *Ohio*[106] (see "Theory Into Practice" Box on Peremptory Challenges and Race in this chapter), the Court found in favor of a white defendant who claimed that his constitutional rights were violated by the intentional exclusion of blacks from his jury through the use of peremptory challenges. In *Powers*, the Court held that "[a]lthough an individual juror does not have the right to sit on any particular petit jury, he or she does possess the right not to be excluded from one on account of race." In a civil case with significance for the criminal justice system, the Court held in *Edmonson* v. *Leesville Concrete Co., Inc.* (1991)[107] that peremptory challenges in *civil* suits were not acceptable if based upon race: "The importance of [*Edmonson*] lies in the Court's significant expansion of the scope of state action—the traditionally held doctrine that private attorneys are immune to constitutional requirements because they do not represent the government." Justice Anthony Kennedy, writing for the majority, said that race-based juror exclusions are forbidden in civil lawsuits because jury selection is a "unique governmental function delegated to private litigants" in a public courtroom.

In the 1992 case of *Georgia* v. *McCollum,*[108] the Court barred defendants and their attorneys from using peremptory challenges to exclude potential jurors on the basis of race. In *McCollum*, Justice Harry Blackmun writing for the majority said, "Be it at the hands of the state or defense, if a court allows jurors to be excluded because of group bias, it is a willing participant in a scheme that could only undermine the very foundation of our system of justice—our citizen's confidence in it." Soon thereafter, peremptory challenges based upon gen-

"[N]inety-five percent of the time, the only black thing a black defendant sees in the courtroom is the judge's robe."

—*Delano Stewart, former chairman, Florida chapter of the National Bar Association*

"The highest act of citizenship is jury service."

—*Abraham Lincoln*

der were similarly restricted (*J.E.B.* v. *Alabama*, 1994), although at the time of this writing the Court has refused to ban peremptory challenges which exclude jurors because of religious or sexual orientation.[109] Also, in 1996 the Court refused "to review whether potential jurors can be stricken from a trial panel because they are too fat."[110] The case involved Luis Santiago-Martinez, a drug defendant whose lawyer objected to the prosecution's use of peremptory challenges "because the government," he said, "had used such strikes to discriminate against the handicapped, specifically the obese." The attorney, who was himself obese, claimed that thin jurors might have been unfairly biased against his arguments.

Finally, in the 1998 case of *Campbell* v. *Louisiana*,[111] the Court held that a white criminal defendant can raise equal protection and due process objections to discrimination against black persons in the selection of *grand jurors*. Campbell, who was white, objected to an apparent pattern of discrimination in the selection of grand jury forepersons. The foreperson of the Evangeline Parish, Louisiana, grand jury that heard second-degree murder charges against him (in the killing of another white man) was white, as had been all such forepersons for the last 16 years. The Supreme Court reasoned that "regardless of skin color, an accused suffers a significant 'injury in fact' when the grand jury's composition is tainted by racial discrimination . . ." and, "The integrity of the body's decisions depends on the integrity of the process used to select the grand jurors."

After wrangling over jury selection has run its course, the jury is sworn in and alternates are selected. At this point the judge will decide whether the jury is to be sequestered during the trial. Members of **sequestered juries,** like those in the O. J. Simpson criminal trial, are not permitted to have contact with the public and are often housed in a motel or hotel until completion of the trial. Anyone who attempts to contact a sequestered jury or to influence members of a nonsequestered juror may be held accountable for jury tampering. Following jury selection, the stage is set for opening arguments[112] to begin.

Sequestered Jury

One which is isolated from the public during the course of a trial and throughout the deliberation process.

Opening Statement

The initial statement of an attorney (or of a defendant representing himself or herself) made in a court of law to a judge, or to a judge and jury, describing the facts that he or she intends to present during trial in order to prove his or her case.

Opening Statements

The presentation of information to the jury begins with opening statements made by the prosecution and defense. The purpose of opening statements is to advise the jury of what the attorneys intend to prove and to describe how such proof will be offered. Evidence is not itself offered during opening statements. Eventually, however, the jury will have to weigh the evidence presented during trial and decide between the effectiveness of the arguments made by both sides. When a defendant has little evidence to present, the main job of the defense attorney will be to dispute the veracity of the prosecution's version of the facts. Under such circumstances, defense attorneys may choose not to present any evidence or testimony at all, focusing instead on the burden of proof requirement facing the prosecution. Such plans will generally be made clear during opening statements. At this time the defense attorney is also

This pen-and-ink drawing depicts one of the first jury trials on which both blacks and whites served. Circa 1867. **Courtesy of the Library of Congress.**

Theory Into Practice

Pre- and Posttrial Motions

A *motion* is defined by the *Dictionary of Criminal Justice Data Terminology*[1] as "[a]n oral or written request made to a court at any time before, during, or after court proceedings, asking the court to make a specified finding, decision, or order." Written motions are called petitions. This box lists the typical kinds of motions that may be made by both sides in a criminal case before and after trial.

Motion for Discovery

A motion for discovery, filed by the defense, asks the court to allow the defendant's lawyers to view the evidence which the prosecution intends to present at trial. Physical evidence, lists of witnesses, documents, photographs, and so on, which the prosecution plans to introduce in court, will usually be made available to the defense as a result of such a motion.

Motion to Suppress Evidence

In the preliminary hearing, or through pretrial discovery, the defense may learn of evidence which the prosecution intends to introduce at the trial. If some of that evidence has been, in the opinion of the defense counsel, unlawfully acquired, a motion to suppress the evidence may be filed.

Motion to Dismiss Charges

A variety of circumstances may result in the filing of a motion to dismiss. They include (1) an opinion, by defense counsel, that the indictment or information is not sound; (2) violations of speedy trial legislation; (3) a plea bargain with the defendant (which may require testimony against codefendants); (4) the death of an important witness or the destruction or disappearance of necessary evidence; (5) the confession, by a supposed victim, that the facts in the case have been fabricated; and (6) the success of a motion to suppress evidence which

effectively eliminates the prosecution's case.

Motion for Continuance

This motion seeks a delay in the start of the trial. Defense motions for continuance are often based upon the inability to locate important witnesses, the illness of the defendant, or a change in defense counsel immediately prior to trial.

Motion for Change of Venue

In well-known cases, pretrial publicity may lessen the opportunity for a case to be tried before an unbiased jury. A motion for a **change of venue** asks that the trial be moved to some other area where prejudice against the defendant is less likely to exist.

Motion for Severance of Offenses

Defendants charged with a number of crimes may ask to be tried separately on all or some of the charges. Although consolidating charges for trial saves time and money, some defendants may think that it is more likely to make them appear guilty.

Motion for Severance of Defendants

Similar to the preceding motion, this request asks the court to try the accused separately from any codefendants. Motions for severance are likely to be filed where the defendant believes that the jury may be prejudiced against him or her by evidence applicable only to other defendants.

Motion to Determine Present Sanity

Present sanity, even though it may be no defense against the criminal charge, can delay trial. A person cannot be tried, sentenced, or punished while insane. If a defendant is insane at the time a trial is to begin, this motion may halt the proceedings until treatment can be arranged.

Motion for a Bill of Particulars

This motion asks the court to order the prosecutor to provide detailed information about the charges which the defendant will be facing in court. Defendants charged with a number of offenses, or with a number of counts of the same offense, may make such a motion. They may, for example, seek to learn which alleged instances of an offense will become the basis for prosecution or which specific items of contraband allegedly found in their possession are held to violate the law.

Motion for a Mistrial

A mistrial may be declared at any time, and a motion for mistrial may be made by either side. Mistrials are likely to be declared where highly prejudicial comments are made by either attorney. Defense motions for a mistrial do not provide grounds for a later claim of double jeopardy.

Motion for Arrest of Judgment

After the verdict of the jury has been announced, but before sentencing, the defendant may make a motion for arrest of judgment. Such a motion means the defendant believes that some legally acceptable reason exists as to why sentencing should not occur. Defendants who are seriously ill, hospitalized, or who have gone insane prior to judgment being imposed may file such a motion.

Motion for a New Trial

After a jury has returned a guilty verdict, a defense motion for a new trial may be entertained by the court. Acceptance of such a motion is most often based upon the discovery of new evidence which is of significant benefit to the defense, and will set aside the conviction.

[1]U.S. Department of Justice, *Dictionary of Criminal Justice Data Terminology,* 2nd ed. (Washington, D.C.: U.S. Government Printing Office, 1982).

Change of Venue

The movement of a suit or trial from one jurisdiction to another or from one location to another within the same jurisdiction. A change of venue may be made in a criminal case to assure the defendant a fair trial.

likely to stress the human qualities of the defendant and to remind jurors of the awesome significance of their task.

Lawyers for both sides are bound by a "good faith" ethical requirement in their opening statements. That requirement limits the content of such statements to mentioning only that evidence which the attorneys actually believe can and will be presented as the trial progresses. Allusions to evidence which an attorney has no intention of offering are regarded as unprofessional and have been defined as "professional misconduct" by the Supreme Court.[113] When material alluded to in an opening statement cannot, for whatever reason, later be presented in court, it may offer opposing counsel an opportunity to discredit the other side.

The Presentation of Evidence

The crux of the criminal trial is the presentation of evidence. The state is first given the opportunity to present evidence intended to prove the defendant's guilt. After prosecutors have rested their case, the defense is afforded the opportunity to provide evidence favorable to the defendant.

Evidence is of two types: direct and circumstantial. **Direct evidence** is that which, if believed by the judge or jury, proves a fact without needing to draw inferences. Direct evidence may consist, for example, of the information contained on a photograph or videotape. It might also consist of testimonial evidence provided by a witness on the stand. A straightforward statement by a witness, such as "I saw him do it!" is a form of direct evidence.

Evidence

Anything useful to a judge or jury in deciding the facts of a case. Evidence may take the form of witness testimony, written documents, videotapes, magnetic media, photographs, physical objects, and so on.

Circumstantial evidence is indirect. It requires the judge or jury to make inferences and draw conclusions. At a murder trial, for example, a person who heard gunshots and moments later saw someone run by with a smoking gun in hand might testify to those facts. Even though there may have been no eyewitness to the actual homicide, the jury might later conclude that the person seen with the gun was the one who pulled the trigger and committed the homicide. Contrary to popular belief, circumstantial evidence is sufficient to produce a verdict and conviction in a criminal trial. In fact, some prosecuting attorneys claim to prefer working entirely with circumstantial evidence, weaving a tapestry of the criminal act in their arguments to the jury.

Direct Evidence

Evidence which, if believed, directly proves a fact. Eyewitness testimony (and, more recently, videotaped documentation) account for the majority of all direct evidence heard in the criminal courtroom.

Real evidence consists of physical material or traces of physical activity. Weapons, tire tracks, ransom notes, and fingerprints all fall into the category of physical evidence. Real or physical evidence is introduced into the trial process by means of exhibits. *Exhibits* are objects or displays which, once formally accepted as evidence by the judge, may be shown to members of the jury. *Documentary evidence* is another type of real evidence that includes writings such as business records, journals, written confessions, and letters. Documentary evidence can extend beyond paper and ink to include magnetic and optical storage devices used in computer operations and video and voice recordings.

Circumstantial Evidence

Evidence which requires interpretation or which requires a judge or jury to reach a conclusion based upon what the evidence indicates. From the close proximity of a smoking gun to the defendant, for example, the jury might conclude that she pulled the trigger.

One of the most significant decisions a trial court judge makes is deciding what evidence can be presented to the jury. In making that decision, judges will examine the relevance of the information in question to the case at hand. Relevant evidence is that which has a bearing on the facts at issue. For example, a decade or two ago, it was not unusual for a woman's sexual history to be brought out in rape trials. Under "rape shield statutes," most states today will not allow such a practice, recognizing that these details often have no bearing on the case. Rape shield statutes have been strengthened by recent U.S. Supreme Court decisions, including the 1991 case of *Michigan* v. *Lucas*.[114] In this case, the defendant, Lucas, had been charged with criminal sexual conduct involving his ex-girlfriend. Lucas had forced the woman into his apartment at knifepoint, beat her, and forced her to engage in several nonconsensual sex acts. At his trial, Lucas asked to have evidence introduced demonstrating that a prior sexual relationship had existed between the two. At the time, however, Michigan law required that a written motion to use such information had to be made within 10 days following arraignment—a condition Lucas failed to meet. Lucas was convicted and sentenced to a term of from 44 to 180 months in prison, but appealed his conviction, claiming that the Sixth Amendment to the U.S. Constitution guaranteed him the right to confront witnesses against him. The U.S. Supreme Court disagreed, however, and ruled that the Sixth Amendment guarantee does not necessarily extend to evidence of a prior sexual relationship between a rape victim and a criminal defendant.

Real Evidence

Evidence consisting of physical material or traces of physical activity.

Theory Into Practice

Peremptory Challenges and Race

"[A] peremptory challenge to a juror means that one side in a trial has been given the right to throw out a certain number of possible jurors before the trial without giving any reasons."[1]

Historically, as the definition—borrowed from a legal dictionary—indicates, attorneys had been able to remove unwanted potential jurors from a criminal case during jury selection procedures through the use of a limited number of peremptory challenges without having to provide any reason whatsoever for the choices they made. (Challenges for cause, on the other hand, although not limited in number, require an acceptable rationale for juror removal.) The understanding of peremptory challenges was changed forever by the 1991 landmark U.S. Supreme Court case of *Powers* v. *Ohio*.[2] The *Powers* case dealt with a white defendant's desire to ensure a racially balanced jury. In *Powers* the Supreme Court identified three reasons why peremptory challenges may not be issued if based on race. The Court provided the following rationale for its decision:

First, the discriminatory use of peremptory challenges causes the defendant cognizable injury, and he or she has a concrete interest in challenging the practice, because racial discrimination in jury selection casts doubt on the integrity of the judicial process and places the fairness of the criminal proceeding in doubt.

Second, the relationship between the defendant and the excluded jurors is such that ... both have a common interest in eliminating racial discrimination from the courtroom....

Third, it is unlikely that a juror dismissed because of race will possess sufficient incentive to set in motion the arduous process needed to vindicate his or her own rights.[3]

The Court continued:

The very fact that [members of a particular race] are singled out and expressly denied ... all right to participate in the administration of the law, as jurors, because of their color, though they are citizens, and may be in other respects fully qualified, is practically a brand upon them, affixed by the law, an assertion of their inferiority, and a stimulant to that race prejudice which is an impediment to securing to individuals of that race equal justice which the law aims to secure to all others.

In a move that surprised many court watchers, the Supreme Court, near the end of its 1991 term, extended its ban on racially motivated peremptory challenges to civil cases. In *Edmonson* v. *Leesville Concrete Co., Inc.,*[4] the Court ruled: "The harms we recognized in *Powers* are not limited to the criminal sphere. A civil proceeding often implicates significant rights and interests. Civil juries, no less than their criminal counterparts, must follow the law and act as impartial fact-finders. And, as we have observed, their verdicts, no less than those of their criminal counterparts, become binding judgments of the court. Racial discrimination has no place in the courtroom, whether the proceeding is civil or criminal."

Following *Powers* and *Edmonson* v. *Leesville Concrete Co., Inc.,* it is clear that neither prosecuting nor civil attorneys in the future will be able to ex-

clude minority potential jurors consistently unless they are able to articulate clearly credible race-neutral rationales for their actions.

Even so, recent dissenting opinions indicate that considerable sentiment may exist among the justices which could lead to the return of a broader use of peremptory challenges. In a dissenting opinion in *J.E.B.* v. *Alabama* (1994),[5] Justices Scalia, Rehnquist, and Thomas wrote: "[T]he core of the Court's reasoning [banning peremptory challenges based upon gender] is that peremptory challenges on the basis of any group characteristic subject to heightened scrutiny are inconsistent with the guarantee of the Equal Protection Clause.... Since all groups are subject to the peremptory challenge ... it is hard to see how any group is denied equal protection."

❓ QUESTIONS FOR DISCUSSION

1. Do you agree with the Court's reasoning in *Powers* that peremptory challenges based upon race should not be permitted in the selection of criminal trial juries? Why or why not?

2. Review the Constitution in the appendix to this book. What support do you find in the Constitution for the *Powers* ruling? Be as specific as possible.

[1] Daniel Oran, *Oran's Dictionary of the Law* (St. Paul, MN: West, 1983), p. 312.

[2] *Powers v. Ohio*, 499 U.S. 400 (1991).

[3] Ibid., online syllabus of the majority opinion.

[4] *Edmonson v. Leesville Concrete Co., Inc.*, 500 U.S. (1991).

[5] *J.E.B. v. Alabama ex rel. T.B.*, 114 S.Ct. 1419, 128 L. Ed. 2d 89 (1994).

In evaluating evidence, judges must also weigh the probative value of an item of evidence against its potential inflammatory or prejudicial qualities. Evidence has probative value when it is useful and relevant. Even useful evidence, however, may unduly bias a jury if it is exceptionally gruesome or presented in such a way as to imply guilt. For example, gory photographs, especially in full color, may be withheld from the jury's eyes. In one recent case, a new trial was ordered when 35mm slides of the crime scene were projected on a wall over the head of the defendant as he sat in the courtroom and were found by an appellate court to have prejudiced the jury.

On occasion, some evidence will be found to have only limited admissibility. *Limited admissibility* means that the evidence can be used for a specific purpose, but that it might not be accurate in other details. Photographs, for example, may be admitted as evidence for the narrow purpose of showing spatial relationships between objects under discussion, even though the photographs themselves may have been taken under conditions that did not exist (such as daylight) when the offense was committed.

When judges err in allowing the use of evidence that may have been illegally or unconstitutionally gathered, grounds may be created for a later appeal if the trial concludes with a guilty verdict. Even when evidence is improperly introduced at trial, however, a number of Supreme Court decisions[115] have held that there may be no grounds for an effective appeal unless such introduction "had substantial and injurious effect or influence in determining the jury's verdict."[116] Called the "harmless error" rule, this standard does place the burden upon the prosecution to show that the jury's decision would most likely have been the same even in the absence of such inappropriate evidence. The rule is not applicable when a defendant's constitutional guarantees are violated by "structural defects in the constitution of the trial mechanism"[117] itself—as when a judge gives constitutionally improper instructions to a jury.

The Testimony of Witnesses

Testimony

Oral evidence offered by a sworn witness on the witness stand during a criminal trial.

Witness **testimony** is generally the chief means by which evidence is introduced at trial. Witnesses may include victims, police officers, the defendant, specialists in recognized fields, and others with useful information to provide. Some of these witnesses may have been present during the commission of the alleged offense, while most will have had only a later opportunity to investigate the situation or to analyze evidence.

Before a witness will be allowed to testify to any fact, the questioning attorney must establish the person's competence. Competency to testify requires that witnesses have personal knowledge of the information they will discuss and that they understand their duty to tell the truth.

One of the defense attorney's most critical decisions is whether to put the defendant on the stand. Defendants have a Fifth Amendment right to remain silent and to refuse to testify. In the precedent-setting case of *Griffin* v. *California* (1965),[118] the U.S. Supreme Court declared that if a defendant refuses to testify, prosecutors and judges are enjoined from even commenting on this fact, other than to instruct the jury that such a failure cannot be held to indi-

---

Theory Into Practice

"Pleading the Fifth"

The Fifth Amendment to the U.S. Constitution is one of the best-known entries in the Bill of Rights. Television shows and crime novels have popularized phrases such as "pleading the Fifth" or "taking the Fifth." As these media recognize, the Fifth Amendment is a powerful ally of any criminal defendant. When the accused, generally upon the advice of counsel, decides to invoke the Fifth Amendment right against self-incrimination, the state cannot require the defendant to testify. In the past, defendants who refused to take the stand were often denigrated by comments the prosecution made to the jury. In 1965 the U.S. Supreme Court, in the case of *Griffin* v. *California*,[1] ruled that the defendant's unwillingness to testify could not be interpreted as a sign of guilt. The Court reasoned that such interpretations forced the defendant to testify and effectively negated Fifth Amendment guarantees. Defendants who choose to testify, however, but who fail to adequately answer the questions put to them, may lawfully find themselves the target of a prosecutorial attack.

[1]*Griffin v. California*, 380 U.S. 609 (1965).

cate guilt. Griffin was originally arrested for the beating death of a woman whose body was found in an alley. Charged with first-degree murder, he refused to take the stand when his case came to trial. At the time of the trial, Article I, Section 13, of the California Constitution provided in part: ". . . in any criminal case, whether the defendant testifies or not, his failure to explain or to deny by his testimony any evidence or facts in the case against him may be commented upon by the court and by counsel, and may be considered by the court or the jury." The prosecutor, remarking on the evidence in closing arguments to the jury, declared: "These things he has not seen fit to take the stand and deny or explain . . . Essie Mae is dead, she can't tell you her side of the story. The defendant won't." The judge then instructed the jury that they might infer from the defendant's silence his inability to deny the evidence which had been presented against him. Griffin was convicted of first-degree murder, and his appeal reached the Supreme Court. The Court ruled that the Fifth Amendment, which the Fourteenth Amendment made applicable to the states, protected the defendant from any inferences of guilt based upon a failure to testify. The verdict of the trial court was voided.

Direct examination of a witness takes place when a witness is first called to the stand. If the prosecutor calls the witness, the witness is referred to as a witness for the prosecution. Where the direct examiner is a defense attorney, witnesses are called witnesses for the defense.

The direct examiner may ask questions which require a "yes" or "no" answer but can also employ narrative questions which allow the witness to tell a story in his or her own words. During direct examination courts generally prohibit the use of leading questions, or those which suggest answers to the witness.[119] Many courts also consider questions which call for "yes" or "no" answers to be inappropriate since they are inherently suggestive.

Cross-examination refers to the examination of a witness by anyone other than the direct examiner. Anyone who offers testimony in a criminal court has the duty to submit to cross-examination.[120] The purpose of cross-examination is to test the credibility and memory of a witness.

Most states and the federal government restrict the scope of cross-examination to material covered during direct examination. Questions about other matters, even though they may relate to the case before the court, are not allowed. A small number of states allow the cross-examiner to raise any issue as long as it is deemed relevant by the court. Leading questions, generally disallowed in direct examination, are regarded as the mainstay of cross-examination. Such questions allow for a concise restatement of testimony which has already been offered and serve to focus efficiently on potential problems that the cross-examiner seeks to address.

Some witnesses offer perjured testimony, or statements which they know to be untrue. Reasons for perjured testimony vary, but most witnesses who lie on the stand probably do so in an effort to help friends accused of crimes. Witnesses who perjure themselves are subject to impeachment, in which either the defense counsel or prosecution demonstrates that they have intentionally offered false testimony. Such a demonstration may occur through the use of prior inconsistent statements whereby previous statements made by the witness are shown to be at odds with more recent declarations. **Perjury** is a serious offense in its own right, and dishonest witnesses may face fines or jail time. When it can be demonstrated that a witness has offered inaccurate or false testimony, the witness has been effectively impeached.

At the conclusion of the cross-examination, the direct examiner may again question the witness. This procedure is called redirect examination and may be followed by a re-cross-examination and so on, until both sides are satisfied that they have exhausted fruitful lines of questioning.

Children as Witnesses

An area of special concern involves the use of children as witnesses in a criminal trial, especially where the children may have been victims. Currently, in an effort to avoid what may be traumatizing direct confrontations between child witnesses and the accused, 37 states allow the use of videotaped testimony in their criminal courtrooms, and 32 permit the use of closed-circuit television—which allows the child to testify out of the presence of the defendant. In 1988, however, the U.S. Supreme Court, in the case of *Coy* v. *Iowa*,[121] ruled that a courtroom screen, used to shield child witnesses from visual confrontation with a defendant in a child sex abuse case, had violated the confrontation clause of the Constitution.

Perjury

The intentional making of a false statement as part of the testimony by a sworn witness in a judicial proceeding on a matter relevant to the case at hand.

On the other hand, in the 1990 case of *Maryland* v. *Craig*,[122] the Court upheld the use of closed-circuit television to shield children who testify in criminal courts. The Court's decision was partially based upon the realization that ". . . a significant majority of States have enacted statutes to protect child witnesses from the trauma of giving testimony in child-abuse cases . . . [which] . . . attests to the widespread belief in the importance of such a policy."

The case involved Sandra Craig, a former preschool owner and administrator in Clarksville, Maryland, who had been found guilty by a trial court of 53 counts of child abuse, assault, and perverted sexual practices, which she had allegedly performed on the children under her care. During the trial, four young children, none past the age of six, had testified against Craig while separated from her in the judge's chambers. Questioned by the district attorney, the children related stories of torture, burying alive, and sexual assault with a screwdriver.[123] Sandra Craig watched the children reply over a TV monitor, which displayed the process to the jury seated in the courtroom. Following the trial, Craig appealed, arguing that her ability to communicate with her lawyer (who had been in the judge's chambers and not the courtroom during questioning of the children) had been impeded and that her right to a fair trial under the Sixth Amendment to the U.S. Constitution had been denied since she was not given the opportunity to be "confronted with the witnesses" against her. In finding against Craig, Justice Sandra Day O'Connor, writing for the Court's majority, stated, ". . . if the State makes an adequate showing of necessity, the State interest in protecting child witnesses from the trauma of testifying in a child-abuse case is sufficiently important to justify the use of a special procedure that permits a child witness in such cases to testify . . . in the absence of face-to-face confrontation with the defendant."[124]

Although a face-to-face confrontation with a child victim may not be necessary in the courtroom, until 1992 the Supreme Court had been reluctant to allow into evidence descriptions of abuse and other statements made by children, even to child-care professionals, when those statements are made outside of the courtroom. The Court, in *Idaho* v. *Wright* (1990),[125] reasoned that such "statements [are] fraught with the dangers of unreliability which the Confrontation Clause is designed to highlight and obviate."

However, in *White* v. *Illinois* (1992),[126] the Court seemed to reverse its stance, ruling that in-court testimony provided by a medical provider and the child's babysitter, which repeated what the child had said to them concerning White's sexually abusive behavior, was permissible. The Court rejected White's claim that out-of-court statements should be admissible only when the witness is unavailable to testify at trial, saying instead: "A finding of unavailability of an out-of-court declarant is necessary only if the out-of-court statement was made at a prior judicial proceeding." Placing *White* within the context of generally established exceptions, the court intoned: "A statement that has been offered in a moment of excitement—without the opportunity to reflect on the consequences of one's exclamation—may justifiably carry more weight with a trier of fact than a similar statement offered in the relative calm of the courtroom. Similarly, a statement made in the course of procuring medical services, where the declarant knows that a false statement may cause misdiagnosis or mistreatment, carries special guarantees of credibility that a trier of fact may not think replicated by courtroom testimony."[127]

The Hearsay Rule

Hearsay

Something which is not based upon the personal knowledge of a witness. Witnesses who testify, for example, about something they have heard are offering hearsay by repeating information about a matter of which they have no direct knowledge.

One aspect of witness testimony bears special mention. **Hearsay** is anything not based upon the personal knowledge of a witness. A witness may say, for example, "John told me that Fred did it!" Such a witness becomes a hearsay declarant, and, following a likely objection by counsel, the trial judge will have to decide whether the witness's statement will be allowed to stand as evidence. In most cases the judge will instruct the jury to disregard such comments from the witness, thereby enforcing the **hearsay rule.** The hearsay rule does not permit the use of "secondhand evidence."

There are some exceptions to the hearsay rule, however, that have been established by both precedent and tradition. One is the dying declaration. *Dying declarations* are statements made by a person who is about to die. When heard by a second party, they may usually be repeated in court, providing that certain conditions have been met. Dying declarations are generally valid exceptions to the hearsay rule when they are made by someone who knows that they are about to die and when the statements made relate to the cause and circumstances of the impending death.

Spontaneous statements provide another exception to the hearsay rule. Statements are considered spontaneous when they are made in the heat of excitement before the person has time to make them up. For example, a defendant who is just regaining consciousness following a crime may make an utterance which could later be repeated in court by those who heard it.

Out-of-court statements made by a witness, especially when they have been recorded in writing or by some other means, may also become exceptions to the hearsay rule. The use of such statements usually requires the witness to testify that the statements were accurate at the time they were made. This "past recollection recorded" exception to the hearsay rule is especially useful in drawn-out court proceedings which occur long after the crime. Under such circumstances, witnesses may no longer remember the details of an event. Their earlier statements to authorities, however, can be introduced into evidence as past recollection recorded.

Closing Arguments

At the conclusion of a criminal trial both sides have the opportunity for a final narrative presentation to the jury in the form of closing arguments. This summation provides a review and analysis of the evidence. Its purpose is to persuade the jury to draw a conclusion favorable to the presenter. Testimony can be quoted, exhibits referred to, and attention drawn to inconsistencies in the evidence which has been presented by the other side.

States vary as to the order of closing arguments. Nearly all allow the defense attorney to speak to the jury before the prosecution makes its final points. A few permit the prosecutor the first opportunity for summation. Some jurisdictions and the Federal Rules of Criminal Procedure[128] authorize a defense rebuttal. Rebuttals are responses to the closing arguments of the other side.

Some specific issues may need to be addressed during summation. If, for example, the defendant has not taken the stand during the trial, the defense attorney's closing argument will inevitably stress that this failure to testify cannot be regarded as indicating guilt. Where the prosecution's case rests entirely upon circumstantial evidence, the defense can be expected to stress the lack of any direct proof, while the prosecutor is likely to argue that circumstantial evidence can be stronger than direct evidence, since it is not as easily affected by human error or false testimony.

The Judge's Charge to the Jury

After closing arguments, the judge will charge the jury to "retire and select one of your number as a foreman . . . and deliberate upon the evidence which has been presented until you have reached a verdict." The words of the charge will vary somewhat between jurisdictions and among judges, but all judges will remind members of the jury of their duty to consider objectively only the evidence which has been presented and of the need for impartiality. Most judges will also remind jury members of the statutory elements of the alleged offense, of the burden of proof which rests upon the prosecution, and of the need for the prosecution to have proven guilt beyond a reasonable doubt before a guilty verdict can be returned.

In their charge many judges will also provide a summary of the evidence presented, usually from notes they have taken during the trial, as a means of refreshing the jurors' memories of events. About half of all the states allow judges the freedom to express their own views as to the credibility of witnesses and the significance of evidence. Other states only permit judges to summarize the evidence in an objective and impartial manner.

Following the charge, the jury will be removed from the courtroom and permitted to begin its deliberations. In the absence of the jury, defense attorneys may choose to challenge portions of the judge's charge. If they feel that some oversight has occurred in the original charge, they may also request that the judge provide the jury with additional instructions or information. Such objections, if denied by the judge, often become the basis for appeals when a conviction is returned.

Hearsay Rule

The long-standing American courtroom precedent that hearsay cannot be used in court. Rather than accepting testimony based upon hearsay, the American trial process asks that the person who was the original source of the hearsay information be brought into court to be questioned and cross-examined. Exceptions to the hearsay rule may occur when the person with direct knowledge is dead or otherwise unable to testify.

Closing Argument

An oral summation of a case presented to a judge, or to a judge and jury, by the prosecution or by the defense in a criminal trial.

Verdict

Jury Deliberations and the Verdict

In criminal case processing, a formal and final finding made on the charges by a jury and reported to the court, or by a trial judge when no jury is used.

In cases where the evidence is either very clear or very weak, jury deliberations may be brief, lasting only a matter of hours or even minutes. Some juries, however, deliberate days or sometimes weeks, carefully weighing all the nuances of the evidence they have seen and heard. Many jurisdictions require that juries reach a unanimous verdict, although the U.S. Supreme Court has ruled that unanimous verdicts are not required in noncapital cases.[129] Even so, some juries are unable to agree upon any verdict. When a jury is deadlocked, it is said to be a hung jury. Where a unanimous decision is required, juries may be deadlocked by the strong opposition of only one member to a verdict agreed upon by all the others.

In some states, judges are allowed to add a boost to nearly hung juries by recharging them under a set of instructions agreed upon by the Supreme Court in the 1896 case of *Allen* v. *United States*.[130] The Allen Charge, as it is known in those jurisdictions, urges the jury to vigorous deliberations and suggests to obstinate jurors that their objections may be ill founded if they make no impression upon the minds of other jurors.

Problems with the Jury System

Judge Harold J. Rothwax, a well-known critic of today's jury system, tells the tale of a rather startling 1991 case over which he presided. The case involved a murder defendant, a handsome young man who had been fired by a New York company that serviced automated teller machines (ATMs). After being fired, the good-looking defendant intentionally caused a machine in a remote area to malfunction. When two former colleagues arrived to fix it, he robbed them, stole the money inside the ATM, and shot both men repeatedly. One of the men survived long enough to identify his former coworker as the shooter. The man was arrested and a trial ensued; but after three weeks of hearing the case the jury deadlocked. Judge Rothwax later learned that the jury had voted 11 to 1 to convict the defendant, but the one holdout jury member just couldn't believe that "someone so good-looking could . . . commit such a crime."[131]

Many everyday cases, like those seen routinely by Judge Rothwax, and some highly publicized cases, like the murder trial of O. J. Simpson, which the whole world watched, have called into question the ability of the American jury system to do its job—that is, to sort through the evidence and accurately determine a defendant's guilt or innocence. Because jurors are drawn from all walks of life, many cannot be expected to understand modern legal complexities and to appreciate all the nuances of trial court practice. Some instructions to the jury are probably poorly understood and rarely observed by even the best-intentioned jurors.[132] In highly charged cases, emotions are often difficult to separate from fact, while during deliberations juries are probably dominated by one or two forceful personalities. Jurors may also become confused over legal technicalities, suffer from inattention, or be unable to understand fully the testimony of expert witnesses or the significance of technical evidence.

> "This is surely the first trial with 95 million jurors."
>
> *—Jess Maghan (University of Illinois at Chicago),* commenting on the O. J. Simpson trial

Many such problems became evident in the trial of Raymond Buckey and his mother, Peggy McMartin Buckey, who were tried in Los Angeles for allegedly molesting dozens of children at their family-run preschool.[133] The trial, which involved 65 counts of child sexual molestation and conspiracy and 61 witnesses, ran for more than three years. Many jurors were stressed to the breaking point by the length of time involved. Family relationships suffered as the trial droned on, and jurors were unable to accompany their spouses and children on vacation. Small-business owners, who were expected to continue paying salaries to employees serving as jurors, faced financial ruin and threatened their absent employees with termination. Careers were put on hold, and at least one juror had to be dismissed for becoming inattentive to testimony. The trial cost taxpayers more than $12 million, but was nearly negated as jury membership and the number of alternate jurors declined due to sickness and personal problems. Ultimately, the defendants were acquitted.

Another trial in which the defendants were similarly acquitted of the majority of charges against them involved state-level prosecution of the officers accused in the now-infamous Rodney King beating. Following the riots in Los Angeles (and elsewhere) which came on the heels of their verdict, jurors in the "Rodney King trial" reported being afraid for their lives.

Some slept with weapons by their side, and others sent their children away to safe locales.[134] Because of the potential for harm jurors faced in the 1993 federal trial of the same officers, U.S. District Judge John G. Davies ruled that the names of jurors be forever kept secret. The secrecy order was called "an unprecedented infringement of the public's right of access to the justice system"[135] by members of the press. Similarly, in the 1993 trial of three black men charged with the beating of white truck driver Reginald Denny during the Los Angeles riots, Los Angeles Superior Court Judge John Ouderkirk ordered that the identities of jurors not be released.

Opponents of the jury system have argued that it should be replaced by a panel of judges who would both render a verdict and impose sentence. Regardless of how well considered such a suggestion may be, such a change could not occur without modification to the Constitution's Sixth Amendment right to trial by jury.

An alternative suggestion for improving the process of trial by jury has been the call for professional jurors. Professional jurors would be paid by the government, as are judges, prosecutors, and public defenders. Their job would be to sit on any jury, and they would be expected to have the expertise to do so. Professional jurors would be trained to listen objectively and would be schooled with the kinds of decision-making skills necessary to function effectively within an adversarial context. They could be expected to hear one case after another, perhaps moving between jurisdictions in cases of highly publicized crimes.

The advantages a professional jury system offers are as follows:

1. *Dependability.* Professional jurors could be expected to report to the courtroom in a timely fashion and to be good listeners, since both would be required by the nature of the job.
2. *Knowledge.* Professional jurors would be trained in the law, would understand what a finding of guilt requires, and would know what to expect from other actors in the courtroom.
3. *Equity.* Professional jurors would understand the requirements of due process and would be less likely to be swayed by the emotional content of a case, having been schooled in the need to separate matters of fact from personal feelings.

A professional jury system would not be without difficulties. Jurors under such a system might become jaded, deciding cases out of hand as routines lead to boredom and suspects are categorized according to whether they "fit the type" for guilt or innocence developed on the basis of previous experiences. Job requirements for professional jurors would be difficult to establish without infringing on the jurors' freedom to decide cases as they understand them. For the same reason, any evaluation of the job performance of professional jurors would be a difficult call. Finally, professional jurors might not truly be peer jurors, since their social characteristics might be skewed by education, residence, and politics.

Improving the Adjudication Process

Courts today are coming under increasing scrutiny, and media-rich trials, such as those of O. J. Simpson, Susan Smith, and the Menendez brothers, have heightened awareness of problems with the American court system. One of today's most important issues involves reducing the number of jurisdictions by unifying courts. The current multiplicity of jurisdictions frequently leads to what many believe are avoidable conflicts and overlaps in the handling of criminal defendants. Problems are exacerbated by the lack of any centralized judicial authority in some states which might resolve jurisdictional and procedural disputes.[136] Proponents of unification suggest the elimination of overlapping jurisdictions, the creation of special-purpose courts, and the formulation of administrative offices in order to achieve economies of scale.[137]

Court-watch citizens groups are also rapidly growing in number. Such organizations focus on the trial court level, but they are part of a general trend toward seeking greater openness in government decision making at all levels.[138] Court-watch groups monitor court proceedings on a regular basis and attempt to document and often publicize inadequacies. They frequently focus on the handling of indigents, fairness in the scheduling of

"My experience was like being in prison."

—*Tracy Hampton,* who was excused from the Simpson criminal jury after four months of sequestration

21st Century CJ

Courtrooms of the Future

A few years ago, the College of William & Mary, in conjunction with the National Center for State Courts (NCSC), unveiled Courtroom 21, the most technologically advanced courtroom in the United States. Courtroom 21, located in the McGlothlin Courtroom of the College of William & Mary, offers anyone concerned with the future of trial practice and with courtroom technology a glimpse at what American courtrooms may be like in the mid-twenty-first century. Courtroom 21 includes the following integrated capabilities:

1. Automatic video recording of proceedings using ceiling-mounted cameras with voice-initiated switching. A sophisticated voice-activation system directs cameras to tape the person speaking, to record what is said, and to tape evidence as it is being presented.

2. Recorded televised evidence display with optical disk storage. Documentary or real evidence may be presented to the judge and jury via television through the use of a video "presenter," which also makes a video record of the evidence as it is being presented for later use.

3. A remote, two-way television arrangement, which allows video and audio signals to be sent from the judge's bench to areas throughout the courtroom, including the jury box.

4. Text-, graphics-, and TV-capable jury computers. Courtroom 21's jury box contains computers for information display and animation so that jury members can easily view documents, live or prerecorded video, and other graphics such as charts, diagrams, and pictures. TV-capable jury computers also allow for the remote appearance of witnesses—that is, for ques-

tioning witnesses who may be unable or unwilling to physically appear in the courtroom—and for the display of crime scene reenactments via computer animation.

5. Access for judge and for counsel on both sides to online legal research databases. Available databases contain an extensive variety of state and federal statutes, case law, and other precedent which allows judges and attorneys to find answers to unanticipated legal questions which might arise during trial.

6. Built-in video playback facilities for out-of-court testimony. Because an increasing number of depositions are being video recorded by attorneys in preparation for trial, Courtroom 21 has capabilities for video deposition playback. To present expert witness testimony or to impeach a witness, video depositions can be played on court monitors.

7. Information storage with software search capabilities. Integrated software programs provide text-searching capabilities to courtroom participants. Previously transcribed testimony, as well as precedent-setting cases from other courts, can be searched and reviewed.

8. Concurrent (real-time) court reporter transcription, including the ability for each lawyer to mark an individual computerized copy for later use. A court reporter uses a self-contained computerized writing machine for real-time capture of testimony in the courtroom. When the reporter writes, the computer translates strokes into English transcripts, which are immediately distributed to the judge and counsel via their personal computers. Using this technology, the judge and attorneys can take a copy of

the day's testimony with them on their laptop computers or on a floppy diskette for evening review and trial preparation.

The technology now being demonstrated in Courtroom 21 suggests many possibilities. For one thing, court video equipment could be used by attorneys for filing remote motions and other types of hearings. As one of Courtroom 21's designers puts it, "Imagine the productivity gains if lawyers no longer need to travel across a city or county for a ten-minute appearance."

Courtroom 21 designers also suggest that the innovative use of audio and video technology can preserve far more evidence and trial detail than written records, making a comprehensive review of cases easier for appellate judges. One study, which has already been conducted by the NCSC, showed that when video records are available, appellate courts are less likely to reverse the original determinations of the trial court. Video court records, analysts say, "might also improve the performance of attorneys and judges. By preserving matters not now apparent on a written record, such as facial expressions, voice inflections, body gestures, and the like, video records may cause trial participants to be more circumspect in their behavior than at present."

High technology can also be expected to have considerable impact on the trial itself. The technology built into Courtroom 21 readily facilitates computer animations and crime scene reenactments. As one of the designers of Courtroom 21 says, "*Jurassic Park* quality computer reenactment may have enormous psychological impact" (on jurors).

While Courtroom 21 shows what a typical courtroom of the near future may be like, it also raises questions about the appropriate use of innovative courtroom technologies. As Fred

(Continued)

21st Century CJ

Courtrooms of the Future

Lederer, one of Courtroom 21's designers, points out, "Modern technology holds enormous promise for our courts. We must recognize, however, that technology's utility often depends upon how people will use it. Although we must continue to improve our courts via technology, we must be sensitive to technology's impact and work to recognize and minimize any negative consequences it might have on our system of justice."

An even more intriguing vision of courtrooms of the future is offered by the Technology of Justice Task Force in its 1997 draft report to the Pennsylvania Futures Commission. The task force predicted that by the year 2020, "There will be 'virtual courtrooms,' where appropriate, to provide hearings without the need for people to come to a physical courthouse." Trials via teleconferencing, public Internet access to many court documents, and payments of fines by credit card are all envisioned by the task force.

? QUESTIONS FOR DISCUSSION

1. How might technologies such as those discussed in this box affect the outcome of criminal trials, if at all?

2. Can you imagine criminal trials in which the use of high-technology courtrooms might not be appropriate? If so, what might they be?

Sources: Court Technology Bulletin, *vol. 6, no. 1, January/February 1994;* Court Technology Bulletin, *vol. 6, no. 2, March/April 1994; the National Center for State Courts World Wide Web site on the Internet (from which some of the material in this box is taken); and the Technology of Justice Task Force,* "Draft Report to the Pennsylvania Futures Commission," *February 21, 1997.*

---

cases for trial, unnecessary court delays, the reduction of waiting time, the treatment of witnesses and jurors, and adequacy of rights advisements for defendants throughout judicial proceedings.

The statistical measurement of court performance is another area which is receiving increased attention. Research has looked at the efficiency with which prosecutors schedule cases for trial, the speed with which judges resolve issues, the amount of time judges spend on the bench, and the economic and other costs to defendants, witnesses, and communities involved in the judicial process.[139] Statistical studies of this type often attempt to measure elements of court performance as diverse as sentence variation, charging accuracy, fairness in plea bargaining, evenhandedness, delays, and attitudes toward the court by lay participants.[140]

In 1994, the Federal Judicial Center, which is the research, education, and planning agency of the federal judicial system, conducted a nationwide survey intended to gather information for the federal Judicial Conference Committee on Long Range Planning. The Center's survey reached nearly all federal judges and covered a wide range of issues. Results of the survey[141] showed that federal judges (1) were convinced that the most serious problem facing federal courts was the huge volume of criminal cases waiting to be processed; (2) believed that criminal case processing needs gravely impacted the ability of federal courts to effectively handle civil cases; (3) hoped that the concerns of federal court judges and administrators would be considered before any new federal criminal legislation was passed; and (4) wanted more discretion in sentencing and fewer rules requiring mandatory minimum sentences for criminal defendants.

Summary

This chapter discussed activities and personnel characteristic of today's criminal courts. Although many individualized courtroom roles can be identified, the criminal trial stands as the hallmark of American criminal justice. The criminal trial owes its legacy to the development of democratic principles in Western society and builds upon an adversarial process which pits prosecution against defense.

Trials have historically been viewed as peer-based fact-finding processes intended to protect the rights of the accused while sifting through disputed issues of guilt or innocence. The adversarial environment, however, which has served American courts for over 200 years, is now being questioned. Well-publicized trials of the last decade or two have demonstrated apparent weaknesses in the trial process. Moreover, a plethora of far-reaching social and technological changes have recently transpired that might at least partially supplant the role of advocacy in the fact-finding process. In many cases, new technologies which were unanticipated by the framers of our present system hold the promise to closely link suspects to criminal activity. Today's electronic media can rapidly and widely disseminate investigative findings. This combination of investigative technologies and readily available public information may eventually make courtroom debates about guilt or innocence obsolete. Whether the current adversarial system can continue to serve the interests of justice in an information-rich and technologically advanced society will be a central question for the twenty-first century.

Discussion Questions

1. We described participants in a criminal trial as working together to bring about a successful close to courtroom proceedings. What do you think a "successful close" might mean to a judge? To a defense attorney? To a prosecutor? To the jury? To the defendant? To the victim?
2. What is a dying declaration? Under what circumstances might it be a valid exception to the hearsay rule? Why do most courts seem to believe that a person who is about to die is likely to tell the truth?
3. Do you think the present jury system is outmoded? Might "professional jurors" be more effective than the present system of "peer jurors"? On what do you base your opinion?
4. What is an expert witness? A lay witness? What different kinds of testimony may both provide? What are some of the difficulties in expert testimony?
5. What are the three forms of indigent defense used throughout various regions of the United States? Why might defendants prefer private attorneys over public counsel?

Web Quest!

Take a Virtual Tour of the U.S. Supreme Court via Northwestern University's multimedia Oyez Project, available on the Web at http://oyez.nwu.edu. Once there you should notice that clickable hot spots on the Quick Time images can help you navigate the site. They, along with other clickable images, and the ability to get a 360-degree view of almost any room by clicking on a picture (hold the mouse button down and drag it) can provide a closer look at almost any area of the Court building. For this assignment you should make use of all navigational features available at the Oyez Project site to move through the Supreme Court building. As you tour the building, write down what you see and print out the images of each room you see. Submit these descriptions and images to your instructor if asked to do so.

Library Extras!

The Library Extras! listed here complement the WebExtras! found throughout this chapter. Library Extras! may be accessed on the Web at CJToday.com.

Library Extra! 8-1. *Felony Defendants in Large Urban Counties* (BJS, current volume).
Library Extra! 8-2. *Federal Pretrial Release and Detention* (BJS, current volume).

Library Extra! 8-3. *Indigent Defense* (BJS, 1996).
Library Extra! 8-4. *NIJ Survey of Prosecutors* (NIJ, 1995).
Library Extra! 8-5. *Trial Court Performance Standards* (BJA, 1997).

References

1. Jill Smolowe, "The Trials of the Public Defender," *Time*, February 8, 1993, p. 46.
2. "Louisiana's Public Defender System Found Unconstitutional," *Criminal Justice Newsletter*, vol. 23, no. 5, (March 3, 1992), p. 1.
3. See, for example, Jeffrey T. Ulmer, *Social Worlds of Sentencing: Court Communities Under Sentencing Guidelines* (Ithaca: State University of New York Press, 1997); and Roy B. Flemming, Peter F. Nardulli, James Eisenstein, *The Craft of Justice: Politics and Work in Criminal Court Communities* (Philadelphia: University of Pennsylvania Press, 1993).
4. See, for example, Edward J. Clynch and David W. Neubauer, "Trial Courts as Organizations," *Law and Policy Quarterly*, vol. 3 (1981), pp. 69–94.
5. American Bar Association, *ABA Standards for Criminal Justice*, 2nd ed. (Chicago: ABA, 1980).
6. In 1940 Missouri became the first state to adopt a plan for the "merit selection" of judges based upon periodic public review.
7. The National Judicial College, "About the NJC," Web posted at www.judges.org/about. Accessed February 2, 2000.
8. The National Judicial College, "Judicial Education," Web posted at www.judges.org/educate. Accessed January 30, 2000.
9. Doris Marie Provine, *Judging Credentials: Nonlawyer Judges and the Politics of Professionalism* (Chicago: University of Chicago Press, 1986).
10. Town and village justices in New York state serve part-time and may or may not be lawyers; judges of all other courts must be lawyers, whether or not they serve full-time. From New York State Commission on Judicial Conduct, *1998 Annual Report*. Web posted at www.scjc.state.ny.us/annual.html. Accessed March 10, 2000.
11. Ibid.
12. "Defendant Claims Judge Bit Him," Associated Press wire services, June 27, 1997.
13. Nationline, "Judge—Show Legs, Pick Up Men," *USA Today*, August 16, 1996, p. 3A.
14. Aminah Franklin, "District Justice Charged with Misconduct," *The Morning Call* (Allentown, PA), July 6, 1995, p. 1A.
15. Allen Baker, "Alaska Justice Steps Down," The Associated Press wire services, July 3, 1997.
16. Debbie Howlett, "Impeachment Sought for 'Arrogant' Judge," *USA Today*, May 6, 1997, p. 3A.
17. *U.S. v. Nixon*, 816 F.2d 1022 (1987).
18. *Nixon v. U.S.*, 506 U.S. 224, 113 S.Ct. 732, 122 L. Ed. 2d 1 (1993).
19. Bureau of Justice Statistics, *Report to the Nation on Crime and Justice: The Data* (Washington, D.C.: U.S. Department of Justice, 1983).
20. For a discussion of the resource limitations of district attorneys in combating corporate crime, see Michael L. Benson, William J. Maakestad, Francis T. Cullen, and Gilbert Geis, "District Attorneys and Corporate Crime: Surveying the Prosecutorial Gatekeepers," *Criminology*, vol. 26, no. 3 (August 1988), pp. 505–517.
21. Carol J. DeFrances and Greg W. Steadman, *Prosecutors in State Courts, 1996* (Washington, D.C.: Bureau of Justice Statistics, 1998).
22. Many large police departments have their own legal counselors who provide advice on civil liability and who may also assist in weighing the quality of evidence which has been assembled.
23. Kenneth Culp Davis, *Discretionary Justice* (Baton Rouge: Louisiana State University Press, 1969), p. 190.
24. Barbara Borland, *The Prosecution of Felony Arrests* (Washington, D.C.: Bureau of Justice Statistics, 1983).
25. *Brady v. Maryland*, 373 U.S. 83 (1963).
26. *U.S. v. Bagley*, 473 U.S. 667 (1985).
27. *Imbler v. Pachtman*, 424 U.S. 409 (1976).
28. *Burns v. Reed*, 500 U.S. 478 (1991).
29. Ibid., complaint, p. 29.
30. Cassia Spohn, John Gruhl, and Susan Welch, "The Impact of the Ethnicity and Gender of Defendants on the Decision to Reject or Dismiss Felony Charges," *Criminology*, vol. 25, no. 1 (1987), pp. 175–191.
31. The same is true under federal law, and in almost all of the states, of communications with clergymen and clergywomen, psychiatrists and psychologists, medical doctors, and licensed social workers in the course of psychotherapy. See, for example, *Jaffee v. Redmond*, 116 S.Ct. 1923 (1996).
32. Richard Carelli, "Rehnquist," The Associated Press wire services, May 25, 1996.
33. "Pay the Costs of Justice," *USA Today*, March 30, 1993, p. 8A.
34. *Powell v. Alabama*, 287 U.S. 45 (1932).
35. *Johnson v. Zerbst*, 304 U.S. 458 (1938).
36. *Gideon v. Wainwright*, 372 U.S. 335 (1963).
37. *Argersinger v. Hamlin*, 407 U.S. 25 (1972).
38. *In re Gault*, 387 U.S. 1 (1967).

39. Bureau of Justice Statistics, *Criminal Defense for the Poor, 1986.* As a 1999 BJS publication says, "Basic data on indigent defense systems in each of the 50 States were last collected in 1986. Over the past decade much has changed in the delivery of indigent defense services as States and local defender systems have begun relying more on contract and private services." BJS is currently planning a new national survey of indigent defense systems to be conducted in conjunction with American Bar Association, the National Association of Criminal Defense Lawyers, and the National Legal Aid and Defenders Association. See www.ojp.usdoj.gov/bjs/abstract/nsids.htm.

40. Steven K. Smith and Carol J. DeFrances, *Indigent Defense,* (Washington, D.C.: Bureau of Justice Statistics, Feb. 1996).

41. Ibid.

42. "Pay the Costs of Justice," *USA Today,* March 30, 1993, p. 8A.

43. Smolowe, "The Trials of the Public Defender," p. 46.

44. Ibid.

45. *Faretta* v. *California,* 422 U.S. 806 (1975).

46. "Indigent Defense," pp. 2–3.

47. "Killings Spotlight Lawyers' Ethics," *Fayetteville Observer-Times* (North Carolina), September 13, 1992, p. 11A.

48. *Nix* v. *Whiteside,* 475 U.S. 157 (1986).

49. Ibid.

50. "Courtroom Killings Verdict," *USA Today,* February 15, 1993, p. 3A.

51. "How Crucial Is Courtroom Security?" *Security Management* (August 1992), p. 78.

52. "Courtroom Firebomb," *USA Today,* April 9, 1997, p. 3A.

53. President's Commission on Law Enforcement and Administration of Justice, *The Challenge of Crime in a Free Society* (Washington, D.C.: U.S. Government Printing Office, 1967), p. 129.

54. National Advisory Commission on Criminal Justice Standards and Goals, *Courts* (Washington, D.C.: U.S. Government Printing Office, 1973), Standard 9.3.

55. See, for example, Joan G. Brannon, *The Judicial System in North Carolina* (Raleigh, NC: The Administrative Office of the United States Courts, 1984), p. 14.

56. *Daubert* v. *Merrell Dow Pharmaceuticals, Inc.,* 113 S.Ct. 2786 (1993).

57. Joseph L. Peterson, "Use of Forensic Evidence by the Police and Courts," *Research in Brief* (Washington, D.C.: National Institute of Justice, 1987), p. 3.

58. Ibid., p. 6.

59. Jennifer Bowles, "Simpson-Paid Experts," The Associated Press wire services, August 12, 1995.

60. *California* v. *Green,* 399 U.S. 149 (1970).

61. Patrick L. McCloskey and Ronald L. Schoenberg, *Criminal Law Deskbook* (New York: Matthew Bender, 1988), Section 17, p. 123.

62. Florida Statutes (Supplement 1996), Chapter 92: Witnesses, Records, and Documents, for example, read: "Witnesses in all cases, civil and criminal, in all courts, now or hereafter created, and witnesses summoned before any arbitrator or master in chancery shall receive for each day's actual attendance $5 and also 6 cents per mile for actual distance traveled to and from the courts. A witness in a criminal case required to appear in a county other than the county of his or her residence and residing more than 50 miles from the location of the trial shall be entitled to per diem and travel expenses at the same rate provided for state employees. . . ."

63. *Demarest* v. *Manspeaker et al.,* 498 U.S. 184, 111 S.Ct. 599, 112 L. Ed. 2d 608 (1991).

64. *Report to the Nation,* p. 82.

65. *Williams* v. *Florida,* 399 U.S. 78, 90 S.Ct. 1893, 26 L. Ed. 2d 446 (1970).

66. *Smith* v. *Texas,* 311 U.S. 128 (1940). That right does not apply when the defendants are facing the possibility of a prison sentence less than six months in length or even when the potential aggregate sentence for multiple petty offenses exceeds six months [see *Lewis* v. *U.S.* (1996)].

67. *Thiel* v. *Southern Pacific Co.,* 328 U.S. 217 (1945).

68. Speaking from a personal experience, the author was himself the victim of a felony some years ago. My car was stolen in Columbus, Ohio, and recovered a year later in Cleveland. I was informed that the person who had taken it was in custody, but I never heard what happened to him nor could I learn where or whether a trial was to be held.

69. *Crosby* v. *U.S.,* 113 S.Ct. 748, 122 L. Ed. 2d 25 (1993).

70. *Zafiro* v. *U.S.,* 113 S.Ct. 933, 122 L. Ed. 2d 317 (1993).

71. Dale Russakoff, "N.Y. Defendant Keeps His Own Counsel; Alleged Killer of Six Commuter Train Passengers Shuns His Lawyers' Advice," The *Washington Post* wire services, January 27, 1995.

72. Larry McShane, "Ferguson—Why?" The Associated Press wire services, February 18, 1995.

73. *Nebraska Press Association* v. *Stuart,* 427 U.S. 539 (1976).

74. However, it is generally accepted that trial judges may issue limited gag orders aimed at trial participants.

75. *Press Enterprise Company* v. *Superior Court of California, Riverside County,* 478 U.S. 1 (1986).

76. *Caribbean International News Corporation* v. *Puerto Rico,* 508 U.S. 147 (1993).

77. Dennis Cauchon, "Federal Courts Camera-Less," *USA Today,* March 10, 1993, p. 2A.

78. See Radio-Television News Directors Association, "Summary of State Camera Coverage Rules," Web posted at www.rtnda.org/issues/cameras_summary.htm. Accessed February 9, 2000.

79. *Chandler* v. *Florida,* 499 U.S. 560 (1981).

80. Ibid.

81. Harry F. Rosenthal, "Courts-TV," The Associated Press wire services, September 21, 1994. See also "Judicial Conference Rejects Cameras in Federal Courts," *Criminal Justice Newsletter,* September 15, 1994, p. 6.

82. See Radio-Television News Directors Association, "Cameras and Microphones in the Courtroom," Web posted at www.rtnda.org /news/cameras.htm. Accessed February 9, 2000.

83. Marc G. Gertz and Edmond J. True, "Social Scientists in the Courtroom: The Frustrations of Two Expert Witnesses," in Susette M. Talarico, ed., *Courts and Criminal Justice: Emerging Issues* (Beverly Hills, CA: Sage Publications, 1985), pp. 81–91.

84. *Klopfer* v. *North Carolina,* 386 U.S. 213 (1967).

85. *Barker* v. *Wingo,* 407 U.S. 514 (1972).

86. *Strunk* v. *U.S.,* 412 U.S. 434 (1973).

87. The federal Speedy Trial Act, 18 U.S.C. 3161 (1974).

88. *U.S.* v. *Brainer,* 515 F. Supp. 627, 630 (D. Md. 1981).

89. *U.S.* v. *Taylor,* U.S. 487 U.S. 326, 108 S.Ct. 2413, 101 L. Ed. 2d 297 (1988).

90. *Fex* v. *Michigan,* 113 S.Ct. 1085, 122 L. Ed. 2d 406 (1993).

91. *Doggett* v. *U.S.,* 112 S.Ct. 2686 (1992).

92. William U. McCormack, "Supreme Court Cases: 1991–1992 Term," *FBI Law Enforcement Bulletin,* November, 1992, pp. 28–29.

93. See, for example, the U.S. Supreme Court's decision in the case of *Murphy* v. *Florida,* 410 U.S. 525 (1973).

94. *Witherspoon* v. *Illinois,* 391 U.S. 510 (1968).

95. *Mu'Min* v. *Virginia,* 500 U.S. 415 (1991).

96. Rule 24(6) of the *Federal Rules of Criminal Procedure.*

97. "Are Juries Colorblind?" *Newsweek,* December 5, 1988, p. 94.

98. Ibid.

99. Ibid.

100. Ibid.

101. Supreme Court majority opinion in *Powers* v. *Ohio,* 499 U.S. 400 (1991), citing *Strauder* v. *West Virginia,* 100 U.S. 303 (1880).

102. *Swain* v. *Alabama,* 380 U.S. 202 (1965).

103. *Batson* v. *Kentucky,* 476 U.S. 79, 106 S.Ct. 1712 (1986).

104. *Ford* v. *Georgia,* 498 U.S. 411 (1991), footnote 2.

105. Ibid.

106. *Powers* v. *Ohio,* 499 U.S. 400 (1991).

107. *Edmonson* v. *Leesville Concrete Co., Inc.,* 500 U.S. 614, 111 S.Ct. 2077, 114 L. Ed. 2d 660 (1991).

108. *Georgia* v. *McCollum,* 505 U.S. 42 (1992).

109. See, for example, *Davis* v. *Minnesota,* 511 U.S. 1115 (1994).

110. Michael Kirkland, "Court Rejects Fat Jurors Case," United Press International wire services, January 8, 1996. The case was *Santiago-Martinez* v. *U.S.,* No. 95-567, (1996).

111. *Campbell* v. *Louisiana,* 523 U.S. 392 (1998).

112. Although the words *argument* and *statement* are sometimes used interchangeably in alluding to opening remarks, defense attorneys are enjoined from drawing conclusions or "arguing" to the jury at this stage in the trial. Their task, as described in the section which follows, is simply to provide information to the jury as to how the defense will be conducted.

113. *U.S.* v. *Dinitz,* 424 U.S. 600, 612 (1976).

114. *Michigan* v. *Lucas,* 500 U.S. 145 (1992).

115. *Kotteakos* v. *United States,* 328 U.S. 750 (1946); *Becht* v. *Abrahamson,* 113 S.Ct. 1710, 123 L. Ed. 2d 353 (1993); and *Arizona* v. *Fulminante,* 111 S.Ct. 1246 (1991).

116. The Court, citing *Kotteakos* v. *United States,* 328 U.S. 750 (1946) in *Brecht* v. *Abrahamson,* 113 S.Ct. 1710, 123 L. Ed. 2d 353 (1993).

117. *Sullivan* v. *Louisiana,* 113 S.Ct. 2078, 124 L. Ed. 2d 182 (1993).

118. *Griffin* v. *California,* 380 U.S. 609 (1965).

119. Leading questions may, in fact, be permitted for certain purposes, including refreshing a witness's memory, impeaching a hostile witness, introducing nondisputed material, and helping a witness with impaired faculties.

120. *In re Oliver,* 333 U.S. 257 (1948).

121. *Coy* v. *Iowa,* 487 U.S. 1012, 108 S.Ct. 2798 (1988).

122. *Maryland* v. *Craig,* 497 U.S. 836, 845–847 (1990).

123. "The Right to Confront Your Accuser," The *Boston Globe* magazine, April 7, 1991, pp. 19, 51.

124. *Maryland* v. *Craig.*

125. *Idaho* v. *Wright,* 497 U.S. 805 (1990).

126. *White* v. *Illinois,* 112 S.Ct. 736 (1992).

127. *White* v. *Illinois,* Project Hermes online decision.

128. Rule 29.1 of the *Federal Rules of Criminal Procedure.*

129. See *Johnson* v. *Louisiana,* 406 U.S. 356 (1972), and *Apodaca* v. *Oregon,* 406 U.S. 404 (1972).

130. *Allen* v. *U.S.,* 164 U.S. 492 (1896).

131. Judge Harold J. Rothwax, *Guilty: The Collapse of Criminal Justice* (New York: Random House, 1996).

132. Amiram Elwork, Bruce D. Sales, and James Alfini, *Making Jury Instructions Understandable* (Charlottesville, VA: Michie, 1982).

133. "Juror Hardship Becomes Critical as McMartin Trial Enters Year 3," *Criminal Justice Newsletter,* vol. 20 (May 15, 1989), pp. 6–7.

134. "King Jury Lives in Fear from Unpopular Verdict," *Fayetteville Observer-Times* (North Carolina), May 10, 1992, p. 7A.

135. "Los Angeles Trials Spark Debate over Anonymous Juries," *Criminal Justice Newsletter,* February 16, 1993, pp. 3, 4.

136. Some states have centralized offices called Administrative Offices of the Courts, or something similar. Such offices, however, are often primarily data-gathering agencies which have little or no authority over the day-to-day functioning of state or local courts.

137. See, for example, Larry Berkson and Susan Carbon, *Court Unification: Its History, Politics, and Implementation* (Washington, D.C.: U.S. Government Printing Office, 1978), and Thomas Henderson et al., *The Significance of Judicial Structure: The Effect of Unification on Trial Court Operators* (Alexandria, VA: Institute for Economic and Policy Studies, 1984).

138. See, for example, Kenneth Carlson et al., *Citizen Court Watching: The Consumer's Perspectives* (Cambridge, MA: Abt Associates, 1977).

139. See, for example, Thomas J. Cook and Ronald W. Johnson et al., *Basic Issues in Court Performance* (Washington, D.C.: National Institute of Justice, 1982).

140. See, for example, Sorrel Wildhorn et al., *Indicators of Justice: Measuring the Performance of Prosecutors, Defense, and Court Agencies Involved in Felony Proceedings* (Lexington, MA: Lexington Books, 1977).

141. Federal Judicial Center, *Planning for the Future: Results of a 1992 Federal Judicial Center Survey of United States Judges,* (Washington, D.C.: Federal Judicial Center 1994).

CHAPTER 9

Sentencing

"Punishment, that is justice for the unjust."
—Saint Augustine (345–430 A.D.)

—Bob Daemmrich, Stock Boston.

CHAPTER OUTLINE

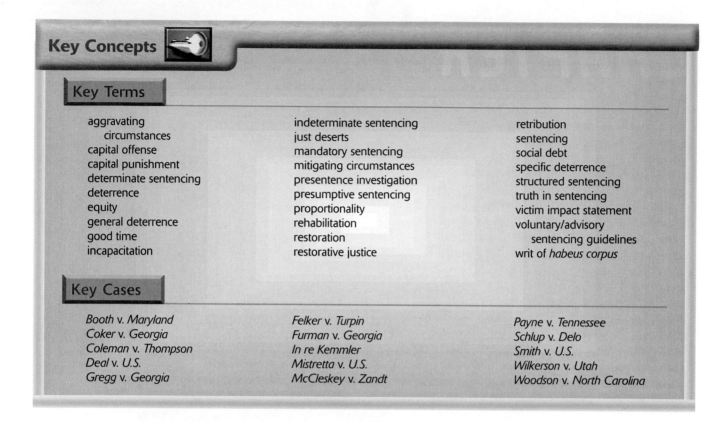

Key Concepts

Key Terms

aggravating circumstances
capital offense
capital punishment
determinate sentencing
deterrence
equity
general deterrence
good time
incapacitation

indeterminate sentencing
just deserts
mandatory sentencing
mitigating circumstances
presentence investigation
presumptive sentencing
proportionality
rehabilitation
restoration
restorative justice

retribution
sentencing
social debt
specific deterrence
structured sentencing
truth in sentencing
victim impact statement
voluntary/advisory sentencing guidelines
writ of *habeus corpus*

Key Cases

Booth v. *Maryland*
Coker v. *Georgia*
Coleman v. *Thompson*
Deal v. *U.S.*
Gregg v. *Georgia*

Felker v. *Turpin*
Furman v. *Georgia*
In re Kemmler
Mistretta v. *U.S.*
McCleskey v. *Zandt*

Payne v. *Tennessee*
Schlup v. *Delo*
Smith v. *U.S.*
Wilkerson v. *Utah*
Woodson v. *North Carolina*

Hear the author discuss this chapter at **cjtoday.com**

Crime and Punishment: Introduction

A few years ago, John Angus Smith and a friend went from Tennessee to Florida to buy cocaine. They hoped to resell it at a profit. While in Florida, they met an acquaintance of Smith's, Deborah Hoag. Hoag purchased cocaine for Smith and then accompanied him and his friend to her motel room, where they were joined by a drug dealer. While Hoag listened, Smith and the dealer discussed Smith's MAC-10 firearm, which had been modified to operate as an automatic. The MAC-10, small, compact, and lightweight, can be equipped with a silencer and is a favorite among criminals. A fully automatic MAC-10 can be devastating. It can fire more than 1,000 rounds per minute. The dealer expressed his interest in becoming the owner of a MAC-10, and Smith promised that he would discuss selling the gun if his arrangement with another potential buyer fell through.

Unfortunately for Smith, Hoag had contacts not only with narcotics traffickers but also with law enforcement officials. She was a confidential informant, and she informed the Broward County Sheriff's Office of Smith's activities. The sheriff's office responded quickly, sending an undercover officer to Hoag's motel room. Several other officers were assigned to keep the motel under surveillance. Upon arriving at Hoag's room, the undercover officer presented himself to Smith as a pawnshop dealer. Smith, in turn, presented the officer with a proposition: He had an automatic MAC-10 and silencer with which he might be willing to part if a good price could be arranged. Smith then pulled the MAC-10 out of a black canvas bag and showed it to the officer. The officer examined the gun and asked Smith what he wanted for it. Rather than asking for money, however, Smith asked for drugs. He was willing to trade his MAC-10, he said, for two ounces of cocaine. The officer told Smith that he was just a pawnshop dealer and did not distribute narcotics. Nonetheless, he indicated that he wanted the MAC-10 and would try to get the cocaine.

The undercover officer then left, promising to return within an hour, and went to the sheriff's office to arrange for Smith's arrest. But Smith did not wait. The officers who were conducting surveillance saw him leave the motel room carrying a gun bag; he then climbed into his van and drove away. The officers reported Smith's departure and began following him. When law enforcement authorities tried to stop Smith, he led them on a high-speed

"To make punishments efficacious, two things are necessary. They must never be disproportioned to the offense, and they must be certain."

—William Sims (1806–1870)

chase, which ended in his apprehension. Smith, it turns out, was well armed. A search of his van revealed the MAC-10, a silencer, ammunition, and a "fast-feed" mechanism. In addition, police found a MAC-11 machine gun, a loaded .45-caliber pistol, and a .22-caliber pistol with a scope and homemade silencer. Smith also had a loaded 9-mm handgun in his waistband.

A grand jury for the Southern District of Florida returned an indictment charging Smith with, among other offenses, two drug-trafficking crimes—conspiracy to possess cocaine with intent to distribute and attempt to possess cocaine with intent to distribute. More importantly, the indictment alleged that Smith knowingly used the MAC-10 and its silencer during and in relation to a drug-trafficking crime. Under federal law, a defendant who so uses a firearm must be sentenced to five years incarceration. And where, as here, the firearm is a "machine gun" or is fitted with a silencer, the sentence is 30 years. The jury convicted Smith on all counts.

This story is taken directly from the majority opinion in the 1993 U.S. Supreme Court case of *Smith* v. *U.S.*,[1] which held that "[a] criminal who trades his firearm for drugs 'uses' it within the meaning" of federal sentencing guidelines. The plain language of the statute, the high court explained, imposes no requirement that the firearm be used as a weapon. Smith's appeal of his 30-year sentence was denied.[2]

Sentencing is the imposition of a penalty upon a person convicted of a crime. Most sentencing decisions are made by judges, although in some cases, especially where a death sentence is possible, juries may be involved in a special sentencing phase of courtroom proceedings. The sentencing decision is one of the most difficult made by any judge or jury. Not only does it involve the future, and perhaps the very life, of the defendant, but society looks to sentencing to achieve a diversity of goals—some of which may not be fully compatible.

This chapter examines sentencing in terms of both philosophy and practice. We will describe the goals of sentencing as well as the historical development of various sentencing models in the United States. The role of victims in contemporary sentencing practices will also be discussed. This chapter contains a detailed overview of victimization and victims' rights in general—especially as they relate to courtroom procedure and to sentencing practice. Finally, federal sentencing guidelines and the significance of presentence investigations are described. For a good overview of sentencing issues, visit the Sentencing Project via **WebExtra! 9-1** at CJToday.com.

> **Sentencing**
>
> *The imposition of a criminal sanction by a judicial authority.*

The Philosophy of Criminal Sentencing

Traditional sentencing options have included imprisonment, fines, probation, and—for very serious offenses—death. Limits on the range of options available to sentencing authorities are generally specified by law. Historically, those limits have shifted as understanding of crime and the goals of sentencing have changed. Sentencing philosophies, or the justifications upon which various sentencing strategies are based, are manifestly intertwined with issues of religion, morals, values, and emotions.[3] Philosophies which gained ascendancy at a particular point in history were likely to be reflections of more deeply held social values. The mentality of centuries ago, for example, held that crime was due to sin, and suffering was the culprit's due. Judges were expected to be harsh. Capital punishment, torture, and painful physical penalties served this view of criminal behavior.

An emphasis on rehabilitation became more prevalent around the time of the American and French revolutions, brought about, in part, by Enlightenment philosophies. Offenders came to be seen as highly rational beings who, more often than not, intentionally and somewhat carefully chose their courses of action. Sentencing philosophies of the period stressed the need for sanctions which outweighed the benefits to be derived from making criminal choices. Severity of punishment became less important than quick and certain penalties.

Recent thinking has emphasized the need to limit offenders' potential for future harm by separating them from society. We still also believe that offenders deserve to be punished, and we have not entirely abandoned hope for their rehabilitation. Modern sentencing practices are influenced by five goals, which weave their way through widely disseminated professional

> "We will not punish a man because he hath offended, but that he may offend no more; nor does punishment ever look to the past, but to the future; for it is not the result of passion, but that the same thing be guarded against in time to come."
>
> *—Seneca (B.C. 3–65 A.D.)*

and legal models, continuing public calls for sentencing reform, and everyday sentencing practice. Each goal represents a quasi-independent sentencing philosophy, since each makes distinctive assumptions about human nature and holds implications for sentencing practice. The five goals of contemporary sentencing are as follows:

1. Retribution
2. Incapacitation
3. Deterrence
4. Rehabilitation
5. Restoration

Retribution

Retribution

The act of taking revenge upon a criminal perpetrator.

Retribution is a call for punishment predicated upon a felt need for vengeance. Retribution is the earliest known rationale for punishment. Most early societies punished offenders whenever they could catch them. Early punishments were swift and immediate—often without the benefit of a hearing—and they were often extreme, with little thought given to whether the punishment "fit" the crime. Death and exile, for example, were commonly imposed, even on relatively minor offenders. In contrast, the Old Testament dictum of "An eye for an eye, a tooth for a tooth"—often cited as an ancient justification for retribution—was actually intended to reduce the severity of punishment for relatively minor crimes.

Just Deserts

As a model of criminal sentencing, one which holds that criminal offenders deserve the punishment they receive at the hands of the law and that punishments should be appropriate to the type and severity of crime committed.

In its modern guise, retribution corresponds to the **just deserts** model of sentencing. The just deserts philosophy holds that offenders are responsible for their crimes. When they are convicted and punished, they are said to have gotten their "just deserts." Retribution sees punishment as deserved, justified, and even required,[4] by the offender's behavior. The primary sentencing tool of today's just deserts model is imprisonment, but in extreme cases capital punishment (that is, death) may become the ultimate retribution.

Although it may be an age-old goal of criminal sentencing, retribution is very much in the forefront of public thinking and political policy-making today. Within the last few years, as the social order perspective with its emphasis on individual responsibility has gained ascendancy, public demands for retribution-based criminal punishments have been loud and clear. In 1994, for example, the Mississippi legislature, encouraged by Governor Kirk Fordice, voted to ban prison air conditioning, remove privately owned television sets from prison cells and dormitories, and prohibit weight lifting by inmates. Governor Fordice sent a "get-tough" proposal to the legislature, which was quickly dubbed the "Clint Eastwood Hang 'em High Bill,"[5]

Modern-day retribution in practice: A counselor in a prison boot camp program tells a robber what it feels like to have a gun pointed at his head.
Steve Starr, Stock Boston.

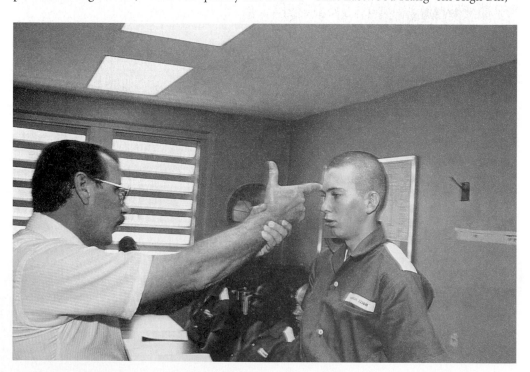

and required inmates to wear striped uniforms with the word "CONVICT" stamped on the back. State Representative Mac McInnis explained the state's retribution-inspired fervor this way: "We want a prisoner to look like a prisoner, to smell like a prisoner."[6]

With public anticrime sentiment at what may be an all-time high, says Jonathan Turley, director of the Prison Law Project, "It's difficult to imagine a measure draconian enough to satisfy the public desire for retribution."[7] As critics say, however, the fact that none of these measures will likely deter crime is beside the point. The goal of retribution, after all, is not deterrence, but satisfaction.[8]

Incapacitation

Incapacitation, the second goal of criminal sentencing, seeks to protect innocent members of society from offenders who might do them harm if they were not prevented in some way. In ancient times mutilation and amputation of the extremities were sometimes used to prevent offenders from repeating their crimes. Modern incapacitation strategies separate offenders from the community in order to reduce opportunities for further criminality. Incapacitation is sometimes called the "lock 'em up approach" and forms the basis for the movement toward prison "warehousing," discussed later in Chapter 11.

Both incapacitation and retribution are used as justifications for imprisonment. A significant difference between the two perspectives, however, lies in the fact that incapacitation requires only restraint—and not punishment. Hence advocates of the incapacitation philosophy of sentencing are sometimes also active prison reformers, seeking to humanize correctional institutions. At the forefront of technology, confinement innovations are now offering ways to achieve the goal of incapacitation without the need for imprisonment. Electronic confinement (discussed shortly) and biomedical intervention (such as "chemical castration") may be able to achieve the goals of incapacitation without the need for imprisonment.

Incapacitation
The use of imprisonment or other means to reduce the likelihood that an offender will be capable of committing future offenses.

Deterrence

Deterrence uses punishment as an example to convince people that criminal activity is not worthwhile. Its overall goal is crime prevention. **Specific deterrence** seeks to reduce the likelihood of recidivism (repeat offenses) by convicted offenders, while **general deterrence** strives to influence the future behavior of people who have not yet been arrested and who may be tempted to turn to crime.

Deterrence is one of the more rational goals of sentencing. It is rational because it is an easily articulated goal, and also because it is possible to investigate objectively the amount of punishment required to deter. It is generally agreed today that harsh punishments can virtually eliminate many minor forms of criminality.[9] Few traffic tickets would have to be written, for example, if minor driving offenses were punishable by death. A free society such as our own, of course, is not willing to impose extreme punishments on petty offenders, and even harsh punishments are not demonstrably effective in reducing the incidence of serious crimes such as murder and drug running.

Deterrence is compatible with the goal of incapacitation, since at least specific deterrence can be achieved through incapacitating offenders. Hugo Bedau,[10] however, points to significant differences between retribution and deterrence. Retribution is oriented toward the past, says Bedau. It seeks to redress wrongs already committed. Deterrence, in contrast, is a strategy for the future. It aims to prevent new crimes. But as H.L.A. Hart has observed,[11] retribution can be the means through which deterrence is achieved. By serving as an example of what might happen to others, punishment may have an inhibiting effect.

Deterrence
A goal of criminal sentencing which seeks to prevent others from committing crimes similar to the one for which an offender is being sentenced.

Specific Deterrence
A goal of criminal sentencing which seeks to prevent a particular offender from engaging in repeat criminality.

General Deterrence
A goal of criminal sentencing which seeks to prevent others from committing crimes similar to the one for which a particular offender is being sentenced by making an example of the person sentenced.

Rehabilitation

Rehabilitation seeks to bring about fundamental changes in offenders and their behavior. As in the case of deterrence, the ultimate goal of rehabilitation is a reduction in the number of criminal offenses. Whereas deterrence depends upon a "fear of the law" and the consequences of violating it, rehabilitation generally works through education and psychological treatment to reduce the likelihood of future criminality.

Rehabilitation
The attempt to reform a criminal offender. Also, the state in which a reformed offender is said to be.

The term *rehabilitation,* however, may actually be a misnomer for the kinds of changes that its supporters seek. Rehabilitation literally means to return a person (or thing) to its previous condition. Hence, medical rehabilitation programs seek to restore functioning to atrophied limbs, rejuvenate injured organs, and mend shattered minds. In the case of criminal offenders, however, it is unlikely that restoring many to their previous state will result in anything other than a more youthful type of criminality.

In the past, rehabilitation as a sentencing strategy, if it existed at all, was primarily applied to youths. One of the first serious efforts to reform adult offenders was begun by the Pennsylvania Quakers, who initiated the development of the late-eighteenth-century penitentiary. The penitentiary, which attempted to combine enforced penance with religious instruction, proved to be something of an aberration. Within a few decades it had been firmly supplanted by a retributive approach to corrections.

It was not until the 1930s that rehabilitation achieved a primary role in the sentencing of adult offenders in the United States. At the time, the psychological world view of therapists such as Sigmund Freud was entering popular culture. Psychology held out, as never before, the possibility of a structured approach to rehabilitation through therapeutic intervention. The rehabilitative approach of the mid-1900s became known as the medical model of corrections, since it was built around a prescriptive approach to the treatment of offenders which provided at least the appearance of clinical predictability.

The primacy of the rehabilitative goal in sentencing fell victim to a "nothing works" philosophy in the late 1970s. The nothing works doctrine was based upon studies of recidivism rates, which consistently showed that rehabilitation was more an ideal than a reality. With as many as 90 percent of former convicted offenders returning to lives of crime following release from prison-based treatment programs, public sentiments in favor of incapacitation grew. Although the rehabilitation ideal has clearly suffered in the public arena, emerging evidence has begun to suggest that effective treatment programs do exist and may be growing in number.[12]

Restoration

Victims of crime or their survivors are frequently traumatized by their experiences. Some are killed, and others receive lasting physical injuries. For many, the world is never the same. The victimized may live in constant fear—reduced in personal vigor and unable to form trusting relationships. Restoration is a sentencing goal that seeks to address this damage by making the victim and the community "whole again."

A recent report by the U.S. Department of Justice explains restoration this way: "Crime was once defined as a 'violation of the State.' This remains the case today, but we now recognize that crime is far more. It is—among other things—a violation of one person by another. While retributive justice may address the first type of violation adequately, **restorative justice** is required to effectively address the latter. . . . Thus [through restorative justice] we seek to attain a balance between the legitimate needs of the community, the . . . offender, and the victim."[13]

The "healing" of victims involves many aspects, ranging from victim assistance initiatives to legislation supporting victim compensation. Sentencing options which seek to restore the victim have focused primarily on restitution payments which offenders are ordered to make, either to their victims or to a general fund, which may then go to reimburse victims for suffering, lost wages, and medical expenses. In support of these goals, the 1984 Federal Comprehensive Crime Control Act specifically requires: "If sentenced to probation, the defendant must also be ordered to pay a fine, make restitution, and/or work in community service."[14]

Texas provides one example of a statewide strategy to utilize restitution as an alternative to prison.[15] The Texas Residential Restitution Program operates community-based centers, which house selected nonviolent felony offenders. Residents work at regular jobs in the community, pay for support of their families, make restitution to their victims, and pay for room and board. During nonworking hours they are required to perform community service work.

Vermont, which in 1995 began a new Sentencing Options Program built around the concept of reparative probation, provides a second example. According to state officials, the Ver-

Restoration

A goal of criminal sentencing which attempts to make the victim "whole again."

Restorative Justice

A sentencing model which builds upon restitution and community participation in an attempt to make the victim "whole again."

A defendant stands before a judge in Austin, Texas, for sentencing.
Bob Daemmrich, Stock Boston.

mont reparative options program, which "requires the offender to make reparations to the victim and to the community, marks the first time in the United States that the Restorative Justice model has been embraced by a state department of corrections and implemented on a statewide scale."[16] Vermont's reparative program builds upon "community reparative boards" consisting of five or six citizens from the community where the crime was committed and requires face-to-face public meetings between the offender and board representatives. Keeping in mind the program's avowed goals of "making the victim(s) whole again" and having the offender "make amends to the community," board members determine the specifics of the offender's sentence. Options include restitution, community service work, victim-offender mediation, victim empathy programs, driver improvement courses, and the like.

Some advocates of the restoration philosophy of sentencing point out that restitution payments and work programs which benefit the victim can also have the added benefit of rehabilitating the offender. The hope is that such sentences may teach offenders personal responsibility through structured financial obligations, job requirements, and regularly scheduled payments. Learn more about restorative justice by visiting WebExtra! 9-2 at CJToday.com.

Indeterminate Sentencing

Indeterminate Sentencing

A model of criminal punishment which encourages rehabilitation via the use of general and relatively unspecific sentences (such as a term of imprisonment of "from one to 10 years").

While the *philosophy* of criminal sentencing is reflected in the goals of sentencing we have just discussed, different sentencing *practices* have been linked to each goal. During most of the twentieth century, for example, the rehabilitative goal has been influential. Since rehabilitation required that individual offenders' personal characteristics be closely considered in defining effective treatment strategies, judges were generally permitted wide discretion in choosing from among sentencing options. Although incapacitation is increasingly becoming the sentencing strategy of choice, many state criminal codes still allow judges to impose fines, probation, or widely varying prison terms, all for the same offense. These sentencing practices, characterized primarily by vast judicial choice, constitute an *indeterminate sentencing model.*

Indeterminate sentencing has both an historical and a philosophical basis in the belief that convicted offenders are more likely to participate in their own rehabilitation if they can reduce the amount of time they have to spend in prison. Inmates on good behavior will be released early, while recalcitrant inmates will remain in prison until the end of their terms. For that reason, parole generally plays a significant role in states which employ the indeterminate sentencing model.

Indeterminate sentencing relies heavily upon judges' discretion to choose among types of sanctions and set upper and lower limits on the length of prison stays. Indeterminate sentences are typically imposed with wording such as "The defendant shall serve not less than five, not more than twenty-five years in the state's prison, under the supervision of the state department of correction...." Judicial discretion under the indeterminate model also extends to the imposition of concurrent or consecutive sentences, where the offender is convicted on more than one charge. Consecutive sentences are served one after the other, while concurrent sentences expire simultaneously.

The indeterminate model was also created to take into consideration detailed differences in degrees of guilt. Under this model judges could weigh minute differences among cases, situations, and offenders. All of the following could be considered before sentence was passed: (1) whether the offender committed the crime out of a need for money, for the thrill it afforded, out of a desire for revenge, or for the "hell of it"; (2) how much harm the offender intended; (3) how much the victim contributed to his or her own victimization; (4) the extent of the damages inflicted; (5) the mental state of the offender; (6) the likelihood of successful rehabilitation; (7) the degree of the offender's cooperation with authorities; and (8) a near infinity of other individual factors.

Under the indeterminate sentencing model, the inmate's behavior (while incarcerated) is the primary determinant of the amount of time served. State parole boards wield great discretion under the model, acting as the final arbiters of the actual sentence served.

A few states employ a partially indeterminate sentencing model. Partially indeterminate sentencing systems allow judges to specify only the maximum amount of time to be served. Some minimum is generally implied by law but is not under the control of the sentencing authority. General practice is to set one year as a minimum for all felonies, while a few jurisdictions assume no minimum time at all—making persons sentenced to imprisonment eligible for immediate parole.

Problems with the Indeterminate Model

Indeterminate sentencing is still the rule in many jurisdictions, including Georgia, Hawaii, Iowa, Kentucky, Massachusetts, Michigan, Nevada, New York, Oklahoma, Rhode Island, South Carolina, Texas, Utah, Vermont, West Virginia, Wyoming, and North and South Dakota.[17] By the 1970s, however, the model had come under fire for contributing to inequality in sentencing. Critics claimed that the indeterminate model allowed divergent judicial personalities, and the often too-personal philosophies of judges, to produce a wide range of sentencing practices from very lenient to very strict. The "hanging judge," who still presides in some jurisdictions, was depicted as tending to impose the maximum sentence allowable under law on anyone who comes before the bench, regardless of circumstances. Worse still, the indeterminate model was criticized for perpetuating a system under which offenders might be sentenced, at least by some judges, more on the basis of social characteristics, such as race, gender, and social class, rather than culpability.

Because of the personal nature of judicial decisions under the indeterminate model, offenders—in jurisdictions where the model is still used—often depend upon the advice and ploys of their attorneys to appear before a judge who is thought to be a good sentencing risk. Requests for delays are a commonly used defense strategy in indeterminate sentencing states where they are used in attempts to manipulate the selection of judicial personalities involved in sentencing decisions.

Another charge leveled against indeterminate sentencing is that it tends to produce dishonesty in sentencing. Because of sentence cutbacks for good behavior and other reductions available to inmates through involvement in work and study programs, punishments rarely mean what they say. A sentence of five to 10 years, for example, might actually see an inmate released in a matter of months after all "gain time," "**good time,**" and other special allowances have been calculated. (Some of the same charges can be leveled against determinate sentencing schemes under which correctional officials can administratively reduce the time served by an inmate.) To ensure long prison terms within indeterminate jurisdictions, some court officials have been led to extremes. In 1994, for example, a judge in Oklahoma, an indeterminate sentencing state, followed a jury's recommendation and sentenced convicted child molester Charles Scott Robinson, aged 30, to 30,000 years in prison.[18] Judge Dan Owens, complying with the jury's efforts to ensure that Robinson would spend the rest of his life behind bars, sentenced him to serve six consecutive 5,000-year sentences. Robinson had 14 previous felony convictions.

Due largely to indeterminate sentencing practices, time served in prison is generally far less than sentences would seem to indicate. A recent survey[19] by the Bureau of Justice Statistics found that even violent offenders, the most serious of all, who were released from state prisons during the study period served, on average, only 53 percent of the sentences they originally received. Nonviolent offenders serve even smaller portions of their sentences. Table 9-1 shows the percentage of imposed sentences that can be expected to be served in prison by offenders sentenced to prison in 1996 by type of offense.

The Rise of Structured Sentencing

Until the 1970s, all 50 states used some form of indeterminate (or partially indeterminate) sentencing. Soon, however, calls for **equity** and **proportionality** in sentencing, heightened by claims of racial disparity in the sentencing practices[20] of some judges, led many states to move toward closer control over their sentencing systems.

Critics of the indeterminate model called for the recognition of three fundamental sentencing principles: proportionality, equity, and **social debt.** *Proportionality* refers to the belief that the severity of sanctions should bear a direct relationship to the seriousness of the crime committed. *Equity* is based upon a concern with social equality and means that similar crimes should be punished with the same degree of severity, regardless of the general social or personal characteristics of offenders. According to the principle of equity, for example, two bank robbers in different parts of the country, who use the same techniques and weapons, with the same degree of implied threat, even though they are tried under separate circumstances, should receive roughly the same kind of sentence. The equity principle needs to be balanced, however, against the notion of social debt. In the case of the bank robbers, the offender who has a prior criminal record can be said to have a higher level of social debt than the one-time robber, where all else is equal. Greater social debt, of course, would suggest a heightened severity of punishment or a greater need for treatment, and so on.

Good Time

The amount of time deducted from time to be served in prison on a given sentence(s) and/or under correctional agency jurisdiction, at some point after a prisoner's admission to prison, contingent upon good behavior and/or awarded automatically by application of a statute or regulation.

Proportionality

A sentencing principle which holds that the severity of sanctions should bear a direct relationship to the seriousness of the crime committed.

Equity

A sentencing principle, based upon concerns with social equity, which holds that similar crimes should be punished with the same degree of severity, regardless of the social or personal characteristics of offenders.

Social Debt

A sentencing principle which objectively counts an offender's criminal history in sentencing decisions.

TABLE 9-1 ■ Percent of Sentence to Be Served by New Court Commitments to State Prison	
OFFENSE TYPE	PERCENT
Violent	51
Property	46
Drug	46
Public-order	49
Average for all felonies	**49**

Source: Paula M. Ditton and Doris James Wilson, Truth in Sentencing in State Prisons *(Washington, D.C.: Bureau of Justice Statistics, January 1999).*

Structured Sentencing

A model of criminal punishment that includes determinate and commission-created presumptive sentencing schemes, as well as voluntary/advisory sentencing guidelines.

Determinate Sentencing (also called Fixed Sentencing)

A model of criminal punishment in which an offender is given a fixed term that may be reduced by good time or earned time. Under the model, for example, all offenders convicted of the same degree of burglary would be sentenced to the same length of time behind bars.

Voluntary/Advisory Sentencing Guidelines

Recommended sentencing policies that are not required by law.

Presumptive Sentencing

A model of criminal punishment that meets the following conditions: (1) the appropriate sentence for an offender in a specific case is presumed to fall within a range of sentences authorized by sentencing guidelines that are adopted by a legislatively created sentencing body, usually a sentencing commission; (2) sentencing judges are expected to sentence within the range to provide written justification for departure; (3) the guidelines provide for some review, usually appellate, of the departure.

Beginning in the 1970s, a number of states moved to address these concerns by developing a different model of sentencing known as **structured sentencing.** One form of structured sentencing, called **determinate sentencing,** requires that a convicted offender be sentenced to a fixed term that may be reduced by good time or earned time. Determinate sentencing states eliminated the use of parole and created explicit standards to specify the amount of punishment appropriate for a given offense. Determinate sentencing practices also specify an anticipated release date for each sentenced offender.

In a 1996 report[21] that traced the historical development of determinate sentencing, the National Council on Crime and Delinquency (NCCD) observed that

> . . . [t]he term 'determinate sentencing' is generally used to refer to the sentencing reforms of the late 1970s. In those reforms, the legislatures of California, Illinois, Indiana, and Maine abolished the parole release decision and replaced the indeterminate penalty structure with a fixed (flat) sentence that could be reduced by a significant good-time provision. The only state that has adopted a true determinate sentencing system since 1980 is Arizona, which enacted a 'truth in sentencing law' on January 1, 1994. These five states have retained their determinate sentencing models, although no other states have adopted such a structured sentencing scheme.

The NCCD report continues:[22]

> In three of the states (California, Illinois, and Indiana), the legislators provided presumptive ranges of confinement. But those in Illinois and Indiana were so wide that they provided the court with extensive discretion on sentence length. For many offenses, there was no presumptive lead as to whether the sentence should be for, or against, incarceration. Thus, courts were left with extensive discretion in deciding both whether to incarcerate and the length of incarceration. It is arguable that the discretion attacked in these reforms was mainly that of parole boards and that the discretion lost by parole boards was largely shifted to the courts or to the prosecutors who control the charging function.

In response to the then-growing determinate sentencing movement, a few states developed **voluntary/advisory sentencing guidelines.** Such guidelines consist of recommended sentencing policies that are not required by law. They are usually based upon past sentencing practices and serve as guides to judges. Voluntary/advisory sentencing guidelines may build upon either determinate or indeterminate sentencing structures. Florida, Maryland, Massachusetts, Michigan, Rhode Island, Utah, and Wisconsin all experimented with voluntary/advisory guidelines during the 1980s. Voluntary/advisory guidelines constitute a second form of structured sentencing.

A third model of structured sentencing employs what NCCD calls "commission-based **presumptive sentencing** guidelines." Presumptive sentencing schemes became common in the 1980s as states began to experiment with approaches using sentencing guidelines developed by sentencing commissions. These models differed from both determinate and voluntary/advisory guidelines in three respects. First, presumptive sentencing guidelines were not developed by the legislature but by a sentencing commission that often represented a diverse array of criminal justice and sometimes private-citizen interests. Second, presumptive sentencing guidelines were explicit and highly structured, typically relying on a quantitative scoring instrument to classify the offense for which a person was to be sentenced. Third, the guidelines were not voluntary/advisory in that judges had to adhere to the sentencing system or provide a written rationale for departures. NCCD observes, "[a]s in the move to determinate sentencing and voluntary/advisory guidelines, the driving forces stimulating presumptive sentencing guidelines were issues of fairness (including disparity, certainty, and proportionality) and prison crowding. These concerns provided the impetus for states to adopt guidelines, replace indeterminate sentencing with determinate sentencing, and abolish or curtail discretionary parole release."[23]

The first four states to adopt presumptive sentencing guideline systems were Minnesota (1980), Pennsylvania (1982), Washington (1983), and Florida (1983). The Minnesota model in particular, with its focus on controlling prison population growth, has often been cited as a successful example of controlling disparity and rising corrections costs through sentencing guidelines. The American Bar Association has endorsed sentencing commission-based guidelines through its Criminal Justice Standards Committee's *Sentencing Alternatives and Procedures* (adopted by the ABA House of Delegates). In making such an endorsement, the Standards Committee relied heavily upon the system of presumptive sentencing pioneered in Minnesota.

The federal government and 16 states have now established commission-based sentencing guidelines. Ten of the 16 states can be classified as using presumptive sentencing guidelines. The remaining six have voluntary/advisory guideline models. As a consequence, sentencing guidelines authored by legislatively created sentencing commissions are now the most popular form of structured sentencing.

Guideline jurisdictions, which specify a presumptive sentence for a given offense, generally allow for "aggravating" or "mitigating" factors—indicating greater or lesser degrees of culpability—which judges can take into consideration in imposing a sentence somewhat at variance from the presumptive term. **Aggravating circumstances** are those which appear to call for a tougher sentence and may include especially heinous behavior, cruelty, injury to more than one person, and so on. In death penalty cases, however, the U.S. Supreme Court has held that aggravating factors must "provide specific and detailed guidance and make rationally reviewable the death sentencing process. . . . In order to decide whether a particular aggravating circumstance meets these requirements, a federal court must determine whether the statutory language defining the circumstance is itself too vague to guide the sentencer. . . ."[24]

Mitigating circumstances, or those which indicate that a lesser sentence is called for, are generally similar to legal defenses, although in this case they only reduce criminal responsibility, not eliminate it. Mitigating factors include such things as cooperation with the investigating authority, surrender, good character, and so on. Common aggravating and mitigating factors are listed in a "Theory into Practice" box in this chapter.

Critiques of Structured Sentencing

Structured sentencing models, which have generally sought to address the shortcomings of indeterminate sentencing by curtailing judicial discretion in sentencing, are not without their critics. Detractors charge that structured sentencing is (1) overly simplistic, (2) based upon a primitive concept of culpability, and (3) incapable of offering hope for rehabilitation and change. For one thing, they say, structured sentencing has built-in limitations, which render it far less able to judge the blameworthiness of individual offenders. Legislatures and sentencing commissions, say critics, simply cannot anticipate all the differences that individual cases can present. Aggravating and mitigating factors, while intended to cover most circumstances, will inevitably shortchange some defendants who don't fall neatly into the categories they provide.

A second critique of structured sentencing is that while it may reduce judicial discretion substantially, it may do nothing to hamper the huge discretionary decision-making power of prosecutors.[25] In fact, federal sentencing reformers, who have adopted a structured sentencing model, have specifically decided not to modify the discretionary power of prosecutors, citing the large number of cases which are resolved through plea bargaining. Such a shift in discretionary authority, away from judges and into the hands of prosecutors, say critics, may be misplaced.

Another criticism of structured sentencing questions its fundamental purpose. Advocates of structured sentencing inevitably cite greater equity in sentencing as the primary benefits of such a model. Reduced to its essence, this means that "those who commit the same crime get the same time." Sentencing reformers have thus couched the drive toward structured sentencing in progressive terms. Others, however, have pointed out that the philosophical underpinnings of the movement may be quite different. Albert Alschuler,[26] for example, suggests that structured sentencing is a regressive social policy which derives from American weariness with considering offenders as individuals. Describing this kind of thinking, Alschuler writes: "Don't tell us that a robber was retarded. We don't care about his problems. We don't know what to *do* about his problems, and we are no longer interested in listening to a criminal's sob stories. The most important thing about this robber is simply that he *is* a robber."[27]

A different line of thought is proposed by Christopher Link and Neal Shover[28] who found in a study of state-level economic, political, and demographic data that structured sentencing may ultimately be the result of declining economic conditions and increasing fiscal strain on state governments rather than any particular set of ideals.

Aggravating Circumstances

Those elements of an offense or of an offender's background which could result in a harsher sentence under the determinate model than would otherwise be called for by sentencing guidelines.

Mitigating Circumstances

Those elements of an offense or of an offender's background which could result in a lesser sentence under the determinate model than would otherwise be called for by sentencing guidelines.

"[Unless the Constitution is amended] we will never correct the existing imbalance in this country between [a] defendant's irreducible constitutional rights and the current haphazard patchwork of victims' rights."

—Former U.S. Attorney General Janet Reno (1997)

Aggravating and Mitigating Factors

Listed here are some typical aggravating and mitigating factors which judges may take into consideration in arriving at sentencing decisions in presumptive sentencing jurisdictions.

Aggravating Factors

◆The defendant induced others to participate in the commission of the offense.

◆The offense was especially heinous, atrocious, or cruel.

◆The defendant was armed with or used a deadly weapon at the time of the crime.

◆The offense was committed for the purpose of avoiding or preventing a lawful arrest or effecting an escape from custody.

◆The offense was committed for hire.

◆The offense was committed against a present or former law enforcement officer or correctional officer while engaged in the performance of official duties, or because of the past exercise of official duties.

◆The defendant took advantage of a position of trust or confidence to commit the offense.

Mitigating Factors

◆The defendant has no record of criminal convictions punishable by more than 60 days of imprisonment.

◆The defendant has made substantial or full restitution.

◆The defendant has been a person of good character or has had a good reputation in the community.

◆The defendant aided in the apprehension of another felon or testified truthfully on behalf of the prosecution.

◆The defendant acted under strong provocation, or the victim was a voluntary participant in the criminal activity, or otherwise consented to it.

◆The offense was committed under duress, coercion, threat, or compulsion which was insufficient to constitute a defense but significantly reduced the defendant's culpability.

◆The defendant was suffering from a mental or physical condition that was insufficient to constitute a defense but significantly reduced culpability for the offense.

? QUESTIONS FOR DISCUSSION

1. What aggravating factors, if any, might you add to the list in this box? Why?

2. What mitigating factors, if any, might you add to the list in this box? Why?

A fifth critique of structured sentencing centers on its alleged inability to promote effective rehabilitation. Under indeterminate sentencing schemes, offenders have the opportunity to act responsibly and thus to participate in their own rehabilitation.[29] Lack of responsible behavior results in denial of parole and extension of the sentence. Structured sentencing schemes, by virtue of dramatic reductions in good-time allowances and parole opportunities, leave little incentive for offenders to participate in educational programs, to take advantage of opportunities for work inside of correctional institutions, to seek treatment, or to contribute in any positive way to their own change.

While these critiques may be valid, they will probably do little to stem the rising tide of structured sentencing. The growth of structured sentencing over the past few decades represents the ascendancy of the "just deserts" perspective over other sentencing goals. In a growing number of jurisdictions, punishment, deterrence, and incapacitation have replaced rehabilitation and restitution as the goals which society seeks to achieve through sentencing practices.

Mandatory Sentencing

A structured sentencing scheme which allows no leeway in the nature of the sentence required and under which clearly enumerated punishments are mandated for specific offenses or for habitual offenders convicted of a series of crimes.

Mandatory Sentencing

Mandatory sentencing, which is actually another form of structured sentencing,[30] deserves special mention. **Mandatory sentencing** is just what its name implies—a structured sentencing scheme which allows no leeway in the nature of the sentence required and under which clearly enumerated punishments are mandated for specific offenses or for habitual offenders convicted of a series of crimes. Mandatory sentencing, because it is truly *mandatory*, differs from presumptive sentencing (discussed earlier) which allows for at least a limited amount of judicial discretion within ranges established by published guidelines. Some mandatory sentencing laws require only modest mandatory prison terms (for example, 3 years for armed robbery), while others are much more far-reaching.

Typical of far-reaching mandatory sentencing schemes are three-strikes laws, discussed in a box in this chapter. Three-strikes laws (and, in some jurisdictions, two-strikes laws) require mandatory sentences (sometimes life in prison without the possibility of parole) for offenders convicted of a third serious felony. Such mandatory sentencing enhancements are aimed at deterring known and potentially violent offenders and are intended to incapacitate convicted criminals through long-term incarceration.

Three-strikes laws impose longer prison terms than most earlier mandatory minimum sentencing laws. California's three-strikes law, for example, requires that offenders who are convicted of a violent crime and who have had two prior convictions serve a minimum of 25 years in prison. The law doubles prison terms for offenders convicted of a second violent felony.[31] Three-strikes laws also vary in breadth. The laws of some jurisdictions stipulate that both of the prior convictions and the current offense be violent felonies; others require only that the prior felonies be violent. Some three-strikes laws count only prior adult violent felony convictions, while others permit consideration of juvenile adjudications for violent crimes.

By passing mandatory sentencing laws, legislators convey the message that certain crimes are deemed especially grave and that people who commit them deserve, and may expect, harsh sanctions. These laws are sometimes passed in response to public outcries following heinous or well-publicized crimes.

Mandatory sentencing has had significant consequences that deserve close attention. Among them are its impact on crime and the operation of the criminal justice system. The possible differential consequences for certain groups of people also bears examination. Evaluations of mandatory sentencing have focused on two types of crimes—those committed with handguns and those related to drugs (the offenses most commonly subjected to mandatory minimum penalties in state and federal courts). An evaluation[32] of a Massachusetts law, for example, that imposed mandatory jail terms for possession of an unlicensed handgun, concluded that the law was an effective deterrent of gun crime—at least in the short term. Studies of similar laws in Michigan[33] and Florida,[34] however, found no evidence that crimes committed with firearms had been prevented by similar laws. An evaluation of mandatory gun-use sentencing enhancements in six large cities (Detroit, Jacksonville, Tampa, Miami, Philadelphia, and Pittsburgh) indicated that such laws deterred homicide but not other violent crimes.[35] A similar assessment of New York's Rockefeller drug laws was unable to support claims for their efficacy as a deterrent to drug crime.[36] None of the studies, however, examined the incapacitation effects of these laws on individual offenders.

Mandatory sentencing has also been evaluated in terms of its impact on the criminal justice system. Traditionally, criminal courts have relied on a high rate of guilty pleas to speed case processing and to avoid logjams. Officials have been able to offer inducements (by way of lowered sentences) to defendants to obtain bargained pleas. Mandatory sentencing laws, it has been found, can disrupt established plea-bargaining patterns by preventing a prosecutor from offering a short prison term in exchange for a guilty plea. However, unless policymakers enact long-term mandatory sentences that apply to many related categories of crimes, prosecutors can usually shift strategies and bargain on charges rather than on sentences—thus retaining plea bargaining as a valid option in most courtrooms.

Research findings on the impact of mandatory sentencing laws on the criminal justice system have been summarized by Michael Tonry.[37] Tonry found that under mandatory sentencing, officials tend to make earlier and more selective arrest, charging, and diversion decisions. They also tend to bargain less and to bring more cases to trial. Specifically, Tonry found that (1) criminal justice officials and practitioners (police, lawyers, and judges) exercise discretion to avoid application of laws they consider unduly harsh; (2) arrest rates for target crimes tend to decline soon after mandatory sentencing laws take effect; (3) dismissal and diversion rates increase at early stages of case processing after mandatory sentencing laws become effective; (4) for defendants whose cases are not dismissed, plea-bargain rates decline and trial rates increase; (5) for convicted defendants, sentencing delays increase; (6) enactment of mandatory sentencing laws has little impact on the probability that offenders will be imprisoned (when the effects of declining arrests, indictments, and convictions are taken into account); and (7) sentences become longer and more severe. Mandatory sentencing laws may also occasionally result in unduly harsh punishments for marginal offenders, who nonetheless meet the minimum requirements for sentencing under such laws.

In an analysis of federal sentencing guidelines, other researchers[38] found that blacks receive longer sentences than whites, not because of differential treatment by judges but because they constitute the large majority of those convicted of trafficking in crack cocaine—a crime Congress has singled out for especially harsh mandatory penalties. This pattern can be seen as constituting a "disparity in results" and, partly for this reason, the U.S. Sentencing Commission recommended to Congress that it eliminate the legal distinction between crack and regular cocaine for purposes of sentencing (a recommendation that Congress has so far rejected).

An alternative to mandatory minimum sentencing provisions, which would protect sentencing policy, preserve legislative control, and still toughen sentences for repeat violent offenders, is the use of presumptive sentences. Other possibilities include (1) directing mandatory sentencing laws at only a few especially serious crimes and requiring "sunset" provisions (for example, requiring geriatric inmates who have reached a specified age to be released after serving a certain minimum); (2) subjecting long mandatory sentences to periodic administrative review to determine the advisability of continued confinement in individual cases; (3) building a funding plan into sentencing legislation to ensure awareness of and responsibility for the costs of long-term imprisonment; and (4) developing policies that make more effective and systematic use of intermediate sanctions.

Truth in Sentencing

Truth in Sentencing

A close correspondence between the sentence imposed upon those sent to prison and the time actually served prior to prison release.

In 1984, with passage of the Comprehensive Crime Control Act, the federal government adopted presumptive sentencing for nearly all federal offenders.[39] The act also addressed the issue of honesty in sentencing. Under the old federal system, a sentence of 10 years in prison might actually have meant only a few years spent behind bars before the offender was released. On average, good-time credits and parole reduced time served to about one-third of actual sentences.[40] At the time, sentencing practices of most states reflected the federal model. While sentence reductions may have benefited offenders, they often outraged victims who felt betrayed by the sentencing process. The 1984 act nearly eliminated good-time credits[41] and targeted 1992 (which was later extended to 2002, with further extensions anticipated) as the date for phasing out federal parole and eliminating the U.S. Parole Commission.[42] The emphasis on honesty in sentencing created, in effect, a sentencing environment of "what you get is what you serve."

More recently, the movement toward "truth in sentencing" has accelerated. Truth in sentencing, which has been described as "a close correspondence between the sentence imposed upon those sent to prison and the time actually served prior to prison release,"[43] has become an important policy focus of many state legislatures and the federal Congress. The Violent Crime Control and Law Enforcement Act of 1994 set aside $4 billion in federal prison construction funds (called Truth in Sentencing Incentive Funds) for states which adopt truth in sentencing laws and are able to guarantee that certain violent offenders will serve 85 percent of their sentences. By 1999 twenty-seven states and the District of Columbia had met the 85 percent requirement.[44] Although most other states are moving toward practices which support truth in sentencing, there are some notable exceptions. Texas and Maryland, for example, retain 50 percent requirements for violent offenders, and Nebraska and Indiana require all offenders to serve only 50 percent of their sentences.

Federal Sentencing Guidelines

Title II of the Comprehensive Crime Control Act, called the Sentencing Reform Act of 1984,[45] established the nine-member U.S. Sentencing Commission. The commission is composed of presidential appointees, including three federal judges. First to head the sentencing commission was William W. Wilkins, Jr., U.S. circuit judge for the Fourth Circuit.

The Sentencing Reform Act established mandatory minimum sentences for certain federal crimes, including drug offenses, and limited the discretion of federal judges by mandating the creation of federal sentencing guidelines, which federal judges are required to follow. The sentencing commission was given the task of developing structured sentencing guidelines in order to reduce disparity in sentencing, promote consistency and uniformity in sentencing, and increase sentencing fairness and equity. To guide the commission, Congress specified the purposes of sentencing to include (1) deterring criminals, (2) incapacitating and/or rehabilitating offenders, and (3) providing "just deserts" in punishing criminals. Congress also charged the commission with eliminating sentencing disparities and reducing confusion, and asked for a system which would permit flexibility in the face of mitigating or aggravating elements.

While developing federal sentencing guidelines, the commission analyzed thousands of past cases and enacted a scale of punishments considered typical for given types of offenses.[46] It came up with a series of federal guidelines intended to provide predictability in sentencing, but which also allow individual judges to deviate from the guidelines when specific aggravating or mitigating factors are present. The Commission also considered relevant federal law, parole guidelines, and the anticipated impact of changes upon federal prison populations. One boundary was set by statute: In creating the Sentencing Commission, Congress had also specified that the degree of discretion available in any one sentencing category could not exceed 25 percent of the basic penalty for that category or six months, whichever might be greater.

Guidelines established by the commission took effect in November 1987 but quickly became embroiled in a series of legal disputes, some of which challenged Congress's authority to form the Sentencing Commission. On January 18, 1989, in the case of *Mistretta* v. *U.S.*,[47] the U.S. Supreme Court held that Congress had acted appropriately in establishing the Sentencing Commission and that the guidelines developed by the commission could be applied in federal cases nationwide. The federal Sentencing Commission continues to meet at least once a year in order to review the effectiveness of the guidelines it created. Visit the U.S. Sentencing Commission via WebExtra! 9-3 at CJToday.com.

Federal Guideline Provisions

Federal sentencing guidelines specify a sentencing range for each criminal offense from which judges must choose. If a particular case has "atypical features," judges are allowed to depart from the guidelines. Departures are generally expected to be made only in the presence of mitigating or aggravating factors—a number of which are specified in the guidelines.[48] Aggravating circumstances may include the possession of a weapon during the commission of a crime, the degree of criminal involvement (whether the defendant was a leader or a follower in the criminal activity), and extreme psychological injury to the victim. Punishments also increase where a defendant violates a position of public or private trust, uses special skills to commit or conceal offenses, or has a criminal history. Defendants who express remorse, cooperate with authorities, or willingly make restitution may have their sentences reduced under the guidelines. Any departure from the guidelines may, however, become the basis for appellate review concerning the reasonableness of the sentence imposed, and judges who deviate from the guidelines must provide written reasons for doing so.

Federal sentencing guidelines are built around a table containing 43 rows, each corresponding to one offense level. Penalties associated with each level overlap those of levels above or below in order to discourage unnecessary litigation. A person charged with a crime involving $11,000, for example, upon conviction is unlikely to receive a penalty substantially greater than if the amount involved had been somewhat less than $10,000—a sharp contrast to the old system. A change of six levels roughly doubles the sentence imposed under the guidelines, regardless of the level at which one starts. Because of their matrix-like quality, federal sentencing provisions have also been referred to as "structured sentencing." The federal sentencing table is available at WebExtra! 9-4 at CJToday.com.

The sentencing table also contains six rows, corresponding to the criminal history category into which an offender falls. Criminal history categories are determined on a point basis. Offenders earn points through previous convictions. Each prior sentence of imprison-

ment for more than one year and one month counts as three points. Two points are assigned for each prior prison sentence over six months, or if the defendant committed the offense while on probation, parole, or work release. The system also assigns points for other types of previous convictions and for offenses committed less than two years after release from imprisonment. Points are added together to determine the criminal history category into which an offender falls. Thirteen points or more are required for the highest category. At each offense level, sentences in the highest criminal history category are generally two to three times as severe as for the lowest category.

Defendants may also move into the highest criminal history category (VI) by virtue of being designated career offenders. Under the sentencing guidelines, a defendant is a career offender if "(1) the defendant was at least 18 years old at the time of the . . . offense, (2) the . . . offense is a crime of violence or trafficking in a controlled substance, and (3) the defendant has at least two prior felony convictions of either a crime of violence or a controlled substance offense."[49]

According to the U.S. Supreme Court, an offender may be adjudged a career offender in a single hearing—even when previous convictions are lacking. In *Deal* v. *U.S.* (1993),[50] the defendant, Thomas Lee Deal, was convicted in a single proceeding of six counts of carrying and using a firearm during a series of bank robberies which occurred in the Houston, Texas, area. A federal district court sentenced him to 105 years in prison as a career offender—five years for the first count and 20 years each on the five other counts, with sentences to run consecutively. In the words of the Court, "[w]e see no reason why [the defendant should not receive such a sentence], simply because he managed to evade detection, prosecution, and conviction for the first five offenses and was ultimately tried on all six in a single proceeding."

Plea Bargaining under the Guidelines

Plea bargaining plays a major role in the federal judicial system. Approximately 90 percent of all federal sentences are the result of guilty pleas,[51] and the large majority of those stem from plea negotiations. In the words of Commission Chairman Wilkins, "With respect to plea bargaining, the commission has proceeded cautiously . . . the commission did not believe it wise to stand the federal criminal justice system on its head by making too drastic and too sudden a change in these practices."[52]

Although the commission allowed plea bargaining to continue, it did require that the agreement (1) be fully disclosed in the record of the court (unless there is an overriding and demonstrable reason why it should not) and (2) detail the actual conduct of the offense. Under these requirements defendants will no longer be able to "hide" the actual nature of their offense behind a substitute plea. The thrust of the federal rules concerning plea bargaining is to reduce the veil of secrecy that had previously surrounded the process. Information on the decision-making process itself is available to victims, the media, and the public.

In 1996, in the case of *Melendez* v. *United States*,[53] the U.S. Supreme Court held that a government motion requesting that a trial judge depart below minimum federal sentencing guidelines as part of a cooperative plea agreement does not permit imposition of a sentence below a statutory minimum specified by law. In other words, while federal judges may depart from the guidelines, they cannot accept plea bargains which would result in sentences lower than the minimum required by law for a particular type of offense.

The Sentencing Environment

A number of studies have attempted to investigate the decision-making process that leads to imposition of a particular sentence. Early studies[54] found a strong relationship between the informal influence of members of the courtroom work group and the severity, or lack thereof, of sentences imposed. A number suggested that minorities ran a much greater risk of imprisonment.[55] Other studies have found that sentencing variations are responsive to extralegal conditions[56] and that public opinion can play a role in the type of sentence handed down.[57] If these findings about public opinion are true, they might explain some of the increase in prison populations. A public opinion study conducted by Bowling

Green State University, for example, found that 71 percent of respondents identified incarceration as the preferred punishment for serious offenses.[58]

More recent analyses, especially in structured sentencing jurisdictions, however, have begun to show that sentences in a number of jurisdictions are becoming more objective and, hence, predictable. A California study[59] of racial equity in sentencing, for example, found that the likelihood of going to prison was increased by the following factors:

- Having multiple current conviction counts, prior prison terms, and juvenile incarcerations

- Being on adult and/or juvenile probation or parole at the time of the offense

- Having been released from prison within 12 months of the current offense

- Having a history of drug and/or alcohol abuse

- Being over 21 years of age

- Going to trial

- Not being released prior to trial

- Not being represented by a private attorney

The same study found that, perhaps partly because of the 1977 California Determinate Sentencing Act, "California courts are making racially equitable sentencing decisions."[60] Findings applied only to the crimes of assault, robbery, burglary, theft, forgery, and drug abuse, but held for sentences involving both prison and probation. Similarly, no disparities were noted in the lengths of sentences imposed.[61] Other studies have found that female felons are not treated substantially differently by sentencing authorities than are their male counterparts.[62]

The Presentence Investigation Report

Before imposing sentence, a judge may request information on the background of a convicted defendant. This is especially true in indeterminate sentencing jurisdictions, where judges retain considerable discretion in selecting sanctions. Traditional wisdom has held that certain factors increase the likelihood of rehabilitation and reduce the need for lengthy prison terms. These factors include a good job record, satisfactory educational attainment, strong family ties, church attendance, an arrest history of only nonviolent offenses, and psychological stability.

Information about a defendant's background often comes to the judge in the form of a presentence report. The task of preparing presentence reports usually falls to the probation/parole office. Presentence reports take one of three forms: (1) a detailed written report on the defendant's personal and criminal history, including an assessment of present conditions in the defendant's life (often called the "long form"); (2) an abbreviated written report summarizing the type of information most likely to be useful in a sentencing decision (the "short form"); and (3) a verbal report to the court made by the investigating officer based on field notes but structured according to categories established for the purpose. A presentence report is much like a résumé, or *vitae,* except that it focuses on what might be regarded as negative as well as positive life experiences.

The length of the completed form is subject to great variation. One survey[63] found that Texas used one of the shortest forms of all—a one-page summary supplemented by other materials which the report writer thought might provide meaningful additional details. Orange County, California, provides an example of the opposite kind and may use the most detailed form of any jurisdiction in the country. The instructions for completing the form consist of a dozen single-spaced pages.[64]

A typical long form is divided into 10 major informational sections, as follows: (1) personal information and identifying data describing the defendant; (2) a chronology of the current offense and circumstances surrounding it; (3) a record of the defendant's previous convictions, if any; (4) home life and family data; (5) educational background; (6) health history and current state of health; (7) military service; (8) religious preference; (9) financial condition; and (10) sentencing recommendations made by the probation/parole officer completing the report.

Presentence Investigation

The examination of a convicted offender's background prior to sentencing. Presentence examinations are generally conducted by probation/parole officers and submitted to sentencing authorities.

The data on which a presentence report is based come from a variety of sources. Since the 1960s modern computer-based criminal information clearinghouses, such as the FBI's National Crime Information Center (NCIC), have simplified at least a part of the data-gathering process. The NCIC began in 1967 and contains information on people wanted for criminal offenses throughout the United States. Individual jurisdictions also maintain criminal records repositories which are able to provide comprehensive files on the criminal history of persons processed by the justice system. In the late 1970s the federal government encouraged states to develop criminal records repositories utilizing computer technology.[65] The years that followed have been described as "the focus of a data gathering effort more massive and more coordinated than any other in criminal justice."[66]

In a presentence report, almost any third-party data are subject to ethical and legal considerations. The official records of almost any agency or organization, while they may prove to be an ideal source of information, are often protected by state and federal privacy requirements. In particular, the Federal Privacy Act of 1974[67] may limit records access. Investigators should first check on the legal availability of all records before requesting them and should receive in writing the defendant's permission to access records. Other public laws, among them the federal Freedom of Information Act,[68] may make the presentence report itself available to the defendant, although courts and court officers have generally been held to be exempt from the provision of such statutes.

Sometimes the defendant is a significant source of much of the information which appears in the presentence report. When such is the case, efforts should be made to corroborate the information provided by the defendant. Unconfirmed data will generally be marked on the report as "defendant-supplied data" or simply "unconfirmed."

The final section of a presentence report is usually devoted to the investigating officer's recommendations. A recommendation may be made in favor of probation, split sentencing, a term of imprisonment, or any other sentencing options available in the jurisdiction. Participation in community service programs may be recommended for probationers, and drug or substance abuse programs may be suggested as well. Some analysts have observed that a "judge accepts an officer's recommendation in an extremely high percentage of cases."[69] Most judges are willing to accept the report writer's recommendation because they recognize the professionalism of presentence investigators and because they know that the investigator may well be the supervising officer assigned to the defendant should a community alternative be the sentencing decision.

Jurisdictions vary in their use of presentence reports and in the form they take. Federal law mandates presentence reports in federal criminal courts and specifies 15 topical areas which each report must contain. The 1984 federal Determinate Sentencing Act directs report writers to include information on the classification of the offense and of the defendant under the offense-level and criminal history categories established by the statute.

Some states require presentence reports only in felony cases, and others in cases where defendants face the possibility of incarceration for six months or more. Still others may have no requirement for presentence reports beyond those ordered by a judge. Even so, report writing, rarely anyone's favorite, may seriously tax the limited resources of probation agencies. In 1998, New York City Department of Probation officers wrote more than 52,000 presentence investigation reports for adult offenders, and 7,000 investigations for juvenile offenders—averaging over 40 reports per probation officer per month.

Presentence reports may be useful sentencing tools. Many officers who prepare them take their responsibility seriously. One study,[70] however, shows a tendency among presentence investigators to satisfy judicial expectations about defendants by tailoring reports to fit the image the defendant projects. Prior criminal record and present offense may influence the interpretation of all the other data gathered.[71]

The Victim—Forgotten No Longer

Thanks to a grass-roots resurgence of concern for the plight of victims, which began in this country in the early 1970s, the sentencing environment now frequently includes consideration of the needs of victims and their survivors.[72] Unfortunately, in times past the concerns

Theory Into Practice

Three Strikes and You're Out—The Tough New Movement in Criminal Sentencing

In the spring of 1994 California legislators passed the state's now-famous "three strikes and you're out" bill. Amid much fanfare, Governor Pete Wilson signed the "three-strikes" measure into law, calling it "the toughest and most sweeping crime bill in California history."

California's law, which is retroactive (in that it counts offenses committed before the date the legislation was signed) requires a 25-year-to-life sentence for three-time felons with convictions for two or more serious or violent prior offenses. Criminal offenders facing a "second strike" can receive up to double the normal sentence for their most recent offense. Parole consideration is not available until at least 80 percent of the sentence has been served.

Today, 23 states have passed three-strikes legislation—and other states are considering it. At the federal level, the Violent Crime Control and Law Enforcement Act of 1994 contains a three-strikes provision, which mandates life imprisonment for federal criminals convicted of three violent felonies or drug offenses.

Questions remain, however, as to the effectiveness of three-strikes legislation, and many are concerned about its impact on the justice system. One year after it was signed into law, the California three-strikes initiative was evaluated by the RAND Corporation. RAND researchers found that, in the first year, more than 5,000 defendants were convicted and sentenced under the law's provisions. The large majority of those sentenced, however, had committed nonviolent crimes such as petty theft and drug possession, causing critics of the law to argue that the law is too broad. Eighty-four percent of "two-strikes" cases and nearly 77 percent of "three-strikes" convictions resulted from nonviolent, drug, or property crimes. A similar 1997 study of three-strikes laws in 22 states, conducted by the Campaign for An Effec-

tive Crime Policy (CECP), concluded that such legislation results in clogged court systems and crowded correctional facilities, while encouraging three-time felons to take dramatic risks to avoid capture. A 1998 study found that only California and Georgia are making widespread use of three-strikes laws. Other states, the study found, have narrowly written laws that are applicable only in rare circumstances.

Supporters of three-strikes laws argue that those convicted under them are career criminals who will be denied the opportunity to commit more violent crimes. "The real story here is the girl somewhere that did not get raped," said Mike Reynolds, a Fresno, California, photographer whose 18-year-old daughter was killed by a paroled felon. "The real story is the robbery that did not happen," he added.

Practically speaking, California's three-strikes law has had a dramatic impact on the state's criminal justice system. By 1999 more than 40,000 people had been sentenced under the law. "But the law has its critics. 'Three strikes and you're out' sounds great to a lot of people," says Alan Schuman, president of the American Probation and Parole Association. "But no one will cop a plea when it gets to the third time around. We will have more trials, and this whole country works on plea bargaining and pleading guilty, not jury trials," Schuman said at a recent meeting of the association. Some California district attorneys have responded by choosing to prosecute fewer misdemeanants in order to concentrate on the more serious three-strikes defendants. According to RAND, full enforcement of the law could cost as much as $5.5 billion annually—or $300 per California taxpayer.

Researchers at RAND conclude that while California's sweeping three-

strikes legislation holds the potential to cut serious adult crime by as much as one-third throughout the state, the high cost of enforcing the law may keep it from ever being fully implemented. In 1998, in the case of *Monge v. California* (524 U.S. 721, 1998), the U.S. Supreme Court upheld a crucial provision of California's three-strikes law. On March 7, 2000, California voters passed Proposition 21, broadening legal categories for determining which felonies can count under that state's three-strikes law. Proposals to amend California's law continue to be made, with many suggesting that three-strikes sentences should only be imposed on offenders who commit violent crimes such as murder, rape, armed robbery, and certain types of arson.

? QUESTIONS FOR DISCUSSION

1. Do you think three-strikes laws serve a useful purpose? If so, what is that purpose? Might other sentencing arrangements meet that same purpose? If so, what arrangements might those be?

2. How will three-strikes laws impact state and federal spending on the criminal justice system? Do you think that such shifts in spending can be justified? If so, how?

Sources: Walter Dickey and Pam Stiebs Hollenhorst, "Three-Strikes Laws: Massive Impact in California and Georgia, Little Elsewhere," *Overcrowded Times*, vol. 9, no. 6 (December 1998), pp. 2–8; The Campaign for an Effective Crime Policy, *The Impact of Three Strikes and You're Out Laws: What Have We Learned?* (Washington, D.C.: CECP, 1997); Bruce Smith, "Crime Solutions," The Associated Press wire services, January 11, 1995; Michael Miller, "California Gets 'Three Strikes' Anti-Crime Bill," Reuters wire services, March 7, 1994; Dion Nissenbaum, "Three-Strikes First Year Debated," United Press wire services northern edition, March 6, 1995.

of victims were often forgotten. Although victims might testify at trial, other aspects of the victimization experience were frequently downplayed by the criminal justice system—including the psychological trauma engendered by the victimization process itself. That changed in 1982 when the President's Task Force on Victims of Crime[73] gave focus to a burgeoning victims' rights movement and urged the widespread expansion of victim assistance programs during what was then their formative period. Victim assistance programs today tend to offer services in the areas of crisis intervention and follow-up counseling and help victims secure their rights under the law.[74] Following successful prosecution, some victim assistance programs also advise victims in the filing of civil suits in order to recoup financial losses directly from the offender. In the mid-1990s, a survey of 319 full-service victim assistance programs based in law enforcement agencies and prosecutors offices was conducted by the National Institute of Justice.[75] The survey found that "the majority of individuals seeking assistance were victims of domestic assault and the most common assistance they received was information about legal rights." Other common forms of assistance included help in applying for state victim compensation aid and referrals to social service agencies.

The 1982 President's Task Force on Victims of Crime[76] also recommended 68 programmatic and legislative initiatives for states and concerned citizens to pursue on behalf of crime victims. About the same time, voters in California approved "Proposition 8," a resolution which called for changes in the state's constitution to reflect concern for victims. A continuing thrust of victim advocacy groups turns in the direction of an amendment to the U.S. Constitution, which such groups say is needed to provide the same kind of fairness to victims that is routinely accorded to defendants. The National Victims' Constitutional Amendment Network (NVCAN), for example, has sought to add the phrase—"likewise, the victim, in every criminal prosecution, shall have the right to be present and to be heard at all critical stages of judicial proceedings"—to the Sixth Amendment. NVCAN now advocates the addition of a new twenty-eighth amendment to the U.S. Constitution. Visit NVCAN via WebExtra! 9-5 at CJToday.com.

In September 1996, a victims' rights constitutional amendment—Senate Joint Resolution 65—was proposed by a bipartisan committee in the U.S. Congress.[77] Although the plan had the support of both President Clinton and his Republican challenger, Bob Dole, problems of wording and terminology prevented its passage. A revised amendment was again proposed in 1998,[78] but its wording was too restrictive for it to gain endorsement from victim's organizations.[79] In 1999 a new amendment was proposed by the Senate Judiciary Committee's Subcommittee on the Constitution, Federalism, and Property and is pending further action in the Senate as this book goes to press. The text of the proposed 1999 amendment, known as Senate Joint Resolution 3, is reproduced in a box in this chapter.

Although a victims' rights amendment to the federal Constitution may not yet be reality, 32 states had passed their own victims' rights amendments as of January 1, 2000,[80] and significant federal legislation has already been adopted. The 1982 Victim and Witness Protection Act (VWPA),[81] for example, requires victim impact statements to be considered at federal sentencing hearings and places responsibility for their creation on federal probation officers. In 1984 the federal Victims of Crime Act (VOCA) was enacted with substantial bipartisan support. VOCA authorized federal funding to help states establish victim assistance and victim compensation programs. Under VOCA the U.S. Department of Justice's Office for Victims of Crime provides a significant source of both funding and information for victim assistance programs. The rights of victims were further strengthened under the Violent Crime Control and Law Enforcement Act of 1994, which created a federal right of allocution for victims of violent and sex crimes, permitting victims to speak at the sentencing of their assailants. The 1994 law also requires sex offenders and child molesters convicted under federal law to pay restitution to their victims and prohibits the diversion of federal victims' funds to other programs. Still more provisions of the 1994 law provide civil rights remedies for victims of felonies motivated by gender bias and extend "rape shield law" protections to civil cases and to all criminal cases as a bar to irrelevant inquiries into a victim's sexual history. A significant feature of the 1994 law can be found in a subsection titled the Violence Against Women Act (VAWA). VAWA provides financial support for police, prosecutors, and victims' services in cases involving sexual violence or domestic abuse.

Much of the philosophical basis of today's victims' movement can be found in the restorative justice model, which was discussed briefly earlier in this chapter. Restorative justice emphasizes offender accountability and victim reparation. Restorative justice also provides the basis for victim compensation programs—which are another means of recognizing the needs of crime victims (see Table 9-2 for a comparison of restorative justice with retributive justice). Today, all 50 states have passed legislation providing for monetary payments to victims of crime. Such payments are primarily designed to compensate victims for medical expenses and lost wages. All existing programs require that applicants meet certain eligibility criteria, and most set limits on the maximum amount of compensation that can be received. Generally disallowed are claims from victims who are significantly responsible for their own victimization.

Victim Impact Statements

Another consequence of the national victim-witness rights movement has been a call for the use of **victim impact statements** prior to sentencing. A victim impact statement generally takes the form of a written document which describes the losses, suffering, and trauma experienced by the crime victim or the victim's survivors. Judges are expected to consider such statements in arriving at an appropriate sanction for the offender.

The drive to mandate inclusion of victim impact statements in sentencing decisions, already mandated in federal courts by the 1982 Victim and Witness Protection Act, was substantially enhanced by the "right of allocution" provision of the Violent Crime Control and Law Enforcement Act of 1994 (mentioned earlier). As a consequence, victim impact statements played a prominent role in the sentencing of Timothy McVeigh, who was convicted of the 1995 bombing of the Murrah Federal Building in Oklahoma City and sentenced to die. Some states, however, have gone the federal government one better. In 1984 the state of California, for example, passed legislation[82] giving victims a right to attend and participate in sentencing and parole hearings. Approximately 20 states now have laws mandating citizen involvement in sentencing, and all 50 states and the District of Columbia "allow for some form of submission of a victim impact statement either at the time of sentencing or to be contained in the presentence investigation reports" made by court officers.[83] Where written victim impact statements are not available, courts may invite the victim to testify directly at sentencing.

An alternative to written impact statements, and to the appearance of victims at sentencing hearings, is the emerging use of victim impact videos. Victim impact videos are available nationally through Victims' Impact Video, Inc. (VIVD). Based in Owing Mills, Maryland, VIVD, a nonprofit organization, asks producers and editing facilities nationwide to contribute a portion of the time required to produce a victim's impact statement video. The remainder of the time is paid for by VIVD from contributions made to the organization. VIVD believes that the ability to present a victim's impact statement on video during the sentencing phase of a trial and/or during an appeal or hearing is an aid that should be available to all victims of violent crime. The company says that "conveying the victim's sense of loss and despair should not be limited by the presenter's command of the language, communications skills or ability to pay."[84]

Hearing from victims, however, does not guarantee that a sentencing court will be sympathetic. On April 3, 1995, for example, a court in Berlin, Germany, refused to imprison Guenter Parche—the unemployed German machinist who stabbed 19-year-old tennis superstar Monica Seles in the back with a kitchen knife at the 1993 Hamburg Open. Even though Seles told the court that Parche "ruined my life" and ended my career "as the world's best tennis player,"[85] the judge ruled that a suspended sentence was appropriate because the man apparently had not intended to kill Seles—only disable her so that German star Steffi Graf could regain the number one world ranking in women's tennis. At the hearing, Seles's American psychologist had testified that Seles "felt like a bird trapped in a cage and was terrified that Parche would strike again."[86] Seles was not able to play professional tennis for more than two years following the attack, and has never regained full championship standing.

One study of the efficacy of victim impact statements found that sentencing decisions are rarely affected by them. In the words of the study: "These statements did not produce sentenc-

Victim Impact Statement

The in-court use of victim- or survivor-supplied information by sentencing authorities wishing to make an informed sentencing decision.

"Too often, we bend over backward to protect the right of criminals, but pay no attention to those who are hurt the most. Victims should have a voice in trial and other proceedings. Their safety should be a factor in the sentencing and release of their attackers. They should be notified when an offender is released back into their community. And they should have a right to compensation from their attacker."

—Former Vice-President Al Gore

21st Century CJ

Is a Victims' Rights Amendment at Hand?

In 1999 Senators Dianne Feinstein and Jon Kyl proposed a victims' rights amendment to the U.S. Constitution in the form of Senate Joint Resolution 3. SJR 3 was the third such attempt to pass such an amendment in recent times. As this book goes to press it is still being debated. The text of the Kyl-Feinstein resolution follows.

Joint Resolution 3

Proposing an amendment to the Constitution of the United States to protect the rights of crime victims

Resolved by the Senate and the House of Representatives of the United States of America in Congress assembled (*two-thirds of each House concurring therein*), That the following article is proposed as an amendment to the Constitution of the United States, which shall be valid for all intents and purposes as part of the Constitution when ratified by the legislatures of three-fourths of the several States within seven years from the date of its submission by the Congress:

Article

Section 1. A victim of a crime of violence, as these terms may be defined by law, shall have the rights:

◆ to reasonable notice of, and not to be excluded from, any public proceedings relating to the crime;

◆ to be heard, if present, and to submit a statement at all such proceedings to determine a conditional release from custody, an acceptance of a negotiated plea, or a sentence;

◆ to the foregoing rights at a parole proceeding that is not public, to the extent those rights are afforded to the convicted offender;

◆ to reasonable notice of a release or escape from custody relating to the crime;

◆ to consideration of the interest of the victim that any trial be free from unreasonable delay;

◆ to an order of restitution from the convicted offender;

◆ to consideration for the safety of the victim in determining any conditional release from custody relating to the crime; and

◆ to reasonable notice of the rights established by this article.

Section 2. Only the victim or the victim's lawful representative shall have standing to assert the rights established by this article. Nothing in this article shall provide grounds to stay or con-

tinue any trial, reopen any proceeding or invalidate any ruling, except with respect to conditional release or restitution or to provide rights guaranteed by this article in future proceedings, without staying or continuing a trial. Nothing in this article shall give rise to or authorize the creation of a claim for damages against the United States, a State, a political subdivision, or a public officer or employee.

Section 3. The Congress shall have the power to enforce this article by appropriate legislation. Exceptions to the rights established by this article may be created only when necessary to achieve a compelling interest.

Section 4. This article shall take effect on the 180th day after the ratification of this article. The right to an order of restitution established by this article shall not apply to crimes committed before the effective date of this article.

Section 5. The rights and immunities established by this article shall apply in Federal and State proceedings, including military proceedings to the extent that the Congress may provide by law, juvenile justice proceedings, and proceedings in the District of Columbia and any commonwealth, territory, or possession of the United States.

Source: S. J. Res. 3, 106th Congress.

---

ing decisions that reflected more clearly the effects of crime on victims. Nor did we find much evidence that—with or without impact statements—sentencing decisions were influenced by our measures of the effects of crime on victims, once the charge and the defendant's prior record were taken into account."[87] The authors concluded that victim impact statements have little effect upon courts because judges and other "officials have established ways of making decisions which do not call for explicit information about the impact of crime on victims."

The Constitutionality of Victim Impact Statements

In 1987 the constitutionality of victim impact statements was called into question by the U.S. Supreme Court in the case of *Booth* v. *Maryland*.[88] The case involved Irvin Bronstein, age 78, and his wife Rose, age 75, who were robbed and brutally murdered in their home in Baltimore, Maryland, in 1983. The killers were John Booth and Willie Reid, acquaintances of the Bronstein's, caught stealing to support heroin habits. After being convicted of murder, Booth decided to allow the jury (rather than the judge) to set his sentence. The jury considered, as required by state law, a victim impact statement which was part of a presentence report prepared by probation officers. The victim impact statement used in the case was a powerful

TABLE 9-2 ■ Differences between Restorative and Retributive Justice	
RETRIBUTIVE JUSTICE	**RESTORATIVE JUSTICE**
Crime is an act against the state, a violation of a law, an abstract idea.	Crime is an act against another person or the community.
The criminal justice system controls crime.	Crime control lies primarily with the community.
Offender accountability is defined as taking punishment.	Accountability is defined as assuming responsibility and taking action to repair harm.
Crime is an individual act with individual responsibility.	Crime has both individual and social dimensions of responsibility.
Victims are peripheral to the process.	Victims are central to the process of resolving a crime.
The offender is defined by deficits.	The offender is defined by the capacity to make reparation.
Emphasis is on adversarial relationships.	Emphasis is on dialogue and negotiation.
Pain is imposed to punish and deter/prevent.	Restitution is a means of restoring both parties; goal of reconciliation/restoration.
Community is on sidelines, represented abstractly by the state.	Community is facilitator in restorative process.
Response is focused on offender's past behavior.	Response is focused on harmful consequences of offender's behavior; emphasis on the future and on reparation.
Dependence is upon proxy professionals.	There is direct involvement by both the offender and the victim.

Source: Adapted from Gordon Bazemore and Mark S. Umbreit, Balanced and Restorative Justice: Program Summary *(Washington, D.C.: Office of Justice and Juvenile Delinquency Prevention, Oct. 1994), p. 7.*

one, describing the wholesome personal qualities of the Bronsteins and the emotional suffering their children had experienced as a result of the murders.

After receiving a death sentence, Booth appealed to the U.S. Supreme Court. The Court overturned his sentence, reasoning that victim impact statements, at least in capital cases, violate the Eighth Amendment ban on cruel and unusual punishments. In a close (5-to-4) decision, the majority held that information in victim impact statements leads to the risk that the death penalty might be imposed in an arbitrary and capricious manner.

Tennis superstar Monica Seles grimaces in pain after being stabbed in the back during a 1993 German tennis tournament by a knife-wielding man. German courts refused to sentence her attacker to time behind bars even though Seles complained that the attack shattered her career and left her unable to compete on the professional circuit for years.
AP, Wide World Photos.

In a complete about face, affected in no small part by the gathering conservative majority among its justices, the Supreme Court held in the 1991 case of *Payne* v. *Tennessee*[89] that the *Booth* ruling had been based upon "a misreading of precedent."[90] The *Payne* case began with a 1987 double-murder, in which a 28-year-old mother and two-year-old daughter were stabbed to death in Millington, Tennessee.[91] A second child, three-year-old Nicholas Christopher, himself severely wounded in the incident, witnessed the deaths of his mother and young sister. In a trial following the killings, the prosecution claimed that Pervis Tyrone Payne, a 20-year-old retarded man, had killed the mother and child after the woman resisted his sexual advances. Payne was convicted of both murders. At the sentencing phase of the trial Mary Zvolanek, Nicholas's grandmother, testified that the boy continued to cry out daily for his dead sister. Following *Booth,* Payne's conviction was upheld by the Tennessee supreme court in an opinion which did little to disguise the Tennessee court's contempt for the precedent set by *Booth.*

This time, however, the Supreme Court agreed with the Tennessee justices, holding that "[v]ictim impact evidence is simply another form or method of informing the sentencing authority about the specific harm caused by the crime in question, evidence of a general type long considered by sentencing authorities." As Chief Justice Rehnquist wrote for the majority, "[C]ourts have always taken into consideration the harm done by the defendant in imposing sentence." In a concurring opinion, Justice Antonin Scalia held that "*Booth* significantly harms our criminal justice system . . ." and had been decided with "plainly inadequate rational support."

Traditional Sentencing Options

Sentencing is fundamentally a risk management strategy designed to protect the public while serving the ends of rehabilitation, deterrence, retribution, and restoration. Because the goals of sentencing are difficult to agree upon, so too are sanctions. Lengthy prison terms do little for rehabilitation, while community release programs can hardly protect the innocent from offenders bent on continuing criminality.

Assorted sentencing philosophies continue to permeate state-level judicial systems. Each state has its own sentencing laws, and frequent revisions of those statutes are not uncommon. Because of huge variation from one state to another in the laws and procedures which control the imposition of criminal sanctions, sentencing has been called "the most diversified part of the Nation's criminal justice process."[92]

There is at least one common ground, however, that can be found in the four traditional sanctions which continue to dominate the thinking of most legislators and judges. The four traditional sanctions are

- Imprisonment
- Probation
- Fines
- Death

In the case of indeterminate sentencing, the first three options are widely available to judges. The option selected generally depends upon the severity of the offense and the judge's best guess as to the likelihood of future criminal involvement on the part of the defendant. Sometimes two or more options are combined, as when an offender might be fined and sentenced to prison or placed on probation and fined in support of restitution payments.

Jurisdictions that operate under presumptive sentencing guidelines generally limit the judge's choice to only one option and often specify the extent to which that option can be applied. Dollar amounts of fines, for example, are rigidly set, and prison terms are specified for each type of offense. The death penalty remains an option in a fair number of jurisdictions, but only for a highly select group of offenders.

A 1999 report by the Bureau of Justice Statistics on the sentencing practices of trial courts[93] found that state courts convicted 997,970 persons of felonies in 1996. Another 43,839 felony convictions occurred in federal courts. Of all persons convicted of felonies (see Figure 9-1),

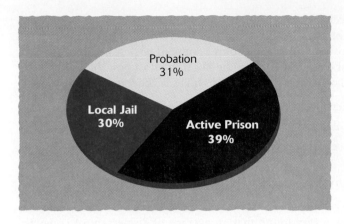

FIGURE 9-1 ■ *The sentencing of convicted felons in state and federal courts by type of sentence.*

Source: *Jodi M. Brown and Patrick A. Langan,* Felony Sentences in the United States, 1996 *(Washington, D.C.: Bureau of Justice Statistics, 1999).*

- ▣ Thirty-nine percent were sentenced to active prison terms.
- ▣ Thirty percent received jail sentences, usually involving less than a year's confinement.
- ▣ Thirty-one percent were sentenced to probation (often with fines or other special conditions).
- ▣ The average prison sentence imposed on convicted felons was just over five years.
- ▣ Those sent to jail received an average sentence of six months.
- ▣ Straight probation sentences averaged about three and one-half years.

The same survey revealed that 84 percent of those convicted of drug-trafficking offenses in federal courts were sentenced to prison, while 39 percent of convicted drug traffickers in state courts received prison sentences. Although the number of active sentences handed out to felons may seem low to some, the number of criminal defendants receiving active prison time has increased dramatically. Figure 9-2 shows that the number of court-ordered prison commitments have increased nearly eightfold in the past 40 years.

Fines

The fine is one of the oldest forms of punishment, predating even the Code of Hammurabi.[94] Until recently, however, the use of fines as criminal sanctions suffered from built-in inequities and a widespread failure to collect them. Inequities arose when offenders with vastly different financial resources were fined similar amounts. A fine of $100, for example, can place a painful economic burden upon a poor defendant but is only laughable when imposed on a wealthy offender.

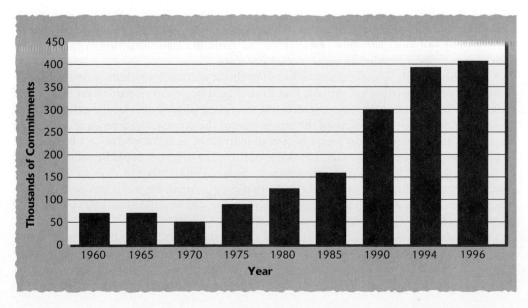

FIGURE 9-2 ■ *Court-ordered prison commitments 1960–1996.*

Source: *Jodi M. Brown and Patrick A. Langan,* Felony Sentences in the United States, 1996 *(Washington, D.C.: BJS, 1999), and Other Years.*

Today, fines are once again receiving attention as serious sentencing alternatives. One reason for the renewed interest is the stress placed upon state resources by burgeoning prison populations. The extensive imposition of fines not only results in less crowded prisons but can contribute to state and local coffers and lower the tax burden of law-abiding citizens. Other advantages of the use of fines as criminal sanctions include the following:

- ■ Fines can deprive offenders of the proceeds of criminal activity.
- ■ Fines can promote rehabilitation by enforcing economic responsibility.
- ■ Fines can be collected by existing criminal justice agencies and are relatively inexpensive to administer.
- ■ Fines can be made proportionate to both the severity of the offense and the ability of the offender to pay.

A National Institute of Justice survey found that an average of 86 percent of convicted defendants in courts of limited jurisdiction receive fines as sentences, some in combination with another penalty.[95] Fines are also experiencing widespread use in courts of general jurisdiction, where the National Institute of Justice study found judges imposing fines in 42 percent of all cases which came before them for sentencing. Some studies estimate that over $1 billion in fines are collected nationwide each year.[96]

Fines are often imposed for relatively minor law violations, such as driving while intoxicated, reckless driving, disturbing the peace, disorderly conduct, public drunkenness, and vandalism. Judges in many courts, however, report the use of fines for relatively serious violations of the law, including assault, auto theft, embezzlement, fraud, and the sale and possession of various controlled substances. Fines are much more likely to be imposed, however, where the offender has both a clean record and the ability to pay.[97]

Opposition to the use of fines is based upon the following arguments:

- ■ Fines may result in the release of convicted offenders into the community but do not impose stringent controls on their behavior.
- ■ Fines are a relatively mild form of punishment and are not consistent with "just deserts" philosophy.
- ■ Fines discriminate against the poor and favor the wealthy.
- ■ Indigent offenders are especially subject to discrimination since they entirely lack the financial resources with which to pay fines.
- ■ Fines are difficult to collect.

A number of these objections can be answered by procedures which make available to judges complete financial information on defendants. Studies have found, however, that courts of limited jurisdiction, which are the most likely to impose fines, are also the least likely to have adequate information on offenders' economic status.[98] Perhaps as a consequence, judges themselves are often reluctant to impose fines. Two of the most widely cited objections by judges to the use of fines are (1) fines allow more affluent offenders to "buy their way out" and (2) poor offenders cannot pay fines.[99]

A solution to both objections can be found in the Scandinavian system of day fines. The day-fine system is based upon the idea that fines should be proportionate to the severity of the offense but also need to take into account the financial resources of the offender. Day fines are computed by first assessing the seriousness of the offense, the defendant's degree of culpability, and his or her prior record as measured in "days." The use of days as a benchmark of seriousness is related to the fact that, without fines, the offender could be sentenced to a number of days (or months or years) in jail or prison. The number of days an offender is assessed is then multiplied by the daily wages that person earns. Hence, if two persons were sentenced to a five-day fine, but one earned only $20 per day, and the other $200 per day, the first would pay a $100 fine, and the second $1,000.

The National Institute of Justice reported on an experimental day-fine program conducted by the Richmond County Criminal Court in Staten Island, New York, in the early 1990s.[100] The program was designed to introduce and assess the use of day fines in the United States. The institute also reported on a similar 12-week experimental program involving the use of day fines by the Milwaukee Municipal Court. Both studies concluded that "the day fine can play a major . . . role as an intermediate sanction"[101] and that "the day-fine concept could be implemented in a typical American limited-jurisdiction court."[102] Those conclusions were supported by a 1996 RAND Corporation report that examined ongoing day-fine demonstration projects in Maricopa County, Arizona; Des Moines, Iowa; Bridgeport, Connecticut; and in four counties in Oregon.[103]

Death: The Ultimate Sanction

Some crimes are especially heinous and seem to cry out for extreme punishment. In 1996, for example, in what some saw as an especially atrocious murder, a Norman, Oklahoma, man decapitated his neighbor and then walked naked down an alleyway to toss the victim's head into a trash dumpster.[104] Witnesses who watched the accused killer, 33-year-old Cameron Smith, throw the head of 44-year-old Roydon Dale Major into the dumpster called police. Responding officers discovered the rest of Major's body in a room at a boarding house where both Smith and Major had lived. Major had been stabbed repeatedly before his head was severed from his body. Smith was still naked when police found him and took him into custody.

Many states today have statutory provisions that provide for a sentence of **capital punishment** for especially repugnant crimes. The death penalty itself, however, has a long and gruesome history. Civilizations have almost always put criminals to death for a variety of offenses. As times changed, so did accepted methods of execution. Under the Davidic monarchy, biblical Israel institutionalized the practice of stoning convicts to death.[105] In that practice, the entire community could participate in dispatching the offender. As an apparent aid to deterrence, the convict's deceased body could be impaled on a post at the gates of the city or otherwise exposed to public view.[106]

Athenian society, around 200 B.C., was progressive by the standards of its day. The ancient Greeks restricted the use of capital punishment and limited the suffering of the condemned through the use of poison derived from the hemlock tree. Socrates, the famous Greek orator, accused of being a political subversive, died this way.

The Romans were far less sensitive. They used beheading most often, although the law provided that arsonists should be burned alive and false witnesses thrown from a high rock.[107] Suspected witches were clubbed to death, and slaves were strangled. Even more brutal sanctions included drawing and quartering, and social outcasts, Christians, and rabble rousers were thrown to the lions or crucified. Although many people think that crucifixion was a barbarous practice that ended around the time of Christ, it survives into the present day. In 1997, for example, courts in Yemeni (a country at the southern tip of the Arabian peninsula) sentenced two convicted murders to be publicly crucified. It was the second time in three months that Yemeni courts, in an effort to combat a spate of violent crimes, imposed crucifixion sentences.[108]

After the fall of the Roman Empire, Europe was plunged into the Dark Ages, a period of superstition marked by widespread illiteracy and political turmoil. The Dark Ages lasted from A.D. 126 until the early thirteenth century. During the Dark Ages, executions were institutionalized through the use of ordeals designed to both judge and punish. Suspects were submerged in cold water, dumped in boiling oil, crushed under huge stones, forced to do battle with professional soldiers, or thrown into bonfires. Theological arguments prevalent at the time held that innocents, protected by God and heavenly forces, would emerge from any ordeal unscathed, while guilty parties would perish. Trial by ordeal was eliminated through a decree of the Fourth Lateran Council of 1215, under the direction of Pope Innocent III, after later evidence proved that many who died in ordeals could not have committed the crimes of which they were accused.[109]

Following the Fourth Lateran Council, trials, much as we know them today, became the basis for judging guilt or innocence. The death penalty remained in widespread use. As recently as a century and a half ago, 160 crimes were punishable in England by death.[110] The young received no special privilege. In 1801 a child of 13 was hanged in Tyburn, England, for stealing a spoon.[111]

Sophisticated techniques of execution were in use by the nineteenth century. One engine of death was the guillotine, invented in France around the time of the French Revolution. The

Capital Punishment

Another term for the death penalty. Capital punishment is the most extreme of all sentencing options.

"There is only one basic human right, the right to do as you please unless it causes others harm. With it comes the only basic human duty, the duty to take the consequences."

—*P. J. O'Rourke*

guillotine was described by its creator, Dr. Joseph-Ignace Guillotin, as "a cool breath on the back of the neck"[112] and found widespread use in eliminating opponents of the Revolution.

In America, hanging became the preferred mode of execution. It was especially popular on the frontier, since it required little by way of special materials and was a relatively efficient means of dispatch. By the early 1890s electrocution had replaced hanging as the preferred form of capital punishment in America. The appeal of electrocution was that it stopped the heart without visible signs of gross bodily trauma.

Executions: The Grim Facts

> "If I were king, I would make every inmate that enters the system pay restitution. Citizens will not have faith in the criminal justice system until restitution is a centerpiece of our efforts."
>
> —*Samuel F. Saxton,*
> *Director, Prince George's County (Maryland) Department of Corrections*

Since 1608, when records on capital punishment first became available, estimates are that more than 18,800 legal executions have been carried out in America.[113] Although capital punishment was widely used throughout the eighteenth and nineteenth centuries, the twentieth century saw a constant decline in the number of persons legally executed in the United States. Between 1930 and 1967, when the U.S. Supreme Court ordered a nationwide stay of pending executions, nearly 3,800 persons were put to death. The years 1935 and 1936 were peak years, with nearly 200 legal killings each year. Executions declined substantially every year thereafter. Between 1967 and 1977 a de facto moratorium existed, with no executions carried out in any U.S. jurisdiction. Following the lifting of the moratorium, executions increased (see Figure 9-3). In 1993, 38 offenders were put to death, while 56 were executed nationwide in 1995. The year 1999 set a modern record for executions, with 98 executions—35 in Texas alone.

In 1995, the state of New York reinstated the death penalty after a 30-year hiatus. Today, 38 of the 50 states and the federal government have capital punishment laws.[114] All but New York permit execution for first-degree murder, while treason, kidnapping, the murder of a police or correctional officer, and murder while under a life sentence are punishable by death in selected jurisdictions.[115] New York allows for the imposition of a death sentence in cases involving the murder of law enforcement officers, judges, and witnesses and their families and applies the punishment to serial killers, terrorists, murderers-for-hire, and those who kill while committing another felony such as robbery or rape.

The number of crimes punishable by death under federal jurisdiction increased dramatically with passage of the Violent Crime Control and Law Enforcement Act of 1994—and now includes a total of about 60 offenses. State legislators are also moving to expand the types of crime for which a sentence of death can be imposed. In 1997, for example, the Louisiana

CRIME IN THE NEWS

I Watched a Murderer Die

FLORENCE, Ariz.—A young, blonde television reporter standing next to me noisily shook one of those thin, plastic grocery bags a few times until it took a gulp of air and ballooned open.

She looked at me somewhat sheepishly to answer my unasked question: "It's in case I get sick."

No one else in the witness room of Arizona State Prison gas chamber that March 3 night was as well-prepared, but we all had the same fear. Frankly, we weren't thinking so much about the man we were about to see put to death; we were more worried about how we'd react to watching it happen.

We remembered the emotional testimonies of those who attended Arizona's last gas chamber execution seven years ago. Their descriptions of the contortions of a condemned man struggling against death for a dozen minutes helped persuade voters to replace cyanide tablets with more "humane" lethal drugs.

Anyone sentenced to death in Arizona after 1992 gets lethal injection, but the 75 men sentenced before 1992 get to choose: gas chamber or lethal injection. Of the 15 inmates executed since the law changed, none chose the gas chamber.

"Make Sure They're Dead"

Until Walter LaGrand. LaGrand and his brother, Karl, both German nationals, sat on death row for 14 years for killing a bank manager during a botched robbery near Tucson. The LaGrands—armed with a toy pistol—tied 63-year-old Ken Hartsock and bank clerk Dawn Lopez, then 21, to office chairs. When Hartsock couldn't open the safe, the brothers repeatedly stabbed and slashed him with a letter opener from Hartsock's desk. Karl always claimed he alone did the stabbings. Dawn Lopez remembers both of them stabbing and slashing. She also remem-

bers Walter telling Karl to "make sure they're dead."

Attorneys for the brothers tried to save them by claiming in their last-minute legal appeals that the judge in 1984 sentenced them to die in the gas chamber but that the gas chamber is "cruel and unusual," and, therefore, their death sentences should be vacated. The attorneys' carefully worded plea avoided mentioning the lethal injection option.

The U.S. Supreme Court didn't buy it. It reasoned that if the brothers thought the gas chamber was cruel, they could choose lethal injection.

International Controversy

The case of the two German brothers drew international attention. Germany's ambassador came to Arizona to personally appeal to Gov. Jane Hull, offering to take the LaGrands back to Germany to serve out life terms. Even the World Court tried unsuccessfully to intervene.

Karl, the younger of the brothers, went first—a week before his brother. In a final letter to his former foster parents, he explained that he chose the gas chamber, not because of his attorneys' legal strategy, but "to atone for what I did."

Yet, just an hour before, he skipped atonement and asked prison officials to let him die by lethal injection. They did. And he did.

A Victim Watches

Among those who watched Karl LaGrand's execution was Lopez, the former bank clerk who survived the attack. She is now a law enforcement officer—and married to the sheriff's detective who arrested the LaGrands.

Less than a week after his brother died, Walter LaGrand appeared before a clemency board. Though his attorneys urged a reprieve, Walter said he wanted to die now that his brother

was dead. Shackled and separated from a bank of TV cameras by a glass and wire wall, LaGrand talked for 45 minutes.

He argued that the murder he and his brother committed was done in a flash of rage when the bank robbery went sour. You don't carry a toy gun if you plan to kill, he reasoned. The state of Arizona, on the other hand, has been planning to murder him for 17 years, and that's premeditation, he said. He charged that as its final act of "barbarism," the state asked him to chose the method of his own death: gas or injection.

"It's not so much the act [of execution] being completed; that just takes a minute. It's the process of years and years leading up to it. That's where the brutality comes," he said.

He failed to mention that his own appeals had something to do with the length of the process.

Reporter As Execution Witness

I've had numerous opportunities during my career to be included on the execution witness list. I've always declined.

This one was different because I had done a number of stories about Walter LaGrand's crimes in and out of prison. I talked to him a time or two, got to know people on the outside who loved him, saw some of his extraordinary artwork and caught glimpses of his wry sense of humor (he asked for Rolaids with his last meal). I concluded he was a sociopath.

I agreed to watch him die before I found out it might be in the gas chamber.

At the same time, the prospect that this could be the last gas chamber execution in Arizona, along with the international media attention swirling around the German inmate, made it a major media event.

(Continued)

CRIME IN THE NEWS

I Watched a Murderer Die

Last Minute Rush of Witnesses

The number of witnesses nearly doubled at the last minute. Prison officials finally cut it off at 50.

The final act began as we were checked with a hand-held metal detector and then escorted into the prison's main yard and into a sparsely furnished multipurpose education building. Hand-lettered signs indicated the room doubles as a chapel. We sat nervously for an hour on plastic chairs. A deputy warden gave us a handout that described the execution process. He took pains to explain what would happen as Walter LaGrand died.

"As the inmate inhales," the warden explained, "he will experience conditions which have been cited as being similar to a heart attack."

He added: "You are free to leave at any time if you feel queasy. Medical staff will be available to help."

Into the Death House

At 9 p.m., we walked out into the prison yard. The multi-story concrete cellblocks surrounding the yard were painted sodium-vapor orange. Just below a guard tower in one corner of the prison yard sat The Death House. Battleship-gray paint covered its cheap stuccoed exterior. It had no windows, no signs. A couple of vent pipes stuck out of the roof.

We were led through a side door into a small rectangular room. Nearly everything inside was gray also: the walls, the ceilings and the indoor-outdoor carpeting that covered the floor and a set of risers with three steps. We were the first group in. We're directed to the top row in the back.

Behind us was a curtain. It hid a large window that looked into the lethal injection execution room. When someone dies in that room, the risers are turned around and pushed back against the gas chamber.

That night, we faced the gas chamber. It looks like an old-time diving bell, with thick walls and large bolts spaced every few inches. It's as if it was intended to withstand great pressures. A wall bisects the chamber so its three observation windows are on one side of the wall, and the door and another window are on the other side. At the moment, the windows on our side were covered with metal Venetian blinds.

The blinds glowed in our darkened room because of a bright light inside the gas chamber.

Strapped in the Chair

We knew from our briefing that LaGrand was already strapped to the chair inside, and the submarine-style door was sealed shut. We could hear muffled shouting and banging inside the chamber. We couldn't tell why.

The reporter next to me noisily got her plastic bag ready in case she got sick.

Other witnesses began filing in. The state's attorney general. Prosecutors, defense attorneys. Officers who investigated the original crime. The murder victim's daughter arrived holding a 5-by-7 portrait of her late father. She moved in close to one of the windows with the picture.

Apparently, she wanted to make sure LaGrand's last vision was that of her dad, just as his last vision was that of Walter LaGrand. That's only a guess though, because the prison wouldn't let us talk to other witnesses, particularly the victims' families. I guess their belief is that witnessing a public execution is a private thing.

Absolute Silence

The room was packed but absolutely silent. We faced the gas chamber and stared at the glowing window blinds. It was like we were all on some large elevator, quietly facing forward, waiting for the doors to open.

Electronic voices crackled over the radios of uniformed corrections officers manning the venetian blinds. They pulled down on cords, and the blinds shot up.

The pale-yellow interior of the dome-shaped gas chamber made its walls glow brightly. It was like peering into a light bulb.

At the center sat a thronelike metal chair, full of tiny holes. The condemned man's back was to us, so we couldn't see his face.

LaGrand tried to twist around to see those of us who had come to watch him die, but his wrists were held firmly by leather straps bolted to the chair's armrests. A chest strap held him back. He could see through the two side windows: In one direction was the woman holding a photo of a man dead for 17 years. In the other, the attorney general. She graduated from law school the year LaGrand was sent to death row.

Straight ahead of him was another window. He and we could see a deputy corrections director, Chuck Ryan, standing at a microphone. Ryan read the death warrant, a legal document that recites the chronology of events—the crime, trial, conviction, sentencing and appeals that lead to this moment.

He ended with "Do you have any last words?"

Murderer's Last Words

Unlike the day before, LaGrand's comments were brief; he didn't attack the state for being a premeditated killer. His voice was steady and strong.

"I just wanted to say sorry to the Hartsock family," he said, still twisting so he could face them. "It's the first time I really got to see that picture.

"I am truly sorry. I hope you find peace. I want to thank Helen [Ken Hartsock's widow] for forgiving us. I want to say to her kids and Dawn Lopez, I hope you find peace.

(Continued)

CRIME IN THE NEWS

I Watched a Murderer Die

"To all my loved ones, I hope they find peace. To all of you here today, I forgive you. I hope I can be forgiven in my next life.

"That's all I have to say."

LaGrand's microphone switched off. And the warden said those ominous words: "Let the execution begin."

Inside the chamber, an electric fan somewhere in the ceiling began to whir. LaGrand flinched and looked around wildly for the source of the noise.

Cyanide Pellets Drop

A couple seconds later we heard a solid metallic clunk beneath his chair. A lever opened a cone-shaped bowl that dropped several cyanide pellets into a small metal vat of distilled water and sulfuric acid.

A light fog rose quickly from the floor, pulled upward by the fan. Just as quickly, LaGrand started violently coughing. He pulled himself up, stretching his neck as if to get above the toxic mist that was enveloping him.

He didn't gasp for breath as if he was suffocating. Instead, he gagged forcefully as if trying to expel something from his throat. I suspect his airways were swelling shut. This was not like any heart attack I'd ever seen.

The coughing ceased quickly, but he flailed from side to side, forward and back as far as the leather restraints would allow.

I could see the side of his face, but not his eyes.

That lasted less than two minutes. His movements slowed as he lost consciousness. He slumped forward. Slight movement of denim shirt indicated he was still breathing. Otherwise he didn't move. Mist continued to swirl around him.

The reporter who was prepared to vomit was instead on her tiptoes, stretching for a better view while furiously making notes of what she saw. I did the same. The non-media witnesses were like statues. The only sound came from the whirring fan, until Dawn Lopez choked out several sobs and darted toward the door, followed by a relative.

LaGrand did not move again, but his upturned hands remained clenched tightly in fists.

LaGrand Dead

Eighteen minutes after it began, Ryan announced that the execution was complete.

The uniformed officers tugged on the Venetian blinds' cords, and LaGrand disappeared from our view forever. He and his brother requested a burial in unmarked graves in the prison cemetery.

We filed outside in reverse order of how we came in. Reporters left last to make sure we couldn't talk to anyone.

Walking through the prison yard toward the free world, I thought about how ceremonial the whole process of life-taking was. It was scripted, organized, clean and unremarkable. I felt disturbed. Not by what I'd seen, but disturbed that I wasn't bothered.

How could I just watch someone be deliberately killed and not have any particular feeling about it?

Had I successfully dehumanized LaGrand in my mind, so that his death was inconsequential? Is that how killers view their victims: They don't deserve to live, so there's nothing to feel bad about?

Thinking About His Victims

Or did I just heed the advice of others who said, "Keep thinking about his victims"? I had to. They were right in front of me.

I had to do a live report at 10 p.m. Hardly enough time to sort out my own feelings. On the air, the anchor asked me what it was like. 'Surreal' was the best I could do. The rest was babble.

The hour's drive home was quiet.

About two weeks later, an investigator from the federal public defender's office called asking lots of questions. How did I feel now? Have I had any bad dreams?

No. I felt fine. I guess they wanted to build a case that capital punishment is uncivilized because it offends basic human sensibilities.

I'm afraid my answers didn't help that argument.

Source: Rich Robertson, "I Watched a Murderer Die," *APB News, May 22, 1999. Reprinted with permission.*

supreme court upheld the state's year-old child rape death penalty statute, which allows for the imposition of a capital sentence when the victim is under 12 years of age. The case involved an AIDS-infected father who raped his three daughters, aged five, eight, and nine years old. In upholding the father's death sentence, the Louisiana court ruled that child rape is "like no other crime."[116]

A total of 3,682 persons were under sentence of death throughout the United States on July 1, 2000. The latest statistics show that 98 percent of those on death row are male, 49 percent are classified as white, 8 percent are Hispanic, 42 percent are black, and 1 percent are of other races (mostly Native American and Pacific Islander).[117] Finally, methods of imposing death vary by state. The majority of death penalty states authorize execution through lethal

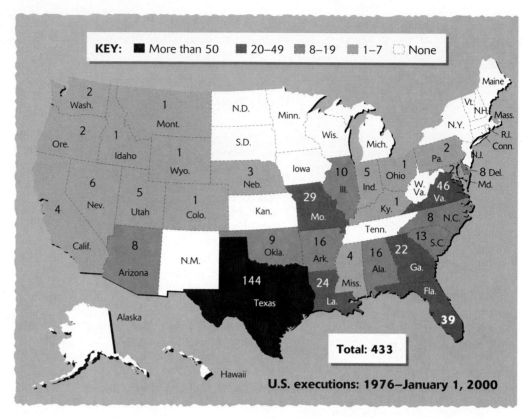

KEY: ■ More than 50 ■ 20–49 ■ 8–19 ■ 1–7 ☐ None

Total: 433

U.S. executions: 1976–January 1, 2000

FIGURE 9-3 ■ *U.S. executions 1976–January 1, 2000, by state.*

Source: *Death Penalty Information Center. Data as of January 2, 2000.*

injection. Electrocution is the second most common means of dispatch, while hanging, the gas chamber, and firing squads have survived, at least as options available to the condemned, in a few states. For the most contemporary statistical information on capital punishment visit **WebExtra!** 9-6 at CJToday.com.

Habeas Corpus Review

The legal process through which a capital sentence is carried to conclusion is fraught with problems. One serious difficulty centers on the fact that automatic review of all death sentences by appellate courts and constant legal maneuvering by defense counsel often lead to a dramatic delay between the time sentence is passed and the time it is carried out. Today, an average of 11 years and 11 months[118] passes between the time a sentence of death is imposed and it is carried out. Such lengthy delays, compounded with uncertainty over whether a sentence will ever be finally imposed, directly contravene the generally accepted notion that punishment should be swift and certain.

Typical of delayed executions, on April 18, 1995 the Louisiana Supreme Court granted two-time killer Antonio James his fourteenth stay of execution just four hours before he was scheduled to die by lethal injection. The 39-year-old James had been sentenced to death 15 years earlier for shooting 70-year-old Henry Silver in the head during an armed robbery on New Year's Day, 1979.[119] He was later sentenced to 99 more years in prison for killing Alvin Adams, 74, during an armed robbery two weeks after the Silver killing. In granting the stay, the Louisiana Supreme Court ruled that a state district court had erred a few days earlier by not granting a hearing on new evidence James's attorneys said could prove he was not the triggerman in either killing. Before the court's ruling, Governor Edwin Edwards had refused to block the execution. James was finally executed in 1996. He had been on Louisiana's death row since 1981.

Delays in the imposition of capital sanctions have been the source of much anguish for condemned prisoners as well as for the victims and the family members of both. In a final statement just before his client was executed, for example, the attorney for 30-year-old Dorsie Johnson-Bey told witnesses, "If the jury trying this case could see what has happened to him in the 11 years he's been on death row, they would say that he certainly doesn't pose a continuing threat to society."[120] A few minutes later, Johnson-Bey was put to death by lethal injection at the Walls Unit in Huntsville, Texas. A one-time janitor in the West Texas community of Colorado City, he had been sentenced to die for the March 1986 murder of Jack Huddleston, a 53-year-old convenience store clerk who had been shot in the head with a .25-caliber pistol after being forced to lie in the store's cooler. Huddleston had been robbed of $161 and cigarettes.

In a speech before the American Bar Association a few years ago, Chief Justice of the U.S. Supreme Court William H. Rehnquist called for reforms of the federal *habeas corpus* system which, at the time, allowed condemned prisoners virtually limitless opportunities for appeal. **Writs of *habeas corpus*** (Latin for "you have the body") require that a prisoner be brought into court to determine whether he or she is being legally held and form the basis for many federal appeals made by prisoners on state death rows. In 1968, Chief Justice Earl Warren called the right to file *habeas* petitions, as guaranteed under the U.S. Constitution, the "symbol and guardian of individual liberty." Nearly 30 years later, however, Rehnquist claimed that writs of *habeas corpus* were being used indiscriminately by death row inmates seeking to delay executions even where grounds for such delay do not exist. "The capital defendant does not need to prevail on the merits in order to accomplish his purpose," said Rehnquist. "He wins temporary victories by postponing a final adjudication."[121]

In a move to reduce delays in the conduct of executions, the U.S. Supreme Court, in the case of *McCleskey* v. *Zandt* (1991),[122] limited the number of appeals a condemned person may lodge with the courts. Saying that repeated filings for the sole purpose of delay promotes "disrespect for the finality of convictions" and "disparages the entire criminal justice system," the Court established a two-pronged criterion for future appeals. According to *McCleskey*, in any petition beyond the first, filed with the federal court, capital defendants must demonstrate (1) good cause why the claim now being made was not included in the first filing and (2) how the absence of that claim may have harmed the petitioner's ability to mount an effective defense. Two months later, the Court reinforced *McCleskey*, when it ruled, in *Coleman* v. *Thompson*,[123] that state prisoners could not cite "procedural default," such as a defense attorney's failure to meet a state's filing deadline for appeals, as the basis for an appeal to federal court.

In 1995, in the case of *Schlup* v. *Delo*,[124] the Court continued to define standards for continued appeals from death row inmates, ruling that before appeals based upon claims of new evidence could be heard, "a petitioner must show that, in light of the new evidence, it is more likely than not that no reasonable juror would have found him guilty beyond a reasonable doubt." A "reasonable juror" was defined as one who "would consider fairly all of the evidence presented and would conscientiously obey the trial court's instructions requiring proof beyond a reasonable doubt."

Opportunities for federal appeals by death row inmates were further limited by the Antiterrorism and Effective Death Penalty Act of 1996 (AEDPA), which sets a one-year postconviction deadline for state inmates filing federal *habeas corpus* appeals. The deadline is six months for state death row inmates who were provided a lawyer for *habeas* appeals at the state level. The Act also requires federal courts to presume that the factual findings of state courts are correct, does not permit use of state court misinterpretations of the U.S. Constitution as a basis for *habeas* relief unless those misinterpretations are "unreasonable," and requires that all petitioners must show, prior to obtaining a hearing, facts sufficient to establish by clear and convincing evidence that but for constitutional error, no reasonable fact finder would have found the petitioner guilty. The act also requires approval by a three-judge panel before an inmate can file a second federal appeal raising newly discovered evidence of innocence. In 1996, in the case of *Felker* v. *Turpin*,[125] the U.S. Supreme Court ruled that limitations on the authority of federal courts to consider successive *habeas corpus* petitions imposed by the Antiterrorism and Effective Death Penalty Act of 1996 are permissible since they do not deprive the U.S. Supreme Court of its original jurisdiction over such petitions.

Some recent statements by Supreme Court justices have indicated that long delays in carrying out executions that are caused by the government may render the punishment unconstitutionally cruel and unusual. One example comes from the 1998 case of *Elledge* v. *Florida*,[126] where the execution of William D. Elledge had been delayed for 23 years. Although the full Court refused to hear the case, Justice Breyer observed that: "Twenty-three years

Writ of *Habeas Corpus*

The writ which directs the person detaining a prisoner to bring him or her before a judicial officer to determine the lawfulness of the imprisonment.

"There can be no doubt that the taking of the life of the President creates much more societal harm than the taking of the life of a homeless person."

—*Tennessee Attorney General Charles Burson*, arguing before the U.S. Supreme Court in Payne v. Tennessee (1991)

under sentence of death is unusual—whether one takes as a measuring rod current practice or the practice in this country and in England at the time our Constitution was written." Moreover, wrote Breyer, execution after such a long delay could be considered cruel, because Elledge "has experienced that delay because of the State's own faulty procedures and not because of frivolous appeals on his own part."

Opposition to Capital Punishment

Thirty years ago David Magris, who was celebrating his 21st birthday with a crime spree, shot Dennis Tapp in the back during a holdup, leaving Tapp a paraplegic. Tapp had been working a late-night shift, tending his father's quick-serve gas station. Magris went on to commit more robberies that night, killing 20-year-old Steven Tompkins in a similar crime. Although sentenced to death by a California court, the U.S. Supreme Court overturned the state's death penalty law in 1972, opening the door for Magris to be paroled in 1985. Long before Magris was freed from prison, however, Tapp had already forgiven him. A few minutes after the shooting happened, Tapp regained consciousness, dragged himself to a telephone, and called for help. The next thing he did was ask "God to forgive the man who did this to me."[127] Today, both Tapp and Magris are staunch death-penalty opponents. And he and Magris, who is president of the Northern California Coalition to Abolish the Death Penalty, have become friends. They are united by a crime that happened 30 years ago and by a heartfelt need to fight against capital punishment. "Don't get me wrong . . ." says Tapp, "David has a good personality. What he did was wrong . . . he did something stupid and he paid for it."[128]

Because of the strong emotions that state-imposed death wrings from the hearts of varied constituencies, many attempts have been made to abolish capital punishment since the founding of the United States. The first recorded effort to abolish the death penalty occurred at the home of Benjamin Franklin in 1787.[129] At a meeting on March 9 of that year, Dr. Benjamin Rush, a signer of the Declaration of Independence and leading medical pioneer, read a paper against capital punishment to a small but influential audience. Although his immediate efforts came to naught, his arguments laid the groundwork for many debates which followed. Michigan, widely regarded as the first abolitionist state, joined the Union in 1837 without a death penalty. A number of other states, including Massachusetts, West Virginia, Wisconsin, Minnesota, Alaska, and Hawaii, have since spurned death as a possible sanction for criminal acts. Many Western European countries have also rejected the death penalty. As noted earlier, it remains a viable sentencing option in 38 of the states and all federal jurisdictions. As a consequence, arguments continue to rage over its value.

Today, five main rationales for abolishing capital punishment are heard:

1. The death penalty can and has been inflicted on innocent people.
2. Evidence has shown that the death penalty is not an effective deterrent.
3. The imposition of the death penalty is, by the nature of our legal system, arbitrary and even discriminatory.
4. Imposition of the death penalty is far too expensive to justify its use.
5. Human life is sacred, and killing at the hands of the state is not a righteous act, but rather one which is on the same moral level as the crimes committed by the condemned.

The first four abolitionist claims are pragmatic; that is, they can be measured and verified (or disproved) by looking at the facts. The last claim is primarily philosophical and therefore not amenable to scientific investigation. Hence, we shall briefly examine only the first four.

While some evidence does exist that a few innocent people have been executed,[130] most research by far has centered on examining the deterrent effect of the death penalty. During the 1970s and 1980s[131] the deterrent effect of the death penalty became a favorite subject for debate in academic circles. Studies[132] of states which had eliminated the death penalty failed to show any increase in homicide rates. Similar studies[133] of neighboring states, in which jurisdictions retaining capital punishment were compared with those which had abandoned it, also failed to demonstrate any significant differences. Although death penalty advocates remain numerous, few any longer argue for the penalty based on its deterrent effects. Deterrent studies continue, however. In 1988, for example, a comprehensive review[134] of capital punishment in Texas, which correlated executions since 1930 with homicide rates, again failed to find any support for the use of death as a deterrent. The study was especially significant because Texas had been very active in the capital punishment arena, executing 317 persons between 1930 and 1986.[135]

The abolitionist claim that the death penalty is arbitrary is based upon the belief that access to effective representation and to the courts themselves is differentially available to people with varying financial and other resources. Access to the courts has also been restricted by a number of new state and federal laws (discussed in greater detail in Chapter 12), leading the American Bar Association's House of Delegates in 1997 to cite what it called "an erosion of legal rights of death row inmates," and to urge an immediate halt to executions in the United States until the judicial process could be overhauled.[136] ABA delegates were expressing concerns that Congress and the states have unfairly limited death row appeals through restrictive legislation. The ABA resolution also called for a halt to executions of people under 18 years old and of those who are mentally retarded.

The claim that the death penalty is discriminatory is harder to investigate. While there may be past evidence that blacks and other minorities in the United States have been disproportionately sentenced to death,[137] the present evidence is not so clear. At first glance, as one study puts it, disproportionality seems apparent: 45 of the 98 prisoners executed between January 1977 and May 1988 were black or Hispanic; 84 of the 98 had been convicted of killing whites.[138] A 1996 Kentucky study found that blacks accused of killing whites in that state between 1976 and 1991 had a higher than average probability of being charged with a **capital offense** and of being sentenced to die than did homicide offenders of other races.[139] For an accurate appraisal to be made, however, any claims of disproportionality must go beyond simple comparisons with racial representation in the larger population and must somehow measure both frequency and seriousness of capital crimes between and within racial groups. Following that line of reasoning, the Supreme Court, in the 1987 case of *McCleskey* v. *Kemp*[140] held that a simple showing of racial discrepancies in the application of the death penalty does not constitute a constitutional violation.

The fourth claim, that the death penalty is too expensive, is difficult to explore. Although the "official" costs associated with capital punishment are high, many death penalty supporters argue that no cost is *too* high if it achieves justice. Death penalty opponents, on the other hand, point to the huge costs to taxpayers associated with judicial appeals and with executions themselves. According to the Death Penalty Information Center (DPIC), which maintains a national database on such costs, "the death penalty costs North Carolina $2.16 million per execution *over* the costs of a non-death penalty murder case with a sentence of imprisonment for life."[141] The DPIC also says that an average execution in Florida costs $3.2 million to carry out, and that "in Texas, a death penalty case costs an average of $2.3 million—about three times the cost of imprisoning someone in a single cell at the highest security level for 40 years."

> **Capital Offense**
>
> *A criminal offense punishable by death.*

Justifications for Capital Punishment

Shortly before Christmas 1996, New York state judge Thomas Demakos sentenced 23-year-old Joshua Torres to 58 years-to-life in prison, saying he wished that he could impose the death penalty. Torres had been convicted of abducting and burning 20-year-old Kimberly Antonakos alive after he and his partners bungled an attempt to extort ransom monies from the young woman's father. The father failed to respond to a $75,000 ransom demand made by the kidnappers because his answering machine didn't record the call. According to witnesses, Torres then tied the college student to a pole, doused her with gasoline, lit a match, and set her on fire. At sentencing, Judge Demakos told those gathered in the courtroom: "I must admit that hearing this testimony (about how Kimberly was set afire) almost brought me to tears."[142] Demakos said that although the case cried out for the death penalty, he could not impose it because it was not in effect in New York state at the time the murder took place.

Judge Demakos, like many others in today's society, feels that "cold-blooded murder" justifies a sentence of death. Justifications for the death penalty are collectively referred to as the retentionist position. The three retentionist arguments are (1) revenge, (2) just deserts, and (3) protection. Those who justify capital punishment as revenge attempt to appeal to the visceral feeling that survivors, victims, and the state are entitled to "closure." Only after execution of the criminal perpetrator, they say, can the psychological and social wounds engendered by the offense begin to heal.

The just deserts argument makes the simple and straightforward claim that some people deserve to die for what they have done. Death is justly deserved; anything less cannot suffice as a sanction for the most heinous crimes. As Justice Potter Stewart once wrote, "[T]he decision that capital punishment may be the appropriate sanction in extreme cases is an expression of the community's belief that certain crimes are themselves so grievous an affront to humanity that the only adequate response may be the penalty of death."[143]

The third retentionist claim, that of protection, asserts that offenders, once executed, can commit no further crimes. Clearly the least emotional of the retentionist claims, the protectionist argument may also be the weakest, since societal interests in protection can also be met in other ways, such as incarceration. In addition, various studies have shown that there is little likelihood of repeat offenses among people convicted of murder and later released.[144] One reason for such results, however, may be that murderers generally serve lengthy prison sentences prior to release and may have lost whatever youthful propensity for criminality they previously possessed. For an intriguing dialogue between two U.S. Supreme Court Justices over the constitutionality of the death penalty, see WebExtra! 9-7 at CJToday.com.

The Future of the Death Penalty

Because of the nature of the positions that both sides advocate, there is little common ground even for discussion between retentionists and abolitionists. Foes of the death penalty hope that its demonstrated lack of deterrent capacity will convince others that it should be abandoned. Their approach, based as it is upon statistical evidence, appears on the surface to be quite rational. However, it is doubtful that many capital punishment opponents could be persuaded to support the death penalty even if statistics showed it to be a deterrent. Likewise, the tactics of death penalty supporters are equally instinctive. Retentionists could probably not be swayed by statistical studies of deterrence, no matter what they show, since their support is bound up with emotional calls for retribution.

The future of the death penalty rests primarily with state legislatures. Short of renewed Supreme Court intervention, the future of capital punishment may depend more upon popular opinion than it does on arguments pro or con. Elected legislatures, because the careers of their members lie in the hands of their constituencies, are likely to follow the public mandate. Hence, it may be that studies of public attitudes toward the death penalty may be the most useful in predicting the sanction's future. At the moment, it appears that the American public, as a whole, favors the imposition of capital punishment in the case of heinous crimes. Support for the death penalty, however, varies considerably from state to state, and from one region of the country to another.[145]

Changes in public opinion could conceivably come quickly, however. Citing the First Amendment to the U.S. Constitution, California TV station KQED filed suit in 1990 in U.S. District Court in San Francisco asking that it be allowed to provide broadcast coverage of executions. The lawsuit claimed that the current state policy of barring cameras at executions, "impedes effective reporting of executions which are events of major public and political significance."[146] The station's request was denied by the court. About the same time, Phil Donahue unsuccessfully petitioned for an opportunity to videotape the execution of North Carolina death row inmate David Lawson. Lawson was scheduled to die for killing a man during a burglary, and Donahue argued that it would be a public service to televise his death—showing people what an execution is like to help them decide whether they could morally support the penalty.

The Courts and the Death Penalty

The U.S. Supreme Court has served as a constant sounding board for issues surrounding the death penalty. One of the court's earliest cases in this area was *Wilkerson* v. *Utah* (1878),[147] which questioned shooting as a method of execution and raised Eighth Amend-

"Life is sacred. It's about the only sacred thing on earth—and no one has a right to do away with it."

—Aldona DeVetsco, mother of a murder victim, commenting on the execution of her son's killer

Drug smugglers executed in China. Signs describe the offenders' crimes.
Xinhua, Liaison Agency, Inc.

ment claims that firing squads constituted a form of cruel and unusual punishment. The Court disagreed, however, contrasting the relatively civilized nature of firing squads with the various forms of torture often associated with capital punishment around the time the Bill of Rights was written.

In similar fashion, electrocution was supported as a permissible form of execution in *In re Kemmler* (1890).[148] In *Kemmler,* the Court defined cruel and unusual methods of execution as follows: "Punishments are cruel when they involve torture or a lingering death; but the punishment of death is not cruel, within the meaning of that word as used in the Constitution. It implies there something inhuman and barbarous, something more than the mere extinguishing of life."[149] Almost 60 years later, the Court ruled that a second attempt at the electrocution of a convicted person, when the first did not work, did not violate the Eighth Amendment.[150] The Court reasoned that the initial failure was the consequence of accident or unforeseen circumstances and not the result of an effort on the part of executioners to be intentionally cruel.

It was not until 1972, however, in the landmark case of *Furman* v. *Georgia,*[151] that the Court recognized "evolving standards of decency"[152] which might necessitate a reconsideration of Eighth Amendment guarantees. In a 5-to-4 ruling, the *Furman* decision invalidated Georgia's death penalty statute on the basis that it allowed a jury unguided discretion in the imposition of a capital sentence. The majority of justices concluded that the Georgia statute, which permitted a jury to decide simultaneously issues of guilt or innocence while it weighed sentencing options, allowed for an arbitrary and capricious application of the death penalty.

Many other states with statutes similar to Georgia's were affected by the *Furman* ruling, but moved quickly to modify their procedures. What evolved was a two-step procedure to be used in capital cases. As a consequence, death penalty trials today involve two stages. In the first stage, guilt or innocence is decided. If the defendant is convicted of a crime for which execution is possible, a second, or penalty phase, ensues. The penalty phase generally permits the introduction of new evidence that may have been irrelevant to the question of guilt but which may be relevant to punishment, such as drug use or childhood abuse. While in most death penalty jurisdictions juries determine the punishment, the trial judge sets the sentence in the second phase of capital murder trials in Arizona, Idaho, Montana, and Nebraska. Alabama, Delaware, Florida, and Indiana allow juries only to recommend a sentence to the judge.

The two-step trial procedure was specifically approved by the Court in *Gregg* v. *Georgia* (1976).[153] In *Gregg* the Court upheld the two-stage procedural requirements of Georgia's new capital punishment law as necessary for ensuring the separation of the highly personal information needed in a sentencing decision from the kinds of infor-

"Excessive bail shall not be required, nor excessive fines imposed, nor cruel and unusual punishments inflicted."

—Eighth Amendment to the U.S. Constitution

mation reasonably permissible in a jury trial where issues of guilt or innocence alone are being decided. In the opinion written for the majority, the Court for the first time recognized the significance of public opinion in deciding upon the legitimacy of questionable sanctions.[154] Its opinion cited the strong showing of public support for the death penalty following *Furman* to mean that death was still a socially and culturally acceptable penalty.

Post-*Gregg* decisions set limits upon the use of death as a penalty for all but the most severe crimes. In 1977, in the case of *Coker* v. *Georgia*,[155] the Court struck down a Georgia law imposing the death penalty for the rape of an adult woman. The Court concluded that capital punishment under such circumstances would be "grossly disproportionate" to the crime. Somewhat later, in *Woodson* v. *North Carolina*,[156] a law requiring mandatory application of the death penalty for specific crimes was overturned.

In two 1990 rulings, *Blystone* v. *Pennsylvania*[157] and *Boyde* v. *California*,[158] the Court upheld state statutes which had been interpreted to dictate that death penalties must be imposed where juries find a lack of mitigating factors that could offset obvious aggravating circumstances. Similarly, in the 1990 case of R. Gene Simmons, an Arkansas mass murderer convicted of killing 16 relatives during a 1987 shooting rampage, the Court granted inmates under sentence of death the right to waive appeals. Prior to the *Simmons* case, any interested party could file a brief on behalf of condemned persons—with or without their consent.

Recently, death row inmates and those who file cases on behalf of such inmates as sounding boards to test the boundaries of statutory acceptability, have been busy bringing challenges to state capital punishment laws. Most such challenges focus upon the procedures involved in sentencing decisions. In 1995, for example, in *Harris* v. *Alabama*,[159] the U.S. Supreme Court upheld Alabama's capital sentencing system, which allows juries to recommend sentences but judges to decide them. A challenge to the constitutionality of California's capital sentencing law, which requires the jury to consider, among other things, the circumstances of the offense, prior violent crimes by the defendant, and the defendant's age, was rejected in *Tuilaepa* v. *California* (1995).[160]

The majority on today's high court seems largely convinced of the constitutionality of a sentence of death. Open to debate, however, is the constitutionality of questionable *methods* for its imposition. In a 1993 hearing, *Poyner* v. *Murray*,[161] the U.S. Supreme Court hinted at the possibility of reopening questions first raised in *Kemmler*. The case challenged Virginia's use of the electric chair as a form of cruel and unusual punishment. Syvasky Lafayette Poyner, who originally brought the case before the Court, lost his bid for a stay of execution and was electrocuted in March 1993. Nonetheless, in *Poyner*, Justices Souter, Blackmun, and Stevens wrote: "The Court has not spoken squarely on the underlying issue since *In re Kemmler* . . . and the holding of that case does not constitute a dispositive response to litigation of the issue in light of modern knowledge about the method of execution in question." In a still more recent ruling, members of the Court questioned the constitutionality of hanging, suggesting that it may be a form of cruel and unusual punishment. In that case, *Campbell* v. *Wood* (1994),[162] the defendant, Charles Campbell, raped a woman, got out of prison, then came back and murdered her. His request for a stay of execution was denied since Washington state law (the state in which the murder occurred) offered Campbell a choice between various methods of execution and, therefore, an alternative to hanging. Similarly, in 1996 the Court upheld California's death penalty statute which provides for lethal injection as the primary method of capital punishment in that state.[163] The constitutionality of the statute had been challenged by two death row inmates who claimed that a provision in the law which permitted condemned prisoners the choice of lethal gas in lieu of injection brought the statute within the realm of allowing cruel and unusual punishments.

Questions about the constitutionality of electrocution as a means of execution again came to the fore in 1997 when flames shot from the head and leather mask covering the face of Pedro Medina during his Florida execution. Similarly, in 1999, blood poured from behind the mask covering Allen Lee "Tiny" Davis's face as he was put to death in Florida's electric chair. State officials claimed that the 344-pound Davis suffered a nosebleed brought on by hypertension and blood-thinning medication that he had been taking. Photographs of Davis

"The absence of a noticeable reduction in adult crime rates as incarceration rates have climbed raises serious questions about the efficacy of America's sentencing policies."

—*The American Correctional Association*

taken during and immediately after the execution showed him grimacing while bleeding profusely onto his chest and neck.

Summary

The goals of criminal sentencing are many and varied, and include retribution, incapacitation, deterrence, rehabilitation, and restoration. The just deserts model, with its emphasis on retribution and revenge, is the ascendant sentencing philosophy in the United States today. Many citizens, however, still expect sentencing practices to provide for the other general sentencing goals. This ambivalence toward the purpose of sentencing reflects a more basic cultural uncertainty regarding the root causes of crime, the true nature of justice, and the fundamental goals of the criminal justice system.

Structured sentencing, embodied in the Federal Sentencing Guidelines and in many state sentencing programs of today, is a child of the just deserts philosophy. The structured sentencing model, however, while apparently associated with a reduction in biased and inequitable sentencing practices which had characterized previous sentencing models, may not be the panacea it once seemed. Inequitable practices under the indeterminate model may never have been as widespread as opponents of that model claimed them to be. Worse still, the practice of structured sentencing may not reduce sentencing discretion but merely move it out of the hands of judges and into the ever widening sphere of plea bargaining. Doubly unfortunate, structured sentencing, by its deemphasis of parole, weakens incentives among the correctional population for positive change and tends to swell prison populations until they're overflowing. Even so, as societywide sentiments and the social policies they support swing further in the direction of social responsibility, the interests of crime victims and the concerns of those who champion them will increasingly be recognized.

Discussion Questions

1. Outline the various sentencing goals discussed in this chapter. Which of these rationales do you find most acceptable as the primary goal of sentencing? How might your choice of goals vary with type of offense? Can you envision any other circumstances which might make your choice less acceptable?
2. In your opinion, is the return to just deserts consistent with the structured sentencing model? Why or why not?
3. Trace the differences between structured and indeterminate sentencing. Which model holds the best long-term promise for crime reduction? Why?
4. What is a victim impact statement? Do you think victim impact statements should be admissible at the sentencing stage of criminal trials? If so, what material should they contain? What material should not be permitted in such reports? How could the information in victim impact statements be best verified?

Web Quest!

Visit the U.S. Sentencing Commission on the Web at www.ussc.gov. Review the most recent "publications" and "reports to Congress" available at that site in order to identify the most current issues in federal sentencing today. List and describe these issues. Also view the "USSC Employment Opportunities" listed at the site, and read the information about the Judicial Fellows Program posted there.

Now visit the Sentencing Project at www.sentencingproject.org (you may also use the Cybrary to find sites that have moved since they were listed in this book). What is the mission of the Sentencing Project? How does that mission coincide with the interests of the National Association of Sentencing Advocates and the Campaign for an Effective Crime Policy? (Hint: Sites for both of these organizations should be listed on the Sentencing Project

home page, or you can find them at the Cybrary.) Summarize what you have learned and submit your findings to your instructor if requested to do so.

Library Extras!

The Library Extras! listed here complement the WebExtras! found throughout this chapter. Library Extras! may be accessed on the Web at CJToday.com.

Library Extra! 9-1. *1996 National Survey of State Sentencing Structures* (NIJ, September 1998).

Library Extra! 9-2. *Balanced and Restorative Justice Philosophy* (OJJDP, not dated).

Library Extra! 9-3. *Capital Punishment* (BJS, current volume).

Library Extra! 9-4. *Effects of Judges' Sentencing Decisions on Criminal Careers* (NIJ, 1999).

Library Extra! 9-5. *Felony Sentences in the United States* (BJS, current volume).

Library Extra! 9-6. *National Assessment of Structured Sentencing* (BJA, 1996).

Library Extra! 9-7. *New Directions from the Field: Victim's Rights and Services in the 21st Century* (OVC, 1998).

Library Extra! 9-8. "Restorative Justice: Key Questions and Answers," *The National Institute of Justice Journal* (March 1998).

Library Extra! 9-9. *Three Strikes and You're Out: A Review of State Legislation* (NIJ, September 1997).

References

1. *Smith v. U.S.,* 113 S.Ct. 1178, 122 L. Ed. 2d 548 (1993).

2. This case, and others like it, turn upon interpretation of the phrase "uses or carries a firearm" during and in relation to a "drug trafficking crime" [18 U.S.C. Section 924(c)(1)]. In the 1995 case of *Bailey* v. *U.S.* [516 U.S. 137 (1996)], the U.S. Supreme Court held that mere "proximity and accessibility of the firearm to drugs or drug proceeds is not alone sufficient to support a conviction for 'use'...." In *Bailey,* "use" was interpreted to mean "active use" connoting more than mere possession of a firearm. In the 1998 case of *Muscarello* v. *U.S.* [524 U.S. 125 (1998)], however, the Court held that "the phrase 'carries a firearm' applies to a person who knowingly possesses and conveys firearms in a vehicle, including in the locked glove compartment or trunk of a car, which the person accompanies."

3. For a thorough discussion of the philosophy of punishment and sentencing, see David Garland, *Punishment and Modern Society: A Study in Social Theory* (Chicago: University of Chicago Press, 1990); Ralph D. Ellis and Carol S. Ellis, *Theories of Criminal Justice: A Critical Reappraisal* (Wolfeboro, NH: Longwood Academic, 1989); and Colin Summer, *Censure, Politics, and Criminal Justice* (Bristol, PA: Open University Press, 1990).

4. The requirement for punishment is supported by the belief that social order (and the laws which represent it) could not exist for long if transgressions went unsanctioned.

5. "Back to the Chain Gang," *Newsweek,* October 17, 1994, p. 87.

6. Ibid.

7. Ibid.

8. For an excellent review of the new "get-tough" attitudes influencing sentencing decisions, see

Tamasak Wicharaya, *Simple Theory, Hard Reality: The Impact of Sentencing Reforms on Courts, Prisons, and Crime* (Albany: State University of New York Press, 1995).

9. For a thorough review of the literature on deterrence, see Raymond Paternoster, "The Deterrent Effect of the Perceived Certainty and Severity of Punishment: A Review of the Evidence and Issues," *Justice Quarterly,* vol. 4, no. 2 (June 1987), pp. 174–217.

10. Hugo Adam Bedau, "Retributivism and the Theory of Punishment," *Journal of Philosophy,* vol. 75 (November 1978), pp. 601–620.

11. H.L.A. Hart, *Punishment and Responsibility: Essays in the Philosophy of Law* (Oxford: Clarendon Press, 1968).

12. See, for example, Lawrence W. Sherman et al., *Preventing Crime: What Works, What Doesn't, What's Promising* (Washington, D.C.: National Institute of Justice, 1997).

13. Gordon Bazemore and Mark S. Umbreit, *Balanced and Restorative Justice: Program Summary* (Washington, D.C.: Office of Juvenile Justice and Delinquency Prevention, October 1994), foreword.

14. 18 U.S.C. 3563 (a) (2).

15. See Joan Petersilia, *Expanding Options for Criminal Sentencing* (Santa Monica, CA: The Rand Corporation, 1987).

16. E-mail communications with the Office of Reparative Programs, Department of Corrections, State of Vermont, July 3, 1995.

17. Donna Hunzeker, "State Sentencing Systems and 'Truth in Sentencing,'" *State Legislative Report,* vol. 20, no. 3 (Denver, CO: National Conference of State Legislatures, 1995).

18. "Oklahoma Rapist Gets 30,000 Years," United Press International wire services, southwest edition, December 23, 1994.

19. Paula M. Ditton and Doris James Wilson, "Truth in Sentencing in State Prisons," *BJS Special Report,* January 1999.

20. For a thorough consideration of alleged disparities, see G. Kleck, "Racial Discrimination in Criminal Sentencing: A Critical Evaluation of the Evidence with Additional Evidence on the Death Penalty," *American Sociological Review,* no. 46 (1981), pp. 783–805, and G. Kleck, "Life Support for Ailing Hypotheses: Modes of Summarizing the Evidence for Racial Discrimination in Sentencing," *Law and Human Behavior,* no. 9 (1985), pp. 271–285.

21. National Council on Crime and Delinquency, *National Assessment of Structured Sentencing* (Washington, D.C.: Bureau of Justice Assistance, 1996).

22. Ibid.

23. Ibid.

24. *Arave* v. *Creech,* 113 S.Ct. 1534, 123 L. Ed. 2d 188 (1993). See also *Richmond* v. *Lewis,* 113 S.Ct. 538, 121 L. Ed. 2d 411 (1992).

25. For an early statement of this problem, see Franklin E. Zimring, "Making the Punishment Fit the Crime: A Consumer's Guide to Sentencing Reform," in Gordon Hawkins and F. E. Zimring, eds., *The Pursuit of Criminal Justice* (Chicago: University of Chicago Press, 1984) pp. 267–275.

26. Albert W. Alschuler, "Sentencing Reform and Prosecutorial Power: A Critique of Recent Proposals for 'Fixed' and 'Presumptive' Sentencing," in Sheldon L. Messinger and Egon Bittner, eds., *Criminology Review Yearbook,* vol. 1 (Beverly Hills, CA: Sage Publications, 1979), pp. 416–445.

27. Ibid., p. 422.

28. Christopher T. Link and Neal Shover, "The Origins of Criminal Sentencing Reforms," *Justice Quarterly,* vol. 3, no. 3 (September 1986), pp. 329–342.

29. For a good discussion of such issues, see Hans Toch, "Rewarding Convicted Offenders," *Federal Probation* (June 1988), pp. 42–48.

30. Much of the material in this section is derived from Dale Parent, Terence Dunworth, Douglas McDonald, and William Rhodes, "Mandatory Sentencing," *NIJ Research in Action Series* (Washington, D.C.: NIJ, January 1997).

31. In mid-1996 the California Supreme Court ruled the state's three-strikes law an undue intrusion on judges' sentencing discretion.

32. G. L. Pierce and W. J. Bowers, "The Bartley-Fox Gun Law's Short-Term Impact on Crime in Boston," *Annals of the American Academy of Political and Social Science,* vol. 455 (1981), pp. 120–132.

33. Colin Loftin, Milton Heumann, and David McDowall, "Mandatory Sentencing and Firearms Violence: Evaluating an Alternative to Gun Control," *Law and Society Review,* vol. 17 (1983), pp. 287–318.

34. Colin Loftin and David McDowall, "The Deterrent Effects of the Florida Felony Firearm Law," *Journal of Criminal Law and Criminology,* vol. 75 (1984), pp. 250–259.

35. David McDowall, Colin Loftin, and Brian Wiersema, "A Comparative Study of the Preventive Effects of Mandatory Sentencing Laws for Gun Crimes," *Journal of Criminal Law and Criminology,* vol. 83, no. 2 (Summer 1992), pp. 378–394.

36. Joint Committee on New York Drug Law Evaluation, *The Nation's Toughest Drug Law: Evaluating the New York Experience, a project of the Association of the Bar of the City of New York, the City of New York and the Drug Abuse Council, Inc.* (Washington, D.C.: U.S. Government Printing Office, 1978).

37. Michael Tonry, *Sentencing Reform Impacts* (Washington, D.C.: National Institute of Justice, 1987).

38. D. C. McDonald and K. E. Carlson, *Sentencing in the Courts: Does Race Matter? The Transition to Sentencing Guidelines, 1986–90* (Washington, D.C.: Bureau of Justice Statistics, 1993).

39. As discussed later in this chapter, federal sentencing guidelines did not become effective until 1987 and still had to meet many court challenges.

40. U.S. Sentencing Commission, *Federal Sentencing Guidelines Manual* (Washington, D.C.: U.S. Government Printing Office, 1987), p. 2.

41. A maximum of 54 days per year of good-time credit can still be earned.

42. The Parole Commission Phaseout Act of 1996 requires the Attorney General to report to Congress yearly as to whether it is cost-effective for the Parole Commission to remain a separate agency or whether its functions (and personnel) should be assigned elsewhere. Under the law, if the Attorney General recommends incorporating the Parole Commission's functions in another component of the Department of Justice, they will continue as long as necessary without respect to the November 1, 2002, expiration date provided elsewhere in the legislation.

43. Lawrence A. Greenfeld, *Prison Sentences and Time Served for Violence* (Washington, D.C.: Bureau of Justice Statistics, April 1995).

44. Ditton and Wilson, "Truth in Sentencing in State Prisons."

45. For an excellent review of the act and its implications, see Gregory D. Lee, "U.S. Sentencing Guidelines: Their Impact on Federal Drug Offenders," *FBI Law Enforcement Bulletin* (Washington, D.C.: FBI, May 1995) pp. 17–21.

46. U.S. Sentencing Commission, *Guidelines,* p. 10.

47. *Mistretta* v. *U.S.,* 488 U.S. 361, 371 (1989).

48. For an engaging overview of how mitigating factors might be applied under the guidelines, see *Koon* v. *U.S.,* 116 S.Ct. 2035, 135 L. Ed. 2d 392 (1996).

49. U.S. Sentencing Commission, *Guidelines,* p. 207.

50. *Deal* v. *U.S.,* 113 S.Ct. 1993, 124 L. Ed. 2d 44 (1993).

51. U.S. Sentencing Commission, *Guidelines,* p. 8.

52. "Sentencing Commission Chairman Wilkins Answers Questions on the Guidelines," National Institute of Justice, *Research in Action Report* (September 1987), p. 7.

53. *Melendez* v. *U.S.,* 117 S.Ct. 383, 136 L. Ed. 2d 301 (1996).

54. James Eisentein and Herbert Jacob, *Felony Justice* (Boston: Little, Brown, 1977).

55. Joan Petersilia, *Racial Disparities in the Criminal Justice System* (Santa Monica, CA: The Rand Corporation, 1983).

56. Anthony J. Ragona and John P. Ryan, *Beyond the Courtroom: A Comparative Analysis of Misdemeanor Sentencing—Executive Summary* (Chicago: American Judicature Society, 1983).

57. James H. Kuklinski and John E. Stanga, "Political Participation and Government Responsiveness: The Behavior of California Superior Courts," *American Political Science Review,* vol. 73 (1979), pp. 1090–1099.

58. See Joseph Jacoby and Christopher Dunn, *National Survey on Punishment for Criminal Offenses—Executive Summary* (Washington, D.C.: Bureau of Justice Statistics, 1987). For a critique of this survey, see Barry Krisberg, "Public Attitudes About Criminal Sanctions," *The Criminologist,* vol. 13, no. 2 (March/April 1988), pp. 12, 16.

59. Stephen P. Klein, Susan Turner, and Joan Petersilia, *Radical Equity in Sentencing* (Santa Monica, CA: The Rand Corporation, 1988). See also, S. Klein, J. Petersilia, and S. Turner, "Race and Imprisonment Decisions in California," *Science* vol. 247 (February, 1990), pp. 812–816.

60. *Radical Equity in Sentencing,* p. 11.

61. Ibid.

62. William Wilbanks, "Are Female Felons Treated More Leniently by the Criminal Justice System?" *Justice Quarterly,* vol. 3, no. 4 (December 1986), pp. 517–529.

63. Andrew Klein, *Alternative Sentencing: A Practitioner's Guide* (Cincinnati, OH: Anderson 1988), p. 23.

64. Ibid.

65. National Criminal Justice Information and Statistics Service, *Privacy and Security Planning Instructions* (Washington, D.C.: U.S. Government Printing Office, 1976).

66. U.S. Department of Justice, "State Criminal Records Repositories," Bureau of Justice Statistics, *Technical Report* (1985).

67. Privacy Act of 1974, 5 U.S.C.A. 522a, 88 Statute 1897, Public Law 93-579, December 31, 1974.

68. Freedom of Information Act, 5 U.S.C. 522, and amendments. The status of presentence investigative reports has not yet been clarified under this act to the satisfaction of all legal scholars, although generally state and federal courts are thought to be exempt from the provisions of the act.

69. Alexander B. Smith and Louis Berlin, *Introduction to Probation and Parole* (St. Paul, MN: West, 1976), p. 75.

70. John Rosecrance, "Maintaining the Myth of Individualized Justice: Probation Presentence Reports," *Justice Quarterly,* vol. 5, no. 2 (June 1988), pp. 237–256.

71. Ibid.

72. For a good review of the issues involved, see Robert C. Davis, Arthur J. Lurigio, and Wesley G. Skogan, *Victims of Crime,* 2nd ed. (Thousand Oaks, CA: Sage, 1997), and Leslie Sebba, *Third Parties: Victims and the Criminal Justice System* (Columbus: Ohio State University Press, 1996).

73. President's Task Force on Victims of Crime, *Final Report* (Washington, D.C.: U.S. Government Printing Office, 1982).

74. Peter Finn and Beverly N. W. Lee, *Establishing and Expanding Victim-Witness Assistance Programs* (Washington, D.C.: National Institute of Justice, August 1988).

75. "Victim Assistance Programs: Whom They Service, What They Offer," A National Institute of Justice *Update* (May, 1995).

76. President's Task Force on Victims of Crime, *Final Report.*

77. SJR 65 is a major revision of an initial proposal, Sen. J. Res. 52 which Senators Kyl and Feinstein introduced on April 22, 1996. Rep. Henry Hyde introduced House Joint Resolution 174, a companion to Sen. J. Res. 52, and a similar proposal, H. J. Res. 173 on April 22, 1996.

78. Senate Joint Resolution 44, 105th Congress.

79. See the National Center for Victim of Crime's critique of the 1998 amendment at www. ncvc.org/law/Nvc_ca.htm.

80. As of this writing, the last three states to adopt victim's rights constitutional amendments were Mississippi, Montana, and Tennessee. See the National Victim's Constitutional Amendment Network news page at www.nvcan.org/news.htm. Accessed January 10, 2000.

81. Public Law 97-291.

82. Proposition 8, California's Victim's Bill of Rights.

83. National Victim Center/Mothers Against Drunk Driving/American Prosecutors Research Institute, *Impact Statements: A Victim's Right to Speak: A Nation's Responsibility to Listen,* July 1994.

84. Web posted at www.g-s-j.org/video.htm. Accessed January 20, 2000. VIVD can be contacted at 9722 Groffs Mill Drive, Suite 223, Owings Mills, MD 21117.

85. Rick Atkinson, "Seles Says Attacker Has 'Ruined My Life': Retrial of Parche Aims at Tougher Sentence," *Washington Post,* March 22, 1995.

86. Rick Atkinson, "Suspended Sentence Upheld for Seles' Attacker," *Washington Post,* April 4, 1995.

87. Robert C. Davis and Barbara E. Smith, "The Effects of Victim Impact Statements on Sentencing Decisions: A Test in an Urban Setting," *Justice Quarterly,* vol. 11, no. 3 (September 1994), pp. 453–469.

88. *Booth* v. *Maryland,* 107 S.Ct. 2529 (1987).

89. *Payne* v. *Tennessee,* 501 U.S. 808 (1991).

90. "Supreme Court Closes Term with Major Criminal Justice Rulings," *Criminal Justice Newsletter,* vol. 22, no. 13 (July 1, 1991), p. 2.

91. See "What Say Should Victims Have?" *Time,* May 27, 1991, p. 61.

92. *Report to the Nation on Crime and Justice,* 2nd ed. (Washington, D.C.: U.S. Department of Justice, 1988), p. 90.

93. Jodi M. Brown and Patrick A. Langan, *Felony Sentences in the United States, 1996* (Washington, D.C.: Bureau of Justice Statistics, 1999).

94. Sally T. Hillsman, Barry Mahoney, George F. Cole, and Bernard Auchter, "Fines as Criminal Sanctions," National Institute of Justice, *Research in Brief* (September 1987), p. 1.

95. Ibid., p. 2.

96. Sally T. Hillsman, Joyce L. Sichel, and Barry Mahoney, *Fines in Sentencing* (New York: Vera Institute of Justice, 1983).

97. Ibid., p. 2.
98. Ibid., p. 4.
99. Ibid.
100. Douglas C. McDonald, Judith Greene, and Charles Worzella, *Day Fines in American Courts: The Staten Island and Milwaukee Experiments* (Washington, D.C.: National Institute of Justice, 1992).
101. Ibid., p. 56.
102. Laura A. Winterfield and Sally T. Hillsman, *The Staten Island Day-Fine Project* (Washington, D.C.: National Institute of Justice, 1993), p. 1.
103. S. Turner and J. Petersilia, *Day Fines in Four U.S. Jurisdictions*, (Santa Monica, CA: The Rand Corporation, 1996).
104. "Man Decapitates Neighbor, Tosses Head in Dumpster," Reuters wire services, May 25, 1996.
105. Herbert A. Johnson, *History of Criminal Justice*, (Cincinatti, OH: Anderson, 1988), pp. 30–31.
106. Ibid., p. 31.
107. Ibid., p. 36.
108. "Yemeni Court Upholds Crucifixions," The Associated Press wire services, August 31, 1997.
109. Ibid., p. 51.
110. Arthur Koestler, *Reflections on Hanging* (New York: Macmillan, 1957), p. xi.
111. Ibid., p. 15.
112. Merle Severy, "The Great Revolution," *National Geographic* (July 1989), p. 20.
113. Capital Punishment Research Project, University of Alabama Law School.
114. As of this writing a strong push is under way to institute the death penalty in a number of jurisdictions, including the District of Columbia. A pro-capital-punishment movement is being led in the District of Columbia by U.S. Sen. Kay Bailey Hutchinson (R-Texas).
115. Bureau of Justice Statistics, *Capital Punishment, 1999* (Washington, D.C.: BJS, 2000).
116. Richard Willing, "Expansion of Death Penalty to Nonmurders Faces Challenges," *USA Today*, May 14, 1997, p. 6A.
117. Death Penalty Information Center Web Site, www.deathpenaltyinfo.org, October 31, 2000.
118. *Capital Punishment 1999*.
119. "Killer Spared 14th Date with Execution in Louisiana," Reuters wire services, April 18, 1995.
120. Allan Turner, "Texas Executes Third and Fourth Prisoners in a Week," *Houston Chronicle* via Simon and Schuster's NewsLink service, June 5, 1997.
121. "Chief Justice Calls for Limits on Death Row Habeas Appeals," *Criminal Justice Newsletter*, February 15, 1989, pp. 6–7.
122. *McCleskey* v. *Zandt*, 499 U.S. 467, 493–494 (1991).
123. *Coleman* v. *Thompson*, 501 U.S. 722 (1991).
124. *Schlup* v. *Delo*, 115 S.Ct. 851, 130 L. Ed. 2d 808 (1995).
125. *Felker* v. *Turpin, Warden*, 117 S.Ct. 30, 135 L. Ed. 2d 1123 (1996).
126. *Elledge* v. *Florida*, 119 S.CT 366 (1998).
127. Michelle Locke, "Victim Forgives," The Associated Press wire services, May 19, 1996.
128. Ibid.
129. Koestler, *Reflections on Hanging*, p. xii.
130. See Radelet and Bedau, *In Spite of Innocence* (Boston: Northeastern University Press, 1992),

who claim that 23 innocent people have been executed in the United States since 1900. Also, a House Judiciary Subcommittee found that 59 people have been released from the nation's death rows since 1970 because of innocence (Staff Report, House Judiciary Committee on Civil and Constitutional Rights, October, 1993).
131. Studies include S. Decker and C. Kohfeld, "A Deterrence Study of the Death Penalty in Illinois: 1933–1980," *Journal of Criminal Justice*, vol. 12, no. 4 (1984), pp. 367–379, and S. Decker and C. Kohfeld, "An Empirical Analysis of the Effect of the Death Penalty in Missouri," *Journal of Crime and Justice*, vol. 10, no. 1 (1987), pp. 23–46.
132. See, especially, the work of W. C. Bailey, "Deterrence and the Death Penalty for Murders in Utah: A Time Series Analysis," *Journal of Contemporary Law*, vol. 5, no. 1 (1978), pp. 1–20, and "An Analysis of the Deterrent Effect of the Death Penalty for Murder in California," *Southern California Law Review*, vol. 52, no. 3 (1979), pp. 743–764.
133. B. E. Forst, "The Deterrent Effect of Capital Punishment: A Cross-State Analysis of the 1960's," *Minnesota Law Review*, vol. 61, no. 5 (1977), pp. 743–767.
134. Scott H. Decker and Carol W. Kohfeld, "Capital Punishment and Executions in the Lone Star State: A Deterrence Study," *Criminal Justice Research Bulletin* (Criminal Justice Center, Sam Houston State University), vol. 3, no. 12 (1988).
135. Ibid.
136. "Attorneys Call for Halt to U.S. Executions," Reuters wire services, February 4, 1997.
137. As some of the evidence presented before the Supreme Court in *Furman* v. *Georgia* (408 U.S. 238, 1972) suggested.
138. *USA Today*, April 27, 1989, p. 12A.
139. Thomas J. Keil and Gennaro F. Vito, "Race and the Death Penalty in Kentucky Murder Trials: 1976–1991," *American Journal of Criminal Justice*, vol. 20, no. 1 (1995), pp. 17–36 (published December 1996).
140. *McCleskey* v. *Kemp*, 481 U.S. 279, 107 S.Ct. 1756, 95 L. Ed. 2d 262 (1987).
141. Death Penalty Information Center, World Wide Web site (www.deathpenaltyinfo.org).
142. "Judge Gives Max in Burned Alive Case," United Press International wire services, northeast edition, December 10, 1996.
143. Justice Stewart, as quoted in *USA Today*, April 27, 1989, p. 12A.
144. Koestler, *Reflections on Hanging*, pp. 147–148, and Gennaro F. Vito and Deborah G. Wilson, "Back from the Dead: Tracking the Progress of Kentucky's Furman-Commuted Death Row Population," *Justice Quarterly*, vol. 5, no. 1 (1988), pp. 101–111.
145. For the latest information on public opinion polls, visit the Death Penalty Information Center online at www.deathpenaltyinfo.org.
146. *Criminal Justice Newsletter*, vol. 21, no. 23 (December 3, 1990), p. 1.
147. *Wilkerson* v. *Utah*, 99 U.S. 130 (1878).
148. *In re Kemmler*, 136 U.S. 436 (1890).

149. Ibid., p. 447.
150. *Louisiana ex rel. Francis* v. *Resweber*, 329 U.S. 459 (1947).
151. *Furman* v. *Georgia*, 408 U.S. 238 (1972).
152. A position first ascribed to in *Trop* v. *Dulles*, 356 U.S. 86 (1958).
153. *Gregg* v. *Georgia*, 428 U.S. 153 (1976).
154. Ibid., p. 173.
155. *Coker* v. *Georgia*, 433 U.S. 584 (1977).
156. *Woodson* v. *North Carolina*, 428 U.S. 280 (1976).
157. *Blystone* v. *Pennsylvania*, 494 U.S. 310 (1990).
158. *Boyde* v. *California*, 494 U.S. 370 (1990).
159. *Harris* v. *Alabama*, 513 U.S. 504, 115 S.Ct. 1031, 130 L. Ed. 2d 1004 (1995).
160. *Tuilaepa* v. *California*, 114 S.Ct. 2630, 129 L. Ed. 2d 750 (1994).
161. *Poyner* v. *Murray*, 113 S.Ct. 1573, 123 L. Ed. 2d 142 1993.
162. *Campbell* v. *Wood*, 114 S.Ct. 1337, 127 L. Ed. 2d 685 (1994).
163. U.S. Supreme Court, *Director Gomez, et al* v. *Fierro and Ruiz* (No. 95-1830), 1996.

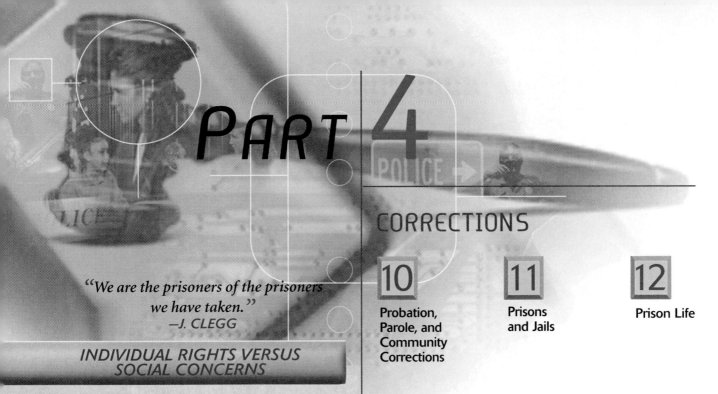

"We are the prisoners of the prisoners we have taken."
—J. CLEGG

INDIVIDUAL RIGHTS VERSUS SOCIAL CONCERNS

THE RIGHTS OF THE CONVICTED AND IMPRISONED

Common law, constitutional, statutory, and humanitarian rights of the convicted and imprisoned:

- A Right Against Cruel or Unusual Punishment
- A Right to Protection from Physical Harm
- A Limited Right to Legal Assistance While Imprisoned
- A Limited Right to Religious Freedom While Imprisoned
- A Limited Right to Freedom of Speech While Imprisoned
- A Right to Sanitary and Healthy Conditions of Confinement
- A Limited Right to Due Process Prior to Denial of Privileges

The individual rights listed must be effectively balanced against these community concerns:

- Punishment of the Guilty
- Safe Communities
- The Reduction of Recidivism
- Secure Prisons
- Control over Convicts
- The Prevention of Escape
- Rehabilitation
- Affordable Prisons

How does our system of justice work toward balance?

The great Christian writer C. S. Lewis (1898–1963) once remarked that if satisfying justice is to be the ultimate goal of Western criminal justice, then the fate of offenders cannot be dictated merely by practical considerations. "The concept of desert is the only connecting link between punishment and justice," Lewis wrote. "It is only as deserved or undeserved that a sentence can be just or unjust," he concluded.

Once a person has been arrested, tried, and sentenced, the correctional process begins. Unlike Lewis's exhortation, however, the contemporary American correctional system—which includes probation, parole, jails, prisons, capital punishment, and a variety of innovative alternatives to traditional sentences—is tasked with far more than merely carrying out sentences. We also ask of our correctional system that it ensures the safety of law-abiding citizens, that it selects the best alternative from among the many available for handling a given offender, that it protects those under its charge, and that it guarantees fairness in the handling of all with whom it comes into contact.

This section of *Criminal Justice: A Brief Introduction* details the development of probation, parole, community corrections, and imprisonment as correctional philosophies; describes the nuances of prison and jail life; discusses special issues in contemporary corrections (including AIDS, geriatric offenders, and female inmates); and summarizes the legal environment which both surrounds and infuses the modern-day practice of corrections. Characteristic of today's correctional emphasis is a societywide push for harsher punishments. The culmination of that strategy, however, is dramatically overcrowded correctional institutions, the problems of which are also described. As you read through this section, encountering descriptions of various kinds of criminal sanctions, you might ask yourself: "When would a punishment of this sort be deserved?" In doing so, remember to couple that thought with another question: "What are the ultimate consequences (for society and for the offender) of the kind of correctional program we are discussing here?" Unlike Lewis, you may also want to ask: "Can we afford it?"

Police

Courts

Corrections

CHAPTER 10

Probation, Parole, and Community Corrections

"Community corrections is an integral part of the criminal justice system and should be fully implemented and promoted in order to save expensive and scarce jail and prison space for violent and serious offenders."
—National Association of Counties, Justice, and Public Safety Steering Committee[1]

—Bob Daemmrich/Stock Boston.

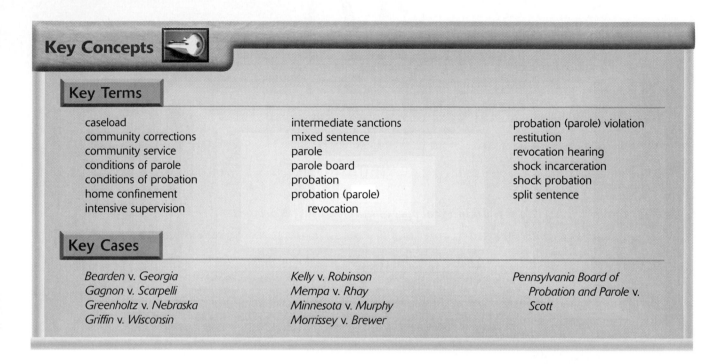

Hear the author discuss this chapter at **cjtoday.com**

Introduction to Community Corrections

In 1996 convicted child molester Larry Don McQuay was released from a Texas prison after serving six years for sexually abusing the six-year-old son of a former girlfriend. McQuay was set free two years before the expiration of an eight-year sentence because of good behavior. His release, however, outraged many Texans because McQuay promised to rape and kill more children, saying that he was helplessly driven to have sex with kids. McQuay added, "I am doomed to eventually rape, then murder my poor little victims to keep them from telling on me."[3] McQuay requested that he be castrated prior to release, but state officials said they were unable to comply with his request. Although not able to prevent his release, officials imposed a number of stringent parole restrictions intended to limit McQuay's movements and mandated that he not associate with anyone under the age of 17.

A few years earlier, another parolee, 39-year-old Leslie Allen Williams, who had a 20-year history of attacks on women, confessed to killing four teenage girls in Pontiac, Michigan. Williams admitted the murders while jailed on charges he had abducted a young woman from a cemetery after she placed a wreath on her mother's grave. Before his arrest for the Pontiac slayings, Williams had been on parole, and had been in and out of prison for abducting and attacking women since 1971. Patrick Urbin, the father of 16- and 14-year-old sisters Michelle and Melissa Urbin—two of Williams's latest victims—said "[t]he system has failed us by letting this person out early . . . [w]e don't personally believe in the death penalty, but he should be behind bars for the rest of his life . . . [w]hy did they let him get so far and do so much in 20 years?"[4]

In August 1999, the shocking case of white supremacist Buford O. Furrow, Jr., splashed across television screens, Internet sites, and newspapers. Brandishing an assault weapon, Furrow attacked a Jewish day-care center in Los Angeles, wounding five people, including three children. He also killed a postal worker whom he encountered following the day-care center shootings. Afterward, authorities learned that Furrow had been on probation following a conviction for second-degree assault as the result of attacking a nurse at a psychiatric hospital in Washington state. As a condition of probation Furrow had been barred from owning guns. An investigation soon uncovered the fact that his probation officer had never checked to see if Furrow had complied with the judge's order, and had not made recommended visits to Furrow's home.[5]

Stories like these, appearing frequently in the media, have cast a harsh light on the early release and poor supervision of criminal offenders. This chapter takes a close look at the

"The abolition of parole has been tried and has failed on a spectacular scale. . . . The absence of parole means that offenders simply walk out the door of prison at the end of a predetermined period of time, no questions asked."

—*Report by the American Probation and Parole Association and the Association of Paroling Authorities International*[2]

A California parole officer lectures a parolee during an office visit. Both parole and probation are forms of supervised release. **State of California Department of Corrections.**

realities behind the practice of what we call "community corrections." **Community corrections,** also called **community-based corrections,** is a sentencing style that represents a movement away from traditional confinement options and an increased dependence upon correctional resources which are available in the community. Community corrections can best be defined as the use of a variety of court-ordered programmatic sanctions permitting convicted offenders to remain in the community under conditional supervision as an alternative to active prison sentences. Community corrections includes a wide variety of sentencing options such as probation, parole, home confinement, the electronic monitoring of offenders, and other new and developing programs—all of which are covered in this chapter.

What Is Probation?

Probation, which is one aspect of community corrections, is "a sentence served while under supervision in the community."[6] Like other sentencing options, probation is a court-ordered sanction. Its goal is to allow for some degree of control over criminal offenders while using community programs to help rehabilitate them. Most of the alternative sanctions discussed later in this chapter are, in fact, predicated upon probationary sentences in which the offender is first placed on probation and then ordered to abide by certain conditions while remaining free in the community—such as participation in a specified program. Although probation can be directly imposed by the court in many jurisdictions, most probationers are technically sentenced first to confinement, but then immediately have their sentences suspended and are remanded into the custody of an officer of the court—the probation officer.

Probation has a long and diverse history. By the 1300s English courts had established the practice of "binding over for good behavior,"[7] in which offenders could be entrusted into the custody of willing citizens. John Augustus (1784–1859), however, is generally recognized as the world's first probation officer. Augustus, a Boston shoemaker, attended sessions of criminal court in the 1850s and would offer to take carefully selected offenders into his home as

---

Community Corrections (also called Community-Based Corrections)

A sentencing style that represents a movement away from traditional confinement options and an increased dependence upon correctional resources which are available in the community.

Probation

A sentence of imprisonment that is suspended. Also, the conditional freedom granted by a judicial officer to an adjudicated adult or juvenile offender, as long as the person meets certain conditions of behavior.

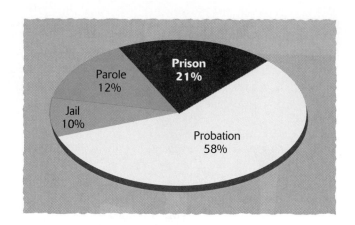

FIGURE 10-1 ■ *Persons under correctional supervision in the United States, by type of Supervision.*

Source: *"Probation and Parole in the United States" (Washington, D.C.: Bureau of Justice Statistics, 2000).*
Note: *Numbers do not total 100 percent due to rounding.*

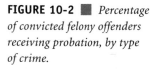

"... Probation and parole services are characteristically poorly staffed and often poorly administered."

—President's Commission on Law Enforcement and Administration of Justice

an alternative to imprisonment.[8] At first he supervised only drunkards, but by 1857 Augustus was accepting many kinds of offenders and devoting all his time to the service of the court.[9] Augustus died in 1859, having bailed out more than 2,000 convicts during his lifetime. In 1878 the Massachusetts legislature enacted a statute which authorized the city of Boston to hire a salaried probation officer. Missouri (1897) followed suit, along with Vermont (1898) and Rhode Island (1899).[10] Before the end of the nineteenth century, probation had become an accepted and widely used form of community-based supervision. By 1925 all 48 states had adopted probation legislation. In the same year the National Probation Act enabled federal district court judges to appoint paid probation officers and impose probationary terms.[11]

The Extent of Probation

Today, probation is the most commonly used form of criminal sentencing in the United States. Between 20 and 60 percent of all persons found guilty of crimes are sentenced to some form of probation. Figure 10-1 shows that 58 percent of all persons under correctional supervision in the United States as of January 1, 2000, were on probation. Not shown is the fact that the number of persons supervised yearly on probation has increased from slightly over 1 million in 1980 to almost 3.8 million today—more than a 300 percent increase.[12] This observation has caused some writers to call "probation crowding" an "immediate threat to the criminal justice process and to community protection."[13]

Even violent offenders stand about a 1-in-5 chance of receiving a probationary term, as Figure 10-2 shows. A 1999 Bureau of Justice Statistics study[14] of felony sentences found that 5 percent of people convicted of homicide were placed on probation, as were 21 percent of convicted sex offenders. Twelve percent of convicted robbers and 30 percent of those com-

FIGURE 10-2 ■ *Percentage of convicted felony offenders receiving probation, by type of crime.*

Source: *Jodi M. Brown and Patrick A. Langan,* Felony Sentences in the United States *(Washington, D.C.: Bureau of Justice Statistics, 1999).*

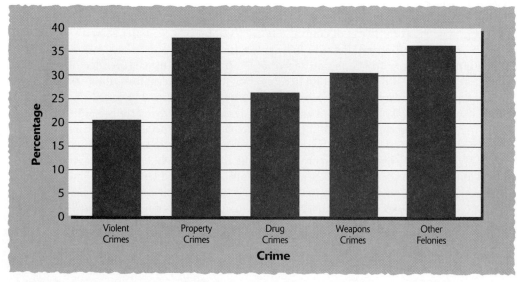

mitting aggravated assault were similarly sentenced to probation rather than active prison time. In a recent example,[15] 47-year-old Carrie Mote of Vernon, Connecticut, was sentenced to probation for shooting her fiancé in the chest with a .38-caliber handgun after he called off their scheduled wedding. Ms. Mote, who faced a maximum of 20 years in prison, claimed to be suffering from diminished psychological capacity at the time of the shooting because of the emotional stress brought on by the canceled wedding.

At the beginning of 2000, a total of 3,773,600 adults were on probation throughout the nation.[16] Individual states, however, made greater or lesser use of probation. North Dakota authorities, with the smallest probationary population, supervised only 2,729 people, while Texas reported 447,100 persons on probation. On a per capita basis, West Virginia had the lowest rate of probation—427 per every 100,000 residents; while the state of Georgia had the highest (5,368 per every 100,000 residents).[17] The national average is 1,864 per every 100,000 residents. Fifty-nine percent of probationers successfully complete their probationary terms, while a small percentage abscond (about 2 percent), and another 3 percent are convicted of new crimes while on probation.[18]

Probation Conditions

Those sentenced to probation must agree to abide by court-mandated conditions of probation. Such conditions are of two types: general and specific. General conditions apply to all probationers in a given jurisdiction and usually include requirements that the probationer "obey all laws," "maintain employment," "remain within the jurisdiction of the court," "possess no firearm," "allow the probation officer to visit at home or at work," and so forth. Figure 10-3 shows a form that judges commonly use to impose general conditions of probation. As a general condition of probation, many probationers are required to pay a fine to the court, usually in a series of installments, that is designed to reimburse victims for damages and to pay lawyers' fees and other costs of court.

Special conditions may be mandated by a judge who feels that the probationary client is in need of particular guidance or control. Figure 10-3 also shows a number of special conditions that are routinely imposed on sizeable subcategories of probationers. Depending upon the nature of the offense, a judge may require that the offender surrender his or her driver's license; submit at reasonable times to warrantless and unannounced searches by a probation officer; supply breath, urine, or blood samples as needed (for drug and alcohol testing); complete a specified number of hours of community service; and complete the General Education Development Test (GED) within a specified time. The judge may also dictate special conditions tailored to the probationary client's situation. Such individualized conditions may prohibit a person from associating with named others (a co-defendant, for example); they may require that the probationer be at home after dark; or they may demand that a particular treatment program be completed within a set time period.

What Is Parole?

Parole is the supervised early release of inmates from correctional confinement. It differs from probation in both purpose and implementation. Whereas probationers generally avoid serving time in prison, offenders who are paroled have already been incarcerated. While probation is a sentencing option available to a judge who determines the form probation will take, parole, in contrast, results from an administrative decision made by a legally designated paroling authority.

States differ as to the type of parole decision-making mechanism they use, as well as the level at which it operates. Two major models prevail: (1) **Parole boards** grant parole based on their judgments and assessments. The parole board's decisions are termed *discretionary parole.* (2) Statutory decrees produce mandatory parole, with release dates usually near the completion of the inmate's prison sentence—minus time off for good behavior and other special considerations. While probation is a sentencing strategy, parole is a correctional strategy whose primary purpose is to return offenders gradually to productive lives. Parole, by making early release possible, can also act as a stimulus for positive behavioral change.

> "I understand that people want violent criminals locked up. We all do. But not every inmate is violent. We must look to supervised probation, to education. We must overcome the fear and think this out."
>
> —*Former Louisiana Governor Edwin Edwards*

Parole

The status of an offender conditionally released from a prison by discretion of a paroling authority prior to expiration of sentence, required to observe conditions of parole, and placed under the supervision of a parole agency.

Parole Board

A state paroling authority. Most states have parole boards (also called commissions) which decide when an incarcerated offender is ready for conditional release and which may also function as revocation hearing panels.

STATE OF NORTH CAROLINA

File No.

______ County ______ Seat Of Court

In The General Court Of Justice
☐ District ☐ Superior Court Division

NOTE:
(This form is not to be used for multiple offenses unless they are consolidated for judgment.)

STATE VERSUS

Defendant

Race	*Sex*	*DOB*

JUDGMENT SUSPENDING SENTENCE AND COMMITMENT ON SPECIAL PROBATION
G.S. 15A-1341, 15A-1342, 15A-1343, 15A-1346

Attorney For State — ☐ *Def. Found Not Indigent* — ☐ *Def. Waived Attorney* — *Attorney For Defendant* ☐ *Appointed* ☐ *Retained*

The defendant ☐ pled guilty to: ☐ was found guilty by the Court of: ☐ was found guilty by a jury of: ☐ pled no contest to:

File No.(s) And Offense(s)	Date of Offense	G.S. No.	Fel./M.	Class	Max. Term	Presumptive

AGGRAVATING/ MITIGATING FACTORS

The Court has considered the aggravating and mitigating factors in G.S. 15A-1340.4(a) and
☐ makes no written findings because the prison term imposed does not require such findings.
☐ makes no written findings because the prison term imposed is pursuant to a plea arrangement as to sentence.
☐ makes the Findings Of Factors In Aggravation And Mitigation Of Punishment set forth on the attached AOC-CR-303.

The Court, having considered evidence, arguments of counsel and statement of defendant, finds that the defendant's plea was freely, voluntarily, and understandingly entered, and Orders the above offenses be consolidated for judgment and the defendant be imprisoned.

for a term of ______ in the custody of the ☐ N.C. Dept. of Correction ☐ Sheriff of ______ County

The defendant shall be given credit for ______ days spent in confinement prior to the date of this Judgment as a result of this charge, to be applied toward the ☐ sentence imposed above. ☐ imprisonment required for special probation below.

SUSPENSION OF SENTENCE

With the consent of the defendant and subject to the conditions set out below, the execution of this sentence is suspended and the defendant is placed on ☐ supervised probation for ______ years. ☐ unsupervised probation for ______ years.

☐ The above period of probation shall begin: ☐ when the defendant is paroled or otherwise released from incarceration in the case referred to below. ☐ at the expiration of the sentence in the case referred to below.
(**NOTE:** *List Case Number, Date, County And Court In Which Prior Sentence Imposed.*)

SPECIAL PROBATION – G.S. 15A-1351

SPECIAL PROBATION ORDER

☐ As a condition of special probation, the defendant shall ☐ serve an active term of ______ ☐ days ☐ months in the custody of the ☐ N.C. DOC. ☐ Sheriff of this County. ☐ submit to IMPACT imprisonment per attached CR-302, Page Two. ☐ pay jail fees.
(**NOTE:** *This term shall NOT be reduced by good time, gain time or parole, or, unless provided above, by time in jail awaiting trial.*)

The defendant shall report in a sober condition to begin serving his term on:	*Day*	*Date*	*Hour*	☐ AM ☐ PM	and shall remain in custody until:	*Day*	*Date*	*Hour*	☐ AM ☐ PM

☐ The defendant shall again report in a sober condition to continue serving this term on the same day of the week for the next ______ consecutive weeks, and shall remain in custody during the same hours each week.

MONETARY CONDITIONS

The defendant shall pay to the Clerk of Superior Court the "Total Amount Due" shown below, plus the probation supervision fee set by law ☐ pursuant to a schedule determined by the probation officer. ☐ at the rate of $ ______ per ______, beginning on ______ and continuing on the same day of each ______ thereafter until paid in full. ☐ Other:

Fine	Costs	Restitution*	Attorney's Fee	Community Service Fee	Total Amount Due
$	$	$	$	$	$

*The name(s) and address(es) and amount(s) due the person(s) to receive this restitution are:

☐ All payments received by the Clerk shall first be disbursed pro rata among the persons entitled to restitution.
☐ Upon payment of the "Total Amount Due", the probation officer may transfer the defendant to unsupervised probation.

AOC-CR-302, Rev. 7/95 — Material opposite unmarked squares is to be disregarded as surplusage.

FIGURE 10-3 ■ *Probation agreement form. (Courtesy of the North Carolina Administrative Office of the Courts, and the North Carolina Department of Correction, Division of Adult Probation and Parole. Reprinted with permission.)*

(Continued)

REGULAR CONDITIONS OF PROBATION – G.S. 15A-1343(b)

The defendant shall: 1. Commit no criminal offense in any jurisdiction. 2. Possess no firearm, explosive device or other deadly weapon listed in G.S. 14-269. 3. remain gainfully and suitably employed or faithfully pursue a course of study or of vocational training that will equip him for suitable employment. 4. Satisfy child support and family obligations, as required by the Court. If the defendant is on supervised probation, he shall also: 5. Remain within the jurisdiction of the Court unless granted written permission to leave by the Court or his probation officer. 6. Report as directed by the Court or his probation officer to the officer at reasonable times and places and in a reasonable manner, permit the officer to visit him at reasonable times, answer all reasonable inquiries by the officer, and obtain prior approval from the officer for, and notify the officer of, any change in address or employment. 7. Notify the probation officer if he fails to obtain or retain satisfactory employment. 8. At a time to be designated by his probation officer, visit with his probation officer at a facility maintained by the Division of Prisons. If the defendant is to serve an active sentence as a condition of special probation, he shall also: 9. Obey the rules and regulations of the Department of Correction governing the conduct of inmates while imprisoned. 10. Report to a probation officer in the State of North Carolina within 72 hours of his discharge from the active term of imprisonment.

GENERAL CONDITIONS

SPECIAL CONDITIONS OF PROBATION – G.S. 15A-1343(b1), 143B-262(c)

The defendant shall also comply with the following special conditions which the Court finds are reasonably related to his rehabilitation:

☐ 11. Surrender his driver's license to the Clerk of Superior Court for transmittal to the Division of Motor Vehicles and not operate a motor vehicle for a period of _____ or until relicensed by the Division of Motor Vehicles, whichever is later.

☐ 12. Submit at reasonable times to warrantless searches by a probation officer of his person, and of his vehicle and premises while he is present, for the following purposes which are reasonably related to his probation supervision:
☐ stolen goods ☐ controlled substances ☐ contraband ☐ _____

☐ 13. Not use, possess, or control any illegal drug or controlled substance unless it has been prescribed for him by a licensed physician and is in the original container with the prescription number affixed on it; not knowingly associate with any known or previously convicted users, possessors, or sellers of any illegal drugs or controlled substances; and not knowingly be present at or frequent any place where illegal drugs or controlled substances are sold, kept, or used.

☐ 14. Supply a breath, urine, and/or blood specimen for analysis of the possible presence of a prohibited drug or alcohol, when instructed by his probation officer.

☐ 15. Successfully pass the General Education Development Test (G.E.D.) during the first _____ months of the period of probation.

☐ 16. Complete _____ hours of community or reparation service during the first _____ days of the period of probation, as directed by the community service coordinator, and pay the fee prescribed by G.S. 143B-475. 1(b) ☐ pursuant to the schedule set out under monetary conditions above. ☐ within _____ days of this Judgment and before beginning service.

☐ 17. Report for initial evaluation by _____ , participate in all further evaluation, counseling, treatment, or education programs recommended as a result of that evaluation, and comply with all other therapeutic requirements of those programs until discharged.

☐ 18. Other:

☐ 19. Comply with the Additional Conditions Of Probation which are set forth on AOC-CR-302, Page Two.

SPECIAL CONDITIONS

☐ A hearing was held in open court in the presence of the defendant at which time a fee, including expenses, was awarded the defendant's appointed counsel or assigned public defender.

ORDER OF COMMITMENT/APPEAL ENTRIES

☐ It is ORDERED that the Clerk deliver three certified copies of this Judgment and Commitment to the Sheriff or other qualified officer, and that the officer cause the defendant to be delivered with these copies to the custody of the agency named on the reverse to serve the sentence imposed or until he shall have complied with the conditions of release pending appeal.

☐ The defendant gives notice of appeal from the judgment of the District Court to the Superior Court. The current pretrial release order shall remain in effect. ☐ except that:

☐ The defendant gives notice of appeal from the judgment of the Superior Court to the Appellate Division. Appeal entries and any conditions of post conviction release are set forth on Form AOC-CR-350.

SIGNATURE OF JUDGE

Date	Name Of Presiding Judge (Type Or Print)	Signature Of Presiding Judge

CERTIFICATION

I certify that this Judgment and the attachment(s) marked below are true copies of the originals.
☐ Judgment Suspending Sentence, Page Two [Additional Conditions Of Probation (AOC-CR-302, Page Two)]
☐ Findings Of Factors In Aggravation And Mitigation Of Punishment (AOC-CR-303)

Date Of Certification	Date Certified Copies Delivered To Sheriff	Signature And Seal
		☐ Deputy CSC ☐ Assistant CSC ☐ Clerk Of Superior Court

NOTE: *Defendant signs the following statement in all cases except unsupervised probation without community or reparation service.*
I have received a copy of this Judgment which contains all of the conditions of my probation, and I agree to them. I understand that no person who supervises me or for whom I work while performing community or reparation service is liable to me for any loss or damage which I may sustain unless my injury is caused by that person's gross negligence or intentional wrongdoing.

Date Signed	Signature Of Defendant	Witnessed By:

AOC-CR-302, Side Two, Rev. 7/95   Material opposite unmarked squares is to be disregarded as surplusage.

Probation (or Parole) Violation

An act or a failure to act by a probationer (or parolee), which does not conform to the conditions of probation (or parole).

Conditions of Probation and Parole

The general (state-ordered) and special (court- or board-ordered) limits imposed upon an offender who is released on either probation or parole. General conditions tend to be fixed by state statute, while special conditions are mandated by the sentencing authority and take into consideration the background of the offender and the circumstances surrounding the offense.

Probation (or Parole) Revocation

The administrative action of a probation (or paroling) authority removing a person from probationary (or parole) status in response to a violation of lawfully required conditions of probation (or parole) including the prohibition against commission of a new offense and usually resulting in a return to prison.

The use of parole in this country began with the Elmira Reformatory in 1876. As you may recall from Chapter 9, indeterminate sentences are a key part of a philosophy that stresses rehabilitation. The indeterminate sentence was made possible by an innovative New York law following the call of leading correctional innovators. Parole was a much-heralded tool of nineteenth-century corrections, whose advocates had been looking for a behavioral incentive to motivate youthful offenders to reform. Parole, through its promise of earned early release, seemed the ideal innovation.

Parolees comprise the smallest of the correctional categories shown in Figure 10-1 (other than "jail"). A growing reluctance to use parole seems due to the expanding realization that today's correctional routines have been generally ineffective at producing any substantial reformation among many offenders prior to their release back into the community. The abandonment of the rehabilitation goal, combined with a return to determinate sentencing in many jurisdictions—including the federal judicial system—has substantially reduced the amount of time the average correctional client spends on parole.

The Extent of Parole

Although time spent on parole is far less than it used to be, most inmates who are freed from prison are still paroled (about 75 percent) or are granted some other form of conditional release (about 5.5 percent).[19] Some states operating under determinate sentencing guidelines require that inmates serve a short period of time, such as 90 days, on reentry parole—a form of mandatory release. Mandatory releases have increased fivefold—from 6 percent of all releases in 1977 to over 40 percent today.[20] As a result, determinate sentencing schemes have changed the face of parole in America, resulting in a dramatic reduction of the average time spent under postprison supervision, while having little impact upon the number of released inmates who experience some form of parole.

At the beginning of 2000, 712,713 people were on parole throughout the United States.[21] States vary considerably in the use they make of parole, influenced as they are by the legislative requirements of sentencing schemes. For example, on January 1, 2000, Maine, a state which is phasing out parole, reported only 31 people under parole supervision (the lowest of all the states), and North Dakota only 157, while California (the highest of all) had a parole population in excess of 114,000, and Texas officials were busy supervising almost 110,000 persons. The rate at which parole is used varies considerably by region. Only 3 out of every 100,000 Maine residents are on parole, whereas 1,201 out of every 100,000 District of Columbia residents are on parole. The national average is 352 per 100,000.[22]

Approximately 49 percent of parolees successfully complete parole, while about 26 percent are returned to prison for **parole violations** and another 12 percent go back to prison for new offenses during their parole period (others may be transferred to new jurisdictions, abscond and not be caught, or die—bringing the total to 100 percent).[23]

Parole Conditions

In those jurisdictions which retain discretionary parole, the **conditions of parole** remain very similar to the conditions agreed to by probationers. Figure 10-4 shows both sides of a typical parole agreement form, which parolees must sign before their release. General conditions of parole usually include agreements not to willfully leave the state, as well as a blanket agreement to extradition requests from other jurisdictions. Parolees must also periodically report to parole officers, and parole officers may visit parolees at their homes and places of business—often arriving unannounced.

The successful and continued employment of parolees is one of the major concerns of parole boards and their officers, and studies have found that successful employment is a major factor in reducing the likelihood of repeat offenses.[24] Hence, the importance of continued employment is typically stressed on parole agreement forms, with the stricture that failure to find employment within 30 days may result in **revocation** of parole. As with probationers, parolees who are working can be ordered to pay fines and penalties. A provision for making **restitution** payments is also frequently included as a condition of parole.

As with probation, special parole conditions may be added by the judge, and might require the parolee to pay a "parole supervisory fee" (often around $15–$20 per month). A relatively new innovation, parole supervision fees shift some of the expenses of community corrections to the offender.

Federal Parole

Federal parole decisions are made by the U.S. Parole Commission, which uses hearing examiners to visit federal prisons. Examiners typically ask inmates to describe why, in their opinion, they are ready for parole. The inmate's job readiness, home plans, past record, accomplishments while in prison, good behavior, and previous experiences on probation or parole form the basis for a report made by the examiners to the parole commission. The 1984 Comprehensive Crime Control Act, which mandated federal fixed sentencing and abolished parole for offenses committed after November 1, 1978, began a planned phaseout of the U.S. Parole Commission. Under the act, the Commission was to be abolished by 1992. The Parole Commission Phaseout Act of 1996,[25] however, extended the continued existence of the commission until 2002, with more extensions expected. Under the law, the U.S. Attorney General must annually certify to Congress that continuation of the commission beyond 2002 is the most effective and cost-efficient method for carrying out the functions assigned to it, or the Attorney General will have to propose to Congress an alternative plan for a transfer of those functions.[26] Visit the Commission's Web site via **WebExtra!** 10-1 at CJToday.com.

Restitution

A court requirement that an alleged or convicted offender pay money or provide services to the victim of the crime or provide services to the community.

Probation and Parole: The Pluses and Minuses

Advantages of Probation and Parole

Probation is used to meet the needs of offenders who require some correctional supervision short of imprisonment, while at the same time providing a reasonable degree of security to the community. Parole fulfills a similar purpose for offenders released from prison. Both probation and parole provide a number of advantages over imprisonment, including

1. *Lower cost.* Imprisonment is expensive. One study found that incarcerating a single offender in Georgia costs approximately $7,760 per year while the cost of intensive probation is as little as $985 per probationer.[27] The expense of imprisonment in some other states may be nearly three times as high as it is in Georgia. Not only do probation and parole save money, they may even help fill the public coffers. Some jurisdictions require that offenders pay a portion of the costs associated with their own supervision. Georgia, for example, charges clients between $10 and $50 per month while they are being supervised,[28] while Texas, in an innovative program which uses market-type incentives to encourage probation officers to collect fees,[29] has been able to annually recoup monies totaling more than half of the total that the state spends on probation services.

2. *Increased employment.* Few people in prison have the opportunity to work. Work-release programs, correctional industries, and inmate labor programs operate in most states, but they usually provide only low-paying jobs and require few skills. At best, such programs include only a small portion of the inmates in any given facility. Probation and parole, on the other hand, make it possible for offenders under correctional supervision to work full time at jobs in the "free" economy. They can contribute to their own and their families' support, stimulate the local economy by spending their wages, and support government through the taxes they pay.

3. *Restitution.* Offenders who are able to work are candidates for court-ordered restitution. Society's interest in restitution (sometimes called "making the victim whole again") may be better served by a probationary sentence or parole than by imprisonment. Restitution payments to victims may help restore their standard of living and personal confidence while teaching the offender responsibility.

PC -104a
10/92

STATE OF NORTH CAROLINA
PAROLE AGREEMENT BETWEEN THE NORTH CAROLINA PAROLE COMMISSION
AND

_____ , PAROLEE

In accepting this parole, I understand that the North Carolina Parole Commission may modify its terms. I also understand that I am under the legal custody of the Parole Commission until duly discharged by the Commission. I understand that should I violate parole, the Commission may cause me to be returned to custody for further action as provided by law. I understand that my term of parole shall be for no less than either (1) the remainder of the maximum term if the maximum term is less than one year, or (2) one year if the remainder of the maximum term is one year or more. I understand that I shall receive no credit for time spent on parole against the remainder of my sentence, and that in the event my parole is revoked I will be reimprisoned for the unserved portion of the maximum term of imprisonment imposed by the court. I understand that in the event of an alleged violation of parole, my parole time may be frozen at the time of the alleged violation. If my parole time is frozen, it may remain frozen until such time as the alleged violations are disposed of, even if it becomes necessary to extend my release date beyond its normal period. I further understand that if I abide by the terms and conditions of this parole, the Parole Commission will unconditionally discharge me no later than my maximum release date. In accepting this parole, I agree to abide by the following rules:

GENERAL CONDITIONS

1. I will report promptly to my Probation/Parole Officer when instructed to do so, and in the manner prescribed by my Probation/Parole Officer and the Parole Commission.
2. I will work steadily at an approved job, and not change my job or my residence without permission from my Probation/Parole Officer. If I am discharged from my job or evicted from my home, I will notify my Probation/Parole Officer. I will also support any persons dependent on me to the best of my ability.
3. I will obey all municipal, county, and state and federal laws, ordinances, and orders. If I am arrested or receive a citation to appear in court while on parole, I will report this fact to my Probation/Parole Officer within 24 hours of such arrest or citation.
4. I will not leave my county of residence without obtaining permission from my Probation/Parole Officer. I will not leave the State of North Carolina without permission from the Parole Commission or my Probation/Parole Officer.
5. I will not consume alcoholic beverages to excess or use or possess drugs in violation of state and federal laws.
6. I will not own or possess any firearms or deadly weapon without written permission from the Parole Commission.
7. I will notify my Probation/Parole Officer in writing three weeks in advance of any plans to alter my marital status (marriage, separation, divorce).
8. I will allow my Probation/Parole Officer to visit my home or place of employment at any time.
9. I do hereby waive extradition to the State of North Carolina from any state of the United States and also agree that I will not contest any effort by any state to return me to the State of North Carolina.
10. I will not enter into any agreement to act as an "informer" or special agent for any law enforcement agency without permission from the Parole Commission.
11. I will not assault, or harm, or threaten to assault or harm, any person.
12. I will comply with the following Special Conditions which have been imposed by the Parole Commission:

☐ In the event (1) I do not have a plan of employment at this time, or (2) my employment plan has been found to be only temporarily suitable, I understand and agree that I must diligently seek employment which is satisfactory to the Parole Commission, and I will use my best efforts to secure the same, and will report the progress of my efforts to my Probation/Parole Officer twice weekly until satisfactory employment is obtained. I further understand and agree that if I have not obtained satisfactory employment within 30 days from today, I may be returned to prison and my parole or conditional release may be revoked, in the discretion of the Commission.

☐ I, _____ , will pay to the Department of Correction the sum

of _____ per week/month to be used to make restitution to the following named payee(s) in the following amounts:

Name of Payee	Address	Amount to be Paid
_____	_____	_____
_____	_____	_____
_____	_____	_____

It shall be my responsibility to send my weekly/monthly payments to the Department of Correction at the following address: WORK RELEASE ACCOUNTING OFFICE, 831 West Morgan St., Raleigh, N.C. 27603.

PAYMENTS SHALL BE MADE EITHER BY CASHIER CHECK, CERTIFIED CHECK, OR POSTAL MONEY ORDER (NO PERSONAL CHECKS ACCEPTED). CHECKS SHALL BE MADE PAYABLE TO THE _DEPARTMENT OF CORRECTION_ AND INCLUDE THE NAME AND ADDRESS OF THE PAROLEE LISTED ABOVE.

FIGURE 10-4 ■ _Parole agreement form. (Courtesy of the North Carolina Parole Commission, and the North Carolina Department of Correction, Division of Adult Probation and Parole. Reprinted with permission.)_

(Continued)

I will accept counseling and/or treatment for drug and/or alcohol abuse at the discretion of the supervising officer.

I will not associate with known drug offenders, users, and/or pushers.

I will consent to a warrantless search of my person, premises, or any vehicle under my control by my supervising officer for any purpose reasonably related to parole supervision.

I will stay away from places where the selling and/or serving of alcohol is the primary business.

I will submit to any physical, chemical, or breathalyzer test when requested to do so by the Parole Commission, or by supervising PPO, for detection of alcohol and/or controlled substances, and pay costs thereof.

I will abide by curfew at discretion of PPO.

I will pay a parole supervision fee of $15 within 30 days after my release on parole and each month thereafter until my parole is terminated unless the Parole Commission relieves me of this obligation because of undue economic burden. I will send my parole supervision fee to the Clerk of Superior Court, Wake County, Raleigh, N.C.

I agree to:

1. Be under the Intensive Parole Supervision Program for a minimum of 6 months.

2. Obey any curfew imposed by the Parole Commission or by my Supervising Officer.

3. Submit to request for blood and urine samples for possible presence of drugs.

4. Attend and participate in counseling, treatment, or educational programs as directed by the Parole Commission or the Intensive/Parole Officer as approved by the Parole Commission, and abide by all rules, regulations, and directives of such programs.

5. Submit at reasonable times to warrantless searches by a Parole Officer of my person, vehicle, or premises while I am present for purposes which are reasonably related to parole supervision.

I will remain at ▮▮▮▮▮▮▮▮▮▮▮▮ School until completion of course.

I will have no contact with ▮▮▮▮▮▮▮▮▮▮▮▮ (co-defendant).

SPECIAL CONDITIONS–USUALLY TYPED ONTO FORM

If I violate any of the conditions or Special Conditions of parole, I may be arrested and held as a parole violator. In this event, I will be given a hearing at which time I may be represented by counsel and, if the Commission decides that I am in violation of one or more of the conditions of my parole, I may be returned to prison.

I have read or have had read to me the foregoing conditions of my parole. I fully understand them and will strictly follow them, and I understand and know what I am doing. No promises or threats have been made to me, and no pressure of any kind has been used against me at the time of signing this Parole Agreement.

DATE _____ SIGNED _____

DATE _____ WITNESS _____

DATE _____ WITNESS _____

NOTE TO CONVICTED FELONS: *The possession of a firearm by a convicted felon is a violation of both federal and state law. Also, the act of registering or voting is punishable by law until such time as these rights are restored.

PROVISION FOR PARTIAL "CIVIL DEATH"

4. *Community support.* The decision to release a prisoner on parole, or to sentence a convicted offender to a probationary term, is often partially based upon considerations of family and other social ties. Such decisions are made in the belief that offenders will be more subject to control in the community if they participate in a web of positive social relationships. An advantage of both probation and parole is that it allows the offender to continue personal and social relationships. Probation avoids splitting up families, while parole may reunite family members separated from each other by time in prison.

5. *Reduced risk of criminal socialization.* Prison has been called a "school in crime." Probation insulates adjudicated offenders, at least to some degree, from the kinds of criminal values which permeate prison. Parole, by virtue of the fact that it follows time served in prison, is less successful than probation in reducing the risk of criminal socialization.

6. *Increased use of community services.* Probationers and parolees can take advantage of services offered through the community, including psychological therapy, substance abuse counseling, financial services, support groups, church outreach programs, and social services. While a few similar opportunities may be available in prison, the community environment itself can enhance the effectiveness of treatment programs by reducing the stigmatization of the offender and allowing the offender to participate in a more "normal" environment.

7. *Increased opportunity for rehabilitation.* Probation and parole can both be useful behavioral management tools. They reward cooperative offenders with freedom and allow for the opportunity to shape the behavior of offenders who may be difficult to reach through other programs.

Disadvantages of Probation and Parole

Any honest appraisal of probation and parole must recognize that they share a number of strategic drawbacks, such as the following:

1. *A relative lack of punishment.* The "just deserts" model of criminal sentencing insists that punishment should be a central theme of the justice process. While rehabilitation and treatment are recognized as worthwhile goals, the model suggests that punishment serves both society's need for protection and the victim's need for revenge. Probation, however, is seen as practically no punishment at all and is coming under increasing criticism as a sentencing strategy. Parole is likewise accused of unhinging the scales of justice because (1) it releases some offenders early, even when they have been convicted of serious crimes, while other, relatively minor offenders, may remain in prison, and (2) it is dishonest because it does not require completion of the offender's entire sentence behind bars.

2. *Increased risk to the community.* Probation and parole are strategies designed to deal with convicted *criminal* offenders. The release into the community of such offenders increases the risk that they will commit additional offenses. Community supervision can never be so complete as to eliminate such a possibility entirely, and studies on parole have pointed to the fact that an accurate assessment of offender dangerousness is beyond our present capability.[30]

   A 1992 Bureau of Justice Statistics study[31]—the nation's largest ever follow-up survey of felons on probation—found that 43 percent of probationers were rearrested for a felony within three years of receiving a probationary sentence, and while still on probation. Half of the arrests were for a violent crime or a drug offense. An even greater percentage of probationers, 46 percent, were either sent to prison or jail or had absconded.

3. *Increased social costs.* Some offenders placed on probation and parole will effectively and responsibly discharge their obligations. Others, however, will become social liabilities. In addition to the increased risk of new crimes, probation and parole increase the chance that added expenses will accrue to the community in the form of child support, welfare costs, housing expenses, legal aid, indigent health care, and the like.

The Legal Environment

Ten especially significant U.S. Supreme Court decisions provide a legal framework for probation and parole supervision. Among recent cases, that of *Griffin* v. *Wisconsin* (1987)[32] may be the most significant. In *Griffin,* the U.S. Supreme Court ruled that probation officers may conduct searches of a probationer's residence without the need for either a search warrant or probable cause. According to the Court, "[a] probationer's home, like anyone else's, is protected by the Fourth Amendment's requirement that searches be 'reasonable.' " However, "[a] State's operation of a probation system . . . presents 'special needs' beyond normal law enforcement that may justify departures from the usual warrant and probable cause requirements." Probation, the Court concluded, is similar to imprisonment because it is a "form of criminal sanction imposed upon an offender after a determination of guilt."

Similarly, in the 1998 case of *Pennsylvania Board of Probation and Parole* v. *Scott,*[33] the Court declined to extend the exclusionary rule to apply to searches by parole officers, even where such searches yield evidence of parole violations. In the words of the Court: "[T]he Court has repeatedly declined to extend the [exclusionary] rule to proceedings other than criminal trials. . . . The social costs of allowing convicted criminals who violate their parole to remain at large are particularly high . . . and are compounded by the fact that parolees . . . are more likely to commit future crimes than are average citizens."

Other court cases focus on the conduct of parole or probation **revocation hearings.** Revocation is a common procedure. Annually, about 22 percent of adults on parole and 7.5 percent of those on probation throughout the United States have their conditional release revoked.[34] Revocation of probation or parole may be requested by the supervising officer if a client has allegedly violated the conditions of community release or has committed a new crime. The most frequent violations for which revocation occurs are (1) failure to report as required to a probation or parole office, (2) failure to participate in a stipulated treatment program, and (3) alcohol or drug abuse while under supervision.[35] Revocation hearings may result in an order that a probationer's suspended sentence be made "active" or that a parolee return to prison to complete his or her sentence in confinement.

In a 1935 decision (*Escoe* v. *Zerbst*)[36] which has since been greatly modified, the Supreme Court held that probation "comes as an act of grace to one convicted of a crime . . ." and that the revocation of probation without hearing or notice to the probationer was acceptable practice. By 1967, however, the case of *Mempa* v. *Rhay*[37] found the Warren court changing direction as it declared that both notice and a hearing were required. It also said that the probationer should have the opportunity for representation by counsel before a deferred prison sentence could be imposed.[38] Jerry Mempa had been convicted of riding in a stolen car at age 17 in 1959 and sentenced to prison, but his sentence was deferred and he was placed on probation. A few months later he was accused of burglary. A hearing was held, and Mempa admitted his involvement in the burglary. An active prison sentence was then imposed. At the hearing Mempa had not been offered the chance to have a lawyer represent him nor was he given the chance to present any evidence or testimony in his own defense.

Two of the most widely cited cases affecting parolees and probationers are *Morrissey* v. *Brewer* (1972)[39] and *Gagnon* v. *Scarpelli* (1973).[40] In *Morrissey,* the Court declared a need for procedural safeguards in revocation hearings involving *parolees.* After *Morrissey,* revocation proceedings would require that (1) the parolee be given written notice specifying the alleged violation; (2) evidence of the violation be disclosed; (3) a neutral and detached body constitute the hearing authority; (4) the parolee have the chance to appear and offer a defense, including testimony, documents, and witnesses; (5) the parolee have the right to cross-examine witnesses; and (6) a written statement be provided to the parolee at the conclusion of the hearing that includes the hearing body's decision, the testimony considered, and reasons for revoking parole, if such occurs.[41]

In 1973 the Court extended the procedural safeguards of *Morrissey* to *probationers* in *Gagnon* v. *Scarpelli* (1973). John Gagnon had pleaded guilty to armed robbery in Wisconsin and was sentenced to 15 years in prison. His sentence was suspended, and the judge ordered him to serve a seven-year probationary term. One month later, and only a day after having been transferred to the supervision of the Cook County, Illinois, Adult Probation Department, Gagnon was arrested by police in the course of a burglary. He was advised of his rights

Revocation Hearing

A hearing held before a legally constituted hearing body (such as a parole board) in order to determine whether a probationer or parolee has violated the conditions and requirements of his or her probation or parole.

CRIME IN THE NEWS

The Bloody Saga of Leo Gonzales Wright

WASHINGTON—On Dec. 16, 1995, a young human rights lawyer, Bettina Pruckmayr, was brutally murdered near an ATM machine in Washington after coming home from an afternoon of Christmas shopping.

Her killer, a convicted murderer and repeat parole violator named Leo Gonzales Wright, robbed her and stabbed her 38 times. There was no excuse for what he did, but there was also no excuse for a criminal justice system that made it easy for him.

Just how easy was laid out in chilling detail in a 47-page inspector general's report that Pruckmayr's angry parents forced out of the D.C. government with a wrongful death lawsuit. They accused the city of gross negligence. The inspector general, E. Barrett Prettyman Jr., found that to be an appalling understatement.

Even more chilling, Prettyman pointed out that "there are a lot of Leo Wrights out there."

No One Did Their Job

The parole officials, the police and the corrections officers who dealt with Wright all failed to do their job, the family charged. "If even one of those individuals had done their duty, Bettina would still be alive," her father, Gerfried Pruckmayr, said Jan. 25 when Prettyman's report was released. "We hold them directly responsible for the murder of our daughter."

It was a savage killing. Wright, a 41-year-old previously convicted murderer released before his time was up for killing a D.C. cabdriver, had been looking in cars for something to steal when he saw Pruckmayr drive up to park near her apartment building. He abducted her, forced her to give him her ATM pass code, and killed her when she tried to escape, stabbing her 38 times with a butcher knife that left wounds 6 inches deep. Covered with

blood, he then went to an ATM machine, tried twice to withdraw more money than she had in her account, and returned to the car, pushing her out while she was still gasping for air. He took her belongings—jewelry, driver's license, even her bar association membership card—with him.

She Tried to Flee

Police arrested him nine days later. He pleaded guilty in 1996. When asked at his sentencing why he killed her, Wright gave the same excuse he had given for the 1976 murder of the cabby: She'd "bucked" him by trying to escape, he said.

"You are the most violent, dangerous person I've ever encountered," the judge said of Wright in sentencing him to life without possibility of parole.

A Violent Past, Ignored

Under the sentence he'd gotten in 1976 for the cabdriver's killing—consecutive sentences for second-degree murder and armed robbery with a minimum of 20 years in prison—Wright should still have been behind bars when he accosted Pruckmayr. His prison record at the Lorton Correctional Complex showed what a bad bet he was, with almost 40 disciplinary reports for assaults on fellow inmates and staff, possession of shanks (weapons) and use and possession of drugs. He was repeatedly transferred to maximum security at Lorton for his "hostile and aggressive behavior."

Nevertheless, Wright was admitted in 1990 to a permissive, and since-terminated, drug treatment program entitling inmates to dormitory space, better food "and less pressure from institutional staff."

Discipline Reports Overlooked

At least five disciplinary reports on Wright were overlooked when the

assignment was made; others were evidently destroyed. One former correctional officer who knew Wright said Wright's inmate record—which included stabbing other inmates, assaulting officers with bricks, and throwing urine and feces on officers—was less than "half its original size" when he inspected it in 1996 for the prosecutors in Pruckmayr's case.

The officer, Arthur Hood, said inmates often had access to their own records. Another witness told Prettyman she had heard of correctional officers and others "being paid by inmates" to remove documents from their files. Exactly how Wright's file shrank remains unknown.

A "Model Inmate"

At the treatment program, however, Wright was regarded as a "model inmate," and in 1992, one senior Lorton official, now an acting deputy warden whom Prettyman assailed in his report, recommended early parole. In the process, Wright was credited with almost five more months' good time than he should have received. A parole analyst still recommended denial of early parole, but a Parole Board member impressed by Wright's "mild-mannered, soft-spoken" demeanor overruled her.

Wright was paroled in February 1993. Had he served the full 20-year minimum imposed in 1976, Prettyman pointed out, "Wright still would have been incarcerated on Dec. 16, 1995, the day he murdered Bettina Pruckmayr."

The System Fails

After his release, police and parole officers demonstrated how inept and inattentive the justice system can be. Wright was supposed to have a job, report to his supervisor once a month, and undergo periodic drug testing. He was

(Continued)

CRIME IN THE NEWS

The Bloody Saga of Leo Gonzales Wright

fired from his job at a thrift store, failed to report for months and when he finally did turn up, was allowed to leave without a test. A warrant for his arrest should have been issued. None was. His parole officer, Anthony Hill, didn't even notice when Wright was arrested on May 24, 1995, and charged with auto theft. The two cops who made the arrest said somebody should have reported it to the Parole Board but nobody did.

The mindless system grew more mindless. The auto theft charge was dismissed for lack of evidence, but Wright was arrested again June 28 on a felony drug charge. That time, the Parole Board was notified so that it could issue a parole violation warrant prior to a July 7, 1995, preliminary hearing, but Hill waited too long. The court wasn't informed of any warrant and it dismissed the charge when the arresting officers, one of them a child-hood friend of Wright named Wayne Stancil, failed to show up.

Cop Neglects Duty

That wasn't unusual for Stancil. Pretty-man's investigators found he was put on leave with pay for "neglect of duty" in July of 1997, charged with seven failures to make court appearances that year, none of them related to Wright. It amounted to a paid vacation.

Stancil was returned to full duty in April 1998, the same month that the Pruckmayr family's lawsuit was settled with the city promising that Inspector General Prettyman would conduct "an independent and impartial review" of the sordid case.

Changes Coming

Some changes are on the way. The D.C. Parole Board is about to be abolished, and federal authorities are now making most parole decisions. Lorton is supposed to shut down in August 2000. Prettyman recommended "appropriate administrative action" against Hill, Stancil

and the Lorton supervisor who glossed over Wright's disciplinary record.

But senior officials who knew or should have known of the total disarray of their parole and correctional systems have been given a pass, at least in part, Prettyman says, "because of perfectly proper rulings by the courts mandating sufficient cell space and other prison facilities to accommodate the growing prison population."

All of that is another way of saying that all too often the criminal justice system still protects the criminals more than it protects the victims. Even today, Prettyman emphasized, inmates are being released "prior to serving their proper terms" to make way for more inmates. "This means that more Leo Wrights are or soon will be on the streets."

Source: George Lardner, Jr., "The Bloody Saga of Leo Gonzales Wright," APB News, Feb. 28, 1999. Reprinted with permission.

Visit WebExtra! 10-2 to learn more about efforts that are being made to keep potentially dangerous offenders in prison.

but confessed to officers that he was in the process of stealing money and property when discovered. His probation was revoked without a hearing. Citing its own decision a year earlier in *Morrissey* v. *Brewer*, the Supreme Court ruled that probationers, because they face a substantial loss of liberty, were entitled to two hearings—the first, a preliminary hearing, to determine whether there is "probable cause to believe that he has committed a violation of his parole," and the second, "a somewhat more comprehensive hearing prior to the making of the final revocation decision." The Court also ruled that probation revocation hearings were to be held "under the conditions specified in *Morrissey* v. *Brewer.*"

The Court also dealt with a separate question centered on Gagnon's indigent status. While being careful to emphasize the narrowness of the particulars in this case, the Court added to the protections granted under *Morrissey* v. *Brewer,* ruling that probationers have the right to a lawyer, even if indigent, provided they claimed that either (1) they had not committed the alleged violation or (2) they had substantial mitigating evidence to explain their violation. In *Gagnon* and later cases, however, the Court reasserted that probation and parole revocation hearings were not a stage in the criminal prosecution process, but a simple adjunct to it, even though they might result in substantial loss of liberty. The difference is a crucial one, for it permits hearing boards and judicial review officers to function, at least to some degree, outside of the adversarial context of the trial court and with lessened attention to the rights of the criminally accused guaranteed by the Bill of Rights.

In 1997, the U.S. Supreme Court extended the rationale found in *Morrissey* and *Gagnon* to inmates set free from prison under early-release programs. In a unanimous decision, the Court held that "an inmate who has been released under a program to relieve prison crowding cannot be reincarcerated without getting a chance to show at a hearing that he has met the conditions of the program and is entitled to remain free."[42] The case involved former Oklahoma inmate Ernest E. Harper, who had been released in 1990 after serving 15 years in Oklahoma prisons for murder. The program under which Harper had been set free was governed by a formula requiring the release of a certain number of inmates as the state's prison system approached capacity. Months after being released, Harper received a call from his parole officer at 5:30 A.M. telling him to report back to prison by ten o'clock that morning. Although Harper had been living according to the rules of the program under which he had been released, state officials argued that he was still a prisoner and said that they were only changing the conditions of his confinement by "recalling" him to an institution. The Supreme Court, however, disagreed, finding that Harper's release from prison was akin to parole—and that it "differed from parole in name alone." As in other situations, said the Court, inmates have a right to challenge, in a formal proceeding, any "grievous loss of liberty" under the Fourteenth Amendment's due process guarantee.

Years ago, but in a related area, the case of *Greenholtz* v. *Nebraska* (1979)[43] established that parole boards do not have to specify the evidence used in deciding to deny parole. The *Greenholtz* case focused on a Nebraska statute which required that inmates denied parole be provided with reasons for the denial. The Court held that reasons for parole denial might be provided in the interest of helping inmates prepare themselves for future review but that to require the disclosure of evidence used in the review hearing would turn the process into an adversarial proceeding.

The 1983 Supreme Court case of *Bearden* v. *Georgia*[44] established that probation could not be revoked for failure to pay a fine and make restitution if it could not be shown that the defendant was responsible for the failure. The Court also held that alternative forms of punishment must be considered by the hearing authority and be shown to be inadequate before the defendant can be incarcerated. Bearden had pleaded guilty to burglary and had been sentenced to three years probation. One of the conditions of his probation required that he pay a fine of $250 and make restitution payments totaling $500. Bearden successfully made the first two payments but then lost his job. His probation was revoked, and he was imprisoned. The Supreme Court decision stated, "If the State determines a fine or restitution to be the appropriate and adequate penalty for the crime, it may not thereafter imprison a person solely because he lacked the resources to pay it."[45] The Court held that if a defendant lacks the capacity to pay a fine or make restitution, then the hearing authority must consider any viable alternatives to incarceration prior to imposing a term of imprisonment.

In another ruling affecting restitution, *Kelly* v. *Robinson* (1986),[46] the Court held that a restitution order cannot be vacated by a filing of bankruptcy. In the *Kelly* case, a woman convicted of illegally receiving welfare benefits was ordered to make restitution in the amount of $100 per month. Immediately following the sentence, the defendant filed for bankruptcy and listed the court-ordered restitution payment as a debt from which she sought relief. The bankruptcy court discharged the debt, and a series of appeals found the U.S. Supreme Court ruling that fines and other financial penalties ordered by criminal courts are not capable of being voided by bankruptcy proceedings.

A probationer's incriminating statements to a probation officer may be used as evidence if the probationer did not specifically claim a right against self-incrimination, according to *Minnesota* v. *Murphy* (1984).[47] Marshall Murphy was sentenced to three years probation in 1980 on a charge of "false imprisonment" (kidnapping) stemming from an alleged attempted sexual attack. One condition of his probation required him to be entirely truthful with his probation officer "in all matters." Some time later Murphy admitted to his probation officer that he had confessed to a rape and murder in conversations with a counselor. He was later convicted of first-degree murder, partially on the basis of the statements made to his probation officer. Upon appeal, Murphy's lawyers claimed that their client should have been advised of his right against self-incrimination during his conversation with the probation officer. Although the Minnesota Supreme Court agreed, the U.S. Supreme Court found for the state, saying that the burden of invoking the Fifth Amendment privilege against self-incrimination in this case lay with the probationer.

"Probation and parole have essentially shifted from legitimate correctional options in their own right to temporary diversionary strategies that we are using while we are trying to figure out how to get tough on crime, (pay) no new taxes, and not pay for any prisons at all, or to pay as little as we can, or pass it off to another generation."

—*Dr. Charles M. Friel*, *Sam Houston State University*

An emerging legal issue today surrounds the potential liability of probation officers and parole boards and their representatives for the criminal actions of offenders they supervise or whom they have released. Some courts have held that officers are generally immune from suit because they are performing a judicial function on behalf of the state.[48] Other courts, however, have indicated that parole board members who do not carefully consider mandated criteria for judging parole eligibility could be liable for injurious actions committed by parolees.[49] In general, however, most experts agree that parole board members cannot be successfully sued unless release decisions are made in a grossly negligent or wantonly reckless manner.[50] Discretionary decisions of individual probation and parole officers which result in harm to members of the public, however, may be more actionable under civil law, especially where their decisions were not reviewed by judicial authority.[51]

In 1995, for example, Pennsylvania state officials faced lawsuits resulting from the release of Robert "Mudman" Simon by parole board officials. "Mudman," a member of the Warlocks motorcycle gang, had been imprisoned for the murder of 19-year-old Beth Smith Dusenberg, who was shot in the face after she refused to let gang members rape her.[52] His release on parole after serving 12 years on a 10- to 20-year sentence was approved by former Pennsylvania Board of Probation and Parole member Mary Ann Stewart and parole board chairman Allen Castor, even though the sentencing judge recommended that "Mudman" not be released; a psychiatrist wrote that "he was a sociopath, lacking in remorse, and prone to kill again."[53] Three months after he was set free, "Mudman" killed New Jersey policeman Ippolito "Lee" Gonzalez, shooting the officer twice in the face at point-blank range after a routine traffic stop. Convicted of first-degree murder, and sent to Pennsylvania's death row, Simon was stomped to death by another death row inmate in 1999.[54]

The Federal Probation System

The federal probation system is just over 70 years old.[55] In 1916 the U.S. Supreme Court, in the *Killets* case,[56] ruled that federal judges did not have the authority to suspend sentences and order probation. After a vigorous campaign by the National Probation Association, Congress finally passed the National Probation Act in 1925, authorizing the use of probation in federal courts. The bill came just in time to save a burgeoning federal prison system from serious overcrowding. The Mann Act, prohibition legislation, and the growth of organized

An automated probation kiosk. Kiosks such as this are being placed in large cities across the country. Probationers use them to make regular reports to probation officers, report changes in their personal status, and even pay installment fines. The kiosks use advanced technology to verify probationers' identities.
Automon Corporation.

crime had all led to increased arrests and a dramatic growth in the number of federal probationers in the early years of the system.

Although the 1925 act authorized one probation officer per federal judge, it allocated only $25,000 for officers' salaries. As a consequence, only eight officers were hired to serve 132 judges, and the system came to rely heavily upon voluntary probation officers. Some sources indicate that as many as 40,000 probationers were under the supervision of volunteers at the peak of the system.[57] By 1930, however, Congress provided adequate funding, and a corps of salaried professionals began to provide probation services to the U.S. courts.

In recent years the work of federal probation officers has been dramatically affected by new rules of federal procedure. Presentence investigations have been especially affected. Revised Rule 32 of the *Federal Rules of Criminal Procedure,* for example, now mandates that federal probation officers who prepare presentence reports must[58]

- ☐ Evaluate the evidence in support of facts.
- ☐ Resolve certain disputes between the prosecutor and defense attorney.
- ☐ Testify when needed to provide evidence in support of the administrative application of sentencing guidelines.
- ☐ Utilize an addendum to the report which, among other things, demonstrates that the report has been disclosed to the defense attorney, defendant, and government counsel.

Some authors have argued that these new requirements demand previously unprecedented skills from probation officers. Officers must now be capable of drawing objective conclusions based upon the facts they observe, and they must be able to make "independent judgments in the body of the report regarding which sets of facts by various observers the

---

CAREERS IN JUSTICE

Working for the Administrative Office of the U.S. Courts

TYPICAL POSITIONS:

U.S. probation officer, pretrial services officer, statistician, defender services officer, and defense investigator.

EMPLOYMENT REQUIREMENTS:

To qualify for the position of probation officer at the GS-5 level, an applicant must possess a bachelor's degree from an accredited college or university and have a minimum of two years of general work experience. General experience must have been acquired after obtaining the bachelor's degree and cannot include experience as a police, custodial, or security officer unless work in such positions involved criminal investigative experience. In lieu of general experience, a bachelor's degree from an accredited college or university in an accepted field of study

(including criminology, criminal justice, penology, correctional administration, social work, sociology, public administration, and psychology) will qualify an applicant for immediate employment at the GS-5 level, providing that at least 32 semester-hours or 48 quarter-hours were taken in one or more of the accepted fields of study. One year of graduate study qualifies applicants for appointment at the GS-7 level, while a master's degree in an appropriate field or a law degree may qualify the applicant for advanced placement.

OTHER REQUIREMENTS:

Applicants must be less than 37 years of age at the time of hiring and be in excellent physical health.

SALARY:

Appointees are typically hired at federal pay grade GS-5 or GS-7, depend-

ing on education and prior work history. Experienced statisticians with bachelor's degrees earned between $36,000 and $68,000 in mid-1999.

BENEFITS:

U.S. probation and pretrial services officers are included in the federal hazardous-duty law enforcement classification and are covered by liberal federal health and life insurance programs. A comprehensive retirement program is available to all federal employees.

DIRECT INQUIRIES TO:

Administrative Office of the U.S. Courts, Personnel Office, Washington, DC 20544. Phone: (202) 273-1297. Web site: www.uscourts.gov.

Source: Administrative Office of the United States Courts.

court should rely upon in imposing sentence."[59] They must also be effective witnesses in court during the trial phase of criminal proceedings. While in the past officers have often been called upon to provide testimony during revocation hearings, the informational role now mandated throughout the trial itself is relatively new.

The Job of a Probation/Parole Officer

Correctional personnel involved in probation/parole supervision totaled 43,198 (including approximately 2,500 federal officers) throughout the United States in 1996 according to the American Correctional Association (ACA).[60] Some 15,352 of these officers supervised probationers only, while 13,833 supervised both probationers and parolees.

The tasks performed by probation and parole officers are often quite similar. Some jurisdictions combine the roles of both into one job. This section describes the duties of probation and parole officers, whether separate or performed by the same individuals. Probation/parole work consists primarily of four functions: (1) presentence investigations, (2) intake procedures, (3) needs assessment and diagnosis, and (4) the supervision of clients.

Where probation is a possibility, intake procedures may include presentence investigations, as described in Chapter 9, which examine the offender's background in order to provide the sentencing judge with facts needed to make an informed sentencing decision. Intake procedures may also involve a dispute settlement process during which the probation officer works with the defendant and victim to resolve the complaint prior to sentencing. Intake duties tend to be more common among juvenile probation officers than they are in adult criminal court, but all officers may find themselves in the position of having to recommend to the judge what sentencing alternative would best answer the needs of the case.

Diagnosis refers to the psychological inventorying of the probation/parole client and may be done on either a formal basis involving the use of written tests administered by certified psychologists, or through informal arrangements, which typically depend upon the observational skills of the officer. Needs assessment, another area of officer responsibility, extends beyond the psychological needs of the client to a cataloging of the services necessary for a successful experience on probation or parole.

Supervision of sentenced probationers or released parolees is the most active stage of the probation/parole process, involving months (and sometimes years) of periodic meetings between the officer and client and an ongoing assessment of the success of the probation/parole endeavor in each individual case.

One special consideration affecting the work of all probation/parole officers is the need for confidentiality. The details of the presentence investigation, psychological tests, needs assessment, conversations between the officer and client, and so on should not be public knowledge. On the other hand, courts have generally held that communications between the officer and client are not privileged, as they might be between a doctor and patient or between a social worker and his or her client.[61] Hence, incriminating evidence related by a client can be shared by officers with appropriate authorities.

Difficulties with the Parole/Probation Officer Job

Perhaps the biggest difficulty that probation and parole officers face is their need to walk a fine line between two conflicting sets of duties—one of which is to provide quasi-social work services and the other to handle custodial responsibilities. In effect, two conflicting images of the officer's role coexist. The social work model stresses a service role for officers and views probationers and parolees as "clients." Officers are seen as "caregivers," who attempt to assess accurately the needs of their clients and, through an intimate familiarity with available community services—from job placement, indigent medical care, and family therapy, to psychological and substance abuse counseling—match clients and community resources. The social work model depicts probation/parole as a "helping profession," wherein officers assist their clients in meeting the conditions imposed upon them by their sentences.

The other model for officers is correctional. It sees probation/parole clients as "wards" whom officers are expected to control. This model emphasizes community protection, which officers are supposed to achieve through careful and close supervision. Custodial supervision means that officers will periodically visit their charges at work and at home, often arriving unannounced. It also means that they will be ready and willing to report clients for new offenses and for violations of the conditions of their release.

Most officers, by virtue of their personalities and experiences, probably identify more with one of the two models than with the other. They think of themselves either primarily as caregivers or as correctional officers. Regardless of the emphasis which appeals most to individual officers, however, demands of the job are bound to generate role conflict at one time or another.

A second problem in probation/parole work is high **caseloads.** The President's Commission on Law Enforcement and the Administration of Justice recommended that probation/parole caseloads should average around 35 clients per officer.[62] However, caseloads of 250 clients are common in some jurisdictions. Various authors have found that high caseloads, combined with limited training and time constraints forced by administrative and other demands, culminate in stopgap supervisory measures.[63] "Postcard probation," in which clients mail in a letter or card once a month to report on their whereabouts and circumstances, is an example of one stopgap measure that harried agencies with large caseloads use to keep track of their wards.[64]

Another difficulty with probation/parole work is the lack of opportunity for career mobility.[65] Probation and parole officers are generally assigned to small agencies, serving limited geographical areas, with one or two lead officers (usually called chief probation officers). Unless retirement or death claims the supervisors, there will be little chance for other officers to advance. Learn more about working as a probation or parole officer via the American Probation and Parole Association's site accessible at WebExtra! 10-3 at CJToday.com.

Caseload

The number of probation or parole clients assigned to one probation or parole officer for supervision.

Intermediate Sanctions (also called Alternative Sanctions)

The use of split sentencing, shock probation and parole, home confinement, shock incarceration, and community service in lieu of other, more traditional, sanctions, such as imprisonment and fines.

Intermediate Sanctions

In 1996, 32-year-old Sia Ye Vang, a Hmong tribesman and Vietnamese immigrant living in La Crosse, Wisconsin, was convicted of sexually molesting his young stepdaughters, aged 10 and 11. Judge Ramona Gonzalez, apparently influenced by defense arguments that sex with girls is accepted practice in Vietnam, sentenced Vang to 24 years probation and ordered him to continue English classes and perform 1,000 hours of community service. The judge decided to allow Vang "the opportunity to continue his education, and his assimilation into our culture."[66] Vang could have received 80 years in prison.

Although Vang's case may be an extreme example, it illustrates the fact that significant new sentencing options have become available to judges in innovative jurisdictions over the past few decades. Many such options are called "intermediate sanctions" because they employ sentencing alternatives which fall somewhere between outright imprisonment and simple probationary release back into the community. They are also sometimes termed "alternative sentencing strategies." Michael J. Russell, former director of the National Institute of Justice, says that "intermediate punishments are intended to provide prosecutors, judges, and corrections officials with sentencing options that permit them to apply appropriate punishments to convicted offenders while not being constrained by the traditional choice between prison and probation. Rather than substituting for prison or probation, however, these sanctions—which include intensive supervision, house arrest with electronic monitoring, and shock incarceration—bridge the gap between those options and provide innovative ways to ensure swift and certain punishment."[67]

A number of citizen groups and special interest organizations are working to widen the use of sentencing alternatives. One organization of special note is the Washington, D.C.-based Sentencing Project. The Sentencing Project was formed in 1986[68] through support from foundation grants.[69] The Project is dedicated to promoting a greater use of alternatives to incarceration and provides technical assistance to public defenders, court officials, and other community organizations.

The Sentencing Project and other groups like it have contributed to the development of over 100 locally based alternative sentencing service programs. Most alternative sentencing services work in conjunction with defense attorneys to develop written sentencing plans.

Such plans are basically well-considered citizen suggestions as to what appropriate sentencing in a given instance might entail. Plans are often quite detailed and may include letters of support from employers, family members, the defendant, and even victims. Sentencing plans may be used in plea bargaining sessions or presented to judges following trial and conviction. A decade ago, for example, lawyers for country and western singer Willie Nelson successfully proposed an alternative option to tax court officials, which allowed the singer to pay huge past tax liabilities by performing in concerts for that purpose. Lacking such an alternative, the tax court might have seized Nelson's property or even ordered the singer confined to a federal facility.

The basic philosophy behind intermediate sanctions is this: When judges can be offered well-planned alternatives to imprisonment, the likelihood of a prison sentence can be reduced. An analysis of alternative sentencing plans such as those sponsored by the Sentencing Project shows that they are accepted by judges in up to 80 percent of the cases in which they are recommended, and that as many as two-thirds of offenders who receive alternative sentences successfully complete them.[70]

Intermediate, or alternative, sanctions have three distinct advantages:[71] (1) They are less expensive to operate on a per offender basis than imprisonment; (2) they are "socially cost-effective," because they keep the offender in the community, thus avoiding both the breakup of the family and the stigmatization which accompanies imprisonment; and (3) they provide flexibility in terms of resources, time of involvement, and place of service. Some of these new options are described in the paragraphs that follow.

Split Sentencing

In jurisdictions where **split sentencing** is an option, judges may impose a combination of a brief period of imprisonment and probation. Defendants sentenced under split sentencing are often ordered to serve time in a local jail rather than in a long-term confinement facility. "Ninety days in jail, together with two years of supervised probation," would be a typical split sentence. Split sentences are frequently used with minor drug offenders and serve notice that continued law violations may result in imprisonment for much longer periods.

Shock Probation/Shock Parole

Shock probation bears a considerable resemblance to split sentencing. Again, the offender serves a relatively short period of time in custody (usually in a prison rather than jail) and is released on probation by court order. The difference is that shock probation clients must *apply* for probationary release from confinement and cannot be certain of the judge's decision. In shock probation, the court in effect makes a resentencing decision. Probation is only a statutory possibility and often little more than a vague hope of the offender as imprisonment begins. If probationary release is ordered, it may well come as a "shock" to the offender who, facing a sudden reprieve, may forswear future criminal involvement. Shock probation was first begun in Ohio in 1965[72] and is used today in about half the United States.[73]

New Jersey runs a model modern shock probation program which is administered by a specially appointed Screening Board composed of correctional officials and members of the public. The New Jersey program has served as an example to many other states. It has a stringent set of selection criteria which allow only inmates serving sentences for nonviolent crimes to apply to the Screening Board for release.[74] Inmates must have served at least 30 days before applying. Those who have served over 60 days are ineligible. Offenders must submit a personal plan describing what they will do when released, what their problems are, what community resources they need or intend to use, and what people can be relied upon to provide assistance. Part of the plan involves a community sponsor with whom the inmate must reside for a fixed period of time (usually a few months) following release. The New Jersey program is especially strict because it does not grant outright release, but rather allows only a 90-day initial period of freedom. If the inmate successfully completes the 90-day period, continued release may be requested.

Shock probation lowers the cost of confinement, maintains community and family ties, and may be an effective rehabilitative tool.[75] Similar to shock probation is shock parole.

Split Sentence

A sentence explicitly requiring the convicted person to serve a period of confinement in a local, state, or federal facility followed by a period of probation.

Shock Probation

The practice of sentencing offenders to prison, allowing them to apply for probationary release, and enacting such release in surprise fashion. Offenders who receive shock probation may not be aware of the fact that they will be released on probation and may expect to spend a much longer time behind bars.

Whereas shock probation is ordered by judicial authority, shock parole is an administrative decision made by a paroling authority. Parole boards or their representatives may order an inmate's early release, hoping that brief exposure to prison may have reoriented the offender's life in a positive direction.

Shock Incarceration

Shock incarceration is the newest of the alternative sanctions discussed here.[76] Shock incarceration, designed primarily for young, first offenders, utilizes military-style "boot camp" prison settings to provide a highly regimented program involving strict discipline, physical training, and hard labor. Shock incarceration programs are of short duration, lasting for only 90 to 180 days. Offenders who successfully complete these programs are generally placed under community supervision. Program "failures" may be moved into the general prison population for longer terms of confinement.

The first shock incarceration program began in Georgia in 1983.[77] Since then, other programs have opened in 28 other states, and four more states are scheduled soon to begin operating shock incarceration programs.[78] The federal government and some Canadian provinces also operate shock incarceration programs. New York's program is the largest, with a capacity for 1,390 participants, while programs in Rhode Island and Wyoming can handle only 30.[79] There are other differences among the states, as well. About half provide for voluntary entry into their shock incarceration programs. A few allow inmates to decide when and whether they want to quit. Although most states allow judges to place offenders into such programs, some delegate that authority to corrections officials. Two states, Louisiana and Texas, authorize judges and corrections personnel joint authority in the decision-making process.[80] Some states, such as Massachusetts, have begun to accept classes of female inmates into boot camp settings. The Massachusetts program, which first accepted women in 1993, requires inmates to spend nearly four months undergoing the rigors of training.

The most comprehensive study of boot camp prison programs to date examined shock incarceration programs in eight states: Florida, Georgia, Illinois, Louisiana, New York, Oklahoma, South Carolina, and Texas. The report,[81] which was issued in 1995, found that boot camp programs are especially popular today because "they are . . . perceived as being tough on crime," and "have been enthusiastically embraced as a viable correctional option." The report concluded, however, that "the impact of boot camp programs on offender recidivism is at best negligible."

More limited studies, such as one which focused on shock incarceration in New York state, have found that boot camp programs save money in two ways: "first by reducing expenditures for care and custody" (since the intense programs reduce time spent in custody, and participation in them is the only way New York inmates can be released from prison before their minimum parole eligibility dates) and "second, by avoiding capital costs for new prison construction."[82] A 1995 study of Oregon's Summit boot camp program reached a similar conclusion. Although they did not study recidivism, Oregon researchers found that "the Summit boot camp program is a cost-effective means of reducing prison overcrowding by treating and releasing specially selected inmates earlier than their court-determined minimum period of incarceration."[83]

Mixed Sentencing and Community Service

Mixed sentences require that offenders serve weekends in jail and receive probation supervision during the week. Other types of mixed sentencing require participation in treatment or community service programs while a person is on probation. Community service programs began in Minnesota in 1972 with the Minnesota Restitution Program,[84] which gave property offenders the opportunity to work and turn over part of their pay as restitution to their victims. Courts throughout the nation quickly adopted the idea and began to build restitution orders into suspended-sentence agreements.

Community service is more an adjunct to, rather than a type of, correctional sentence. Community service is compatible with most other forms of innovation in probation and parole, except, perhaps for home confinement (discussed shortly). Even there, however,

A boot camp correctional officer greets a new arrival. Shock incarceration programs—also called boot camp prisons—provide a sentencing alternative which is growing rapidly in popularity.
R. Maiman, Corbis/SYGMA.

offenders could be sentenced to community service activities which might be performed in the home or at a job site during the hours they are permitted to be away from their homes. Washing police cars, cleaning school buses, refurbishing public facilities, and assisting in local government offices are typical forms of community service. Some authors have linked the development of community service sentences to the notion that work and service to others are good for the spirit.[85] Community service participants are usually minor criminals, drunk drivers, and youthful offenders.

One problem with community service sentences is that authorities rarely agree on what they are supposed to accomplish. Most people admit that offenders who work in the community are able to reduce the costs of their own supervision. There is little agreement, however, over whether such sentences reduce recidivism, provide a deterrent, or act to rehabilitate offenders.

Intensive Supervision

Intensive probation supervision (IPS), first implemented by Georgia in 1982, has been described as the "strictest form of probation for adults in the United States."[86] The Georgia program involves a minimum of five face-to-face contacts between the probationer and supervising officer per week, mandatory curfew, required employment, a weekly check of local arrest records, routine and unannounced alcohol and drug testing, 132 hours of community service, and automatic notification of probation officers via the State Crime Information Network whenever an IPS client is arrested.[87] Caseloads of probation officers involved in IPS are much lower than the national average. Georgia officers work as a team with one probation officer and two surveillance officers supervising about 40 probationers.[88] IPS is designed to achieve control in a community setting over offenders who would otherwise have gone to prison.

North Carolina's Intensive Supervision Program follows the model of the Georgia program and adds a mandatory "prison awareness visit" within the first three months of

Intensive Supervision

A form of probation supervision involving frequent face-to-face contacts between the probationary client and probation officers.

supervision. North Carolina selects candidates for the Intensive Supervision Program on the basis of six factors: (1) the level of risk the offender is deemed to represent to the community; (2) assessment of the candidate's potential to respond to the program; (3) existing community attitudes toward the offender; (4) the nature and extent of known substance abuse; (5) the presence or absence of favorable community conditions, such as positive family ties, the possibility of continuing meaningful employment, constructive leisure-time activities, and adequate residence; and (6) the availability of community resources relevant to the needs of the case (such as drug treatment services, mental health programs, vocational training facilities, and volunteer services).[89] Some states have extended intensive supervision to parolees, allowing the early release of some who would otherwise serve lengthy prison terms.

Home Confinement and Electronic Monitoring

Home Confinement

House arrest. Individuals ordered confined to their homes are sometimes monitored electronically to be sure they do not leave during the hours of confinement (absence from the home during working hours is often permitted).

Home confinement, also referred to as house arrest, has been defined as "a sentence imposed by the court in which offenders are legally ordered to remain confined in their own residences."[90] They may leave only to attend to medical emergencies, go to their jobs, or buy household essentials. House arrest has been cited as offering a valuable alternative to prison for offenders with special needs. Pregnant women, geriatric convicts, offenders with special handicaps, seriously or terminally ill offenders, and the mentally retarded might all be better supervised through home confinement than traditional incarceration.

Florida's Community Control Program, authorized by the state's Correctional Reform Act of 1983, is the most ambitious home confinement program in the country.[91] On any given day in Florida, as many as 5,000 offenders are restricted to their homes and supervised by community control officers who visit unannounced. Candidates for the program are required to agree to specific conditions, including (1) restitution, (2) family support payments, and (3) supervisory fees (around $50 per month). They are also obligated to fill out daily logs about their activities. Community control officers have a minimum of 20 contacts per month with each offender. Additional discussions are held by the officer with neighbors, spouses, friends, landlords, employers, and others in order to allow the earliest possible detection of program violations or renewed criminality.

Florida's most serious home confinement offenders are monitored via a computerized system of *electronic bracelets*. Random telephone calls require the offender to insert a computer chip worn in a wrist band into a specially installed modem in the home, verifying his or her presence. More modern units make it possible to record the time a supervised person

Via an alternative sentencing program, juvenile offenders in Bellflower, California, work with children who are physically challenged.
Bart Barthalomew, Black Star.

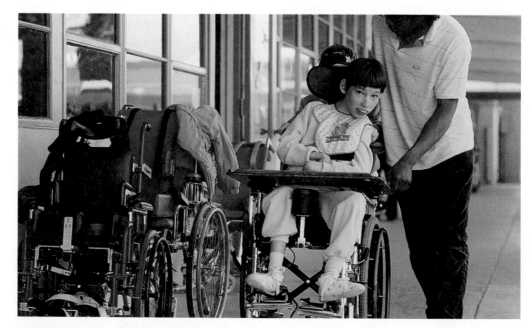

enters or leaves the home and whether the phone line or equipment has been tampered with, and to send or receive messages.[92] Electronic monitoring of offenders has undergone dramatic growth both in Florida and across the nation. A survey by the National Institute of Justice,[93] as the use of electronic monitoring was just beginning, showed only 826 offenders being monitored electronically in mid-1987. By 1989, only two years later, the number had jumped to around 6,500, while by the end of 1997 it stood at 21,375.[94] Of these, 15,373 were serving probationary sentences, and 6,002 were parolees.

In 1999 South Carolina's Probation and Parole Department began using satellites to track felons recently freed from state prisons. The satellite-tracking plan, which makes use of 21 satellites in the Global Positioning System (GPS), allows the agency's officers to keep track of every move made by convicts wearing electronic bracelets.[95] The system, which also notifies law enforcement officers when bracelet-wearing offenders leave their assigned areas, can electronically alert anyone holding a restraint order whenever the offenders enter a two-mile radius surrounding them.

Many states view house arrest as a cost-effective response to the rising expense of imprisonment. Estimates show that traditional home confinement programs cost about $1,500 to $7,000 per offender per year, while electronic monitoring increases the costs by at least $1,000.[96] Advocates of house arrest argue that it is also socially cost-effective,[97] as it provides no opportunity for the kinds of negative socialization which occur in prison. Opponents have pointed out that house arrest may endanger the public, that it may be illegal,[98] and that it may provide little or no actual punishment.

Individualized Innovations

In an ever growing number of cases, innovative judges have begun to use the wide discretion in sentencing available to them under the laws of certain jurisdictions to impose truly unique punishments. In Memphis, Tennessee, for example, Judge Joe Brown recently began escorting burglary victims to thieves' homes, inviting them to take whatever they wanted.[99] An Arkansas judge made shoplifters walk in front of the stores they stole from, carrying signs describing their crimes. At least one Florida court began ordering those convicted of drunk driving to put a "Convicted DUI" sticker on their license plates. Similarly, two years ago, Thomas Jache, a Manchester, New Hampshire, child molester who admitted his guilt, got two years of a minimum five-year sentence suspended—but was ordered to place an advertisement in two local newspapers that included his picture, an apology, and a plea for other potential molesters to get help. In 1997, Boston courts began ordering men convicted of the crime of "sexual solicitation" to spend four hours sweeping the streets of Chinatown—an area known for prostitution. The public was invited to watch men sentenced to the city's "John Sweep" program clean up streets and alleyways littered with used condoms and sexual paraphernalia.

A common theme that carries through individualized sentencing innovations such as these is that of public shaming. The rise in shame-as-punishment harks back to "scarlet letter" days, when sentences were meant not only to punish, but also to deter wrongdoers through public humiliation. Some of today's innovative judges, faced with prison overcrowding, high incarceration costs, and public calls for retribution, have begun to employ the kinds of shaming strategies described here.

Shaming as a crime reduction strategy finds considerable support in criminal justice literature. Australian criminologist John Braithwaite,[100] for example, found shaming to be a particularly effective strategy because, he said, it holds the potential to enhance moral awareness among offenders—thereby building conscience and increasing inner control. Braithwaite distinguishes, however, between "disintegrative" (or "stigmatic") and "reintegrative" shaming. Disintegrative shaming, says Braithwaite, treats offenders like outcasts, while reintegrative shaming includes communal forgiveness and attempts to reintegrate the offender back into the community. Reintegrative shaming, which Braithwaite says is inherent in Japanese culture but not in American society, is said to be more effective at reducing recidivism. The results of a 1997 Australian study by Braithwaite and others, called the Reintegrative Shaming Experiments (RISE), appear to show that reintegrative shaming can be far more effective at producing feelings of guilt and shame in offenders than traditional criminal court processing. The RISE experiment induced feelings of shame in offenders through the use of diversionary conferencing—a technique that builds upon an intensive form of moderated interaction between victim and offender.[101]

Braithwaite is quick to point out that judges in American society are far more likely to employ disintegrative shaming techniques rather than reintegrative ones. Perhaps for that reason, critics argue that contemporary efforts at shaming by justice system officials in the United States don't work. "It's an embarrassment to the criminal justice system and all done in the guise of law and order to appease the victims,"[102] says Knoxville lawyer Jim A. H. Bell. Bell, who serves on the board of the National Association of Criminal Defense Lawyers, says, "It's all done for shock value." On the other hand, Dan Kahan, a professor at the University of Chicago Law School, points out that "shame supplies the main motive why people obey the law, not so much because they're afraid of formal sanctions, but because they care what people think about them."[103]

Whether public shaming as an alternative sentencing strategy will continue to grow in popularity is unclear. What is clear, however, is that the American public and an ever growing number of judicial officials are now looking for workable alternatives to traditional sentencing options.

Questions about Alternative Sanctions

As prison populations continue to rise, alternative sentencing strategies are likely to become increasingly attractive. Many questions remain to be answered, however, before most alternative sanctions can be employed with confidence. These questions have been succinctly stated in a Rand Corporation study authored by Joan Petersilia.[104] Unfortunately, while the questions can be listed, few definitive answers are yet available. Some of the questions Petersilia poses are as follows:

- Do alternative sentencing programs threaten public safety?
- How should program participants be selected?
- What are the long-term effects of community sanctions on people assigned to them?
- Are alternative sanctions cost-effective?
- Who should pay the bill for alternative sanctions?
- Who should manage stringent community-based sanctions?
- How should program outcomes be judged?
- What kind of offenders benefit most from alternative sanctions?

In order to address some of the problems raised by alternative sentencing strategies, and especially by those programs that make use of community resources and community placement, Todd R. Clear suggests reframing the idea of community corrections to include the notion of a *corrections of place*. Clear notes that although community corrections sounds much like community policing, there are important differences. "In corrections," says Clear, "the term 'community' does not stand for the problem-solving focus but instead often merely indicates that an offender happens to be living outside a correctional facility."[105] In order to develop a true corrections of place, says Clear, it is necessary to take into consideration the needs of the local community as well as the demands of the wider society for retribution, punishment, and rehabilitation. In an example from Vermont, Clear points to community boards that now assist in determining the conditions of supervision for offenders sentenced to probation and placed on parole. Suggesting that correctional officials should embrace the spirit underlying the community policing movement, Clear says that "[w]hen community members feel they can shape correctional policy by direct participation, they will also feel less estranged from the decisions made by officials, and they will feel inclined to shape their participation to be meaningful rather than antagonistic." Learn more about innovations in community corrections by visiting the International Community Corrections Association via WebExtra! 10-4 at CJToday.com.

The Future of Probation and Parole

Parole has been widely criticized in recent years. Citizen groups claim that it unfairly reduces prison sentences imposed on serious offenders. Academicians allege that parole programs can provide no assurance that criminals will not commit further crimes. Media attacks upon parole have centered on recidivism and have highlighted the so-called revolving prison door as representative of the failure of parole.

Some years ago, the case of Larry Singleton came to represent all that is wrong with parole. Singleton was convicted of raping 15-year-old Mary Vincent, then hacking off her forearms and leaving her for dead on a California hillside.[106] When an apparently unrepentant[107] Singleton was paroled after eight years in prison, public outcry was tremendous. Communities banded together to deny him residence, and he had to be paroled to the grounds of San Quentin prison until public concern lessened. Singleton's story did not end there, however. He soon moved to Florida where, in 1997, he was rearrested and charged with the murder of 31-year-old Roxanne Hayes, an alleged prostitute. Hayes' nude body was discovered in Singleton's Tampa apartment by police alerted by neighbors who heard a woman screaming. She had been stabbed many times. "It's a sad commentary on the criminal justice system that a person who committed a crime this heinous was out on the street," said Tampa police spokesman Lieutenant David Gee.[108] In 1998 Singleton was found guilty of first-degree murder.[109]

Official attacks upon parole have come from some powerful corners. Senator Edward Kennedy has called for the abolition of parole, as did former Attorney General Griffin Bell and former U.S. Bureau of Prisons Director Norman Carlson.[110] Prisoners have also challenged the fairness of parole, saying it is sometimes arbitrarily granted and creates an undue amount of uncertainty and frustration in the lives of inmates. Parolees have complained about the unpredictable nature of the parole experience, citing their powerlessness in the parole contract. Against the pressure of official attacks and despite cases like that of Singleton, parole advocates struggle to clarify and communicate the value of parole in the correctional process.

As more and more states move toward the elimination of parole, other voices call for moderation. A 1995 report by the Center for Effective Public Policy, for example, concludes that those states which have eliminated parole "have jeopardized public safety and wasted tax dollars." In the words of the report, "Getting rid of parole dismantles an accountable system

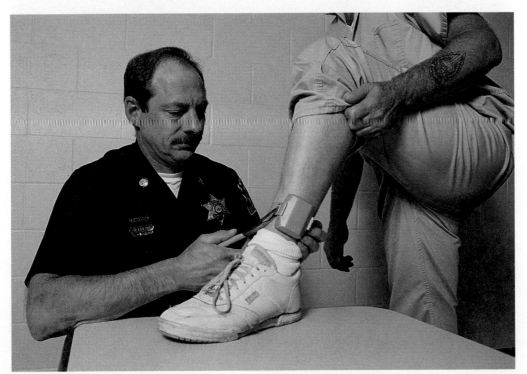

Commonly called "house arrest," the electronic monitoring of convicted offenders appears to have the capacity to dramatically reduce correctional costs for nondangerous offenders. This photograph demonstrates the use of an electronic "ankle bracelet," capable of answering a computer's call to verify that the wearer is at home.
Larry Downing, Corbis/SYGMA.

21st Century CJ

Chemical Castration Becomes Law in California

In September 1996, then-Governor Pete Wilson signed legislation making California the first state in the nation to require regular hormone injections for convicted child molesters upon their release from prison. "Chemical castration," which went into effect in the state on January 1, 1997, requires twice-convicted child molesters to receive weekly injections of a synthetic female hormone known as Depo-Provera. The laboratory-manufactured chemical is said to lower sex drive in males. There are about 16,000 convicted child molesters in California prisons, and approximately 200 are released from custody each week. Under the law, however, judges can also mandate injections for first offenders. Treatment is to continue until state authorities determine that it is no longer necessary.

With passage of the bill, California joined Georgia, Texas, Montana, and Florida—which have similar legislation in place. Other states are considering chemical castration laws. California Assemblyman Bill Hoge (R-Pasadena), the bill's author, encouraged other states to pass castration legislation. "We have now set the stage for America—and we hope you are listening America," Hoge said. "We can do this all over the country. This is going to have the biggest impact on this horrible, horrible crime of any legislation ever seen."

If chemical castration survives the court challenges which are certain to come, it may establish itself in the twenty-first century as a widely used form of alternative sentencing. Opposition to the new law, however, is plentiful. Shortly after the law was signed, a spokeswoman for the American Civil Liberties Union said that the group was considering a legal challenge because the legislation supposedly mandates an unproven remedy for child molesta-

tion and is a violation of civil rights. "There is no evidence, absolutely no evidence, that chemical castration will alleviate the problem," said Ann Bradley, a Los Angeles ACLU spokeswoman. "We see this as a violation of prisoners' civil liberties," she said.

Proponents of the legislation, on the other hand, cite studies in Canada and Europe where repeat offender rates of more than 80 percent were reduced to less than 4 percent among criminals treated with Depo-Provera. "I would have to say to the ACLU that there is no right to molest a child," said Governor Wilson.

Source: "Castration 1998–2000+," Web posted at *http://members.aol.com/USCCCN/castration.index.html* (accessed February 20, 2000); and Dave Lesher, "Molester Castration Measure Signed: California Becomes the First State to Require That Offenders Get Periodic Injections to Suppress Sex Drive," Los Angeles Times, *September 18, 1996.*

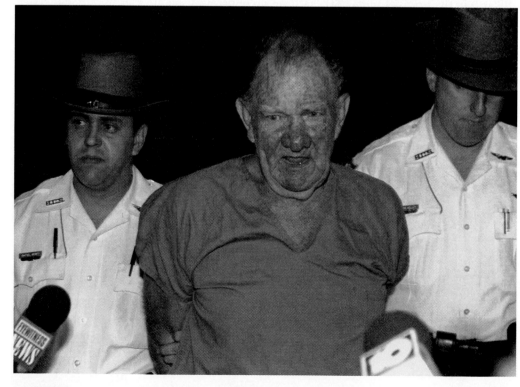

Lawrence Singleton, shown here following his 1997 arrest for the murder of a prostitute whose naked and bloody body was discovered in his Tampa apartment by police officers responding to a neighbor's call. Singleton caused a national uproar when he was paroled in California in 1986 after spending eight years in prison for the rape and mutilation of a 15-year-old girl, whose arms he cut off.
AP/Wide World Photos.

Probation Kiosks: High-Tech Supervision

In 1997, probation authorities in New York City began experimenting with the use of "probation kiosks" designed to lower probation officer caseloads. Fifteen electronic kiosks, similar in design to automatic teller machines, are now scattered throughout the city and allow probationers to check in with probation officers by placing their palms on a specially designed surface while answering questions presented on a flashing screen.

The kiosks identify probationers by the shape and size of their hands—which have been previously scanned into the system. Probationers are then prompted to press "yes" or "no" in response to questions such as, "Have you moved recently?" "Have you been arrested again?" "Do you need to see a probation officer?" Meetings with officers can be scheduled directly from the kiosk. Probation officers use a computer to monitor data sent from the kiosks and can zero in on individual probationers who are having problems—prompting more personal attention. By the time the system is fully operational, as many as 30,000 "low-

risk" probationers—about one-third of New York City's total—will report through kiosks.

Kiosks have already yielded positive results according to NYC probation officer Genée Bogans. Before the kiosks, says Bogans, she was swamped by administrative details required to track the 250 offenders in her caseload. Kiosks allow her to track nonviolent, older offenders with a minimum of time and effort, and she now focuses most of her personal attention on the relatively few violent youths who are also part of her caseload—meeting with them and their families twice weekly in small group sessions. Bogans even goes to family funerals and graduations, making youthful offenders feel like they are getting special attention. "But it can be done only when you have 30 cases as opposed to 200," says Bogans.

New York's use of kiosks is being watched closely by other probation and parole agencies around the country as they face swelling probation caseloads and shrinking budgets. Some cities have taken other steps to automate their probation systems.

Some, like Denver and Seattle, are using 900-numbers by which probationers can report in.

Critics charge that without personal supervision probationers are more likely to reoffend—an assertion which is essentially untested. Others say kiosks are far removed from meaningful "punishment" and that offenders deserve stricter treatment. Supporters, on the other hand, say that kiosks and 900-numbers will soon become more commonplace. "New York City had no choice; it had to do something like that," says Todd Clear, associate dean of the School of Criminology at Florida State University. Clear assisted the city in restructuring its probation program. "No one wants probationers reporting to kiosks, but the alternative was even more unthinkable—a system in which nobody receives quality service," said Clear.

Source: Isabelle de Pommereau, "N.Y.C. Probation Officers To Get High-Tech Helper," The Christian Science Monitor, *February 8, 1997, and Rice County, Minnesota, World Wide Web site.*

of releasing prisoners back into the community and replaces it with a system that bases release decisions solely on whether a prison term has been completed."[111]

Probation, although it has generally fared better than parole, is not without its critics. The primary purpose of probation has always been rehabilitation. Probation is a powerful rehabilitative tool because, at least in theory, it allows the resources of a community to be focused on the offender. Unfortunately for advocates of probation, however, the rehabilitative ideal holds far less significance today than it has in the past. The contemporary demand for "just deserts" appears to have reduced the tolerance society as a whole feels for even relatively minor offenders. Also, the image of probation has not benefited from its all-too-frequent and inappropriate use with repeat or relatively serious offenders. Probation advocates themselves have been forced to admit that it is not a very powerful deterrent because it is far less punishing than a term of imprisonment. Arguments in support of probation have been weakened because some of the positive contributions probation had to offer are now being made available from other sources. Victims' compensation programs, for example, have taken the place of probationers' direct restitution payments to victims.

In an intriguing 1997 task force report on community corrections,[112] Joan Petersilia notes that the current "get-tough on criminals" attitude now sweeping the nation has resulted in increased funding for prisons, but has left stagnating budgetary allotments for probation and parole services in its wake. This result has been especially unfortunate, Petersilia says, because "[I]t has been continually shown that there is a 'highly significant statistical relationship between the extent to which probationers received needed services and the success of probation.' " "As services have dwindled," says Petersilia, "recidivism rates have climbed." Some jurisdictions, notes Petersilia, spend only a few hundred dollars per year on each probation/parole client, while successful treatment in therapeutic settings is generally acknowledged to cost nearly $15,000 per person per year. The investment of such sums in the treatment of correctional clients, argues Petersilia, is potentially worthwhile because diverting probationers and parolees from lives of continued crime will save society even more money in terms of the costs of crime and the expenses associated with eventual imprisonment.

The solution to the crisis that now exists in the probation/parole field, says Petersilia, is to "first regain the public's trust that probation and parole can be meaningful, credible sanctions." Petersilia concludes: "Once we have that in place, we need to create a public climate to support a reinvestment in community corrections. Good community corrections cost money, and we should be honest about that."

Summary

Probation, simply put, is a sentence of imprisonment that is suspended. Parole, in contrast, is the conditional early release of a convicted offender from prison. Both probation and parole impose "conditions" upon defendants, requiring them to obey the law, meet with probation/parole officers, hold a job, and the like. Failure to abide by the conditions of probation or parole can result in rearrest and imprisonment.

Viewed historically, probation and parole are two of the most recent large-scale innovations in the correctional field. Both provide opportunities for the reintegration of offenders into the community through the use of resources not readily available in institutional settings. Unfortunately, however, increased freedom for criminal offenders also means some degree of increased risk for other members of society. As a consequence, contemporary "get-tough" attitudes have resulted in a lessening use of probation and parole in many jurisdictions—and an increased use of imprisonment. Until and unless probation and parole solve the problems of accurate risk assessment, reduced recidivism, and adequate supervision, they are likely to continue to be viewed with suspicion by a crimeweary public.

Discussion Questions

1. Probation is a sentence served while under supervision in the community. Do you believe that a person who commits a crime should be allowed to serve all or part of his or her sentence in the community? If so, what conditions would you impose on the offender?
2. Can you think of any other "general conditions" of probation or parole that you might add to the list of those found in the sample probation and parole forms in this chapter? If so, what would they be? Why would you want to add them?
3. Do you believe that ordering an offender to make restitution to his or her victim will teach the offender to be a more responsible person? Offer support for your opinion.
4. Do you believe that "role conflict" is a real part of most probation and parole officers' jobs? If so, do you see any way to reduce the role conflict experienced by probation and parole officers? How might you do it?
5. Do you think home confinement is a good idea? What do you think is the future of home confinement? In your opinion, does it discriminate against certain kinds of offenders? How might it be improved?

Web Quest!

Use the Cybrary to research the World Wide Web in order to learn as much as you can about the future of probation and parole. In particular, you might want to focus on the use of satellite technology to monitor offenders placed on probation, the extent of the use of home confinement, and public and media attitudes toward probation and parole. Studies on the future of probation and parole should also be gathered. Group your findings under headings (i.e., "innovative options," "alternative sanctions," "probation in (your home state)," "the future of probation and parole," etc.).

Also visit the American Probation and Parole Association (www.appa-net.org). The organization is also listed in the Cybrary. What is the mission of the APPA? What are its goals and objectives? What organizations are affiliated with it? How many of them have Web sites? Submit your findings to your instructor if requested to do so.

Library Extras!

The Library Extras! listed here complement the WebExtras! found throughout this chapter. Library Extras! may be accessed on the Web at CJToday.com.

Library Extra! 10-1. *Characteristics of Adults on Probation* (BJS, current volume).
Library Extra! 10-2. *Correctional Populations in the United States* (BJS, current volume).
Library Extra! 10-3. "Job Placement for Offenders: A Promising Approach to Reducing Recidivism and Correctional Costs," *The National Institute of Justice Journal* (NIJ, July 1999).
Library Extra! 10-4. "Probation in the United States: Practices and Challenges," *The National Institute of Justice Journal* (NIJ, September 1997).
Library Extra! 10-5. State Court Sentencing of Convicted Felons (NIJ, March 1998).

References

1. As quoted in *Criminal Justice Newsletter*, January 19, 1993, p. 1.
2. American Probation and Parole Association and the Association of Paroling authorities International, *Abolishing Parole: Why the Emperor Has No Clothes* (Lexington, KY: AAPA, 1995).
3. Sam Howe Verhovek, "Texas Frees Child Molester Who Warned of Backsliding," *New York Times*, April 9, 1996, p. B7.
4. "Parolee Confesses to Killing 4 Girls," *The Robesonian* (Lumberton, NC), May 29, 1992, p. 1A.
5. "Report: Probation Officer Ignored Furrow's Arsenal," APB Online, August 14, 1999. Web posted at www.apbonline.com/911/1999/08/14/jewish0814_01.html. Accessed January 20, 2000.
6. The President's Commission on Law Enforcement and Administration of Justice, *The Challenge of Crime in a Free Society* (Washington, D.C.: U.S. Government Printing Office, 1967).
7. Alexander B. Smith and Louis Berlin, *Introduction to Probation and Parole* (St. Paul, MN: West, 1976), p. 75.
8. John Augustus, *John Augustus, First Probation Officer: John Augustus' Original Report on His Labors—1852* (Montclair, NJ: Patterson-Smith, 1972).
9. Smith and Berlin, *Introduction to Probation and Parole*, p. 77.
10. Ibid., p. 80.
11. George C. Killinger, Hazel B. Kerper, and Paul F. Cromwell, Jr., *Probation and Parole in the Criminal Justice System* (St. Paul, MN: West, 1976), p. 25.
12. Bureau of Justice Statistics, "Probation and Parole Statistics." Web posted at www.djp:usdot.gov/bjs/pandp.htm. Accessed November 3, 2000.
13. James M. Byrne *Probation, a National Institute of Justice Crime File Series Study Guide* (Washington, D.C.: U.S. Department of Justice, 1988), p. 1.
14. Jodi M. Brown and Patrick A. Langan, *Felony Sentences in the United States, 1996* (Washington, D.C.: Bureau of Justice Statistics, 1999).
15. "Woman Gets Probation for Shooting Fiance," *Fayetteville Observer-Times* (North Carolina), April 16, 1992, p. 9A.
16. "Probation and Parole Statistics."
17. Ibid.
18. Bureau of Justice Statistics, *Correctional Populations in the United States 1995* (Washington, D.C.: BJS, 1997).

19. Stephanie Minor-Harper and Christopher A. Innes, "Time Served in Prison and on Parole, 1984," Bureau of Justice Statistics Special Report (1987).

20. Bureau of Justice Statistics, *Correctional Populations in the United States 1995* (Washington, D.C.: BJS, 1997).

21. "Probation and Parole Statistics."

22. Ibid.

23. Ibid.

24. "The Effectiveness of Felony Probation: Results from an Eastern State," *Justice Quarterly* (December 1991), pp. 525–543.

25. Public Law 104–232.

26. For additional information see the U.S. Parole Commission home page at www.usdoj.gov/uspc. Accessed January 20, 2000.

27. Byrne, *Probation.*

28. Ibid., p. 3.

29. Peter Finn and Dale Parent, *Making the Offender Foot the Bill: A Texas Program* (Washington, D.C.: National Institute of Justice, 1992), and "Benefits of Probation Fees Cited in Texas Program," *Criminal Justice Newsletter* (January 19, 1993), p. 5.

30. See Andrew von Hirsch and Kathleen J. Hanrahan, *Abolish Parole?* (Washington, D.C.: Law Enforcement Assistance Administration, 1978).

31. Patrick A. Langan and Mark A. Cunniff, *Recidivism of Felons on Probation 1986–1989* (Washington, D.C.: Bureau of Justice Statistics, 1992).

32. *Griffin* v. *Wisconsin,* 483 U.S. 868, 107 S.Ct. 3164 (1987).

33. *Pennsylvania Board of Probation and Parole* v. *Scott,* 118 S.CT. 2014 (1998).

34. Jamie Lillis, "Twenty-two Percent of Adult Parole Cases Revoked in 1993," *Corrections Compendium* (August 1994), pp. 7–8.

35. *Escoe* v. *Zerbst,* 295 U.S. 490 (1935).

36. *Mempa* v. *Rhay,* 389 U.S. 128 (1967).

37. A deferred sentence involves postponement of the sentencing decision, which may be made at a later time, following an automatic review of the defendant's behavior in the interim. A suspended sentence requires no review unless the probationer violates the law or conditions of probation. Both may result in imprisonment.

38. *Morrissey* v. *Brewer,* 408 U.S. 471 (1972).

39. *Gagnon* v. *Scarpelli,* 411 U.S. 778 (1973).

40. Smith and Berlin, *Introduction to Probation and Parole,* p. 143.

41. See Linda Greenhouse, *N.Y. Times* News Service, March 18, 1997 (no headline). The case is *Young* v. *Harper,* 520 U.S. 143 (1997).

42. *Greenholtz* v. *Inmate of Nebraska Penal and Correctional Complex,* 442 U.S. 1 (1979).

43. *Bearden* v. *Georgia,* 461 U.S. 660, 103 S.Ct. 2064, 76 L. Ed. 2d 221 (1983).

44. Ibid.

45. *Kelly* v. *Robinson,* 479 U.S. 36, 107 S.Ct. 353, 93 L. Ed. 2d 216 (1986).

46. *Minnesota* v. *Murphy,* 465 U.S. 420, 104 S.Ct. 1136, 79 L. Ed. 2d 409 (1984).

47. *Harlow* v. *Clatterbuick,* 30 CLr. 2364 (VA S.Ct. 1986); *Santangelo* v. *State,* 426 N.Y.S. 2d 931 (1980); *Welch* v. *State,* 424 N.Y.S. 2d 774 (1980); and *Thompson* v. *County of Alameda,* 614 P. 2d. 728 (1980).

48. *Tarter* v. *State of New York,* 38 CLr. 2364 (NY S.Ct. 1986); *Grimm* v. *Arizona Board of Pardons and Paroles,* 115 Arizona 260, 564 P. 2d 1227 (1977); and *Payton* v. *United States,* 636 F. 2d 132 (5th Cir.).

49. *Rolando* v. *del Carmen, Potential Liabilities of Probation and Parole Officers* (Cincinnati, OH: Anderson, 1986), p. 89.

50. See, for example, *Semler* v. *Psychiatric Institute,* 538 F. 2d 121 (4th Cir. 1976).

51. Mario F. Cattabiani, "Panel Opens Parole System Probe," *The Morning Call* (Allentown, PA), May 20, 1995, p. A6.

52. Ibid.

53. Mario F. Cattabiani, "Murderer 'Mudman' Dies in Death-Row Brawl," *The Morning Call* (Allentown, PA), September 8, 1999, p. 1A.

54. This section owes much to Sanford Bates, "The Establishment and Early Years of the Federal Probation System," *Federal Probation* (June 1987), pp. 4–9.

55. *Ex parte United States,* 242 U.S. 27.

56. Bates, "The Establishment and Early Years of the Federal Probation System," p. 6.

57. As summarized by Susan Krup Grunin and Jud Watkins, "The Investigative Role of the United States Probation Officer Under Sentencing Guidelines," *Federal Probation* (December 1987), pp. 43–49.

58. Ibid., p. 46.

59. American Correctional Association, *Vital Statistics in Corrections* (Lanham, MD: ACA, 2000).

60. *Minnesota* v. *Murphy,* U.S. 104 S.Ct. 1136, 1143 (1984).

61. National Advisory Commission on Criminal Justice Standards and Goals, *Task Force Report: Corrections* (Washington, D.C.: U.S. Government Printing Office, 1973).

62. James P. Levine, Michael C. Musheno, and Dennis J. Palumbo, *Criminal Justice in America: Law in Action* (New York: John Wiley, 1986), p. 548.

63. Ibid.

64. James A. Inciardi, *Criminal Justice,* 2nd ed. (New York: Harcourt Brace Jovanovich, 1987), p. 638.

65. "Molester Sentenced to Classes," The Associated Press, August 29, 1996.

66. From the introduction to James Austin, Michael Jones, and Melissa Bolyard, *The Growing Use of Jail Boot Camps: The Current State of the Art* (Washington, D.C.: National Institute of Justice, October 1993), p. 1.

67. Although now an independent nonprofit corporation, The Sentencing Project has its roots in a 1981 project of the National Legal Aid and Defender Association.

68. The Sentencing Project, *1989 National Directory of Felony Sentencing Services* (Washington, D.C.: The Project, 1989).

69. The Sentencing Project, *Changing the Terms of Sentencing: Defense Counsel and Alternative Sentencing Services* (Washington, D.C.: The Project, no date).

70. Joan Petersilia, *Expanding Options for Criminal Sentencing* (Santa Monica, CA: The Rand Corporation, 1987).

71. *Ohio Revised Code*, Section 2946.06.1 (July 1965).

72. Lawrence Greenfield, Bureau of Justice Statistics, *Probation and Parole 1984* (Washington, D.C.: U.S. Government Printing Office, 1986).

73. For a complete description of this program, see Petersilia, *Expanding Options for Criminal Sentencing*.

74. Harry Allen, Chris Eskridge, Edward Latessa, and Gennaro Vito, *Probation and Parole in America* (New York: The Free Press, 1985), p. 88.

75. For a good overview of such programs, see William N. Osborne, Jr., "Shock Incarceration and the Boot Camp Model: Theory and Practice," *American Jails* (July/August 1994), pp. 27–30.

76. Doris Layton MacKenzie and Deanna Bellew Ballow, "Shock Incarceration Programs in State Correctional Jurisdictions—An Update," *NIJ Reports* (May/June 1989), pp. 9–10.

77. "Shock Incarceration Marks a Decade of Expansion," *Corrections Compendium* (September 1996), pp. 10–28.

78. Ibid.

79. MacKenzie and Ballow, "Shock Incarceration Programs in State Correctional Jurisdictions."

80. National Institute of Justice, *Multisite Evaluation of Shock Incarceration* (Washington, D.C.: NIJ, 1995).

81. Cherie L. Clark, David W. Aziz, and Doris L. MacKenzie, *Shock Incarceration in New York: Focus on Treatment* (Washington, D.C.: National Institute of Justice, August 1994), p. 8.

82. "Oregon Boot Camp Is Saving the State Money, Study Finds," *Criminal Justice Newsletter* (May 1, 1995), pp. 5–6.

83. Douglas C. McDonald, "Restitution and Community Service," National Institute of Justice, *Crime File Study Guide* (1988).

84. Richard J. Maher and Henry E. Dufour, "Experimenting with Community Service: A Punitive Alternative to Imprisonment," *Federal Probation* (September 1987), pp. 22–27.

85. James P. Levine et al., *Criminal Justice in America: Law in Action* (New York: John Wiley, 1986), p. 549.

86. Billie S. Erwin and Lawrence A. Bennett, "New Dimensions in Probation: Georgia's Experience with Intensive Probation Supervision," National Institute of Justice, *Research in Brief* (1987).

87. Ibid., p. 2.

88. North Carolina Department of Correction, *Intensive Supervision Manual* (Raleigh, NC: Division of Adult Probation and Parole, 1988), pp. 3–5.

89. Joan Petersilia, "House Arrest," National Institute of Justice, *Crime File Study Guide* (1988).

90. Ibid.

91. Ibid.

92. Marc Renzema and David T. Skelton, *The Use of Electronic Monitoring by Criminal Justice Agencies 1989*, Grant Number OJP-89-M-309 (Washington, D.C.: National Institute of Justice, 1990).

93. Bureau of Justice Statistics, *Correctional Populations in the United States 1995* (Washington, D.C.: BJS, 1997).

94. "Satellites Tracking People on Parole," The Associated Press, April 13, 1999.

95. Petersilia, "House Arrest."

96. *BI Home Escort: Electronic Monitoring System*, advertising brochure, BI Incorporated, Boulder, Colorado (no date).

97. For additional information on the legal issues surrounding electronic home confinement, see Bonnie Berry, "Electronic Jails: A New Criminal Justice Concern," *Justice Quarterly*, vol. 2, no. 1 (1985), pp. 1–22, and J. Robert Lilly, Richard A. Ball, and W. Robert Lotz, Jr., "Electronic Jail Revisited," *Justice Quarterly*, vol. 3, no. 3 (September 1986), pp. 353–361.

98. Much of the information in this section is taken from Haya El Nasser, "Paying for Crime With Shame: Judges Say 'Scarlet Letter' Angle Works," *USA Today*, June 26, 1996, p. 1A.

99. John Braithwaite, *Crime, Shame, and Reintegration* (Cambridge, MA: Cambridge University Press, 1989).

100. Four papers have been released in the RISE series to date. They are Lawrence W. Sherman and Heather Strang, *The Right Kind of Shame for Crime Prevention* (Canberra, Australia: Australian National University, 1997); Heather Strang and Lawrence W. Sherman, *The Victim's Perspective* (Canberra, Australia: Australian National University, 1997); Lawrence W. Sherman and Geoffrey C. Barnes, *Restorative Justice and Offenders' Respect for the Law* (Canberra, Australia: Australian National University, 1997); and Lawrence W. Sherman and Heather Strang, *Restorative Justice and Deterring Crime* (Canberra, Australia: Australian National University, 1997).

101. Ibid.

102. Such evidence does, in fact, exist. See, for example, Harold G. Grasmick, Robert J. Bursik, Jr., and Bruce J. Arneklev, "Reduction in Drunk Driving as a Response to Increased Threats of Shame, Embarrassment, and Legal Sanctions," *Criminology*, vol. 31, no. 1 (1993), pp. 41–67.

103. Petersilia, "House Arrest."

104. Todd R. Clear, "Toward a Corrections of Place: The Challenge of 'Community' in Corrections," *National Institute of Justice Journal* (August 1996), pp. 52–56.

105. "A Victim's Life Sentence," *People*, April 25, 1988.

106. Ibid., p. 40.

107. Steve Morrell, "Convicted California Rapist, Mutilator, Arrested," Reuters wire services, February 20, 1997.

108. Lisa Holewa, "Lawrence Singleton Guilty of First-Degree Murder," *Naples Daily News*, February 20, 1998. Web posted at www.naplesnews.com/today/florida/a38459o.htm. Accessed February 20, 2000.

109. Inciardi, *Criminal Justice*, 2nd ed., p. 664.

110. The Center for Effective Public Policy, *Abolishing Parole: Why the Emperor Has No Clothes,* 1995.

111. Joan Petersilia, "A Crime Control Rationale for Reinvesting in Community Corrections," in *Critical Criminal Justice Issues: Task Force Reports From the American Society of Criminology* (Washington, D.C.: National Institute of Justice, 1997).

CHAPTER 11

Prisons and Jails

"To put people behind walls and bars and do little or nothing to change them is to win a battle but lose a war. It is wrong. It is expensive. It is stupid."
—Former Chief Justice Warren E. Burger (1907–1995)[1]

"Infinite are the nine steps of a prison cell, and endless is the march of him who walks between the yellow brick wall and the red iron gate, thinking things that cannot be chained and cannot be locked. . . ."
—Arturo Giovannitti (1884–1959)

"Years ago I began to recognize my kinship with all living beings. . . . I said then, and I say now, that while there is a lower class I am in it; while there is a criminal element, I am of it; while there is a soul in prison, I am not free."
—Eugene V. Debs, American Socialist Leader (1855–1926)

—Richard Falco, Black Star.

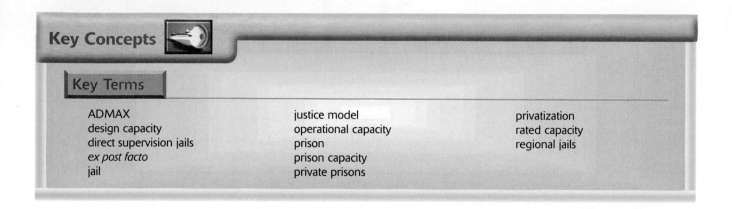

Key Concepts

Key Terms

ADMAX
design capacity
direct supervision jails
ex post facto
jail

justice model
operational capacity
prison
prison capacity
private prisons

privatization
rated capacity
regional jails

Prisons Today

Hear the author discuss this chapter at **cjtoday.com**

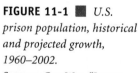

Prison

A state or federal confinement facility having custodial authority over adults sentenced to varying terms of confinement.

There are approximately 1,000 state and 80 federal **prisons** in operation across the country today. More are quickly being built as both the states and the federal government scramble to fund and construct new facilities. America's prison population has tripled since 1980, and its growth shows no signs of slowing. On January 1, 2000, the nation's state and federal prisons held 1,366,721 inmates.[2] Slightly over 6.6 percent (or 90,688) of those imprisoned were women.[3] Figure 11-1 shows the rise in U.S. prison populations over the past 40 years.

The size of prison facilities varies greatly. One out of every four state institutions is a large, maximum-security prison, with a population approaching a thousand inmates. A few exceed that figure, but the average state prison is small, with an inmate population of less than 500, while community-based facilities average around 50 residents. The typical state prison system (in relatively populous states) consists of[4]

■ One high-security prison for long-term, high-risk cases,

■ One or more medium-security institutions for the bulk of offenders who are not high risks,

FIGURE 11-1 ■ *U.S. prison population, historical and projected growth, 1960–2002.*

Sources: *Greg Wees, "Inmate Population Expected to Increase 43% by 2002," Corrections Compendium, April 1996; and A. Beck, Prisoners in 1999 (Washington, D.C.: Bureau of Justice Statistics, 2000).*

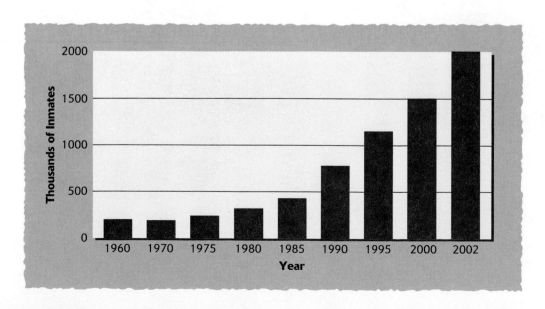

- One institution for adult women,
- One or two institutions for young adults (generally under age 25),
- One or two specialized mental hospital-type security prisons for mentally ill prisoners, and
- One or more open-type institutions for low-risk nonviolent populations.

Most people sentenced to state prisons have been convicted of violent crimes (46 percent), while property crimes (24 percent) are the second most common category for which inmates have been sentenced, and drug crimes are the reason for which 23 percent of "active" sentences are imposed.[5] In contrast, prisoners sentenced for drug law violations are the single largest group of federal inmates (60 percent), and the increase in the imprisonment of drug offenders accounts for three quarters of the total growth in the number of federal inmates since 1980. The inmate population in general suffers from a low level of formal education, comes from a socially disadvantaged background, and lacks significant vocational skills.[6] Most adult inmates have served some time in juvenile correctional facilities.[7]

An examination of imprisonment statistics by race highlights the huge disparity between blacks and whites in prison. While only an estimated 868 white males are imprisoned in the United States for every 100,000 white males in their late 20s, latest figures show an incarceration rate of 8,630 black men for every 100,000 black males of the same age—*10 times* greater than the figure for whites![8] Worse yet, the rate of growth in such figures shows that the imprisonment rate of blacks increased dramatically over the past 10 years, while the rate of white imprisonment has grown far less. Figure 11-2 shows historical U.S. incarceration rates by race and sex.

Approximately 350,000 staff members are employed in corrections,[9] with the majority performing direct custodial tasks in state institutions. Females account for 20 percent of all correctional officers, with the proportion of women officers increasing at around 19 percent per year.[10] In an effort to encourage the increased employment of women in corrections, the American Correctional Association formally adopted a statement,[11] which reads: "Women have a right to equal employment. No person who is qualified for a particular position/assignment or for job-related opportunities should be denied such employment or opportunities because of gender." The official statement goes on to encourage correctional agencies to "ensure that recruitment, selection, and promotion opportunities are open to women."

According to a recent report by the American Correctional Association, 70 percent of correctional officers are white, 22 percent are black, and slightly over 5 percent are Hispanic.[12] The inmate/custody staff ratio in state prisons averages around 4.1 to 1. Incarceration costs the states an average of $11,302 per inmate per year, while the federal government spends about $13,162 to house one inmate for a year.[13]

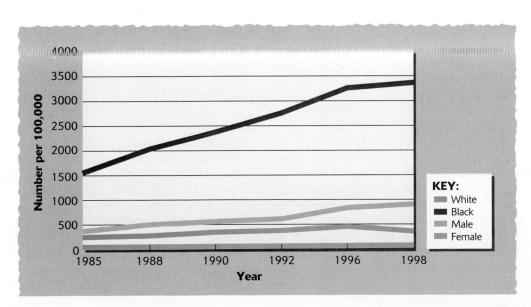

FIGURE 11-2 ■ *U.S. incarceration rates by race and sex.*

Source: *Bureau of Justice Statistics.*

The Philosophy of Imprisonment

Prisons in this country were originally built primarily for the purpose of rehabilitation and as an alternative to the corporeal punishments of earlier times.[14] Although many correctional administrators continue to avow a philosophy of rehabilitation, and although American corrections continues to serve a variety of purposes, the ascendant policy influencing the course of our nation's prisons today is one of retribution. Today's overcrowded prisons are largely the result of "get tough on crime" attitudes that have swept the nation for the past decade. These attitudes are based on a perspective that is sometimes referred to as the **justice model.** The justice model, which emphasizes individual responsibility and the punishment of offenders, has become the operative principle underlying many of today's correctional initiatives. Justice model philosophy is grounded squarely upon a just deserts theme, in which imprisonment is seen as a fully *deserved* consequence of criminal behavior.

The Justice Model

A contemporary model of imprisonment in which the principle of just deserts forms the underlying social philosophy.

While many would probably agree that get-tough philosophies come and go, the current wave of such feelings is far from exhausted. State legislatures everywhere, encouraged in large part by their constituencies, are scrambling to place limits on inmate privileges and to increase the pains of imprisonment. In 1995, for example, Alabama became the first state in modern times to reinstitute use of the prison chain gang.[15] Under the Alabama system, shotgun-armed guards oversaw prisoners, who were chained together by the ankles while they worked the state's roadsides—picking up trash, clearing brush, and filling ditches. Inmates served up to 90 days on chain gangs, during which they worked 12-hour shifts and remained chained even while using portable toilet facilities. Following a lawsuit brought by the Southern Policy Law Center, Alabama officials stopped the use of chains in 1996.

Proponents of chain gangs are adamant about the purpose such punishment serves. "If a person knows they're going to be out on the highway in chains, they are going to think twice about committing a crime," says state prison commissioner Ron Jones.[16] And, Jones says, officials from many other states have contacted him about beginning chain gangs elsewhere. Opponents of the chain gang, however, such as ACLU National Prison Project spokeswoman Jenni Gainsborough, call it "a giant step backward"[17] or "a return to the dark ages." Some even view it as a return to slavery, especially since blacks are overrepresented (on a per capita basis) among Alabama's prison population. Following Alabama's lead, in 1995, Arizona became the second state to field prison chain gangs and was followed shortly thereafter by Florida.[18] John Hallahan, warden of the prison at Douglas, Arizona, explained chain gangs this way: "The lesson is, you go to prison in Arizona and you're going to do hard labor."[19] Florida state senator Charlie Crist, nicknamed "Chain Gang Charlie" for writing the legislation reviving shackling in Florida, echoed similar sentiments. "What we want to do is tell people that if you commit a crime in Florida, if you're convicted of committing that crime in Florida, Florida will punish you, you will do your time, and it will not be pleasant."[20]

In another example of the move toward greater punishments and longer prison terms, the state of Virginia abolished parole as of January 1, 1995, increased sentences for certain violent crimes by as much as 700 percent, and announced that it would build a dozen new prisons over the next decade. Changes in state law, initiated by the administration of Governor George Allen, were intended to move the state further in the direction of truth in sentencing and to appease the state's voters, who—reflecting a groundswell of public opinion nationwide—demanded a "get tough toward criminals" stance. William P. Barr, a former U.S. attorney general under President Bush and cochairman of the Virginia commission that developed the state's plan, explained why no provisions for rehabilitation and crime prevention were included: "The most effective method of prevention," he said, "is to take the rapist off the street for 12 years instead of four."[21]

Symptomatic of the shift in public attitudes in favor of the just deserts model of corrections is the virtual avalanche of state and federal legislation (much of it still pending as of this writing) intended to clamp down on prison comforts such as weight training, adults-only films, premium cable TV channels, pornographic materials by mail, miniature golf courses, individual cells with television sets and coffeepots, personally owned computers and modems, and expensive electronic musical instruments. All would be banned under some proposed federal legislation now pending. "Some criminals have come to view jail as an

The "Big House" of the Future

STERLING, Colo.—When the Sterling Correctional Facility opens later this year here in the eastern portion of the state, inmates will have two stunning views: the Rocky Mountains and a 6,000-volt perimeter fence programmed to kill them if they try to escape.

The state is building the 13-foot-high, death-dealing fence at a cost of $1.7 million. But the fence is not just being installed to deter escapes. It is also being built to save money by replacing a longstanding icon of prison life: the tower guard armed with a high-powered rifle.

"The state of Colorado, as with most other states, has always had the authority to use lethal force to keep felons from escape," said Liz McDonough, a spokeswoman for the state Department of Corrections. "This is a technology that allows us to do this with considerable savings."

Prisons have been moving toward high-tech equipment in an attempt to reduce staffing costs. The lethal fence being installed here is just one way state authorities are attempting to contain costs. Visitation via video terminals, the bar-coding of inmates and even the construction of so-called mega-prisons are just a few of the ways prisons and jails across the United States are eliminating the need for more prison guards and related services.

But as America's prison population continues to balloon, some concerned corrections officers are saying the technology, by removing the human guards, threatens prison safety.

Fence Saves More Than $1 Million

When it opens, Sterling will have the capacity to hold nearly 2,450 inmates, ranging from minimum- to maximum-security prisoners. The prison is scheduled to open its first 1,200 beds in May and the remainder in 2000.

Sterling will be twice as large as any other prison in the state and is costing $170 million to build. McDonough said the electrified fence was built to help save money, replacing the need for five guard towers. This will save the state $1.2 million in construction costs and $750,000 a year in reduced staffing costs, prison officials said.

"This is an expensive facility, and it's very large, so we were concerned about any cost savings to the state," McDonough said.

Colorado also plans to install the fatal fences at another prison currently under construction in Trinidad, a town about 180 miles south of Denver.

Death-Dealing Fencing Rare

California is reportedly the only other state that has installed electrified fences capable of killing fleeing inmates. Beginning in 1993, California built the fences around 23 medium- and high-security prisons, two-thirds of its 33-prison total. Since then, the state has had no escapes through the fences but no fatalities either.

"California has the largest prison system in the United States, so we're on the cutting edge in a lot of different areas," said Terry Thornton, a spokeswoman for the California Department of Corrections. "Maybe this is one such area."

According to Thornton, the fences have also saved California money by reducing the number of guards. "We turned on the first fence in November 1993. Since then, we've saved more than $33.9 million," Thornton said. "They pay for themselves pretty much in the first year."

Technology Races Ahead Nationwide

From 1990 to mid-year 1997, the incarcerated population rose an average of 7.7 percent a year. Jails and prisons now hold 1,218,256 prisoners—577,100 more than they did at the beginning of the decade. And prison growth has been fastest in the West. From 1996 to 1997, the national prison population grew 4.7 percent. But in California, prison population grew 7.9 percent in that same year; in Colorado, the prison population grew 8.2 percent. As a result, corrections officials have turned to technology to keep costs low. Here are some examples:

◆ Bayside State Prison in New Jersey is now constructing a fence that also detects motion, tampering and tunneling underneath the fence. The fence is scheduled to go on line in the spring.

◆ The Jackson County, Mo., jail has begun a $627,000 program that forces prisoners to wear bar-coded wristbands that allow corrections officers to track their movement throughout the prison. Corrections officers will also wear bar-coded badges. The system will allow prison officials to know at all times the location of both prisoners and corrections officers, streamlining operations and eliminating the need to hire 80 additional corrections officers.

"It's my belief that this can make a very significant contribution to reducing the cost in safe, accountable correctional institutions," said Jim Cleaveland, the president of QuaTel, the company that developed the technology. "The most intensive part of day-to-day inmate operations is directing and controlling prisoner movement. During the

(Continued)

CRIME IN THE NEWS

The "Big House" of the Future

daytime, inmates are constantly being moved from place to place, and that's quite labor intensive."

◆ Prison officials are finding that video visitation cuts down labor costs. In Arapahoe County, officials have installed two-way video equipment inside their jail so convicts can talk to their visitors in reception areas. In Pinellas County, Fla., prison officials are building a new wing to their 2,500-inmate prison that will feature 54 fiber-optic video booths inside the prison that will be connected to visitor areas. Reducing face-to-face contact eliminates crowds and contraband but also reduces staffing costs as well, prison officials said.

By placing the video equipment in jail dayrooms and other living areas, guards will no longer have to escort prisoners around the jail to meet visitors. In the Pinellas County facility, for example, prisoners must walk up to a quarter-mile from their cells to see visitors—escorted at all times, of course, by prison guards.

"It's going to result in tremendous amounts of savings," said Capt. Frank Henn, division commander for the Arapahoe County Sheriff's Office. In the past, Henn said, "One officer would move the prisoner to the visiting area. But there's four different pods, so you could be affecting four different officers during visitation periods."

Mega-Prison

In South Carolina, a prison design firm is counting on technological innovations, along with economies of scale, to save taxpayers' money.

Built five years ago, the Lee Correc-

tion Facility outside Columbia, S.C., opened with enough beds for 1,400 prisoners. The prison was designed to keep prisoners safe while relying on its size to save money. Prisoners are kept in two different wings with dining, medical and program areas located in the center. Having the same staff in effect serve two distinct prisons results in a 34 percent savings in guard salaries when compared with two separate, smaller prisons, according to the prison's designer, the National Corrections Corporation.

And the firm included several high-tech and low-tech devices to ensure that the savings don't come at the expense of safety for the sprawling prison.

Instead of a tower, armed officers can man emergency posts on prison roofs, and hallways are kept as straight as possible to increase sightlines and reduce the need for extra guards, said Larry Fields, National Corrections Corporation's chief operating officer. Even stairwells have been redesigned. The vertical portions of each stairwell, located between each step, have been made see-through to increase visibility.

When outside, prisoners congregate in small groups, in separate recreation yards attached to each housing unit.

"There is no time when you walk out on the yard and see inmates just standing around congregating," said John Barkley, a spokesman for the South Carolina Department of Corrections. "We have systems that have been implemented that manage the inmates, that make the prison safer. That's a big reason why you can have such large numbers, because you don't have 1,500 inmates standing around the yard at the same time."

Video Surveillance System

High-tech innovations such as camera surveillance also contribute to prison security. "You don't just reduce staff by economies of scale, you reduce it through technology," Fields said. "Cameras are an excellent way of reducing staff and increasing security for the staff."

"Any area where you have a congregation of inmates, you can cut back—not eliminate—the number of officers required," Fields added.

Concern From Corrections Officers

However, not everyone is happy about the idea of electrified fences, video cameras, and bar codes replacing prison guards and guard towers.

"In prisons, it's a visual deterrent when officers are present," said Brian Dawe, director of operations for Corrections USA, an advocacy group for corrections workers. "Cameras cannot respond to emergencies. I've worked in the business for years, and I've never seen a camera jump off the wall and respond to an emergency."

Dawe also criticized the elimination of guard towers as jeopardizing the safety of guards who work in prison yards.

"One of the first things we're told is if the yard gets out of control, go to the tower, because the officers in the tower have weapons, and they will protect you," Dawe said. "Towers serve multiple purposes. They are terrific observation points because they're up high and they offer protection."

Source: Hans H. Chen, "The 'Big House' of the Future," APB News, Jan. 11, 1999. Reprinted with permission.

almost acceptable lifestyle because amenities are better for them on the inside than on the outside. You should pay the price for your crime, not be rewarded with a vacation watching premium cable on your personal TV," says Republican congressman Dick Zimmer of New Jersey, a sponsor of the so-called no-frills legislation.[22]

A nationwide survey of state departments of correction by *Corrections Compendium*, a publication covering all aspects of imprisonment, found that prisons "of the present and near future are being stripped of anything that can be considered a luxury. Prison life is becoming less and less attractive with the elimination of sacred privileges like smoking and the addition of hard labor and humiliating uniforms."[23] The survey found that 60 percent of the 46 states that responded reported a decrease in inmate privileges during the previous 12 months, including reductions in the amount or type of personal property inmates are allowed to keep, restrictions on outside purchases and food packages from home, and the elimination of cable television and rented movies. A number of prison systems reported abolishing family visits, special occasion banquets, and the like. "The elimination of family-oriented privileges," said the publication, "reflects the extremely harsh public view towards prisoners that is currently in vogue."[24]

Other get-tough initiatives can be seen in the "three strikes and you're out" laws that have swept through state legislatures everywhere.[25] Three-strikes legislation, discussed earlier in this book, mandates lengthy prison terms for criminal offenders convicted of a third violent crime or felony. While three-strikes laws have either been enacted or are being considered in more than 30 states and by the federal government (which requires life imprisonment for federal criminals convicted of three violent felonies or drug offenses), critics of such laws say that they will not prevent crime.[26] Jerome Skolnick, of the University of California-Berkeley, for example, criticizes three-strikes legislation because, he says, although it may satisfy society's desire for retribution to "lock 'em up and throw away the key,"[27] such a practice will almost certainly not reduce the risk of victimization—especially the risk of becoming a victim of random violence. That is so, says Skolnick, because most violent crimes are committed by young men between the ages of 13 and 23. "It follows," according to Skolnick, "that if we jail them for life after their third conviction, we will get them in the twilight of their careers, and other young offenders will take their place." Three-strikes programs, says Skolnick, will lead to creation of "the most expensive, taxpayer-supported middle-age and old-age entitlement program in the history of the world," which will provide housing and medical care to older, burned-out, law violators. Another author puts it this way: "The question . . . is whether it makes sense to continue to incarcerate aged prisoners beyond the time they would have served under ordinary sentences. This is unnecessary from the standpoint of public safety, and it is expensive."[28]

Alan Schuman, president of the American Probation and Parole Association, feels much the same way. Although building more prisons may be a popular quick fix to crime, says Schuman, such a strategy will only cost millions of dollars without making streets safer. "The Draconian single-level approach of merely building new institutions will cause us problems for decades," Schuman said during a recent meeting.[29]

Criticisms like these, however, fail to appreciate the new sentiments underlying the correctional era now emerging. Proponents of today's get-tough policies, while no doubt interested in personal safety, lower crime rates, and balanced state and federal budgets, are keenly focused on retribution. And where retribution fuels a correctional policy, deterrence, reformation, and economic considerations play only secondary roles. The real issue for those advocating today's retribution-based correctional policies is *not* whether they deter or whether they lower crime rates, but rather the overriding conviction that criminals *deserve* punishment. As more and more states enact three-strikes and other get-tough legislation, prison populations across the nation will swell even more, eclipsing those of the warehousing era. The new just deserts era of correctional philosophy now provides what has become for many an acceptable rationale for continued prison expansion. Newman Flanagan, executive director of the National District Attorneys Association, puts it this way: "I would venture to say in all probability they [the states] will all start looking at three strikes laws. It's the 'in' thing to do. The public is fed up with criminals."[30] In fact, it is the correctional systems of this country that will bear the burden of housing those imprisoned under such laws. One recent study[31] found that, as a direct consequence of three-strikes and other get-tough legislation now in vogue, the number of persons imprisoned in the United States can be expected to increase to nearly 2 million by the year 2002—adding an avalanche of new inmates on top of correctional systems already struggling to keep pace with court-ordered prison commitments. California officials estimate that by 2004, three-strikes legislation "will account for over 50% of the prison population"[32] in that state. A similar 1997 study of three-strikes laws

An Alabama chain gang sets out to work the roads. In 1995, reflecting a renewed societywide emphasis on punishment which is reminiscent of the punitive era in corrections, Alabama became the first state in modern times to revive use of prison chain gangs.
AP/Wide World Photos.

"The American public is alarmed about crime, and with good reason. For the past generation, state and federal crime control policies have been based on the belief that law enforcement can solve the problem: more police, harsher sentencing laws, greater use of the death penalty. But today, with an unprecedented number of people behind bars, we are no safer than before. We are, however, much less free."

—ACLU (Web site)
www.aclu.org/issues/criminal/iscj.html

"Incarceration is a crash course in extortion and criminal behavior."

—Vincent Schiraldi,
National Center on Institutions and Alternatives

in 22 states concluded that such legislation results in clogged court systems and crowded correctional facilities, and encourages three-time felons to take dramatic risks to avoid capture.[33]

Given studies like these, many now claim that the new retribution-based "lock 'em up" philosophy may bode ill for the future of American corrections. "I am worried there is going to be a disaster in our prisons," says Michael Quinlan, director of the Federal Bureau of Prisons under former presidents Bush and Reagan. The combination of burgeoning prison populations and newly popular restrictions on inmate privileges could soon have a catastrophic and disastrous effect—leading to riots, more prison violence, work stoppages, an increased number of inmate suicides, and other forms of prison disorder, says Quinlan.[34]

Overcrowding

Prisons everywhere are crowded. The incarceration rate for state and federal prisoners sentenced to more than a year has reached a record 476 prisoners per every 100,000 U.S. residents.[35] One out of every 110 men, and 1 in every 1,695 women were sentenced prisoners under the jurisdiction of state or federal authorities in 1998.

Until 1996, the problem of overcrowding was worst in Texas, which has the nation's second highest incarceration rate (after Louisiana) with 700 out of every 100,000 Texans behind prison bars.[36] In 1996 Texas completed a $1.5 billion expansion program, moving more than 20,000 inmates into 28 new facilities across the state. The Texas prison system, which has been described as "by far the largest in the free world," is capable of housing 155,000 regular prison inmates (it now holds 163,190).[37] California has now taken the lead in overcrowding—housing twice the number of inmates in its prisons than those facilities were designed to handle.[38]

Federal prisons tell a similar story. On January 1, 2000, federal prisons held 135,246 inmates in facilities rated to accommodate only 90,075.[39] Statistics on overcrowding are displayed graphically in Figure 11-3.

Experts agree that prison crowding can be measured along a number of dimensions, which include[40]

■ Space available per inmate (such as square feet of floor space)

■ How long inmates are confined in cells or housing units (versus time spent on recreation, etc.)

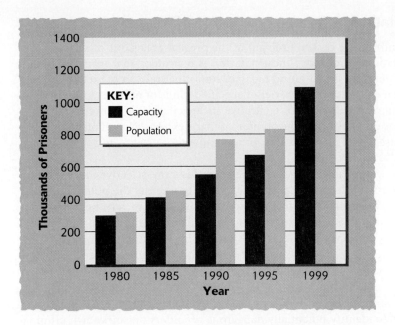

FIGURE 11-3 ■ *State and federal prison populations, inmates versus capacity, 1980–1999.*

Source: *Bureau of Justice Statistics,* Correctional Populations in the United States *(Washington, D.C.: BJS, Various Years).*

- ▣ Living arrangements (i.e., single versus double bunking)
- ▣ Type of housing (use of segregation facilities, tents, etc., in place of general housing)

Complicating the crowding picture still further is the fact that prison officials have developed three definitions of **prison capacity. Rated capacity** refers to the size of the inmate population a facility can handle according to the judgment of experts. **Operational capacity** is the number of inmates that a facility can effectively accommodate based on an appraisal of the institution's staff, programs, and services. **Design capacity** refers to the inmate population the institution was originally built to handle. Rated capacity estimates usually yield the largest inmate capacities, whereas design capacity (upon which observations in this chapter are based) typically shows the highest amount of overcrowding.

Crowding by itself is not cruel and unusual punishment, according to the Supreme Court in *Rhodes* v. *Chapman* (1981),[41] which considered the issue of double bunking among other alleged forms of "deprivation" at the Southern Ohio correctional facility. The Ohio facility, built in 1971, was substantially overcrowded according to the original housing plans on which it was constructed. Designed to house one inmate per cell, the cells were small (only 63 square feet of floor space on the average). However, at the time the suit was filed, the facility held 2,300 inmates, 1,400 of whom were double celled. Kelly Chapman, an inmate serving a sentence as an armed robber and prison escapee, claimed that his portion of a cell was too small—smaller even than the space recommended by Ohio State Veterinarian Services for a five-week-old calf. Thirty-six states joined the case in support of the Ohio practice of double celling, while the American Medical Association and the American Public Health Association took Chapman's side.[42] The court, reasoning that overcrowding is not necessarily dangerous if other prison services are adequate, held that prison housing conditions may be "restrictive and even harsh," for they are part of the penalty that offenders pay for their crimes.

However, overcrowding combined with other negative conditions may lead to a finding against the prison system. The American Correctional Association believes that such a totality-of-conditions approach requires the court to judge the overall quality of prison life while viewing overcrowded conditions in combination with the following:

- ■ The prison's meeting of basic human needs
- ■ The adequacy of the facility's staff
- ■ The program opportunities available to inmates
- ■ The quality and strength of the prison management

Prison Capacity

A general term referring to the size of the correctional population an institution can effectively hold. There are three types of prison capacity: design, rated, and operational.

Rated Capacity

The size of the inmate population a facility can handle according to the judgment of experts.

Operational Capacity

The number of inmates a prison can effectively accommodate based upon management considerations.

Design Capacity

The number of inmates a prison was architecturally intended to hold when it was built or modified.

Selective Incapacitation: A Strategy to Reduce Overcrowding

Some authors have identified the central problem of the present era as one of selective versus collective incapacitation.[43] Collective incapacitation is a strategy that would imprison almost all serious offenders and is still found today in states that rely on predetermined, or fixed, sentences for given offenses or for a series of specified kinds of offenses (as in the case of three-strikes legislation just discussed). Collective incapacitation is, however, prohibitively expensive as well as unnecessary in the opinion of many experts. Not all offenders need to be imprisoned, because not all represent a continuing threat to society—but those who do are difficult to identify.[44]

In most jurisdictions where the just deserts initiative holds sway, selective incapacitation is rapidly becoming the rule. Selective incapacitation seeks to identify the potentially most dangerous criminals with the goal of selectively removing them from society. Repeat offenders with records of serious and violent crimes are the most likely candidates for incapacitation—as are those who will probably commit such crimes in the future even though they have no records. But potentially violent offenders cannot be readily identified, and those thought likely to commit crimes cannot be sentenced to lengthy prison terms for things they have not yet done.

In support of selective incapacitation, many states have enacted career offender statutes that attempt to accurately identify potentially dangerous offenders out of known criminal populations. Selective incapacitation efforts, however, have been criticized for yielding a rate of "false positives" of over 60 percent,[45] and some authors have been quick to call selective incapacitation a "strategy of failure."[46] Nevertheless, in a 1996 analysis of recidivism studies,[47] Canadians Paul Gendreau, Tracy Little, and Claire Goggin found that criminal history, a history of preadult antisocial behavior, and "criminogenic needs"—which were defined as measurable antisocial thoughts, values, and behaviors—were all dependable predictors of recidivism. The article, subtitled "What Works!," was intended as a response to Martinson's "nothing works doctrine," mentioned earlier.

Some state programs designed to reduce overcrowding, however, have run afoul of selective incarceration principles. In 1997, for example, the U.S. Supreme Court[48] ordered the state of Florida to release as many as 2,500 inmates—many of whom had been convicted of violent crimes—under a "gain time" program set up by the state in 1983. Provisions of the program allowed inmates to earn as much as two months off their sentences for every month served. Although the program was originally intended to relieve overcrowding, a change in public sentiment led Florida attorney general Bob Butterworth to revoke gain time that had already been earned. In ordering the inmates' release, however, the U.S. Supreme Court unanimously ruled that Florida had violated constitutional guarantees against **ex post facto** laws and required officials to be bound by the program's original conditions. The release of hundreds of murderers, rapists, robbers, and other felons caused a statewide uproar and media furor. Lee County sheriff John McDougall expressed dismay at the Court's decision. "A hell of a lot of innocent people are going to be robbed, raped, and murdered," he said. "How many people are going to have to die in order to pay for this blunder?"[49]

The Florida experience and others like it, have caused states to tighten restrictions on early release programs. As the just deserts model matures, it is likely that we will see the clear-cut targeting of violent criminals who will be sentenced to lengthy prison stays with little possibility of release, and the increased use of alternative sanctions for minor offenders.

Security Levels

Watch television shows about prison and you'll most likely see maximum-custody institutions. Such institutions tend to be massive old prisons with large inmate populations. Some, such as Central Prison in Raleigh, North Carolina, are much newer and incorporate advances in prison architecture to provide tight security without sacrificing building aesthetics. Such institutions provide a high level of security characterized by high fences, thick walls, secure cells, gun towers, and armed prison guards. Maximum-custody prisons tend to locate cells and other inmate living facilities at the center of the institution and place a variety of barri-

---

"We are likely to see continued record overcrowding no matter how many prisons we build."

—*U.S. Representative Charles B. Rangel (D-N.Y.)*

Ex post facto

Latin for "after the fact." The Constitution prohibits the enactment of ex post facto laws, which make acts punishable as crimes which were committed before the laws in question were passed.

ers between the living area and the institution's outer perimeter. Technological innovations such as electric perimeters, laser motion detectors, electronic and pneumatic locking systems, metal detectors, X-ray machines, television surveillance, radio communications, and computer information systems are frequently used today to reinforce the more traditional maximum-security strategies. These new technologies have helped to lower the cost of new prison construction, although some argue that prison electronic detection devices may be relied upon too heavily and have not yet been adequately tested.[50] Death row inmates are all maximum-security prisoners, although the level of security on death row exceeds even that experienced by most prisoners held in maximum custody. Prisoners on death row must spend much of the day in single cells and are often permitted a brief shower only once a week under close supervision.

Most states today have one large centrally located maximum-security institution. Some of these prisons combine more than one custody level and may be both maximum- and medium-security facilities. Medium security is a custody level that in many ways resembles maximum security. Medium-security prisoners are generally permitted more freedom to associate with one another and can go to the prison yard, exercise room, library, and shower and bathroom facilities under less intense supervision than their maximum-security counterparts. An important security tool in medium-security prisons is the count, which is literally a headcount of inmates taken at regular intervals. Counts may be taken four times a day and usually require inmates to report to designated areas to be counted. Until the count has been "cleared," all other inmate activity must cease. Medium-security prisons tend to be smaller than maximum-security institutions and often have barbed-wire-topped chain-link fences in place of the more secure stone or concrete block walls found in many of the older maximum-security facilities. Cells and living quarters tend to have more windows and are often located closer to the perimeter of the institution than is the case in maximum security. Dormitory-style housing, where prisoners live together in "ward"-like arrangements, may be employed in medium-security facilities. Medium-security facilities generally have more prison programs and opportunities for inmates to participate in recreational and other programs than do maximum-custody facilities.

Minimum-security institutions do not fit the stereotypical conception of prisons. Minimum-security inmates are generally housed in dormitory-like settings and are free to walk the yard and visit most of the prison facilities. Some newer prisons provide minimum-security inmates with private rooms, which they can decorate (within limits) according to their tastes. Inmates usually have free access to a "canteen," which sells personal products such as cigarettes, toothpaste, and candy bars. Minimum-security inmates often wear uniforms of a different color from those of inmates in higher custody levels, and in some institutions may wear civilian clothes. They work under only general supervision and usually have access to recreational, educational, and skills training programs on the prison grounds. Guards are unarmed, gun towers do not exist, and fences, if they are present at all, are usually low and sometimes even unlocked. Many minimum-security prisoners participate in some sort of work or study release program, and some have extensive visitation and furlough privileges. Counts may still be taken, although most minimum-security institutions keep track of inmates through daily administrative work schedules. The primary "force" holding inmates in minimum-security institutions is their own restraint. Inmates live with the knowledge that minimum-security institutions are one step removed from close correctional supervision and that if they fail to meet the expectations of administrators they will be transferred into more-secure institutions, which will probably delay their release. Inmates returning from assignments in the community may be frisked for contraband, but body cavity searches are rare in minimum custody, being reserved primarily for inmates suspected of smuggling.

Upon entry into the prison system, most states assign prisoners to initial custody levels based upon their perceived dangerousness, escape risk, and type of offense. Some inmates may enter the system at the medium- (or even minimum-) custody level. Inmates move through custody levels according to the progress they are judged to have made in self-control and demonstrated responsibility. Serious, violent criminals who begin their prison careers with lengthy sentences in maximum custody have the opportunity in most states to work

"The first two decades of the [twenty-first] century, at least, will see a major growth in prison populations. We have an opportunity now to start doing a better job of handling the responsibilities of the criminal justice system as well as of society. I hope we take both more seriously in the future than we do currently."

—Dr. Alfred Blumstein, *Dean, School of Urban and Public Affairs, Carnegie-Mellon University*

their way up to minimum security, although the process usually takes a number of years. Those who "mess up" and represent continuous disciplinary problems are returned to closer custody levels. Minimum-security prisons, as a result, house inmates convicted of all types of criminal offenses.

The typical American prison today is medium or minimum custody. Some states have as many as 80 or 90 small institutions, which may originally have been located in every county to serve the needs of public works and highway maintenance. Medium- and minimum-security institutions house the bulk of the country's prison population and offer a number of programs and services designed to assist with the rehabilitation of offenders and to create the conditions necessary for a successful reentry of the inmate into society. Most prisons offer psychiatric services, academic education, vocational education, substance abuse treatment, health care, counseling, recreation, library services, religious programs, and industrial and agricultural training.[51] To learn more about all aspects of contemporary prisons, visit The Corrections Connection via **WebExtra!** 11-1 at CJToday.com.

The Federal Prison System

In 1895 the federal government opened a prison at Leavenworth, Kansas, for civilians convicted of violating federal law. Leavenworth had been a military prison, and control over the facility was transferred from the Department of the Army to the Department of Justice. By 1906 the Leavenworth facility had been expanded to a 1,200-inmate capacity, and another prison—in Atlanta, Georgia—had been built. McNeil Island Prison in Washington state was also functioning by the early 1900s. The first federal prison for women opened in 1927 in Alderson, West Virginia. With increasing complexity in the federal criminal code, the number of federal prisoners grew.[52]

On May 14, 1930, the Federal Bureau of Prisons (BOP) was created under the direction of Sanford Bates. The Bureau inherited a system which was dramatically overcrowded. Many federal prisoners were among the most notorious criminals in the nation, and ideals of humane treatment and rehabilitation were all but lacking in the facilities of the 1930s. Director Bates began a program of improvements to relieve overcrowding and to increase the treatment capacity of the system. In 1933 the Medical Center for Federal Prisoners opened in Springfield, Missouri, with a capacity of around 1,000 inmates. Alcatraz Island began operations in 1934.

The federal prison system classifies its institutions according to five[53] security levels: (1) administrative maximum (**ADMAX**), (2) high security, (3) medium security, (4) low security, and (5) minimum security. High-security facilities are called United States Penitentiaries (USPs), medium- and low-security institutions are both called Federal Correctional Institutions (FCIs); and minimum-security prisons are termed Federal Prison Camps (FPCs).[54] Minimum-security facilities (such as Eglin Air Force Base, Florida; and Maxwell Air Force Base, Alabama) are essentially honor-type camps with barracks-like housing and no fencing. Low-security facilities in the federal prison system are surrounded by double chain-link fencing and employ vehicle patrols around their perimeters to enhance security. Medium-security facilities (such as those in Terminal Island, California; Lompoc, California; and Seagoville, Texas) make use of similar fencing and patrols, but supplement them with electronic monitoring of the grounds and perimeter areas. High-security facilities (USPs such as those in Atlanta, Georgia; Lewisburg, Pennsylvania; Terre Haute, Indiana; and Leavenworth, Kansas) are architecturally designed to prevent escapes and to contain disturbances. They also make use of armed patrols and intense electronic surveillance. A separate federal prison category is that of Administrative Facility, consisting of institutions with special missions, which are designed to house all types of inmates. Most administrative facilities are Metropolitan Detention Centers (MDCs). MDCs, which are generally located in large cities close to federal courthouses, are the jails of the federal correctional system and hold inmates awaiting trial in federal court. Another five administrative facilities are termed Medical Centers for Federal Prisoners (MCFPs) and function as hospitals.

As of August 22, 1999, the federal correctional system consisted of 94 facilities existing either as single institutions or as Federal Correctional Complexes—that is, sites consisting of

ADMAX

Administrative maximum; the term used by the federal government to denote ultra-high-security prisons.

"If you don't like the place, don't come here."

—Maricopa County (Arizona) Sheriff Joe Arpaio, offering advice to inmates housed in his desert tent city

more than one type of correctional institution. The Federal Correctional Complex at Allenwood, Pennsylvania, for example, consists of a United States Penitentiary, a Federal Prison Camp, and two Federal Correctional Institutions (one low and one medium security), each with its own warden. Federal institutions can be classified by type as follows: 55 are Federal Prison Camps (holding 34 percent of all federal prisoners), 17 are low-security facilities (with 27 percent of the system's prisoners), 26 are medium-security facilities (23 percent of the population), 8 are high-security prisons (13 percent of prisoners), and 1 is an ADMAX facility (with 1 percent of the prison population). Long-term confinement facilities in the federal correctional system are shown in Figure 11-4.

One of the most recent additions to the system is the $60 million ultra-maximum security federal prison at Florence, Colorado—the federal system's only ADMAX unit. Dubbed by some "the Alcatraz of the Rockies," the new 575-bed facility is designed to be the most secure prison ever built by the government.[55] Opened in 1995, it holds mob bosses, spies, terrorists, murderers, and escape artists. Dangerous inmates are confined to their cells 23 hours per day and are not allowed to see or associate with other inmates. Electronically controlled doors throughout the institution channel inmates to individual exercise sessions, and educational courses, religious services, and administrative matters are conducted via closed-circuit television piped directly into the prisoners' cells. Remote-controlled heavy steel doors within the prison allow correctional staff to section off the institution in the event of rioting, and the system can be controlled from outside if the entire prison is compromised.

With new facilities rapidly coming online, however, crowding in federal prisons is pervasive. The number of inmates held in federal prisons had risen from 24,000 in 1980 to 145,779 by late 2000.[56] Beginning in 1992, and continuing through today, approximately 60 percent of all federal prisoners were serving sentences for drug offenses.[57]

In an effort to combat rising expenses, the U.S. Congress passed legislation in 1992 that imposes a "user fee" on federal inmates able to pay the costs associated with their incarceration.[58] Under the law, inmates may be assessed a dollar amount up to the cost of a year's incarceration—currently around $20,000. The statute, which was designed so as not to impose hardships on poor defendants or their dependents, directs that collected funds, estimated to soon total $48 million per year, are to be used to improve alcohol and drug abuse programs within federal prisons. To learn more about the Federal Bureau of Prisons, visit **WebExtra!** 11-2 at CJToday.com.

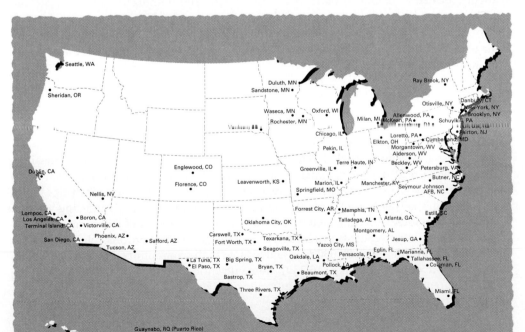

FIGURE 11-4 ■ *Long-term confinement facility locations in the federal correctional system, 2000.*

Source: *Federal Bureau of Prisons.*
Note: *Does not include BOP offices and Community Corrections Management (CCM) offices.*

Recent Improvements

In the midst of frequent lawsuits, court-ordered changes in prison administration, and over-crowded conditions, outstanding prison facilities are being recognized through the American Correctional Association's program of accreditation. The ACA Commission on Accreditation has developed a set of standards which correctional institutions can use in self-evaluation. Those which meet the standards can apply for accreditation under the program. Unfortunately, accreditation of prisons has few "teeth." Although unaccredited universities would not long be in business, few prisoners can choose the institution they want to be housed in.

Another avenue toward improvement of the nation's prisons can be found in the National Academy of Corrections, the training arm of the National Institute of Corrections. The Academy, located in Boulder, Colorado, offers seminars and training sessions for state and local correctional managers, trainers, personnel directors, sheriffs, and state legislators.[59] Issues covered include strategies to control overcrowding, community corrections program management, prison programs, gangs and disturbances, security, and public and media relations, as well as many other topics.[60]

Jails

Jail

A confinement facility administered by an agency of local government, typically a law enforcement agency, intended for adults but sometimes also containing juveniles, which holds persons detained pending adjudication and/or persons committed after adjudication (usually those committed on sentences of a year or less).

Jails are short-term confinement facilities that were originally intended to hold suspects following arrest and pending trial. Today, jails also house those convicted of misdemeanors who are serving relatively short sentences and felony offenders awaiting transportation to long-term confinement facilities. A 2000 report[61] by the Bureau of Justice Statistics found that the nation's jails held a total of 605,943 persons—with 67,487 of them being women. Juveniles held in local jails numbered 9,458. Numerically, 57 percent of jail inmates are pretrial detainees or are defendants involved in some stage of the trial process.[62] Jail authorities also supervised an additional 82,030 men and women in the community under the following programs: electronic monitoring (10,230); home detention without electronic monitoring (518); day reporting (5,080); community service (20,139); and weekender programs (16,089).[63]

A total of 3,304 jails are in operation throughout the United States today, staffed by approximately 165,500 correctional workers—the equivalent of about 1 employee for every 2.8 jail inmates.[64] Overall, the jail budget is huge, and facilities are overflowing. Some $9.6 billion is spent every year by state and local governments to operate the nation's jails,[65] with more than $1 billion in additional monies earmarked for new jail construction and for facilities renovation. On average, approximately $14,667 is spent yearly to house one jail inmate.[66]

While only a few years ago driving under the influence was the most common charge for jailed persons 45 years of age or older (accounting for 10 percent of all jail inmates), persons charged with drug law violations now account for 22 percent of those in jail.[67] Bond has been set by the court, although not yet posted, for almost nine out of 10 jail inmates. Significantly, one of the fastest-growing sectors of today's jail population consists of sentenced offenders serving time in local jails because overcrowded prisons cannot accept them.

Approximately 20 million people are admitted (or readmitted) to the nation's jails each year. Some jail inmates stay for as little as one day, while others serve extended periods of jail time. Most jails are small. Two out of three were built to house 50 or fewer inmates. Most people who spend time in jail, however, do so in larger institutions.[68] According to the National Institute of Justice, "about 6% of jail facilities housed more than half of all jail inmates . . ." in the nation.[69] Although there are many small and medium-sized jails across the country, a handful of "megajails" house thousands of inmates. The largest such facilities can be found in New York City's Riker's Island, the Cook County jail in Chicago, Houston's Harris County Downtown Central Jail, the New Orleans Parish Prison System, Los Angeles County's Pitchess Honor Ranch, and Los Angeles County's Men's Central Jail. Men's Central Jail was to be replaced by the new 4,000-bed Twin Towers Correctional Facility. Twin Towers, which cost $373 million to build, opened in 1997, but budget problems plaguing Los Angeles County have kept it from being fully utilized.[70] The largest employer among these huge jails is the Cook County facility, with over 1,200 personnel on its payroll.[71]

Not surprisingly, the nation's most populous states tend to have the most inmates. Almost half of the nation's jail population are housed in the jails of five states:[72] California, Texas, Florida, New York, and Georgia. Some states, however, report a much higher rate of growth in the use of local confinement facilities than others. NIJ reports that jail populations in Texas grew by 264 percent in the 10 years between 1985 and 1995, and increased 103 percent in Maryland—while growing only slightly in Maine, Missouri, Nebraska, and Wyoming.

CAREERS IN JUSTICE

Working with the Federal Bureau of Prisons

TYPICAL POSITIONS:

Correctional officer, psychologist, physician, nurse, chaplain, correctional/drug treatment specialist, safety specialist, teacher, program officer, vocational instructor, and others.

EMPLOYMENT REQUIREMENTS:

Applicants must (1) be U.S. citizens, (2) be less than 37 years of age (although for some hard-to-fill positions an age waiver may be granted), (3) successfully complete an employee interview, (4) pass a physical examination, and (5) pass a field security investigation. Correctional officer candidates must hold a bachelor's degree.

OTHER REQUIREMENTS:

Successful completion of in-service training at the Federal Law Enforcement Training Academy at Glynco, Georgia.

SALARY:

Correctional officers are appointed at the GS-5 level, while six months or more of graduate education in criminal justice or any social science may qualify the applicant for the GS-6 level or higher. A correctional officer may be advanced to the next higher paygrade level after six months of satisfactory service.

BENEFITS:

Benefits include (1) participation in the Federal Employees' Retirement System, (2) paid annual leave, (3) paid sick leave, (4) low-cost health and life insurance, and (5) paid holidays. Other benefits naturally accrue from what the bureau describes as "strong internal merit promotion practices" and "unlimited opportunities for advancement in one of the fastest-growing government agencies."

DIRECT INQUIRIES TO:

Federal Bureau of Prisons, Room 460, 320 First Street NW, Washington, DC 20534. Phone: (202) 307-3175. Web site: www.bop.gov.

Some states, such as Louisiana (with 377 jail inmates per every 100,000 residents), Georgia (328 per 100,000), and Texas (307 per 100,000), show a high *rate* of jail usage, while other states, such as Iowa, Maine, and North Dakota (with only 57 jail inmates per 100,000 state residents), and Minnesota, Montana, and South Dakota (with around 81 per 100,000), make less use of jail.[73]

Most people processed through the country's jails are members of minority groups (59 percent), with 42 percent of jail inmates classifying themselves as black, 15 percent as Hispanic, and another 2 percent as minorities belonging to other races. Forty-one percent of jail inmates classify themselves as white. Ninety-one percent are male.[74]

Women and Jail

Although women comprise only 9 percent of the country's jail population, they are "virtually the largest growth group in jails nationwide."[75] Jailed women face a number of special problems. Only 25.7 percent of the nation's jails report having a classification system specifically designed to evaluate female inmates,[76] and, although "a large proportion of jurisdictions" report plans "to build facilities geared to the female offender,"[77] not all jurisdictions today even provide separate housing areas for female inmates. Educational levels are very low among jailed women, and fewer than half are high-school graduates.[78] Pregnancy is another problem. Nationally, 4 percent of female inmates are pregnant at the time they come to jail,[79] but as much as 10 percent of the female population of urban jails is reported to be pregnant on any given day.[80] As a consequence, a few hundred children are born in jails each year. Jailed mothers are not only separated from their children, they may have to pay for their support. Twelve percent of all jails in one study group reported requiring employed female inmates to contribute to the support of their dependent children.

Drug abuse is another significant source of difficulty for jailed women. Over 30 percent of women who are admitted to jail have a substance abuse problem at the time of admission, and in some parts of the country, that figure may be as high as 70 percent.[81] Adding to the problem is the fact that substantive medical programs for female inmates, such as obstetrics and gynecological care, are often lacking. In planning medical services for female inmates into the next century, some writers have advised jail administrators to expect to see an

A guard walks alone along a wall at Los Angeles County's new $373 million Twin Towers Correctional Facility. Opened in 1997, it is one of the world's largest jails.
Damian Dovarganes, AP/Wide World Photos.

increasingly common kind of inmate: "[a]n opiate-addicted female who is pregnant with no prior prenatal care having one or more sexually transmitted diseases, and fitting a high-risk category for AIDS (prostitution, IV drug use)."[82]

Female inmates are only half the story. Women working in corrections are the other. In one study[83] Linda Zupan, a member of the new generation of outstanding jail scholars, found that women comprised 22 percent of the correctional officer force in jails across the nation. The deployment of female personnel, however, was disproportionately skewed toward jobs in the lower ranks. Although 60 percent of all support staff (secretaries, cooks, and janitors) were women, only one in every 10 chief administrators was female. Zupan explains this pattern by pointing to the "token-status" of women staff members in some of the nation's jails.[84] Even so, Zupan did find that women correctional employees were significantly committed to their careers and that attitudes of male workers toward female coworkers in jails were generally positive. Zupan's study uncovered 626 jails in which over 50 percent of the correction officer force consisted of women. On the opposite side of the coin, 954 of the nation's 3,316 jails operating at the time of the study had no female officers.[85] Zupan noted that: "An obvious problem associated with the lack of female officers in jails housing females concerns the potential for abuse and exploitation of women inmates by male staff."[86]

Jails which do hire women generally accord them equal footing with male staffers. Although cross-gender privacy is a potential area of legal liability, few jails limit the supervisory areas which may be visited by female officers working in male facilities. In three quarters of the jails studied by Zupan, women officers were assigned to supervise male housing areas. Only one in four jails which employed women restricted their access to unscreened shower and toilet facilities used by men and/or to other areas such as sexual offender units.

Crowding in Jails

Jails have been called the "shame of the criminal justice system." Many are old, overcrowded, poorly funded, scantily staffed by underpaid and poorly trained employees, and given low priority in local budgets. Court-ordered caps on jail populations are increasingly common. One of the first was placed on the Harris County Jail in Houston, Texas, a decade ago. The jail was forced to release 250 inmates after missing a deadline for reducing its resident population of 6,100 people.[87] A nationwide survey, published by the Bureau of Justice Statistics, undertaken around the same time, found that 46 percent of all jails were built more than 25 years ago and of that percentage, over half were more than 50 years old.[88]

Although not all jails are overcrowded, many overcrowded jails still exist in the nation's largest cities and counties, and have become a critical issue for the justice system.[89] A 1983 national census revealed that jails were operating at only 85 percent of their rated capacity.[90] By 1990, however, the nation's jails were running at 108 percent of capacity, and new jails could be found on drawing boards and under construction across the country. By 1999 new facilities had opened, and overall jail occupancy was reported at 93 percent of rated capacity, although some individual facilities were desperately overcrowded.[91] With square footage per inmate averaging only 58.3[92] in jails today, managers still cite crowding and staff shortages as the two most critical problems facing jails today.[93]

The root cause of jail crowding can be found in a growing crime rate coupled with a punitive public attitude, which has heavily influenced correctional practice. In 1995, for example, Maricopa County, Arizona, sheriff Joe Arpaio added 25 tents to 42 others he had ordered erected two years earlier in the desert outside of Phoenix to relieve overcrowding in the county jail.[94] Arpaio, faced with 1,900 more inmates than his 3,900-capacity jail could handle, built the tent city with help from a volunteer posse, whose members work for free and pay for their own uniforms and guns. Temperatures in the desert jail, which is without air conditioning, soar to well over 100 degrees in the summer time, and wind-blown sand makes life difficult for inmates. In what some see as adding insult to injury, the tough-talking sheriff runs the desert jail frugally—replacing hot inmate meals with bologna sandwiches and requiring inmates to cut one another's hair in order to save on barber's fees. He's also put an end to violent television, forcing inmates to watch shows like *Lassie* and *Donald Duck,* rather than ones with shoot-'em-up themes.

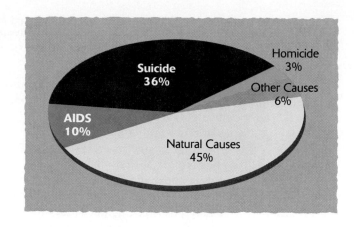

FIGURE 11-5 ■ *Causes of jail deaths in the United States.*
Source: *U.S. Department of Justice.*

Overcrowded prisons have also spilled over into jails. During the last few years, many states have begun using jails instead of prisons for the confinement of convicted felons, exacerbating the jail crowding problem still further. In 1999, for example, approximately 70,000 inmates were being held in local jails because of overcrowding in state prisons.[95] Another problem arises from the sentencing of individuals who are unable to make restitution, alimony, or child support payments to jail time—a practice which has made the local lockup at least partially a debtor's prison. Symptomatic of problems brought on by overcrowding, the National Institute of Justice reported 234 suicides in jails across the nation during a recent year.[96] Jail deaths from all causes (which total about 650 annually) are shown in Figure 11-5.

Other factors also conspire to keep at least some jails overcrowded. They include the following.[97]

■ The inability of jail inmates to make bond due to institutionalized bail bond practices and lack of funding sources for indigent defendants

■ Unnecessary delays between arrest and final case disposition

■ Unnecessarily limited access to vital information about defendants which could be useful in facilitating court-ordered pretrial release

■ The limited ability of the criminal justice system to handle cases expeditiously due to a lack of needed resources (judges, assistant prosecuting attorneys, etc.)

■ Inappropriate attorney delays in moving cases through court (motions to delay cases as part of an attorney's strategy, etc.)

■ Unproductive statutes requiring that specified nonviolent offenders be jailed (including those requiring mandatory pretrial jailing of DWIs, minor drug offenders, second-offense shoplifting, etc.)

Some innovative jurisdictions have already substantially reduced jail crowding. San Diego, California, for example, uses a privately operated detoxification reception program in order to divert many inebriates from the proverbial "drunk tank."[98] Officials in Galveston County, Texas, routinely divert mentally ill arrestees directly to a mental health facility.[99] Other areas use pretrial services and magistrates' offices, which are open 24 hours a day, for the purpose of setting bail, making release possible.

Direct Supervision Jails

Some authors have suggested that the problems found in many jails today stem from "mismanagement, lack of fiscal support, heterogeneous inmate populations, overuse and misuse of detention, overemphasis on custodial goals, and political and public apathy."[100] Others propose that environmental and organizational elements inherent in traditional jail architecture and staffing have given rise to today's difficulties.[101] Traditional jails, say these observers, were built upon the assumption that inmates are inherently violent and potentially destructive. Hence, most of today's jails were constructed to give staff maximum control over inmates—through the use of thick walls, bars, and other architectural barriers to

Children whose mothers are behind bars in a Rhode Island facility await their turn to visit. Women in jail face special problems, many of which are associated with child care.
Gale Zucker, Stock Boston.

the free movement of inmates. Such institutions, however, also limit the correctional staff's visibility and access to many confinement areas. As a consequence, they tend to encourage just the kinds of inmate behavior that jails were meant to control. Efficient hallway patrols and expensive video technology help in overcoming the limits that old jail architecture places on supervision.

In an effort to solve many of the problems which have dogged jails in the past, a new jail management strategy emerged during the 1980s. Called **direct supervision** (or podular/ direct supervision, or PDS) this contemporary approach "joins podular/unit architecture with a participative, proactive management philosophy."[102] Often built in a system of "pods," or modular self-contained housing areas linked to one another, direct supervision jails eliminate the old physical barriers which separated staff and inmates. Gone are bars and isolated secure observation areas for officers. They are replaced by an open environment, in which inmates and correctional personnel mingle with relative freedom. In a growing number of such "new-generation" jails, large reinforced Plexiglas panels have supplanted walls and serve to separate activity areas, such as classrooms and dining halls, from one another. Soft furniture is often found throughout these institutions, and individual rooms take the place of cells, allowing inmates at least a modicum of personal privacy. In today's direct supervision jails, 16 to 46 inmates typically live in one pod, with correctional staffers present among the inmate population on an around-the-clock basis.

The first direct supervision jail opened in the 1970s in Contra Costa County, California. This 386-bed facility became a model for the nation, and other new-generation jails soon opened in Las Vegas; Portland; Reno; New York City; Bucks County, Pennsylvania; Vancouver, British Columbia; and Miami. The federal prison system opened PDS facilities in 1974–1975 in the Metropolitan Correctional Centers (MCCs) of San Diego, New York, and Chicago.

Direct supervision jails have been touted for their tendency to reduce inmate dissatisfaction and for their ability to deter rape and violence among the inmate population. By eliminating architectural barriers to staff/inmate interaction, direct supervision facilities are said to place officers back in control of institutions. While these innovative facilities are still too

Direct Supervision Jails

Temporary confinement facilities which eliminate many of the traditional barriers between inmates and correctional staff. Physical barriers in direct supervision jails are far less common than in traditional jails, allowing staff members the opportunity for greater interaction with, and control over, residents.

new to assess fully, a number of studies have already demonstrated their success at reducing the likelihood of inmate victimization. One such study[103] found that staff morale in direct supervision jails was far higher than in traditional institutions, while inmates reported reduced stress levels, and fewer inmate-on-inmate and inmate-on-staff assaults occurred in podular jails. Similarly, sexual assault, jail rape, suicide, and escape have all been found to occur far less frequently in direct supervision facilities than in traditional institutions.[104] Significantly, new-generation jails appear to reduce substantially the number of lawsuits brought by inmates and lower the incidence of adverse court-ordered judgments against jail administrators.

The most comprehensive study of direct supervision jails to date found that 114 confinement facilities across the country could be classified as direct supervision facilities.[105] The study, which attempted to survey all such jails, found that direct supervision jails had the following attributes:

1. Range in size from small jails with 24 inmates (and 12 officers on staff), to large facilities with 2,737 (and 600 correctional officers).
2. Average 591 inmates and employ 148 officers, with an inmate-to-officer ratio of 16.8:1 during a given shift.
3. Are podular in design, with an average of 47 inmates and one officer per pod at any given time.
4. Hold local, state, and federal prisoners. About 45 percent of the institutions surveyed held only local inmates, while the rest held mixed groups of inmates.
5. Varied by security level. The majority (about 59 percent) held mixed-security levels, while 26 percent were maximum-security jails. About 13 percent described themselves as medium-security facilities, and another 2 percent fit within the minimum-security category.
6. Were usually unionized. About 70 percent of direct supervision jails reported unionized staffs.

While the number of direct supervision jails seems to be rapidly growing, such facilities are not without their problems. In 1993, for example, the 238-bed Rensselaer County PDS jail in Troy, New York, experienced a disturbance "that resulted in a total loss of control . . . removal of officers from the pods—and the escape of two inmates."[106] Somewhat later, the 700-bed San Joaquin County Jail in Stockton, California, experienced numerous problems, including the escape of seven inmates.

Some authors[107] have recognized that new-generation jails are too frequently run by old-style managers and that correctional personnel sometimes lack the training needed to make the transition to the new style of supervision. Others[108] have suggested that managers of direct supervision jails, especially those at the midlevel, could benefit from clearer job descriptions and additional training. In the words of one Canadian advocate of direct supervision,[109] "[T]raining becomes particularly critical in direct supervision jails where relationships are more immediate and are more complex." Finally, recommendations have arisen from those tasked with hiring[110] that potential new staff members should be psychologically screened and that intensive use be made of preemployment interviews in order to determine the suitability of applicants for correctional officer positions in direct supervision jails.

Jails and the Future

In contrast to more visible issues confronting the justice system, such as the death penalty, gun control, the war on drugs, and big-city gangs, jails have received relatively little attention from the media and have generally escaped close public scrutiny.[111] National efforts, however, to improve the quality of jail life are under way. Some changes involve adding crucial programs for inmates. A recent American Jail Association study of drug treatment programs in jails, for example, found that "a small fraction (perhaps fewer than 10%) of inmates needing drug treatment actually receive these services."[112] Follow-up efforts were aimed at developing standards to guide jail administrators in increasing the availability of drug treatment services to inmates.

Jail industries are another growing programmatic area. The best of them serve the community while training inmates in marketable skills.[113] In an exemplary effort to humanize its megajails,[114] for example, the Los Angeles County Sheriff's Department recently opened an inmate telephone-answering service. Many calls are received by the Sheriff's Department daily, requesting information about a significant number of the county's 22,000 jail inmates. These requests for information were becoming increasingly difficult to handle due to the growing fiscal constraints facing local government. To handle the huge number of calls effectively without tying up sworn law enforcement personnel, the department began using inmates specially trained to handle incoming calls. Eighty inmates were assigned to the project, with groups of different sizes covering shifts throughout the day. Each inmate staffer went through a program designed to provide coaching in proper telephone procedures and to teach each operator how to run computer terminals containing routine data on the department's inmates. The new system is now fully in place and handles 4,000 telephone inquiries a day. The time needed to answer a call and provide information has dropped from 30 minutes under the old system to a remarkable 10 seconds today.

Another innovative program operates out of the Jackson County Detention Center (JCDC) in Kansas City, Missouri.[115] The JCDC began using citizen volunteers more than a decade ago. Today, 123 volunteers work in the facility—many of them are tutors in the general education program. Others offer substance abuse counseling, marriage counseling, and chaplain's services. Citizen volunteers have contributed 50,000 hours of service time during the past six years, at a value of over half a million dollars.

Jail boot camps, such as that run by the Harris County, Texas, probation department, are also growing in popularity. Boot camps in jail serve to give offenders who are sentenced to probationary terms a taste of confinement and the rigors of life behind bars. The Harris County CRIPP (Courts Regimented Intensive Probation Program) facility began operation in May 1991 and is located in Humble, Texas. Separate CRIPP programs are run for about 400 male and 50 female probationers.[116] The most recent comprehensive study[117] of jail boot camps found only 10 such jail-based programs in the country, although current numbers are probably higher.

Also capturing much recent attention are **regional jails**—that is, jails that are built and run using the combined resources of a variety of local jurisdictions and that have begun to replace smaller and often antiquated local jails in at least a few locations. One example of a regional jail is the Western Tidewater Regional Jail, serving the cities of Suffolk and Franklin, and the county of Isle of Wright in Virginia.[118] Regional jails, which are just beginning to come into their own, may develop more quickly in Virginia—where the state, recognizing the economies of consolidation, offers to reimburse localities up to 50 percent of the cost of building regional jails.

One final element in the unfolding saga of jail development should be mentioned: the emergence of state jail standards. Thirty-two states have set standards for municipal and county jails.[119] In 25 states, those standards are mandatory. The purpose of jail standards is to identify some basic minimum level of conditions necessary for inmate health and safety. On a national level, the Commission on Accreditation for Corrections, operated jointly by the American Correctional Association and the federal government, has developed its own set of jail standards,[120] as has the National Sheriff's Association. Both sets of standards are designed to ensure a minimal level of comfort and safety in local lockups. Increased standards, though, are costly. Local jurisdictions, already hard pressed to meet other budgetary demands, will probably be slow to upgrade their jails to meet such external guidelines, unless forced to. Ken Kerle, in a study[121] of 61 jails which was designed to test compliance with National Sheriff's Association guidelines, discovered that in many standards areas—especially those of tool control, armory planning, community resources, release preparation, and riot planning—the majority of jails were sorely out of compliance. Lack of a written plan was the most commonly cited reason for failing to meet the standards.

In what may be one of the best sets of recommendations for the future development of jails, Joel A. Thompson and G. Larry Mays[122] suggest that (1) states should provide financial aid and/or incentives to local governments for jail construction and renovation, (2) all states must develop mandatory jail standards, (3) mandatory jail inspections should become commonplace in the enforcement of standards, (4) citizens should be educated about the function and significance of jails to increase their willingness to fund new jail construction, (5)

Regional Jails

Jails that are built and run using the combined resources of a variety of local jurisdictions.

all jails need to have written policies and procedures to be used in training and to serve as a basis for a defense against lawsuits, and (6) "[c]ommunities should explore alternatives to incarceration [because] . . . [m]any jail detainees are not threats to society and should not occupy scarce and expensive cell space." Learn more about jails by visiting the American Jail Association via WebExtra! 11-3 at CJToday.com.

Private Prisons

Private Prisons

Correctional institutions operated by private firms on behalf of local and state governments.

Privatization

The movement toward the wider use of private prisons.

Throughout our nation's history, state-run prison systems have contracted with private industries for food, psychological testing, training, recreational, and other services, and it is estimated that more than three dozen states today rely on private businesses to serve a variety of correctional needs. It was only logical, therefore, that states would at some point turn to private industry for the provision of prison space. Beginning in the early 1980s, that's exactly what they did. Although the **privatization** movement was slow to catch on, it has since grown at a rapid pace. In 1986 only 2,620 prisoners could be found in privately run confinement facilities.[123] But by 1999 more than 71,000 prisoners were being held in 130 privately operated secure correctional facilities throughout 18 states and the District of Columbia—and the number of prisoners held in such institutions is expected to double over the next five years.[124] Today's privately run prisons are operated by Corrections Corporation of America (CCA), U.S. Corrections Corporation, Wackenhut Corrections Corporation, and numerous other smaller companies. According to one source, the growth rate of the private prison "industry" is over 35 percent annually[125]—comparable to the highest growth rates anywhere in the corporate sector.

Most states that use private firms to supplement their prison resources contract with such companies to provide a full range of custodial and other correctional services. (Interest in the privatization of jails is also on the increase, although space does not permit a full discussion of the issue.[126]) States contract with private companies in order to reduce overcrowding, lower operating expenses, and avoid lawsuits targeted at state officials and employees.[127] As Dale K. Sechrest and David Shichor observe, "The major arguments for privatization in the current era are economic and administrative. It is repeatedly stated that the private sector can operate prisons cheaper by providing at least the same quality of service as the public sector and [by] demonstrating more flexibility in terms of anticipating needs and devising ways to meet them."[128] A 1996 study[129] by the United States General Accounting Office, however, questioned such claims. As Sechrest and Shichor note, "The GAO study found neither cost savings nor substantial differences in the quality of services . . ."[130] between private and publicly run prisons.

Many hurdles remain before the privatization movement can effectively provide large-scale custodial supervision. The Theory into Practice box in this section addresses some of the questions about the movement toward private prisons. One of the most significant barriers to privatization lies in the fact that some states have old laws which prohibit private involvement in correctional management. Other practical hurdles exist as well. States which do contract with private firms may face the specter of strikes by guards who do not come under state laws restricting the ability of employees to strike. Moreover, since responsibility for the protection of inmate rights still lies with the state, their liability will not transfer to private corrections.[131] In today's legal climate, it is unclear whether a state can shield itself or its employees through private prison contracting, but it would appear that such shielding is unlikely to be recognized by the courts. To limit their own liability, states will probably have to oversee private operations as well as set standards for training and custody. In 1997 the U.S. Supreme Court, in the case of *Richardson* v. *McNight,*[132] made it clear that prison guards employed by a private firm are not entitled to qualified immunity from suits by prisoners charging a violation of Section 1983 of Title 42 of the U.S. Code. In the words of the Court: "While government employed prison guards may have enjoyed a kind of immunity defense arising out of their status as public employees at common law . . . [t]here is no conclusive evidence of an historical tradition of immunity for private parties carrying out these functions."[133]

Some of the potentially most serious legal issues face states that contract to hold inmates outside of their own jurisdiction. In 1996, for example, two inmates escaped from a 240-man sex offender unit run by Corrections Corporation of America under contract with the state

21st Century CJ

Jails and the Future

A number of new directions are beginning to emerge as America's jails move into the twenty-first century. Among them are the following:

1. A shift away from traditional publicly run facilities to jails that are operated by private corporations under contracts with local governments. More information on the privatization of prisons and jails is provided in this chapter.

2. An increase in the proportion of inmates who are expected to pay for at least a portion of the expenses associated with their incarceration. In 1996, for example, pretrial inmates in the Broward County (Florida) jail system began paying a $2.00 per day fee for housing and meals. Charges are deducted from inmates' commissary funds, which are contributed by themselves or family members. Inmates who feel they are unable to pay the fee are required to petition jail administrators and to demonstrate why they should not be required to pay.

3. The growing use of computer-based inmate information systems that are integrated with networks used for the administration of court schedules, docket monitoring, and for coordination with other criminal justice agencies. One jail consultant has gone so far as to claim that, because of efficient and integrated information management systems, "paperwork will be a thing of the past in the 21st century jail."[1]

4. A movement toward the professionalization of jail facilities, made possible through growing opportunities for accreditation. Accreditation programs, such as those offered through the American Correctional Association, the Commission on Accreditation for Law Enforcement Agencies, and the National Commission on Correctional Health Care, are already helping shield jail administrators and local governments from the threat of lawsuits by demonstrating adherence to professional standards.

5. A movement toward the increased professionalization of jail personnel, made possible by certification programs such as the new Jail Manager Certification Program operated by the American Jail Association. "Certified Jail Manager" status became possible for the first time in 1997, when applications and certification handbooks were distributed at the AJA's annual meeting in Salt Lake City.

6. A changing public climate—one which may soon shift away from the "get-tough" policies of the past decade toward a more pragmatic emphasis on the needs of both inmates and administrators. Inmate needs in the areas of mental health counseling, suicide prevention, and opportunities for meaningful employment will be met in an effort to facilitate institutional administration.

7. A greater use of direct supervision jails, resulting in fewer internal problems and easier administration. The increased use of direct supervision jails will heighten both inmate and staff morale in most locations where such facilities are deployed.

8. A growing use of inmate labor, as counties, communities, the nonprofit sector, and corporations begin to more fully recognize the advantages to be gained from the meaningful employment of inmates. As a consequence, more inmates will work, and those who do will be involved in an ever widening sphere of activities. The increase in inmate labor will lead to a widening of partnerships among jails, their administrators, and other community groups. Corporate employers, for example, will begin to operate more and more training programs in jails with the goal of increasing workforce efficiency.

9. A greater use of research in the field of jail operations, which will lead to better-informed and more effective programs and strategies. Research showing that more female officers mean fewer assaults overall, for example, should lead to the hiring of more women in the correctional field.

Sources: Ron Carroll, "Jails and the Criminal Justice System in the 21st Century," American Jails (March/April 1997), pp. 26–31; Susan W. McCampbell, "The Paying Prisoner," American Jails (March/April 1997), pp. 37–43; Cindy Malm, "AJA Jail Manager Certification Program," American Jails (March/April 1997), p. 99; Rod Miller, "Inmate Labor in the 21st Century," American Jails (March/April 1997), pp. 45–49; Joseph R. Rowan, "Corrections in the 21st Century," American Jails (March/April 1997), pp. 32–36.

Theory Into Practice

American Jail Association Code of Ethics for Jail Officers

As an officer employed in a detention/correctional capacity, I swear (or affirm) to be a good citizen and a credit to my community, state, and nation at all times. I will abstain from all questionable behavior which might bring disrepute to the agency for which I work, my family, my community, and my associates. My lifestyle will be above and beyond reproach and I will constantly strive to set an example of a professional who performs his/her duties according to the laws of our country, state, and community and the policies, procedures, written and verbal orders, and regulations of the agency for which I work.

On the job I promise to:

Keep The institution secure so as to safeguard my community and the lives of the staff, inmates, and visitors on the premises.

Work With each individual firmly and fairly without regard to rank, status, or condition.

Maintain A positive demeanor when confronted with stressful situations of scorn, ridicule, danger, and/or chaos.

Report Either in writing or by word of mouth to the proper authorities those things which should be reported, and keep silent about matters which are to remain confidential according to the laws and rules of the agency and government.

Manage And supervise the inmates in an evenhanded and courteous manner.

Refrain At all times from becoming personally involved in the lives of the inmates and their families.

Treat All visitors to the jail with politeness and respect and do my utmost to ensure that they observe the jail regulations.

Take Advantage of all education and training opportunities designed to assist me to become a more competent officer.

Communicate With people in or outside of the jail, whether by phone, written word, or word of mouth, in such a way so as not to reflect in a negative manner upon my agency.

Contribute To a jail environment which will keep the inmate involved in activities designed to improve his/her attitude and character.

Support All activities of a professional nature through membership and participation that will continue to elevate the status of those who operate our nation's jails.

Do my best through word and deed to present an image to the public at large of a jail professional, committed to progress for an improved and enlightened criminal justice system.

Source: *The American Jail Association,* Code of Ethics for Jail Officers *as adopted January 10, 1991 (Hagerstown, MD: The Association, 1991). Reprinted with permission.*

Inside a direct supervision jail. Inmates and officers can mingle in this Hillsborough County, New Hampshire, jail. **Rick Friedman, Black Star.**

Theory Into Practice

The Debate over Private Prisons—Some Questions Which Remain

◆Can the government delegate its powers to incarcerate persons to a private firm?

◆Can a private firm deprive persons of their liberty and exercise coercive authority, perhaps through use of deadly force?

◆Who would be legally liable in the event of lawsuits?

◆Who would be responsible for maintaining the prison if the private employees go on strike?

◆Would a private company have the right to refuse to accept certain

types of inmates, for example, those with AIDS?

◆If a private firm went bankrupt, who would be responsible for the inmates and the facility?

◆Could a private company reduce staff salaries or hire nonunion members as a way of reducing costs?

◆Would the "profit motive" operate to the detriment of the government or the inmates, either by keeping inmates in prison who should be released or by reducing services to a

point at which inmates, guards, and the public were endangered?

◆What options would a government with no facility of its own have if it became dissatisfied with the performance of the private firm?

◆Is it appropriate for the government to circumvent the public's right to vote to increase its debt ceiling (to build new prisons)?

Source: *Bureau of Justice Statistics,* Report to the Nation on Crime and Justice, *2nd ed. (Washington, D.C.: U.S. Department of Justice, 1988).*

of Oregon. Problems immediately arose because the CCA unit was located near Houston, Texas—not in Oregon, where the men had been originally sentenced to confinement. Following the escape, Texas officials were unsure whether they even had arrest power over the former prisoners, since they had not committed any crimes in Texas. Moreover, while prison escape is a crime under Texas law, the law only applies to state-run facilities—not to private facilities where correctional personnel are not employed by the state nor empowered in any official capacity by state law. Harris County (Texas) prosecutor John Holmes explained the situation this way: "They have not committed the offense of escape under Texas law . . . and

The Corrections Corporation of America's Houston Processing Center—one of a growing number of private prison facilities across the country. Private prisons may be the way of the future. **Brett Coomer, AP/Wide World Photos.**

the only reason at all that they're subject to being arrested and were arrested was because during their leaving the facility, they assaulted a guard and took his motor vehicle. That we can charge them with and have."[134]

Opponents of the movement toward privatization cite these and many other issues. They claim that, aside from legal concerns, cost reductions via the use of private facilities can only be achieved by lowering standards. They fear a return to the inhumane conditions of early jails, as private firms seek to turn prisons into profitmaking operations. For states that do choose to contract with private firms, the National Institute of Justice recommends a "regular and systematic sampling" of former inmates to appraise prison conditions, as well as "on-site inspections at least every year" of each privately run institution. State personnel serving as monitors should be stationed in large facilities, says NIJ, and a "meticulous review" of all services should be conducted prior to the contract renewal date.[135] You can learn more about prison privatization via WebExtra! 11-4 at CJToday.com

Summary

Prisons are long-term secure confinement facilities in which convicted offenders serve time as punishment for breaking the law. Jails, in contrast, are short-term confinement facilities which were originally intended to hold suspects following arrest and pending trial. Differences between the two types of institutions have begun to blur, however, as large and medium-size jails across the country are being increasingly called upon to house offenders who have been convicted of relatively minor crimes and to accommodate a portion of our country's overflowing prison population.

Today's overcrowded prisons are largely the result of historical efforts to humanize the treatment of offenders. "Doing time for crime" is our modern answer to the corporeal punishments of centuries past. Even so, contemporary corrections is far from a panacea, and questions remain about the conditions of imprisonment in today's correctional facilities. Many prisons are dangerously overcrowded, and new ones are expensive to build. The emphasis upon security, which is so characteristic of correctional staff members and prison administrators, leaves little room for capable treatment programs. Moreover, an end to crowding is nowhere in sight, and a new just deserts philosophy strongly influences today's correctional policy. The just deserts philosophy is characterized by a "get-tough" attitude which continues to swell prison populations even as it reduces opportunities for change among individual inmates. It is also a highly pragmatic philosophy, based as it is upon studies demonstrating the clear likelihood of recidivism among correctional clients and upon a strong belief that "nothing works" to rehabilitate criminal offenders.

As a result of all these considerations, today's imprisonment practices rest upon a policy of frustration. Prisons exist in a kind of limbo, continuing their role as warehouses for the untrusted and the unreformable. The return of prison industries, heightened interest in efficient technologies of secure imprisonment, and court-ordered reforms are all signs that society has given up any hope of successful large-scale reformation among inmate populations.

Discussion Questions

1. What do you think will be the future of the prison industry? Describe the future you envision. On what do you base your predictions?
2. What do you see as the role of private prisons? What will be the state of private prisons two or three decades from now?
3. Explain the pros and cons of the present just deserts model of corrections. Do you believe that new rehabilitative models will be developed which will make just deserts a thing of the past? If so, on what will they be based?
4. What solutions, if any, do you see to the present overcrowded conditions of many prison systems? How might changes in the law help ease overcrowding? Are such changes a workable strategy? Why or why not?

Web Quest!

Visit the Corrections Connection on the World Wide Web (www.corrections.com). What are some of the many features available at this site?

Explore the "Legal Issues" bulletin board available at the Corrections Connection in order to learn about the latest legal issues of concern to corrections professionals. What are some of those issues?

Select, enter, and participate in one of the "Live Interaction" chat rooms available at the site. What topics are being discussed?

If no one is in the chat room when you enter, then visit the "Message Boards" and list the most recent topics being discussed. Submit this information to your instructor if requested to do so.

Library Extras!

The Library Extras! listed here complement the WebExtras! found throughout this chapter. Library Extras! may be accessed on the Web at CJToday.com.

Library Extra 11-1. *Census of State and Federal Correctional Facilities* (BJS, current volume).
Library Extra! 11-2. *Prison and Jail Inmates* (BJS, current volume).
Library Extra! 11-3. *Two Views of Imprisonment Policies* (NIJ, July 1997).

References

1. As cited in the National Conference on Prison Industries, *Discussions and Recommendations* (Washington, D.C.: U.S. Government Printing Office, 1986), p. 23.
2. Allen J. Beck, *Prisoners in 1999* (Washington, D.C.: Bureau of Justice Statistics, 2000).
3. Ibid.
4. Robert M. Carter, Richard A. McGee, and E. Kim Nelson, *Corrections in America* (Philadelphia: J. B. Lippincott, 1975), pp. 122–123.
5. Department of Justice press release, "The Nation's Prison Population Grew by 60,000 Inmates Last Year," August 15, 1999.
6. Bureau of Justice Statistics, *National Corrections Reporting Program 1985* (Washington, D.C.: BJS, December 1990), p. 54.
7. Ibid.
8. "The Nation's Prison Population Grew by 60,000 Inmates Last Year."
9. American Correctional Association, "Correctional Officers in Adult Systems," in *Vital Statistics in Corrections* (Laurel, MD: ACA, 2000).
10. Ibid.
11. Ibid.
12. Ibid. *Note:* "Other" minorities round out the percentages to a total of 100 percent.
13. Ibid.
14. See, for example, Harry Elmer Barnes and Negley K. Teeters, *New Horizons in Criminology*, 3rd ed. (Englewood Cliffs, NJ: Prentice Hall, 1959).
15. Although many other states require inmates to work on road maintenance, and such inmates are typically supervised by armed guards, Alabama became the first state in modern times to shackle workers.
16. Lori Sharn and Shannon Tangonan, "Chain

Gangs Back in Alabama," *USA Today*, May 4, 1995, p. 3A.
17. Ibid.
18. See "Back on the Chain Gang: Florida Becomes Third State to Resurrect Forced Labor," Associated Press, November 22, 1995.
19. "Chain Gang Hits the Road in Arizona," *USA Today*, May 16, 1995, page 3A.
20. "Back on the Chain Gang."
21. Peter Baker, "Allen Crime Plan Ends Parole; Expensive Va. Proposal Would Strain Budget, Require More Prisons," *Washington Post* online, August 17, 1994.
22. "U.S. House Votes to Make Life Tougher for Prisoners," Reuters wire services, February 10, 1995.
23. "The Extinction of Inmate Privileges," *Corrections Compendium*, June 1995, p. 5.
24. Ibid.
25. The state of Washington is generally credited with having been the first state to pass a three-strikes law by voter initiative (in 1993).
26. For a good overview of the topic, see David Shichor and Dale K. Sechrest, *Three Strikes and You're Out: Vengeance as Public Policy* (Thousand Oaks, CA: Sage, 1996).
27. David S. Broder, "When Tough Isn't Smart," *Washington Post* online, March 24, 1994.
28. "The Klaas Case and the Crime Bill" *Washington Post* online, February 21, 1994.
29. Bruce Smith, "Crime Solutions," Associated Press online, January 11, 1995.
30. Mark Jewell, "Three Strikes Laws," Associated Press online, northern edition, February 21, 1994.
31. Greg Wees, "Inmate Populations Expected to

Increase 43% by 2002," *Corrections Compendium,* April 1996.

32. Amanda Wunder, "Corrections Systems Must Bear the Burden of New Legislation," *Corrections Compendium,* March 1995.

33. The Campaign for an Effective Crime Policy, *The Impact of Three Strikes and You're Out Laws: What Have We Learned?* (Washington, D.C.: CECP, 1997).

34. David Lawsky, "Prison Wardens Decry Overcrowding, Survey Says," Reuters online, December 21, 1994.

35. Beck, *Prisoners in 1999.*

36. Darrell K. Gillard, "Prison and Jail Inmates at Midyear 1998" (Washington, D.C.: Bureau of Justice Statistics, 1999).

37. Beck, *Prisoners in 1999;* and "Prison Expansion Nears Completion," United Press International wire services, southwest edition, June 12, 1995.

38. Beck, *Prisoners in 1999.*

39. Beck, *Prisoners in 1999.*

40. Adapted from U.S. Department of Justice, *Report to the Nation on Crime and Justice,* 2nd ed. (Washington, DC: U.S. Government Printing Office, 1988), p. 108.

41. *Rhodes* v. *Chapman,* 452 U.S. 337 (1981).

42. James Lieber, "The American Prison: A Tinderbox," *New York Times* magazine, March 8, 1981.

43. D. Greenberg, "The Incapacitative Effect of Imprisonment, Some Estimates," *Law and Society Review,* vol. 9 (1975), pp. 541–580. See also Jacqueline Cohen, "Incapacitating Criminals: Recent Research Findings," *Research in Brief* (Washington, D.C.: National Institute of Justice, December 1983).

44. For information on identifying dangerous repeat offenders, see M. Chaiken and J. Chaiken, "Selecting Career Criminals for Priority Prosecution," final report (Cambridge, MA: Abt Associates, 1987).

45. J. Monahan, *Predicting Violent Behavior: An Assessment of Clinical Techniques* (Beverly Hills, CA: Sage Publications, 1981).

46. S. Van Dine, J. P. Conrad, and S. Dinitz, *Restraining the Wicked: The Incapacitation of the Dangerous Offender* (Lexington, MA: Lexington Books, 1979).

47. Paul Gendreau, Tracy Little, and Claire Goggin, "A Meta-Analysis of the Predictors of Adult Offender Recidivism: What Works!" *Criminology,* vol. 34, no. 4 (November 1996), pp. 575–607.

48. In the case of *Lynce* v. *Mathis,* No. 95-7452 (1997).

49. "Florida Releases Prisoners, Issues Warnings to Victims," Associated Press, March 12, 1997.

50. G. Camp, "Stopping Escapes: Perimeter Security," *Prison Construction Bulletin* (Washington, D.C.: National Institute of Justice, 1987).

51. Adapted from Grizzle et al., "Measuring Corrections Performance," NIJ Grant, 78-NI-AX-0130 (1980), p. 31.

52. U.S. Bureau of Prisons, *Facilities,* Web posted at www.bop.gov/map.html.

53. An older system, in which the terms "Level 1," "Level 2," and so on were used, was abandoned around 1990 and officially replaced with the new terminology used here.

54. Most of the information in this section comes from telephone conversations with and faxed information from the Federal Bureau of Prisons, August 25, 1995.

55. For additional information, see Dennis Cauchon, "The Alcatraz of the Rockies," *USA Today,* November 16, 1994, p. 6A.

56. *Source:* BOP World Wide Web site, www.bop. gov. Accessed, November 3, 2000.

57. Ibid.

58. "Congress OKs Inmates Fees to Offset Costs of Prison," *Criminal Justice Newsletter* (October 15, 1992), p. 6.

59. National Institute of Corrections, "National Academy of Corrections: Outreach Training Programs" (July 1987).

60. National Institute of Corrections, "Correctional Training Programs" (July 1987).

61. Much of the information in this section comes from Allen J. Beck, *Prison and Jail Inmates at Midyear 1999* (Washington, D.C.: Bureau of Justice Statistics, 2000).

62. Ibid.

63. Department of Justice press release, "Incarceration Rate More Than Doubles in Dozen Years," March 14, 1999.

64. Craig A. Perkins, James J. Stephan, and Allen J. Beck, *Jails and Jail Inmates 1993–94* (Washington, D.C.: Bureau of Justice Statistics, 1995).

65. Ibid.

66. Ibid.

67. Caroline Wolf Harlow, *Profile of Jail Inmates, 1996* (Washington, D.C.: Bureau of Justice Statistics, 1998).

68. U.S. Department of Justice, *Report to the Nation on Crime and Justice,* 2nd ed., p. 106.

69. Ibid.

70. See Gale Holland, "L.A. Jail Makes Delayed Debut," *USA Today,* January 27, 1997, p. 3A.

71. See Dale Stockton, "Cook County Illinois Sheriff's Office," *Police* (October 1996), pp. 40–43. The Cook County Department of Correction operates 10 separate jails which house approximately 9,000 inmates. More than 2,800 correctional officers are employed by the department.

72. U.S. Department of Justice, press release, *The Nation's Jails Hold Record 490,442 Inmates,* May 1, 1995.

73. Ibid.

74. *Prison and Jail Inmates at Midyear 1999.*

75. William Reginald Mills and Heather Barrett, "Meeting the Special Challenge of Providing Health Care to Women Inmates in the '90's," *American Jails,* vol. 4, no. 3 (September/October 1990), p. 55.

76. Ibid.

77. Ibid., p. 21.

78. Ibid.

79. American Correctional Association, *Vital Statistics in Corrections.*

80. Mills and Barrett, "Meeting the Special Challenge," p. 55.

81. Ibid.

82. Ibid.

83. Linda L. Zupan "Women Corrections Officers in the Nation's Largest Jails," *American Jails* (January/February 1991), pp. 59–62.

84. Ibid., p. 11.

85. Linda L. Zupan, "Women Corrections Officers

in Local Jails," paper presented at the annual meeting of the Academy of Criminal Justice Sciences, Nashville, Tennessee, March 1991.

86. Ibid., p. 6.

87. "Jail Overcrowding in Houston Results in Release of Inmates," *Criminal Justice Newsletter,* October 15, 1990, p. 5.

88. Bureau of Justice Statistics, *Census of Local Jails 1988* (Washington, D.C.: BJS, 1991), p. 31.

89. Kathleen Maguire and Ann L. Pastore, *Sourcebook of Criminal Justice Statistics 1994* (Washington, D.C.: U.S. Government Printing Office, 1995).

90. Ibid.

91. *Prison and Jail Inmates at Midyear 1999.*

92. Bureau of Justice Statistics, *Census of Local Jails 1988* (Washington, D.C.: BJS, 1991), p. 15.

93. Randall Guynes, *Nation's Jail Managers Assess Their Problems* (Washington, D.C.: National Institute of Justice, 1988).

94. Carol J. Casteneda, "Arizona Sheriff Walking Tall, But Some Don't Like His Style," *USA Today,* May 26, 1995, p. 7A.

95. Beck, *Prisoners in 1999.*

96. U.S. Department of Justice, *The Nation's Jails Hold Record 490,442 Inmates.*

97. As identified in George P. Wilson and Harvey L. McMurray, *System Assessment of Jail Overcrowding Assumptions,* paper presented at the annual meeting of the Academy of Criminal Justice Sciences, Nashville, Tennessee, March 1991.

98. Andy Hall, *Systemwide Strategies to Alleviate Jail Crowding* (Washington, D.C.: National Institute of Justice, 1987).

99. Ibid.

100. Linda L. Zupan and Ben A. Menke, "The New Generation Jail: An Overview," in Joel A. Thompson and G. Larry Mays, eds., *American Jails: Public Policy Issues* (Chicago: Nelson-Hall, 1991), p. 180.

101. Ibid.

102. Herbert R. Sigurdson, Billy Wayson, and Gail Funke, "Empowering Middle Managers of Direct Supervision Jails," *American Jails* (Winter 1990), p. 52.

103. Byron Johnson, "Exploring Direct Supervision: A Research Note," *American Jails* (March/April 1994), pp. 63–64.

104. H. Sigurdson, *The Manhattan House of Detention: A Study of Modular Direct Supervision* (Washington, D.C.: National Institute of Corrections, 1985). For similar conclusions, see Robert Conroy, Wantland J. Smith, and Linda L. Zupan, "Officer Stress in the Direct Supervision Jail: A Preliminary Case Study," *American Jails* (November/December 1991), p. 36.

105. Brian Dawe and James Kirby, "Direct Supervision Jails and Minimum Staffing," *American Jails* (March/April 1995), pp. 97–100.

106. W. Raymond Nelson and Russell M. Davis, "Popular Direct Supervision: The First Twenty Years," *American Jails* (July/August 1995), p. 17.

107. Jerry W. Fuqua, "New Generation Jails: Old Generation Management," *American Jails* (March/April 1991), pp. 80–83.

108. Sigurdson, Wayson, and Funke, "Empowering Middle Managers."

109. Duncan J. McCulloch and Time Stiles, "Technology and the Direct Supervision Jail," *American Jails* (Winter 1990), pp. 97–102.

110. Susan W. McCampbell, "Direct Supervision: Looking for the Right People," *American Jails* (November/December 1990), pp. 68–69.

111. For a good review of the future of American jails, see Ron Carroll, "Jails and the Criminal Justice System in the 21st Century," *American Jails* (March/April 1997), pp. 26–31.

112. Robert L. May II, Roger H. Peters, and William D. Kearns "The Extent of Drug Treatment Programs in Jails: A Summary Report," *American Jails* (September/October 1990), pp. 32–34.

113. See, for example, John W. Dietler, "Jail Industries: The Best Thing That Can Happen to a Sheriff," *American Jails* (July/August 1990), pp. 80–83.

114. Robert Osborne, "Los Angeles County Sheriff Opens New Inmate Answering Service," *American Jails* (July/August 1990), pp. 61–62.

115. Nancy E. Bond and Dave Smith, "The Challenge: Community Involvement in Corrections," *American Jails* (November/December 1992), pp. 19–20.

116. Robert J. Hunter, "A Locally Operated Boot Camp," *American Jails* (July/August 1994), pp. 13–15.

117. James Austin, Michael Jones, and Melissa Bolyard, *The Growing Use of Jail Boot Camps: The Current State of the Art* (Washington, D.C.: National Institute of Justice, October 1993).

118. See J. R. Dewan, "Regional Jail—The New Kid on the Block," *American Jails* (May/June 1995), pp. 70–72.

119. Tom Rosazza, "Jail Standards: Focus on Change," *American Jails* (November/December 1990), pp. 84–87.

120. American Correctional Association, *Manual of Standards for Adult Local Detention Facilities,* 3rd ed. (College Park, MD: ACA, 1991).

121. Ken Kerle, "National Sheriff's Association Jail Audit Review," *American Jails* (Spring 1987), pp. 13–21.

122. Joel A. Thompson and G. Larry Mays, "Paying the Piper but Changing the Tune: Policy Changes and Initiatives for the American Jail," in Joel A. Thompson and G. Larry Mays, eds., *American Jails: Public Policy Issues* (Chicago: Nelson-Hall, 1991), pp. 240–246.

123. Bureau of Justice Statistics, *Report to the Nation on Crime and Justice,* p. 119. See also Judith C. Hackett et al., "Contracting for the Operation of Prisons and Jails," National Institute of Justice, *Research in Brief* (June 1987), p. 2.

124. *Prisoners in 1999,* and Eric Bates, "Private Prisons: Over the Next 5 Years Analysts Expect the Private Share of the Prison 'Market' to More than Double," *The Nation,* vol. 266, no. 1 (1998), pp. 11–18.

125. Professor Charles Thomas, as cited in Joan Thompson, "Private Prisons," The Associated Press wire services, November 5, 1996.

126. See, for example, G. Larry Mays and Tara Gray, *Privatization and the Provision of Correctional Services: Context and Consequences* (Cincinnati, OH: Anderson, 1996); Dale K. Sechrest and

David Shichor, "Private Jails: Locking Down the Issues," *American Jails* (March/April 1997), pp. 9–18; R. K. Walla, "Privatization of Jails: Is It A Good Move?" *American Jails,* (September/ October 1995), pp. 73–74.

127. Gary Fields, "Privatized Prisons Pose Problems," *USA Today,* November 11, 1996, p. 3A.

128. Dale K. Sechrest and David Shichor, "Private Jails: Locking Down the Issues," *American Jails* (March/April 1997), pp. 9–18.

129. U.S. General Accounting Office, *Private and Public Prisons: Studies Comparing Operational Costs and/or Quality of Service* (Washington, D.C.: U.S. Government Printing Office, 1996).

130. Sechrest and Shichor, "Private Jails: Locking Down the Issues," p. 10.

131. For a more detailed discussion of this issue, see Ira Robbins, *The Legal Dimensions of Private Incarceration* (Chicago: American Bar Foundation, 1988).

132. *Richardson* v. *McKnight,* 117 S.Ct. 2100, 138 L. Ed 2d 540 (1997).

133. Ibid., syllabus.

134. As quoted in Joan Thompson, "Private Prisons," Associated Press wire services, November 5, 1996.

135. Hackett et al., "Contracting for the Operation of Prisons and Jails," p. 6.

CHAPTER 12

Prison Life

"Our policy of confining large numbers of offenders seems to have been ineffective in reducing the violent crime rate."
—John H. Kramer, Executive Director, Pennsylvania Commission on Sentencing

"The person of a prisoner sentenced to imprisonment in the State prison is under the protection of the law, and any injury to his person, not authorized by law, is punishable in the same manner as if he were not convicted or sentenced."
—California Penal Code, Section 2650

We Must Remember Always That The "Doors Of Prisons Swing Both Ways."
—Mary Belle Harris, First Federal Woman Warden[1]

CHAPTER OUTLINE

- Realities of Prison Life: The Male Inmate's World
- Realities of Prison Life: The Staff World
- Prison Riots
- Realities of Prison Life: Women in Prison
- Prisoner Rights
- Issues Facing Prisons Today

—Armineh Johannes, SIPA Press.

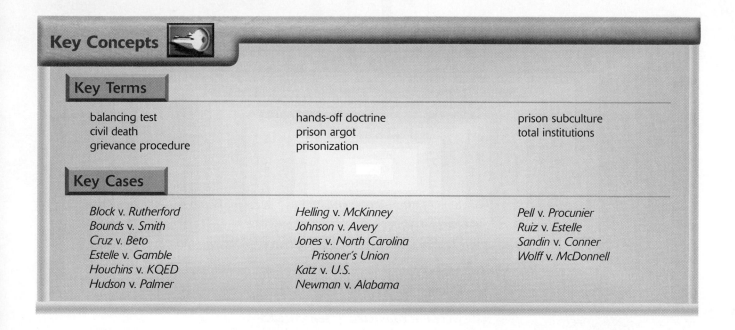

Key Concepts

Key Terms

balancing test
civil death
grievance procedure

hands-off doctrine
prison argot
prisonization

prison subculture
total institutions

Key Cases

Block v. Rutherford
Bounds v. Smith
Cruz v. Beto
Estelle v. Gamble
Houchins v. KQED
Hudson v. Palmer

Helling v. McKinney
Johnson v. Avery
Jones v. North Carolina
    Prisoner's Union
Katz v. U.S.
Newman v. Alabama

Pell v. Procunier
Ruiz v. Estelle
Sandin v. Conner
Wolff v. McDonnell

AUDIO EXTRA! Hear the author discuss this chapter at **cjtoday.com**

Realities of Prison Life: The Male Inmate's World

For the first 150 years of their existence, prisons and prison life could be described by the phrase "out of sight, out of mind." Very few citizens cared about prison conditions, and those unfortunate enough to be locked away were regarded as lost to the world. By the mid-1900s, beginning with the treatment era, such attitudes started to change. Concerned citizens began to offer their services to prison administrations, neighborhoods began accepting work-release prisoners and halfway houses, and social scientists initiated a serious study of prison life.

This chapter describes the realities of prison life today, including prisoner lifestyles, prison subcultures, sexuality in prison, prison violence, and inmate "rights" and grievance procedures. We will discuss both the world of the inmate and the staff world. A separate section on women in prison details the social structure of women's prisons, daily life in such facilities, and the various types of female inmates. We turn now to early research on prison life and will quickly move on to a discussion of the inmate world.

Research on Prison Life—Total Institutions

In 1935 Hans Reimer, then chairman of the Department of Sociology at Indiana University, set the tone for studies of prison life when he voluntarily served three months in prison as an incognito participant observer.[2] Reimer reported the results of his studies to the American Prison Association, stimulating many other, albeit less spectacular, efforts to examine prison life. Other early studies include Donald Clemmer's *The Prison Community* (1940),[3] Gresham M. Sykes's *The Society of Captives: A Study of a Maximum Security Prison* (1958),[4] Richard A. Cloward and Donald R. Cressey's *Theoretical Studies in Social Organization of the Prison* (1960),[5] and Donald R. Cressey's *The Prison: Studies in Institutional Organization and Change* (1961).[6]

These studies and others focused primarily on maximum-security prisons for men. They treated correctional institutions as formal or complex organizations and employed the analytical techniques of organizational sociology, industrial psychology, and administrative science.[7] As modern writers on prisons have observed, "[T]he prison was compared to a primitive society, isolated from the outside world, functionally integrated by a delicate system of mechanisms, which kept it precariously balanced between anarchy and accommodation."[8]

Another approach to the study of prison life was developed by Erving Goffman who coined the term **total institutions** in a 1961 study of prisons and mental hospitals.[9] Goffman described total institutions as places where the same people work, play, eat, sleep, and recreate together on a daily basis. Such places include prisons, concentration camps, mental hospitals, seminaries, and other facilities in which residents are cut off from the larger society either forcibly or willingly. Total institutions are small societies. They evolve their own distinctive values and styles of life and place pressures on residents to fulfill rigidly proscribed behavioral roles.

Generally speaking, the work of prison researchers built upon findings of other social scientists who discovered that any group with similar characteristics, subject to confinement in the same place at the same time, develops its own subculture with specific components that govern hierarchy, behavioral patterns, values, and so on. Prison subcultures, described in the next section, also provide the medium through which prison values are communicated and expectations made known.

Prison Subcultures

Two social realities coexist in prison settings. One is the official structure of rules and procedures put in place by the wider society and enforced by prison staff. The other is the more informal but decidedly more powerful inmate world.[10] The inmate world, best described by its pervasive immediacy in the lives of inmates, is controlled by **prison subculture.** The realities of prison life—including a large and often densely packed inmate population which must look to the prison environment for all its needs—mean that prison subculture is not easily subject to the control of prison authorities.

Prison subcultures develop independently of the plans of prison administrators, and inmates entering prison discover a social world not mentioned in the handbooks prepared by correctional staff. Inmate concerns, values, roles, and even language weave a web of social reality into which new inmates step and in which they must participate. Those who try to remain aloof soon find themselves subjected to dangerous ostracism and may even be suspected of being in league with the prison administration.

The socialization of new inmates into the prison subculture has been described as a process of prisonization.[11] **Prisonization** refers to the learning of convict values, attitudes, roles, and even language. When the process is complete, new inmates have become "cons." The values of the inmate social system are embodied in a code whose violations can produce sanctions ranging from ostracism and avoidance to physical violence and homicide.[12] Sykes and Messinger[13] recognize five elements of the prison code:

1. Don't interfere with the interests of other inmates. Never rat on a con.
2. Don't lose your head. Play it cool and do your own time.
3. Don't exploit inmates. Don't steal. Don't break your word. Be right.
4. Don't whine. Be a man.
5. Don't be a sucker. Don't trust the guards or staff.

Stanton Wheeler closely examined the concept of prisonization in a study of the Washington State Reformatory.[14] Wheeler found that the degree of prisonization experienced by inmates tends to vary over time. He described changing levels of inmate commitment to prison norms and values by way of a "U-shaped" curve. When an inmate first enters prison, Wheeler said, the conventional values of outside society are of paramount importance. As time passes, the lifestyle of the prison is adopted. However, within the half-year prior to release, most inmates begin to demonstrate a renewed appreciation for conventional values.

Different prisons share aspects of a common inmate culture,[15] so that prison-wise inmates who enter a new facility far from their home will already know the ropes. **Prison argot,** or language, provides one example of how widespread prison subculture can be. The terms used to describe inmate roles in one institution are generally understood in others. The word *rat,* for example, is prison slang for an informer. Popularized by crime movies of the 1950s, the term *rat* is understood today by members of the wider society. Other words common to prison argot are shown in the accompanying Theory Into Practice box.

Total Institutions

Enclosed facilities, separated from society both socially and physically, where the inhabitants share all aspects of their lives on a daily basis.

Prison Subculture

The values and behavioral patterns characteristic of prison inmates. Prison subculture has been found to have surprising consistencies across the country.

Prisonization

The process whereby newly institutionalized individuals come to accept prison lifestyles and criminal values. While many inmates begin their prison experience with only a modicum of values supportive of criminal behavior, the socialization experience they undergo while incarcerated leads to a much wider acceptance of such values.

Prison Argot

The slang characteristic of prison subcultures and prison life.

Theory Into Practice

Prison Argot—The Language of Confinement

Writers who have studied prison life often comment on the use by prisoners of a special language or slang, which is termed prison *argot*. This language generally refers to the roles assigned by prison culture to types of inmates as well as to prison activities. This box lists a few of the many words and phrases identified in various studies by different authors. The first group of words are characteristic of male prisons; the last few have been used in prisons for women.

Men's Prison Slang

Ace duce: Best friend

Badge (or bull, hack, "the man," or screw): A correctional officer

Banger (or burner, shank, or sticker): A knife

Billys: White men

Boneyard: Conjugal visiting area

Cat-J (or J-cat): A prisoner in need of psychological or psychiatric therapy or medication

Cellie: Cellmate

Chester: Child molester

Dog: Homeboy or friend

Fag: A male inmate who is believed to be a "natural" or "born" homosexual

Featherwood: A peckerwood's woman

Fish: A newly arrived inmate

Gorilla: An inmate who uses force to take what he wants from others

Homeboy: A prisoner from one's hometown or neighborhood

Ink: Tattoos

Lemon squeezer: An inmate who has an unattractive "girlfriend"

Man walking: A phrase used to signal that a guard is coming

Merchant (or peddler): One who sells when he should give

Peckerwood (or wood): A white prisoner

Punk: A male inmate who is forced into a submissive or feminine role during homosexual relations

Rat (or snitch): An inmate who squeals (provides information about other inmates to the prison administration)

Schooled: Knowledgeable in the ways of prison life

Shakedown: A search of a cell or of a work area

Tree jumper: Rapist

Turn out: To rape or make into a punk

Wolf: A male inmate who assumes the aggressive masculine role during homosexual relations

Women's Prison Slang

Cherry (or Cherrie): A female inmate who has not yet been introduced to lesbian activities

Fay Broad: A white female inmate

Femme (or Mommy): A female inmate who plays the female role during lesbian relations

Safe: The vagina, especially when used for hiding contraband

Stud Broad (or Daddy): A female inmate who assumes the role of a male during lesbian relations

Sources: Gresham Sykes, The Society of Captives *(Princeton, NJ: Princeton University Press, 1958); Rose Giallombardo*, Society of Women: A Study of a Woman's Prison *(New York: John Wiley, 1966); and Richard A. Cloward et al.*, Theoretical Studies in Social Organization of the Prison *(New York: Social Science Research Council, 1960). For a more contemporary listing of prison slang terms, see Reinhold Aman*, Hillary Clinton's Pen Pal: A Guide to Life and Lingo in Federal Prison *(Santa Rosa, CA: Maledicta Press, 1996); Jerome Washington*, Iron House: Stories from the Yard *(Ann Arbor, MI: QED Press, 1994); Morrie Camhi*, The Prison Experience *(Boston: Charles Tuttle Co., 1989); and Harold Long*, Survival In Prison *(Port Townsend, WA: Loompanics Unlimited, 1990).*

Some criminologists have suggested that inmate codes are simply a reflection of general criminal values. If so, they are brought to the institution rather than created there. Either way, the power and pervasiveness of the inmate code require convicts to conform to the worldview held by the majority of prisoners. View an online prisoner's dictionary (which is frequently updated) via **WebExtra!** 12-1 at CJToday.com.

The Evolution of Subcultures

Prison subculture is constantly changing. Like any other American subculture, it evolves to reflect the concerns and experiences of the wider culture, reacting to new crime-control strategies and embracing novel opportunities for crime and its commission. The AIDS epidemic of the last two decades, for example, has brought about changes in prison sexual behavior, at least for a segment of the inmate population, while the emergence of a high-tech criminal group has further differentiated convict types. Because of such changes, John Irwin, by the time he was about to complete his now-famous study entitled *The Felon* (1970), expressed worry that his book was already obsolete.[16] *The Felon,* for all its insights into prison subculture, follows in the descriptive tradition of works by Clemmer and Reimer. Irwin recognized that by 1970 prison subcultures had begun to reflect cultural changes sweeping America. A decade later other investigators of prison subculture were able to write, "It was no longer meaningful to speak of a single inmate culture or even subculture. By the time we began our field research . . . it was clear that the unified, oppositional convict culture, found in the sociological literature on prisons, no longer existed."[17]

Stastny and Tyrnauer, describing prison life at Washington State Penitentiary in 1982, discovered four clearly distinguishable subcultures: (1) official, (2) traditional, (3) reform, and (4) revolutionary. Official culture was promoted by the staff and by administrative rules of the institution. Enthusiastic participants in official culture were mostly correctional officers and other staff members, although inmates were also well aware of the normative expectations official culture imposed on them. Official culture impacted the lives of inmates primarily through the creation of a prisoner hierarchy based upon sentence length, prison jobs, and the "perks" which cooperation with the dictates of official culture could produce. Traditional prison culture, described by early writers on the subject, still existed, but its participants spent much of their time lamenting the decline of the convict code among younger prisoners. Reform culture was unique at Washington State Penitentiary. It was the result of a brief experiment with inmate self-government during the early 1970s. Elements of prison life which evolved during the experimental period sometimes survived the termination of self-government and were eventually institutionalized in what Stastny and Tyrnauer call reform culture. Such elements included inmate participation in civic-style clubs, citizen involvement in the daily activities of the prison, banquets, and inmate speaking tours. Revolutionary culture built upon the radical political rhetoric of the disenfranchised and found a ready audience among minority prisoners who saw themselves as victims of society's basic unfairness. Although they did not participate in it, revolutionary inmates understood traditional prison culture and generally avoided running afoul of its rules.

The Functions of Prison Society

How do social scientists and criminologists explain the existence of prison societies? Although people around the world live in groups and create their own cultures, in few cases does the intensity of human interaction approach the level found in prisons. As we discussed in Chapter 11, today's prisons are overcrowded places where inmates can find no retreat from the constant demands of staff and the pressures brought by fellow prisoners. Prison subculture, according to some authors, is fundamentally an adaptation to deprivation and confinement. It is a way of addressing the psychological, social, physical, and sexual needs of prisoners living within the context of a highly controlled and regimented institutional setting.

What are some of the deprivations prisoners experience? In *The Society of Captives,* Gresham Sykes calls felt deprivations the "pains of imprisonment."[18] The pains of imprisonment—the frustrations induced by the rigors of confinement—form the nexus of a deprivation model of prison culture. Sykes said that prisoners are deprived of (1) liberty, (2) goods and services, (3) heterosexual relationships, (4) autonomy, and (5) personal security and that these deprivations lead to the development of subcultures intended to ameliorate the personal pains which accompany them.

In contrast to the deprivation model, the importation model of prison culture suggests that inmates bring with them values, roles, and behavior patterns from the outside world. Such external values, second nature as they are to career offenders, depend substantially upon the criminal worldview. When offenders are confined, these external elements shape the inmate social world.

The social structure of the prison, a concept that refers to accepted and relatively permanent social arrangements, is another element which shapes prisoner subculture. Donald Clemmer's early prison study recognized nine structural dimensions of inmate society. He said that prison society could be described in terms of the following:[19]

1. The prisoner/staff dichotomy
2. The three general classes of prisoners

3. Work gangs and cellhouse groups
4. Racial groups
5. Type of offense
6. The power of inmate "politicians"
7. Degree of sexual abnormality
8. The record of repeat offenses
9. Personality differences due to preprison socialization

Clemmer's nine structural dimensions are probably still descriptive of prison life today. When applied in individual situations, they designate an inmate's position in the prison pecking order and create expectations of the appropriate role for that person. Prison roles serve to satisfy the needs of inmates for power, sexual performance, material possessions, individuality, and personal pleasure—and to define the status of one prisoner relative to another. For example, inmate leaders, sometimes referred to as "real men" or "toughs" by prisoners in early studies, offer protection to those who live by the rules. They also provide for a redistribution of wealth inside of prison and see to it that the rules of the complex prison-derived economic system—based on barter, gambling, and sexual favors—are observed. To learn more about prison life visit **WebExtra!** 12-2 at CJToday.com.

Homosexuality in Prison

Homosexual behavior inside of prisons is an important area which is both constrained and encouraged by prison subculture. One Houston woman, whose son is serving time in a Texas prison, explained the path to prison homosexuality this way: "Within a matter of days, if not hours, an unofficial prison welcome wagon sorts new arrivals into those who will fight, those who will pay extortion cash of up to $60 every two weeks, and those who will be servants or slaves. You're jumped on by two or three prisoners to see if you'll fight," said the woman. "If you don't fight, you become someone's girl, until they're tired of you and they sell you to someone else."[20]

Sykes's early study of prison argot found many words describing homosexual activity. Among them were the terms "wolf," "punk," and "fag." Wolves were aggressive men who assumed the masculine role in homosexual relations. Punks were forced into submitting to the female role, often by wolves. Fags described a special category of men who had a natural proclivity toward homosexual activity and effeminate mannerisms. While both wolves and punks were fiercely committed to their heterosexual identity and participated in homosexuality only because of prison conditions, fags generally engaged in homosexual lifestyles before their entry into prison and continued to emulate feminine mannerisms and styles of dress once incarcerated.

Prison homosexuality depends to a considerable degree upon the naivete of young inmates experiencing prison for the first time. Even when newly arrived inmates are protected from fights, older prisoners looking for homosexual liaisons may ingratiate themselves by offering cigarettes, money, drugs, food, or protection. At some future time these "loans" will be "called in," with payoffs demanded in sexual favors. Because the inmate code requires the repayment of favors, the "fish" who tries to resist may quickly find himself face to face with the brute force of inmate society.

Prison rape represents a special category of homosexual behavior behind bars. Estimates of the incidence of prison rape are both rare and dated. Those that are survey-based vary considerably in their findings. One such study found 4.7 percent of inmates in the Philadelphia prison system willing to report sexual assaults.[21] Another survey found that 28 percent of prisoners had been targets of sexual aggressors at least once during their institutional careers.[22]

While not greatly different from other prisoners, a large proportion of sexual aggressors are characterized by low education and poverty, having grown up in a broken home headed by the mother, and having a record for violent offenses. Victims of prison rape tend to be physically slight, young, white, nonviolent offenders from nonurban areas.[23] Lee Bowker, summarizing studies of sexual violence in prison,[24] provides the following observations:

1. Most sexual aggressors do not consider themselves to be homosexuals.
2. Sexual release is not the primary motivation for sexual attack.

3. Many aggressors must continue to participate in gang rapes in order to avoid becoming victims themselves.
4. The aggressors have themselves suffered much damage to their masculinity in the past.

As in cases of heterosexual rape, sexual assaults in prison are likely to leave psychological scars long after the physical event is over.[25] The victims of prison rape live in fear, may feel constantly threatened, and can turn to self-destructive activities.[26] At the very least victims question their masculinity and undergo a personal devaluation. In some cases victims of prison sexual attacks turn to violence. Frustrations, long bottled up through abuse and fear, may explode and turn the would-be rapist into a victim of prison homicide.

Prison Lifestyles and Inmate Types

Prison society is strict and often unforgiving. Even so, inmates are able to express some individuality through the choice of a prison lifestyle. John Irwin was the first well-known author to describe prison lifestyles, viewing them (like the subcultures of which they are a part) as adaptations to the prison environment.[27] Other writers have since elaborated on these coping mechanisms. Following are some of the types of prisoners described by commentators.

The Mean Dude

Some inmates adjust to prison by being mean. They are quick to fight, and when they fight, they fight like wild men (or women). They give no quarter and seem to expect none in return. Other inmates know that such prisoners are best left alone. The mean dude receives frequent write-ups and spends much time in solitary confinement.

The mean dude role is supported by the fact that some prisoners occupy it in prison as they did when they were free. Similarly, certain personality types, such as the psychopathic, may feel a natural attraction to this role. On the other hand, prison culture supports the role of the mean dude in two ways: (a) by expecting inmates to be tough and (b) through the prevalence of a type of wisdom which says that "only the strong survive" inside prison.

A psychologist might say that the mean dude is acting out against the fact of captivity, striking out at anyone he (or she) can. This type of role performance is more common in male institutions and in maximum-security prisons. It tends to become less common as inmates progress to lower-security levels.

"Whilst we have prisons it matters little which of us occupies the cells."
—George Bernard Shaw

The Hedonist

Some inmates build their lives around the limited pleasures which can be had within the confines of prison. The smuggling of contraband, homosexuality, gambling, drug running, and other officially condemned activities provide the center of interest for prison hedonists. Hedonists generally have an abbreviated view of the future, living only for the "now." Such a temporal orientation is probably characteristic of the personality type of all hedonists and exists in many persons, incarcerated or not.

The Opportunist

The opportunist takes advantage of the positive experiences prison has to offer. Schooling, trade training, counseling, and other self-improvement activities are the focal points of the opportunist's life in prison. Opportunists are the "do-gooders" of the prison subculture. They are generally well liked by prison staff, but other prisoners shun and mistrust them because they come closest to accepting the role which the staff defines as "model prisoner." Opportunists may also be religious, a role adaptation worthy of a separate description which follows.

The Retreatist

Prison life is rigorous and demanding. Badgering by the staff and actual or feared assaults by other inmates may cause some prisoners to attempt psychological retreat from the realities of imprisonment. Such inmates may experience neurotic or psychotic episodes, become heavily involved in drug and alcohol abuse, or even attempt suicide. Depression and mental illness are the hallmarks of the retreatist personality in prison. The best hope for the retreatist, short of release, is protective custody combined with therapeutic counseling.

The Legalist

The legalist is the "jail house lawyer." Just like the mean dude, the legalist fights confinement. The weapons in this fight are not fists or clubs, however, but the legal "writ." Convicts facing long sentences, with little possibility for early release through the correctional system, are most likely to turn to the courts in their battle against confinement.

The Radical

Radical inmates picture themselves as political prisoners. Society, and the successful conformists who populate it, are seen as oppressors who have forced criminality upon many "good people" through the creation of a system which distributes wealth and power inequitably. The radical inmate speaks a language of revolution and may be versed in the writings of the "great" revolutionaries of the past.

    The inmate who takes on the radical role is unlikely to receive much sympathy from prison staff. Radical rhetoric tends to be diametrically opposed to staff insistence on accepting responsibility for problematic behavior.

The Colonist

Some inmates think of prison as their home. They "know the ropes," have many "friends" inside, and may feel more comfortable institutionalized than on the streets. They typically hold either positions of power or respect (or both) among the inmate population. These are the prisoners who don't look forward to leaving prison. Most colonizers grow into the role gradually and only after already having spent years behind bars. Once released, some colonizers have been known to attempt new crimes in order to return to prison.

The Religious

Some prisoners profess a strong religious faith. They may be born-again Christians, committed Muslims, or even Satanists or witches (perhaps affiliated with the Church of Wicca). Religious inmates frequently attend services, may form prayer groups, and sometimes ask the prison administration to allocate meeting facilities or create special diets to accommodate their claimed spiritual needs.

A San Diego, California, inmate shows off his physique. Some inmates attempt to adapt to prison life by acting tough. Recent attempts by both the states and the federal government to ban weight-lifting programs in prison, however, may put a crimp in such styles of adaptation.
Armineh Johannes, SIPA Press.

While it is certainly true that some inmates have a strong religious faith, staff members are apt to be suspicious of the overly religious prisoner. The tendency is to view such prisoners as "faking it" in order to demonstrate a fictitious rehabilitation and thereby gain sympathy for an early release.

The Realist

The realist is a prisoner who sees confinement as a natural consequence of criminal activity. Time spent in prison is an unfortunate "cost of doing business." This stoic attitude toward incarceration generally leads the realist to "pull his (or her) own time" and to make the best of it. Realists tend to know the inmate code, are able to avoid trouble, and continue in lives of crime once released.

Realities of Prison Life: The Staff World

The flip side of inmate society can be found in the world of the prison staff, which includes many more people and professions than guard. Staff roles encompass those of warden, psychologist, counselor, area supervisor, program director, instructor, and correctional officer—and in some large prisons, physician and therapist. Officers, generally considered the bottom of the staff hierarchy, may be divided into cellblock and tower guards, while some are regularly assigned to administrative offices where they perform clerical tasks.

Like prisoners, correctional officers undergo a socialization process that helps them to function by the official and unofficial rules of staff society. Lucien Lombardo has described the process by which officers are socialized into the prison work world.[28] Lombardo interviewed 359 correctional personnel at New York's Auburn Prison and found that rookie officers had to quickly abandon preconceptions of both inmates and other staff members. According to Lombardo, new officers learn that inmates are not the "monsters" much of the public makes them out to be. On the other hand, rookies may be seriously disappointed in their experienced colleagues when they realize that ideals of professionalism, often stressed during early training, are rarely translated into reality. The pressures of the institutional work environment, however, soon force most correctional personnel to adopt a united front in relating to inmates.

One of the leading formative influences on staff culture is the potential threat that inmates pose. Inmates far outnumber correctional personnel in any institution, and the hostility they feel for guards is only barely hidden even at the best of times. Correctional personnel know that however friendly inmates may appear, a sudden change in institutional climate—as can happen in anything from simple disturbances on the yard to full-blown riots—can quickly and violently unmask deep-rooted feelings of mistrust and hatred.

As in years past, prison staffers are still most concerned with custody and control. Society, especially under the emerging just deserts philosophy of criminal sentencing, expects correctional staff to keep inmates in custody as the basic prerequisite of successful job performance. Custody is necessary before any other correctional activities, such as instruction or counseling, can be undertaken. Control, the other major staff concern, ensures order, and an orderly prison is thought to be safe and secure. In routine daily activities, control over almost all aspects of inmate behavior becomes paramount in the minds of most correctional officers. It is the twin interests of custody and control that lead to institutionalized procedures for ensuring security in most facilities. The use of strict rules, body and cell searches, counts, unannounced shakedowns, the control of dangerous items, materials, and contraband, and the extensive use of bars, locks, fencing, cameras, and alarms all support the human vigilance of the staff in maintaining security.

Types of Correctional Officers

Staff culture, in combination with naturally occurring personality types, gives rise to a diversity of officer types. Like the inmate typology we've already discussed, correctional staff can be classified according to certain distinguishing characteristics. Among the most prevalent types are the following.

The Dictator

Some officers go by the book; others go beyond it, using prison rules to enforce their own brand of discipline. The guard who demands signs of inmate subservience, from constant use of the word "sir" or "ma'am" to frequent free shoeshines, is one type of dictator. Another goes beyond legality, beating or "macing" inmates even for minor infractions or perceived insults. Dictator guards are bullies. They find their counterpart in the "mean dude" inmate described earlier.

Dictator guards may have sadistic personalities and gain ego satisfaction through the feelings of near omnipotence which come from the total control of others. Some may be fundamentally insecure and employ a false bravado to hide their fear of inmates. Officers who fit the dictator category are the most likely to be targeted for vengeance should control of the institution temporarily revert to the inmates.

The Friend

Friendly officers try to fraternize with inmates. They approach the issue of control by trying to be "one of the guys." They seem to believe that they can win inmate cooperation by being nice. Unfortunately, such guards do not recognize that fraternization quickly leads to unending requests for special favors—from delivering mail to bending "minor" prison rules. Once a few rules have been "bent," the officer may find that inmates have the upper hand through the potential for blackmail.

Many officers have amiable relationships with inmates. In most cases, however, affability is only a convenience which both sides recognize can quickly evaporate. Friendly officers, as the term is being used here, are *overly* friendly. They may be young and inexperienced. On the other hand, they may simply be possessed of kind and idealistic personalities built on successful friendships in free society.

The Merchant

Contraband could not exist in any correctional facility without the merchant officer. The merchant participates in the inmate economy, supplying drugs, pornography, alcohol, and sometimes even weapons to inmates who can afford to pay for them.

Probably only a very few officers consistently perform the role of merchant, although a far larger proportion may occasionally turn a few dollars by smuggling some item through the gate. Low salaries create the potential for mercantile corruption among many otherwise "straight arrow" officers. Until salaries rise substantially, the merchant will remain an institutionalized feature of most prisons.

The Turnkey

The turnkey officer cares little for what goes on in the prison setting. Officers who fit this category may be close to retirement, or they may be alienated from their jobs for various reasons. Low pay, the view that inmates are basically "worthless" and incapable of changing, and the monotonous ethic of "doing time" all combine to numb the professional consciousness of even young officers.

The term *turnkey* comes from prison argot where it means a guard who is there just to open and shut doors and who cares about nothing other than getting through his or her shift. Inmates do not see the turnkey as a threat nor is such an officer likely to challenge the status quo in institutions where merchant guards operate.

The Climber

The climber is apt to be a young officer with an eye for promotion. Nothing seems impossible to the climber, who probably hopes eventually to be warden or program director or to hold some high-status position within the institutional hierarchy. Climbers are likely to be involved in schooling, correspondence courses, and professional organizations. They may lead a movement toward unionization for correctional personnel and tend to see the guard's role as a "profession" which should receive greater social recognition.

Climbers have many ideas. They may be heavily involved in reading about the latest confinement or administrative technology. If so, they will suggest many ways to improve prison routine, often to the consternation of other complacent staff members.

Like the turnkey, climbers turn a blind eye toward inmates and their problems. They are more concerned with improving institutional procedures and with their own careers than they are with the treatment or day-to-day control of inmates.

The Reformer

The reformer is the "do-gooder" among officers, the person who believes that prison should offer opportunities for personal change. The reformer tends to lend a sympathetic ear to the personal needs of inmates and is apt to offer "arm-chair" counseling and suggestions. Many reformers are motivated by personal ideals, and some of them are highly religious. Inmates tend to see the reformer guard as naive, but harmless. Because the reformer actually tries to help, even when help is unsolicited, he or she is the most likely of all the guard types to be accepted by prisoners.

The Professionalization of Correctional Officers

Correctional officers have generally been accorded low occupational status. Historically, the role of prison guard required minimal formal education and held few opportunities for professional growth and career advancement. Such jobs were typically low-paying, frustrating, and often boring. Growing problems in our nation's prisons, including emerging issues of legal liability, however, increasingly require a well-trained and adequately equipped force of professionals. As correctional personnel have become better trained and more proficient, the old concept of *guard* has been supplanted by that of *corrections officer*.

A Broad River Correctional Institution (South Carolina) inmate is subdued following a riot in 1995. A new rule requiring collar-length hair sparked the riot, which resulted in five staff members being stabbed. Three others were taken hostage.
Jamie Francis, Pool, AP/Wide World Photos.

Many states and a growing number of large-city correctional systems make efforts to eliminate individuals with potentially harmful personality characteristics from correctional officer applicant pools. New York, New Jersey, Ohio, Pennsylvania, and Rhode Island, for example, all use some form of psychological screening in assessing candidates for prison jobs.[29]

Although only some states utilize psychological screening, all make use of training programs intended to prepare successful applicants for prison work. New York, for example, requires trainees to complete six weeks of classroom-based instruction, as well as 40 hours of rifle range practice, followed by another six weeks of on-the-job training. Training days begin around 5 A.M. with a mile run and conclude after dark with study halls for students who need extra help. To keep pace with rising inmate populations, the state has often had to run a number of simultaneous training academies.[30]

On the federal level, a developmental model for correctional careers addresses many of the problems of correctional staffing. The Federal Bureau of Prisons' Career Development Model stands as an example of what state departments of correction can do in the area of staff training and development. The model establishes five sequential phases for the development of career correctional officers:[31] (1) Phase I, Career Assessment; (2) Phase II, Career Path Development; (3) Phase III, Career Enhancement and Management Development; (4) Phase IV, Advanced Management Development; and (5) Phase V, Senior Executive Service Development. Using a psychological personality inventory, the model seeks to identify the skills, abilities, and interests of officers and matches them with career opportunities in the federal correctional system.

Prison Riots

The 10 years between 1970 and 1980 have been called the "explosive decade" of prison riots.[32] The decade began with a massive uprising at Attica Prison in New York state in September 1971. The Attica riot resulted in 43 deaths. More than 80 men were wounded. The explosive decade ended in 1980 at Santa Fe, New Mexico. There, in a riot at the New Mexico penitentiary, 33 inmates died, the victims of vengeful prisoners out to eliminate rats and informants. Many of the deaths involved mutilation and torture. More than 200 other inmates were beaten and sexually assaulted, and the prison was virtually destroyed.

Prison riots did not stop with the end of the explosive 1970s. For 11 days in 1987, the Atlanta (Georgia) Federal Penitentiary fell into the hands of inmates. The institution was "trashed," and inmates had to be temporarily relocated while it was rebuilt. The Atlanta riot followed closely on the heels of a similar, but less intense, disturbance at the federal detention center at Oakdale, Louisiana. Both outbreaks were attributed to the dissatisfaction of Cuban inmates, most of whom had arrived on the Mariel boat lift.[33] A two-night rampage in October 1989 left more than 100 people injured and the Pennsylvania prison at Camp Hill in shambles. At the time of the riot, the State Correctional Institution at Camp Hill was 45 percent over its capacity of 2,600 inmates.[34] Easter Sunday 1993 saw the beginning of an 11-day rebellion at the 1,800-inmate Southern Ohio Correctional Facility in Lucasville, Ohio—one of the country's toughest maximum-security prisons. The riot ended with nine inmates and one correctional officer dead. The officer had been hung. Paul W. Goldberg, executive director of the Ohio Civil Service Employees Association, told an Ohio senate panel, "[T]hose of us who deal with our prisons every day—the men and women on the front lines—know that overcrowding and understaffing are at the heart of Ohio's prison crisis. . . ." "Lucasville is not an aberration," said Goldberg. "Every prison in Ohio is a powder keg."[35] The close of the riot—involving a parade of 450 inmates—was televised as prisoners had demanded. Among other demands were (1) no retaliation by officials, (2) review of medical staffing and care, (3) review of mail and visitation rules, (4) review of commissary prices, and (5) better enforcement against what the inmates called "inappropriate supervision."[36]

Riots related to inmate grievances over perceived disparities in federal drug sentencing policies and the possible loss of weight-lifting equipment occurred throughout the federal prison system in October 1995. The riots, which began at Allenwood Correctional Facility in Pennsylvania and the federal prison at Talladega, Alabama, quickly spread to eight other federal prisons. Within a few days, the unrest led to a nationwide lockdown of 73 federal prisons. Although fires were set and a number of inmates and guards were injured, no deaths resulted.

Causes of Riots

It is difficult to explain satisfactorily why prisoners riot, despite study groups which attempt to piece together the "facts" leading up to an incident. After the riot at Attica, the New York State Special Commission of Inquiry filed a report which recommended the creation of inmate advisory councils, changes in staff titles and uniforms, and other institutional improvements. The report emphasized "enhancing [the] dignity, worth, and self-confidence" of inmates. The New Mexico attorney general, in a final report on the violence at Santa Fe, placed blame upon a breakdown in informal controls and the subsequent emergence of a new group of violent inmates among the general prison population.[37]

A number of authorities[38] have suggested a variety of causes for prison riots. Among them are the following:

1. An insensitive prison administration and neglected inmates' demands. Calls for "fairness" in disciplinary hearings, better food, more recreational opportunities, and the like may lead to riots when ignored.

Theory Into Practice

Code of Ethics—American Correctional Association

The American Correctional Association expects of its members unfailing honesty, respect for the dignity and individuality of human beings, and a commitment to professional and compassionate service. To this end we subscribe to the following principles:

◆Members will respect and protect the civil and legal rights of all individuals.

◆Members will treat every professional situation with concern for the person's welfare and with no intent of personal gain.

◆Relationships with colleagues will be such that they promote mutual respect within the profession and improve the quality of service.

◆Public criticisms of colleagues or their agencies will be made only when warranted, verifiable, and constructive in purpose.

◆Members will respect the importance of all disciplines within the criminal justice system and work to improve cooperation with each segment.

◆Subject to the individual's rights to privacy, members will honor the public's right to know and share information with the public to the extent permitted by law.

◆Members will respect and protect the right of the public to be safeguarded from criminal activity.

◆Members will not use their positions to secure personal privileges or advantages.

◆Members will not, while acting in an official capacity, allow personal interest to impair objectivity in the performance of duty.

◆No member will enter into any activity or agreement, formal or informal, which presents a conflict of interest or is inconsistent with the conscientious performance of his or her duties.

◆No member will accept any gift, service, or favor that is or appears to be improper or implies an obligation inconsistent with the free and objective exercise of his or her professional duties.

◆In any public statement, members will clearly distinguish between personal views and those statements or positions made on behalf of an agency or the Association.

◆Each member will report to the appropriate authority any corrupt or unethical behavior where there is sufficient cause to initiate a review.

◆Members will not discriminate against any individual because of race, gender, creed, national origin, religious affiliation, age, or any other type of prohibited discrimination.

◆Members will preserve the integrity of private information; they will neither seek data on individuals beyond that needed to perform their responsibilities nor reveal nonpublic data unless expressly authorized to do so.

◆Any member who is responsible for agency personnel actions will make all appointments, promotions, or dismissals in accordance with established civil service rules, applicable contract agreements, and individual merit, and not in furtherance of partisan interests.

Adopted August 1975 at the 105th Congress of Correction.
Revised August 1990 at the 120th Congress of Correction.

Source: *American Correctional Association, Code of Ethics (Laurel, MD: American Correctional Association, 1990). Reprinted with permission.*

Visit the American Correctional Association at www.corrections.com/aca.

2. The lifestyles most inmates are familiar with on the streets. It should be no surprise that prisoners use organized violence when many of them are violent people anyway.

3. Dehumanizing prison conditions. Overcrowded facilities, the lack of opportunity for individual expression, and other aspects of total institutions culminate in explosive situations of which riots are but one form.

4. The way that riots regulate inmate society and redistribute power balances among inmate groups. Riots provide the opportunity to "cleanse" the prison population of informers and rats and to resolve struggles among power brokers and ethnic groups within the institution.

5. "Power vacuums" created by changes in prison administration, the transfer of influential inmates, or court-ordered injunctions which significantly alter the informal social control mechanisms of the institution.

Although riots are difficult to predict in specific institutions, some state prison systems appear ripe for disorder. Texas, for example, has an overcrowded system that exhibits a number of the preceding characteristics. Making matters worse, Texas prisons house a number of rapidly expanding gangs among whom turf violations can easily lead to widespread disorder. Gang membership among inmates in the Texas prison system, practically nonexistent in 1983, is now estimated at over 1,200.[39] The Texas Syndicate, the Aryan Brotherhood of Texas, and the Mexican Mafia (sometimes known as "La Eme," Spanish for the letter *M*) are probably the largest gangs functioning in the Texas prison system. Each has around 300 members.[40] Other gangs known to operate in some Texas prisons include Aryan Warriors; Black Gangster Disciples (mostly in the Midwest); the Black Guerrilla Family, an African-American prison gang; the Confederate Knights of America; and the Nuestra Familia, an organization of Hispanic prisoners.

Gangs in Texas grew rapidly in part because of the "power vacuum" created when a court ruling ended the "building tender" system.[41] *Building tenders* were tough inmates who were given an almost free reign by prison administrators in keeping other inmates in line, especially in many of the state's worst prisons. The end of the building tender system dramatically increased demands on the Texas Department of Corrections for increased abilities and professionalism among its guards and other prison staff.

The real reasons for any riot are probably institution-specific and may not allow for easy generalization. However, it is no simple coincidence that the explosive decade of prison riots coincided with the growth of revolutionary prisoner subcultures referred to earlier. As the old convict code began to give way to an emerging perception of social victimization among inmates, it was probably only a matter of time until those perceptions turned to militancy. Seen from this perspective, riots are more a revolutionary activity undertaken by politically motivated cliques rather than spontaneous and disorganized expressions stemming from the frustrations of prison life.

Stages in Riots and Riot Control

Rioting cannot be predicted.[42] Riots are generally unplanned and tend to occur spontaneously, the result of some relatively minor precipitating event. Once the stage has been set, prison riots tend to evolve through five phases:[43] (1) explosion, (2) organization (into inmate-led groups), (3) confrontation (with authority), (4) termination (through negotiation or physical confrontation), and (5) reaction and explanation (usually by investigative commissions). Donald Cressey[44] points out that the early explosive stages of a riot tend to involve "binges" during which inmates exult in their newfound freedom with virtual orgies of alcohol and drug use or sexual activity. Buildings are burned, facilities are wrecked, and old grudges between individual inmates and inmate groups are settled, often through violence. After this initial explosive stage, leadership changes tend to occur. New leaders emerge who, at least for a time, may effectively organize inmates into a force that can confront and resist officials' attempts to regain control of the institution. Bargaining strategies then develop and the process of negotiation begins.

In the past, many correctional facilities depended upon informal procedures to quell disturbances—and often drew upon the expertise of seasoned correctional officers who were veterans of past skirmishes and riots. Given the large size of many of today's institutions, the

The number of women in prison is growing steadily. Because of disciplinary problems, this woman is housed in the segregation unit of a Rhode Island correctional facility.
Gale Zucker, Stock Boston.

rapidly changing composition of inmate and staff populations, and increasing tensions caused by overcrowding and the movement toward reduced inmate privileges, the "old guard" system can no longer be depended upon to quell disturbances. Hence, most modern facilities have incident management procedures and systems in place which are designed to be implemented in the event of disturbances. Such systems remove the burden of riot control from the individual officer, depending instead upon a systematic and deliberate approach developed to deal with a wide variety of correctional incidents.

Realities of Prison Life: Women in Prison

As of January 1, 2000, 90,688 women were imprisoned in state and federal correctional institutions throughout the United States[45]—accounting for 6.6 percent of all prison inmates. A recent survey found that California has the largest number of female prisoners, exceeding even the federal government.[46] Figure 12-1 provides a breakdown of the total American prison population by gender and ethnicity. Most women inmates are housed in centralized state facilities known as women's prisons, which are dedicated exclusively to the holding of female felons. Many states, however, particularly those with small populations, continue to keep women prisoners in special wings of what are otherwise institutions for men.

While there are still far more men imprisoned across the nation than women (approximately 16 men for every woman), the number of female inmates is rising quickly.[47] In 1981 women comprised only 4 percent of the nation's overall prison population, but the number of female inmates nearly tripled during the 1980s and is continuing to grow at a rate greater than that shown by male inmates.

Professionals working with imprisoned women attribute the rise in female prison populations largely to drugs.[48] Figure 12-2 shows, in relative graphics, the proportion of men and women imprisoned for various kinds of offenses. While the figure shows that approximately 35 percent of all women in prison are there explicitly for drug offenses, other estimates say that the impact of drugs on the imprisonment of women is far greater than a simple reading

FIGURE 12-1 ■ *Prison inmates by gender and ethnicity, state and federal prisons, 1999.*

Source: *Allen J. Beck,* Prisoners in 1999 *(Washington, D.C.: Bureau of Justice Statistics, 2000).*

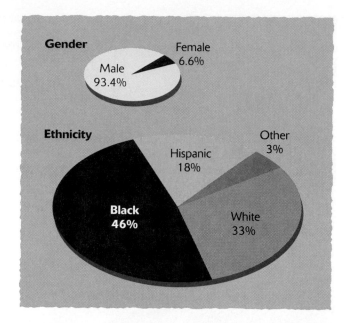

of the figures would show. Warden Robert Brennan of New York City's Rose M. Singer jail for women estimates that drugs—either directly or indirectly—account for the imprisonment of around 95 percent of the inmates there. Drug-related offenses committed by women include larceny, burglary, fraud, prostitution, embezzlement, and robbery, as well as other crimes stimulated by the desire for drugs. In fact, incarcerated women most frequently list (1) trying to pay for drugs, (2) attempts to relieve economic pressures, and (3) poor judgment as the reasons for their arrest.[49]

Another reason for the rapid growth in the number of women behind bars may be the demise, over the last decade or two, of the "Chivalry Factor." The Chivalry Factor, so called because it was based upon an archaic cultural stereotype that depicted women as helpless or childlike compared to men, allegedly lessened the responsibility of female offenders in the eyes of some male judges and prosecutors—resulting in fewer active prison sentences for women involved in criminal activity. Recent studies show that the Chivalry Factor is now primarily of historical interest. In jurisdictions examined, the gender of convicted offenders no longer affects sentencing practices except insofar as it may be tied to other social variables. B. Keith Crew,[50] for example, in a comprehensive study of gender differences in sentencing observes, "[A] woman does not automatically receive leniency because of her status of wife or mother, but she may receive leniency if those statuses become part of the official

FIGURE 12-2 ■ *Men and women in prison by type of offense.*

Source: *Allen J. Beck,* Prisoners in 1999 *(Washington, D.C.: Bureau of Justice Statistics, 2000).*

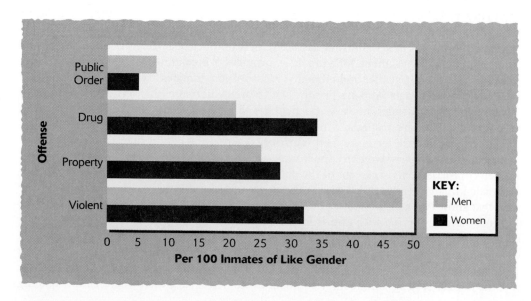

explanation of her criminal behavior (for example, she was stealing to feed her children, or an abusive husband forced her to commit a crime)."

Although there may be no one typical prison for women and no perfectly average female inmate, the American Correctional Association's 1990 report by the Task Force on the Female Offender found that women inmates and the institutions which house them could be generally described as follows:[51]

1. Most prisons for women are located in towns with fewer than 25,000 inhabitants.
2. A significant number of facilities were not designed to house female inmates.
3. The number of female offenders being sent to prison is rising.
4. Most facilities that house female inmates also house males.
5. Not many facilities for women have programs especially designed for female offenders.
6. Very few major disturbances or escapes are reported among female inmates.
7. Substance abuse among female inmates is very high.
8. Very few work assignments are available to female inmates.
9. The number of female inmates without a high-school education is very high.

Statistics[52] show that the average age of female inmates is 29–30, most are black or Hispanic (57 percent), most come from single-parent or broken homes, and 50 percent have other family members who are incarcerated. The typical female inmate is a high-school dropout (50 percent), who left school either because she was bored or because of pregnancy (34 percent). She has been arrested an average of two to nine times (55 percent) and has run away from home between one and three times (65 percent). Thirty-nine percent report using drugs to make them feel better emotionally, while 28 percent have attempted suicide at least once. Sixty-two percent were single parents with one to three children prior to incarceration, and many have been physically and/or sexually abused.[53]

> "It is better to prevent crimes than to punish them."
>
> —*Cesare Bonesana,*
> *Marchese Di Beccaria*

Eighty percent of women entering prison are mothers, and 85 percent of those women retain custody of their children at the time of prison admission. One out of four women entering prison has either recently given birth or is pregnant. Critics charge that women inmates face a prison system designed for male inmates and run by men. Hence, pregnant inmates, many of whom are drug users, malnourished, or sick, often receive little prenatal care—a situation that risks additional complications. Separation from their children is a significant deprivation facing incarcerated mothers. Although husbands and/or boyfriends may assume responsibility for the children of imprisoned spouses/girlfriends, such an outcome is the exception to the rule. Eventually, a large proportion of children are released by their imprisoned mothers into foster care or put up for adoption.

Some states do offer parenting classes for women inmates with children. In a national survey[54] of prisons for women, 36 states responded that they provide parenting programs which deal with caretaking, reducing violence toward children, visitation problems, and related issues. Some offer facilities as diverse as play areas complete with toys, while others attempt to alleviate difficulties attending mother/child visits. The typical program studied lasts from four to nine weeks and provides for a meeting time of two hours per week.

Other meaningful prison programs for women are often lacking—perhaps because the ones which are in place were originally based upon traditional models of female roles which left little room for substantive employment opportunities. Many trade training programs still emphasize low-paying jobs, such as cook, beautician, or laundry machine operator. Classes in homemaking are not uncommon.

Social Structure in Women's Prisons

Most studies of women's prisons have revealed a unique feature of such institutions: the way that women inmates construct organized families. Typical of such studies are Ward and Kassebaum's *Women's Prison: Sex and Social Structure,*[55] E. Heffernan's *Making It in Prison: The Square, The Cool, and the Life,*[56] and Rose Giallombardo's *Society of Women: A Study of Women's Prisons.*[57]

Giallombardo, for example, examined the Federal Reformatory for Women at Alderson, West Virginia, spending a year in gathering data (1962–1963). Focusing closely on the formation of families, she entitled one of her chapters "The Homosexual Alliance as a Marriage Unit." In it she describes in great detail the sexual identities assumed by women at Alderson and the symbols they chose to communicate those roles. Hair style, dress, language, and mannerisms were all used to signify "maleness" or "femaleness." Giallombardo details "the anatomy of the marriage relationship from courtship to 'fall out,' that is, from inception to the parting of the ways, or divorce."[58] Romantic love at Alderson was seen as of central importance to any relationship between inmates, and all homosexual relationships were described as voluntary. Through marriage the "stud broad" became the husband and the "femme" the wife.

Studies attempting to document the extent of inmate involvement in prison "families" produce varying results. Some have found as many as 71 percent of women prisoners involved in the phenomenon, while others have found none.[59] The kinship systems described by Giallombardo and others, however, extend beyond simple "family" ties to the formation of large, intricately related groups involving a large number of nonsexual relationships. In these groups the roles of "children," "in-laws," "grandparents," and so on may be explicitly recognized. Even "birth order" within a family can become an issue for kinship groups.[60] Kinship groups sometimes occupy a common household—usually a prison cottage or dormitory area. The description of women's prisons provided by such authors as Giallombardo show a closed society in which social interaction—including expectations, normative forms of behavior, and emotional ties—is regulated by an inventive system of artificial relationships which mirror the outside world.

Some authors have suggested that this emphasis on describing family structures in women's prisons is unfortunate because it tends to deny other structural features of those institutions.[61] The family emphasis may, in fact, be due to traditional explanations of female criminality which were intertwined with narrow understandings of the role of women in society.

Types of Female Inmates

As in institutions for men, the subculture of women's prisons is multidimensional. Esther Heffernan, for example, found that three terms used by women prisoners she studied—the "square," the "cool," and the "life"—were indicative of three styles of adaptation to prison life.[62] Square inmates had few early experiences with criminal lifestyles and tended to sympathize with the values and attitudes of conventional society. Cool prisoners were more likely to be career offenders. They tended to keep to themselves and were generally supportive of inmate values. Women who participated in the "life" subculture were well familiar with lives of crime. Many had been arrested repeatedly for prostitution, drug use, theft, and so on. "Life" group members were full participants in the economic, social, and familial arrangements of the prison. Heffernan believed that "the life" offered an alternative lifestyle to women who had experienced early and constant rejection by conventional society. Within "the life" women could establish relationships, achieve status, and find meaning in their lives. The square, the "life," and the cool represented subcultures to Heffernan because individuals with similar adaptive choices tended to closely relate to one another and to support the lifestyle characteristic of that type.

Square inmates are definitely in the minority in prisons for both men and women. Perhaps for that reason they have rarely been studied. In an insightful self-examination, however, one such inmate, Jean Harris, published her impressions of prison life after more than seven years in the maximum-security Bedford Hills (New York) Correctional Facility. Harris was convicted of killing the "Scarsdale Diet Doctor," Herman Tarnower, over a romance gone sour. A successful socialite in her early fifties at the time of the crime, Harris had an eye-opening experience in prison. Her book, *They Always Call Us Ladies,*[63] argues hard for prison reform. Sounding like the square she was, Harris says other inmates are "hard for you and me to relate to"[64] and describes them as "childlike women without social skills."[65] Speaking to a reporter, Harris related, "There's really nobody for me to talk to here."[66] Harris was granted clemency by New York Governor Mario Cuomo on December 29, 1992—after having served 12 years in prison.[67]

Recently, the social structure of women's prison has become dichotomized by the advent of "Crack kids," as they are called in prison argot. "Crack kids," whose existence

Theory Into Practice

The Language of Women's Prisons

When a stud and a femme have established their union, they are said to be "making it" or to "be tight," which is to say that other inmates recognize them socially as a "married" pair. Since the prisoners attach a positive value to sincerity, the "trick"—one who is simply exploited sexually or economically—is held in low esteem by the inmate subculture. Tricks are also regarded as "suckers" and "fools"

because their lovers dangle unkept promises in front of them. The "commissary hustler" is the woman who establishes more than one relationship; besides an alliance with an inmate in the same housing unit, she also maintains relations with one or more inmates in other housing units for economic advantage. The other women, labeled tricks in the prison argot, supply her with coveted material items which she shares only with

the "wife" in her own unit. The femme may even encourage and guide the stud in finding and exploiting the tricks. The legitimacy of the primary pseudomarriage is not contested, though the tricks may anticipate replacing the femme when a suitable opportunity arises.

Source: Stephen Donaldson, "Prisons, Jails, and Reformatories," Encyclopedia of Homosexuality, *Wayne R. Dynes, ed., (New York: Garland, 1990).*

highlights generational differences among female offenders, are streetwise young women with little respect for traditional prison values, for their elders, or even for their own children. Known for frequent fights and for their lack of even simple domestic skills, these young women quickly estrange many older inmates, some of whom call them "animalescents."

Violence in Women's Prisons

Some authors have suggested that violence in women's prisons is less frequent than it is in institutions for men. Bowker observes that "[e]xcept for the behavior of a few 'guerrillas,' it appears that violence is only used in women's prisons to settle questions of dominance and subordination when other manipulative strategies fail to achieve the desired effect."[68] It appears that few homosexual liaisons are forced, perhaps representing a general aversion among women to such victimization in wider society. At least one study, however, has shown the use of sexual violence in women's prisons as a form of revenge against inmates who are overly vocal in their condemnation of such practices among other prisoners.[69]

Not all abuse occurs at the hands of inmates. On November 15, 1992, 14 correctional officers, 10 men and 4 women, were indicted for the alleged abuse of female inmates at the 900-bed Women's Correctional Institute in Hardwick, Georgia. The charges resulted from affidavits filed by 90 female inmates alleging "rape, sexual abuse, prostitution, coerced abortions, sex for favors, and retaliation for refusal to participate"[70] in such activities. One inmate who was forced to have an abortion after becoming pregnant by a male staff member said, "[A]s an inmate, I simply felt powerless to avoid the sexual advances of staff and to refuse to have an abortion."[71]

The Task Force on the Female Offender[72] recommends a number of changes in the administration of prisons for women. Among them are the following:

1. Substance abuse programs should be available to women inmates.
2. Women inmates need to acquire greater literacy skills, and literacy programs should form the basis upon which other programs are built.
3. Female offenders should be housed in buildings independent of male inmates.
4. Institutions for women should develop programs for keeping children in the facility in order to "fortify the bond between mother and child."
5. To ensure equal access to assistance, institutions should be built to accommodate programs for female offenders.

Prisoner Rights

Until the 1960s American courts took a neutral approach—commonly called the **hands-off doctrine**—toward the running of prisons. Judges assumed that prison administrators were sufficiently professional in the performance of their duties to balance institutional needs with humane considerations. The hands-off doctrine rested upon the belief that defendants lost most of their rights upon conviction, suffering a kind of **civil death.** Many states defined the concept of civil death through legislation which denied inmates the right to vote, hold public office, or even marry. Some states made incarceration for a felony a basis for uncontested divorce at the request of the noncriminal spouse.

The hands-off doctrine ended in 1969 when a federal court declared the entire Arkansas prison system unconstitutional after hearing arguments that it constituted a form of cruel and unusual punishment.[73] The court's decision resulted from what it judged to be pervasive overcrowding and primitive living conditions. Stories about the system by longtime inmates claimed that a number of other inmates had been beaten or shot to death by guards and buried over the years in unmarked graves on prison property. An investigation did unearth some skeletons in old graves, but their origin was never resolved.

Detailed media coverage of the Arkansas prison system gave rise to suspicions about correctional institutions everywhere. Within a few years federal courts intervened in the running of prisons in Florida, Louisiana, Mississippi, New York City, and Virginia.[74] In 1975, in a precedent-setting decision, U.S. District Court Judge Frank M. Johnson issued an order which banned the Alabama Board of Corrections from accepting any more inmates. Citing a population which was more than double the capacity of the state's system, Judge Johnson enumerated 44 standards to be met before additional inmates could be admitted to prison. Included in the requirements were specific guidelines on living space, staff/inmate ratios, visiting privileges, the racial makeup of staff, and food service modifications.

The Legal Basis of Prisoners' Rights

In 1974, the Supreme Court case of *Pell* v. *Procunier*[75] established a "balancing test" which, although it was at the time addressed only to First Amendment rights, served to define a guideline generally applicable to all prison operations. In *Pell* the Court ruled that the "prison inmate retains those First Amendment rights that are not inconsistent with his status as a prisoner or with the legitimate penological objectives of the corrections system."[76] In other words, inmates have rights much the same as people who are not incarcerated, provided that the legitimate needs of the prison for security, custody, and safety are not compromised. Other court decisions have declared that order maintenance, security, and rehabilitation are all legitimate concerns of prison administration, but that financial exigency and convenience are not. As the **balancing test** makes clear, we see reflected in prisoner rights a microcosm of the due process versus social order dilemma found in wider society.

Prisoner rights, because they are constrained by the legitimate needs of imprisonment, are more conditional rights than they are absolute rights. The Second Amendment to the U.S. Constitution, for example, grants citizens the right to bear arms. The right to arms is, however, necessarily compromised by the need for order and security in prison, and we would not expect a court to rule that inmates have a right to weapons. Conditional rights, because they are subject to the exigencies of imprisonment, bear a strong resemblance to privileges, which should not be surprising since "privileges" were all that inmates officially had until the modern era. The practical difference between a privilege and a conditional right stems from the fact that privileges exist only at the convenience of granting institutions and can be revoked at any time for any reason. The rights of prisoners, on the other hand, have a basis in the Constitution and in law external to the institution. Although the institution may change them for legitimate correctional reasons, they may not be infringed without good cause that can be demonstrated in a court of law.

The past two decades have seen many lawsuits brought by prisoners challenging the constitutionality of some aspect of confinement. Suits filed by prisoners with the courts are generally called writs of *habeas corpus* and formally request that the person detaining a prisoner bring him or her before a judicial officer to determine the lawfulness of imprisonment. The

American Correctional Association says that most prisoner lawsuits have been based upon: "1. the Eighth Amendment prohibition against cruel and unusual punishment; 2. the Fourteenth Amendment prohibition against the taking of life, liberty, or property without due process of law; and 3. the Fourteenth Amendment provision requiring equal protection of the laws."[77] Aside from appeals by inmates which question the propriety of their convictions and sentences, such constitutional challenges represent the bulk of legal action initiated by those imprisoned. State statutes and federal legislation, however, including Section 1983 of the Civil Rights Act of 1871, provide other bases for challenges to the legality of specific prison conditions and procedures.

"The Privilege of the Writ of *Habeas Corpus* shall not be suspended, unless when in Cases of Rebellion or Invasion the public Safety may require it."

—*U.S. Constitution*, Article I, section 9, clause 2.

Precedents in Inmate Rights

To date, the Supreme Court has not spoken with finality on many questions of inmate rights, and there is some evidence of a trend back to a modified hands-off doctrine.[78] However, high-court decisions of the last few decades can be interpreted along with a number of lower-court findings to enumerate the conditional rights of prisoners shown in Table 12-1. A number of especially significant Court decisions are discussed in the following sections.

Communications

As previously mentioned, the rights listed in Table 12-1 are not absolute but must be balanced against the security, order maintenance, and treatment needs of the institution. The Supreme Court has indicated that institutional exigency can in fact abbreviate any right. In the case of *Procunier* v. *Martinez* (1974),[79] for example, the Court ruled that a prisoner's mail may be censored if it is necessary to do so for security purposes. On the other hand, mere institutional convenience does not provide a sufficient basis for the denial of rights. In *McNamara* v. *Moody* (1979),[80] a federal court upheld the right of an inmate to write vulgar letters to his girlfriend in which he made disparaging comments about the prison staff. The court reasoned that the letters may have been embarrassing to prison officials but that they did not affect the security or order of the institution. However, libelous materials have generally not been accorded First Amendment protection in or out of institutional contexts.

Concerning inmate publications, legal precedent has held that prisoners have no inherent right to publish newspapers or newsletters for use by other prisoners, although many institutions do permit and finance such periodicals.[81] Publications originating from outside of prison, such as newspapers, magazines, and special interest tracts, have generally been protected when mailed directly from the publisher, although magazines which depict deviant sexual behavior can be banned according to *Mallery* v. *Lewis* (1983)[82] and other precedents. Nudity by itself is not necessarily obscene, and federal courts have held that prisons cannot ban nude pictures of inmates' wives and girlfriends.[83]

Religious Practice

The early Supreme Court case of *Cruz* v. *Beto* (1972)[84] established that inmates must be given a "reasonable opportunity" to pursue their faith even if it differs from traditional forms of worship. Meeting facilities must be provided for religious use when those same facilities are made available to other groups of prisoners for other purposes,[85] but no group can claim exclusive use of a prison area for religious reasons.[86] The right to assemble for religious purposes, however, can be denied to inmates who use such meetings to plan escapes or who take the opportunity to dispense contraband. Similarly, prisoners in segregation do not have to be permitted the opportunity to attend group religious services.[87]

Although prisoners cannot be made to attend religious services,[88] records of religious activity can be maintained in order to administratively determine dietary needs and eligibility for passes to religious services outside of the institution.[89] In *Dettmer* v. *Landon* (1985),[90] a federal district court held that an inmate who claimed to practice witchcraft must be provided with the artifacts necessary for his worship services. Included were items such as sea salt, sulfur, a quartz clock, incense, candles, and a white robe without a hood. The district court's opinion was later partially overturned by the U.S. Court of Appeals for the Fourth Circuit.

TABLE 12-1 ■ The Conditional Rights of Inmates

RELIGIOUS FREEDOM

The Right of Assembly for Religious Services and Groups
The Right to Attend Services of Other Religious Groups
The Right to Receive Visits from Ministers
The Right to Correspond with Religious Leaders
A Right to Observe Religious Dietary Laws
The Right to Wear Religious Insignia

FREEDOM OF SPEECH

The Right to Meet with Members of the Press[1]
The Right to Receive Publications Directly from the Publisher
The Right to Communicate with Nonprisoners

ACCESS TO LEGAL ASSISTANCE

A Right of Access to the Courts[2]
A Right to Visits from Attorneys
A Right to Mail Communications with Lawyers[3]
A Right to Communicate with Legal Assistance Organizations
A Right to Consult "Jail House Lawyers"[4]
A Right to Assistance in Filing Legal Papers, which should include one of the following:
    Access to an Adequate Law Library
    Paid Attorneys
    Paralegal Personnel or Law Students

MEDICAL TREATMENT

A Right to Sanitary and Healthy Conditions
A Right to Medical Attention for Serious Physical Problems
A Right to Needed Medications
A Right to Treatment in Accordance with "Doctor's Orders"

PROTECTION

A Right to Food, Water, and Shelter
A Right to Protection from Foreseeable Attack
A Right to Protection from Predictable Sexual Abuse
A Right to Protection Against Suicide

INSTITUTIONAL PUNISHMENT AND DISCIPLINE

An Absolute Right Against Corporal Punishments (unless *sentenced* to such punishments)
A Limited Right to Due Process Prior to Punishment, including:
    Notice of Charges
    A Fair and Impartial Hearing
    An Opportunity for Defense
    A Right to Present Witnesses
    A Written Decision

[1]*But not beyond the opportunities afforded for inmates to meet with members of the general public.*
[2]*As restricted by the Prison Litigation Reform Act of 1996.*
[3]*Mail communications are generally designated as privileged or nonprivileged. Privileged communications include those between inmates and their lawyers or court officials and cannot legitimately be read by prison officials. Nonprivileged communications include most other written communications.*
[4]*Jail house lawyers are inmates with experience in the law, usually gained from filing legal briefs on their own behalf or on the behalf of others. Consultation with jail house lawyers was ruled permissible in the Supreme Court case of Johnson v. Avery, 393 U.S. 483 (1968), unless inmates are provided with paid legal assistance.*

The appellate court recognized the Church of Wicca as a valid religion, but held that concerns over prison security could preclude inmates' possession of dangerous items of worship.[91]

Drugs and dangerous substances have not been considered permissible even when inmates claimed they were a necessary part of their religious services.[92] Prison regulations prohibiting the wearing of beards, even those grown for religious reasons, were held acceptable for security considerations in the 1985 federal court case of *Hill* v. *Blackwell*.[93]

Visitation

Visitation and access to the news media are other areas which have come under court scrutiny. Maximum-security institutions rarely permit "contact" visits, and some have on occasion suspended all visitation privileges. In the case of *Block* v. *Rutherford* (1984),[94] the Supreme Court upheld the policy of the Los Angeles County Central Jail which prohibited all visits from friends and relatives. The Court agreed that the large jail population and the conditions under which visits might take place could combine to threaten the security of the jail.

In *Pell* v. *Procunier* (1974),[95] cited in the balancing test, the Court found in favor of a California law which denied prisoners the opportunity to hold special meetings with members of the press. The Court reasoned that media interviews could be conducted through regular visitation arrangements and that most of the information desired by the media could be conveyed through correspondence. In *Pell*, the Court also held that any reasonable policy of media access was acceptable so long as it was administered fairly and without bias.

In a later case, the Court ruled that news personnel cannot be denied correspondence with inmates, but also ruled that they have no constitutional right to interview inmates or to inspect correctional facilities beyond the visitation opportunities available to others.[96] This equal-access policy was set forth in *Houchins* v. *KQED, Inc.* (1978), by Justice Stewart who wrote, "The Constitution does no more than assure the public and the press equal access once government has opened its doors."[97]

Legal Access to the Courts

A well-established right of prisoners is access to the courts[98] and to legal assistance. The right of prisoners to petition the court was recognized in *Bounds* v. *Smith* (1977),[99] which, at the time, was a far-reaching Supreme Court decision. While attempting to define *access,* the Court in *Bounds* imposed upon the states the duty of assisting inmates in the preparation and filing of legal papers. Assistance could be provided through trained personnel knowledgeable in the law or via law libraries in each institution, which all states have since built. In 1996, however, in the case of *Lewis* v. *Casey,* the U.S. Supreme Court repudiated part of the *Bounds* decision, saying, "[S]tatements in *Bounds* suggesting that prison authorities must also enable the prisoner to discover grievances, and to litigate effectively once in court . . . have no antecedent in this Court's pre-*Bounds* cases, and are now disclaimed." In *Lewis,* the Court overturned earlier decisions by a federal district court and by the Ninth Circuit Court of Appeals. Both lower courts had found in favor of Arizona inmates who had complained that state prison law libraries provided inadequate legal research facilities, thereby depriving them of their right of legal access to the courts as established by *Bounds.* In turning back portions of *Bounds,* the majority in *Lewis* wrote that inmates raising such claims need to demonstrate "widespread actual injury" to their ability to access the courts, not merely "isolated instances of actual injury." "Moreover," wrote the Justices, "*Bounds* does not guarantee inmates the wherewithal to file any and every type of legal claim, but requires only that they be provided with the tools to attack their sentences . . . and to challenge the conditions of their confinement."

In an earlier case, *Johnson* v. *Avery* (1968),[100] the Court had ruled that persons under correctional supervision have a right to consult "jail house lawyers" for advice when assistance from trained professionals is not available. Other court decisions have established that inmates have a right to correspond with their attorneys[101] and with legal assistance organizations. Such letters, however, can be opened and inspected for contraband[102] (but not read) by prison authorities in the presence of the inmate. The right to meet with hired counsel for reasonable lengths of time has also been upheld.[103] Indigent defendants must be provided with stamps for the purpose of legal correspondence,[104] and inmates cannot be disciplined for communicating with lawyers or requesting legal help. Conversations between inmates and their lawyers can be monitored, although any evidence obtained through such a process cannot be used in court.[105] Inmates do not, however, have the right to an appointed lawyer, even when indigent, if no judicial proceedings against them have been initiated.[106]

Medical Care

The historic Supreme Court case of *Estelle* v. *Gamble* (1976)[107] specified prison officials' duty to provide for inmates' medical care. In *Estelle,* the Court concerned itself with "deliberate indifference" on the part of the staff toward a prisoner's need for serious medical attention. "Deliberate indifference" can mean a wanton disregard for the health of inmates. Hence, while poor treatment, misdiagnosis, and the like may constitute medical malpractice, they do not necessarily constitute deliberate indifference.[108]

More recently, in *Farmer* v. *Brennan* (1994),[109] the Court clarified the concept of "deliberate indifference" by holding that it required both actual knowledge and disregard of risk of harm. The case involved Dee Farmer, a preoperative transsexual with obvious feminine characteristics who had been incarcerated with other males in the federal prison system. Farmer was sometimes held in the general prison population but was more often in segregation. While mixing with other inmates, however, Farmer was beaten and raped by a fellow prisoner. Subsequently, he sued correctional officials, claiming that they had acted with deliberate indifference to his safety because they knew that the penitentiary had a violent environment as well as a history of inmate assaults, and because they should have known that Farmer would be particularly vulnerable to sexual attack.

The Court sent Farmer's case back to a lower court for rehearing, after clarifying what it said was necessary to establish deliberate indifference. "Prison officials," wrote the Justices, "have a duty under the Eighth Amendment to provide humane conditions of confinement. They must ensure that inmates receive adequate food, clothing, shelter, and medical care and must protect prisoners from violence at the hands of other prisoners. However, a constitutional violation occurs only where . . . the official has acted with 'deliberate indifference' to inmate health or safety." The Court continued: "A prison official may be held liable under the Eighth Amendment for acting with 'deliberate indifference' to inmate health or safety only if he knows that inmates face a substantial risk of serious harm and disregards that risk by failing to take reasonable measures to abate it."[110]

Two other cases, *Ruiz* v. *Estelle* (1982)[111] and *Newman* v. *Alabama* (1972)[112] have had substantial impact concerning the rights of prisoners to medical attention. In *Ruiz,* the Texas Department of Corrections was found lacking in its medical treatment programs. The court ordered an improvement in record keeping, physical facilities, and general medical care, while it continued to monitor the progress of the department. In *Newman,* Alabama's prison medical services were found so inadequate as to be "shocking to the conscience." Problems with the Alabama program included the following:[113]

- Not enough medical personnel
- Poor physical facilities for medical treatment
- Poor administrative techniques for dispersal of medications
- Poor medical records
- A lack of medical supplies
- Poorly trained or untrained inmates who provided some medical services and performed minor surgery
- Medically untrained personnel who determined the need for treatment

Part of the issue of medical treatment is the question of whether inmates can be forced to take medication or can refuse to eat. A 1984 federal court case held that inmates could be medicated in emergency situations against their wills.[114] The court did recognize that unwanted medications designed to produce only psychological effects, such as tranquilizers, might be refused more readily than life-sustaining drugs.[115] Similarly, other courts have held that inmates do not have a right to starve themselves to death.

In 1993, the Court gave indication that environmental conditions of prison life which pose a threat to inmate health may have to be corrected. In *Helling* v. *McKinney*,[116] Nevada inmate William McKinney claimed that exposure to secondary cigarette smoke circulating in his cell was threatening his health, in violation of the Eighth Amendment's prohibition on cruel and unusual punishment. The Court, in ordering that a federal district court provide McKinney with the opportunity to prove his allegations, held that "[A]n injunction cannot be denied to inmates who plainly prove an unsafe, life-threatening condition on the ground that nothing yet has happened to them." In effect, the *Helling* case gave notice to prison officials that they are responsible not only for "inmates' current serious health problems," but also for maintaining environmental conditions under which health problems might be prevented from developing.

Privacy

Many court decisions, including the Tenth Circuit case of *U.S.* v. *Ready* (1978)[117] and the U.S. Supreme Court decisions of *Katz* v. *U.S.* (1967)[118] and *Hudson* v. *Palmer* (1984)[119] have held that inmates cannot have a reasonable expectation to privacy while incarcerated. Palmer, an inmate in Virginia, claimed that Hudson, a prison guard, had unreasonably destroyed some of his personal (noncontraband) property following a cell search. Palmer's complaint centered on the lack of due process which accompanied the destruction. The Court disagreed, saying that the need for prison officials to conduct thorough and unannounced searches precludes inmate privacy in personal possessions.

In *Block* v. *Rutherford* (1984)[120] the Court established that prisoners do not have a right to be present during a search of their cells. Some lower courts, however, have begun to indicate that body cavity searches may be unreasonable unless based upon a demonstrable suspicion or conducted after prior warning has been given to the inmate.[121] They have also indicated that searches conducted simply to "harass or humiliate" inmates are illegitimate.[122] These cases may be an indication that the Supreme Court will soon recognize a limited degree of privacy in prison cell searches, especially those which uncover legal documents and personal papers prepared by the prisoner.[123]

Disciplinary and Grievance Procedures

A major area of inmate concern is the hearing of grievances. Complaints may arise in areas as diverse as food service (quality of food or special diets for religious purposes or health regimens), interpersonal relations between inmates and staff, denial of privileges, and accusations of misconduct levied against an inmate or a guard.

In 1972 the National Council on Crime and Delinquency developed a Model Act for the Protection of Rights of Prisoners, which included the opportunity for grievances to be heard. The 1973 National Advisory Commission on Criminal Justice Standards and Goals called for the establishment of responsible practices for the hearing of inmate grievances. Finally, in 1977, in the case of *Jones* v. *North Carolina Prisoners' Labor Union, Inc.*,[124] the Supreme Court held that prisons must establish some formal opportunity for the airing of inmate grievances. Soon, formal grievance plans were established in prisons in an attempt to divert inmate-originated grievances away from the courts.

Today all sizable prisons have an established **grievance procedure** whereby an inmate files a complaint with local authorities and receives a mandated response. Modern grievance procedures range from the use of a hearing board composed of staff members and inmates to a single staff appointee charged with the resolution of complaints. Inmates who are dissatisfied with the handling of their grievance can generally appeal beyond the level of the local prison unit.

Disciplinary actions by prison authorities may also require a formalized hearing process, especially when staff members bring charges of rule violations against inmates, which might result in some form of punishment being imposed on them. In a precedent-setting decision, the Supreme Court decided, in the case of *Wolff* v. *McDonnell* (1974),[125] that sanctions could not be levied against inmates without appropriate due process. The *Wolff* case involved an inmate who had been deprived of previously earned good-time credits because of misbehavior. The Court established that good-time credits were a form of "state-created

Grievance Procedure

Formalized arrangements, usually involving a neutral hearing board, whereby institutionalized individuals have the opportunity to register complaints about the conditions of their confinement.

right(s)," which, once created, could not be "arbitrarily abrogated."[126] *Wolff* was especially significant because it began an era of court scrutiny of what came to be called "state-created liberty interests." State-created liberty interests were said to be based upon the language used in published prison regulations, and were held, in effect, to confer due process guarantees upon prisoners. Hence, if a prison regulation said that a disciplinary hearing should be held before a prisoner could be sent to solitary confinement, and that such a hearing should permit a discussion of the evidence for and against the prisoner, courts interpreted that regulation to mean that the prisoner had a state-created right to a hearing and sending him or her to solitary confinement in violation of the regulation was a violation of a state-created liberty interest. State-created rights and privileges were also called "protected liberties" in later court decisions and were interpreted to include any significant change in a prisoner's status.

In the interest of due process, and especially where written prison regulations governing the hearing process exist, courts have generally held that inmates going before disciplinary hearing boards are entitled to (1) notice of the charges brought against them, (2) the chance to organize a defense, (3) an impartial hearing, and (4) the opportunity to present witnesses and evidence on their behalf. A written statement of the hearing board's conclusions should be provided to the inmate.[127] More recently, in the case of *Ponte* v. *Real* (1985),[128] the Supreme Court held that prison officials must provide an explanation to inmates who are denied the opportunity to have a desired witness at their hearing. The case of *Vitek* v. *Jones* (1980) extended the requirement of due process to inmates about to be transferred from prisons to mental hospitals.[129]

So that inmates can know what is expected of them as they enter prison, the American Correctional Association recommends: "A rulebook that contains all chargeable offenses, ranges of penalties and disciplinary procedures [be] posted in a conspicuous and accessible area; [and] a copy . . . given to each inmate and staff member."[130]

A Return to the Hands-Off Doctrine?

Many state-created rights and "protected liberties" may soon be a thing of the past. In June 1991, an increasingly conservative U.S. Supreme Court signaled the beginning of what appears to be at least a partial return to the hands-off doctrine of earlier times. The case, *Wilson* v. *Seiter*,[131] involved a 1983 suit brought against Richard P. Seiter, director of the Ohio Department of Rehabilitation and Correction, and Carl Humphreys, warden of the Hocking Correctional Facility (HCF) in Nelsonville, Ohio. In the suit, Pearly L. Wilson, a felon incarcerated at HCF, alleged that a number of the conditions of his confinement—specifically, overcrowding, excessive noise, insufficient locker storage space, inadequate heating and cooling, improper ventilation, unclean and inadequate restrooms, unsanitary dining facilities and food preparation, and housing with mentally and physically ill inmates—constituted cruel and unusual punishment in violation of the Eighth and Fourteenth Amendments to the U.S. Constitution. Wilson asked for a change in prison conditions and sought $900,000 from prison officials in compensatory and punitive damages.

Both the federal district court in which Wilson first filed affidavits and the Sixth Circuit Court of Appeals held that no constitutional violations existed because the conditions cited by Wilson were not the result of malicious intent on the part of officials. The U.S. Supreme Court agreed, noting that the "deliberate indifference" standard applied in *Estelle* v. *Gamble*[132] to claims involving medical care is similarly applicable to other cases in which prisoners challenge the conditions of their confinement. In effect, the Court created a standard which effectively means that all future challenges to prison conditions by inmates, which are brought under the Eighth Amendment, must show "deliberate indifference" by the officials responsible for the existence of those conditions before the Court will hear the complaint.

The written opinion of the Court in *Wilson* v. *Seiter* is telling. Writing for the majority, Justice Scalia observed that "if a prison boiler malfunctions accidentally during a cold winter, an inmate would have no basis for an Eighth Amendment claim, even if he suffers objectively significant harm. If a guard accidentally stepped on a prisoner's toe and broke it, this would not be punishment in anything remotely like the accepted meaning of the word."

Although the criterion of deliberate indifference is still evolving, it is likely that such indifference could be demonstrated by petitioners able to show that prison administrators have done nothing to alleviate life-threatening prison conditions after those conditions had been called to their attention. Even so, critics of *Wilson* are concerned that the decision may excuse prison authorities from the need to improve living conditions within institutions on the basis of simple budgetary constraints. Four of the justices themselves recognized the potential held by *Wilson* for a near-return to the days of the hands-off doctrine. Although concurring with the Court's majority, Justices White, Marshall, Blackmun, and Stevens noted their fear that "[t]he ultimate result of today's decision, [may be] that 'serious deprivations of basic human needs' . . . will go unredressed due to an unnecessary and meaningless search for 'deliberate indifference.' "

In the 1995 case of *Sandin* v. *Conner*,[133] the U.S. Supreme Court took a much more definitive stance in favor of a new type of hands-off doctrine and voted 5 to 4 to reject the argument that any state action taken for a punitive reason encroaches upon a prisoner's constitutional due process right to be free from the deprivation of liberty. The Court effectively set aside substantial portions of earlier decisions such as *Wolff* v. *McDonnell* (1974)[134] and *Hewitt* v. *Helms* (1983),[135] which, wrote the Justices, focused more on procedural issues than on those of "real substance." As a consequence, the majority opinion held, past cases such as these have "impermissibly shifted the focus" away from the *nature* of a due process deprivation to one based on the language of a particular state or prison regulation. "This shift in focus," the Justices wrote, "has encouraged prisoners to comb regulations in search of mandatory language on which to base entitlements to various state-conferred privileges." As a result, the Court said, cases such as *Wolff* and *Hewitt* "created disincentives for States to codify prison management procedures in [order to avoid lawsuits by inmates], and . . . led to the involvement of federal courts in the day-to-day management of prisons."

In *Sandin*, Demont Conner, an inmate at the Halawa Correctional Facility in Hawaii, was serving an indeterminate sentence of 30 years to life for numerous crimes, including murder, kidnapping, robbery, and burglary. Conner alleged in a lawsuit in federal court that prison officials had deprived him of procedural due process when a hearing committee refused to allow him to present witnesses during a disciplinary hearing and then sentenced him to segregation for alleged misconduct. An appellate court agreed with Conner, concluding that an existing prison regulation which instructed the hearing committee to find guilt in cases where a misconduct charge is supported by substantial evidence, meant that the committee could not impose segregation if it did not look at all the evidence available to it.

The Supreme Court, however, reversed the decision of the appellate court, holding that while "such a conclusion may be entirely sensible in the ordinary task of construing a statute defining rights and remedies available to the general public, [i]t is a good deal less sensible in the case of a prison regulation primarily designed to guide correctional officials in the administration of a prison." The Court concluded that "such regulations [are] not designed to confer rights on inmates," but are meant only to provide *guidelines* to prison staff members. Hence, based upon *Sandin*, it appears that inmates in the future will have a much more difficult time challenging the administrative regulations and procedures imposed upon them by prison officials, even when stated procedures are not explicitly followed. "The *Hewitt* approach," wrote the majority in *Sandin*, "has run counter to the view expressed in several of our cases that federal courts ought to afford appropriate deference and flexibility to state officials trying to manage a volatile environment. . . . The time has come," said the Court, "to return to those due process principles that were correctly established and applied in" earlier times.

The Prison Litigation Reform Act (1996)

While only about 2,000 petitions per year concerning inmate problems were being filed with the courts in 1961, by 1975 the number of filings had increased to around 17,000, and by 1996 prisoners filed 68,235 civil-rights lawsuits in federal courts nationwide.[136] Some inmate-originated suits seemed patently ludicrous and became the subject of much media coverage in the mid-1990s.[137] One such suit involved Robert Procup, a Florida State Prison inmate serving time for the murder of his business partner. Procup repeatedly sued Florida prison officials—once because he got only one roll with his dinner; again because he once didn't get a luncheon salad; a third time because prison-provided TV dinners didn't come with a drink; and a fourth time because his cell had no television. Two other well-publicized cases involved an inmate who went to court asking to be allowed to exercise religious freedom by attending prison chapel services in the nude; and an inmate who, thinking he could become pregnant via homosexual relations, sued prison doctors who wouldn't provide him with birth control pills. An infamous example of seemingly frivolous inmate lawsuits was one brought by inmates claiming religious freedoms and demanding that members of the Church of the New Song, or CONS, be provided steak and Harvey's Bristol Cream every Friday in order to celebrate communion. The CONS suit stayed in various courts for 10 years before finally being thrown out.[138]

The huge number of inmate-originated lawsuits created a backlog of cases in many federal courts and was targeted by the media and some citizen's groups as an unnecessary waste of taxpayer money. The National Association of Attorneys General, which supports efforts to restrict frivolous inmate lawsuits, estimates that lawsuits filed by prisoners cost states more than $81 million a year in legal fees alone.[139]

In 1996, in an effort to restrict inmate filings to worthwhile cases and to reduce the number of suits brought by state prisoners in federal courts, Congress enacted the federal Prison Litigation Reform Act (PLRA).[140] The Act was signed into law by President Clinton in April of that year. It

- Requires inmates to pay a $120 federal-court filing fee.
- Limits the award of attorneys' fees in successful lawsuits brought by inmates.
- Requires judges to screen all inmate complaints against the federal government and to immediately dismiss those deemed frivolous or without merit.
- Revokes the good-time credits earned by federal prisoners toward early release if they file a malicious lawsuit.
- Bars prisoners from suing the federal government for mental or emotional injury unless there was also an associated physical injury.
- Mandates that court orders affecting prison administration cannot go any further than necessary to correct a violation of a particular inmate's civil rights.
- Makes it possible for state officials to have court orders lifted after two years unless there is a new finding of a continuing violation of federally guaranteed civil rights.
- Mandates that any court order requiring the release of prisoners due to overcrowding be approved by a three-member court before it can become effective.

A number of states have filed suit under PLRA, seeking to wrest control of their prison systems back from federal authorities. Federal oversight of prisons in 40 states and in the District of Columbia had been ordered during the 1980s by federal courts as a result of overcrowding or poor administration by local officials. The first successful bid to end federal oversight of an entire state system came in 1996 when control of the South Carolina prison system reverted back to state authorities. The state had yielded to federal oversight in a 1985 agreement. Iowa and Wisconsin have also sought relief under PLRA, and, as of this writing, New York, Michigan, Illinois, and Connecticut are considering filing challenges.

Opponents of PLRA fear that it might stifle the filing of meritorious suits by inmates facing real deprivations. "Although the act was advertised as an attack on frivolous litigation, it actually is an attack on litigation of great merit," says Elizabeth Alexander of the American Civil Liberties Union's national prison project.[141] Ira Robbins, an American University law professor, adds: "A lot of the changes that have to be made to bring prisons up to minimum levels of decency aren't going to occur." In passing the Prison Litigation Reform Act, Robbins is concerned that "Congress has focused on efficiency at the expense of fairness."[142] Prisoners' rights organizations have vowed to challenge the PLRA in court, and Elizabeth Alexander, executive director of the ACLU Foundation's Prison Project, says, "We believe that the major provisions of the PLRA are unconstitutional and will be held so as a violation of the separation of powers and the due process clause of the Constitution."

Alexander promised that the ACLU would "challenge PLRA in every court in which it comes up."[143]

Issues Facing Prisons Today

Prisons are society's answer to a number of social problems. They house outcasts, misfits, and some highly dangerous people. While prisons provide a part of the answer to the question of crime control, they also face problems of their own. A few of those special problems are described in what follows.

AIDS

An earlier chapter discussed the steps being taken by police agencies to deal with health threats represented by AIDS. In 1997 the Justice Department reported finding 24,881 cases of AIDS among inmates of the nation's prisons[144]—a 12-fold increase over 1987. At the time of the survey, 3.5 percent of all female state prison inmates were HIV-positive, as were 2.3 percent of male prisoners. Positive seroprevalence rates have been found to vary from region to region—ranging between 2.1 and 7.6 percent of all men entering prison and between 2.5 and 14.7 percent of women. Some states have especially high rates. Almost 14 percent of New York prison inmates, for example, are HIV-positive. Of all HIV-positive inmates, 24 percent exhibit symptoms of AIDS.[145] Jail populations exhibit a similar prevalence of HIV infection. In both prisons and jails, the highest incidence of infection is found among inmates being held on drug charges (2.9 percent), while property (2.4 percent) and violent offenders (1.9 percent) have somewhat lower rates. Those who reported having shared a needle to use drugs prior to arrest had the highest infection rate (7.7 percent).

The incidence of HIV infection among the general population stands at 8.6 cases per 100,000 according to a recent report by the Centers for Disease Control. Among inmates, however, best estimates place the reported HIV-infection rate at 2,300 cases per 100,000[146]— many times as great. AIDS, in fact, has become the leading cause of death among prison inmates.[147] While not all inmates are infected in prison, authorities say the virus is spread behind bars through homosexual activity (including rape), intravenous drug use, and the sharing of tainted tattoo and hypodermic needles. The fact that inmates tend to have histories of high-risk behavior before entering prison, especially intravenous drug use, however, probably means that many are infected before coming to prison and helps to explain much of the huge difference in infection rates.

Early studies have shown that, contrary to popular opinion, AIDS transmission inside of prisons appears minimal. In a test of inmates at a U.S. Army military prison, 542 prisoners who upon admission had tested negative for exposure to the AIDS virus were retested two years later. None showed any signs of exposure to the virus.[148] On the other hand, some authorities suggest that it is only a matter of time before widespread forms of high-risk behavior inside of prisons begin to make a more visible contribution to the spread of AIDS.[149] Similarly, prison staffers fear infection from AIDS through routine activities, such as cell searches, responding to fights, performing body searches, administering CPR, and confiscating needles or weapons.

A recent report by the National Institute of Justice[150] suggests that there are two types of strategies available to correctional systems to reduce the transmission of AIDS. One strategy relies upon medical technology to identify seropositive inmates and segregate them from the rest of the prison population. Mass screening and inmate segregation, however, may be prohibitively expensive. They may also be illegal. Some states specifically prohibit HIV antibody testing without the informed consent of the person tested.[151] The related issue of confidentiality may be difficult to manage, especially where the purpose of testing is to segregate infected inmates from others. In addition, civil liability may result where inmates are falsely labeled as infected or where inmates known to be infected are not prevented from spreading the disease. Only a few state prison systems[152] segregate all known HIV-infected inmates, but more limited forms of separation can be practiced. In 1994, for example, a federal appeals court upheld a California prison policy which bars inmates who are HIV-positive from working in food service jobs.[153]

Many state prison systems routinely deny HIV-positive inmates jobs, educational opportunities, visitation privileges, conjugal visits, and home furloughs, causing some researchers to conclude that "inmates with HIV and AIDS are routinely discriminated against and denied equal treatment in ways that have no accepted medical basis."[154] Theodore Hammett, the nation's leading researcher on AIDS in prison, says, "The point is, people shouldn't be punished for having a certain medical condition."[155]

The second strategy is one of prevention through education. Educational programs teach both inmates and staff members about the dangers of high-risk behavior and offer suggestions on how to avoid HIV infection. An NIJ model program[156] recommends the use of simple, straightforward messages presented by knowledgeable and approachable trainers. Alarmism, says NIJ, is to be avoided. A recent survey[157] found that 98 percent of state and federal prisons provide some form of AIDS/HIV education, and that 90 percent of jails do as well—although most such training is oriented toward correctional staff rather than inmates.

In anticipation of court rulings which will likely prohibit the mass testing of inmates for the AIDS virus, the second strategy seems best. A third, but controversial, strategy involves issuing condoms to prisoners. Although this alternative is sometimes rejected because it implicitly condones sexual behavior among inmates, six correctional systems within the United States report that they make condoms available to inmates upon request.[158]

Geriatric Offenders

As determinate sentencing and the just deserts model take greater hold and more and more criminals are sentenced to longer prison terms, there will be increasing numbers of older prisoners among the general prison population. Although some prisoners grow old behind bars, others are old before they get there. American prisons, serving an aging population, are seeing more geriatric prisoners than ever before. At the moment, however, "It's a middle-aged bulge, rather than an increasing proportion of elderly prisoners," says Allen Beck of the Bureau of Justice Statistics.[159] The proportion of state prisoners aged 35 to 54 increased from 25 percent in 1986 to 40 percent in 1998. The proportion aged 55 and older increased only slightly (and remains around 3.3 percent).[160]

Many persons already in prison, including those in their middle years, will be serving longer sentences because of harsher sentencing laws which have been passed over the last decade. Hence, longer sentences and mandatory life without parole laws will soon bring a relentless increase in the number of elderly prisoners being held at both the federal and state levels. Some experts are predicting an explosion in the number of elderly prisoners in coming decades. A small but growing number of inmates (10 percent) will serve 20 years or more in prison, and 5 percent will never be released.[161]

The graying of America's prison population has a number of causes: "(1) the general aging of the American population, which is reflected inside prisons; (2) new sentencing policies such as 'three strikes,' 'truth in sentencing' and 'mandatory minimum' laws that send more criminals to prison for longer stretches; (3) a massive prison building boom that, since the 1980s, has provided space for more inmates, reducing the need to release prisoners to alleviate overcrowding; and (4) dramatic changes in parole philosophies and practices,"[162] with state and federal authorities phasing out or canceling parole programs, thereby forcing jailers to hold inmates with life sentences until they die.

Crimes of violence are what bring most older inmates into the correctional system. According to one study, 52 percent of inmates who were over the age of 50 at the time they entered prison had committed violent crimes, compared with 41 percent of younger inmates.[163] Violent crimes are also what keep them there. Ronald Wikberg and Burk Foster provide a snapshot of long-termers in their study of Angola prison.[164] Wikberg and Foster described 31 inmates at the Louisiana State Penitentiary at Angola who had served a continuous sentence of 25 years or longer, as of early 1988. They found the typical long-termer to be black (27 out of 31), with many of them sentenced for raping or killing a white. Inmate ages ranged from 42 to 71. A common thread linking most of these inmates was that their release was opposed by victims' families and friends. Some had a record as prison trouble-makers, but a few had been near-model prisoners.

Long-termers and geriatric inmates have special needs. They tend to suffer from handi-caps, physical impairments, and illnesses not generally encountered among their more youthful counterparts. Unfortunately, few prisons are equipped to deal adequately with the medical needs of aging offenders. Some large facilities have begun to set aside special sec-tions to care for elderly inmates with typical disorders, such as Alzheimer's disease, cancer, or heart disease. Unfortunately, such efforts have barely kept pace with problems. The number of inmates requiring round-the-clock care is expected to increase dramatically over the next two decades.[165]

Even the idea of rehabilitation takes on a new meaning where geriatric offenders are con-cerned. What kinds of programs are most likely to be useful in providing the older inmate with the needed tools for success on the outside? Which counseling strategies hold the great-est promise for introducing socially acceptable behavior patterns into the long-established lifestyles of elderly offenders about to be released? There are few answers to these questions. To date, no in-depth federal studies to answer such questions have been done which might help prepare the nation's prison system for handling the needs of older inmates.[166] Learn about some of the oldest prisoners in America via WebExtra! 12-3 at CJToday.com. Read a letter from William Heirens via WebExtra! 12-4 at CJToday.com. Heirens has been locked up for over 50 years.

Mentally Ill Inmates

The mentally ill are another inmate category with special needs. Some mentally ill inmates are neurotic or have personality problems, which increase tension in prison. Others have serious psychological disorders which may have escaped earlier diagnosis (at trial) or which did not provide a legal basis for the reduction of criminal responsibility. A fair number of offenders develop psychiatric symptoms while in prison. Some news accounts of modern prisons have focused squarely on the problem: "Raging mental illness is so common it's ignored," wrote a *Newsweek* staffer visiting a women's prison.[167]

Unfortunately, few states have any substantial capacity for the psychiatric treatment of mentally disturbed inmates. In 1982 Hans Toch described the largely ineffective practice of bus therapy, whereby disturbed inmates are shuttled back and forth between mental health centers and correctional facilities.[168] In February 1990, the U.S. Supreme Court, in the case of *Washington State* v. *Harper,*[169] ruled that mentally ill inmates could be required to take antipsychotic drugs, even against their wishes. The ruling stipulated that such a requirement would apply where "the inmate is dangerous to himself or others, and the treatment is in the inmate's medical interest." A 1999 study by the Bureau of Justice Statistics found that the nation's prisons and jails hold an estimated 283,800 mentally ill inmates (16 percent of those confined), and that 547,800 such offenders are on probation.[170] The government study also found that 10 percent of mentally ill inmates receive no treatment. For more details about the report, visit WebExtra! 12-5 at CJToday.com.

Mentally deficient inmates constitute still another group with special needs. Some studies estimate the proportion of mentally deficient inmates at about 10 percent.[171] Retarded inmates are less likely to complete training and rehabilitative programs successfully than are other inmates. They also evidence difficulty in adjusting to the routines of prison life. As a consequence, they are likely to exceed the averages in proportion of sentence served.[172] Only seven states report special facilities or programs for the mentally retarded inmate.[173] Other state systems "mainstream" such inmates, making them participate in regular activities with other inmates.

Texas, one state which does provide special services for retarded inmates, began a Men-tally Retarded Offender Program (MROP) in 1984. Inmates in Texas are given a battery of tests that measure intellectual and social adaptability skills, and prisoners who are identified as retarded are housed in special satellite correctional units. The Texas MROP program pro-vides individual and group counseling, along with training in adult life skills. Learn more about prison issues via WebExtra! 12-6 at CJToday.com.

Should Elderly Convicts Be Kept in Prison?

BRIDGETON, N.J.—On the outskirts of this time-forgotton coastal town, South Woods State Prison rises above the salt marshes in a symphony of concrete, bulletproof glass and pyramids of razor wire coils.

This $240 million prison, which costs $200,000 per day to operate, holds some of the state's most infirm inmates. Among them is 80-year-old jewel thief John Seybold. He may not be dangerous anymore, nor much of an escape risk, but Seybold readily acknowledges that he's still a drain on society.

"If I was 40 years old and still out stealing diamonds, that's a different story," said Seybold, whose face and hands are spotted with age. "But I can barely walk. It's not sensible to consider us a risk to the social structure anymore. We're beyond that point."

If Seybold were an average prisoner, his 12 years in prison would have cost taxpayers about $240,000. But he's an old man who needs expensive medical care—and gets it from his jailers.

Pulling open his tan prison smock, he shows off the white scar above his left breast where taxpayer-paid surgeons inserted a pacemaker to correct a heart problem. In the outside world, the cost of a pacemaker operation ranges from $15,000 to $50,000.

When the jewel thief was serving time in federal prison, doctors gave him a titanium replacement knee in an operation that he said cost $22,000. In separate operations, doctors also repaired his prostate and aorta.

"It's a real imposition on the taxpayer," he said.

Prisons As Old-Age Homes

Seybold's case is far from unique. As prison systems grow, some are metamorphosing into old-age homes providing sophisticated elder care and medical services. Prison nurses now routinely attend to patients in their 80s and 90s, operating dialysis machines, emptying bedpans and helping inmates brush their teeth and get undressed. Some corrections authorities have been forced to build custom facilities for prisoners who've gone blind, deaf or mute.

In Louisiana, Warden Burl Cain keeps watch over 5,100 inmates at Angola prison, 88 percent of whom will never leave. Cain said the practice is a waste of space, lives and tax dollars. "We've long said prison should be for predators and not old men," Cain said.

If Cain had his way, as many as 200 of his inmates would be released immediately. "They're getting older and older because nobody gets out," he said. "They just stay here until they die."

Growing Old in the Joint

Kentucky's oldest prisoner, 87-year-old Creed Warren, waxes lyrical about ending his days inside the joint.

"I know that I've got to leave this world one way or the other," said Warren, a convicted sex offender and former moonshiner housed in the Kentucky State Reformatory.

"I've got to leave it and go to Jesus when he calls me out on the cloud," he said. "If I die here, I'll just die. It won't bother me a bit, not a bit in the world."

In West Virginia, aging murderer James Lee Burkhammer is more realistic.

"I don't think I could make it out there by myself," Burkhammer said by telephone from the Huttonsville Correctional Center.

"I'm 65," said Burkhammer. "It'd be hard to get a job out there. I've got high blood pressure and arthritis. I couldn't do much. I wouldn't want to be a burden upon anybody."

As an inmate's age rises, so does the cost of keeping him in prison. The U.S. Justice Department reports the average prisoner costs about $20,000 a year to house. But the price of housing an elderly inmate can rise many times that much. A 1996 report of the National Criminal Justice Commission (NCJC) reported it cost $69,000 per year to house geriatric prisoners.

But as the cost of imprisonment rises, the danger to society retreats.

According to the U.S. Parole Commission, age is the single most reliable indicator in predicting recidivism. Within a year of release, inmates between the ages of 18 and 24 have a recidivism rate of 22 percent. For inmates over the age of 43—which the parole commission's Tom Kowalski called "the magic burnout date"—the rate drops to 2 percent.

Special Parole for the Elderly?

In the face of such statistics, many corrections analysts believe penning the elderly in expensive prison cells may serve as punishment for a crime, but doesn't give society much payback in public safety. Many are calling for parole of the elderly.

"It doesn't make sense in terms of crime control. If someone committed armed robbery at 30, he's not terribly likely to commit armed robbery at 60 if you let him out of prison," said Marc Mauer, assistant director of the Sentencing Project, a group advocating alternative sentences.

Some go further. At George Washington University's Project for Older Prisoners, coordinator Ann Burdick has successfully lobbied for the release of more than 200 infirm, well-behaved older prisoners who've admitted guilt for their crimes.

"We think they're more of a burden on society by being incarcerated than a threat to society if they're outside," said Burdick.

(Continued)

CRIME IN THE NEWS

Should Elderly Convicts Be Kept in Prison?

Not one prisoner represented by Burdick's group has returned to commit a crime, she said.

"And we want to keep it that way," she said.

"Prison Is Punishment"

There is another side to the debate, of course. Many tough sentencing advocates believe convicted felons belong in prison because they require punishment, regardless of their health or age.

For Louisiana Gov. Mike Foster, who has yet to grant pardons to any of the state's life-without-parole inmates, a lifetime behind bars is a proper penalty for a heinous crime.

"Gov. Foster falls into the 'just deserts' category," said Cheny Joseph, Foster's legal counsel. "He does believe that prison is punishment. You have to impose a penalty that's just and punishes someone for what they've done."

Prison-Building Boom

Many states have addressed the long-term implications of such tough sentencing policies with an unprecented prison-building boom. Texas, for example, has added almost 100,000 beds, tripling its capacity.

"We called it the greatest construction project since the pyramids," said Glen Castlebury of the Texas Department of Criminal Justice (TDCJ). He said the average prisoner's age is creeping up by six months a year. Currently it's 33. In a decade, the average jailed Texan will be 38.

In 30 years, Castlebury conceded, some Texas prisons will resemble nursing homes.

California is headed down the same road. There, the Department of Corrections is involved in the largest building program in the country—worth $5.3 billion—to keep up with an inmate population that more than doubled in 10 years, reaching almost 160,000 last year.

In Ohio, a corrections report estimated that its 1997 population of 3,000 older inmates would grow 50 percent over the next two decades. Now, growth is ahead of that pace. The report called for construction of a second prison for the elderly and new elder "pods" at existing institutions.

Death As the Only Way Out

Meanwhile, thousands of inmates across the country already must face the fact that they'll grow old and die in prison.

With the average inmate's age now in the mid-30s, many prisoners locked up in the late '80s and early '90s won't emerge until they're 60 or 70 years old.

"Under the new laws, there's no compassionate grounds for release, even for the very ill," said Herbert Rosefield, assistant director for health services in North Carolina's Division of Prisons.

"I'm still hopeful, but the way it looks now, I can't see no out," said Virgil Lee Evans, an 85-year-old murderer serving his 27th year of a life sentence in Michigan. Evans' next parole hearing won't come until 2003, when he's 89. "That's telling me that they want me to die in prison," he said.

Source: Jim Krane, "Should Elderly Convicts Be Kept in Prison?" APB News), April 12, 1999. Reprinted with permission.

Summary

Prisons are small, self-contained societies, which are sometimes described as total institutions. Studies of prison life have detailed the existence of prison subcultures, or inmate worlds, replete with inmate values, social roles, and lifestyles. New inmates who are socialized into prison subculture are said to undergo the process of prisonization. Prisonization involves, among other things, learning the language of prison—commonly called prison argot.

Prison subcultures are very influential and must be reckoned with by both inmates and staff. Given the large and often densely packed inmate populations which characterize many of today's prisons, however, prison subcultures are not easily subject to the control of prison authorities. Complicating life behind bars are numerous conflicts of interest between inmates and staff. Lawsuits, riots, violence, and frequent formal grievances are symptoms of such differences.

For many years courts throughout the nation assumed a hands-off approach to prisons, rarely intervening in the day-to-day administration of prison facilities. That changed in the late 1960s when the hands-off era ended and the U.S. Supreme Court began to identify inmate rights mandated by the U.S. Constitution. Rights identified by the Court include the right to physical integrity, an absolute right to be free from unwarranted corporeal punish-

Geriatric inmates are becoming an increasingly large part of the inmate population. Here, Jonathan Turley, founder of the Project for Older Prisoners (POPS), speaks with two Angola, Louisiana, inmates.
Mark Sultz, AP/Wide World Photos.

ments, certain religious rights, and procedural rights such as those involving access to attorneys, to the courts, and so on. The conditional rights of prisoners, which have been repeatedly supported by the U.S. Supreme Court, mandate professionalism among prison administrators and require vigilance in the provision of correctional services. The era of prisoner rights was sharply curtailed, however, with passage of the 1996 Prison Litigation Reform Act, and by a growing recognition of the legal morass resulting from unregulated access to federal courts by inmates across the nation. The Prison Litigation Reform Act, in concert with other restrictions sanctioned by the U.S. Supreme Court, has substantially limited inmate access to courts at the federal level.

Today's prisons remain miniature societies—reflecting the problems and challenges which exist in the larger society of which they are a part. HIV-infected inmates, geriatric offenders, homosexual inmates, and the mentally ill all constitute special groups within the inmate population which require additional attention.

Discussion Questions

1. Explain the concept of prison subcultures. What purpose do you think prison subcultures serve? Why do they develop?
2. What does *prisonization* mean? Describe the U-shaped curve developed by Stanton Wheeler as it relates to prisonization. Why do you think the curve is U-shaped?
3. What are the primary concerns of prison staff? Do you agree that those concerns are important? What other goals might staff members focus on?
4. What does it mean to say that inmates have "rights"? Where do such rights come from? Do you think that inmates have too many rights? Why or why not?
5. What does the term *state-created rights* mean within the context of corrections? What do you think might be the future of state-created rights?
6. Explain the balancing test established by the Supreme Court in deciding issues of prisoners' rights. How might such a test apply to the emerging area of inmate privacy?
7. What are some of the special problems facing prisons today which are discussed in this chapter? What new problems do you think the future might bring?

Web Quest!

Visit the Cybrary and search for "jobs," "careers," and "employment." What criminal justice–related employment sites can you find? Explore some of the sites you find in order to explore the possibility of a career in corrections. Document the sources you used, and list their URLs, along with the date you accessed each. Then answer these questions:

What is the difference between a job and a career?

What career opportunities are available in corrections?

Why is career planning important? How can you develop an effective career plan?

What is the difference between education and training?

Why are education and training important to building a career in corrections?

What role might professionalism play in building your career?

What traits must you have to achieve your goals and to be successful in a career in corrections?

You should e-mail your answers to your instructor if requested to do so. *Note:* The questions in this Web Quest have been adapted from "Building your Career in Corrections," *The Keeper's Voice,* vol. 18, no. 1. Web posted at www.acsp.uic.edu/iaco/kv1801/180127.shtml. Accessed July 5, 1999.

Library Extras!

The Library Extras! listed here complement the WebExtras! found throughout this chapter. Library Extras! may be accessed on the Web at CJToday.com.

Library Extra! 12-1. "Can Telemedicine Reduce Spending and Improve Prisoner Health Care?" *The National Institute of Justice Journal* (NIJ, April 1999).

Library Extra! 12-2. *HIV in Prisons and Jails* (BJS, current volume).

Library Extra! 12-3. *Resolution of Prison Riots* (NIJ, October 1995).

Library Extra! 12-4. *Women Offenders: Programming Needs and Promising Approaches* (NIJ, August 1998).

Library Extra! 12-5. *Work in American Prisons: Joint Ventures with the Private Sector* (NIJ, not dated).

Library Extra! 12-6. *Women in Prison* (BJS, current volume).

References

1. Joseph W. Rogers, "Mary Belle Harris: Warden and Rehabilitation Pioneer," *Criminal Justice Research Bulletin,* vol. 3, no. 9 (Huntsville, TX: Sam Houston State University, 1988), p. 8.

2. Hans Reimer, "Socialization in the Prison Community," *Proceedings of the American Prison Association 1937* (New York: American Prison Association, 1937), pp. 151–155.

3. Donald Clemmer, *The Prison Community* (Boston: Holt, Rinehart, Winston, 1940).

4. Gresham M. Sykes, *The Society of Captives: A Study of a Maximum Security Prison* (Princeton, NJ: Princeton University Press, 1958).

5. Richard A. Cloward et al., *Theoretical Studies in Social Organization of the Prison* (New York: Social Science Research Council, 1960).

6. Donald R. Cressey, ed., *The Prison: Studies in Institutional Organization and Change* (New York: Holt, Rinehart, and Winston, 1961).

7. Lawrence Hazelrigg, ed., *Prison Within Society: A Reader in Penology* (Garden City, NY: Anchor Books, 1969), preface.

8. Charles Stastny and Gabrielle Tyrnauer, *Who Rules the Joint? The Changing Political Culture of Maximum-Security Prisons in America* (Lexington, MA: Lexington Books, 1982), p. 131.

9. Erving Goffman, *Asylums: Essays on the Social Situation of Mental Patients and Other Inmates* (Garden City, NY: Anchor Books, 1961).

10. For a firsthand account of the prison experience, see Victor Hassine, *Life Without Parole: Living in Prison Today* (Los Angeles: Roxbury, 1996); and W. Rideau and R. Wikberg, *Life Sentences: Rage and Survival Behind Prison Bars* (New York: Times Books, 1992).

11. The concept of prisonization is generally attributed to Clemmer, *The Prison Community,* although Quaker penologists of the late 1700s were actively concerned with preventing "contamination" (the spread of criminal values) among prisoners.

12. Gresham M. Sykes and Sheldon L. Messinger, "The Inmate Social System," in Richard A. Cloward et al., *Theoretical Studies in Social Organization of the Prison* (New York: Social Science Research Council, 1960), pp. 5–19.

13. Ibid., p. 5.

14. Stanton Wheeler, "Socialization in Correctional Communities," *American Sociological Review,* vol. 26 (October 1961), pp. 697–712.

15. Sykes, *The Society of Captives,* p. xiii.

16. Stastny and Tyrnauer, *Who Rules the Joint?,* p. 135.

17. Ibid.

18. Sykes, *The Society of Captives.*

19. Clemmer, *The Prison Community* (New York: Holt, Rinehart, and Winston, 1940), pp. 294–296.

20. Joseph L. Galloway, "Into the Heart of Darkness," *U.S. News,* March 8, 1999. Web posted at

www.usnews.com/usnews/issue/990308/8pris.htm. Accessed March 20, 2000.

21. Alan J. Davis, "Sexual Assaults in the Philadelphia Prison System and Sheriff's Vans," *Trans-Action,* vol. 6 (December 1968), pp. 8–16.

22. Daniel Lockwood, "Sexual Aggression Among Male Prisoners," unpublished dissertation (Ann Arbor, MI: University Microfilms International, 1978).

23. Lee H. Bowker, *Prison Victimization* (New York: Elsevier, 1980).

24. Ibid., p. 42.

25. Ibid., p. 1.

26. Hans Toch, *Living in Prison: The Ecology of Survival* (New York: The Free Press, 1977), p. 151.

27. John Irwin, *The Felon* (Englewood Cliffs, NJ: Prentice Hall, 1970).

28. Lucien X. Lombardo, *Guards Imprisoned: Correctional Officers at Work* (New York: Elsevier, 1981), pp. 22–36.

29. Leonard Morgenbesser, "NY State Law Prescribes Psychological Screening for CO Job Applicants," *Correctional Training* (Newsletter of the American Association of Correctional Training Personnel, Winter 1983), p. 1.

30. "A Sophisticated Approach to Training Prison Guards," *Newsday,* August 12, 1982.

31. Rosalie Rosetti, "Charting Your Course: Federal Model Encourages Career Choices," *Corrections Today* (August 1988), pp. 34–38.

32. Stastny and Tyrnauer, *Who Rules the Joint?* p. 1.

33. See Frederick Talbott, "Reporting from Behind the Walls: Do It Before the Siren Wails," *The Quill* (February 1988), pp. 16–21.

34. "Prison Riot Leaves Injuries," *Fayetteville Observer-Times* (North Carolina), October 28, 1989, p. 1A.

35. Lee Leonard, "Lucasville Guards Were Outnumbered 50–1 Before Riot," *Columbus Dispatch,* May 12, 1993.

36. "Ohio Prison Rebellion Is Ended," *USA Today,* April 22, 1993, p. 2A.

37. *Report of the Attorney General on the February 2 and 3, 1980 Riot at the Penitentiary of New Mexico* (two parts), June and September 1980.

38. See, for example, American Correctional Association, *Riots and Disturbances in Correctional Institutions* (College Park, MD: ACA, 1981); Michael Braswell et al., *Prison Violence in America* (Cincinnati, OH: Anderson, 1985); and R. Conant, "Rioting, Insurrectional and Civil Disorderliness," *American Scholar,* vol. 37 (Summer 1968), pp. 420–433.

39. Robert S. Fong, Ronald E. Vogel, and S. Buentello, "Prison Gang Dynamics: A Look Inside the Texas Department of Corrections," in A. V. Merlo and P. Menekos, eds., *Dilemmas and Directions in Corrections* (Cincinnati, OH: Anderson, 1992).

40. Ibid.

41. *Ruiz* v. *Estelle,* 503 F.Supp. 1265 (S.D. Texas, 1980).

42. Steve Dillingham and Reid Montgomery, "Prison Riots: A Corrections Nightmare Since 1774," in Braswell et al., *Prison Violence in America,* pp. 19–36.

43. Vernon Fox, "Prison Riots in a Democratic Society," *Police,* vol. 26, no. 12 (December 1982), pp. 35–41.

44. Donald R. Cressey, "Adult Felons in Prison," in Lloyd E. Ohlin, ed., *Prisoners in America* (Englewood Cliffs, NJ: Prentice Hall, 1972), pp. 117–150.

45. Allen J. Beck, *Prisoners in 1999* (Washington, D.C.: Bureau of Justice Statistics, 2000).

46. Ibid.

47. This section owes much to the American Correctional Association, Task Force on the Female Offender, *The Female Offender: What Does the Future Hold?* (Washington, D.C.: St. Mary's Press, 1990), and "The View from Behind Bars," *Time,* Fall 1990 (special issue), pp. 20–22.

48. For greater insight into the criminality of incarcerated women, see Evelyn K. Sommers, *Voices from Within: Women Who Have Broken the Law* (Toronto: University of Toronto Press, 1995).

49. American Correctional Association, *The Female Offender.*

50. B. Keith Crew, "Sex Differences in Criminal Sentencing: Chivalry or Patriarchy?" *Justice Quarterly,* vol. 8, no. 1 (March 1991), pp. 59–83.

51. American Correctional Association, *The Female Offender.*

52. Ibid.

53. Mary Jeanette Clement, "National Survey of Programs for Incarcerated Women," paper presented at the Academy of Criminal Justice Sciences annual meeting, Nashville, Tennessee, March 1991.

54. Ibid., pp. 8–9.

55. D. Ward and G. Kannebaum, *Women's Prison: Sex and Social Structure* (London: Weidenfeld and Nicolson, 1966).

56. Esther Heffernan, *Making It in Prison: The Square, the Cool and the Life* (London: Wiley-Interscience, 1972).

57. Rose Giallombardo, *Society of Women: A Study of Women's Prisons* (New York: John Wiley, 1966).

58. Ibid., p. 136.

59. For a summary of such studies (including some previously unpublished), see Lee H. Bowker, *Prisoner Subcultures* (Lexington, MA: Lexington Books, 1977), p. 86.

60. Giallombardo, *Society of Women,* p. 162.

61. Russell P. Dobash, P. Emerson Dobash, and Sue Gutteridge, *The Imprisonment of Women* (Oxford: Basil Blackwell, 1986), p. 6.

62. Heffernan, *Making It in Prison.*

63. Jean Harris, *They Always Call Us Ladies* (New York: Scribners, 1988).

64. "The Lady on Cell Block 112A," *Newsweek,* September 5, 1988, p. 60.

65. Ibid.

66. Ibid.

67. "Scarsdale Diet Doctor's Killer Given Clemency," *USA Today,* December 30, 1992, p. 3A.

68. Bowker, *Prison Victimization,* p. 53.

69. Giallombardo, *Society of Women.*

70. "Georgia Indictments Charge Abuse of Female Inmates," *USA Today,* November 16, 1992, p. 3A.

71. Ibid.

72. American Correctional Association, *The Female Offender,* p. 39.

73. *Holt* v. *Sarver,* 309 F.Supp. 362 (E.D. Ark 1970).

74. Vergil L. Williams, *Dictionary of American Penology: An Introduction* (Westport, CT: Greenwood, 1979), pp. 6–7.

75. *Pell* v. *Procunier,* 417 U.S. 817, 822 (1974).

76. Ibid.

77. American Correctional Association, *Legal Responsibility and Authority of Correctional Officers: A Handbook on Courts, Judicial Decisions and Constitutional Requirements* (College Park, MD: ACA, 1987), p. 8.

78. According to the ACA, *Legal Responsibility,* p. 57, "A trend may be developing in favor of less intrusive remedial orders in conditions cases in favor of allowing institutional official an opportunity to develop and implement relief with as little court involvement as possible." For further information on this and other issues in the area of prisoners' rights, see Barbara B. Knight and Stephen T. Early, Jr., *Prisoner's Rights in America* (Chicago: Nelson-Hall, 1986).

79. *Procunier* v. *Martinez,* 416 U.S. 396 (1974).

80. *McNamara* v. *Moody,* 606 F.2d 621 (5th Cir. 1979).

81. *The Luparar* v. *Stoneman,* 382 F.Supp. 495 (D. Vt. 1974).

82. *Mallery* v. *Lewis,* 106 Idaho 227 (1983).

83. See, for example, *Pepperling* v. *Crist,* 678 F.2d 787 (9th Cir. 1981).

84. *Cruz* v. *Beto,* 405 U.S. 319 (1972).

85. *Aziz* v. *LeFevre,* 642 F.2d 1109 (2nd Cir. 1981).

86. *Glasshofer* v. *Thornburg,* 514 F.Supp. 1242 (E.D. Pa. 1981).

87. See, for example, *Smith* v. *Coughlin,* 748 F.2d 783 (2d Cir. 1984).

88. *Campbell* v. *Cauthron,* 623 F.2d 503 (8th Cir. 1980).

89. *Smith* v. *Blackledge,* 451 F.2d 1201 (4th Cir. 1971).

90. *Dettmer* v. *Landon,* 617 F.Supp. 592, 594 (D.C. Va. 1985).

91. *Dettmer* v. *Landon,* 799 F.2d 929 (4th Cir. 1986).

92. *Lewellyn (L'Aquarius)* v. *State,* 592 P.2d 538 (Okla. Crim. App. 1979).

93. *Hill* v. *Blackwell,* 774 F.2d 338, 347 (8th Cir. 1985).

94. *Block* v. *Rutherford,* 486 F.2d 576 (1984).

95. *Pell* v. *Procunier,* 417 U.S. 817, 822 (1974).

96. *Houchins* v. *KQED, Inc.,* 438 U.S. 11 (1978).

97. Ibid.

98. For a Supreme Court review of the First Amendment right to petition the courts, see *McDonald* v. *Smith,* 105 S.Ct. 2787 (1985).

99. *Bounds* v. *Smith,* 430 U.S. 817, 821 (1977).

100. *Johnson* v. *Avery,* 393 U.S. 483 (1968).

101. *Bounds* v. *Smith.*

102. *Taylor* v. *Sterrett,* 532 F.2d 462 (5th Cir. 1976).

103. *In re Harrell,* 87 Cal. Rptr. 504, 470 P.2d 640 (1970).

104. *Guajardo* v. *Estelle,* 432 F.Supp. 1373 (S.D. Texas, 1977).

105. *O'Brien* v. *United States,* 386 U.S. 345 (1967); and *Weatherford* v. *Bursey,* 429 U.S. 545 (1977).

106. *U.S.* v. *Gouveia,* 104 S.Ct. 2292, 81 L. Ed. 2d 146 (1984).

107. *Estelle* v. *Gamble,* 429 U.S. 97 (1976).

108. Ibid.

109. *Farmer* v. *Brennan,* 114 S.Ct. 1970, 128 L. Ed. 2d 811 (1994).

110. Ibid.

111. *Ruiz* v. *Estelle,* 679 F.2d 1115 (5th Cir. 1982).

112. *Newman* v. *Alabama,* 349 F.Supp. 278 (M.D. Ala. 1972).

113. Adapted from American Correctional Association, *Legal Responsibility and Authority of Correctional Officers,* pp. 25–26.

114. *In re Caulk,* 35 CrL 2532 (New Hampshire S.Ct. 1984).

115. Ibid.

116. *Helling* v. *McKinney,* 113 S.Ct. 2475, 125 L. Ed. 2d 22 (1993).

117. *U.S.* v. *Ready,* 574 F.2d 1009 (10th Cir. 1978).

118. *Katz* v. *U.S.,* 389 U.S. 347, 88 S.Ct. 507, 19 L. Ed. 2d 576 (1967).

119. *Hudson* v. *Palmer,* 468 U.S. 517 (1984).

120. *Block* v. *Rutherford,* 104 S.Ct. 3227, 3234–35 (1984).

121. *U.S.* v. *Lilly,* 576 F.2d 1240 (5th Cir. 1978).

122. *Palmer* v. *Hudson,* 697 F.2d 1220 (4th Cir. 1983).

123. William H. Erickson et al., *United States Supreme Court Cases and Comments* (New York: Matthew Bender, 1987), Section 10.02 2 (c), pp. 10–38.

124. *Jones* v. *North Carolina Prisoners' Labor Union, Inc.,* 433 U.S. 119, 53 L. Ed. 2d 629, 641 (1977).

125. *Wolff* v. *McDonnell,* 94 S.Ct. 2963 (1974).

126. Ibid.

127. Ibid.

128. *Ponte* v. *Real,* 471 U.S. 491, 105 S.Ct. 2192, 85 L. Ed. 2d 553 (1985).

129. *Vitek* v. *Jones,* 445 U.S. 480 (1980).

130. American Correctional Association, Standard 2-4346. See ACA, *Legal Responsibility and Authority of Correctional Officers,* p. 49.

131. *Wilson* v. *Seiter et al.,* 501 U.S. 294 (1991).

132. *Estelle* v. *Gamble,* 429 U.S. 97, 106 (1976).

133. *Sandin* v. *Conner,* 63 U.S.L.W. 4601 (1995).

134. *Wolff* v. *McDonnell,* 94 S.Ct. 2963 (1974).

135. *Hewitt* v. *Helms,* 459 U.S. 460 (1983).

136. Laurie Asseo, "Inmate Lawsuits," The Associated Press wire services, May 24, 1996; and "State and Federal Prisoners Filed 68,235 Petitions in U.S. Courts in 1996," BJS Press Release, October 29, 1997.

137. See, for example, "The Great Prison Pastime," *20/20,* ABC News, September 24, 1993, which is part of the video library available to instructors using this textbook.

138. Ibid.

139. Asseo, "Inmate Lawsuits."

140. Public Law 104-134. Although the PLRA was signed into law on April 26, 1996, and is frequently referred to as the "Prison Litigation Reform Act of 1996," the official name of the act is the Prison Litigation Reform Act of 1995.

141. Ibid.

142. Ibid.

143. "Inmate Litigation and the PLRA," *Corrections Compendium,* December 1996, p. 2.

144. Bureau of Justice Statistics, *1996–1997 Update: HIV/AIDS, STDs, and TB in Correctional Facilities Series* (Washington, D.C.: BJS, 1998).

145. Ibid.

146. Laura Maruschak, *HIV in Prisons and Jails* (Washington, D.C.: Bureau of Justice Statistics, 1997).

147. Dennis Cauchon, "AIDS in Prison: Locked Up and Locked Out," *USA Today,* March 31, 1995, p. 6A.

148. Theodore M. Hammett, *AIDS in Correctional Facilities: Issues and Options,* 3rd ed. (Washing-

ton, D.C.: National Institute of Justice, 1988), p. 29.

149. M.A.R. Kleiman and R. W. Mockler, "AIDS, the Criminal Justice System, and Civil Liberties," *Governance: Harvard Journal of Public Policy* (Summer/Fall 1987), pp. 48–54.

150. Hammett, *AIDS in Correctional Facilities,* p. 37.

151. At the time of writing, California, Wisconsin, Massachusetts, New York, and the District of Columbia were among such jurisdictions.

152. Cheryl A. Crawford, "Health Care Needs in Corrections: NIJ Responds," (Washington, D.C.: National Institute of Justice).

153. See "Court Allows Restriction on HIV-Positive Inmates," in *Criminal Justice Newsletter,* vol. 25, no. 23 (December 1, 1994), pp. 2–3.

154. Cauchon, "AIDS in Prison."

155. Hammett, *AIDS in Correctional Facilities,* pp. 47–49.

156. Ibid.

157. Darrell Bryan, "Inmates, HIV and the Constitutional Right to Privacy: AIDS in Prison Facilities," *Corrections Compendium,* vol. 19, no. 9 (September 1994), pp. 1–3.

158. Cheryl A. Crawford, "Health Care Needs in Corrections: NIJ Responds."

159. As quoted in Paula Mergenhagen, "The Prison Population Bomb," *American Demographics,* (February 1996). Available on the World Wide Web at www.demographics.com/Publications/AD/96_AD/9602_AD/ad880.htm.

160. Beck and Mumola, *Prisoners in 1998.*

161. BJS press release, "The Nation's Prison Population Grew by 60,000 Inmates Last Year," August 15, 1999.

162. Jim Krane, "Demographic Revolution Rocks U.S. Prisons," APB Online, April 12, 1999. Web posted at www.apbonline.com/safestreets/old-prisoners/mainpris0412.html. Accessed January 5, 2000.

163. Lincoln J. Fry, "The Older Prison Inmate: A Profile," *The Justice Professional,* vol. 2, no. 1 (Spring 1987), pp. 1–12.

164. Ronald Wikbert and Burk Foster, "The Longtermers: Louisiana's Longest Serving Inmates and Why They've Stayed So Long," paper presented at the annual meeting of the Academy of Criminal Justice Sciences, Washington, D.C., 1989.

165. Ibid., p. 51.

166. S. Chaneles, "Growing Old Behind Bars," *Psychology Today,* vol. 21, no. 10 (October 1987), p. 51.

167. "The Lady in Cell Block 112A," *Newsweek,* September 5, 1988, p. 60.

168. Hans Toch, "The Disturbed Disruptive Inmate: Where Does the Bus Stop?" *The Journal of Psychiatry and Law,* vol. 10 (1982), pp. 327–349.

169. *Washington* v. *Harper,* 494 U.S. 210 (1990).

170. Paula M. Ditton, "Mental Health and Treatment of Inmates and Probationers," (Washington, D.C.: Bureau of Justice Statistics, 1999).

171. Robert O. Lampert, "The Mentally Retarded Offender in Prison," *The Justice Professional,* vol. 2, no. 1 (Spring 1987), p. 61.

172. Ibid., p. 64.

173. George C. Denkowski and Kathryn M. Denkowski, "The Mentally Retarded Offender in the State Prison System: Identification, Prevalence, Adjustment, and Rehabilitation," *Criminal Justice and Behavior,* vol. 12 (1985), pp. 55–75.

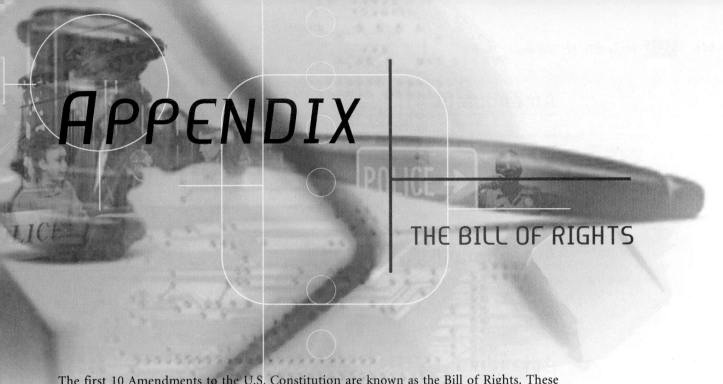

APPENDIX

THE BILL OF RIGHTS

The first 10 Amendments to the U.S. Constitution are known as the Bill of Rights. These amendments have special relevance to criminal justice and are reproduced here.

Amendment I. (1791)

Congress shall make no law respecting an establishment of religion, or prohibiting the free exercise thereof; or abridging the freedom of speech, or of the press; or the right of the people peaceably to assemble, and to petition the Government for a redress of grievances.

Amendment II. (1791)

A well regulated Militia, being necessary to the security of a free State, the right of the people to keep and bear Arms, shall not be infringed.

Amendment III. (1791)

No Soldier shall, in time of peace be quartered in any house, without the consent of the Owner, nor in time of war, but in a manner to be prescribed by law.

Amendment IV. (1791)

The right of the people to be secure in their persons, houses, papers, and effects, against unreasonable searches and seizures, shall not be violated, and no Warrants shall issue, but upon probable cause, supported by Oath or affirmation, and particularly describing the place to be searched, and the persons or things to be seized.

Amendment V. (1791)

No person shall be held to answer for a capital, or otherwise infamous crime, unless on a presentment or indictment of a Grand Jury, except in cases arising in the land or naval forces, or in the Militia, when in actual service in time of War or public danger; nor shall any person be subject for the same offence to be twice put in jeopardy of life or limb; nor shall be compelled in any criminal case to be a witness against himself, nor be deprived of life, liberty, or property, without due process of law; nor shall private property be taken for public use, without just compensation.

Amendment VI. (1791)

In all criminal prosecutions, the accused shall enjoy the right to a speedy and public trial, by an impartial jury of the State and district wherein the crime shall have been committed, which district shall have been previously ascertained by law, and to be informed of the nature and cause of the accusation; to be confronted with the witnesses against him; to have compulsory process for obtaining Witnesses in his favor, and to have the Assistance of Counsel for his defence.

Amendment VII. (1791)

In Suits at common law, where the value in controversy shall exceed twenty dollars, the right of trial by jury shall be preserved, and no fact tried by a jury, shall be otherwise reexamined in any Court of the United States, than according to the rules of the common law.

Amendment VIII. (1791)

Excessive bail shall not be required, nor excessive fines imposed, nor cruel and unusual punishments inflicted.

Amendment IX. (1791)

The enumeration of the Constitution, of certain rights, shall not be construed to deny or disparage others retained by the people.

Amendment X. (1791)

The powers not delegated to the United States by the Constitution, nor prohibited by it to the States, are reserved to the States respectively, or to the people.

INDEX

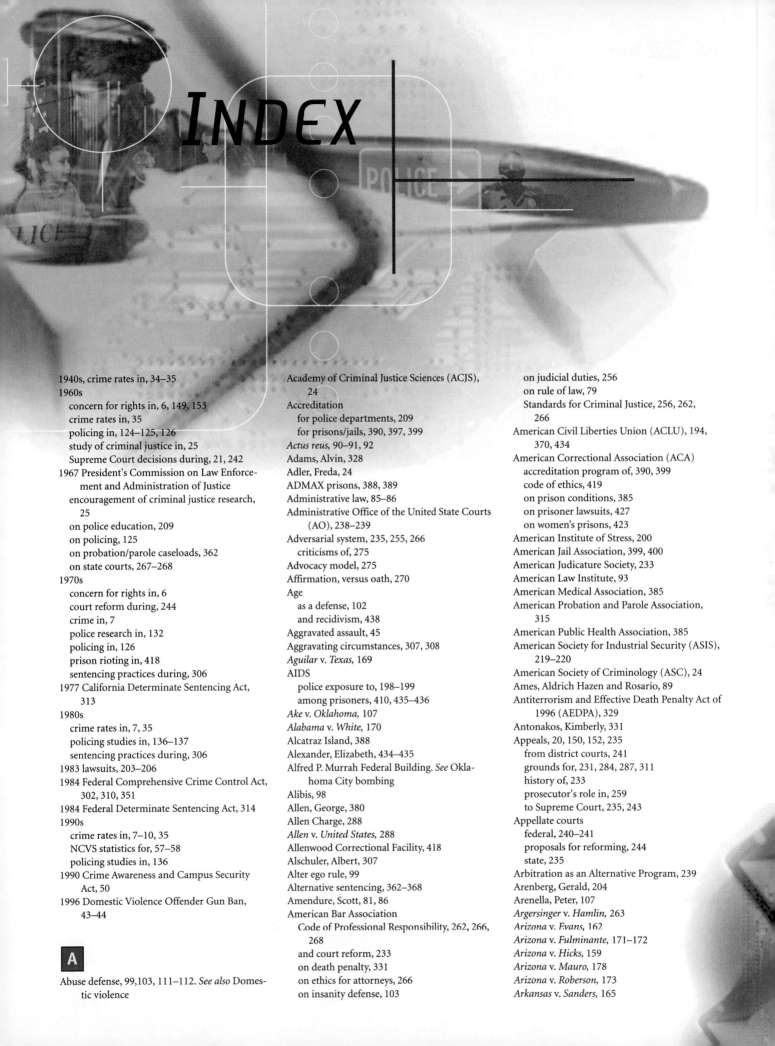